HOLOGRAPHY – BASIC PRINCIPLES AND CONTEMPORARY APPLICATIONS

Edited by **Emilia Mihaylova**

Holography – Basic Principles and Contemporary Applications
http://dx.doi.org/10.5772/46111
Edited by Emilia Mihaylova

Contributors

Anette Gjörloff Wingren, Olga Andreeva, Yuri Leonidovich Korzinin, Boris Glebovich Manuhin, Ngoc Diep Lai, Vladimir A. Postnikov, Aleksander Kraiskii, Valeri Sergienko, Francisco Palacios, Ligia Ferreira, Oneida Font, Guillermo Palacios, Jorge Ricardo, Miriela Escobedo, Isis Vasconcelos, Mikiya Muramatsu, Diogo Soga, José Valin, Aline Ambrogi, Flavia Oliveira, Young-Ho Seo, Dong-Wook Kim, Hyun-Jun Choi, Gabriel Martinez-Niconoff, Elena Stoykova, Hoonjong Kang, Jiyung Park, Sung Hee Hong, Youngmin Kim, David Brotherton-Ratcliffe, Eduardo Acedo Barbosa, Danilo Silva, Merilyn Ferreira, Dagmar Senderakova, Luciano Lamberti, Cesar A. Sciammarella, Federico Sciammarella, Izabela Naydenova, Emilia Mihaylova

Published by InTech

Janeza Trdine 9, 51000 Rijeka, Croatia

Publishing Process Manager Iva Simcic
Technical Editor InTech DTP team
Cover InTech Design team

Additional hard copies can be obtained from orders@intechopen.com

Holography – Basic Principles and Contemporary Applications, Edited by Emilia Mihaylova
p. cm.
ISBN 978-953-51-1117-7

For EU product safety concerns:
IN TECH d.o.o., Prolaz Marije Krucifikse Kozulić 3, 51000 Rijeka, Croatia,
info@intechopen.com or visit our website at intechopen.com.

Meet the editor

Emilia Mihaylova is Associate Professor of Physics at the Agricultural University of Plovdiv, Bulgaria. She received her Ph. D. from the Bulgarian Academy of Sciences. She has published more than 60 papers in leading international journals.
Current research interests of Emilia Mihaylova include holography, with focus on new holographic photopolymers for specific applications, digital holography with focus on microscopy and metrology, electronic speckle pattern interferometry and shearography, white light interferometry and profilometry.

Contents

Preface

Holography – Basic Principles and Contemporary Applications is a collection of fifteen chapters, describing the basic principles of holography and some recent innovative developments in the field. The book is divided into three sections. The first, Understanding Holography, presents the principles of hologram recording illustrated with practical examples. A comprehensive review of diffraction in volume gratings and holograms is also presented. The second section, Contemporary Holographic Applications, is concerned with advanced applications of holography including sensors, holographic gratings, white-light viewable holographic stereograms. The third section of the book Digital Holography is devoted to digital hologram coding and digital holographic microscopy.

The following paragraphs give a brief summary of contents.

Understanding Diffraction in Volume Gratings and Holograms presents two analytical methods for describing diffraction in loss-free volume holographic gratings: Kogelnik's model and the Parallel Stacked Mirrors (PSM) model. The overall conclusion is that for index modulations characteristic of modern display and optical element holograms, both Kogelnik's coupled wave theory and the PSM model provide a rather good description of diffraction in a volume grating.

Volume Transmission Hologram Gratings - Basic Properties, Energy Channelizing, Effect of Ambient Temperature and Humidity discusses properties and specific features of volume holograms. The authors present a study of the effect of ambient temperature and humidity on parameters of polymeric hologram gratings, produced in laboratory conditions on the base of silicate glass.

White Light Reconstructed Holograms describes some basic principles of recording holograms, including Denisyuk and Benton types. Some popular applications of white light reconstructed holograms are presented.

Research on Holographic Sensors and Novel Photopolymers at the Centre for Industrial and Engineering Optics reviews recent developments in holographic sensors technology at the Centre for Industrial and Engineering Optics (IEO) at Dublin Institute of Technology. The authors also report the development of a novel environmentally friendly holographic photopolymer. Diffraction efficiencies greater than 90% are achievable in 80μm layers at 1000 l/mm, and a refractive index modulation of 3.3x10-3 has been obtained.

Holographic Sensors for Detection of Components in Water Solutions reports the development of a method for manufacturing holographic sensors of different types. The authors demonstrate that holographic sensors can be used to determine the quality of water, acidity of media, ethanol concentration, metal ions concentration, and glucose concentration in blood serum.

Photopolymer Holographic Optical Elements for Application in Solar Energy Concentrators consists of two parts. The first reviews developments in the design and fabrication of solar concentrators utilising holographic optical elements. The second presents experimental results from the recording of simple focusing holographic optical elements in a photopolymer layer. The authors report that five gratings and five cylindrical lenses were successfully recorded in the same photopolymer layer.

Optically Accelerated Formation of One and Two-Dimensional Holographic Surface Relief Gratings on DR1/PMMA describes the fabrication of one and two-dimensional holographic surface relief gratings (SRGs) based on single or multiple exposure of the azobenzene copolymer to two and/or three-beam interference patterns. In this chapter, simple fabrication techniques based on two-beam and three-beam interference were theoretically studied and experimentally demonstrated as efficient methods for the creation of desired SRGs on azo-copolymer. In addition the authors propose to enhance the formation of SRGs, employing an incoherent ultraviolet or visible wavelength beam.

Holographic Printing of White-Light Viewable Holograms and Stereograms starts with a review of the research on the printing of holographic stereograms (HSs) followed by a survey of recent achievements in printing large-format full-color HSs. The next section is devoted to direct printing of a holographic fringe patterns on a photo-sensitive material. The authors describe the principle of a wavefront printer for production of white-light viewable computer-generated holograms. The chapter concludes with an outline of future trends in the holographic printing.

Microscopic Interferometry by Reflection Holography with Photorefractive Sillenite Crystals exploits Denisiuk reflection holography using anisotropic diffraction in sillenite crystals. The realization of this idea allows the construction of two types of simple and compact in-line interferometric microscopes.

Bifurcation Effects Generated with Holographic Rough Surfaces describes how interference between speckle patterns with controlled statistical parameters can be used for the generation of bifurcation effects.

Holography at the Nano Level with Visible Light Wavelengths presents a new method for recording nano-sized diffraction patterns of the observed objects. The authors show an application of the suggested approach to measure the topography of nano-sized sodium chloride crystals and spherical polystyrene particles.

Digital Hologram Coding presents a review of the coding techniques for digital holograms with the main emphasis on lossy coding techniques. The overall process of coding a digital holographic video and the whole architecture of the service system for digital holograms are also explained.

Applications of Holographic Microscopy in Life Sciences reviews the recent advances in the application of digital holographic microscopy to the study of biological specimens. The authors also describe the development of a digital holographic microscope at the Agricultural University of Plovdiv and report some of its life science applications.

Cells and holograms - Holograms and Digital Holographic Microscopy as a Tool to Study the Morphology of Living Cells utilizes digital holographic microscopy (DHM) to study the morphology of living, dividing and dying cells. Cell morphology studied by DHM can be very useful in toxicology, stem cell and cancer research.

Phase and Polarization Contrast Methods by Use of Digital Holographic Microscopy: Applications to Different Types of Biological Samples presents the application of Digital Polarization Holographic Microscopy for the study of linear dichroism and birefringence of transparent samples. The authors also report results from Digital Holographic Microscopy (DHM) analysis of different biological samples. A comparative study of DHM and bright-field optical microscopy in visualization and analysis of microscopic structures is presented and discussed.

I would like to thank all of the authors for making this book an absorbing read for a wide audience – everybody with an interest in holography will find a chapter or more to enjoy.

Associate Prof. Dr. Emilia Mihaylova
Agricultural University Plovdiv
Bulgaria

Section 1

Understanding Holography

Chapter 1

Understanding Diffraction in Volume Gratings and Holograms

Brotherton-Ratcliffe David

Additional information is available at the end of the chapter

http://dx.doi.org/10.5772/53413

1. Introduction

Kogelnik's Coupled wave theory [1], published in 1969, has provided an extremely successful approach to understanding diffraction in sinusoidal volume gratings and in providing analytic formulae for the calculation of diffractive efficiency. N-coupled wave theory [2] has extended Kogelnik's approach to provide a useful analytic model of diffraction in spatially multiplexed gratings and in monochromatic holograms.

A more recent and alternative approach to Kogelnik's coupled wave theory, known as the PSM model [3], short for "Parallel Stacked Mirrors", is based on a differential formulation of the process of Fresnel reflection occurring within the grating. This theory has the advantage of providing a particularly useful and more intuitively natural description of diffraction in the reflection volume grating. It also deals with the π-polarisation, which requires significantly greater work under Kogelnik's approach, in a simpler and more natural way.

Although the PSM model is itself a type of coupled-wave theory, it is nevertheless based on an alternative and distinct set of assumptions to standard coupled-wave theory. This in itself is extremely useful as it allows one to look at the problem of diffraction in volume gratings from two relatively separate perspectives. In some cases the PSM assumptions are clearly somewhat superior to Kogelnik's as evidenced by rigorous computational solutions of the Helmholtz equation. But this is not always the case and in various albeit rather extreme cases Kogelnik's theory can provide the superior estimate of diffractive efficiency.

The PSM model naturally treats polychromatic index modulation profiles. This is not to say that Kogelnik's formulism cannot be extended to treat the polychromatic case. Indeed Ning has demonstrated this [4]. But the mathematics and their meaning here is more transparent in the PSM case. Like standard coupled-wave theory, the PSM model can be generalised to an N-coupled wave theory, capable of describing spatially multiplexed gratings and holograms. Again the PSM model provides a simple and trivially transparent generalisation to the polychromatic spatially multiplexed grating allowing a very clear understanding of diffraction in the full-colour reflection volume hologram.

Despite the utility and analytic nature of both Kogelnik's coupled wave theory and the PSM model, a completely accurate description of diffraction in gratings can only be offered by a rigorous solution of the underlying wave equation. Moharam and Gaylord [5] first tackled this problem in 1989 and provided numerical solutions for both transmission and reflection gratings as index modulation increased. Glytis and Gaylord [6] extended this work to cover anistropic media and simple multiplexed gratings.

2. Kogelnik's coupled wave theory

Kogelnik's theory [1] assumes that only two plane waves propagate inside and outside a finite thickness grating. The Helmholtz equation is then used to calculate how a specific modulation in the dielectric permittivity intrinsically couples these waves. The approach has its origins in the field of acousto-optics. The first wave is assumed to be the illuminating reference wave and the second wave is the hologram's response or "signal" wave. The adoption of just two waves is made on the assumption that coupling to higher order modes will be negligible. There is no rigorous mathematical proof for this per se; we therefore look to the results of this two-wave theory to see whether they are sensible and consistent. In addition we shall review a rigorous formulation of the coupled wave equations in section 5 and here we shall see that for the kind of index modulations present in modern holography, the two-wave assumption is pretty good.

2.1. Derivation of the coupled wave equations

Assuming a time dependence of $\sim \exp(i\omega t)$ Maxwell's equations and Ohm's law can be used to write down the general wave equation for a dielectric in SI units:

$$\nabla \times (\nabla \times \boldsymbol{E}) - \gamma^2 \boldsymbol{E} = 0 \tag{1}$$

$$\text{where } \gamma^2 = i\omega\mu\sigma - \omega^2\mu\varepsilon \tag{2}$$

Here μ is the permeability of the medium, ε its permittivity and σ represents its electrical conductivity. Two important assumptions are now made. The first is that the grating is lossless so that $\sigma = 0$. The second is that the polarization of the two waves is perpendicular to the grating vector or $\boldsymbol{E} \cdot \nabla \varepsilon = 0$. This allows (1) to be simplified to the Helmholtz equation

$$\nabla^2 \boldsymbol{E} - \gamma^2 \boldsymbol{E} = 0 \tag{3}$$

The assumption of small conductivity means that our analysis is restricted to lossless phase holograms with no absorption. The assumption that $\boldsymbol{E}\cdot\nabla\varepsilon=0$ leads us to study the σ-polarisation.

2.1.1. One-dimensional grating

A one-dimensional grating extending from $x=0$ to $x=d$ is now assumed. The relative permittivity is also assumed to vary within the grating according to the following law:

$$\varepsilon_r=\varepsilon_{r0}+\varepsilon_{r1}\cos\boldsymbol{K}\cdot\boldsymbol{r} \tag{4}$$

The grating vector $\boldsymbol{K}$ is defined by its slope, ϕ and its pitch, Λ

$$\boldsymbol{K}=\frac{2\pi}{\Lambda}\begin{pmatrix}\cos\phi\\ \sin\phi\end{pmatrix} \tag{5}$$

We may write the γ parameter in (2) as

$$\gamma^2\sim-\beta^2-4\kappa\beta\cos\boldsymbol{K}\cdot\boldsymbol{r} \tag{6}$$

$$\text{with }\ \beta=\omega(\mu\varepsilon_0\varepsilon_{r0})^{1/2} \tag{7}$$

Here we have also introduced Kogelnik's coupling constant

$$\kappa\equiv\frac{1}{4}\frac{\varepsilon_{r1}}{\varepsilon_{r0}}\beta\sim\frac{1}{2}(\frac{n_1}{n_0})\beta \tag{8}$$

2.1.2. Solution at Bragg resonance

At Bragg resonance the signal and reference wavevectors are related by the condition

$$\boldsymbol{k}_i=\boldsymbol{k}_c-\boldsymbol{K} \tag{9}$$

The magnitude of both $\boldsymbol{k}_c$, the reference wavevector, and of $\boldsymbol{k}_i$, the signal wavevector is also exactly $\beta=2\pi n/\lambda_c$. Accordingly (6) may be written as

$$\gamma^2=-\beta^2-4\kappa\beta\cos(\boldsymbol{k}_c-\boldsymbol{k}_i)\cdot\boldsymbol{r} \tag{10}$$

$$\text{with}\boldsymbol{k}_c=\beta\begin{pmatrix}\cos\theta_c\\ \sin\theta_c\end{pmatrix} \quad ; \quad \boldsymbol{k}_i=\beta\begin{pmatrix}\cos\theta_i\\ \sin\theta_i\end{pmatrix}=\beta\begin{pmatrix}\cos\theta_c\\ \sin\theta_c\end{pmatrix}-\frac{2\pi}{\Lambda}\begin{pmatrix}\cos\phi\\ \sin\phi\end{pmatrix} \tag{11}$$

We now choose a very particular trial solution of the form

$$E_z=R(x)e^{-i\boldsymbol{k}_c\cdot\boldsymbol{r}}+S(x)e^{-i\boldsymbol{k}_i\cdot\boldsymbol{r}} \tag{12}$$

The first term represents the illumination or "reference" wave and the second term, the response or "signal" wave. Both are plane waves. Figure 1(a) illustrates how these waves propagate in a reflection grating and Figure 1(b) illustrates the corresponding case of the transmission hologram. Note that the complex functions R and S are functions of x only - even though the wave-vectors $\boldsymbol{k}_c$ and $\boldsymbol{k}_i$ both possess x and y components. The grating is assumed to be surrounded by a dielectric having the same permittivity and permeability as the average values within the grating so as not to unduly complicate the problem with boundary reflections. Within the external dielectric both R and S are constants. The choice of just using two waves in the calculation - clearly the absolute minimum - and with only a one-dimensional behaviour was inspired by the work of Bhatia and Noble [7] and Phariseau [8] in the field of acousto-optics.

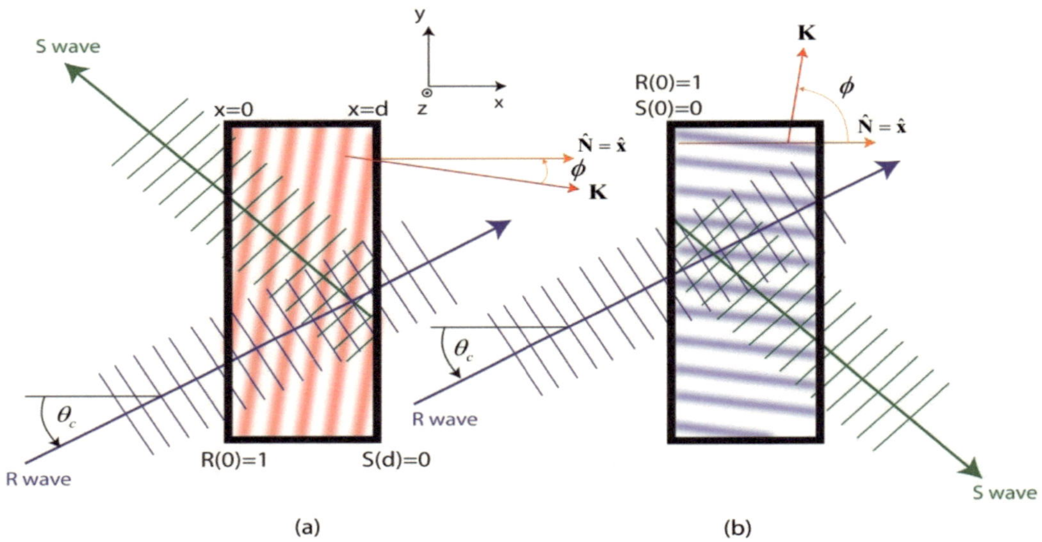

Figure 1. The "R" and "S" waves of Kogelnik's Coupled Wave Theory for the case of (a) a reflection grating and (b) a transmission grating.

Substituting (12) into (3) we obtain

$$e^{-i\mathbf{k}_c\cdot\mathbf{r}}\left\{\frac{d^2R}{dx^2}-2ik_{cx}\frac{dR}{dx}+2\beta\kappa S\right\}+e^{-i\mathbf{k}_i\cdot\mathbf{r}}\left\{\frac{d^2S}{dx^2}-2ik_{ix}\frac{dS}{dx}+2\beta\kappa R\right\}$$
$$+2\beta\kappa Se^{-i(2\mathbf{k}_i-\mathbf{k}_c)\cdot\mathbf{r}}+2\beta\kappa Re^{-i(2\mathbf{k}_c-\mathbf{k}_i)\cdot\mathbf{r}}=0 \tag{13}$$

Since only two waves are assumed to exist in the solution we must now disregard the third and fourth term of this expression on the pretext that they inherit only negligible energy from the primary modes. Next, second-order derivatives are neglected on the premise that R and S are slowly varying functions. Then (13) reduces to the two coupled first-order ordinary differential equations:

$$\frac{k_{cx}}{\beta}\frac{dR}{dx}+i\kappa S=0 \tag{14}$$

$$\frac{k_{ix}}{\beta}\frac{dS}{dx}+i\kappa R=0 \tag{15}$$

We can then use (14) and (15) to derive identical uncoupled second order differential equations for R and S:

$$\frac{d^2R}{dx^2}+(\kappa^2\sec\theta_c\sec\theta_i)R=0;\ \frac{d^2S}{dx^2}+(\kappa^2\sec\theta_c\sec\theta_i)S=0 \tag{16}$$

Here the x component of the Bragg condition tells us that

$$\sec\theta_i=\left\{\cos\theta_c-\frac{\lambda_c K_x}{2\pi n_0}\right\}^{-1} \tag{17}$$

And if the grating has been written using a reference and object wave of angles of incidence of respectively θ_r and θ_o and at a wavelength of λ_r then

$$K_x=\frac{2\pi n_0}{\lambda_r}(\cos\theta_r-\cos\theta_o) \tag{18}$$

2.1.3. Boundary conditions

It has been assumed that the R wave is the driving wave and that the S wave is the response or "signal" wave. Clearly, and without loss of generality, the input amplitude of the driving wave can be normalised to unity. Then different boundary conditions can be written down for transmission and reflection gratings. For transmission gratings the choice of normalisation means that $R(0)=1$. In addition we demand that $S(0)=0$ as the power of the transmitted signal wave must be zero at the input boundary as evidently no conversion has yet taken place at this point. For reflection holograms we demand once again that $R(0)=1$ but now the second boundary condition is $S(d)=0$. This is because the reflected response wave travels in the direction $x=d$ to $x=0$ and its amplitude must clearly be zero at the far boundary.

With these boundary conditions in hand we can now solve (14) - (15) for the transmission and reflection cases. For the transmission grating we obtain

$$\begin{aligned} R &= \cos\{\kappa x(\sec\theta_c \sec\theta_i)^{1/2}\} \\ S &= -i\sqrt{\frac{\cos\theta_c}{\cos\theta_i}}\sin\{\kappa x(\sec\theta_c \sec\theta_i)^{1/2}\} \end{aligned} \tag{19}$$

And for the reflection grating we have

$$\begin{aligned} R &= \operatorname{sech}\{\kappa d(\sec\theta_c \,|\sec\theta_i|\,)^{1/2}\}\cosh\{\kappa(d-x)(\sec\theta_c \,|\sec\theta_i|\,)^{1/2}\} \\ S &= -i\sqrt{\frac{\cos\theta_c}{|\cos\theta_i|}}\operatorname{sech}\{\kappa d(\sec\theta_c \,|\sec\theta_i|\,)^{1/2}\}\sinh\{\kappa(d-x)(\sec\theta_c \,|\sec\theta_i|\,)^{1/2}\} \end{aligned} \tag{20}$$

These are very simple solutions which paint a rather logical picture. For the transmission case we see that as the reference wave enters the grating it slowly donates power to the signal wave which grows with increasing x. When the argument of the cosine function in (19) reaches $\pi/2$ all of the power has been transferred to the S wave which is now at a maximum. As x increases further the waves change roles; the S wave now slowly donates power to a newly growing R wave. This process goes on until the waves exit the grating at $x=d$.

In the reflection case the behaviour is rather different. Here, as one might well expect, there is simply a slow transfer of energy from the reference driving wave to the reflected signal wave. If the emulsion is thin then the signal wave is weak and most of the energy escapes as a transmitted R wave. If the emulsion is thick on the other hand then the amplitudes of both waves become exponentially small as x increases and all the energy is transferred from the R wave to the reflected S wave.

2.1.4. Power balance and diffraction efficiency

Using Poynting's theorem it can be shown that power flowing along the x direction is given by

$$P = \cos\theta_c RR^* + \cos\theta_i SS^* \tag{21}$$

Multiplying (21) by respectively R^* and S^* and then adding these equations and taking the real part results in the equation

$$\frac{dP}{dx} = 0 \tag{22}$$

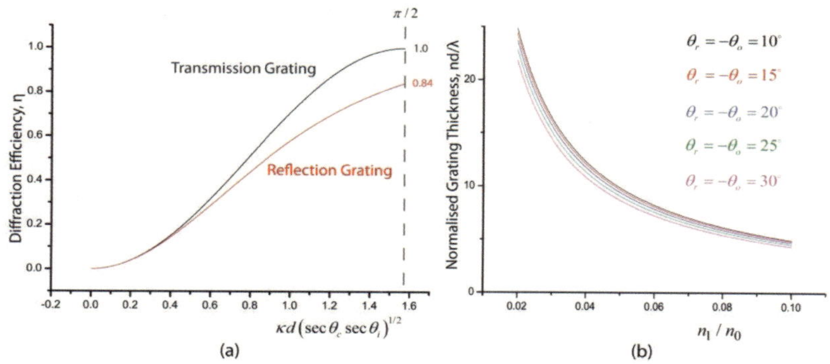

Figure 2. Perfect Bragg Compliance: (a) Diffractive replay efficiencies (σ-polarisation) of the transmission grating and the reflection grating versus the normalised grating thickness according to Kogelnik's coupled wave theory. (b) Optimal value of the normalised grating thickness (providing $\eta_T = 1$) at Bragg Resonance versus the modulation, n_1 / n_0 for the unslanted transmission grating recorded at various (internal) angles, $\theta_r = -\theta_o$.

This tells us that at each value of x the power in the R wave and in the S wave change but that the power in both waves taken together remains a constant. Now it is of particular interest to understand the efficiency of a holographic grating. With this in mind we define the diffraction efficiency of a grating illuminated by a reference wave of unit amplitude as

$$\eta = \frac{|\cos\theta_i|}{\cos\theta_c} SS^* \tag{23}$$

where S is evaluated on the exit boundary which for a reflection hologram will be at $x = 0$ and for a transmission hologram at $x = d$.

It is now simple to use the forms for R and S given in (19) and (20) to calculate the expected diffractive efficiencies for the transmission and reflection grating:

$$\eta_T = \sin^2\{\kappa d(\sec\theta_c \sec\theta_i)^{1/2}\} \tag{24}$$

$$\eta_R = \tanh^2\{\kappa d(\sec\theta_c |\sec\theta_i|)^{1/2}\} \tag{25}$$

Figure 2(a) shows this graphically for $0 \le \kappa d(\sec\theta_c |\sec\theta_i|)^{1/2} \le \pi/2$. Clearly for a small emulsion thickness or for a small permittivity modulation, the diffractive efficiencies of the reflection and transmission types of hologram are identical. As the parameter $\kappa d(\sec\theta_c \sec\theta_i)^{1/2}$ increases towards $\pi/2$ the transmission hologram becomes slightly more diffractive than its corresponding reflection counterpart. However, as we have remarked above, when $\kappa d(\sec\theta_c \sec\theta_i)^{1/2} > \pi/2$, the transmission hologram decreases in diffractive response whereas the corresponding reflection hologram continues to produce an increasing response. Figure 2(b) shows the relationship between the optimum grating thickness at which the diffractive response of the (un-slanted) transmission grating peaks and the grating modulation, n_1/n_0.

2.1.5. Behaviour away from Bragg resonance

To study the case of a small departure from the Bragg condition Kogelnik continues to use (9) but relaxes the condition that $|\boldsymbol{k}_i| = \beta$. This choice, which is certainly not unique, has the effect that the phases of the contributions of the signal wave from each Bragg plane no longer add up coherently and leads naturally to the definition of an "off-Bragg" parameter; this allows us in turn to easily quantify how much the Bragg condition is violated either in terms of wavelength or in terms of angle. Proceeding in this fashion, equation (14) remains the same but equation (15) generalizes to

$$\frac{k_{ix}}{\beta}\frac{dS}{dx} + i\left(\frac{\beta^2 - |k_i|^2}{2\beta}\right)S + i\kappa R = 0 \tag{26}$$

We then define the "Off-Bragg" or "dephasing" parameter

$$\vartheta = \frac{\beta^2 - |k_i|^2}{2\beta} = |\boldsymbol{K}|\cos(\phi - \theta_c) - \frac{|\boldsymbol{K}|^2}{2\beta} \tag{27}$$

where ϕ represents the slant angle between the grating normal and the grating vector (see Figure 1). The value of ϑ is determined by the angle of incidence on reconstruction (θ_c) and by the free-space wavelength of the illuminating light ($\lambda_c = 2\pi n_0/\beta$). Clearly when $\vartheta = 0$ the Bragg condition is satisfied and $|\boldsymbol{k}_i| = \beta$. We define the obliquity factors

$$\begin{aligned} k_{ix}/\beta &= (|k_{ix}|/\beta)\cos\theta_i \equiv c_S \\ k_{cx}/\beta &= \cos\theta_c \equiv c_R \end{aligned} \tag{28}$$

Then, as before, we can solve equations (14) and (26) to arrive at expressions for the diffractive efficiency[1]. For the transmission grating the result is

$$\eta_T = \frac{\sin^2\left(\frac{\kappa^2 d^2}{c_R c_S} + \frac{d^2\vartheta^2}{4c_S^2}\right)^{1/2}}{1 + \frac{\vartheta^2 c_R}{4c_S\kappa^2}} \tag{29}$$

1 Note that equation 23 is modified away from Bragg resonance in Kogelnik's theory to the more general form $\eta = \frac{|c_S|}{c_R} SS^*$

whereas for the reflection grating we have

$$\eta_R = \left\{ 1 + \frac{1 - \dfrac{\vartheta^2 c_R}{4|c_S|\kappa^2}}{\sinh^2\left(\dfrac{\kappa^2 d^2}{c_R|c_S|} - \dfrac{d^2\vartheta^2}{4{c_S}^2}\right)^{1/2}} \right\}^{-1} \tag{30}$$

Clearly for $\vartheta = 0$ these equations revert respectively to (24) and (25). Figures 3 (a) and (b) show the behaviour of (29) and (30) for several values of $\kappa d / (c_R \mid c_S \mid)^{1/2}$.

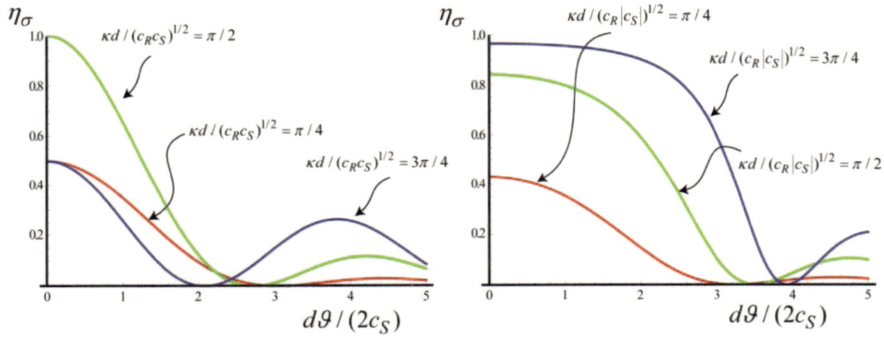

(a) (b)

Figure 3. (a) Diffraction Efficiency for the transmission grating according to Kogelnik's theory versus the normalised Off-Bragg Parameter, $d / (2c_S)$ for different values of $\kappa d / (c_R c_S)^{1/2}$. (b) Corresponding graph for the reflection grating.

We can understand better the parameter ϑ if we imagine having recorded the grating, which we are now seeking to play back, with an object beam at angle of incidence θ_o and with a reference beam at angle θ_r. The recording wavelength is λ_r and we assume that there is no emulsion shrinkage and no change in average emulsion index on recording the grating. Then the various wave-vectors can be written as

$$\boldsymbol{k}_r = \frac{2\pi n}{\lambda_r}\begin{pmatrix}\cos\theta_r \\ \sin\theta_r\end{pmatrix}; \boldsymbol{k}_o = \frac{2\pi n}{\lambda_r}\begin{pmatrix}\cos\theta_o \\ \sin\theta_o\end{pmatrix} \tag{31}$$

$$\boldsymbol{k}_c = \frac{2\pi n}{\lambda_c}\begin{pmatrix}\cos\theta_c \\ \sin\theta_c\end{pmatrix}; \boldsymbol{k}_i = \mid k_i \mid \begin{pmatrix}\cos\theta_i \\ \sin\theta_i\end{pmatrix} \tag{32}$$

Then (27) can be written as

$$\vartheta = \frac{2\pi n}{\lambda_r}\{\cos(\theta_r - \theta_c) - \cos(\theta_o - \theta_c)\} - \frac{2\pi n \lambda_c}{\lambda_r{}^2}\{1 - \cos(\theta_r - \theta_o)\} \tag{33}$$

This tells us how the parameter ϑ behaves when $\lambda_c \neq \lambda_r$ and when $\theta_c \neq \theta_r$. Direct substitution of (33) into (29) and (30) leads trivially to general expressions for the diffractive response of a lossless holographic grating recorded with parameters (θ_r, θ_o, λ_r) and replayed with (θ_c, λ_c). These expressions often provide an extremely useful computational estimation of the diffractive response of many modern holographic gratings.

2.1.6. Sensitivity to wavelength and replay angle

We can understand the replay angle and wavelength behaviour of the transmission and reflection gratings by an analysis of equations (29) and (30).

To this end we assume that the illumination wave on playback is of magnitude $|k_i| = 2\pi n / \lambda_r + \Delta\beta$ and that its angle of incidence is $\theta_c = \theta_r + \Delta\theta$. Then equations (9), (11) and (27) lead to the following simple expression which relates ϑ to $\Delta\theta_c$ and $\Delta\beta$

$$\vartheta = \frac{2\pi n}{\lambda_r}\Delta\theta \sin(\theta_r - \theta_o) + \Delta\beta\{1 - \cos(\theta_r - \theta_o)\} \tag{34}$$

We will now adopt a value of $\kappa d / \sqrt{c_R | c_S |} = \pi / 2$. You may recall that this gives us perfect conversion from the R wave to the S wave in the transmission grating when $\vartheta = 0$. It also corresponds to a diffractive efficiency for the reflection hologram of 0.84. We use (29) and (30) to calculate the value of the dephasing parameter ϑ which is required to bring the diffraction to its first zero. This is given by

$$\vartheta_T = \sqrt{3}\pi \frac{c_S}{d}; \vartheta_R = \sqrt{5}\pi \frac{| c_S |}{d} \tag{35}$$

We may then use (34) to show that for the un-slanted transmission grating[2],

$$\Delta\theta_T \sim \frac{\sqrt{3}}{2}\frac{\Lambda}{d} = \frac{\sqrt{3}}{4}\frac{\lambda}{dn}\csc\theta_r \tag{36}$$

$$\left(\frac{\Delta\lambda}{\lambda}\right)_T \sim \frac{\sqrt{3}}{2}\frac{\Lambda}{d}\cot\theta_r = \frac{\sqrt{3}}{4}\frac{\lambda}{dn}\cos\theta_r \csc^2\theta_r \tag{37}$$

and for the corresponding reflection grating,

2 Note that Kogelnik gives the following formulae for the FWHM: ; $.\Delta\theta_{FWHM} = \Lambda / d \; \Delta\lambda_{FWHM} = \cot\theta_c \cdot \Lambda / d$

$$\Delta\theta_R \sim \frac{\sqrt{5}}{2}\frac{\Lambda\cot\theta_r}{d} = \frac{\sqrt{5}}{4}\frac{\lambda}{dn}\csc\theta_r \tag{38}$$

$$\left(\frac{\Delta\lambda}{\lambda}\right)_R = \frac{\sqrt{5}}{2}\frac{\Lambda}{d} = \frac{\sqrt{5}}{4}\frac{\lambda\sec\theta_r}{dn} \tag{39}$$

This shows that a transmission grating is generally more selective in angle than a reflection grating: $\Delta\theta_R / \Delta\theta_T = \sqrt{5/3}$, independent of wavelength and angle! Similarly $\Delta\lambda_R / \Delta\lambda_T \sim \sqrt{5/3}\tan^2\theta_r$, which for small θ_r makes the reflection grating much more wavelength selective than the corresponding transmission case.

3. The PSM theory of gratings

The PSM model [3] offers an alternative method to Kogelnik's coupled wave theory for the analysis of diffraction in planar gratings. PSM stands for "Parallel Stacked Mirrors". As might be expected from this name, the theory models a holographic grating as an infinite stack of mirrors, each one parallel to the next. Each mirror is formed by a "jump" or discontinuity in the permittivity profile which constitutes the grating; the process of diffraction is then described entirely by Fresnel reflection. In many ways the PSM model can be thought of as a differential representation of the chain matrix approach of Abeles [9] as described by various authors [10,11] and which was derived from the ideas of Rouard[12]. These ideas, in turn, extend back to Darwin's 1914 work on X-ray diffraction [13]. Early attempts at an analytical formulation of diffraction in the planar grating in terms of Fresnel reflection are also due to Ludman [14] and Heifetz, Shen and Shariar [15].

3.1. The simplest model - The unslanted reflection grating at normal incidence

An unslanted holographic grating with the following index profile is assumed

$$n = n_0 + n_1\cos\left(\frac{4\pi n_0}{\lambda_r}y\right) = n_0 + \frac{n_1}{2}\left\{e^{\frac{4i\pi n_0}{\lambda_r}y} + e^{-\frac{4i\pi n_0}{\lambda_r}y}\right\} \tag{40}$$

Here, n_0 is the average index and n_1 is generally a small number representing the index modulation[3]. We can imagine that this grating was created by the interference of two counter propagating normal-incidence plane waves within a photosensitive material, each of wavelength λ_r.

Now we wish to understand the response of the grating to a plane reference wave of the form

3 Note that this is equivalent to the grating of (4) for zero slant - but note the change of coordinates.

$$R^{ext} = e^{i\beta y} \tag{41}$$

$$\text{where} \beta = \frac{2\pi n_0}{\lambda_c} \tag{42}$$

As before we shall assume that the grating is surrounded by a zone of constant index, n_0 to circumvent the complication of refraction/reflection at the grating interface. We start by modelling the grating of (40) by a series of many thin constant-index layers, N_0, N_1, N_2, ..., N_M, between each of which exists an index discontinuity (see Figure 4(a)). Across each such discontinuity we can derive the well-known Fresnel formulae [e.g.16] for the amplitude reflection and transmission coefficients from Maxwell's equations by demanding that the tangential components of the electric and magnetic fields be continuous. An illuminating plane wave will in general generate many mutually interfering reflections from each discontinuity. We therefore imagine two plane waves within the grating - the driving reference wave, $R(y)$ and a created signal wave, $S(y)$. Using the Fresnel formulae we may then write, for either the σ or the π-polarisation, the following relationship:

$$\begin{aligned} R_J &= 2e^{i\beta n\delta y/n_0}\left\{\frac{N_{J-1}}{N_J + N_{J-1}}\right\}R_{J-1} + e^{i\beta n\delta y/n_0}\left\{\frac{N_{J-1} - N_J}{N_J + N_{J-1}}\right\}S_J \\ S_J &= 2e^{i\beta n\delta y/n_0}\left\{\frac{N_{J+1}}{N_{J+1} + N_J}\right\}S_{J+1} + e^{i\beta n\delta y/n_0}\left\{\frac{N_{J+1} - N_J}{N_{J+1} + N_J}\right\}R_J \end{aligned} \tag{43}$$

Here the terms in brackets are just the Fresnel amplitude reflection and transmission coefficients and the exponential is a phase propagator which advances the phase of the R and S waves as they travel the distance δy between discontinuities. We now let

$$X_{J-1} = X_J - \frac{dX}{dy}\delta y - ... \tag{44}$$

and consider the limit $\delta y \to 0$. Further expanding the exponential terms as Taylor series and ignoring quadratic terms in δy we arrive at the differential counterpart to (43)

$$\begin{aligned} \frac{dR}{dy} &= \frac{R}{2}\left(2i\beta\frac{n}{n_0} - \frac{1}{n}\frac{dn}{dy}\right) - \frac{1}{2n}\frac{dn}{dy}S \\ \frac{dS}{dy} &= -\frac{S}{2}\left(\frac{1}{n}\frac{dn}{dy} + 2i\beta\frac{n}{n_0}\right) - \frac{1}{2n}\frac{dn}{dy}R \end{aligned} \tag{45}$$

These equations are an *exact* representation of Maxwell's equations for an arbitrary index profile, $n(y)$ - as letting $u(y) = R(y) - S(y)$ we see that they simply reduce to the Helmholtz equation

$$\frac{d^2u}{dy^2} + \frac{\beta^2 n^2}{n_0^2}u = 0 \tag{46}$$

and the conservation of energy

$$\frac{d}{dy}(nR^*R - nS^*S) = 0 \tag{47}$$

When $dn/dy=0$ equations (45) describe two counter propagating and non-interacting plane waves. A finite index gradient couples these waves.

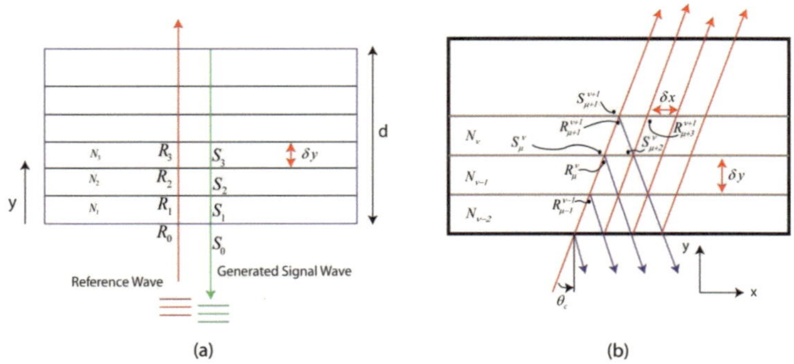

Figure 4. The PSM model of the unslanted reflection grating for (a) normal incidence and (b) for oblique incidence. In the case of normal incidence both the R and S fields have one index whereas for the case of oblique incidence the fields have two indices. In both cases the grating is modelled as a stack of dielectric layers of differing index.

We now make the transformation

$$R \to R'(y)e^{i\beta y}; S \to S'(y)e^{-i\beta y} \tag{48}$$

where the primed quantities are slowly varying compared to $e^{i\beta y}$. Since they are slowly-varying we can write

$$\langle R' \rangle \sim R; \langle S' \rangle \sim S \tag{49}$$

where the operator $\langle\rangle$ takes an average over several cycles of $e^{i\beta y}$. Substituting (48) in (45) and using (49) we then arrive at the following differential equations

$$\frac{dR}{dy} = -i\alpha\kappa S e^{2i\beta y(\alpha-1)}; \frac{dS}{dy} = i\alpha\kappa R e^{-2i\beta y(\alpha-1)} \tag{50}$$

$$\text{where}\alpha = \frac{\lambda_c}{\lambda_r} \tag{51}$$

which is just the ratio of the replay wavelength to the recording wavelength. Introducing the pseudo-field,

$$\hat{S} = Se^{2\beta iy(\alpha-1)} \tag{52}$$

these equations may now be written in the form of Kogelnik's equations for the normal-incidence sinusoidal grating

$$c_R \frac{dR}{dy} = -i\kappa\hat{S};\, c_S \frac{d\hat{S}}{dy} = -i\vartheta\hat{S} - i\kappa R \tag{53}$$

where Kogelnik's constant, κ is the same as defined previously in equation (8) but now the obliquity constants and off-Bragg parameter are a little different

$$c_R = \frac{1}{\alpha};\, c_S = -\frac{1}{\alpha};\, \vartheta = 2\frac{\beta}{\alpha}(1-\alpha) \tag{54}$$

For comparison, Kogelnik's coefficients are

$$c_R = 1;\, c_S = (2\alpha - 1);\, \vartheta = 2\alpha\beta(1-\alpha) \tag{55}$$

By imposing boundary conditions appropriate for the reflection hologram

$$R(y=0) = 1;\, \hat{S}(y=d) = 0 \tag{56}$$

where d is the grating thickness, equations (53) may be solved analytically. We can then define the diffraction efficiency for both the PSM and Kogelnik models as

$$\eta = \left| \frac{c_S}{c_R} \right| \hat{S}(0)\hat{S}^*(0) = \left\{ 1 - \frac{c_R c_S}{\kappa^2}\, {}^2 csh^2(d) \right\}^{-1} \tag{57}$$

$$\text{where}\ {}^2 = -\frac{\vartheta^2}{4c_S^2} - \frac{\kappa^2}{c_R c_S} \tag{58}$$

Note that we should ensure that

$$d = m\left(\frac{\pi}{2\alpha\beta}\right) \tag{59}$$

where m is a non-zero integer to prevent a discontinuity in index at $y = d$ (see [17] for a detailed discussion of the starting and ending conditions of a grating).

For cases of practical interest for display and optical element holography, substitution of (54) (the PSM coefficients) or (55) (Kogelnik's coefficients) into (57) / (58) yield very similar results. However one should note that the only approximation made in deriving the PSM equations, (53) - (54) and (57) has been that of equation (49). This is an assumption which one would reasonably expect to hold in most gratings of interest. Equation (57) in conjunction with (55) is of course exactly equivalent to (30) for the case of zero grating slant and normal incidence.

At Bragg resonance, when $\alpha = 1$, both the Kogelnik and PSM models reduce to

$$\eta = \tanh^2(\kappa d) \tag{60}$$

However the PSM model provides a useful insight into what is happening within the grating: multiple reflections of the reference wave simply synthesise the signal wave by classical Fresnel reflection and transmission at each infinitesimal discontinuity. This is a rigorous picture for the normal incidence unslanted reflection grating as equations (45) are an exact representation of Maxwell's equations. The fact that we explicitly need to introduce a "pseudo-field", $\hat{S}$ in order to get the PSM equations into the same form as Kogelnik's equations reminds us that indeed Kogelnik's signal wave is not the physical electric field of the signal wave for $\alpha \neq 1$. Kogelnik's theory models the dephasing away from Bragg resonance by letting the non-physical wave propagate differently to the physical signal wave. In the PSM analytical theory (53) - (54) the pseudo-field is also not the real electric field - but here transformations (49) and (52) make the relationship between the real and the pseudo-field perfectly clear.

3.2. The unslanted panchromatic reflection grating at normal incidence

One of the advantages of the PSM model is that it does not limit the grating to a sinusoidal form. This is an advantage over the simplest variants of standard coupled-wave theories including Kogelnik's.

We start by assuming a general index profile

$$\begin{aligned} n &= n_0 + n_1\cos(2\alpha_1\beta y) + n_2\cos(2\alpha_2\beta y) + \dots \\ &= n_0 + \frac{n_1}{2}\left\{e^{2i\beta\alpha_1 y} + e^{-2i\beta\alpha_1 y}\right\} + \frac{n_2}{2}\left\{e^{2i\beta\alpha_2 y} + e^{-2i\beta\alpha_2 y}\right\} + \dots \end{aligned} \tag{61}$$

Equations (45) then reduce to the following form

$$\begin{aligned} \frac{dR}{dy} &= -S\sum_{j=1}^{N} i\kappa_j\alpha_j e^{2i\beta y(\alpha_j - 1)} \\ \frac{dS}{dy} &= R\sum_{j=1}^{N} i\kappa_j\alpha_j e^{-2i\beta y(\alpha_j - 1)} \end{aligned} \tag{62}$$

Assuming that the individual gratings have very different spatial frequencies these equations then lead to a simple expression for the diffractive efficiency when the reference wave is in Bragg resonance with one or another of the multiplexed gratings:

$$\eta_j = \tanh^2(\kappa_j d) \tag{63}$$

$$\text{where}\kappa_j = \frac{n_j \pi}{\lambda_c} \tag{64}$$

In addition, in the region of the jth Bragg resonance, (62) leads to the approximate analytical form

$$\eta_j = \frac{\alpha_j^2 \kappa_j^2}{\beta^2 (1-\alpha_j)^2 + (\alpha_j^2 \kappa_j^2 - \beta^2 (1-\alpha_j)^2) coth^2 \left\{ d\sqrt{\alpha_j^2 \kappa_j^2 - \beta^2 (1-\alpha_j)^2} \right\}} \tag{65}$$

When the spatial frequencies of the different gratings are too close to one another, these relations break down. For many cases of interest however (63) to (65) provide a rather accurate picture of the normal-incidence unslanted polychromatic reflection phase grating. Indeed the following form can often be used to accurately describe an N-chromatic grating at normal incidence:

$$\eta = \sum_{j=1}^{N} \frac{\alpha_j^2 \kappa_j^2}{\beta^2 (1-\alpha_j)^2 + (\alpha_j^2 \kappa_j^2 - \beta^2 (1-\alpha_j)^2) coth^2 \left\{ d\sqrt{\alpha_j^2 \kappa_j^2 - \beta^2 (1-\alpha_j)^2} \right\}} \tag{66}$$

For example Diehl and George [18] have used a sparse Hill's matrix technique to computationally calculate the diffraction efficiency of a lossless trichromatic phase reflection grating at normal incidence. They used free-space recording wavelengths of 400nm, 500nm and 700nm. The grating thickness was 25 microns and the index parameters were taken as n_0=1.5, n_1=n_2=n_3=0.040533. Comparison of Equation (66) with Diehl and George's published graphical results shows very good agreement. In cases where the gratings are too close to one another in wavelength, equations (45) or (62) must, however, be solved numerically.

3.3. The unslanted reflection grating at oblique incidence

To treat the case of reference wave incidence at finite angle to the grating planes we must redraw Figure 4(a) using two-dimensional fields, *R* and *S* which we now endow with two indices instead of the previous single index (see Figure 4(b)). We shall make the approximation that the index modulation is small enough such that the rays of both the *R* and *S* waves are not deviated in angle. We shall however retain the proper Fresnel amplitude coefficients.

The Fresnel amplitude coefficients for the σ-polarisation may be written as

$$\begin{aligned} r_{k,k+1} &= \frac{N_{k+1}\sqrt{1-\frac{n_0^2}{N_{k+1}^2}\sin^2\theta_c} - N_k\sqrt{1-\frac{n_0^2}{N_k^2}\sin^2\theta_c}}{N_{k+1}\sqrt{1-\frac{n_0^2}{N_{k+1}^2}\sin^2\theta_c} + N_k\sqrt{1-\frac{n_0^2}{N_k^2}\sin^2\theta_c}} \\ t_{k,k+1} &= \frac{2N_k\sqrt{1-\frac{n_0^2}{N_k^2}\sin^2\theta_c}}{N_{k+1}\sqrt{1-\frac{n_0^2}{N_{k+1}^2}\sin^2\theta_c} + N_k\sqrt{1-\frac{n_0^2}{N_k^2}\sin^2\theta_c}} \end{aligned} \tag{67}$$

where r and t pertain respectively to reflection and transmission occurring at the index discontinuity between layers k and k+1. The R and S waves in the exterior medium of index n_0 are assumed to be plane waves of the form

$$R = e^{i(k_{cx}x + k_{cy}y)};\ S = S_0 e^{i(k_{ix}x + k_{iy}y)} \tag{68}$$

where S_0 is a constant. Within the grating we shall assume that R and S are functions of x and y. Using the normal rules of Fresnel reflection, the wave-vectors can be written explicitly as

$$\boldsymbol{k}_c = \beta\begin{pmatrix}\sin\theta_c \\ \cos\theta_c\end{pmatrix};\ \boldsymbol{k}_i = \beta\begin{pmatrix}\sin\theta_c \\ -\cos\theta_c\end{pmatrix} \tag{69}$$

where the angle θ_c is the angle of incidence of the R wave.

We can now use Figure 4 (b) to write down two expressions relating the discrete values of R and S within the grating. These are an equation for $R_{\mu+1}^{\nu+1}$

$$\begin{aligned} R_{\mu+1}^{\nu+1} = {} & e^{i\beta n(\sin\theta_c\delta x + \cos\theta_c\delta y)/n_0} R_\mu^\nu \left\{ \frac{2N_{\nu-1}\sqrt{1-\frac{n_0^2}{N_{\nu-1}^2}\sin^2\theta_c}}{N_{\nu-1}\sqrt{1-\frac{n_0^2}{N_{\nu-1}^2}\sin^2\theta_c} + N_\nu\sqrt{1-\frac{n_0^2}{N_\nu^2}\sin^2\theta_c}} \right\} \\ & + e^{i\beta n(\sin\theta_c\delta x + \cos\theta_c\delta y)/n_0} S_\mu^\nu \left\{ \frac{N_{\nu-1}\sqrt{1-\frac{n_0^2}{N_{\nu-1}^2}\sin^2\theta_c} - N_\nu\sqrt{1-\frac{n_0^2}{N_\nu^2}\sin^2\theta_c}}{N_{\nu-1}\sqrt{1-\frac{n_0^2}{N_{\nu-1}^2}\sin^2\theta_c} + N_\nu\sqrt{1-\frac{n_0^2}{N_\nu^2}\sin^2\theta_c}} \right\} \end{aligned} \tag{70}$$

and the corresponding equation for $S_{\mu+1}^{\nu-1}$

$$\begin{aligned} S_{\mu+1}^{\nu-1} = {} & e^{i\beta n(\sin\theta_c\delta x + \cos\theta_c\delta y)/n_0} S_\mu^\nu \left\{ \frac{2N_\nu\sqrt{1-\frac{n_0^2}{N_\nu^2}\sin^2\theta_c}}{N_{\nu-1}\sqrt{1-\frac{n_0^2}{N_{\nu-1}^2}\sin^2\theta_c} + N_\nu\sqrt{1-\frac{n_0^2}{N_\nu^2}\sin^2\theta_c}} \right\} \\ & + e^{i\beta n(\sin\theta_c\delta x + \cos\theta_c\delta y)/n_0} R_\mu^\nu \left\{ \frac{N_\nu\sqrt{1-\frac{n_0^2}{N_\nu^2}\sin^2\theta_c} - N_{\nu-1}\sqrt{1-\frac{n_0^2}{N_{\nu-1}^2}\sin^2\theta_c}}{N_{\nu-1}\sqrt{1-\frac{n_0^2}{N_{\nu-1}^2}\sin^2\theta_c} + N_\nu\sqrt{1-\frac{n_0^2}{N_\nu^2}\sin^2\theta_c}} \right\} \end{aligned} \tag{71}$$

Since we are assuming that δx and δy are small we can use Taylor expansions for the fields and index profile

$$R_{\mu+1}^{\nu+1} = R_\mu^\nu + \frac{\partial R_\mu^\nu}{\partial x}\delta x + \frac{\partial R_\mu^\nu}{\partial y}\delta y + \dots$$
$$S_{\mu+1}^{\nu-1} = S_\mu^\nu + \frac{\partial S_\mu^\nu}{\partial x}\delta x - \frac{\partial S_\mu^\nu}{\partial y}\delta y + \dots \tag{72}$$
$$N_{\nu-1} = N_\nu - \frac{\partial N_\nu}{\partial y}\delta y + \dots$$

The exponentials are also written using a Taylor expansion. Then using the following additional approximations

$$\sqrt{1 - \frac{n_0{}^2}{N_\nu{}^2}\sin^2\theta_c} = \sqrt{1 - \frac{a}{N_\nu{}^2}} \sim \cos\theta_c = b \tag{73}$$

$$\sqrt{1 - \frac{n_0{}^2}{N_{\nu-1}{}^2}\sin^2\theta_c} \sim b - \frac{\partial N_\nu}{\partial y}\frac{a\delta y}{bN_\nu^3} + O(\delta y^2) \tag{74}$$

$$\text{letting} R_\mu^\nu \to R; S_\mu^\nu \to S; N_\nu \to n \tag{75}$$

and taking the limit $\delta x,\ \delta y \to 0$, we arrive at partial differential equations for the $R$and S fields

$$\frac{\mathbf{k}_c}{\beta} \cdot \nabla R = \sin\theta_c \frac{\partial R}{\partial x} + \cos\theta_c \frac{\partial R}{\partial y} = \frac{R}{2}\left\{2i\beta - \frac{1}{n\cos\theta_c}\frac{\partial n}{\partial y}\right\} - \frac{S}{2n\cos\theta_c}\frac{\partial n}{\partial y} \tag{76}$$

$$\frac{\mathbf{k}_i}{\beta} \cdot \nabla S = \sin\theta_c \frac{\partial S}{\partial x} - \cos\theta_c \frac{\partial S}{\partial y} = \frac{S}{2}\left\{2i\beta + \frac{1}{n\cos\theta_c}\frac{\partial n}{\partial y}\right\} + \frac{R}{2n\cos\theta_c}\frac{\partial n}{\partial y} \tag{77}$$

Note the similarity of (76) and (77) to (45). Note also that if we set $\theta_c = 0$ then we retrieve (45) exactly. Equations (76) and (77) are the PSM equations for an unslanted reflection grating at oblique incidence for the σ-polarisation. Corresponding equations can be derived for the π-polarisation by consideration of the appropriate Fresnel reflection formulae [e.g.16]. These give

$$\frac{\mathbf{k}_c}{\beta} \cdot \nabla R = \sin\theta_c \frac{\partial R}{\partial x} + \cos\theta_c \frac{\partial R}{\partial y} = \frac{R}{2}\left\{2i\beta - \frac{1}{n}\frac{\cos 2\theta_c}{\cos\theta_c}\frac{\partial n}{\partial y}\right\} - \frac{S}{2n}\frac{\cos 2\theta_c}{\cos\theta_c}\frac{\partial n}{\partial y} \tag{78}$$

$$\frac{\mathbf{k}_i}{\beta} \cdot \nabla S = \sin\theta_c \frac{\partial S}{\partial x} - \cos\theta_c \frac{\partial S}{\partial y} = \frac{S}{2}\left\{2i\beta + \frac{1}{n}\frac{\cos 2\theta_c}{\cos\theta_c}\frac{\partial n}{\partial y}\right\} + \frac{R}{2n}\frac{\cos 2\theta_c}{\cos\theta_c}\frac{\partial n}{\partial y} \tag{79}$$

3.3.1. Simplification of the PSM equations to ODEs

The PSM equations may be simplified under boundary conditions corresponding to monochromatic illumination of the grating.

Let

$$R \to R(y)e^{i\beta\sin\theta_c x}; S \to S(y)e^{i\beta\sin\theta_c x} \tag{80}$$

Under this transformation equations (76) - (77) yield the following pair of ordinary differential equations

$$\begin{aligned} \cos\theta_c \frac{dR}{dy} &= \frac{R}{2}\left\{2i\beta\cos^2\theta_c - \frac{1}{n\cos\theta_c}\frac{dn}{dy}\right\} - \frac{S}{2}\left\{\frac{1}{n\cos\theta_c}\frac{dn}{dy}\right\} \\ -\cos\theta_c \frac{dS}{dy} &= \frac{S}{2}\left\{2i\beta\cos^2\theta_c + \frac{1}{n\cos\theta_c}\frac{dn}{dy}\right\} + \frac{R}{2}\left\{\frac{1}{n\cos\theta_c}\frac{dn}{dy}\right\} \end{aligned} \tag{81}$$

Similarly the π-polarisation equations yield

$$\begin{aligned} \cos\theta_c \frac{dR}{dy} &= \frac{R}{2}\left\{2i\beta\cos^2\theta_c - \frac{\cos2\theta_c}{n\cos\theta_c}\frac{dn}{dy}\right\} - \frac{S}{2}\left\{\frac{\cos2\theta_c}{n\cos\theta_c}\frac{dn}{dy}\right\} \\ -\cos\theta_c \frac{dS}{dy} &= \frac{S}{2}\left\{2i\beta\cos^2\theta_c + \frac{\cos2\theta_c}{n\cos\theta_c}\frac{dn}{dy}\right\} + \frac{R}{2}\left\{\frac{\cos2\theta_c}{n\cos\theta_c}\frac{dn}{dy}\right\} \end{aligned} \tag{82}$$

Equations (81) and (82) are approximate only because we have assumed an approximate form for the direction vector of the waves within the grating. We may however approach the problem differently and derive exact equations directly from (45). For example, in the case of the σ-polarisation, we use the optical invariant

$$\beta(y) \to \beta(y)\cos\theta(y) \tag{83}$$

$$\text{where}\beta(y) = \frac{\beta n(y)}{n_0} \tag{84}$$

Then using Snell's law

$$\frac{d\beta(y)}{dy}\sin\theta(y) + \beta(y)\frac{d\theta(y)}{dy}\cos\theta(y) = 0 \tag{85}$$

it is simple to see that (45) reduces to

$$\cos\theta\frac{dR}{dy}=\frac{R}{2}\left\{2i\beta\cos^2\theta-\frac{1}{\beta\cos\theta}\frac{d\beta}{dy}\right\}-\frac{S}{2}\left\{\frac{1}{\beta\cos\theta}\frac{d\beta}{dy}\right\}$$
$$-\cos\theta\frac{dS}{dy}=\frac{S}{2}\left\{2i\beta\cos^2\theta+\frac{1}{\beta\cos\theta}\frac{d\beta}{dy}\right\}+\frac{R}{2}\left\{\frac{1}{\beta\cos\theta}\frac{d\beta}{dy}\right\} \tag{86}$$

where θ is now a function of y throughout the grating. If we now replace (80) with the more general behaviour

$$R\to R(y)e^{i\beta(y)\sin\theta(y)x};S\to S(y)e^{i\beta(y)\sin\theta(y)x} \tag{87}$$

then (86) is seen to be an exact solution of the Helmholtz equation. Therefore the solution of (85) and (86) subject to the boundary conditions (56) and $\theta(0)=\theta_c$ constitute a rigorous solution of the Helmholtz equation. Note that this is independent of periodicity required by a Floquet solution. Since these equations are none other than a differential representation of the chain matrix method of thin films [11], it is simple to show that this implies that the chain matrix method is itself rigorous.

3.3.2. *Analytic solutions for sinusoidal gratings*

We start by defining an unslanted grating with the following index profile

$$n=n_0+n_1\cos(2\alpha\beta\cos\theta_r y)=n_0+\frac{n_1}{2}\left\{e^{2i\alpha\beta\cos\theta_r y}+e^{-2i\alpha\beta\cos\theta_r y}\right\} \tag{88}$$

where we imagine θ_r to be the recording angle of this grating. Then letting

$$R\to R(y)e^{i\beta\cos\theta_c y};S\to S(y)e^{-i\beta\cos\theta_c y} \tag{89}$$

and using (49), equations (81) reduce to

$$\begin{aligned}\cos\theta_c\frac{dR}{dy}&=-\frac{1}{2n}n_1 i\beta\alpha\frac{\cos\theta_r}{\cos\theta_c}\left\langle\left\{e^{2i\beta\alpha\cos\theta_r y}+...\right\}Se^{-2i\beta y\cos\theta_c}\right\rangle\\&=-\frac{n_1 i\beta(\alpha\cos\theta_r)}{2n\cos\theta_c}Se^{2i\beta y(\alpha\cos\theta_r-\cos\theta_c)}\\\cos\theta_c\frac{dS}{dy}&=\frac{1}{2n}n_1 i\beta\alpha\frac{\cos\theta_r}{\cos\theta_c}\left\langle\left\{e^{-2i\beta\alpha\cos\theta_r y}+...\right\}Re^{2i\beta y\cos\theta_c}\right\rangle\\&=\frac{n_1 i\beta(\alpha\cos\theta_r)}{2n\cos\theta_c}Re^{-2i\beta y(\alpha\cos\theta_r-\cos\theta_c)}\end{aligned} \tag{90}$$

As before we now define the pseudo-field

$$\hat{S} = S e^{2i\beta y(\alpha\cos\theta_r - \cos\theta_c)} \tag{91}$$

whereupon equations (90) reduce to the standard form of Kogelnik's equations

$$c_R \frac{dR}{dy} = -i\kappa \hat{S}; c_S \frac{d\hat{S}}{dy} = -i\vartheta \hat{S} - i\kappa R \tag{92}$$

The coefficients for the PSM model and for Kogelnik's model are as follows:

$$\begin{aligned} c_{R(PSM)} &= \frac{\cos^2\theta_c}{\alpha\cos\theta_r} \quad c_{R(KOG)} = \cos\theta_c \\ c_{S(PSM)} &= -\frac{\cos^2\theta_c}{\alpha\cos\theta_r} \quad c_{S(KOG)} = \cos\theta_c - 2\alpha\cos\theta_r \\ \vartheta_{PSM} &= 2\beta\left(1 - \frac{\cos\theta_c}{\alpha\cos\theta_r}\right)\cos^2\theta_c \quad \vartheta_{KOG} = 2\alpha\beta\cos\theta_r(\cos\theta_c - \alpha\cos\theta_r) \end{aligned} \tag{93}$$

Equations (92) in conjunction with the boundary conditions (56) then lead, as before to the general analytic expression for the diffractive efficiency of the unslanted reflection grating:

$$\eta_\sigma = \frac{|c_S|}{c_R}\hat{S}(0)\hat{S}^*(0) = \frac{\kappa^2\sinh^2(d)}{\kappa^2\sinh^2(d) - c_R c_S{}^2} \tag{94}$$

$$\text{where}\ ^2 = -\frac{\vartheta^2}{4c_S{}^2} - \frac{\kappa^2}{c_R c_S} \tag{95}$$

Note that at Bragg resonance both the PSM theory and Kogelnik's theory reduce to the well-known formula

$$\eta_\sigma = \tanh^2(\kappa d \sec\theta_c) \tag{96}$$

The π-polarisation may be treated in an exactly analogous way, leading to the following pair of ordinary differential equations for R and $\hat{S}$:

$$c_R \frac{dR}{dy} = -i\kappa\cos 2\theta_c \hat{S}; c_S \frac{d\hat{S}}{dy} = -i\vartheta \hat{S} - i\kappa\cos 2\theta_c R \tag{97}$$

These are just Kogelnik's equations with a modified κ parameter. The PSM model distinguishes the π and σ-polarisations in exactly the same manner as Kogelnik's theory does! In both theories, in the case of the unslanted grating, Kogelnik's constant is simply transformed according to the rule

$$|\kappa| \rightarrow |\kappa\cos 2\theta_c| \tag{98}$$

The practical predictions of Kogelnik's model and the PSM model are very close for gratings of interest to display and optical element holography. This is largely due to the effect of Snell's law which acts to steepen the angle of incidence in most situations. But at very high angles of incidence within the grating, larger differences appear.

3.3.3. Multi-colour gratings

A multi-colour unslanted reflection grating can be modelled in the following way

$$\begin{aligned} n &= n_0 + n_1\cos(2\alpha_1\beta\cos\theta_{r1}y) + n_2\cos(2\alpha_2\beta\cos\theta_{r2}y) + \ldots \\ &= n_0 + \frac{1}{2}\sum_{j=1}^{N} n_j\left\{e^{2i\alpha_j\beta\cos\theta_{rj}y} + e^{-2i\alpha_j\beta\cos\theta_{rj}y}\right\} \end{aligned} \tag{99}$$

In this case the PSM σ-polarisation equations yield

$$\begin{aligned} \cos\theta_c\frac{dR}{dy} &= -S\sum_{j=1}^{N} i\kappa_j\alpha_j\frac{\cos\theta_{rj}}{\cos\theta_c}e^{2i\beta y(\alpha_j\cos\theta_{rj}-\cos\theta_c)} \\ \cos\theta_c\frac{dS}{dy} &= R\sum_{j=1}^{N} i\kappa_j\alpha_j\frac{\cos\theta_{rj}}{\cos\theta_c}e^{-2i\beta y(\alpha_j\cos\theta_{rj}-\cos\theta_c)} \end{aligned} \tag{100}$$

$$\text{where}\kappa_j = \frac{n_j\pi}{\lambda_c} \tag{101}$$

Once again, if we assume that the individual gratings have very different spatial frequencies, then these equations lead to a simple expression for the diffractive efficiency when the reference wave is in Bragg resonance with one or another of the multiplexed gratings:

$$\eta_{PSM/\sigma_j} = \tanh^2(\kappa_j d\sec\theta_c) \tag{102}$$

The corresponding result for the π-polarisation is

$$\eta_{PSM/\pi_j} = \tanh^2(\kappa_j d\sec\theta_c\cos 2\theta_c) \tag{103}$$

In the region of the jth Bragg resonance, (100) leads to the approximate analytical form[4]

$$\eta_{\sigma j} = \frac{\kappa_{\sigma j}{}^2\sinh^2(d_{\sigma j})}{\kappa_{\sigma j}{}^2\sinh^2(d_{\sigma j}) - c_R c_{S\sigma j}{}^2} \tag{104}$$

---

4 Note that the ${}^2_{\sigma j} = -\frac{\vartheta_{\sigma j}^2}{4c_S{}^2} - \frac{\kappa_j{}^2}{c_R c_S}$ and $\vartheta_{\sigma j} = 2\beta(1 - \frac{\cos\theta_c}{\alpha_j\cos\theta_r})\cos^2\theta_c$

Again, as long as there is sufficient difference in the spatial frequencies of each grating we can add each response to give an convenient analytical expression for the total diffraction efficiency:

$$\eta_\sigma = \sum_{j=1}^{N} \frac{\kappa_{\sigma j}{}^2 \sinh^2(d_{\sigma j})}{\kappa_{\sigma j}{}^2 \sinh^2(d_{\sigma j}) - c_R c_S \sigma_j{}^2} \tag{105}$$

In cases where the individual gratings are too close to one another in wavelength or where small amplitude interaction effects between gratings are to be described, equations (100) must be solved numerically.

3.4. The slanted reflection grating at oblique incidence

We may use the PSM equations for the unslanted grating to derive corresponding equations for the general slanted grating. To do this we define rotated Cartesian coordinates (x', y') which are related to the un-primed Cartesian system by

$$\begin{pmatrix} x' \\ y' \end{pmatrix} = \begin{pmatrix} \cos\psi & -\sin\psi \\ \sin\psi & \cos\psi \end{pmatrix} \begin{pmatrix} x \\ y \end{pmatrix} \tag{106}$$

In the un-primed frame we have

$$\boldsymbol{k}_c = \beta \begin{pmatrix} \sin\theta_c \\ \cos\theta_c \end{pmatrix}; \boldsymbol{k}_i = \beta \begin{pmatrix} \sin\theta_c \\ -\cos\theta_c \end{pmatrix} \tag{107}$$

whereas in the primed frame we have

$$\boldsymbol{k}'_c = \beta \begin{pmatrix} \sin(\theta_c - \psi) \\ \cos(\theta_c - \psi) \end{pmatrix}; \boldsymbol{k}'_i = \beta \begin{pmatrix} \sin(\theta_c + \psi) \\ -\cos(\theta_c + \psi) \end{pmatrix} \tag{108}$$

Derivatives in the primed system are related to those in the un-primed system by Leibnitz's chain rule

$$\begin{aligned} \frac{\partial}{\partial x} &= \frac{\partial x'}{\partial x}\frac{\partial}{\partial x'} + \frac{\partial y'}{\partial x}\frac{\partial}{\partial y'} = \cos\psi \frac{\partial}{\partial x'} + \sin\psi \frac{\partial}{\partial y'} \\ \frac{\partial}{\partial y} &= \frac{\partial y'}{\partial y}\frac{\partial}{\partial y'} + \frac{\partial x'}{\partial y}\frac{\partial}{\partial x'} = -\sin\psi \frac{\partial}{\partial x'} + \cos\psi \frac{\partial}{\partial y'} \end{aligned} \tag{109}$$

The PSM equations for the σ-polarisation may therefore be written as

$$\frac{\boldsymbol{k}'_c}{\beta} \cdot \nabla' R = \frac{\partial R}{\partial x'} \sin(\theta_c - \psi) + \frac{\partial R}{\partial y'} \cos(\theta_c - \psi) = \frac{R}{2}\left\{2i\beta - \frac{1}{n\cos\theta_c}\frac{\partial n}{\partial y}\right\} - \frac{S}{2n\cos\theta_c}\frac{\partial n}{\partial y} \tag{110}$$

and

$$\frac{\boldsymbol{k}'_i}{\beta}\cdot\nabla' S=\frac{\partial S}{\partial x'}\sin(\theta_c+\psi)-\frac{\partial S}{\partial y'}\cos(\theta_c+\psi)=\frac{S}{2}\left\{2i\beta+\frac{1}{n\cos\theta_c}\frac{\partial n}{\partial y}\right\}+\frac{R}{2n\cos\theta_c}\frac{\partial n}{\partial y} \qquad (111)$$

Note that we have kept the un-primed frame on the RHS on purpose as in this system the index profile is one dimensional and so much easier to evaluate.

3.4.1. Analytic solutions for sinusoidal gratings

To study the single colour grating we use the unslanted index profile (88) in the un-primed frame leading to the following profile in the primed frame

$$\begin{aligned} n&=n_0+n_1\cos(2\alpha\beta\cos\theta_r\{\sin\psi x'-\cos\psi y'\})\\ &=n_0+\frac{n_1}{2}\left\{e^{2i\beta\alpha\cos\theta_r\hat{\boldsymbol{K}}.\boldsymbol{r}'}+e^{-2i\beta\alpha\cos\theta_r\hat{\boldsymbol{K}}.\boldsymbol{r}'}\right\}\end{aligned} \qquad (112)$$

Letting

$$R\to \mathrm{R}e^{i\beta\{\sin(\theta_c-\psi)x'+\cos(\theta_c-\psi)y'\}};S\to Se^{i\beta\{\sin(\theta_c+\psi)x'-\cos(\theta_c+\psi)y'\}} \qquad (113)$$

Equations (110) and (111) then become

$$\begin{aligned} &\sin(\theta_c-\psi)\frac{\partial R}{\partial x'}+\cos(\theta_c-\psi)\frac{\partial R}{\partial y'}\\ &=-\frac{S}{2}\left\{\frac{1}{n\cos\theta_c}\frac{\partial n}{\partial y}\right\}e^{i\beta\{[\sin(\theta_c+\psi)-\sin(\theta_c-\psi)]x'-[\cos(\theta_c-\psi)+\cos(\theta_c+\psi)]y'\}}\\ &=-\frac{S}{2}\left\langle\left\{\frac{1}{n_0\cos\theta_c}\frac{\partial}{\partial y}\frac{n_1}{2}\left\{e^{2i\beta\alpha(\cos\theta_r)y}+e^{-2i\beta\alpha(\cos\theta_r)y}\right\}\right\}e^{2i\beta\cos\theta_c\{[\sin\psi]x'-[\cos\psi]y'\}}\right\rangle\\ &=-\frac{i\beta n_1}{2n_0}\alpha\frac{\cos\theta_r}{\cos\theta_c}Se^{2i\beta(\alpha\cos\theta_r-\cos\theta_c)(y'\cos\psi-x'\sin\psi)}\end{aligned} \qquad (114)$$

$$\text{and}\sin(\theta_c+\psi)\frac{\partial S}{\partial x'}-\cos(\theta_c+\psi)\frac{\partial S}{\partial y'}=-\frac{i\beta n_1}{2n_0}\alpha\frac{\cos\theta_r}{\cos\theta_c}Re^{-2i\beta(\alpha\cos\theta_r-\cos\theta_c)(y'\cos\psi-x'\sin\psi)} \qquad (115)$$

Next we make the transformation

$$\hat{S}=S(y')e^{2i\beta(\alpha\cos\theta_r-\cos\theta_c)(y'\cos\psi-x'\sin\psi)};\hat{R}=R(y') \qquad (116)$$

whereupon once again the PSM equations reduce to a simple pair of ordinary differential equations of the form of Kogelnik's equations, (92) with coefficients

http://dx.doi.org/10.5772/53413

$$c_{R(PSM)}=\frac{\cos\theta_c\cos(\theta_c-\psi)}{\alpha\cos\theta_r};c_{S(PSM)}=-\frac{\cos\theta_c\cos(\theta_c+\psi)}{\alpha\cos\theta_r};\vartheta_{PSM}=2\beta(1-\frac{\cos\theta_c}{\alpha\cos\theta_r})\cos^2\theta_c \quad (117)$$

For comparison, Kogelnik's coefficients are

$$c_{R(KOG)}=\cos(\theta_c-\psi);c_{S(KOG)}=\cos(\theta_c-\psi)-2\alpha\cos\theta_r\cos\psi;\vartheta_{KOG}=2\alpha\beta\cos\theta_r(\cos\theta_c-\alpha\cos\theta_r) \quad (118)$$

With the usual reflective boundary conditions $\hat{R}(0)=1$ and $\hat{S}(d)=0$ we can then use the standard formula to describe the diffraction efficiency of the slanted reflection grating:

$$\eta_\sigma=\frac{|c_S|}{c_R}\hat{S}(0)\hat{S}^*(0)=\frac{\kappa^2\sinh^2(d)}{\kappa^2\sinh^2(d)-c_Rc_S{}^2} \quad (119)$$

$$\text{where}{}^2=-\frac{\vartheta^2}{4c_S{}^2}-\frac{\kappa^2}{c_Rc_S} \quad (120)$$

Substitution of either (117) or (118) into (119) gives the required expression for the diffractive efficiency in either the Kogelnik or PSM model. When $\psi=0$, $\eta_{PSM/\sigma}$ reduces to the un-slanted formula which was derived in section 3.3.2. In the case of finite slant and Bragg resonance (where $\cos\theta_c=\alpha\cos\theta_r$) we have

$$\eta_{PSM/\sigma}=\tanh^2(d\kappa\sqrt{\sec(\theta_c-\psi)\sec(\theta_c+\psi)}) \quad (121)$$

which is identical to Kogelnik's solution. Note that the behaviour of the π-polarisation is simply described by making the transformation (98) in all formulae of interest. The PSM model for the slanted grating under either the σ or π polarisations gives expressions very similar to Kogelnik's theory. For most gratings of practical interest to display and optical element holography, the two theories produce predictions which are extremely close.

3.4.2. Polychromatic gratings

As before the formulae (102) - (105) with coefficients (117) give useful expressions for the diffractive efficiency of the general polychromatic slanted reflection grating at oblique incidence.

3.5. Slanted transmission gratings at oblique incidence

The PSM model can be applied to transmission gratings by simply using the appropriate boundary conditions to solve the PSM equations in a rotated frame. We use the transmission boundary conditions

$$R(0)=1;S(0)=0 \quad (122)$$

3.2. Energy channelizing in the volume transmission phase hologram grating

Diffraction of an intensity-uniform monochromatic plane wave by a volume hologram grating structure finds an adequate description in the coupled wave theory (Kogelnik, 1969). Consider propagation of radiation in a "strong" ($\varphi_1 >> \pi/2$) transmission phase hologram grating, recorded symmetrically, under Bragg incidence of reconstruction radiation as shown in Fig. 3.

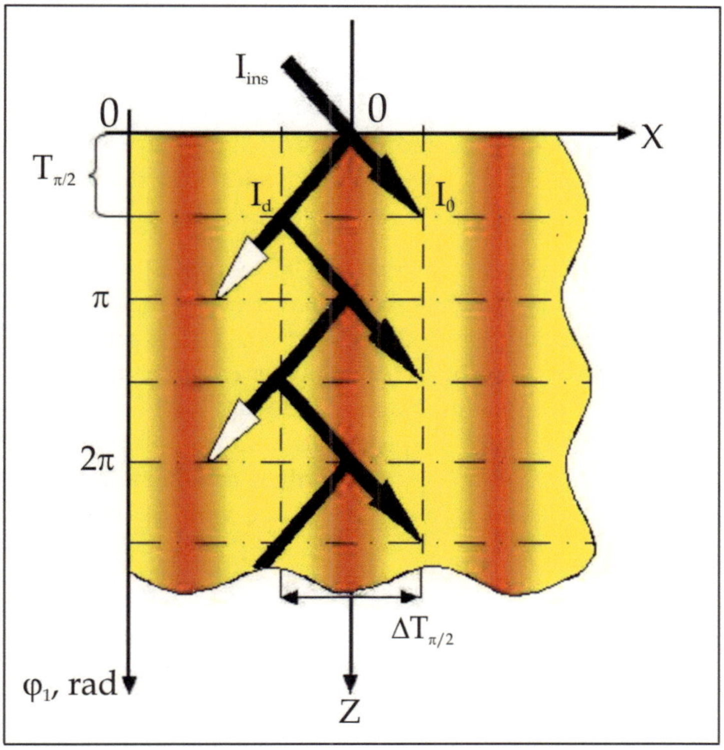

Figure 3. Process of radiation propagation in a "strong" transmission phase hologram grating, recorded symmetrically, under Bragg incidence reconstruction radiation: dot-and-dash lines are hologram planes that correspond to the values $\varphi_1 = k\pi/2$, where k = 1, 2, 3...; $\Delta x_{\pi/2}$ is the cross-section of the channel of radiation energy propagation; $T_{\pi/2}$ is the thickness of hologram layer with $\varphi_1 = \pi/2$.

Of special importance during reconstruction of a "strong" volume hologram grating are the hologram areas, where function $\eta(\varphi_1)$ has extremums (in Fig. 3 the extremum planes appear as dot-and-dash lines) – these are the hologram planes that correspond to the values of phase modulation amplitude of diffracted radiation, $\varphi_1 = k\pi/2$, where k = 1, 2, 3.... In accordance with the concepts of the coupled wave theory, the vector of the radiation propagation in a hologram changes its direction in each extremum plane of function $\eta(\varphi_1)$. The geometrical dimensions of the radiation propagation channel in a hologram are clearly seen to be bounded and less than size $\Delta x_{\pi/2}$, as shown on the diagram in Fig. 3: $\Delta x_{\pi/2}$ is found in extremum plane of function $\eta(\varphi_1)$ with k = 1, where $\varphi_1 = \pi/2$; the thickness of the hologram layer is denoted as $T_{\pi/2}$.

to solve equations (92) with coefficients (117) which at Bragg resonance result in the standard formula given by Kogelnik's theory.

$$\eta_{\sigma T/PSM} = \sin^2(\kappa d / \sqrt{c_R c_S}) = \sin^2(\kappa d / \sqrt{-\cos(\theta_c - \psi)\cos(\theta_c + \psi)}) \tag{123}$$

4. Theory of the spatially-multiplexed reflection grating

Both Kogelnik's Coupled wave model and the PSM model can be extended to model diffraction from spatially multiplexed gratings of the form [19]

$$\begin{aligned} n &= n_0 + \sum_{\mu=1}^{N} n_\mu \cos(2\alpha\beta\cos\theta_{r\mu}\{\sin\psi_\mu x' - \cos\psi_\mu y'\}) \\ &= n_0 + \sum_{\mu=1}^{N} \frac{n_\mu}{2}\left\{e^{iK_\mu . r'} + e^{-iK_\mu . r'}\right\} \end{aligned} \tag{124}$$

In PSM this is done by considering the Fresnel reflections from N grating planes, each having a slant ψ_μ, and assuming that cross-reflections between grating planes do not add up to a significant amplitude. This leads to the N-PSM equations for the spatially multiplexed monochromatic grating

$$\frac{\partial R}{\partial y'} = -i\sum_{\mu=1}^{N} \frac{\kappa_\mu}{c_{R\mu}} \hat{S}_\mu ; c_{S\mu} \frac{\partial \hat{S}_\mu}{\partial y'} = -i\vartheta_\mu \hat{S}_\mu - i\kappa_\mu R \tag{125}$$

where for the σ-polarisation

$$c_{R\mu} = \frac{\cos\theta_{c\mu}\cos(\theta_{c\mu} - \psi_\mu)}{\alpha\cos\theta_{r\mu}} ; c_{S\mu} = -\frac{\cos\theta_{c\mu}\cos(\theta_{c\mu} + \psi_\mu)}{\alpha\cos\theta_{r\mu}} ; \vartheta_\mu = 2\beta(1 - \frac{\cos\theta_{c\mu}}{\alpha\cos\theta_{r\mu}})\cos^2\theta_{c\mu} \tag{126}$$

and where

$$\left.\begin{aligned} \theta_{c\mu} - \psi_\mu = \Phi_c ; \theta_{c\mu} + \psi_\mu = -\Phi_{i\mu} \\ \theta_{r\mu} - \psi_\mu = \Phi_r ; \theta_{r\mu} + \psi_\mu = -\Phi_{o\mu} \end{aligned}\right\} \forall\, \mu \le N \tag{127}$$

Here the θ variables indicate incidence angles with respect to the respective grating plane normals and the Φ variables indicate incidence angles with respect to the physical normal of the grating. These equations may be solved using the boundary conditions appropriate for a reflection multiplexed grating - i.e.

$$R(0) = 1; \hat{S}_\mu(d) = 0 \,\forall\, \mu \le N \tag{128}$$

At Bragg resonance $c_{R\mu}$ becomes a constant

$$c_R = c_{R\mu} = \frac{\cos\theta_{c\mu}\cos(\theta_{c\mu} - \psi_\mu)}{\alpha_\mu \cos\theta_{r\mu}} = \cos\Phi_c \tag{129}$$

and (125) then gives the following expression for the diffractive efficiency of the μth grating:

$$\eta_\mu \equiv \frac{1}{c_R} \mid c_{s\mu} \mid \hat{S}_\mu(0)\hat{S}_\mu{}^*(0) = \frac{1}{c_{s\mu}} \frac{\kappa_\mu^2}{\sum\limits_{k=1}^{N} \frac{\kappa_k^2}{c_{sk}}} \tanh^2\left\{ d\sqrt{-\frac{1}{c_R}\sum_{k=1}^{N}\frac{\kappa_k^2}{c_{sk}}} \right\} \tag{130}$$

The total diffraction efficiency of the entire multiplexed grating is likewise found by summing the diffractive response from each grating:

$$\eta \equiv \sum_{\mu=1}^{N} \eta_\mu = \tanh^2\left\{ d\sqrt{\frac{1}{\cos\Phi_c}\sum_{k=1}^{N}\frac{\kappa_k^2}{\cos\Phi_{ik}}} \right\} \tag{131}$$

Here Φ_c is the incidence angle of the replay reference wave and Φ_{ik} is the incidence angle of the kth signal wave. These results are identical to the expressions obtained from an extension of Kogelnik's theory - the N-coupled wave theory of Solymar and Cooke [2]. At Bragg resonance the N-PSM model of the multiplexed grating therefore gives an identical description to the corresponding N-coupled wave theory just as the simple PSM theory gives an identical description at Bragg resonance to Kogelnik's theory. Away from Bragg resonance however, the predictions of the two models will be somewhat different.

N-PSM can be extended to the polychromatic case in which case (130) generalises to

$$\eta_{mj} \equiv \frac{1}{c_{sj}} \frac{\kappa_{mj}^2}{\sum\limits_{k=1}^{N} \frac{\kappa_{mk}^2}{c_{sk}}} \tanh^2\left\{ d\sqrt{-\frac{1}{c_R}\sum_{k=1}^{N}\frac{\kappa_{mk}^2}{c_{sk}}} \right\} \tag{132}$$

In the limit that $N \to \infty$ the above results also lead to formulae for the diffractive efficiency of the lossless polychromatic reflection hologram

$$\begin{gathered} \eta_m(\Phi_c, \Phi_i) = \frac{\kappa_m^2(\Phi_i)}{L_m \cos\Phi_i} \tanh^2\left\{ d\sqrt{\frac{L_m}{\cos\Phi_c}} \right\} \\ \eta_m = \frac{1}{\Delta\Phi}\int \frac{\kappa_m^2(\Phi')}{L_m \cos\Phi'} \tanh^2\left\{ d\sqrt{\frac{L_m}{\cos\Phi_c}} \right\} d\Phi' = \tanh^2\left\{ d\sqrt{\frac{L_m}{\cos\Phi_c}} \right\} \end{gathered} \tag{133}$$

$$\text{where} L_m = \frac{1}{\Delta\Phi}\int \frac{\kappa_m^2(\Phi)}{\cos\Phi} d\Phi \tag{134}$$

and where Φ is the replay image angle and $\Delta\Phi$ is the total reconstructed image angle range.

5. Rigorous coupled wave theory

Moharam and Gaylord [5] first showed how coupled wave theory could be formulated without approximation. This led to a computational algorithm which could be used to solve the wave equation exactly. Although earlier approaches such as the Modal method [20] were also rigorous they involved the solution of a trancendental equation for which a general unique algorithm could not be defined. This contrasted to the simple Eigen formulation of Maraham and Gaylord. Here we provide a derivation of rigorous coupled wave theory for the more complicated spatially multiplexed case. For brevity we shall limit discussions to the σ-polarisation for which the Helmholtz equation may be written

$$\frac{\partial^2 u}{\partial x^2}+\frac{\partial^2 u}{\partial y^2}-\gamma^2 u=0 \tag{135}$$

where u is the transverse (z) electric field and the parameter

$$\gamma^2=-\beta^2-2\beta\sum_{\mu=1}^{N}\kappa_\mu\left\{e^{iK_\mu\cdot r}+e^{-iK_\mu\cdot r}\right\} \tag{136}$$

defines the multiplexed grating[5]. We consider the case of illumination of the grating by a wave of the form

$$u(y<0)=e^{i(k_x x+k_y y)} \tag{137}$$

$$\text{where}\begin{array}{l} k_x=\beta\sin(\theta_{c\mu}-\psi_\mu) \\ k_y=\beta\cos(\theta_{c\mu}-\psi_\mu) \end{array}\forall\,\mu \tag{138}$$

In both the front region ($y<0$) and the rear region ($y<d$) the average index is assumed to be n_0. Now the Helmholtz field, $u(x,\ y)$ may be consistently expanded in the following way

$$\begin{aligned} u(x,\ y)&=\sum_{l_1=-\infty}^{\infty}\sum_{l_2=-\infty}^{\infty}\sum_{l_3=-\infty}^{\infty}\ldots u_{l_1l_2l_3\ldots}(y)e^{i(k_x+l_1K_{1x}+l_2K_{2x}+\ldots)x} \\ &=\sum_{l_1=-\infty}^{\infty}\sum_{l_2=-\infty}^{\infty}\sum_{l_3=-\infty}^{\infty}\ldots u_{l_1l_2l_3\ldots}(y)e^{ik_x x}\prod_{\sigma=1}^{N}e^{il_\sigma K_{\sigma x}x} \end{aligned} \tag{139}$$

5 This is just the same as (124)

This expression may be substituted into (135) and(136). On taking the Fourier transform and applying orthogonality we then arrive at the following rigorous coupled wave equations:

$$\left\{(k_x+\sum_{\sigma=1}^{N} l_\sigma K_{\sigma x})^2-\beta^2\right\}u_{l_1 l_2 l_3 \ldots l_N}(y)-\frac{\partial^2 u_{l_1 l_2 l_3 \ldots l_N}}{\partial y^2}(y)$$
$$=2\beta\sum_{\sigma=1}^{N}\kappa_\sigma\left\{u_{l_1 l_2 l_3 \ldots (l_\sigma-1)\ldots l_N}(y)e^{iK_{\sigma y}y}+u_{l_1 l_2 l_3 \ldots (l_\sigma+1)\ldots l_N}(y)e^{-iK_{\sigma y}y}\right\} \tag{140}$$

Note that for the case of the simple sinusoidal grating, the transformation

$$u_l(y)=\hat{u}_l(y)e^{i(k_y+lK_y)y} \tag{141}$$

reduces (140) to the more usual form

$$\frac{\partial^2 \hat{u}_l(y)}{\partial y^2}+2i(k_y+lK_y)\frac{\partial \hat{u}_l(y)}{\partial y}=\left\{(k_x+lK_x)^2+(k_y+lK_y)^2-\beta^2\right\}\hat{u}_l(y)-2\beta\kappa\left\{\hat{u}_{l-1}(y)+\hat{u}_{l+1}(y)\right\} \tag{142}$$

5.1. Boundary conditions

In the zones in front of and behind the grating where $\kappa_\sigma=0$ equations (140) reduce to the simpler constant index equations:

$$\left\{(k_x+l_1K_{1x}+l_2K_{2x}+\ldots)^2-\beta^2\right\}u_{l_1 l_2 l_3 \ldots}(y)-\frac{\partial^2 u_{l_1 l_2 l_3 \ldots}}{\partial y^2}(y)=0 \tag{143}$$

These equations define which l modes can propagate in the exterior regions. They have simple solutions of the form

$$u_{l_1 l_2}=Ae^{i\sqrt{\{\beta^2-(k_x+l_1K_{1x}+l_2K_{2x})^2\}}y}+Be^{-i\sqrt{\{\beta^2-(k_x+l_1K_{1x}+l_2K_{2x})^2\}}y} \tag{144}$$

where the square roots are real for un-damped propagation[6]. Accordingly we may deduce that the form of the front solution comprising the illumination wave and any reflected modes must be of the form

$$u(x,\ y)=e^{ik_x x}e^{i\sqrt{\beta^2-k_x^2}y}+\sum_{l_1=-\infty}^{\infty}\sum_{l_2=-\infty}^{\infty}\sum_{l_3=-\infty}^{\infty}\ldots u_{1 l_1 l_2 l_3 \ldots}e^{-i\sqrt{\{\beta^2-(k_x+l_1K_{1x}+l_2K_{2x}+\ldots)^2\}}y}e^{i(k_x+l_1K_{1x}+l_2K_{2x}+\ldots)x} \tag{145}$$

---

6 Note that there are modes which propagate inside the grating but which show damped propagation outside.

Likewise the rear solution comprising all transmitted modes must be of the form

$$u(x, y) = \sum_{l_1=-\infty}^{\infty} \sum_{l_2=-\infty}^{\infty} \sum_{l_3=-\infty}^{\infty} \ldots u_{3 l_1 l_2 l_3 \ldots} e^{i\sqrt{\{\beta^2 - (k_x + l_1 K_{1x} + l_2 K_{2x} + \ldots)^2\}}\, y} e^{i(k_x + l_1 K_{1x} + l_2 K_{2x} + \ldots)x} \tag{146}$$

By demanding continuity of the tangential electric field and the tangential magnetic field at the boundaries $y=0$ and $y=d$ we may now use these expressions to define the boundary conditions required for a solution of (135) within the multiplexed grating. At the front surface these are

$$\begin{aligned} i\sqrt{\beta^2 - k_x^2}(2 - u_{000\ldots}(0)) &= \left.\frac{du_{000\ldots}}{dy}\right|_{y=0} \\ -i\sqrt{\beta^2 - (k_x + l_1 K_{1x} + l_2 K_{2x} + \ldots)^2}\, u_{l_1 l_2 l_3 \ldots}(0) &= \left.\frac{du_{l_1 l_2 l_3 \ldots}}{dy}\right|_{y=0} \end{aligned} \tag{147}$$

And at the rear surface they take the form

$$i\sqrt{\beta^2 - (k_x + l_1 K_{1x} + l_2 K_{2x} +)^2}\, u_{l_1 l_2 l_3 \ldots}(d) = \left.\frac{du_{l_1 l_2 l_3 \ldots}}{dy}\right|_{y=d} \tag{148}$$

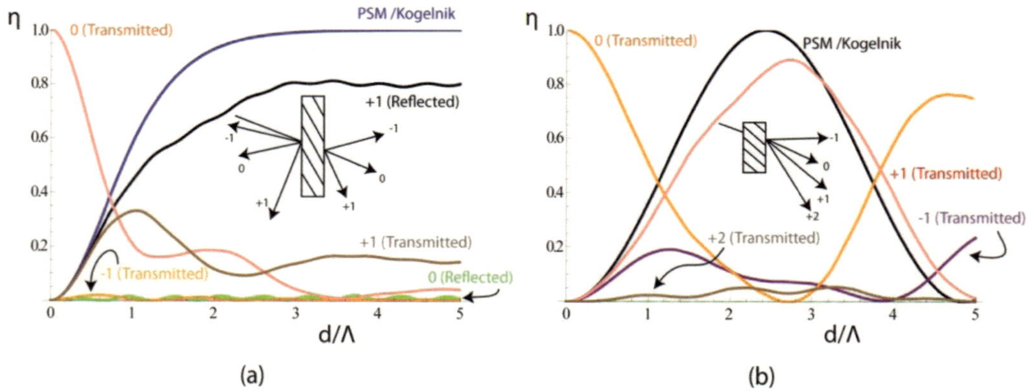

Figure 5. Diffraction Efficiency versus normalised grating thickness according to rigorous coupled wave theory and compared to the PSM and Kogelnik theories at Bragg resonance for (a) the simple reflection grating (n0=1.5, n1/n0=0.331/2, $\theta_c=\theta_r=50°$, $\psi=30°$, $\lambda_c=\lambda_r=532nm$) and (b) the simple transmission grating (n0=1.5, n_1/n_0=0.121/2, $\theta_c=\theta_r=80°$, $\psi=60°$, $\lambda_c=\lambda_r=532nm$).

The modes available for external (undamped) propagation are calculated using the condition

$$\beta^2 > (k_x + l_1 K_{1x} + l_2 K_{2x} + \ldots)^2 \tag{149}$$

Moharam and Gaylord [5] solved the single grating equations (142) using a state-space formulation in which solutions are obtainable through the eigenvalues and eigenvectors of an easily defined coefficient matrix. But one can also solve the more general equations (140), subject to the boundary conditions (147) and (148), using simple Runge-Kutta integration. This is a practical method as long as the number of component gratings within the multiplexed grating is relatively small. Diffraction efficiencies of the various modes are defined as

$$\eta_{l_1 l_2 l_3 \dots} = \frac{\sqrt{\beta^2 - (k_x + l_1 K_{1x} + l_2 K_{2x} + l_3 K_{3x} + \dots)^2}}{k_y} u_{l_1 l_2 l_3 \dots} u_{l_1 l_2 l_3 \dots}{}^* \tag{150}$$

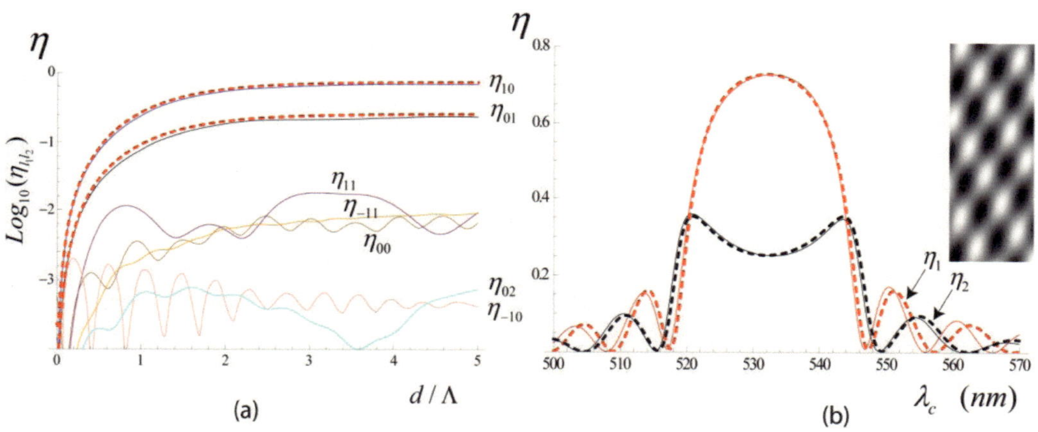

Figure 6. (a) Diffractive Efficiency, η_σ versus normalised grating thickness, d / Λ as predicted by the N-PSM model and by a rigorous coupled wave calculation (RCW) for the case of a twin multiplexed (duplex) reflection grating at Bragg resonance (grating shown in inset photo). The grating is replayed using light of 532nm at an incidence angle of $\Phi_c = 30°$. The grating index modulation of each of the component twin gratings in the duplex has been taken to be $n_1 = 0.2$. The dotted lines indicate the S_1 and S_2 modes of the N-PSM model and the full lines indicate the modes of the RCW calculation. The most prominent RCW modes are the 01 and 10 modes which correspond to the S_1 and S_2modes in N-PSM. The duplex grating has been recorded with a reference beam angle of $\Phi_c = 30°$and with a wavelength of 532nm. One grating in the duplex has a slope of $\psi_1 = 20°$ and the other has a slope of $\psi_2 = -20°$. Note that Λ refers to the larger of the two grating periods. (b) Diffractive Efficiency, η_σ versus replay wavelength, λ_c as predicted by the N-PSM model and by a RCW calculation for the same duplex grating as used in (a) at and away from Bragg resonance. The grating is again illuminated at its recording angle of $\Phi_c = 30°$. A grating index modulation of $n_1 = 0.03$ for each component grating is assumed and a grating thickness of $d = 7\mu m$ is used. The dotted lines indicate the S_1 and S_2 modes of the N-PSM model and the full lines indicate the corresponding 10 and 01 modes of the rigorous coupled wave calculation. In both (a) and (b) the average index inside and outside the grating is $n_0 = 1.5$.

where the fields in this equation are defined either at the front boundary in the case of reflected modes or at the rear boundary in the case of transmitted modes. Note that we are treating the lossless case here and so the sum of all transmitted and reflected efficiencies totals to unity[7].

6. Comparison of PSM and Kogelnik's theory with rigorous CW theory

Equations (140), subject to the boundary conditions (147) and (148) can be solved using either Runge-Kutta integration or through the eigen-method referred to above. This permits the rigorous calculation of the diffraction efficiencies of all modes which are produced by a general grating. Fig.5 shows an example for a simple reflection grating and a simple transmission grating at Bragg Resonance[8]. In the case of the reflection grating a very high index modulation has been assumed. Nevertheless the PSM/Kogelnik estimation is still only 20% out and it is clear that most of the dynamics of the grating is associated with the +1 reflected mode as both PSM and Kogelnik's coupled wave theories assume. In the case of the transmission hologram, a relatively high index modulation is assumed and also a large incidence angle with respect to the grating planes. Here we see again only a small departure from the PSM/Kogelnik estimation but also the presence of the +2 mode.

Fig.6 compares the N-PSM theory with the rigorous equations (140) for the case of a reflection duplex grating formed by the sequential recording of two simple reflection gratings of different slant. The first plot shows the on-Bragg behaviour at high index modulation where evidently good agreement is seen between the two "+1" rigorous modes and the two signal waves in N-PSM despite many other waves being present at much smaller amplitude. The second plot shows the off-Bragg behaviour of the duplex grating at a typical index modulation where excellent agreement is seen between N-PSM and the rigorous calculation.

In general, for the type of index modulations encountered typically in display and optical element holography, the Kogelnik and PSM theories produce fairly accurate estimations of diffractive efficiencies. For multiplexed gratings and for holograms, N-PSM and N-Coupled wave theory similarly produce usefully accurate estimations.

7. Discussion

In this chapter we have presented two analytic methods to describe diffraction in loss-free volume holographic gratings. These are Kogelnik's model and the PSM model. We have shown briefly how the PSM model can be extended to describe spatially multiplexed gratings and holograms. At Bragg resonance the N-PSM model is in exact agreement here with the extension of Kogelnik's model which is known as N-coupled wave theory. Away from Bragg resonance Kogelnik's model and the PSM model give slightly different predictions. But the differences are rather small. This is the same situation when one compares the N-PSM theory with N-coupled wave theory.

We have briefly discussed rigorous coupled wave analysis. Here we have seen that even at high values of index modulation diffraction in the simple reflection grating is controlled

7 In the case of the front reflected 000... mode one uses $\eta_{000...} = \frac{\sqrt{\beta^2 - k_x^2}}{k_y}(u_{000...} - 1)(u_{000...} - 1)^*$.

8 Note that at Bragg resonance the PSM and Kogelnik models give the same predictions.

predominantly by the "+1" mode. In the simple transmission grating, higher order modes such as the "+2" can become significant if index modulation and incidence angle with respect to the grating planes is high. However the overall conclusion is that for index modulations characteristic of modern display and optical element holography both Kogelnik's coupled wave theory and the PSM model provide a rather good description of diffraction in the volume grating. And this is particularly so in the reflection case where Snell's law conspires to reduce the incidence angles and where RCW analysis shows that the dynamics are controlled really by the "+1" mode alone. RCW analysis also shows that this picture extends to the case of the multiplexed grating - with the implication that it should also apply to holograms.

Finally we should point out that all the theories presented here can be extended to cover more complex cases such as the presence of loss and anisotropy.

Author details

Brotherton-Ratcliffe David

Geola Technologies Ltd, UK

References

[1] H. Kogelnik, "Coupled Wave Theory for Thick Hologram Gratings", Bell Syst. Tech. J. 48, 2909-47 (1969).

[2] D.J. Cooke and L. Solymar, "Comparison of Two-Wave Geometrical Optics and N-Wave Theories for Volume Phase Holograms", J.Opt.Soc.Am.70, 1631 (1980).

[3] Brotherton-Ratcliffe, D. "A treatment of the general volume holographic grating as an array of parallel stacked mirrors," *J. Mod. Optic* 59, 1113–1132 (2012).

[4] X. Ning,"Analysis of multiplexed-reflection holograting," J.Opt.Soc.Am. A7, 1436–1440 (1990).

[5] M.G.Moharam and T.K.Gaylord, "Rigorous Coupled Wave Analysis of Planar Grating Diffraction", JOSA, 71, Issue 7, 811-818 (1981).

[6] E.N. Glytis and T.K. Gaylord, "Rigorous 3D Coupled Wave Diffraction Analysis of Multiple Superposed Graings in Ansiotropic Media", Applied Optics, 28, 12, 2401-2421 (1989).

[7] A. B. Bhatia and W. J. Noble, "Diffraction of light by ultrasonic waves," *Proc. Roy. Soc.* A220, 356-385 (1953).

[8] P. Phariseau, "On the diffraction of light by supersonic waves," *Proc. Ind. Acad. Sci.* 44A 165-170 (1956).

[9] F. Abeles, "Recherches sur la propagation des ondes électromagnétiques sinusoïdales dans les milieux stratifiés. Application aux couches minces," Ann. Phys. (Paris) 5, 596–640 (1950).

[10] R. Jacobsson, "Light reflection from films of continuously varying refractive index," *Progress in Optics*, E. Wolf, ed. North-Holland, Amsterdam, Vol. 5, Chap. 5, pp. 247–286. (1966).

[11] O.S.Heavens,"Optical Properties of Thin Films", Reports on Progress in Physics, XXIII, (1960).

[12] M. P. Rouard, "Etudes des propriétés optiques des lames métalliques très minces," Ann. Phys. (Paris) Ser. II 7, 291–384 (1937).

[13] C.G. Darwin, "The Theory of X-Ray Reflection", Phil.Mag.27, 315-333 (1914).

[14] J.E. Ludman," Approximate bandwidth and diffraction efficiency in thick holograms" Am. J. Phys., 50, 244, (1982).

[15] A. Heifetz, J.T. Shen and M.S. Shariar, "A simple method for Bragg diffraction in volume holographic gratings", Am. J. Phys. 77 No. 7, 623-628 (2009).

[16] R. Guenther, "Modern Optics", John Wiley & sons, ISBN 0-471-60538-7 (1990).

[17] M. G. Moharam and T. K. Gaylord, "Chain-matrix analysis of arbitrary-thickness dielectric reflection gratings," J. Opt. Soc.Am. 72, 187–190 (1982).

[18] D.W. Diehl and N.George, "Analysis of Multitone Holographic Interference Filters by Use of a Sparse Hill Matrix Method," Appl. Opt. 43, 88-96 (2004).

[19] Brotherton-Ratcliffe, D. "Analytical treatment of the polychromatic spatially multiplexed volume holographic Grating," *Appl. Opt.* 51, 7188–7199 (2012).

[20] R. S. Chu and J. A. Kong, "Modal theory of spatially periodic media," IEEE Trans. Microwave Theory Tech. MTT-25,18-24 (1977).

Chapter 2

Volume Transmission Hologram Gratings — Basic Properties, Energy Channelizing, Effect of Ambient Temperature and Humidity

O.V. Andreeva, Yu.L. Korzinin and B.G. Manukhin

Additional information is available at the end of the chapter

http://dx.doi.org/10.5772/54253

1. Introduction

Volume holograms of thickness on order of 1 mm are of great interest from the viewpoint of experimental research base in the field of three-dimensional holography and provision for practical applications of holography, which are related to creation of elements and devices with properties unrealizable by traditional optical methods.

The field of research into volume holograms is at its development stage: inception and generation of theoretical methods to describe the properties of volume holograms, and recording media to produce the latter, experimental techniques to study the properties of high-selectivity volume holograms and materials for their recording.

The present paper offers the authors' view of such an important problem as classification of volume holograms, which has currently no generally accepted clear-cut principles and terminology; discussion of parameters of volume recording media that have been developed in S.I. Vavilov State Optical Institute, Russia, and show principal directions in the field of design of volume recording media for holography; description of the results of the authors' experiments to study the impact of ambient temperature and humidity on parameters of polymeric hologram gratings.

Special attention is paid to examining the special features of transmission hologram gratings with high values of phase modulation amplitudes; the experimental results are given to confirm the presence of the energy channelizing effect by so-called "strong" transmission holograms.

The described experiments used the volume recording media manufactured in laboratory conditions on the base of silicate glass (photo-thermo-refractive glass) and polymer (material "Difphen" with phenanthrenequinone in polymethylmethacrylate). The issues, assessments and recommendations in question are dealt with on the basis of many years of the authors' work with volume media for holography.

2. Classification of volume holograms

2.1. Hologram gratings and holograms of complex wave fields

The hologram classification used in literature proceeds according to a number of distinctive signs that include recording conditions, reconstruction conditions, hologram application, specific features of recording media, radiation sources, and so on. The present work concentrates on such distinctive signs as the interference pattern (IP) structure, defined by spatial parameters of interacting waves, the recording medium geometry, and the relationship between them. From this viewpoint, one distinguishes, first of all, hologram gratings and holograms of complex wave fields.

To record a hologram grating, two coherent monochromatic plane waves are used, and the hologram structure represents a grating formed by some recording medium parameter, its change being due to spatial variations of the radiation intensity in the IP under recording (Fig. 1a, b).

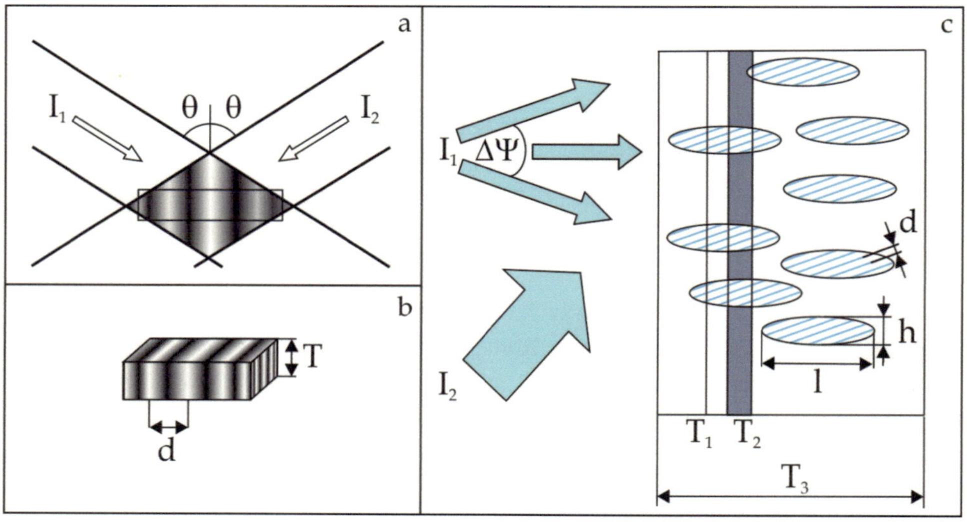

Figure 1. a, b – recording process and structure of hologram gratings: a – formation of interference pattern by interaction of two plane waves I_1 and I_2; b – hologram grating, where the spatial distribution of the light field intensity was transformed into variation of the absorption index of the recording medium (T is the hologram thickness, d is the IP period, 2θ is the angle between interfering beams); c – recording of holograms of complex wave fields: I_1 is the object wave with the angular spectrum half-width Δψ; I_2 is the reference plane wave; d is the characteristic period of the cross-modulation structure; l, h is the characteristic speckle dimensions; T_1, T_2, T_3, is the recording medium thickness corresponding to different types of hologram.

A hologram grating is described with certain value of IP period, d, (or spatial frequency, $\nu = 1/d$), IP orientation with respect to recording medium boundaries, magnitude, localization, and spatial distribution of the hologram modulation amplitude. A hologram grating is the simplest hologram type, useful for practical applications. Such parameters as spatial resolution of the recording material, amplitude of modulation of optical constants in a hologram can be found exactly only for hologram gratings with certain period (spatial frequency).

The coupled wave theory describes the properties of hologram gratings (Kogelnik, 1969), which enables estimation of hologram parameters taking into account of properties of an actual recording medium.

The relationship between the period of optical parameter variation in a hologram (d) and the hologram thickness (T) determines the hologram type that is connected with important hologram properties – selectivity and the number of diffractive orders. At $T/d \rightarrow 0$, a hologram regarded as two-dimensional, at $T/d \rightarrow \infty$ – three-dimensional. As a theoretical criterion of degree of dimensionality, holography uses Klein's parameter $Q = 2\pi\lambda T/(nd^2)$ (Kogelnik, 1969), where λ is the radiation wavelength, T is the hologram thickness, n is the average refractive index of a hologram, d is the spatial period of a hologram. Klein's parameter is applicable only to describe hologram gratings that are classified as follows:

- two-dimensional, 2D, thin gratings: $Q \ll 1$.
- three-dimensional, volume gratings: $Q > 10$.

When complex wave fields composed by superposition of a set of plane components is used to record holograms, the hologram structure becomes more complicated and contains cross-modulation and intermodulation structures. Hologram cross-modulation structure is generated by interference of object and reference waves. In contrast, the intermodulation structure is generated by mutual interference of plane components of either the object wave or reference wave.

Fig. 1c shows schematically the hologram structure at interaction of a complex wave field (object wave, I_1) and a plane reference wave (I_2). The object wave has a bounded angular spectrum, $\Delta\psi$. In this case, the interference pattern generated by a set of the plane components of the object wave forms a speckle pattern (speckles are illuminated areas separated by dark regions). The speckle shape is elongated in the direction of the wave propagation (see Fig. 1c), since a speckle is $l \sim 1/(\Delta\psi)^2$ long and $h \sim 1/\Delta\psi$ wide. The hologram cross-modulation structure in the case can be schematically represented with isophase surfaces crossing the speckles, their section in the plane of drawing being schematically represented with lines with directions coincident with IP intensity maximums and orientated along the bisectrix of the angle between the reference beam and the central direction of the object beam.

Depending on the thickness of the recording medium, one can distinguish the following three hologram types as to the degree of dimensionality and use the corresponding analytical description to examine their properties.

1. 2D hologram (thin hologram): thickness of the medium (T_1) is substantially less than the characteristic dimensions of elements of hologram cross-modulation and intermodulation structures ($T_1 << d, l, h$). Theory – Fresnel-Kirchhoff Integral.
2. Thick film (layer) hologram (Zeldovich et al., 1986): thickness of the medium (T_2) is significantly greater than the characteristic period of cross-modulation structure, but substantially less than the characteristic dimensions of hologram intermodulation structure ($d < T_2 < l, h$). Theory – Local Kogelnick's theory.
3. Volume hologram: thickness of the medium (T_3) is significantly greater than the characteristic dimensions of elements of hologram cross-modulation and intermodulation structures ($T_3 >> d, l, h$). Theory – Mode theory (Sidorovich, 1977, 2012), Speckle-mode theory (Zeldovich et al., 1986), Spatial-frequency version (Korzinin, 1990).

The first successful attempt to analyze the properties of volume holograms of spatially non-uniform wave fields with account of mutual rescattering by structure of a hologram of space-frequency components of wave field was the mode theory, proposed by V. G. Sidorovich. The use of the mode theory methods yielded first ever quantitative interpretation of the effect of phase-conjugate reflection under stimulated scattering (Sidorovich, 1976) and gave impetus to the further advance of theoretical studies of volume holograms.

2.2. Recording media for volume holograms

The experiments on recording volume holograms require a recording medium of physical thickness that should be on order of millimeter (from tenths of mm). Providing experimental studies with recording media is one of the main problems of volume holography, since the property package exhibited by such media cannot be ensured by traditional photomaterials (Sukhanov, 1994). Beside large physical thickness, samples of such media should have high physical and mechanical performance (to ensure invariability of the hologram structure in the course of post-exposure treatment and when operated under impact of external factors); possess high spatial resolution (thousands of lines per millimeter), sufficient energy sensitivity and transparence at the operating wavelength; and secure long-term storage and nondestructive hologram reconstruction.

The first studies in the field of three-dimensional holography made use of photochromic glasses, electro-optical crystals, photochromic and photostructured polymeric compositions (see, e. g., Sukhanov, 1994). Each of the above materials had certain drawbacks and failed to possess the set of required properties. Since the very inception of holography in three-dimensional media (Denisyuk, 1962, 1963), research and development in the field never ceased, yet there is a short line of recording medium samples for recording of volume holograms; they are manufactured in laboratory conditions, as a rule, in single pieces (or small batches) and exhibit no stable and reproducible characteristics.

It is rather difficult to present all works attempting to create recording media for volume holography with a broad spectrum of necessary parameters. The main tendencies in the development of such media were manifested most clearly in the activity of the S.I. Vavilov State Optical Institute, Russia, its staff contributing greatly to development of volume light-sensitive media and elaboration of principles for their design (Sukhanov, 1994, 2007). The more recent of the quoted works presents the results of many years' study in the field, describes the mechanisms of hologram formation in new and original materials (their parameters are given in Table 1, reproduced from the work Sukhanov, 2007). The development of materials listed in Table 1 drew on various substances and mechanisms to create a light-sensitive composition and silicate glasses, crystals and polymeric matrices as the rigid framework. These are the directions that are actively used today.

Materials in Table 1 found their application in creation of HOE, mostly narrowband radiation selectors. Reoxan-based volume reflection hologram was used as a spectral selector (Sukhanov et al., 1984). The diffusion-enhanced medium PQ+PMMA served as a base to develop its modifications by different work groups (e. g., Steckman et al., 1998; Lin et al., 2000; Shelby, 2002; Hsu et al., 2003; Luo et al., 2008; Liu et al., 2010; Yu et al., 2010). Media on porous glass base offer great opportunities in formation of volume holograms and control of their characteristics (Sukhanov et al., 1992), but they are yet to find their application in practice because of complicated technological modes of sample production and parameter control. By virtue of their properties, identical to those of standard glass (K8, Russia), photo-thermo-refractive glass shows promise in creation of high-precision hologram elements (Efimov et al., 2004; Zlatov et al., 2010). The holographic medium on the base of CaF_2 crystals, doped with alkali metals, features high mechanical and radiation stability and damage threshold (Shcheulin et al., 2007) and shows promise in metrological applications. The samples of the material have been the base of optical element "Holographic prism" (Angervaks et al., 2010, 2012).

Characteristic	Polymeric materials		Silicate glass based		Crystal
	Reoxan (PMMA)	PQ+PMMA	Porous Glass	PTR Glass	CaF_2
Spectral sensitivity region	440 ÷ 900	480 ÷ 540	440 ÷ 520	280 ÷ 350	300 ÷ 400
Light sensitivity, J/cm^2	0.5 ÷ 1.5	0.5 ÷ 1.5	0.01 ÷ 1	0.05÷1	≈1
Maximum value of Δn	$2 \cdot 10^{-2}$	$5 \cdot 10^{-3}$	0.1	$5 \cdot 10^{-4}$	$5 \cdot 10^{-5}$
Operating spectral range		Visible, near IR		Long-wave visible, IR	
Hologram thickness, mm	0.1 ÷ 1	0.1 ÷ 10	0.01 ÷ 1	≈1	1 ÷ 10
Thermal stability	70 °C	(70 ÷ 100) °C	500 °C	500 °C	200 °C
Pre-exposure treatment	Oxygen saturation	Not required	Not required	Not required	Not required
Development	Not required	Thermal treatment at (50÷70) °C	Chemical development, pickling	Thermal treatment at 400 and 520 °C	Not required
Fixation	Degassing	Uniform exposure	Not required	Not required	Not required
References	Lashkov & Sukhanov, 1978	Veniaminov et al., 1991	Sukhanov, 1994	Glebov et al., 1990	Shcheulin et al. 2007

Table 1. Volume recording media, developed in State Optical Institute, and their main characteristics. PMMA – polymethylmethacrylate; PQ – phenanthrenequinone; PTR Glass – photo-thermo-refractive glass.

Note that the materials listed in Table 1 are in no competition with one another, while their diversity allows making a reasonable choice proceeding from the priority requirements to be met by a specific product.

3. Some properties of volume transmission hologram gratings

3.1. Phase transmission hologram gratings

Volume hologram gratings are of great practical interest foremost in creation of hologram optical elements (HOE) used as radiation selectors. The main hologram parameters that determine properties of such elements are diffraction efficiency (DE, defined as S•S* in the coupled wave theory) and hologram selectivity, both angular and spectral (defined with mismatch parameter ξ) – see Fig. 2a. In practice, the DE is found as ratio of intensity of diffracted beam (I_d) to the sum of those of zero-order (I_0) and diffracted beams (I_d) behind the hologram: $\eta = I_d/(I_d + I_0)$, and describes the efficiency of the element operation under given experimental conditions.

The limiting values of DE for hologram gratings of different types, estimated under Bragg conditions, are given in Table 2.

Hologram type		Modulated quantity	Maximum DE, % Hologram recording mode: linear	Maximum DE, % Hologram recording mode: nonlinear
3D	transmission	absorption index	3.7	25
		refractive index	100	100
	reflection	absorption index	7.2	60
		refractive index	100	100

Table 2. Estimated limiting values of diffraction efficiency for holograms of different types.

The data for recording of holograms in linear mode are taken from the book (Collier et al., 1971) and are well known. As shown in work (Alekseev-Popov, 1981), recording holograms in nonlinear mode enables realization of the situation that allows considerable improvement of the attainable performance of a volume amplitude hologram. The presence of nonlinear effects in recording amplitude, phase and amplitude-phase holograms has a decisive role in many practical situations, as it can markedly improve the efficiency of recorded holograms.

Of greatest practical interest are volume transmission holograms that have no absorption. The DE of such holograms is described according to the coupled wave theory by expression:

$$\eta = \sin^2\varphi_1, \tag{1}$$

where φ_1 is the phase modulation amplitude, determined by recording conditions and recording medium parameters (for symmetrical gratings):

$$\varphi_1 = \pi n_1 T/\lambda \cos \theta. \quad (2)$$

The limiting values of diffraction efficiency of both transmission and reflection phase holograms amount to 100%. The main feature of transmission holograms as distinct from reflection ones is the oscillatory nature of dependence of DE on magnitude of phase modulation. Quantity φ_1 is an important parameter in development of technology for manufacturing optical elements and in comparative analysis of theoretical calculation results and experiment, for it relates parameters of a hologram and recording medium, (first of all, the value of modulation amplitude of refractive index, n_1).

Evaluation of φ_1 by DE measurements for transmission holograms proceeds as follows. Dependence $\eta(\varphi_1)$ being of oscillatory nature, quantity φ_1 is found by formula $\varphi_1 = k\pi \pm \arcsin\sqrt{\eta}$, where k = 0, 1, 2, 3,...; to find φ_1 by DE values uniquely is possible only for holograms with $\varphi_1 < 0.5\pi$. For high-efficiency holograms, finding φ_1 by measured DE values should involve the selectivity contour shape. The situation gives grounds to divide transmission phase holograms into so-called "weak" holograms with phase modulation less than $\varphi_1 = 0.5\pi$ and "strong" holograms, where phase modulation can substantially exceed $\varphi_1 = 0.5\pi$ (e.g., Steckman et al., 1998). Note that DE values for both "weak" and "strong" holograms can coincide and be rather high. Fig. 2 gives selectivity contours of holograms that have identical DE values: $\eta = 1$ (Fig. 2a, b) and $\eta = 0.5$ (Fig. 2c, d), but different values of the phase modulation amplitude in Bragg reconstruction.

Determination of values of φ_1 for transmission phase holograms uses in addition to the selectivity contour shape also the following factors to describe "strong" hologram gratings with a given value of coefficient k:

- the sign of the first derivative $d\eta/d\varphi_1$ of variation of function $\eta(\varphi_1)$, which describes growth or drop of DE with growing φ_1 at given section;
- the sign of the second derivative $\{d^2(I_d)/(d\theta)^2\}_{Br}$ of variation of function $I_d(\theta)$ at the point of extremum of the function under Bragg conditions, which describes the appearance of selectivity contour – whether the principal maximum is present (Fig. 2c) or not (Fig. 2d);
- the ratio of DE values, measured at different polarization of reconstructing radiation, η^{TM}/η^{TE}.

As known (Kogelnik, 1969), $\varphi_1^{TM}/\varphi_1^{TE} = \cos 2\theta$, where 2θ is the angle between the zero-order and diffracted beams (in the hologram bulk) in hologram reconstruction, therefore, depending on variation interval of φ_1, the ratio $\arcsin(\sqrt{\eta^{TM}})/\arcsin(\sqrt{\eta^{TE}})$ can be either greater or less than unity, so the value of η^{TM}/η^{TE} can be either > 1, or < 1. Note that the characteristic is to be used at wide enough angles between beams, since the difference between values of η^{TM} and η^{TE} at small 2θ is small too and may fall within the limits of measurement accuracy.

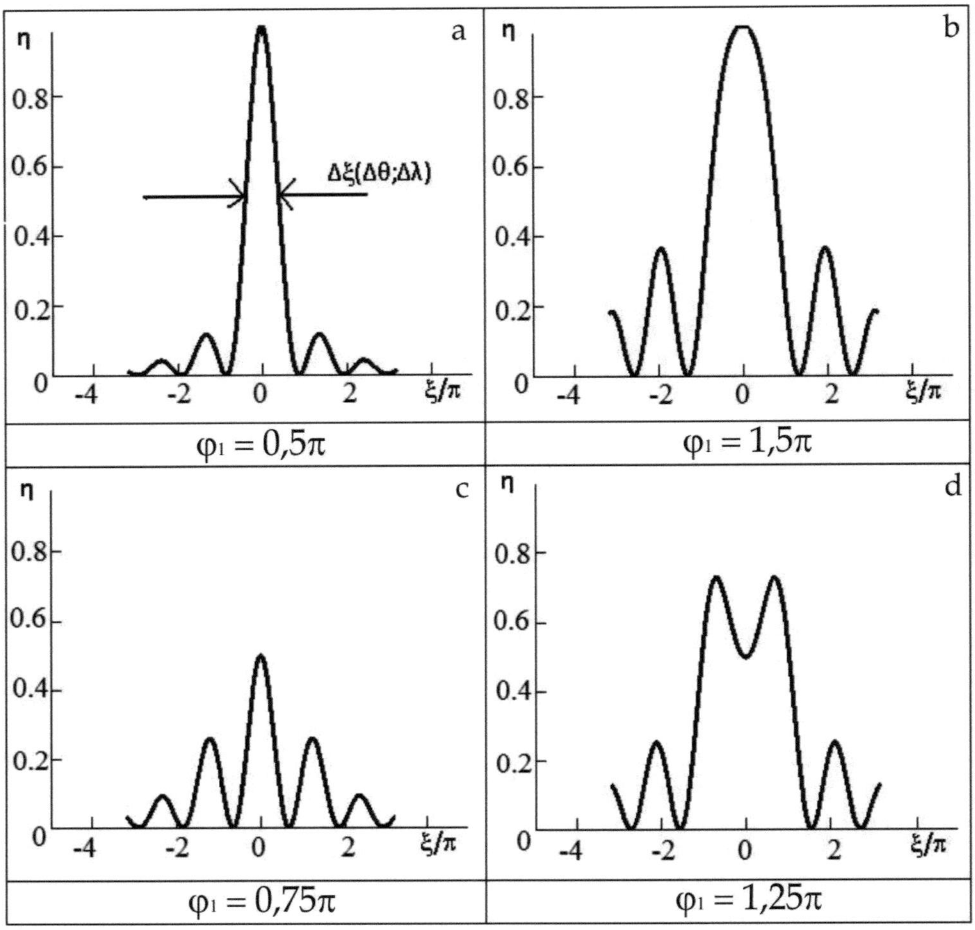

Figure 2. Selectivity contour of a volume transmission phase hologram gratings with $\eta = 1$ at $\varphi_1 = 0.5\pi$ (a) and at $\varphi_1 = 1{,}5\pi$ (b); with $\eta = 0.5$ at $\varphi_1 = 0.75\pi$ (c) and at $\varphi_1 = 1{,}25\pi$ (d). ξ is the mismatch parameter, $\Delta\xi$ is the half-width of selectivity contour of a volume hologram; $\Delta\theta$, $\Delta\lambda$ are the angular and spectral selectivity of a hologram, respectively.

Variation interval of φ_1	k	$\varphi_1(\eta)$	$d\eta/d\varphi_1$	$\{d^2(I_d)/(d\theta)^2\}_{Br}$	η^{TM}/η^{TE}
0.0 – 0.5 π	0	$\mathrm{Arcsin}\sqrt{\eta}$	> 0	> 0	> 1
0.5 – 1.0 π	1	$\pi - \arcsin\sqrt{\eta}$	< 0	> 0	< 1
1.0 – 1.5 π	2	$\pi + \arcsin\sqrt{\eta}$	> 0	< 0	> 1
1.5 – 2.0 π	3	$2\pi - \arcsin\sqrt{\eta}$	< 0	> 0	< 1

Table 3. Additional data for finding the value of phase modulation of transmission holograms by measured DE values and angular selectivity contour shape of a hologram.

Thus, under Bragg incidence of a reconstructing beam at the entrance face of hologram grating, the propagation of the energy of diffracted and zero-order beams occurs along isophase hologram planes, i. e. radiation energy is channelized and the geometrical cross-section of its propagation channel is bounded by value $\Delta x_{\pi/2}$.

As shown by the present author's theoretical calculations, the effect of energy channelizing by "strong" transmission hologram gratings is exhibited also in the diffraction of reconstruction radiation with nonuniform intensity distribution, as it occurs in case of actual light beams. Besides, within the framework of the coupled wave theory, the energy channelizing effect has been shown to reveal itself at its fullest in case of angular spectrum ($\Delta\psi$) of the incident monochromatic wave being much narrower than the width of the angular selectivity contour of a hologram layer of thickness $T_{\pi/2}$, which is equivalent to the requirement of the beam diameter (or its size in the section plane of the hologram considered in Fig. 3) being much greater than the thickness of the hologram layer ($T_{\pi/2}$), where $\varphi_1 = \pi/2$.

The author's experiments in 2008, reported at "Holoexpo-2008" conference, confirmed the manifestation of the energy channelizing effect when reconstructing beam of radiation with nonuniform intensity distribution is used. The experiments involved PTR-glass samples 9 mm thick, where hologram gratings were recorded under symmetrical incidence of interfering beams onto sample surface at a 45-degree angle. Interference planes in a hologram were situated perpendicularly to the front and rear sample surfaces, as shown in Fig. 4a, b. The hologram recording conditions allowed setting the recording regime, needed to obtain a hologram grating with the required value of phase modulation amplitude.

The value of phase modulation amplitude was in one case as low as $\varphi_1 \approx 0.25\pi$ (Fig.4a, c – "weak" hologram, as $\varphi_1 < \pi/2$) and in another as high as $\varphi_1 = 10.25\pi$ (Fig.4 b, d – "strong" hologram). Fig. 4 pre sents the schematic view (a, b) of radiation propagations as well as the radiation energy distribution (c, d) on the front and rear faces of studied samples of identical thickness. The photograph in Fig. 5 a fixates the process of reconstruction of a "strong" hologram (the date are given in Fig. 4 b, d): one can clearly see the energy propagation channel, orientated perpendicularly to the front and rear sample faces, i. e. directed along the isophase surfaces of the hologram.

The energy distributions in radiation beams on the hologram entrance and exit faces (Fig. 4 c, d) are processed experimental results. Parameters of beams on the hologram entrance face correspond to those of reconstructing beams used in the experiment, while the beam intensity distribution on the exit hologram face is calculated with account of the hologram phase modulation. The phase modulation for each hologram was found experimentally by the DE value and the shape of the angular selectivity contour. The calculation for Bragg diffraction of Gaussian beams by periodically modulated media used the technique, published in works (Chu & Tamir, 1976). The calculated results for the beam intensity distribution on the exit hologram face are in qualitative agreement with the picture of beam diffraction, observed in the experiment.

As noted, the terms "weak" hologram and "strong" hologram for a transmission volume phase hologram bear no relation to the DE value, but are defined by the value of phase modulation amplitude φ_1. The DE value for holograms in the experiment, which was attained under Bragg conditions in the two cases is less than 50% for both the "weak" and the "strong" holograms. Despite the close values of DE, the appearance of the spatial intensity distribution for either of the two interacting beams (diffracted and zero-order ones) on the hologram exit face differs markedly. As seen from the data of Fig. 4 a, c, intensity distribution of diffracted and zero-order beams on the exit face of a "weak" hologram 9 mm thick exhibits two peaks that are spaced apart and correspond to the diffracted beam and zero-order diffraction beam (transmitted one). Here, the diffracted beam is appreciably broadened with respect to the incident one and exits the hologram strictly opposite to the incident one, i. e. the diffracted beam energy propagates along antinodes of a hologram grating, which is schematically illustrated in Fig. 4 a. The zero-order diffraction beam propagates practically in the direction, prescribed by ray optics.

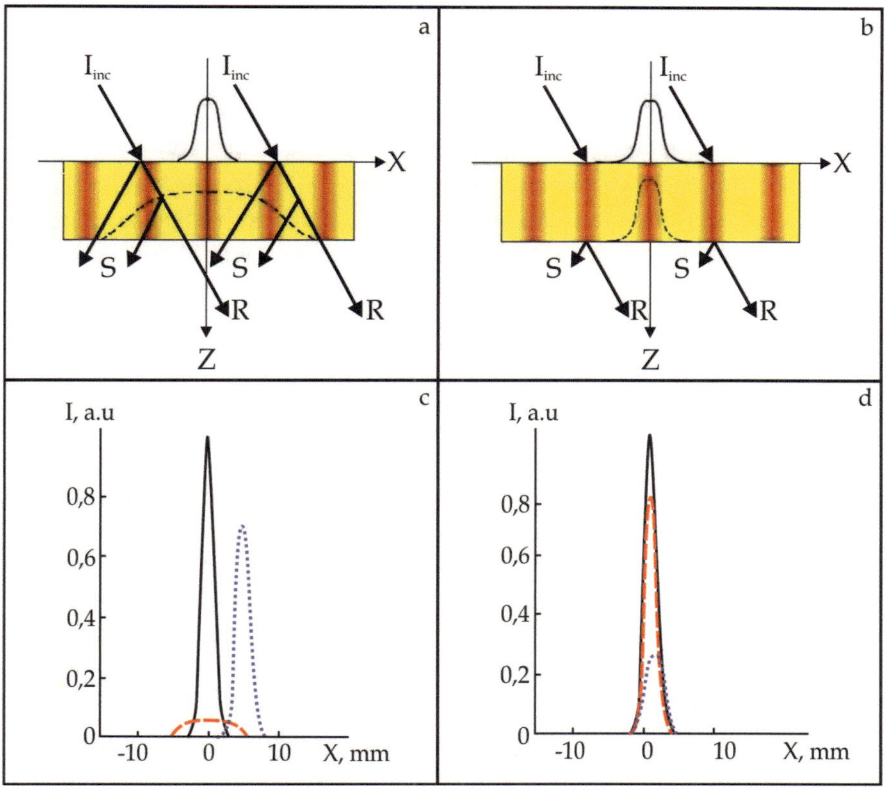

Figure 4. Reconstruction of symmetrically-recorded hologram gratings in samples of identical thickness (T = 9 mm): "weak" hologram with $\varphi_1 \approx 0.25\pi$ (a, c) and "strong" hologram with $\varphi_1 = 10.25\pi$ (b, d); a, b - radiation propagation diagram, where I_{inc} is the incident (reconstructing) beam, S is the diffracted beam, R is the zero-order diffraction beam; c, d - radiation intensity distribution in the reconstructing beam on the entrance hologram face (solid curves), and in zero-order (dot lines) and diffracted (dash lines) beams at the hologram exit face.

On the exit surface of a "strong" hologram, however:

- the diffracted beam and zero-order diffraction beam are spatially aligned with each other;
- the intensity distribution in zero-order and diffracted beams is practically no different from that in the reconstructing radiation beam;
- the spatial position of the beams specifies the direction of isophase surfaces, along which the radiation propagates.

Reconstruction radiation parameters				**Hologram parameters**			**Channelizing conditions**		
Beam D, mm	$\Delta\psi$, mrad	Incid. angle	T, mm	φ_1, rad	$T_{\pi/2}$,mm	$\Delta\theta$, mrad	$\Delta\psi/\Delta\theta$	$D/T_{\pi/2}$	$\Delta x_{\pi/2}$,mm
3	0.3	θ_{Br}	9	10.25π	0.45	> 3	< 0.1	> 7	4

Table 4. The conditions for running the experiment to observe the energy channelizing effect in reconstruction of a hologram grating 9 mm thick.

Table 4 shows hologram grating parameters that enable the observation of the energy channelizing effect.

Special notice should be given to the situation observed in the reconstruction of a "strong" hologram beyond Bragg angle. Fig. 5 b shows dependences, obtained in non-Bragg reconstruction of the "strong" hologram, its reconstruction results at Bragg angle having been given in Fig. 4 d. The deviation from Bragg angle in the case was 0.4 mrad, so, after crossing the entrance sample surface, the zero-order beam propagated in the hologram both within the angular selectivity contour $\Delta\theta$ of the hologram, (see Fig. 2 a) and partially outside its limits.

The data in Fig. 5 b demonstrate a very interesting situation: the channelized radiation intensity in the direction of the isophase surfaces is zero as distinct from Bragg conditions of reconstruction, whereas another two radiation propagation channels emerge symmetrically to the right and the left with respect to the "Bragg" propagation channel.

What is the possible reason behind the emergence of two radiation propagation channels? One can suggest the following general behavior of propagating beams in a volume hologram grating in non-Bragg reconstruction of the "strong" hologram. The reconstructing radiation beam deviated from Bragg reconstruction condition by value 0.4 mrad that is less than the half-width of the angular selectivity contour of a hologram at $\varphi_1 = \pi/2$, which is in the present experiment about $\Delta\theta \approx 3$ mrad. Having passed the plane of the first extremum of function $\eta(\varphi_1)$ (at $T_{\pi/2}$), this so-called "first" zero-order beam (I_{01}) can, by virtue of small deviation from Bragg angle, bifurcate and continue partially propagating in the original position, thus forming the "second" zero-order beam (I_{02}) that can likewise bifurcate after passing the hologram section T_π and from the "third" zero-order beam, propagating at the same angle as I_{02} symmetrically with respect to I_{01}. Each of the zero-order beams can form its "own" propagation channel that should remain, according to theoretical concepts, within the geometrical limits of the cross-sectional area $\Delta x_{\pi/2}$ of the hologram, but may be misaligned with the direction of the radiation propagation under Bragg reconstruction conditions.

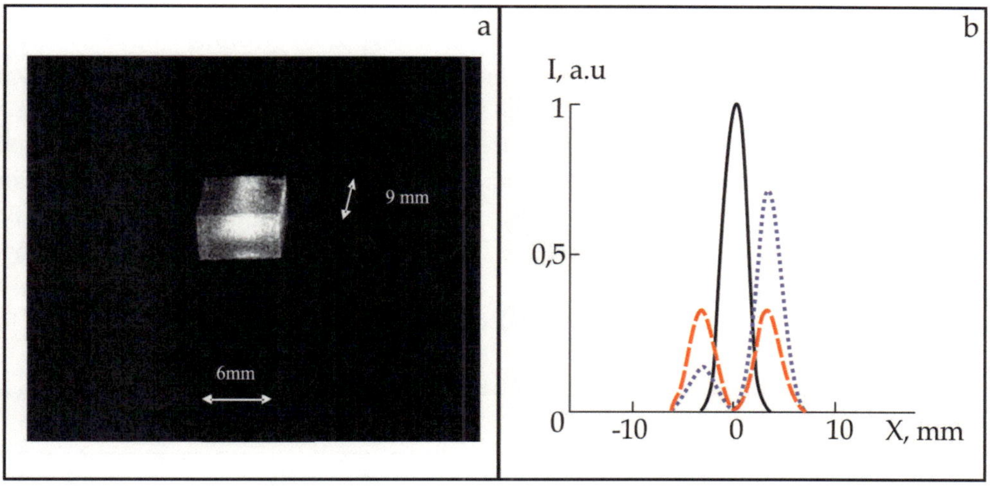

Figure 5. a - observation of the energy channelizing effect in volume hologram grating 9 mm thick with phase modulation amplitude 10.25π, recorded in PTR-glass: incident beam illuminates the sample exit face at a 45-degree angle, beam diameter is 3 mm. b - processed experimental results for reconstruction of a "strong" hologram at a deviation from Bragg angle by 0.4 mrad: radiation intensity distributions in the reconstructing beam on the hologram entrance surface (solid curves); in zero-order (dot line) and diffracted (dash line) beams on the hologram exit face. Hologram parameters are the same as given in Fig4 d and Fig. 5 a.

Thus, the present experiment has realized the scenario of "bifurcation" of radiation propagation channels by way of selection of non-Bragg reconstruction; in addition, intensity distributions of the zero-order and diffracted beams on the hologram exit surface were calculated for the case. The results of intensity distribution calculations are in qualitative agreement with the picture of beam diffraction, observed in the experiment. Theoretically, one can realize the situation with a large number of propagation channels that should theoretically lie within the limits, defined by the conditions of the experiment on observation of the energy channelizing effect (see Fig. 3.).

4. The effect of ambient conditions on volume hologram parameters

4.1. The effect of ambient variations on parameters of recording media

A recording medium to produce volume holograms should, as already mentioned, be about a millimeter thick and ensure the invariability of hologram structure in the course of treatment and operation. The temperature is one of the main ambient parameters with its effect to be allowed for when handling HOE. Temperature variation causes changes in both linear dimensions and refractive index of a sample. Table 5 lists characteristics that enable assessment the temperature-induced changes in parameters of samples of recording materials in use.

Note that the changes occurring in samples at varying ambient temperature are, as a rule, interrelated. i. e. a drop in refractive index is due to an increase in sample dimensions (its expansion), while sample contraction causes the index to grow. At the same time, the processes of hologram recording and post-exposure treatment have a selective effect on sample parameters: either recording or post-exposure treatment necessarily results in a refractive index change, with the geometrical dimensions of the medium remaining practically the same (the media are then called "shrinkproof") or undergoing slight changes (media with "negligible shrinkage"). Media on silicate glass base are commonly believed to be shrinkproof; yet when the holograms are recorded on PTR-Glass samples (see Table 1), the average refractive index changes in the course of thermal post-exposure treatment by a noticeable value ~ 10^{-4} (Glebov, et al., 2002). This is to be allowed for in design of HOE with prescribed performance.

Characteristic	**Material**		
	Polymer	**Silicate glass**	**Crystal, CaF_2**
Linear thermal expansion, dl/dT, K^{-1}	$(3.6 \div 6.5)\ 10^{-5}$	$(5 \div 9)\ 10^{-6}$	$18.9 \bullet 10^{-6}$*
Refractive index, dn/dT, K^{-1}	$-1.05 \bullet 10^{-4}$	$-(10^{-5} \div 10^{-6})$	$-8.7 \bullet 10^{-6}$
References	Marvin, 2003; * Malitson, 1963		

Table 5. The temperature effect on the changes in refractive index and dimensions of samples used to produce volume recording media

As seen from the data of Table 5, the changes in parameters of polymeric media at varying temperature are substantively (severalfold) larger than those of media on the base of silicate glass and crystals. In addition, polymers exhibit a property to take up moisture, which in turn causes changes in sample thickness and average refractive index; therefore, handling the polymeric samples makes it necessary to maintain the ambience stable.

Experiments on recording and reconstruction of holograms, produced on silicate glasses and crystals, are held under ambient conditions, maintained as a rule at the level of standard conditions of a research laboratory (temperature variation is ± 1K, humidity variation is 3÷5%). The accuracy, within which one should maintain the ambient temperature and humidity for the conditions to be considered stable for polymeric samples, is dependent on the recording medium properties and the prescribed requirements to hologram parameters. The present section gives the results of experiments on the temperature and humidity effect on parameters of hologram gratings (1.0 ÷ 1.4) mm thick, which were produced on samples of polymeric material Difphen at recording by radiation with c $\lambda = 488$ nm at spatial frequency $\nu = (300 \div 500)\ mm^{-1}$.

The results obtained for a PMMA-based polymeric recording medium can be used to optimize the conditions of experimental operation of different polymeric samples in recording and reconstruction of information.

4.2. The effect of temperature variation on parameters of polymeric volume holograms

4.2.1. The experimental technique with the use of low-frequency interference pattern

The effect of temperature on parameters of polymeric volume hologram gratings was assessed by observation of behavior of low-frequency interference pattern (IP). The schematic diagram of the experiment is given in Fig. 6. It was carried out with the use of a stand intended for hologram recording, the same where the hologram under study was recorded.

Hologram grating was mounted into the scheme in the position it had had during recording and illuminated by two coherent beams I_1 and I_2. Each of the incident beams was diffracted by the hologram structure with formation of its "own" diffracted beam: beam I_1 formed diffracted beam I_{1d} that propagated in the same direction as beam I_{20}, and beam I_2 formed diffracted beam I_{2d} that propagated in the same direction as beam I_{10}. When the hologram was shifted, an angle, 2φ, was formed between beams that propagated behind the hologram in the same direction (I_{1d} and I_{20}; I_{2d} and I_{10}), and the IP was formed is the space where the beams superimposed. At a turn of the hologram through angle φ = 0.1 mrad, the pattern period, d, has according to Bragg condition the value d ≈ 2.5 mm.

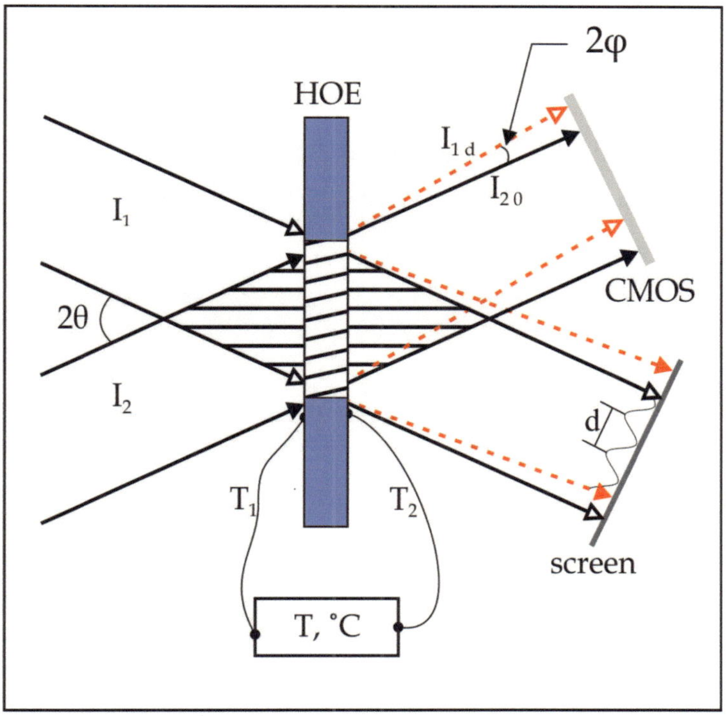

Figure 6. Diagram of the experiment on creation of low-frequency interference pattern: I_1 and I_2 are coherent beams of collimated radiation with λ = 488 nm; 2θ is the angle between beams I_1 and I_2 in the air; HOE is the hologram grating; T_1 and T_2 are temperature sensors; I_{1d}, I_{2d}, I_{10}, I_{20} are beams of radiation diffracted by a hologram grating (first and zero orders); 2φ is the angle between beams that form the low-frequency IP.

The forming interference pattern can be observed in each of propagating beams (I_1 and I_2) with a screen installed perpendicularly to the beam propagation. The IP was recorded using a CMOS matrix of a size that allowed recording the observed interference field in full and obtaining interferograms imaged in Fig.7a, b. The interferograms were shot at actual size simultaneously with temperature control. The temperature sensors, mounted onto the sample on the side 1 (T_1) and on the side 2 (T_2) in close proximity to the observation area, allowed carrying out the control with accuracy 0.1 K.

Before the experiment started, the hologram was set in the position, where the IP had the maximum period that provided the possibility under those conditions to process interferograms and perform quantitative measurements. To measure the temperature, a warm air jet was directed towards the hologram on the side 2 and the sample was heated up to temperature T = 32 ºC. The interferograms were shot in a stationary state of the scheme, with the sample cooling down after the action of warm air; the difference in readings T_1 and T_2 was within the measurements accuracy.

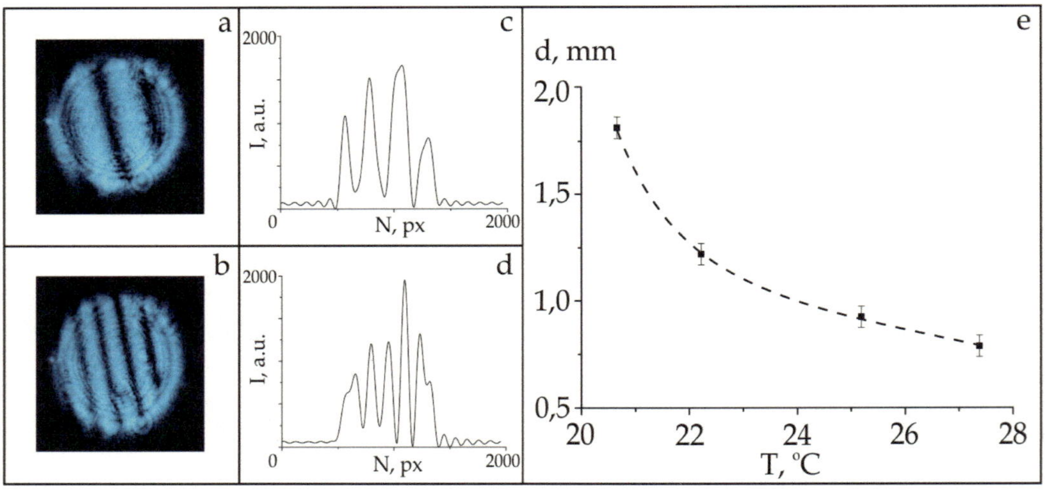

Figure 7. Changes of the period of the low-frequency interference pattern (IP) at variation of the temperature of polymeric hologram grating with v = 350 mm^{-1}, recorded on a sample of Difphen material 1.2.mm thick: a, b – IP images at hologram temperature 21 ºC (a) and 27 ºC (b); c, d – processing of interferograms given in a and b, respectively; e – dependence of IP period, d, on sample temperature, dashed line illustrate the character of process.

4.2.2. The experimental results

The experiment was carried out under the following conditions: interfering beam diameter, D, 8–10 mm; angle between beams I_1 and I_2, 2θ, 10 deg.; λ = 488 nm; angular selectivity of the hologram under study, Δθ, 1.7 mrad; temperature variation interval 21–28 ºC.

The obtained interferograms and the results of their processing are given in Fig. 7 a-d. The dependence of IP period change on sample temperature is given in Fig. 7 e. As seen, with the temperature growing from 21 to 28 deg., the IP period changed from 1.8 mm to 0.7 mm, which corresponds to a change in angle 2φ (θ_{max} shift) by 0.43 mrad. The experiment showed no change (within the measurements accuracy) in the IP period, measured before the start of measurements and after the sample cooled down to the room temperature. Thus, one can estimate the effect of temperature variation on parameters of polymeric hologram 1.2.mm thick with spatial frequency $\nu = 350$ mm^{-1} as follows: with the temperature changing by 1K, the change in the diffraction angle (θ_{max} shift) amounts to $\delta\theta_{max} = 0.06$ mrad, i. e. the hologram under study has thermal shift 0.06 mrad/K.

Note that the temperature effect on parameters of polymeric reflection holograms, recorded on samples of Reoxan material (Sukhanov et al., 1984), demonstrates the magnitude of changes on the same order. With the temperature of Reoxan sample changing from 24 ºC to 29 ºC, the shift of λ_{max} in the spectrum of reflected radiation is from 532.1 nm to 532.6 nm (spectral interval of reconstructing radiation, $\Delta\lambda < 0.01$ nm). Thus, the studied hologram (thickness 1 mm, $\nu > 3000$ mm^{-1}, spectral selectivity, $\Delta\lambda = 0.15$ nm), intended for the use as a narrowband spectral selector, had thermal shift $\delta\lambda_{max} = 0.1$ nm/K.

4.3. The effect of ambient humidity variation on parameters of polymeric volume holograms

4.3.1. The method of assessment of the change in the space position of diffracted beam

It has been established that a Difphen material sample (a disk 40 mm in diameter and 4 mm thick), when immersed in water in the temperature range (20 ÷ 30) ºC, takes up to 1.5% of water with respect to the sample weight in air-dry condition at relative humidity of the ambient air H ≈ 50%. Taking up moisture changes the average refractive index and thickness of the sample and, accordingly, characteristics of recorded holograms.

The effect of varying humidity of the ambient air on the polymeric hologram parameters was studied at an experimental stand of a design that provided for an enclosed volume around the hologram to maintain humidity ≈ 90% (much higher than normal conditions) and for conduct of long-time measurements (several hours). Fig. 8 shows the optical diagram of the stand (Fig. 8 a) and schematic drawing to illustrate possible changes in polymeric sample dimensions under moisture take-up (Fig. 8 b).

The stand was used to measure the angular selectivity contour of a hologram at a one-time fixation of all contour data. The hologram was illuminated with a divergent radiation beam; the intensity distribution of the diffracted radiation (angular selectivity contour) was recorded by a CMOS matrix of a camera – the results of processing the experimental data are given in Fig. 9. The effect of varying humidity on hologram parameters was assessed by a change in the position, θ_{max}, of the intensity maximum of diffracted radiation in a CMOS matrix during the process under study. Position θ_{max} was detected with accuracy ± 1 pixel, which corresponded to angular resolution ≈ 0.02 mrad.

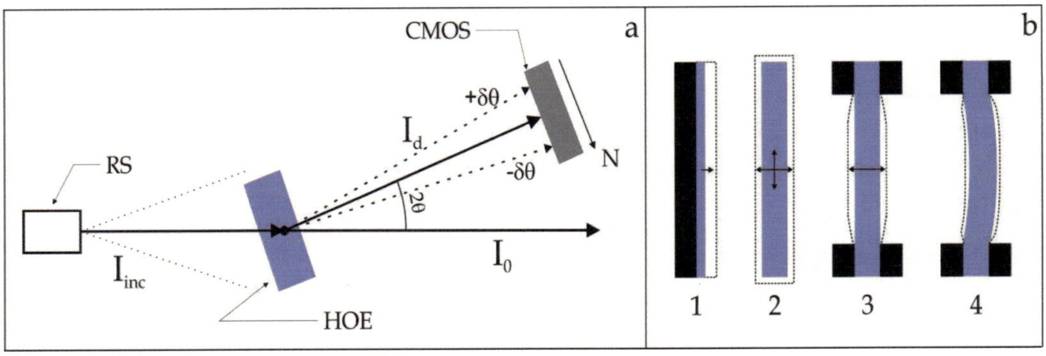

Figure 8. a – optical diagram of experiment to assess the changes of hologram parameters under varying ambient humidity: RS – radiation source, I_{inc} is the incident (reconstructing) beam, I_d is the diffracted beam, I_0 is the zero-order diffraction beam, 2θ is the diffraction angle, ±δθ is the diffraction angle change, N is the readout of pixel number in CMOS matrix (in the arrow direction). b – polymeric sample growing in size upon taking up moisture: 1 – the sample is fixed in a rigid framework, 2 – the sample is in free state, 3, 4 – the sample is fixed in a cartridge, geometrical dimensions of a sample upon taking up moisture are dash lines, arrows show the size growth direction.

4.3.2. The experimental results

The experimental results are presented in Fig.9. Fig. 9 a shows the position θ_{max} of a hologram at ambient humidity 40% and 90%. A change of position θ_{max} in the present experiment corresponded to the increase of the diffraction angle and was as large as $\delta\theta_{max} \approx + 0.25$ mrad. It is this value that characterizes the difference in hologram parameters in two stable states of the sample at different humidity.

The process of hologram relaxation (stabilization of its parameters) at a sudden drop of the ambient humidity from 85% to 50% is illustrated by Fig. 9 b. The stabilization of hologram parameters in changed conditions was accompanied by a change in the position of the selectivity contour maximum, which corresponds to a decrease of the diffraction angle and a shift of θ_{max} by $\delta\theta_{max} \approx$ (0.10-0.18) mrad, fixed in 2.5 hours after the sudden variation of the humidity. As shown by results of experiments on different samples, position θ_{max}, at a sudden drop of the ambient humidity from (85 ÷ 90)% to (40 ÷ 50)%, attains its steady state value, which remains later practically the same, in 2-3 hours (relaxation time is dependent on sample properties), while θ_{max} shifts by $\delta\theta_{max} < 0.3$ mrad.

Thus, one can estimate the change in the diffraction angle at humidity change of 5% (which accords with typical excursions of workroom humidity) to be $(\delta\theta_{max})_{5\%} < 0.03$ mrad and recommend to keep a polymeric hologram in stable conditions for at least two-three hours for stabilization of its internal structure. The effect of changing ambient temperature and humidity on the parameters of polymeric hologram gratings is given in Table 6.

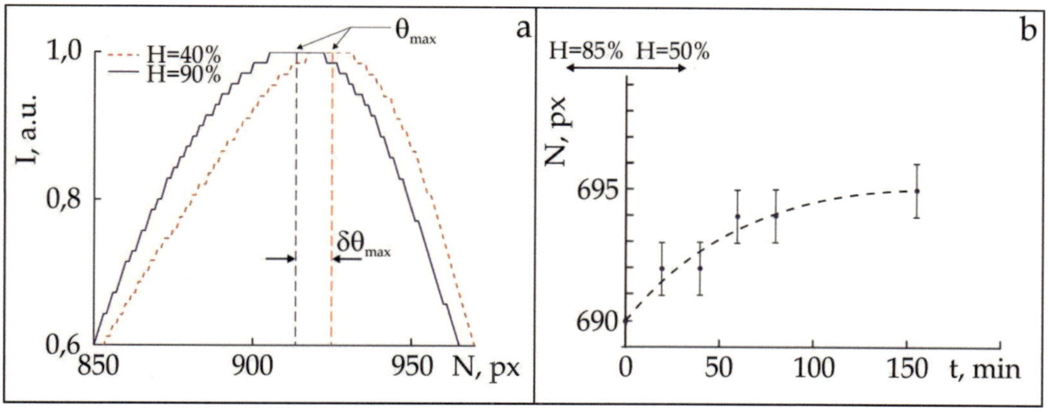

Figure 9. Processing of experimental results: a – the position of the angular selectivity contour maximum, θ_{max}, in CMOS matrix at ambient humidity H ≈ 40% (dot line) and H ≈ 90% (solid line), $\delta\theta_{max}$ is the position θ_{max} shift (hologram with ν ≈ 450 mm^{-1}); b – the relaxation of hologram grating at a sudden change in humidity from 85% to 50% (hologram with ν ≈ 350 mm^{-1}), dashed line illustrate the character of process.

It shall be remembered that the recording of holograms under study took place, as a rule, at the ambient humidity H ≈ (50 ÷ 60)%. With rising humidity, the growing of dimensions of a sample, rigidly fixed in a cartridge (Fig. 8 b, positions 3, 4), is accompanied by some deformation unlike the sample in a rigid framework and that in a free state (Fig. 8 b, positions 1 and 2, respectively). The sample, fixed in a rigid framework is as a rule a film one in silicate glass framework. When such sample takes up moisture, only the change in its thickness is considered (as, e. g., in the work Pandey et al., 2008). Here, side 1 of the sample is rigidly with the framework and never changes its position in space.

Ambience variation		**Hologram parameter variation**		
Property	Amount of change	Parameter	Amount of change	Recording material
Humidity, rel. %	5%	θ_{max} shift	0.03 mrad	Difphen, ν ≈ 450 mm^{-1}
Temperature, K	1 K	θ_{max} shift	0.06 mrad	Difphen, ν ≈ 350 mm^{-1}
		λ_{max} shift	0.1 nm	Reoxan ν > 3000 mm^{-1}

Table 6. The effect of variation of ambient temperature and humidity on the parameters of polymeric volume hologram gratings about 1 mm thick.

The sample in a free state grows in size, when taking up moisture, along all three coordinates. The sample, rigidly fixed in a cartridge (Fig. 8 b, positions 3, 4), grows in volume, when taking up moisture, due to increasing thickness, with position of sides 1 and 2 of the sample changing relative to its center. At lesser deformations, the position of the sample center in space remains the same (Fig. 8 b, position 3). Yet, if the sample volume growth exceeds the threshold deformation values determined by the sample geometry (the ratio of diameter to thickness), the performed calculations have revealed the possibility of the sample bending and the sample center shifting in space, as shown in Fig. 8 b, position 4.

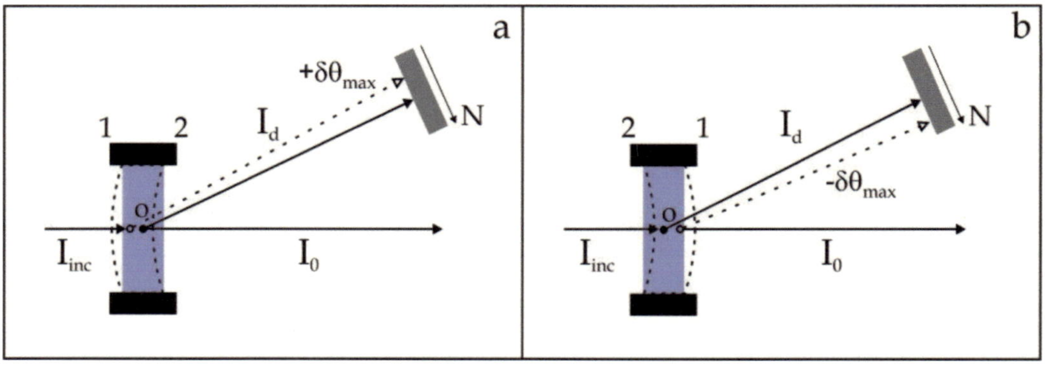

Figure 10. Diagram of experiment on observation of shifts of the diffracted beam (I_d) during hologram reconstruction from side 1 (a) and side 2 (b) - deformation with a shift along the sample axis. I_{inc} is the incident (reconstruction) beam; I_0 is the zero-order diffraction beam; O is the sample center without deformations; 1 and 2 are the sample sides; N is the CMOS matrix (the pixel number is counted in the arrow direction).

The presence of sample deformations due to its bending at taking-up the moisture has been detected in experiments on observation of the shift of the diffracted beam during reconstruction of a hologram from either sample side. The experiment diagram is given in Fig. 10. Its implementation contains five stages. Fig. 11 gives the results of processing of the performed experiment and shows the change in position θ_{max} in CMOS matrix at stages 1, 3, 5. Stage 1: the sample in steady state is mounted in a cartridge (at workroom humidity $H \approx 50\%$), and angular selectivity contours are shot for several scores of minutes (Fig.11 – stage 1). Stage 2: enclosed volume is established around the sample (HOE) using a protective housing, where humidity $H \approx 90\%$ is maintained, the stage duration is about 20 hours. Stage 3: protective housing is removed, and selectivity contours are shot in automatic mode under hologram relaxation in conditions of workroom humidity (Fig. 11 – stage 3). Stage 4: the sample is kept in stable workroom conditions for about 20 hours. Stage 5: angular selectivity contours are shot for a hologram in steady state.

As seen from experimental data of Fig.11, position θ_{max} in steady state of the hologram (stages 1 and 5) is stable and lies within measurement accuracy during reconstruction from both side 1 and side 2. However, position θ_{max} at $H \approx 90\%$ (value N at $t = 0$ at stage 3) as compared to that at $H \approx (40 \div 60)\%$ demonstrates growth of the diffraction angle during hologram reconstruction from side 1 and decrease of the diffraction angle during reconstruction from side 2. Such situation may be due to the presence of sample deformations with a shift of its center in space (sample bending), as shown schematically on Fig. 10 a, b.

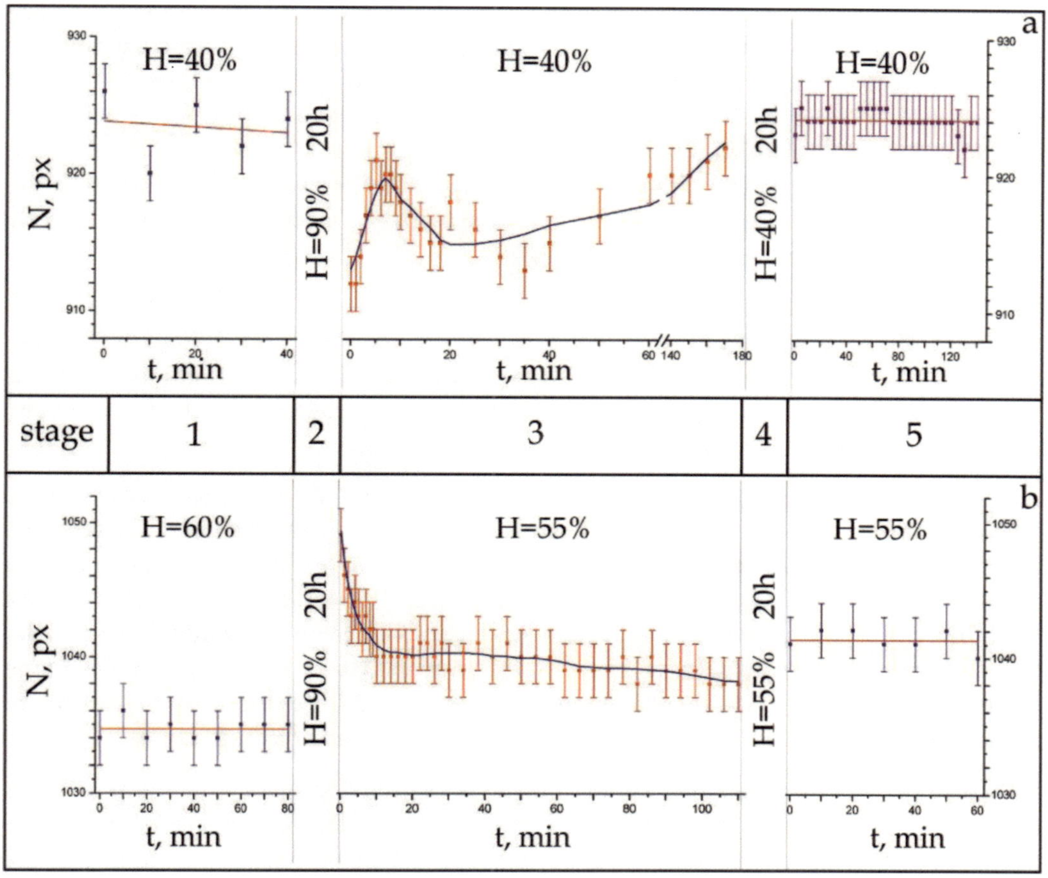

Figure 11. Results of experiment on observation of shifts of θ_{max} during hologram reconstruction from side 1 (a) and side 2 (b): plots show the pixel number in CMOS matrix, N, corresponding to position θ_{max} of a hologram at given instant of time in steady state (stages 1, 5) and out of the critical deformation (stage 3). Hologram with $\nu \approx 450$ mm^{-1}.

5. Conclusion

The present work discusses properties and specific features of volume holograms as well as results of original experiments that demonstrate unique potentiality of such holograms.

The results of examination of parameters are given for phase volume transmission hologram gratings that are of practical importance, and the hologram features are discussed, which are related to radiation propagation in media of great thickness with periodic structure on the order of the radiation wavelength. Practical recommendations are given to allow finding the phase modulation amplitude of "strong" hologram gratings by the value of diffraction efficiency and the shape of selectivity contour.

Experimental results are presented, which prove the existence of the effect of energy channelizing by "strong" transmission hologram gratings when using a reconstruction radiation beam with non-uniform intensity distribution, and the experimental conditions are defined for the effect to be revealed. The energy propagation in such structures has been shown to be confined to area occupied by the interacting beams (zero-order and diffracted) upon attaining $\varphi_1 = 0.5\pi$, the first extremum of function $\eta(\varphi_1)$. An effect was found of beam bifurcation and emergence of two channels for radiation propagation during reconstruction of a "strong" hologram grating beyond Bragg angle.

Parameters are listed for recording media to produce volume holograms, they were developed according to principles of recording media design, proposed in late 80s of the last century by S.I. Vavilov State Optical Institute specialists. The information is still topical as the last two decades saw mostly refinement, modification, and improvement of variants of volume recording media manufactured in laboratory conditions.

The effect of ambient temperature and humidity was studied for parameters of polymeric hologram gratings about 1 mm thick with spatial frequency ~ (350 ÷ 450) mm^{-1}, which were produced on Difphen material samples. The results allow estimating the change in the diffraction angle as ≈ 0.06 mrad at temperature variation by 1°K and as ≈ 0.03 mrad at relative humidity variation 5%. Despite the dependence of the values on the sample physical and mechanical properties, geometry and history, the estimates can be used to plan the working conditions for HOE on base of different polymers and to optimize the experimental conditions for handling polymer samples in information recording and reconstruction.

Experimental data were obtained to substantiate the assumption that taking-up of moisture can result not only in a change in thickness of a sample, rigidly fixed in a cartridge spatial, but also in its deformation, describable as "bending". Bending-type deformation was observed in conditions of high humidity on a sample with the diameter/thickness ratio of about 40:1. Thus, hologram gratings can be used to study deformation of materials under impact of ambient conditions.

The study of the temperature effect on parameters of polymeric hologram gratings employed an original technique for observing hologram deformations with the help of low-frequency interference pattern. The obtained results demonstrated efficiency of the technique and high accuracy of detecting the changes of hologram parameters.

Acknowledgements

The authors express their gratitude for participation in the experiments and assistance in preparation of the publication to A.A. Paramonov, S.A. Chivilikhin, D.A. Gomon, O.V. Bandyuk, V.V. Lesnichy, A.S. Zlatov, P.A. Kudriavcev.

Author details

O.V. Andreeva, Yu.L. Korzinin and B.G. Manukhin

The National Research University of Information Technologies, Mechanics and Optics, Russia

References

[1] Alekseev-Popov, A.V. (1981). *J. Technical Physics,* Vol.51(6), pp. 1275-1278, USSR

[2] Angervaks, A.E. et al (2010, 2012) Holographic Prizm as a New Optical Element . *Optics and Spectroscopy,* Vol.108(5), pp.824-830; Vol.112(2), pp. 312-317.

[3] Chu, R.-Sh. & Tamir (1976). *J. Opt. Soc. Am.,* Vol. 66(3,12), pp. 220-226, 1438-1440

[4] Collier, R.J. et al (1971). *Optical holography,* Academic Press, New York and London

[5] Denisyuk, Yu.N. (1962). *Doclady AN SSSR,* Vol.144(6), pp. 522;

[6] Denisyuk, Yu.N. & Protas, I.R. (1963). *Opt. and Spectrosc.,* Vol.14, pp. 721, USSR

[7] Efimov, O.V. et al (2004). High efficiency volume diffractive elements in photo-thermo-refractive glass. *US Patent.* 6,673,497 B2.

[8] Glebov, L.B. et al (1990). *Doclady AN SSSR,* Vol.314(4), pp.849-853

[9] Hsu, K.Y. et al (2003). *Opt. Eng.,* Vol.42(5), pp. 1390-1396

[10] Kogelnik, H. (1969). *The Bell System Technical Journal,* Vol.48, No9, P.2909-2947.

[11] Korzinin, Yu.L. (1990), *Optics and Spectroscopy,* Vol.68(1,5), pp. 213-215, 1154-1160

[12] Lashkov, G.I. & Sukhanov, V.I. (1978). *Optics and Spectroscopy,* Vol.44, pp. 590-594

[13] Lin, S.N. et al. (2000). *Optics Letters,* Vol.25(7), pp. 451-453

[14] Liu, D. et al. (2010). *Optics Express,* Vol.18(7), pp. 6447-6454

[15] Luo, Yu. et al. (2008). *Optics Letters,* Vol.33(6), pp. 566-568

[16] Malitson, I.H. (1963). A redetermination of some optical properties of calcium fluoride, *Appl. Opt.,* Vol.2, p. 1103

[17] Pandey, N. et al. (2008). *Optics Letters,* Vol.33(17), pp. 1981-1983

[18] Shcheulin, F.S. et al (2007). *Optics and Spectroscopy,* Vol.103(3,4), pp. 496; 664; 668; 673.

[19] Shelby, R.M. (2002). Materials for holographic digital data storage, *Proceedings of SPIE,* Vol.4659, pp. 344-360

[20] Sidorovich, V.G. (1976), *J. Technical Physics,* Vol.46(6), pp. 2168-2174, USSR

[21] Sidorovich, V.G. (1977), *Optics and Spectroscopy*, Vol.42(4), pp. 693-699

[22] Sidorovich, V.G. (2012), *Optics and Spectroscopy*, Vol.112(2), pp. 335-342

[23] Steckman, G.J. et al. (1998), *Opt. Lett.*, Vol.23(16), pp. 1310-1312

[24] Sukhanov, V.I. et al. (1984). Three dimensional hologram on Reoksan as narrow band spectral selector, *Sov. Techn. Phys. Lett.*, Vol.10, pp. 387-390

[25] Sukhanov, V.I. et al (1992). *Optics and Spectroscopy*, Vol.72(3), pp. 716-730

[26] Sukhanov, V.I. (1994). 3-Dimensional Deep Holograms and Materials for Recording Them, *J. Opt. Technol.*, Vol.61(1), pp. 49-56

[27] Sukhanov, V.I. et al. (2007). *Proceedings of meeting "In Memorial of Yu.N Denisyuk "*, Sankt-Petersburg, pp. 262-276

[28] Veniaminov, A.V. et al. (1991). *Optics and Spectroscopy,*. Vol.70, pp. 505-508

[29] Weber, M.J. (Ed) (2003). *Handbook of Optical Materials*, CRC Press LLC

[30] Yu, D. et al. (2010). *Optics Communs*, V.283, pp. 4219-4223

[31] Zeldovich, B. et al. (1986). *Physics-Uspekhi*, Vol.149(3), pp. 511-549

[32] Zlatov, A.S. et al. (2010) , *J. Opt. Technol.*, Vol.77(12), pp. 22-24

Chapter 3

White Light Reconstructed Holograms

Dagmar Senderakova

Additional information is available at the end of the chapter

http://dx.doi.org/10.5772/53592

1. Introduction

I would like to begin the chapter with two quotations, I came across during my study, I like very much and I am certain, they literally express holography, its properties, its beauty and its role today, at the beginning either of the 21st century or the third millenium, we have an opportunity to be eye witnesses.

"Holography is the only visual recording and playback process that can record our 3D world on a two-dimensional recording medium and playback the original object or scene to the unaided eyes, as a 3D image. The image demonstrates complete parallax and depth-of-field. The image floats in space either behind, in front, or straddling the recording medium." – is the first one. It is hard to find its origin, since it can be found at the beginnings of many papers dealing with holography.

"Since its first commercial usage in the 70's the demand has only increased with each passing year. Holography has found its applications in almost all industrial sectors including commercial and residential applications. Next years might bring us to see a new world of holograms in every aspect. The use of holograms is the representation of a new visual language in communication and we are moving into the age of light as the media of the future. Holography will soon be an integral part of the light age of information and communications." [1]

Well, people today come across the term *hologram* and can meet holograms on banknotes, various cards and products. A holographic technology comes along with advertisements, promotions,... People specialized in photonics [2], an interdisciplinary field dealing with utilizing photons, may know that holography is closely related to a special kind of light – laser light, which possesses a special property – *coherence,* i.e. all the light waves coming from a laser have the same properties. It is very important, because there are two basic physical light wave phenomena, enabling *holography*.

To record, i.e. to create a hologram, the phenomenon of *two-wave interference of light* is applied. The term *hologram* tells us that all the information transported by light wave is recorded. What does it mean – *all the information*? Let us repeat some basic terms [3]. Modelling light as a light wave $A(r, t)$ depending on space (r) and time (t) means, that there are two main parameters – the *amplitude* A_0 of a wave and its *phase* Φ

$$A = A_0 \cos\Phi(\boldsymbol{r}, t) = A_0 \cos(\omega t - \boldsymbol{k}.\boldsymbol{r} + \Phi_0) \tag{1}$$

where $\boldsymbol{r}(x, y, z)$ is a displacement vector determining a point in a space and $\boldsymbol{k}(k_x, k_y, k_z)$ denotes for a *wave vector,* determining direction of wave propagation. Its absolute value $k = 2\pi/\lambda$ defines the *wave number*. Φ_0 is the *initial phase* of the wave. The distance between the two neighbouring amplitude peaks of the same kind is *wavelength* λ [m]. ω [rad.s^{-1}], is *angular frequency,* which is related to the linear *frequency,* ν [s^{-1}], by the formula $\omega = 2\pi\nu$. It lasts $T = \lambda/c$ seconds to pass the path λ at the speed c. Such a time interval is called *period* and $T = 1/\nu$.

A *wave front* is another useful term for us, else. It is the surface upon which the wave has equal phase. It is perpendicular to the direction of propagation, i.e. to the wave vector $\boldsymbol{k}$.

For example, considering a wave propagating in the +z direction, the wave vector k is parallel to the z–axis everywhere. Because of that, wave fronts are parallel planes, perpendicular to the z–axis. Such a wave is known as a *plane wave*. When the $\boldsymbol{k}(k_x, k_y, k_z)$ direction is general, the phase in a point determined by a displacement vector $\boldsymbol{r}(x, y, z)$ includes the scalar product of $\boldsymbol{k}.\boldsymbol{r}$.

Let us mention also a *spherical wave*

$$A(\mathbf{r},t) = \frac{A_0}{r}\cos(\omega t - k.r + \varphi_0) \tag{2}$$

which is irradiated from a point light source in homogeneous medium. In such a case wave fronts are centrally symmetrical spheres, so it is enough to consider only radial coordinate r of *spherical* ones. Moreover, $\boldsymbol{k}$ and $\boldsymbol{r}$ are parallel, so $\boldsymbol{k}.\boldsymbol{r} = kr$. Increasing distance from the source the surface of the sphere increases and amplitude A_0 decreases proportionally to $1/r$.

It is more convenient to represent the light wave expression in a complex form

$$\boldsymbol{A} = A_0 \mathrm{e}^{\mathrm{i}\Phi} = A_0 \cos\Phi + \mathrm{i}A_0 \sin\Phi \tag{3}$$

As for light wave recording, one has to realize a special property of light waves. The instantaneous amplitude $\boldsymbol{A}$, which varies with both, time and space, cannot be measured experimentally in a direct way. The frequency of the *light wave* is too high for any known physical mechanism to reply to the changes of the instantaneous amplitude $\boldsymbol{A}$. Any known detector or recording medium replies only to the incident energy. When denoting energy transferred by a wave as E, it can be got as square of the amplitude, i.e. $E = (A_0)^2 = \boldsymbol{A}.\boldsymbol{A}^*$, when using the complex representation, *-symbol represents the complex conjugate quantity.

http://dx.doi.org/10.5772/53592

The value known as *intensity I* of light, is proportional to the energy per unit of surface and unit of time. It is very important to realise that the *time averaged light intensity* is a measurable value, only. Because of that it is said that both, light detection and light recording are *quadratic*.

It is just *holography*, which provides us with a method allowing to record both, the amplitude and phase information despite quadratic recording. Naturally, it is impossible when there is only one light wave. *Dennis Gabor* realized, that there is included the phase information in intensity interference pattern of two waves and it can be utilized in a new – *holographic* method of recording [4].

When two light waves meet and are able to keep a constant phase difference at any point for a proper time interval (long enough to make a record), the interference pattern, i.e. a space redistribution of the resulted energy, can be recorded. Such a situation can come truth only for two coherent waves. Just because of that boom of practical holography started after laser had been invented [5].

To reconstruct, i.e. to see what information is hidden in a hologram, another basic physical phenomenon is applied – *diffraction of light*. There are various types of holograms. Some of them can be reconstructed only by laser light. However, there is also a group of holograms, which can be reconstructed also using common sunlight or another source of *white light*, in which, all the visible spectrum is included. Naturally, that group takes the greatest interest among public and this chapter is going to deal just with such holograms, named here *white light reconstructed holograms* (WLRH).

In the beginning, the basic properties of diffraction of light by a periodic structure are going to be noticed and correlation between diffraction and holographic reconstruction shown. Attention is concentrated especially to the white light diffraction. Understanding of the principles will help the reader to understand problems arising during white light reconstruction of a hologram and also give a hint how to proceed when recording a hologram to avoid such problems. Attention is going to be given to Denisyuk's holograms, image holograms and Benton's rainbow holograms.

The last part of the chapter is focused on some applications of WLRH, especially public ones. To mention also a scientific application, one of our former works, dealing with determination of index of refraction radial profile of a fibre is described briefly.

2. How to record a WLRH

The simple fact that there are two groups of holograms, one of them reconstructed only by coherent light, another one by common white light, tells us that the secret must be hidden in the hologram recording process. To reveal the secret of recording, it would be usable to understand phenomenon of light diffraction, which is the physical principle of hologram reconstruction.

2.1. Diffraction – the physical principle of hologram reconstruction

Firstly - it is said that any deviation from rectilinear propagation of light that cannot be explained because of reflection or refraction is included into diffraction. Such a deviation can be met when light either passes through or reflects from a structure, i.e. a space distribution either of the transmittance, or the refractive index.

Telling more precisely - diffraction is the spreading of waves from a wave-front limited in extent, occurring either when a part of the wave-front is removed by an obstacle, or when all, but a part of the wave-front is removed by an aperture or a stop. The Fraunhofer theory of diffraction, which is interesting for us from the point of view of hologram reconstruction, is concerned with the angular spread of light leaving an aperture of arbitrary shape and size [3].

Secondly – remember that a hologram is, in fact, a two-wave interference pattern recorded, i.e. a kind of structure of intensity distribution. It depends on the type of recording medium and related light-matter interaction mechanism, which of its optical properties distribution follows the interference pattern intensity distribution.

And thirdly – when reconstructing a hologram, it has to be illuminated with light that either passes through or reflects from the hologram. Now, it seems to be obvious to put the equal sign between reconstruction and diffraction.

An introduction to phenomenon of light diffraction and related basic relations can be found in any basic book of optics/photonics, e.g. [3] and even in [6]. Let us show briefly some basic results, related to white light reconstructed holograms.

For the readers, taking a deeper interest - exact solutions of diffraction problems are given by solving Maxwell's equations. However, well-known Kirchhoff's scalar theory gives very good results if period of diffraction structure does not approach a wavelengths size and amplitude vector does not leave a plane.

Let the plane (x_0, y_0) is the plane of a structure and diffraction is observed in the plane (x, y). To find resulting amplitude A_P in $P(x, y)$, amplitudes of spherical waves from all the point sources in the plane of the structure have to be summed (Fig. 1). The idea is expressed by Kirchhoff's diffraction integral

$$A_P(x,y,z) \sim \iint_S \frac{A_0(x_0,y_0)}{r_2} \exp\{-ikr_2\} dx_0 dy_0 \tag{4}$$

where the distance $r_2 = [(x - x_0)^2 + (y - y_0)^2 + z^2]^{1/2}$ and S is size of the illuminated structure. The experimentally observable interference pattern is given by

$I(x, y, z) \sim A_P(x, y, z).[A_P(x, y, z)]^*.$

http://dx.doi.org/10.5772/53592

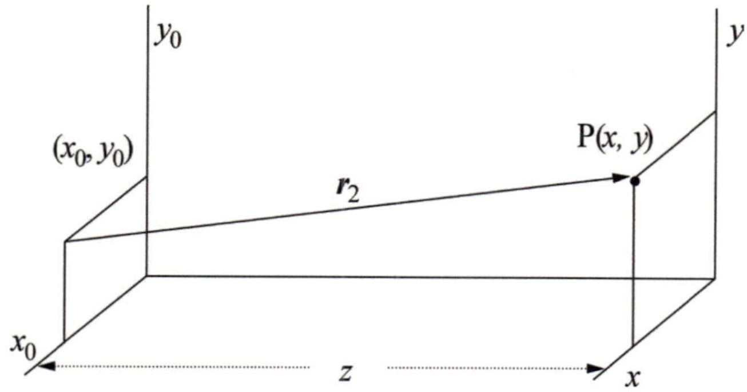

Figure 1. To the principle to solve scalar diffraction problems

To calculate the integral (4), two approximations for r_2 are used – Fresnel's approximation and Fraunhofer's ones. For the purposes of this chapter, let us mention Fraunhofer's aproximation: x_0, y_0, « z, i.e. next mathematical approximation is used to express the phase

$$(x-x_0)^2 \to x^2 - 2x x_0 \quad \text{and} \quad (y-y_0)^2 \to y^2 - 2y y_0$$

and integral (4) turns into

$$A_P(x,y,z) = \\ = \frac{\mathrm{i}}{\lambda z} \exp\left\{-\mathrm{i}k\left(z + \frac{x^2+y^2}{2z}\right)\right\} \iint_S A_0(x_0, y_0, 0)\ \frac{\exp\{-\mathrm{i}k(xx_0 + yy_0)\}}{z}\ \mathrm{d}x_0\ \mathrm{d}y_0 \tag{5}$$

A holographic record can be regarded as a record of a general structure. The light diffraction theory (5) gives us a detail description of light diffraction at a regular plane grating. It is widely used, especially in spectroscopy (looking for various wavelengths).

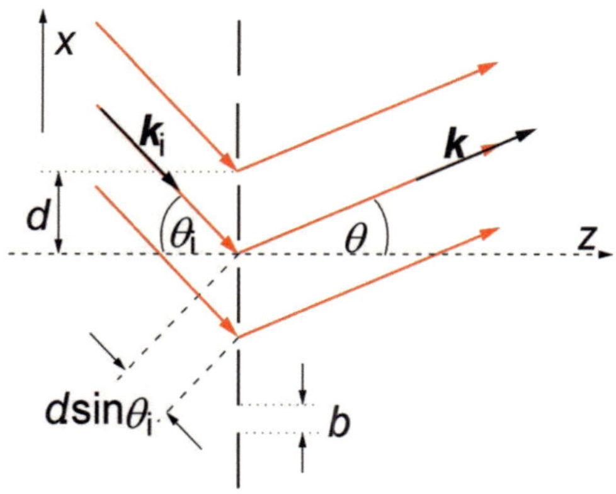

Figure 2. Diffraction by a plane grating (*d* – grating interval, *b* – slit width)

The grating is an ensemble of single equal slits, parallel to each other and having the same distance between each other.

There are two parameters, which define the grating – the *slit width* (b) and the *grating interval* (d) – distance between centres of any two adjacent slits (Fig. 2.). Symbols θ_i and θ denote angles of incident and diffracted waves respectively.

Diffraction at such a grating is, in fact, the interference of many "diffractions" by single slits. The number of interfering "diffractions" depends on the number N of illuminated slits. A detailed calculating of (5) results in the angular intensity distribution

$I \sim \boldsymbol{A_P}.(\boldsymbol{A_P})^*$

and it's normalized value can be get in the form

$$I_R = I_{R1}.I_{R2} = \frac{I(\theta,\lambda,b,d)}{bI_0} = \left\{ \frac{\sin\left[(kb/2)\sin\theta\right]}{(kb/2)\sin\theta} \right\}^2 \left\{ \frac{\sin\left[(Nkd/2)(\sin\theta + \sin\theta_i)\right]}{\sin\left[(kd/2)(\sin\theta + \sin\theta_i)\right]} \right\}^2 \qquad (6)$$

The angle θ appeared because of the Fraunhofer's approximation, where $x/z \sim \sin\theta$. In fact, relation (6) expresses N-wave interference (I_{R2}) modulated by diffraction at a single slit (I_{R1}). Practically usable is especially the condition for interference maxima

$$\frac{kd}{2}(\sin\theta + \sin\theta_i) = m\pi, \quad |m| = 0,1,2,3,... \qquad (7)$$

where $k = 2\pi n/\lambda_0$, n – refractive index of the space of diffraction, λ_0 – wavelength in vacuum and m – order of diffraction. It is obvious that real values of m can be achieved only when grating constant $d > \lambda_0/n = \lambda$. For simplicity, only one-dimensional (x) structure distribution was considered.

Study in the region of X-rays contributed to the phenomenon of diffraction. The short wavelengths of X-rays are not well suited for diffraction by optical gratings. They are, however, conveniently close to the spacing of atoms in crystal lattices, which therefore provide excellent three-dimensional diffraction gratings for X-rays. It was shown, that the diffraction pattern is intimately connected with the arrangement and spacing of atoms within a crystal, so that X-rays can be used for determining the lattice structure [3].

It was Max von Laue who first suggested that a crystal might behave towards a beam of X-rays rather as does a ruled diffraction grating to ordinary light. It is interesting, that at the time it was not certain either crystals really were such regular arrangements, or X-rays were short-wavelength electromagnetic radiation [3]. W. L. Bragg proved the idea in 1912.

It can be derived in a simply way taking into account the result for plane grating and the influence of a thickness h of the grating (Fig. 3). Let us consider angles of incidence θ_i and

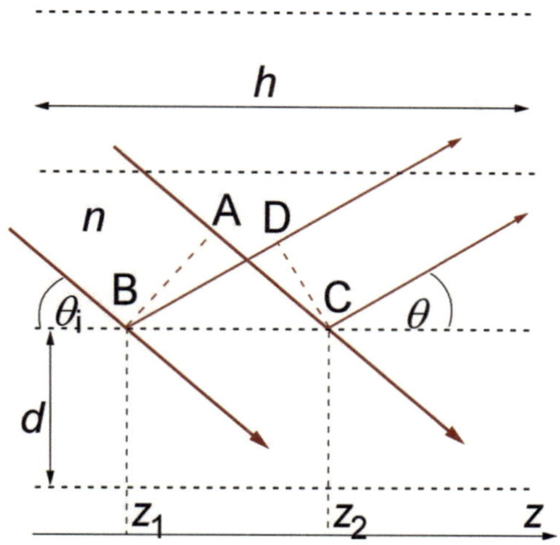

Figure 3. Diffraction by a volume grating (*h* – thickness, *n* – index of refraction)

angle of refraction θ. To get the intensity maximum in passing light, the condition (7) has to be fulfilled, i.e.

$$nd\left(\sin\theta + \sin\theta_i\right) = m\lambda_0 \tag{8}$$

Moreover, because of the thickness of the grating, all the waves irradiated along the *z*-axis should be in phase in direction of the angle θ, i.e.

$$\left(AC - BD\right)n_0 = n_0\left(z_2 - z_1\right)\left[cos\theta_i - cos\theta\right] = m\lambda_0, \;\; where \; \left|m\right| = 0, 1, 2, ... \tag{9}$$

The condition has to be satisfied for all the *z* coordinates. It is possible only for $\theta = \pm\theta_i$ that leads to the well known Bragg's law for X-ray reflection from a crystal

$$2nd\sin\theta_i = m\lambda_0, \quad \left|m\right| = 0, 1, 2, ... \tag{10}$$

used also to describe diffraction at optical volume gratings.

Concluding this paragraph, let us try to describe the diffraction phenomenon using holographic terms. Two coherent plane waves

$$w_1 \sim \exp\left(i\varphi_1\right), \qquad w_2 \sim \exp\left(i\varphi_2\right) \tag{11}$$

interfere (Fig.4a). The interference pattern that will work as a grating can be expressed in the form, which corresponds with the amplitude transmission *t* of produced grating

$$t = (w_1 + w_2)(w_1 + w_2)^* = |w_1|^2 + |w_2|^2 + w_1 w_2^* + w_1^* w_2 \tag{12}$$

Let us suppose the grating to be very thin and illuminated by a plane wave w_0 in the z axis direction (Fig. 4b). The phases of all the waves can be expressed as

$$\varphi_j = kx \sin\phi_j, \quad j = 0,1,2 \tag{13}$$

The light wave w passing the grating consists of three parts

$$w = w_0 t = w_0\left(|w_1|^2 + |w_2|^2\right) + w_0 w_1 w_2^* + w_0 w_1^* w = w_A + w_B + w_C \tag{14}$$

The phases of three waves in (14) are

$$\varphi_A = kx \sin\phi_0, \quad \varphi_B = kx(\sin\phi_0 + \sin\phi_1 - \sin\phi_2), \quad \varphi_C = kx(\sin\phi_0 - \sin\phi_1 + \sin\phi_2) \tag{15}$$

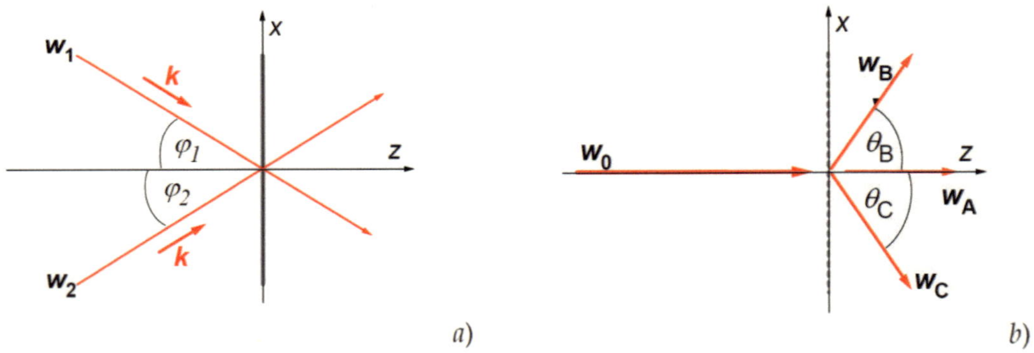

Figure 4. Diffraction as holography. *a* - 2-wave interference produces a grating; *b* - diffraction at the grating

Supposing $\varphi_0 = 0$, $\varphi_1 = \alpha/2$ and $\varphi_2 = -\alpha/2$ one can obtain phases

$$\varphi_A = 0, \quad \varphi_B = 2kx \sin(\alpha/2), \quad \varphi_C = 2kx \sin(-\alpha/2) \tag{16}$$

Let us compare (16) to the light diffraction at a plane grating with the grating interval d. The grating interval in our case is

$$d = \lambda / 2\sin(\alpha/2) \tag{17}$$

Taking into account $\theta_i = 0$, the condition (7) for intensity maximum turns into

$$\sin\theta = m.2\sin(\alpha/2), \quad |m| = 0,1,2,3,... \tag{18}$$

The relation (18) gives the same angles of propagation $\sin\theta_A = 0$, $\sin\theta_B = 2\sin(\alpha/2)$, and $\sin\theta_C = 2\sin(-\alpha/2)$, as relations (16).

2.2. How to avoid problems arising during white-light reconstruction

Now we posses all the knowledge to realize what kind of problems can be met when reconstructing a hologram using white light and even to find a way to avoid them. There are two important results that had been derived above – relation (7) expressing the conditions for existence of a diffracted wave of the order m at a plane grating that can be rewritten into:

$$dn(\sin\theta + \sin\theta_i) = m\lambda_0, \quad |m| = 0,1,2,3,... \tag{19}$$

The second one is the same kind of relation, valid for a volume grating - relation (10)

$$2nd\sin\theta = 2nd\sin\theta_i = m\lambda_0, \quad |m| = 0,1,2,... \tag{20}$$

Let us consider white light reconstruction of a *plane hologram*, which deals with the relation (19). It is obvious that when using waves with various wavelengths λ_j, they will be diffracted at various angles θ_j. When considering reconstruction as a diffraction, m =1. The angle θ of diffraction depends on the wavelength λ_{0j} and various angles $\theta_j(\lambda_{0j})$ will cause various positions of the reconstructed object (Fig. 5.) Naturally, it results in "a blurred" reconstructed object both, horizontally and vertically. However, looking at Fig. 5, it could have occurred to us that if the distance between the object and hologram would have been smaller a less blurred reconstruction could be obtained (image holograms).

Figure 5. White light reconstruction – the scheme and white light & HeNe laser reconstruction

Moreover, not only a colour blur appears. It is also a *space blur* present. Both, lens and hologram create an image, so hologram is often compared to a lens. So-called *hologram formula*

$$\frac{1}{R_2^{(r,v)}} + \frac{1}{R_1} = \frac{1}{R_1}\left(1 + \frac{\lambda_2}{\lambda_1}\right) - \frac{\lambda_2/\lambda_1}{L_1} \pm \frac{1}{L_2} = \frac{1}{f_{\mathrm{H}}^{(\mathrm{r,v})}} \tag{21}$$

similar to the *lens formula* can be derived, too. A hologram also can be characterised by its *focal length* f_{H}. It depends on the wavelength of light when either recording (λ_1), or reconstructing (λ_2), object distance from the hologram (R_1) and distance of the source of both, reference (L_1) and reconstructing (L_2) beam from the hologram [7]. Paraxial approximation is supposed, all the distances are measured perpendicularly to the plane of hologram and indices (signs) r (±→-), v (±→+) in (21) are related to *real* and *virtual* reconstruction.

In fact, the relation (21) defines a space blur (various R_{2j}) because of various wavelengths λ_{0j}. Remembering of various horizontal and vertical resolution of a human eye, it gives us another hint – to try to limit a possibility of the reconstruction *in whole* (Benton's holograms).

Now, let us take an interest in *volume holograms*, where results obtained for diffraction at a volume grating were obtained. Ideally there are only two diffraction grating order numbers relevant – $m = 0, 1$. Intensity of higher diffraction grating orders diminish to zero because of mutual interference and the condition (20) turns into

$$2nd\sin\theta_j = 2nd\sin\theta_{ij} = \lambda_{0j} \tag{22}$$

It is a very interesting and for WLRH important result. According to the relation (22) there is an unambiguous relation among the grating period d, wavelength λ_{0j} and angle $\theta_j = \theta_{ij}$. That means – when reconstructing by white light there is the only special angle for every wavelength. This way, the *volume hologram* picks from the white-light spectrum different reconstruction angle for every wavelength, i.e. prepares time coherent light for reconstruction (Denisyuk's hologram). It depends on the method of hologram recording if the reconstructed object is observed either in single colours or colourfully.

2.3. Denisyuk's holograms

Let us proceed following the history of holography and start with Denisyuk's holograms. In 1962, Yuri Denisyuk combined holography with 1908 Nobel Laureate Gabriel Lippmann's work in natural color photography [8]. Denisyuk's approach produced a white-light reflection hologram which, for the first time, could be viewed in light from an ordinary incandescent light bulb [9].

To explain the principle briefly, at least: Isaac Newton found out colours produced by a very thin layer due to interference of light. Colours in butterflies are the result of interference phenomena, too. And in 1886, when the photography was still struggling to transfer the col-

http://dx.doi.org/10.5772/53592

ours of nature to adequate tonal values in black and white, the French physicist Gabriel Lippmann conceived a method to record and reproduce colour images directly through the wavelengths from the lighted object. He introduced a photographic colour process that demanded no colorants, dyes, or pigments, based on light waves interference principles, too.

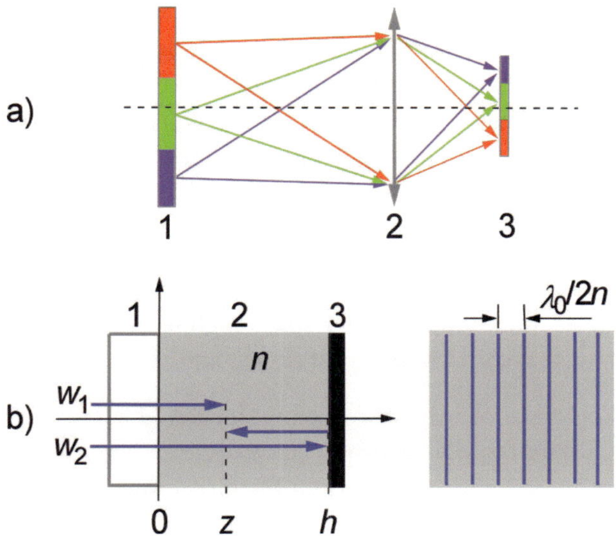

Figure 6. Principle of Lippmann's colour photography. a - colour photography (1-object, 2-lens, 3-image); b - two-wave interference (w_1 and w_2-interfering waves, 1-photographic glass plate, 2-photographic emulsion, 3-mercury mirror, $n(h)$-refractive index (thickness) of the emulsion.

He used a photographic emulsion between a photographic glass plate and a mercury mirror (Fig. 6a). The glass plate and emulsion are nearly transparent. Light waves coming from the object reflect from the HG-mirror (w_1) and interfere with coming light waves (w_2) – Fig. 6b. Since the Hg index of refraction prevails the emulsion index of refraction n, standing waves are created [3]. The interference pattern consists of *nodes*-surfaces and *loops*-surfaces, i.e. dark and bright interference surfaces that are recorded in the fine grain emulsion. Fig. 6b demonstrates a simple section of the interference surfaces to evaluate their spacing $\lambda_0/2n$, which depends on the wavelength λ_0.

It can be derived in a very simply way, when realizing the phase difference $\Delta\Phi(z)$ between two plane waves meeting at the coordinate z

$$\Delta\varphi(z) = \frac{2\pi}{\lambda_0} n\left[h + (h - z) - z\right] = \frac{2\pi}{\lambda_0} 2n\left(h - z\right) \tag{23}$$

If $\Delta\Phi(z_m) = 2m\pi$, where $m = 0, 1, 2,...$ interference maximum is located at z_m. It follows for the spacing between two adjacent maxima the value $\Delta z = z_{m+1} - z_m = \lambda_0/2n$. For simplicity, to point the principle, only, the angle between interfering plane waves was taken to be π.

This way the processed photographic emulsion became a layer where beside an image also volume gratings with various grating intervals, related to the local wavelength, were recorded.

Taking into account the former paragraph (2.2), it is obvious that after the photograph is illuminated by white light, the image in its original colours can be observed because of diffraction of white light at such a structure.

It is hardly imaginable that in the late 1800s such an advanced photographic technique was already conceived and realized. The resemblance with volume holography, published in 1962 by Yuri Denisyuk, is striking. Lippmann photography actually is the ancestor of volume reflection holography or Denisyuk holography, which is sometimes also referred to as Denisyuk-Lippmann-Bragg holography.

Yu. Denisyuk, inspired by the ingenious Lippmann's colour photography technique did extensive theoretical analysis and experimented with mercury lamp sources since 1958 and even enlisted colleagues to develop a special thick, high-resolution, and relatively sensitive photographic emulsion to record the wave pattern in depth [10].

Later, realizing the potential of wave-front reconstruction, devised a different approach to record a hologram. A laser beam illuminated an object through a photographic plate (reference beam) interfered with light reflected from the object (object beam) to produce a hologram in the layer of the photographic emulsion (Fig. 7a).

Reconstruction can be performed by sunlight or another white-light source lighting the hologram. If the direction is the same as when recording, the Bragg's diffractive reflection provides us with a monochromatic reconstructed image of the object in the wavelength used when recording the hologram (e.g. Fig. 7b). Fig. 7c demonstrates a possible two-beam experimental set-up.

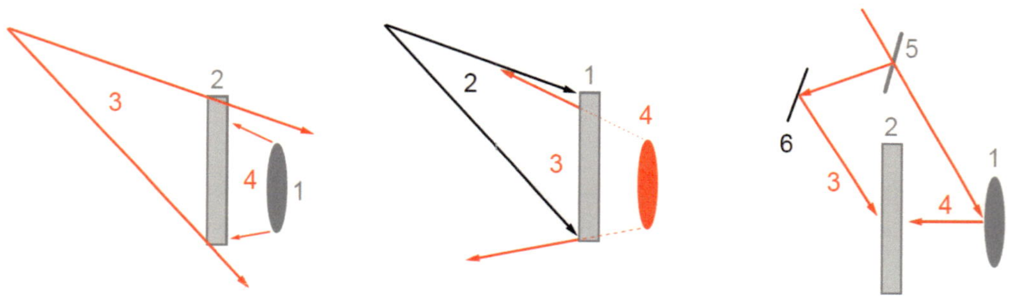

a) *b)* *c)*

Figure 7. Denisyuk's 1-beam holographical set-up. *a* – recording (1-object, 2-recording medium, 3-reference beam, 4-object beam), *b* – reconstruction (1-hologram, 2-reconstructing beam, 3-reconstructed wave, 4-holographic image), *c* – 2-beam set-up (1-object, 2-recording medium, 3-reference beam, 4-object beam, 5-beam splitter, 6-mirror).

However, as mentioned above, such a reconstruction is a monochromatic one, only (Fig. 8). What about colour holograms?

To produce colourful hologram, one needs three lasers generating on three basic wavelengths (red, green, blue) to record such a hologram. Each of the waves creates own interference structure (Fig. 9). After illuminating such a hologram with white light, each structure helps to reconstruct the object wave in related wavelength. The reconstruction can be seen in three colours and thanks to sophisticated activity of our brain as colourful.

Figure 8. Yu. Denisyuk reconstructed from a hologram and alive [11]

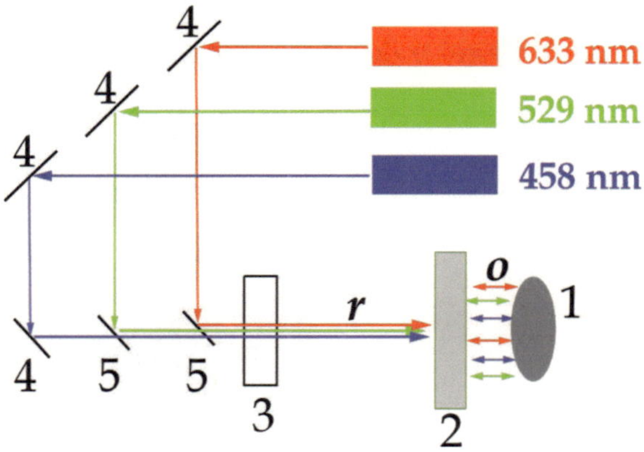

Figure 9. A colourful hologram recording (1-object, 2-recording medium, 3-optics to spread light, 4-mirror, 5-semi-transparent mirrors)

Yu. N. Denisyuk presented his technique as a generalized form of Lippmann photography, or as a colour-dependent optical element. This technique, using reflection holography and the white-light reconstruction technique, seems to be the most promising one as regards the actual recording of colour holograms [12].

2.4. Image hologram

Writing on white-light reconstructed holograms it is necessary to take into account that depending on the relation between the thickness h of the recording medium and the average spacing $\bar{d}$ of the recorded holographic structure fringes, there are defined two types of holograms – *thin* and *thick*, i.e. *volume* ones. They are characterized by a parameter Q

$$Q = \frac{2\pi\lambda_0 h}{n\bar{d}^2} \tag{24}$$

introduced in [13]. $Q < 1$ corresponds to thin gratings, while $Q > 1$ corresponds to volume gratings. Moreover the objects around us can be defined as either 2D or 3D objects.

It is obvious that Denisyuk's method of holography is applicable to any object and the recording media suitable to create a volume hologram. Moreover, it represents a reflection holography, i.e. the reconstructed wave seems like reflection of the reconstructing wave from the hologram. When recording, the reference beam and the object beam come from opposite sides of the recording medium. Because of that, when reconstructing, observer and the source of the reconstructing wave are on the same side of the hologram. The next two paragraphs are dealing with so-called *transmission thin holograms*.

Let us remember of the physical principle of reconstruction of a hologram. It is diffraction of either transmitted or reflected incident, i.e. reconstructing light. Due to that, the white-light reconstruction of transmission thin holograms brings a possible colour and space *blur* of the reconstructed image (Fig. 5). The illustrative Fig.5 gives us a hint to decrease the object – hologram distance when recording the hologram as much as possible to avoid the colour blur. It would be the best to decrease the distance to zero. However, the reference beam must not be blocked.

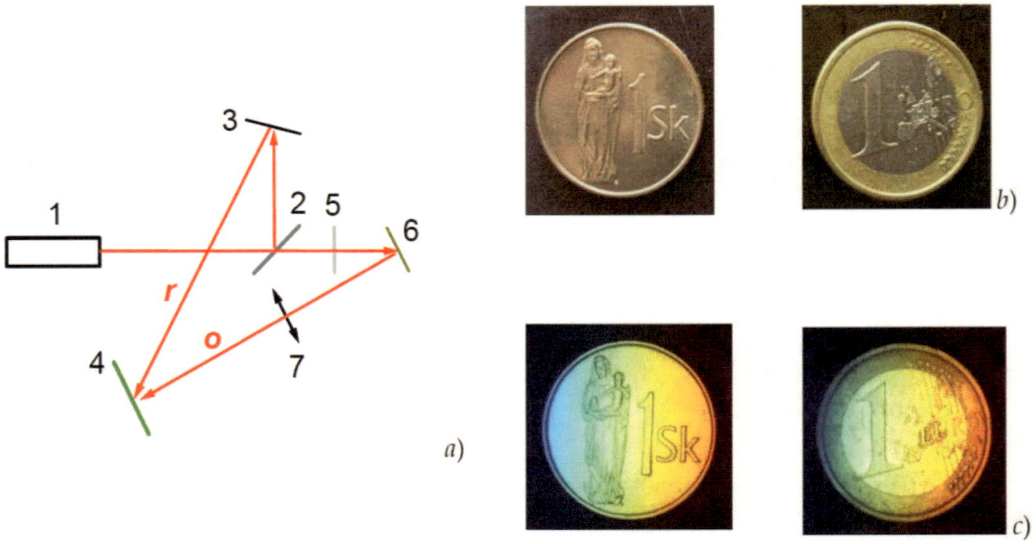

Figure 10. Image holography. *a* – experimental set-up (1-laser & collimator, 2-beam splitter, 3-mirror, 4-hologram, 5-ground glass, 6-object, 7-projecting lens; *b* - objects, *c* - reconstruction

There is a simple possibility to put the recorded object (Fig. 10b) even "into" the recording medium and not to restrict the reference wave while recording the hologram – to *project* it there by a projecting lens (Fig. 10a). When reconstructing in white light the reconstruction is observed in various (rainbow) colours from various directions at the same place (Fig. 10c.).

When the image coincides with the hologram plane, it is perfectly sharp. Naturally, projection of a 3D object has 3D properties, too. In practice, display holograms up to around 2 cm in depth can be acceptable. This type of hologram is called an *open-aperture* hologram [14]. However, such a simple method is used mostly for approximately "2D" objects like medals, coins, photos, and so on.

A more detailed estimation of the image blur can be found in [15]. It can be shown that if the source used to reconstruct the hologram is located at the same position as the reference source used to record it and has very nearly the same wavelength, the blur Δx_{R2} of the reconstructed image along the x axis for a source size Δx_{L2} is

$$\Delta x_{R2} = (R_1 / L_2)\Delta x_{L2} \quad (25)$$

Similarly, if the source used to reconstruct the hologram has a mean wavelength λ_2 very nearly equal to λ_1, the wavelength used to record the hologram, and a spectral bandwidth $\Delta\lambda_2$, the transverse image blur Δx_{R2} due to the finite spectral bandwidth of the source of reconstructing wave, located at x_{L2} can be shown to be

$$|\Delta x_{R2}| = (x_{L2} / L_2) R_1 (\Delta\lambda_2 / \lambda_2) \quad (26)$$

The image blur increases with the depth of the image and the interbeam angle.

It follows from (25) and (26) that if the interbeam angle and the depth of the object are small, it is possible to use an extended white-light source to view the image.

2.5. Benton's holograms

When a real 3D object is recorded the well-known Benton's method [16], which allows us to get rid of vertical blur of the reconstructed image, has to be used. The Benton (rainbow) hologram is a transfer transmission hologram, which reconstructs a bright, sharp, monochromatic image when illuminated with white light [17]. Benton holograms are produced by means of an optical technique that sacrifices the vertical parallax of the holographic image in favour of a sharp monochromatic reconstruction by a white light point source. In other words - the physical basis of this method is to reduce the amount of information on the hologram. The vertical parallax is eliminated. The method relays on the fact that human beings have two eyes in horizontal position, i.e. people are less sensitive to vertical parallax.

In fact, it is a hologram of a hologram. The first (master) hologram H_1 of the object O is produced (Fig. 11a). The object and reference waves are directed around the horizontal plane.

Then, H_1 is masked with a narrow horizontal slit S and wave 1, conjugated to the reference wave 2 from Fig. 11a is used to reconstruct the free part of H_1. The conjugate wave [6] of the original object wave is reconstructed and the real holographic image HI serves as an object to record the second hologram H_2 (the part *a)* in Fig. 11b). The part *b)* of Fig. 11b demonstrates the view to the process of recording H_2 from the side. The 3D object, represented by reconstructed HI straddles the plane of medium to record H_2 and a converging reference wave 3 is now inclined in the vertical plane.

When viewing such a hologram in the same monochromatic light as the recording one, the holographic image from H_2 that straddles the plane of H_2 is reconstructed. However, while recording H_2 the width of the slit S limited the vertical parallax of the object and it will be limited when observing the reconstruction, too. That means, there is a small interval of angles in vertical direction that allows observing the reconstruction of H_2, i.e. the perspective information in vertical axis is lost. The horizontal parallax is much more wider, given by the width of H_1 determined by the length of the slit S.

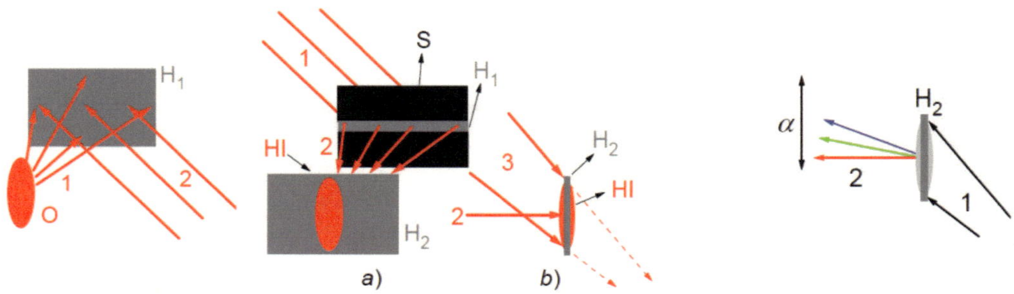

a) *b)* *c)*

Figure 11. Principle of Benton's rainbow hologram. *a* – object O, hologram H_1, object wave 1, reference wave 2; *b* – hologram H_1, slit S, reconstructing wave 1, reconstructed wave 2 as a new object wave, holographic image HI, reference wave 3, hologram H_2; *c* – hologram H_2, reconstructing white light 1, colour reconstructed waves 2 related to various angles *α*.

It seems like a kind of limitation, but remember – when recording H_2, the reference wave 3 was inclined in the vertical plane. This way, the hologram H_2, which is a set of arbitrary gratings with horizontal fringes in principle, became a dispersion element for vertical angle variations. That provides the hologram H_2 with colour dispersion. With a white-light source, located approximately in the convergence point of 3 (Fig. 11c), the reconstruction is dispersed in the vertical plane to form a continuous spectrum (hence the term "rainbow"). An observer whose eyes are positioned at any part of this spectrum then sees a sharp, three-dimensional image of the object in the corresponding colour. In [18] is presented an optical system that permits both steps of the recording process to be carried out with a minimum of adjustment.

The image reconstructed from a rainbow hologram is free from speckle, because it is illuminated with incoherent light. However, it is not free from blur. A more detailed analyse of rainbow holograms can be found in [19].

http://dx.doi.org/10.5772/53592

One cause of image blur is the finite wavelength spread in the image. The maximum wavelength spread observed when the rainbow hologram is illuminated with white light can be estimated as

$$(\Delta\lambda)_{\max} \sim \lambda / \sin\theta / \left(D + b\right) / L \tag{27}$$

where θ is the angle between object and reference waves when recording H_2, L is the distance between H_1 and H_2, D is eye pupil diameter and b is the slite S width. The eyes of the person viewing the image are supposed to be placed in the position, where the image of the slit is formed. The relation (27) leads to the image blur due to wavelength spread of about

$$\delta_{\Delta\lambda} \sim z_0\left(D + b\right) / L \tag{28}$$

where z_0 reprezents the H_2-to-image distance generally, when the image does not straddle the H_2 plane. With $z_0 \to 0$ the image blur (28) also goes to zero.

Another cause of image blur is the finite size of the source used to illuminate the hologram. If the source has the angular subtense Ω_S, as viewed from the hologram, the resultant image blur is approximatelly

$$\delta_S \sim z_0 \Omega_S \tag{29}$$

A final cause of image blur is diffraction at the slit

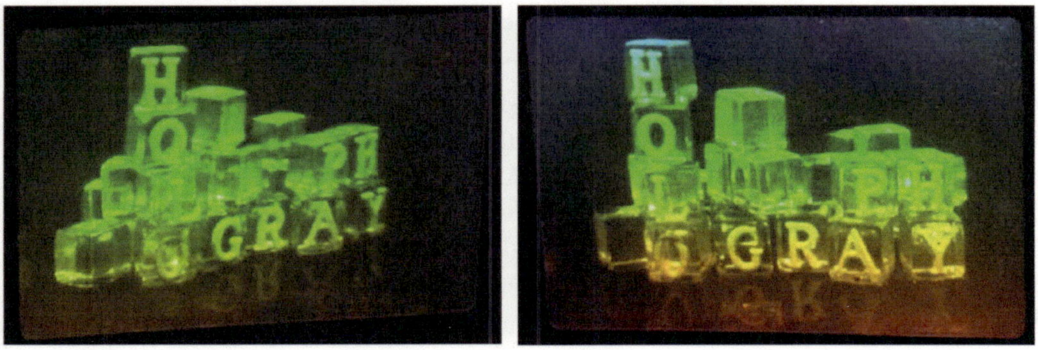

Figure 12. White light reconstruction of Benton's hologram "*Holography Blocks*" (made of tens of 1 inch transparent acrylic cubes) photographed from two directions to demonstrate its 3D property [20].

$$\delta_{diff} \sim 2\lambda\left(z_0 + L\right) / b \tag{30}$$

However, this can be neglected unless the width of the slit is very small.

Concluding this part, I would like to memory the inventor of this kind of holography, Benton S. A., and include the reconstruction of his *Holography Blocks*, the transmission rainbow hologram that he made of tens of 1 inch transparent acrylic cubes (1975). The pictures (Fig. 12) were photographed from his hologram from the left and from the right to demonstrate its 3D property by R. L. van Renesse and published in his monograph written in remembrance of Steve Benton after he passed away, in 2003 [20].

3. Some applications of WLRH

This paragraph consists of two parts. The first one mentions some situations briefly, at least, when anyone can meet white light reconstructed holograms. For those, taking an interest, there is great amount of Internet information accessible now, even pointing to details related to methods and technologies to produce WLRH.

Naturally, there are many scientific applications of WLRH, too. To solve the problem of commercial application can, also, be considered as a scientific application. I decided to use the second part to present short information, at least, on one of our former works, which was published in Slovak, only. It is focused on using the phase-shifting image holographic interferometry to study an optical fibre refractive index radial distribution. The image holography was used for us to be able to profit from possible magnification of the studied region.

3.1. Popular WLRH applications

When considering current applications of holographic technology enabling white light hologram reconstruction, i.e. displaying and viewing holograms using a common white light source, consumer products and advertising materials have to be mentioned firstly [1].

Security and product authentication seem to be the most popular growing areas for the use of holograms, especially of white-light reconstructed holograms. Why is it so?

Generally speaking, holograms can reconstruct one of two waves used to record them, when illuminated by the second one. That means optical reconstruction of 3D space from a 2D record. After four milestones in history of holography, represented by D. Gabor (father of holography), Yu. N. Denisyuk (invented volume reflection holography), E. N. Leith and J. Upatnieks (invented off-axis holography), and S. Benton (invented rainbow holography), the subsequent development of the micro-embossing technique allowed their mass replication [21].

For example a very popular variation became the *embossed hologram*. Such holograms are easily produced in mass quantity and at a very low cost. The holographic structure is recorded on a light sensitive medium (a photo-resistor), which can be processed by etching and a microscopic relief is created. By electro-deposition of a metal (nickel) on the relief a stamper is made and its surface relief is copied by impressing it onto another material (e.g. polyester base film, thermoplastic film).

It was soon realized that holograms might be used as security features on valuable documents and products and this way classical hologram became the first of a manifold of diffractive structures developed to thwart counterfeiting. Many of these diffractive structures can no longer be called holograms in the strict sense and some of them are no longer made by laser interference techniques, but created by advanced electron beam lithographic techniques [21].

These holograms, i.e. diffractive elements provide a powerful obstacle to counterfeiting. One can meet holograms either on various goods itself or in the packaging of products, on banknotes, various types of cards, and so on. For example - almost all credit cards carry a hologram, which is a good sign that security holography has proven to be very effective. There are various kinds of holographic labels and stickers [1].

Holographic labels are firmly affixed on the desired place of a product to verify its genuineness. Such labels cannot be copied, altered, either adapted or manufactured in an easy way. Moreover, hidden information can be embedded, visible at special circumstances, only. To increase the uniqueness of holographic labels, there are used another specific techniques, e.g. custom etching and overwriting of labels. To give some examples, holographic labels are used in various kinds of cards, artwork, banknotes, bank checks, product packaging for brand protection, alcohol, cosmetics, and so on.

Holographic stickers (*HS*) – most of them are self adhesive, providing authentication, security and protection against counterfeit, too. To increase their security level, various techniques are used. Let us mention some of them, like laser beam engraved dots (*dot-matrix HS*), double-exposed hologram of two objects from two directions (*flip-flop HS*) that displays two images from two different viewing angles), combinations of holograms, micro-information included, visible only by magnifier (*micro text/image HS*). Locally different thickness of the hologram layer gives reconstruction in various colours. A hidden text or image invisible to the naked eye but visible by means of a laser reader, serial numbers, overprinting left after the sticker is peeled off, are next examples of holographic stickers security increasing.

To minimise counterfeiting in holograms various methods during recording are used. It is possible to include hidden information or make the image so complicated that it is not worth to duplicate it, considering the time and money involved [1]. However, hidden information is of great value only if the cheater cannot find it or duplicate it. So, effective use of hidden information or any kind of complex images requires some sort of relatively simple and inexpensive reading device or decoding device.

Another possibility profits from using variable processing parameters, like randomly changed exposure, development time or other processing parameters to produce variable shrinkage all over the hologram. This results into a hologram whose colour varies from point to point and when using a monochromatic source - laser the brightness changes dramatically with the shrinkage of the film.

Holograms are not easy to counterfeit either if variable information like serial numbers, encoded personal information or dates are included or they are made of some special materials. Combined countermeasures can be another effective approach, too.

To show another ways of WLRH using, let us remember that in the beginning, holograms, a kind of "windows with a memory" with unfamiliar properties, were regarded as similar to daguerreotypes, photography predecessors [22]. Like early photography, holography was expected to develop technically and become cheaper, more capable and widespread. Where possible, people worked to realize these expectations of progress, especially for trade show displays. A pulse ruby laser had been developed to enable recording a human portrait in a darkened room to create static 3D human scenes for advertising. While such holograms attracted interest their display requirements (laser) made them too unwieldy to be sold or even displayed outside the laboratories.

Some artists, supported by scientists at first, began to take up holography. Inspired by the art and technology movement that was then exploring videotape, architecture, and other influences, they sought to make fine-art holograms. A second group - artisans intended to make holography an expressive medium for anyone.

However, the cost of the laser, needed for both, recording and viewing holograms, was a crucial constraint for artists and advertisers. Moreover, the monochromacity of laser light provided portraits inferior to the panchromatic black-and-white films. For photographers then, holographic portraiture represented problems not progress. These limitations restricted holography to a narrow class of subjects and applications [22].

Denisyuk's holograms offered a solution of the most pressing problem for aesthetic and commercial users - the need for a laser to display the hologram. Then Benton's rainbow hologram also became widespread, which could be viewed in white light in a spectrum of colours.

As mentioned above, embossed holograms provided new audiences, manufactured by the millions on metal foil, they became ubiquitous in packaging, graphic arts, and security applications. Embossed holograms were inexpensive, reducing the cost of copies by a hundredfold. They could be mass-produced reliably by using a number of proprietary techniques. And they were chemically and mechanically stable, unlike most previous hologram materials that were susceptible to breakage, humidity, or aging [22]. Together, these technical advantages promoted the widespread application of embossed holograms.

On the other hand, their flexibility, particularly on magazine covers, caused colour shifts and image distortion. Moreover, the holograms were usually viewed in uncontrolled lighting, images could appear fuzzy or dim. In response to these limitations, their producers progressively simplified the imagery. This way embossed holograms promoted low-cost mass production but had relatively poor image quality. However, these characteristics were deemed to be a serious defect for imaging purposes. Fine-art holograms declined in popularity, with artists complaining that embossed holograms irreparably devalued the aesthetic attraction of the medium [22].

Despite all of that, holograms are used in advertisement to attract potential buyers. They can be met on magazine and book covers. Display holograms are widely used wherever an audience needs to be reached (e.g. at trade fairs, presentations). Holograms found their place in the entertainment industry (movies), became popular in the area of packaging and for promotional purpose. This type of holography can be found as a part of some either pure or combined holographic artist works (in special galleries), too [22, 23].

3.2. An example of WLRH in science - Interferometric analysis of optical fibre profile

There is a special interest focused to optical fibres all over the world. They became of great importance as parts of many photonic devices and various methods are used to study their properties. Radial profile of fibre optical thickness, i.e. of its refractive index is one of the most important fibre characteristics. Many papers arise contemporary. Mostly they are based on classic interferometric microscopy of a fibre located in a wedge shaped layer of an immerse liquid. When applying optical imaging, methods are limited by the diffractive resolution $\lambda/2n.\sin\theta$, where n is the refractive index of the object space, θ is the angle related entrance aperture of the objective. The limit follows from the Rayleigh criterion, applicable in the Fraunhofer approximation. Taking into account a conception of near-field optics it would be a better solution [12].

The experimental method elaborated in our paper is based on double-exposure phase-shifting interferometry. Moreover, the image holographic interferometry was used to profit from both the advantages - lower demands on optical quality of all the set-up elements and also the possibility of white-light reconstruction and magnifying the object size. Moreover, phase-shifting interferometry allows determining both, the size and direction of optical path changes. Fig. 13 demonstrates the experimental set-up. The laser beam is divided into collimated waves, object ($\boldsymbol{o}$) and reference ($\boldsymbol{p}$) ones. The object V is projected on the recording medium with a proper magnification and hologram H is recorded. To apply the phase-shifting interferometry the wedge K inclines the reference beam between two expositions. V represents two states of the object – either a glass cell filled with glycerine (n_K = 1,4534 ± 0.0005) and the fibre embedded into it, or the glass cell filled with glycerine without the fibre.

The glycerine helped to reduce somehow the influence of the basic index of refraction n_0 of the fibre on the interference pattern. Accurately, the cell exit was projected on the plane of hologram. The object wave passes through the fibre perpendicularly to its axis.

The glass wedge K, passed through by the reference wave enabled phase-shifting interferometry. It was a very simple method to change the object-reference-beam angle in the order of the hundredths of a degree [24].

Two fibre specimen of the same kind from Slovak Academy of Sciences were used with radii R_1 = 0.825 mm and R_2 = 0.55 mm. The numerical aperture of them was 0.22 and relation between radii $R_J = 0.9R$ (Fig. 13).

The basic fibre index of refraction was n_0 = 1,45718 (at λ = 632.8 nm).

Interferograms (e.g. Fig. 14) were analysed supposing radial refractive index increment distribution $\Delta n(x, y)$ within the core radius R_J and the thickness of the glycerine layer d. The change of optical thickness Δl at coordinate y (Fig. 13) can be expressed in the form

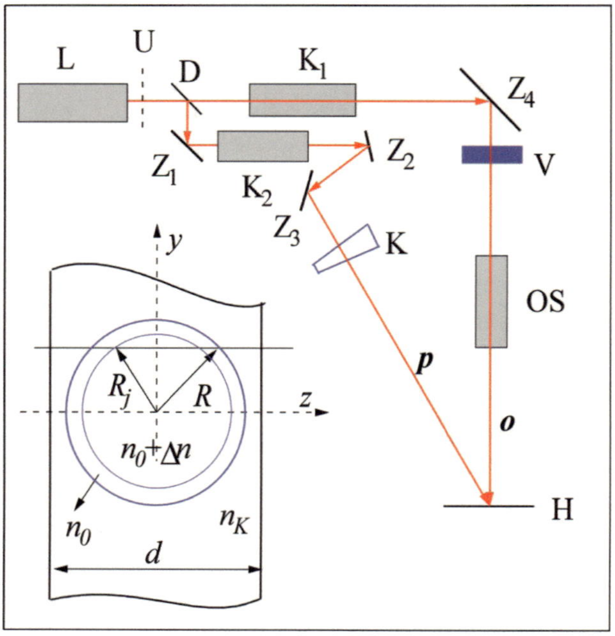

Figure 13. Experimental set-up. L–He-Ne laser, D-beam splitter, U-switch, K_i-collimators, Z_i-mirrors, K-wedge, V-the object, OS-objective, H-hologram, ***o*** (***p***)-object (reference) beam. In left bottom corner - the scheme of the fibre cross-section in a cell.

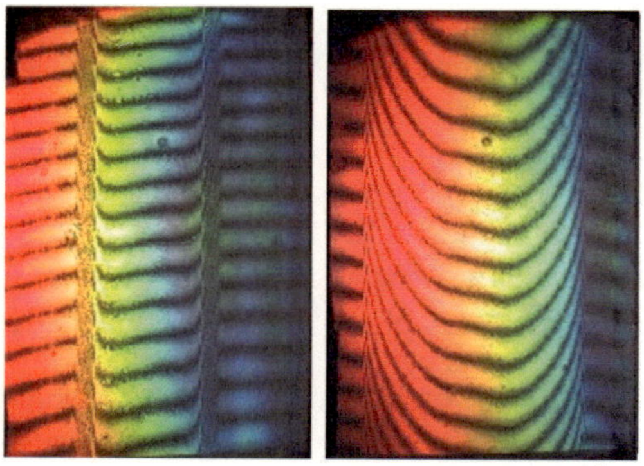

$R_1 = 0.55$ mm;	$R_2 = 0.825$ mm;
$\Delta m_1 \sim 4$	$\Delta m_2 \sim 5.5$
$\Delta n_1 \sim 0.015$	$\Delta n_2 \sim 0.017$

Figure 14. Demonstration of interferograms.

http://dx.doi.org/10.5772/53592

$$\Delta l(y) = 2\int_{0}^{R(y)} [n_0 - \Delta n(r) - n_K]dz + 2\int_{0}^{R_J(y)} \Delta n dz \tag{31}$$

Supposing axially symmetrical refractive index distribution, it is convenient to introduce the substitution

$$z(y) = \sqrt{r^2 - y^2} \tag{32}$$

Interference maxims appear when Δl is equal to an integral number of wavelengths - $m\lambda$. Due to that the interference order m becomes a function of the coordinate y

$$m(y) = \Delta l(y) / \lambda \tag{33}$$

The shift Δm of the interference order was estimated from the interference pattern obtained (Fig. 14), which were digitalized and numerically analysed using the relation (33). Fig. 15 is to demonstrate analysis of one set of experimental data. It is necessary to realize that also the change $\Delta m_C(y)$ caused by the cylindrical shape of the fibre, denoted as $y0$ in Fig. 15, is included in the experimentally obtained distribution of $m(y)$ expressed by ym in Fig. 15. The distribution $\Delta m_C(y) = y0$ was determined theoretically using the known fibre parameters.

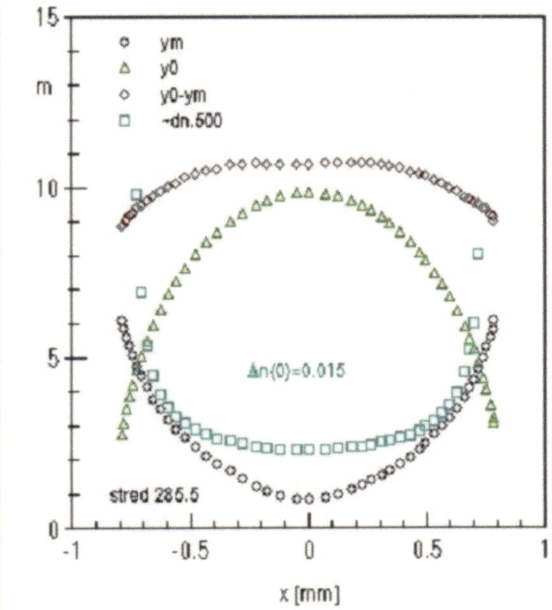

Figure 15. Analysis of experimental data

This way the producer's data, related to the original preform were approved (a stepped-index fibre with core radius $R_J = 0.9R$ and $\Delta n = 0.016$). The results obtained confirmed possibilities provided by holographic interferometry to analyse refractive index profile of an optical fibre in the region of sizes not demanding near-field optics concepts. The numerical analysis had been improved applying method of genetic algorithm and extended to a gradient-index fibre [25].

4. Conclusion

Today, holography seems to be a common method of optical information recording and especially - information advertising. Not only holograms can be met everywhere, moreover, terms, like *"hologram"* and *"holographic"* can be found in many fields of human life.

I suppose white-light reconstructed holograms to be of great interest especially for common public, without a special optical education. However, it is not possible to restrict their usage for public reasons, only. They are applicable as both, scientific and measuring tools, too.

Great amount of information is accessible by the Internet. However, it is important to read patiently, to find the truth. Due to that I tried to explain especially the basic principles to understand the matter.

To conclude, I would like to use another quotation from a very interesting paper, devoted to a historian's view of holography [22]: *„From a historian's point of view, then, holography represents a fascinating case of modern science and technology. It is a complex example of a surprisingly common but little noticed situation in modern science, in which a technical subject has created new communities and grown with them. Its evolution has been distinctly different from what most historians of science-and even holographers-might have expected, which can help us to better understand how modern sciences emerge, and how to more realistically chart their future trajectories. And because of the rich variety of communities that the subject has embraced, ranging from artists to defense contractors, its history is likely to be of enduring interest to broad audiences."*

Acknowledgment

I would like to express this way my sincere thanks to Faculty of Mathematics and Physics, Comenius University at Bratislava, which provided me with a possibility to get familiar with beauty of new, contemporary optics. I, also, would like to express my thanks to all of my close colleagues and students, for transforming the atmosphere of my working place into a home atmosphere, indeed.

Author details

Dagmar Senderakova*

Address all correspondence to: Dagmar.Senderakova@fmph.uniba.sk

Comenius University, Slovakia

References

[1] Shanghai Henglei Hologram Co.,LTD: Hologram Products and Hologram Machines. http://www.hlhologram.com (accessed 18 August 2012).

[2] Saleh B. E. A., Teich M. C. Fundamentals of photonics. New York / Chichester / Brisbane / Toronto / Singapore: John Wiley & Sons, INC.; 1991.

[3] Smith F. G., King T. A., Wilkins D. Optics and Photonics. Great Britain: John Wiley & Sons, Ltd; 2007.

[4] Gabor. D. Microscopy by reconstructed wave front. Proc. Roy. Soc. 1949, A(197) 454-463.

[5] Maiman T. H. Stimulated Optical Radiation in Ruby. Nature 1960, 187 493-495.

[6] Senderakova D. Holography – what is it about? In: Ramirez F. A. M. (ed.) Holography – different fields of application. Rijeka: InTech; 2011. p1-28.

[7] Meier R. W. Magnification and third-order aberrations in holography. Journal of the Optical Society of America 1965; 55, 987-92.

[8] Lippmann G. Photographie des Couleurs. Journal de Physique 1894, 3 97-106.

[9] Denisyuk Yu. N. On the reproduction of optical properties of an object by the wave field of its scattered radiation (in Russian). Doklady Akademii Nauk SSSR 1962; 144(6), 1275-1278.

[10] Denisyuk Yu. N., Protas R. R. Improved Lippmann photographic plates for the record of standing waves (in Russian). Optika i Spektroskopija 1963;14, 721-725.

[11] Van Renesse R. L. Yuri Denisyuk - Pioneer of modern holography. http://www.vanrenesse-consulting.com/index.php?page=photography.htm (accessed 18 August 2012).

[12] Ludman J., Caulfield H. J., Riccobono J. (Eds.). Holography for the New Millenium. New York: Springer-Verlag, Inc.; 2002.

[13] Klein W. R., Cook B. D. Unified approach to ultrasonic light diffraction. IEEE Transactions on Sonics & Ultrasonics 1967; SU-14, 123-34.

[14] Bazargan K. White light transmission holography. http://holographer.org/white-light-transmission-holography/ (accessed 18 August 2012).

[15] Hariharan P. Basics of Holography. New York: Cambridge University Press; 2002.

[16] Benton S. A. Hologram Reconstructions with Extended Incoherent Sources. J. Opt. Soc. Am. 1969; 59 1545-1546.

[17] Benton S. A. (1977). White light transmission/reflection holographic imaging. In Marom E., Friesem A. A., Wiener-Avenar E. (eds.) Applications of Holography and Optical Data Processing. Oxford: The Pergamon Press; 1977. p 401-9.

[18] Hariharan P., Steel W. H., Hegedus Z. S. Multicolor holographic imaging with a white light source. Optics Letters 1977; 1, 8-9.

[19] Wyant J. C. Image blur for rainbow holograms. Optics Letters 1977; 1, 130-2.

[20] Van Renesse R. L. Stephen Benton (1941-2003) – a pioneer in holography. http://www.vanrenesse-consulting.com/index.php?page=photography.htm (accessed 18 August 2012).

[21] Van Renesse R. L. A review of holograms and other microstructures as security features. http://www.vanrenesse-consulting.com/index.php?page=chapter.htm (accessed 18 August 2012).

[22] Johnston S. F. A historian's view of holography.

[23] http://3d-holography.ru/historyholography/ (accessed 18 August 2012).

[24] Gentet Y. Ultimate holography technologies for Museum Applications. http://www.museum-holography.com (accessed 18 August 2012).

[25] Senderakova D., Strba A. Analysis of a wedge prism to perform small-angle beam deviation. In Hrabovsky M., Senderakova D., Tomanek P. (eds.) Photonics Devices, and Systems II: Proceedings of SPIE 5036, 148-151. SPIE, Bellingham, WA; 2003.

[26] Pigosova J. On Solving Optical Problems by Genetic Algorithm. In Strba A., Senderakova D., Hrabovsky M. (eds.) 14th Slovak-Czech-Polish Optical Conference on Wave and Quantum Aspects of Contemporary Optics: Proceedings of SPIE 5945, 1Q1-1Q9. SPIE, Bellingham, WA; 2004.

Section 2

Contemporary Holographic Applications

Chapter 4

Research on Holographic Sensors and Novel Photopolymers at the Centre for Industrial and Engineering Optics

Emilia Mihaylova, Dervil Cody, Izabela Naydenova,
Suzanne Martin and Vincent Toal

Additional information is available at the end of the chapter

http://dx.doi.org/10.5772/56061

1. Introduction

The recent resurgence of interest in photopolymers for commercial holograms is a strong incentive for development of photopolymers that are as environmentally friendly as possible. Photopolymer materials consist of a light-sensitive film which is exposed during production to form the hologram, thereby offering versatility well beyond that of current security holograms, which are mass produced from a master using a foil stamping processes.

Most holographic recording media based on photopolymerizable materials contain monomers such as acrylates or acrylamides as well as an electron donor such as Triethanolamine, a light absorbing dye such as Methylene Blue or Erythrosine B and an inert polymer binder such as Polyvinyl Alcohol.

Like their foil-stamped/embossed counterparts, the finished photopolymer hologram is a thin, solid layer applied to the surface of a product or package and any harmful monomers present in the photosensitive recording material have usually been fully polymerized during the exposure/recording process. Even so, the handling of raw materials during mass production and the disposal of waste produced by the production process must be carefully controlled when harmful monomers are present. Replacement of the current monomers with environmentally friendly constituents is better for the environment and may help to reduce overall production cost.

Photopolymers have been in development since the late 1960s, but development of the embossing technique for mass production of surface relief holograms in the early 1980s led to commercial success for the now familiar surface hologram. Since the early work of Close et al. [1] some photopolymers for holography have been produced commercially. The well known DuPont photopolymer [2-4] and Polaroid DMP-128 [5, 6] emerged in the 1970's and 1980's but commercial use was limited.

As interest in holographic data storage grew, Polaroid spin–out company Aprilis began to commercialize their material, and the Bell Laboratories spin out company, InPhase introduced the new 'Tapestry' medium for holographic data storage. General Electric were also developing a data storage medium.

Currently, the biggest market in commercial holography is security holograms. However, despite the growth in activity in volume materials for data storage, until very recently the security hologram industry focussed almost exclusively on surface relief holograms. Over the last five years we have seen significant activities in developing of volume photopolymer holograms. DuPont has been joined by other large commercial companies including Bayer [7, 8] and Sony [9] in offering commercial holographic photopolymer materials to industry. With the prospect of very high volume production, environmental and cost considerations become even more important.

The photopolymer phase reflection hologram is attractive for security holograms for a number of reasons. The fact that it is relatively thick by hologram standards (tens of microns) means the diffraction efficiency can be very high, leading to eye-catching 3D images, visually quite different to the rainbow effect of the embossed hologram. A second important feature if the photopolymer reflection holograms is the capacity to angularly multiplex several holograms into one layer. In photopolymers with high refractive index modulation, this can produce a moving image effect, which is very striking. Even a small number of multiplexed holograms can enable toggling between two static images, so that text or warnings can be visible in conjunction with the holographic image. A third beneficial characteristic is the broad range of wavelength sensitivity in many photopolymers [10—12], enabling several colour components in the hologram. Finally, most photopolymers are completely self developing and require no chemical processing. This means that they can be exposed individually during production thus introducing the possibility of serialization and individualized data [12, 13] to provide a new level of security.

As well as improving the polymer formulation, this Chapter aims to illustrate some properties, unique to volume photopolymer holograms, that could be developed into innovative products. In a recent overview at HoloPack-HoloPrint 2012, Lancaster and Tidmarsh pointed out that the security market is one of the main drivers for growth and innovation in the industry and the market is changing as customers are demanding more functionality in security technologies [14].

This chapter is divided in two parts. The first part describes some attractive applications of an acrylamide-based photopolymer developed in the Centre for Industrial and Engineering Optics (IEO), at Dublin Institute of Technology. This particular photopolymer is characterised by high diffraction efficiency and self development (immediate) [15], and it can be prepared in thickness ranging from a few microns to 1mm [16]. It has been recently reformulated for

http://dx.doi.org/10.5772/56061

panchromaticity [10] and improved with the addition of nanoparticles [17-22]. This holographic photopolymer is sensitive to humidity [23-26] and to high pressure. It was discovered recently that its pressure sensitivity can be varied using a particular additive and adjusting the polymer's chemical composition accordingly. The second part of the chapter reports results for a novel photopolymer based on diacetone-acrylamide.

2. IEO Holographic sensor technology

Research in IEO has been focused on holography and its applications using, mainly, low cost photopolymers which are water soluble and require no chemical or other form of processing. IEO is one of very few places in the world capable of making acrylamide photopolymer reflection holograms that can be viewed in ordinary light, like the holograms on credit cards. Until recently this was not possible, but IEO researchers have overcome the technical problems.

Holograms are made by exposing the photopolymer film to two beams of coherent laser light. When the finished hologram is illuminated at the playback or reconstruction stage by just one of the beams, the second beam reappears. This is how holographic images are produced. If the second beam was originally reflected from an object before reaching the film then, on reconstruction we'd see an image of the object. Furthermore if the two beams approach the film from opposite sides, the hologram can be played back in white light in which case we'd see a holographic image in the colour of the laser light that was used for the recording. Such holograms are known as reflection holograms. If no object is used and both recording beams illuminate the film directly then we obtain what's known as a holographic grating because the pattern of light formed at the film by the interference of two beams consists of finely spaced bright and dark regions and the recording consists correspondingly of finely spaced regions of photo-polymerised material interspersed with unpolymerised material.

Holographic sensors of three types are under development, both offering a number of advantages including visual, easy interpretation of information by non specialists, low cost, flexible design and small format.

In the first type of sensor a change in the dimensions, or average refractive index or refractive index modulation occurring in the photopolymer layer, when it is exposed to an analyte will cause the brightness or, in the case of a reflection hologram, the colour of the reconstructed light to change. Holographic indicators that change colour when exposed to a change in relative humidity have been developed [23-26]. The device can be calibrated so that a precise reading of the colour enables an accurate measure of relative humidity. The pictures in Fig. 1 show the change from blue to red in the colour of the reconstructed image from a hologram after it is simply breathed on. The colour reverts to the original after a few minutes.

The humidity sensitive hologram may alternatively be used as a security device. Holograms are a common feature on credit cards, banknotes, passports, concert tickets and other high value items and are put there as an authentication device. However it has become fairly easy to counterfeit these mass produced holograms. IEO's new humidity sensitive holograms are particularly difficult to emulate and can be used to provide an added level of authentication.

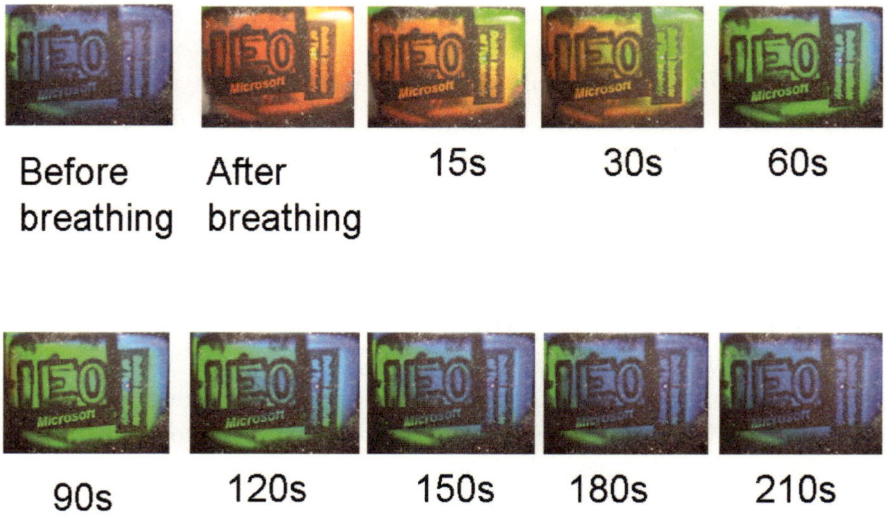

Figure 1. Moisture sensitive colour changing hologram

The second type of sensor relies on a very simple principle. Polymerisation by visible light requires that the monomers, a co-initiator and a sensitiser all be present in order for photopolymerisation to take place. If the sensitiser is absent then photopolymerisation is impossible.

Because the presence of the dye is essential, the film is usually made sensitive to light during its preparation. Here we separate the film preparation and the sensitisation processes (Fig. 2). In this way the photo-polymerisation process is used to detect dye labelled analytes, providing an alternative to fluorescence detection methods.

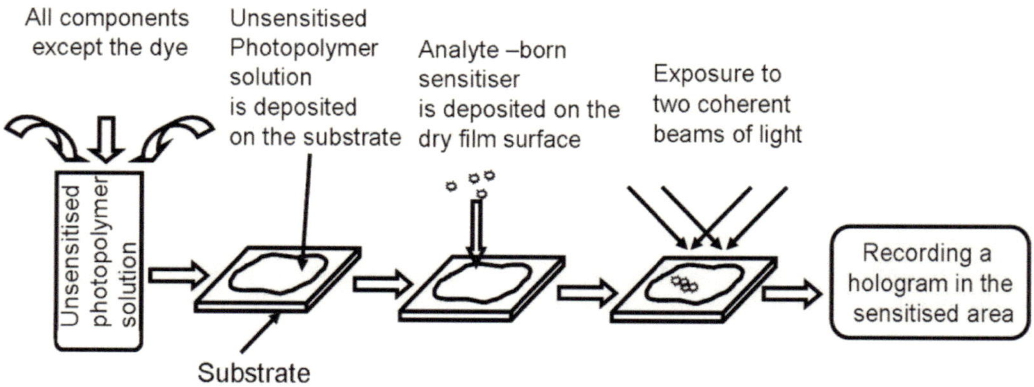

Figure 2. Detection principle based on novel approach to photopolymer sensitisation

We have been successful in the detection of dye-labelled DNA single strand molecules by the recording of a simple holographic grating (Fig.3) [27]. The minimum amount of material that has been detected was 5.10^{-14} mol.

http://dx.doi.org/10.5772/56061

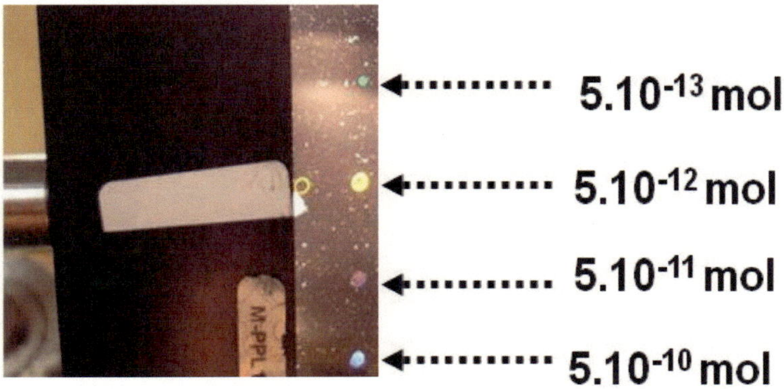

Figure 3. Holographic gratings recorded in photopolymer layer deposited on top of dye-labelled DNA molecules immobilised on a substrate. Arrows indicate areas in contact with dye-labelled DNA exposed to holographic recording

The significance of the principle described above extends beyond holographic sensing. It opens new possibilities in optical device fabrication [27]. Figure 4 shows a Fresnel lens made in this way. The sensitiser was deposited in the pattern of the required device on a photopolymer film, which was then exposed to ordinary light.

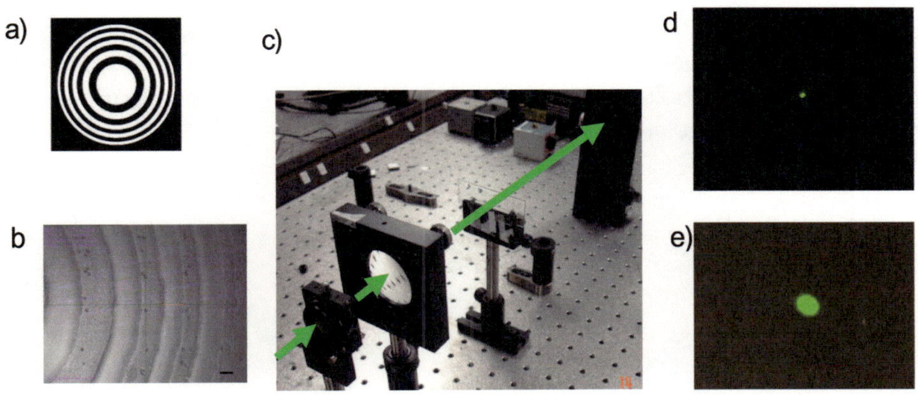

Figure 4. a) Fresnel lens pattern b) deposited sensitiser pattern on photopolymer film c) demonstration experiment using a collimated beam of laser light d) focussed spot with Fresnel lens in place e) lens removed

The third type of sensor is a pressure sensor. A pressure sensitive photopolymer (PSP) for tactile pressure measurements and their colour visualisation was developed recently in IEO. This pressure sensitive material is cheap and easy to produce. Its chemical composition is similar to the standard IEO holographic photopolymer [15-16]. This optimised photopolymer is capable of recording transmission and reflection holograms. The reflection holograms recorded in this novel material are of particular interest for different applications (Fig. 5), because of their ability to produce colour maps of pressure distribution without the need for scanning and digital processing.

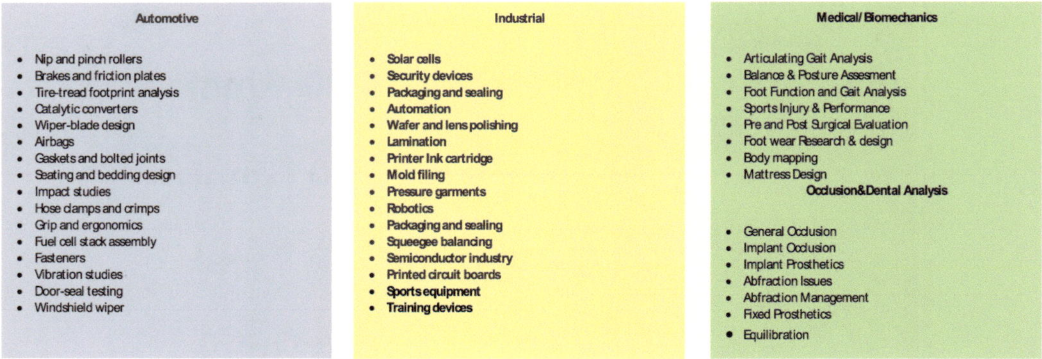

Figure 5. Applications requiring a thin film capable of tactile pressure measurements

The operating principle (Fig. 6) is that the colour of the reconstructed light from a reflection hologram, illuminated by ambient light, depends on the pressure to which the hologram has been subjected. This principle derives from the fact that the hologram is made in an elastic photopolymer, which compresses under pressure, in turn reducing the recorded interference fringe spacing and hence the resonant wavelength of the device.

When a reflection hologram is illuminated with white light, light of a specific colour is diffracted and this is the colour observed. If a red laser is used for recording of the reflection hologram the reconstructed image will be observed in red.

Pressure sensitive photopolymers shrink due to applied pressure, which leads to a change in the fringe spacing of the hologram, and consequently to change in the colour observed (Fig. 6). The colour changes from red to yellow – green – blue as the applied pressure increases.

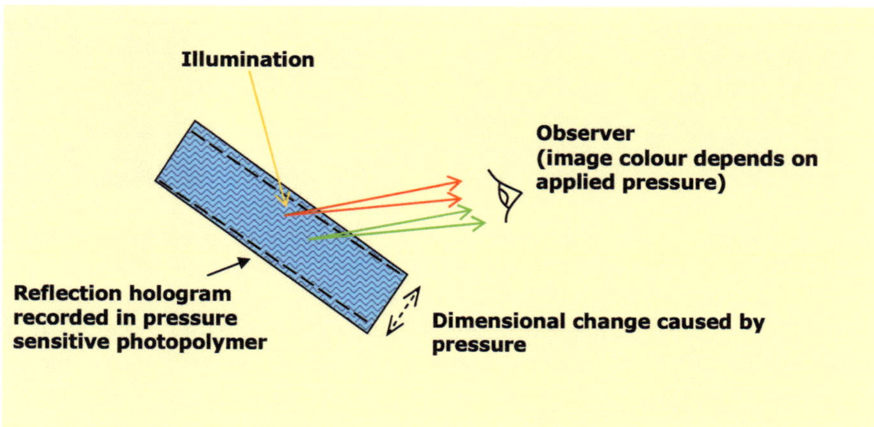

Figure 6. Principle of operation of a holographic pressure sensor

As a first step in the development of a new family of holographic sensors, several photopolymer compositions with different pressure sensitivities were produced. The initial tests

http://dx.doi.org/10.5772/56061

performed with an INSTRON machine show that that the reconstructed images from reflection holograms made in the new PSP material, change colour when pressure is applied. Four different compositions were investigated (PSP1, PSP2, PSP3 and PSP4). Figure 7 and Figure 8 show our results for the pressure sensitivity of different PSPs. Figure 7 presents results for one PSP composition (PSP3) under two different applied pressures.

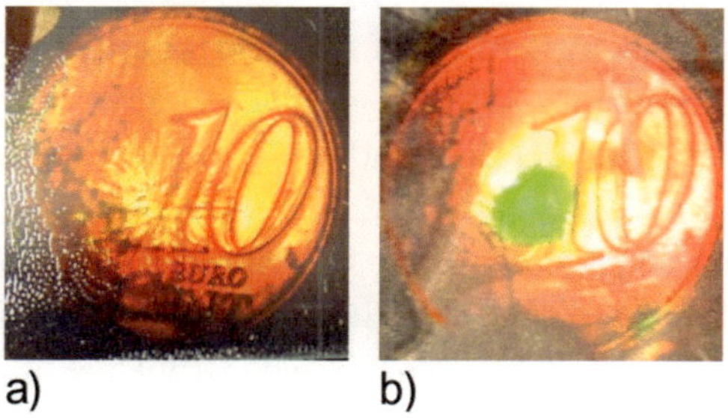

Figure 7. Change in hologram colour in thin films of PSP3 photopolymer under pressure of: a) 10 N/cm^2; b) 50 N/cm^2

Figure 8 present results for one pressure applied to thin films of three different PSP compositions. The results are repeatable and can serve as a basis for development of pressure sensitive thin film material with tuneable pressure sensitivity.

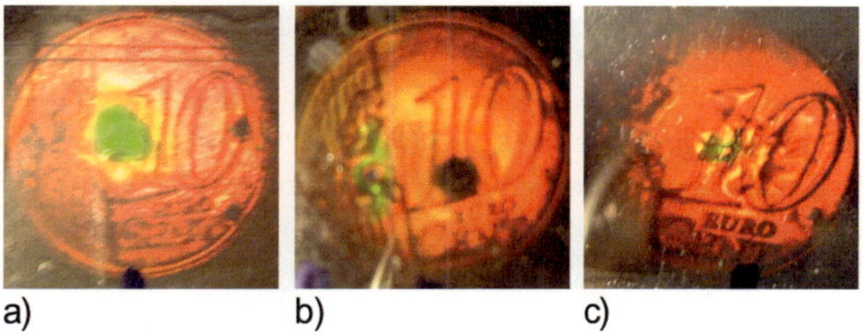

Figure 8. Change in hologram colour under pressure of 80 N/cm^2 in photopolymer thin films of: a) PSP1; b) PSP2, c) PSP4

The pressure sensitivity of the photopolymers diminishes in the direction (highest) PSP2 ⇒ PSP1 ⇒ PSP4 (lowest). The object in all experiments was a 10 cent coin for display purposes.

3. Environmentally friendly holographic photopolymers

The suitability of PVA/Acrylamide photopolymer materials for holographic applications is currently a hot research topic under investigation by numerous research groups [20-33]. However the toxicity of these photopolymer materials is of concern. This toxicity can be attributed to the carcinogenic nature of the monomer acrylamide (AA) [34-37]. As holographic technologies are advanced, there is going to be a need for recording media, which can be produced in bulk with little risk to workers involved in its in manufacture or to the environment. In order for photopolymer recording media to be a viable option for holographic applications, this issue has to be addressed, and a replacement monomer must be used.

Research into the development of non-toxic, water-soluble photopolymers has been reported by Ortuno et al. [38-40]. Sodium Acrylate (NaAO) was chosen as the substitute monomer in the photopolymer composition, the toxicity of which is reported to be lower than AA [41]. A maximum diffraction efficiency of 77% at the Bragg is reported for 900μm thick NaAO photopolymer layers [38] at a spatial frequency of 1125 l/mm, with a recording intensity of $5mW/cm^2$. A refractive index modulation of $\sim 2.24 \times 10^{-4}$ is reported for the NaAO photopolymer. This is a factor of a magnitude lower than the refractive index modulations achieved with the PVA/AA composition [15, 28, 42]. This could be partly due to the difference in the refractive index of the AA and NaAO based materials [39]. The shrinkage of the NaAO photopolymer has been measured at ~3%, making it unsuitable for data storage applications.

A low toxicity water-soluble material using PVA photosensitized with dihydrated copper chloride ($CuCl_2(2H_2O)$) is reported by Olivares-Perez et al. [43]. An attractive feature of this material is its ability to conduct electricity, making it a candidate for opto-electronic applications. However the maximum diffraction efficiency recorded in 200μm thick layers in transmission mode is very low, 3.9%.

IEO has developed a new non-toxic photopolymer using the monomer Diacetone Acrylamide (DA) as the replacement for AA. A cytotoxicity comparison of the two monomers has been carried out. The replacement of AA with DA is justified by a decrease by two orders of magnitude in the Lethal Dose, or LD50, concentration. The results of this study will be published elsewhere. Characterisation of the holographic recording capabilities of the water-soluble material in the transmission mode of recording has been carried out [44]. Diffraction efficiencies greater than 90% were obtained in 80μm layers at 1000 l/mm, and a refractive index modulation of 3.3×10^{-3} has been obtained. This compares favourably to the refractive index modulation achievable with the AA-based photopolymer, as shown in Fig. 9. The DA photopolymer demonstrates a more uniform trend in intensity dependence than the AA photopolymer, which is most likely due to the larger monomer molecule size. As the rate of polymerisation is increased, the refractive index modulation for DA levels out due to a reduced rate of diffusion. This can be compared to the smaller AA monomer molecules which are more easily able to diffuse at higher recording intensities, and therefore the maximum refractive index modulation is greater. The DA photopolymer has also been doped with different additives, such as glycerol, which improves both the optical quality of the layers and its response at low exposure energies [45, 46]. Theoretical models [42] are currently being modified to explain the behaviour of the new non-toxic photopolymer. Initial Raman spectroscopy studies indicate that the mechanism for photo-polymerisation is the same for the DA and AA monomers, as the double peak observed at $\sim 1630cm^{-1}$ for DA and the cross-linker bisacrylamide (BA) matches that observed for AA and BA (Figures 10, 11) [47].

http://dx.doi.org/10.5772/56061

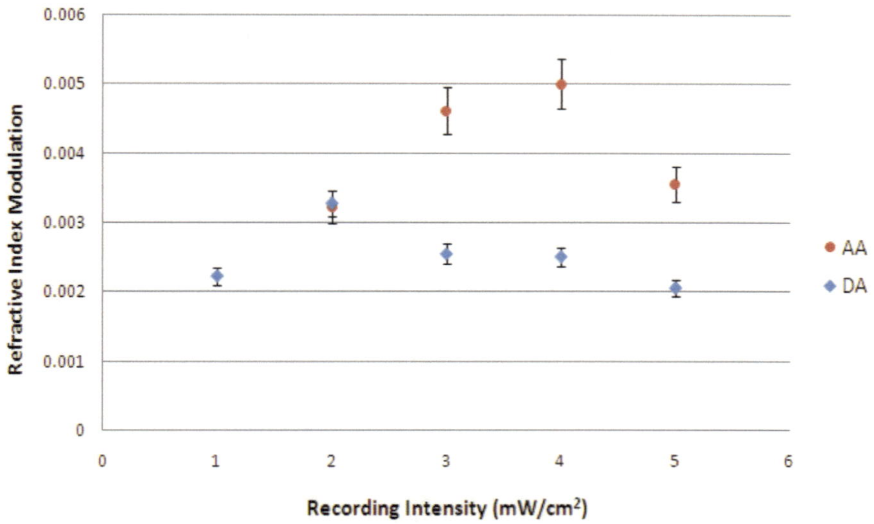

Figure 9. Refractive index modulation vs. recording intensity for the DA and AA photopolymers at 1000 l/mm with an exposure energy 100mJ/cm^2.

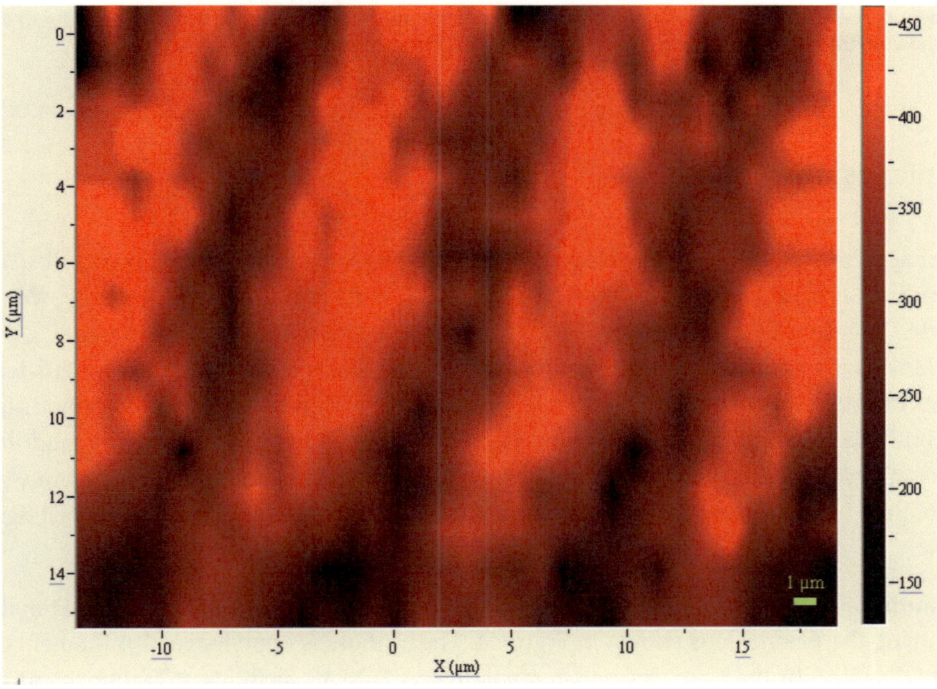

Figure 10. Raman map showing the redistribution of the 1636cm^{-1} DA peak across a holographic grating with a fringe spacing of 10µm, recorded in the DA photopolymer. Measurements were taken at 514nm with a S.A. (Jobin Yvon) LabRam 1B Spectrometer.

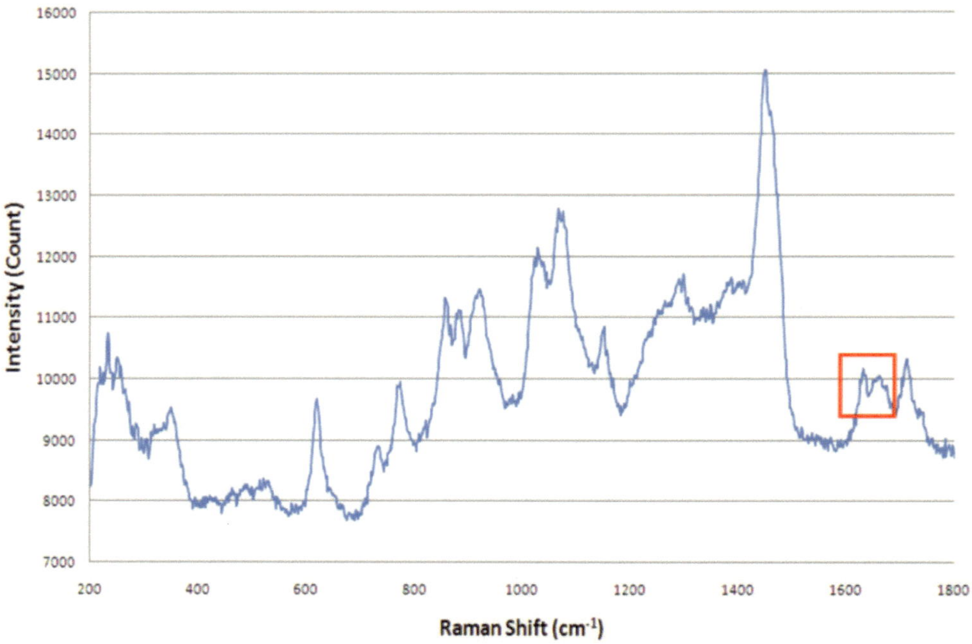

Figure 11. Raman spectrum of the DA photopolymer taken from the map in fig. 2. The peaks at 1636 cm^{-1} and 1658 cm^{-1} (shown in the red box) correspond to the DA and BA C=C bonds respectively.

4. Conclusion

The chapter reviewed recent developments in holographic sensors technology at the Centre for Industrial and Engineering Optics (IEO) at Dublin Institute of Technology. We also reported the development of a novel environmentally friendly holographic photopolymer. Acrylamide is excluded from the composition of this photopolymer. Diffraction efficiencies greater than 90% are achievable in 80μm layers at 1000 l/mm, and a refractive index modulation of $3.3x10^{-3}$ has been obtained. This compares favourably to the refractive index modulation achievable with the acrylamide-based photopolymer. Characterisation of the recording capabilities of the diacetone-based photopolymer in the reflection mode of recording will follow.

The authors acknowledge the assistance of Dr Karl Crowley, Dublin City University in producing the Fresnel lens shown in Figure 4. The authors acknowledge also the help of Dr Luke O'Neill with the Raman measurements using FOCAS facilities at Dublin Institute of Technology.

The work on the development of the diacetone-acrylamide based photopolymer was financially supported by the Irish Research Council Embark Initiative.

http://dx.doi.org/10.5772/56061

Author details

Emilia Mihaylova[1,2], Dervil Cody[1], Izabela Naydenova[1], Suzanne Martin[1] and Vincent Toal[1]

1 Centre for Industrial and Engineering Optics, School of Physics, College of Sciences and Health, Dublin Institute of Technology, Dublin, Ireland

2 Department of Mathematics and Physics, Agricultural University, Plovdiv, Bulgaria

References

[1] D. H. Close, A. D. Jacobson, R. C. Magerum, R. G. Brault, and F. J. McClung, "Hologram recording on photopolymer materials," Appl. Phys. Lett.14(5), 159–160 (1969).

[2] W. S. Colburn and K. A. Haines "Volume Hologram Formation in Photopolymer Materials"Applied Optics, Vol. 10, Issue 7, pp. 1636-1641 (1971)

[3] R. H. Wopschall and T.R. Pampalone "Dry Photopolymer Film for Recording Holograms"Applied Optics, Vol. 11, Issue 9, pp. 2096-2097 (1972)

[4] B. L. Booth, "Photopolymer Material for Holography," Appl. Opt. 11, 2994-2995 (1972)

[5] R. T. Ingwall and H. L. Fielding, "Hologram recording with a new photopolymer system," Opt. Eng. 24, 808–811 (1985).

[6] R. T. Ingwall; M. Troll "Mechanism Of Hologram Formation In DMP-128 Photopolymer" *Opt. Eng.* 28 (6), 586 (1989)

[7] Jurbergs et al "New recording materials for the holographic industry"Practical Holography XXIII: Materials and Applications, edited by Hans I. Bjelkhagen, Raymond K. Kostuk, Proc. of SPIE Vol. 7233, 72330K (2009)

[8] Weiser et al "Self-Processing, Diffusion-Based Photopolymers for Holographic Applications, Macromolecular Symposia, Special Issue: Modern Trends in Polymer Science – EPF'09 – Vol. 296, Issue 1, pages 133–137, October (2010)

[9] Holography News "Dai Nippon and Sony High-Res Animated Holograms", Vol 21, No 7, (July 2007)

[10] Meka, C.,Jallapuram, R., Naydenova, I., Martin, S., Toal, V.: "Development of a panchromatic acrylamide based photopolymer for multicolour reflection holography". Applied Optics, Vol. 49, Issue 8, pp. 1400-1405 (2010)

[11] Pramitha Vayalamkuzhi , Rani Joseph, Krishnapillai Sreekumar, and Cheranellore Sudha Kartha "silver-doped poly(vinyl alcohol)/acrylamide photopolymer" Applied Optics, Vol. 50, Issue 18, pp. 2886-2891 (2011)

[12] T. Facke " New Photopolymer Film Enabling the Next Generation Overt Security Features" presentation at Holo-Pack Holo-Print Holography Conference , 28-30 Oct 2012, Vienna, Austria (2012)

[13] Suzanne Martin, Emilia Mihaylova, Amanda Creane, Vincent Toal, Izabela Naydenova "Digitally Printed Holograms", presentation at Holo-Pack Holo-Print Holography Conference , 28-30 Oct 2012, Vienna, Austria (2012)

[14] I. Lancaster and D. Tidmarsh, "The changing market for security holograms", presentation at Holo-Pack Holo-Print Holography Conference , 28-30 Oct 2012, Vienna, Austria (2012)

[15] S. Martin ; P. E. Leclere ; Y. L. M. Renotte ; V. Toal and Y. F. Lion "Characterization of an acrylamide-based dry photopolymer holographic recording material", Opt. Eng. 33(12), 3942-3946 (1994)

[16] Mahmud, M., Naydenova, I., Pandey, N., Babeva, T., Jallapuram, R., Martin, S., Toal, V.: Holographic recording in acrylamide photopolymers: Thickness limitations. Applied Optics, 48(14), 2642-2648 (2009)

[17] I. Naydenova, H. Sherif, S. Mintova, S. Martin, V. Toal, "Holographic recording in nanoparticle-doped photopolymer", SPIE proceedings of the International Conference on Holography, Optical Recording and Processing of Information, V 6252, 45-50, 2006.

[18] Leite, E., Naydenova*, I., Pandey, N., Babeva, T., Majano, G., Mintova, S., et al. (2009). Investigation of the light induced redistribution of zeolite beta nanoparticles in an acrylamide-based photopolymer. Journal of Optics A: Pure and Applied Optics, 11(2) 024016.

[19] Leite, E., Naydenova, I, Mintova, S. Leclercq, L., Toal, V. "Photopolymerisable Nanocomposites for Holographic Recording and Sensor Application", Appl.Opt. / Vol. 49, No. 19 , 3652-3660 (2010)

[20] E. Leite, Tz. Babeva, E.-P. Ng, V. Toal, S. Mintova, and I. Naydenova, "Optical Properties of Photopolymer Layers Doped with Aluminophosphate Nanocrystals" Journal of Phys. Chem. C, (2010), DOI: 10.1021/jp1060073

[21] I. Naydenova, E. Leite, Tz. Babeva, N. Pandey, T. Baron, T. Yovcheva, S. Sainov, S. Martin, S. Mintova and V. Toal, Optical properties of photopolymerisable nanocomposites containing nanosized molecular sieves, (2011), J. Opt., (2011) 044019 (10pp), doi:10.1088/2040-8978/13/4/044019

[22] Moothanchery, M., Naydenova, I., Mintova, S., Toal, V.: Nanozeolites Doped Photopolymer Layers with Reduced Shrinkage. Optics Express, Vol. 19, Issue 25, pp. 25786-25791 (2011); http://dx.doi.org/10.1364/OE.19.025786

[23] I. Naydenova, R. Jallapuram, V. Toal and S. Martin, "Hologram-based humidity indicator for domestic and packaging applications", SPIE proceedings, V 6528, 652811, 2007.doi:10.1117/12.716242

[24] Izabela Naydenova, Raghavendra Jallapuram, Vincent Toal, and Suzanne Martin, A visual indication of environmental humidity using a color changing hologram recorded in a self-developing photopolymer, Appl. Phys. Lett. 92, 031109 (2008); DOI: 10.1063/1.2837454

[25] I. Naydenova, J. Raghavendra, V.Toal, S. Martin, "Characterisation of the humidity and temperature responses of a reflection hologram recorded in acrylamide-based photopolymer", Sensors and Actuators B: Chemical 139, 35-38 (2009).

[26] I. Naydenova, R. Jallapuram, S. Martin, V. Toal, "Holographic humidity sensors", in "Humidity sensors: Types, Nanomaterials and Environmental monitoring" , Nova Science Publishers, 2011, ISBN: 978-1-61209-246-1

[27] I. Naydenova, S. Martin, V. Toal, (2009) , "Photopolymers –beyond the standard approach to photosensitisation", JEOS Rapid Publications, 4, 09042.

[28] S. Blaya, L. Carretero, R. Mallavia, A. Fimia, R. Madrigal, M. Ulibarrena, D. Levy, "Optimisation of an Acrylamide-based dry film for holographic recording", Applied Optics 37, 7604-7610 (1998).

[29] E. Fernandez, A. Marquez, S. Gallego, R. Fuentes, C. Garcia, I. Pascual, "Hybrid ternary modulation applied to multiplexing holograms in photopolymers for data page storage", Journal of Lightwave Technology 28, 776-783 (2010).

[30] S.Q. Tao, Y.X. Zhao, Y.H. Wan, Q.L Zhai, P.F. Liu, D.Y. Wang, F.P. Wu, "Dual-wavelength sensitized photopolymer for holographic data storage", Japanese Journal of Applied Optics 49, 2010.

[31] F.K. Bruder, F. Deuber, T. Facke, R. Hagen, D. Honel, D. Jurbergs, M. Kogure, T. Rolle, M.S. Weiser, "Full-colour self-processing holographic photopolymers with high sensitivity in red – the first class of instant holographic photopolymers", Journal of Photopolymer Science and Technology 22, 257-260 (2009).

[32] V. Pramitha, K.P. Nimmi, N.V. Subramanyan, R. Joseph, K. Sreekumar, C.S. Kartha, "Silver-doped photopolymer media for holographic recording", Applied Optics 48, 2255-2261 (2009).

[33] S. Liu, J. Sheridan, "Improvement of photopolymer materials for holographic data storage", Journal of Materials Science 44, 6090-6099 (2009).

[34] D. D. McCollister, F. Oyen and V. K. Rowe, "Toxicology of Acrylamide", Toxicology and Applied Pharmacology 6, 172-181 (1964).

[35] A., G. Lawrence, R. Gentry, T. McDonald, H. Bartow, J. Bounds, N. Macdonald, H. Clewell, B. Allen and C. Van Landingham, "Acrylamide: Review of Toxicity Data

and Dose-Response Analyses for Cancer and Noncancer Effects", Critical Reviews in Toxicology 36, 481-608 (2006).

[36] D. J. King and R. R. Noss, "Toxicity of polyacrylamide and acrylamide monomer", Rev. Environ. Health 8, 3-16 (1989).

[37] Health implications of acrylamide in food: report of a joint FAO/WHO consultation, WHO Headquarters, Geneva, Switzerland, 25-27 June, 2002.

[38] M. Ortuno, E. Fernandez, S. Gallego, A. Belendez, I. Pascual, "New photopolymer holographic recording material with sustainable design", Optics Express 15, 12425-12435 (2007).

[39] S. Gallego, A. Marquez, M. Ortuno, S. Marini, J. Frances, "High environmental compatibility photopolymers compared to PVA/AA based materials at zero spatial frequency limit", Optical Materials 33, 531-537 (2011).

[40] M. Ortuno, S. Gallego, A. Marquez, C. Neipp, I. Pascual, A. Belendez, "Biophotopol: A Sustainable Photopolymer for Holographic Data Storage Applications", Materials 5(5), 772-783 (2012).

[41] J. M. Barnes, "Effects on rats of compounds related to Acrylamide", British Journal of Industrial Medicine, 1970.

[42] T. Babeva, I. Naydenova, D. Mackey, S. Martin, V. Toal, "Two-way diffusion model for short-exposure holographic grating formation in Acrylamide-based photopolymer", Journal of Optical Society of America B 27, 197-203 (2010).

[43] A. Olivares-Perez, M.P. Hernandez-Garnay, I. Fuentes-Tapia, J.C. Ibarra-Torres, "Holograms in polyvinyl alcohol photosensitized with $CuCl_2(H_2O)$", Optical Engineering 50, 0658011-0658016 (2011).

[44] D. Cody, I. Naydenova, E. Mihaylova, "New non-toxic holographic photopolymer", Journal of Optics 14, DOI: 10.1088/2040-8978/14/1/015601 (2012).

[45] D. Cody, I. Naydenova, E. Mihaylova, "Effect of glycerol on a diacetone acrylamide-based holographic photopolymer material", Applied Optics 52(3), 489-494 (2013).

[46] D. Cody, I. Naydenova, E. Mihaylova, "Diacetone acrylamide-based non-toxic holographic photopolymer", SPIE Proceedings 8429, Photonics Europe, 16-19 April 2012, Brussels Belgium.

[47] R. Jallapuram, I. Naydenova, H. Byrne, S. Martin, R. Howard, V. Toal, "Raman spectroscopy for the characterization of the polymerization rate in an acrylamide-based photopolymer", Applied Optics 47, 206-212 (2008).

Chapter 5

Holographic Sensors for Detection of Components in Water Solutions

Vladimir A. Postnikov, Aleksandr V. Kraiskii and
Valerii I. Sergienko

Additional information is available at the end of the chapter

http://dx.doi.org/10.5772/53564

1. Introduction

Currently optical sensors for measuring considerable concentrations of specific components of solutions and their parameters attract persistent worldwide interest. One of the advantages of these sensors is that they permit one to determine simply concentrations both instrumentally and visually. These sensors include holographic sensors [1, 2] and photonic crystal sensors [3, 4]. They can be used for measuring the concentration of protons (pH) in water solutions, heavy metal ions [5-8], glucose in blood [7-12] and other biological liquids [13,14], bacterium spores [15,16], metabolites [17] bacterial growth [18,19], humidity and temperature responses [20,21].

Holographic sensors are quite promising because they are highly sensitive, are easy to operate, provide high enough accuracy and can be used for various applications. At present time they belong to sensors with a moderate sensitivity (10^{-5} -10^{-1} mol•L^{-1}), depending on the type of the analyzed component, the design and the composition of the sensor matrix. Such a sensitivity range is required, for example, in measurements of the glucose concentration in blood and other biological liquids. Holographic sensors represent a polymer hydrogel matrix grafted onto the surface of glass or transparent polymer films and doped with nanosize solid grains, so that their concentration changes periodically in space and the mean distance between the grains is much smaller than the visible-light wavelength.

Holographic diffraction gratings [22] are generated within photosensitive polymer-silver halide photographic emulsions upon exposure to a single collimated laser beam, which passes through the polymer film and then reflected back by a plane mirror. Interference between the mutually coherent incident and reflected beams generates a standing wave pattern which, after development and fixing, creates a three-dimensional pattern comprising fringes of ultrafine metallic silver grains embedded within the thickness (from 5 to 50 μm) of the polymer film. Under white light illumination, the holographic fringes reflect light of a specific narrow band of wavelengths, hence acting as a sensitive wavelength filter and recreating a monochromatic image of the original mirror used in their construction. Constructive interference between partial reflections from each plane produces a distinctive spectral peak with a wavelength governed by the Bragg equation ($m\lambda_{max} = 2n\ d\ sin\theta$). Any physical, chemical, or biological reaction that that alters the spacing (d) between fringes or the refractive index (n) will generate visible changes in the wavelength (color) or intensity (brightness) of the reflection hologram. The intensity of holographic diffraction is also determined by the number of planes and the modulation depth of the refractive index. Swelling of the holographic film increases the distance between fringes producing a red-shift in the wavelength of reflected light, whereas film shrinkage results in a blue-shifted light. In essence, the holographic gratings act as a reporter, whose optical properties are dictated by the physical characteristics of the holographic film. Reflection holograms have proven to be advantageous in many aspects, including the simplicity bestowed by the holographic element providing both the analyte-sensitive matrix and the optical transducer. Special components embedded into the hydrogel matrix to cause a change in the swelling (or shrinkage) of hydrogel under the action of component solution to be analyzed. This leads to the change in the period of the structure and, therefore, in the reflected radiation wavelength. By measuring this wavelength with the help of an optofibre spectrometer or observing it visually, we can estimate the concentration of tested components (metal ions, glucose, acidity, etc.).

The main goal at this stage is the development of sensors for measuring the glucose concentration in blood - low-cost and simple to handle of test plates. In addition, we assume the possibility of the development of sensors to control the conditions of transport and storage of vaccines, serums, ferment preparations, food, and also simple test systems in homes. In our opinion, the study of mechanisms of changes in the holographic response will make it possible to perform the precise adjustment of a sensor for particular operating conditions.

2. Results and discussion

Photosensitized nanocrystals of AgBr were synthesized in the hydrogel matrix by diffusion method [2]. By exposing photographic emulsions in water or acetic acid (1%) solution to radiation from a He-Ne (632.8 nm, 15 mW) laser in the counter propagating-beam scheme, we obtained silver nanograins [23-28] with the period of layers providing the location of reflected radiation peaks in the operating region of the spectrometer. A number of matrices of different compositions and designs were investigated. Hydrogel matrices were consisted of three-dimensional polymer of acrylamide (AA), N, N′-methylene-bis-acrylamide (bis) as crosslinking agent and other comonomers: N-ε-methacryloyl-lysin (Lys), 2-(dimethylamino)-ethylmethacrylate (DMA), acrylic acid (AC), N-acryloyl-2-glucosamine (GA), N-acryloyl-3-aminophenylboronic acid (AMPh). Matrices based on copolymers of acrylamide with ionogen comonomers are sensitive to the solution acidity and ionic strength, while matrices based on aminophenylboronic acid are sensitive to glucose.

Figure 1 shows the typical reflection spectrum of the sensitive layer of a sensor. The reflection spectrum for the ideal layer should be described by the function (sin x/x)$^{2.}$ In our case, the spectrum is well described by a Gaussian. This is explained apparently the imperfect arrangement of silver grain layers.

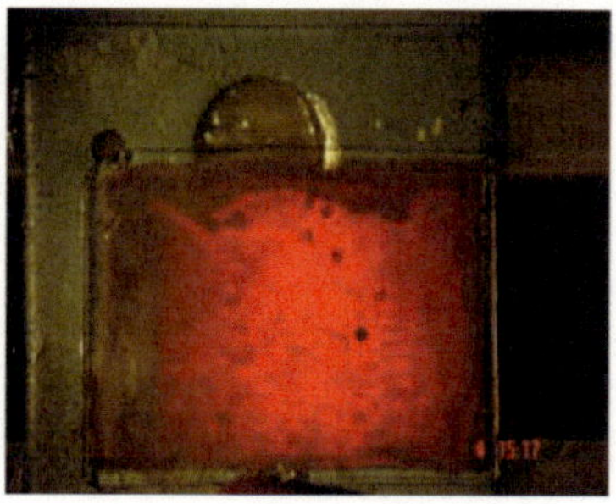
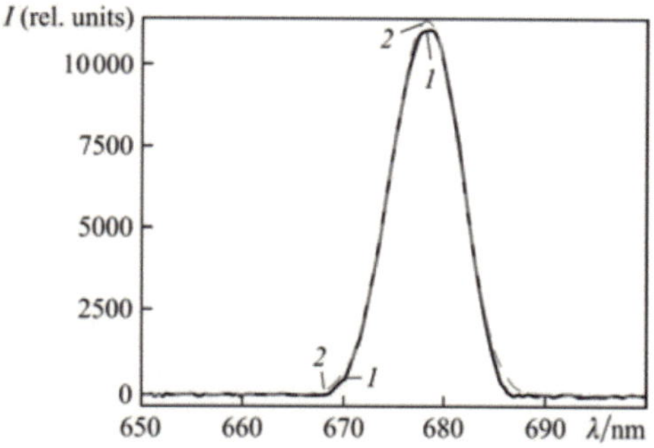

Figure 1. The experimental reflection spectrum of the sensor (1) and its approximation by a Gaussian of width 8 nm (2). (Sensor: AA-AMPh-bis – 87-12-1 mol.%,)

Note that metal silver grains are located in the hologram in a very complex environment containing molecules and ions of solution, elements of the hydrogel matrix. When the solution composition is changed, the composition of ions in solution and the structure of the matrix itself are redistributed. As a result, the sensor response, i.e. the mean wavelength of reflected radiation changes, and the radiation intensity also changes due to the change in the diffraction efficiency of the hologram.

One of the most important properties of holographic sensors is reversibility of the response when changing composition of the solution (Fig.2). Figure 2a shows the time dependence of the reflection line shape during the transfer of the sensor based on aminophenylboronic acid from the citrate buffer to distilled water and back. This change is reversible. The complex shape of the line is explained by the inhomogeneous distribution of the distance between silver layers over depth. One can see that the diffraction efficiency decreases during layer swelling. Figure 2b presents the time dependences of the reflection line wavelength for aminophenylboronic acid sensor after the replacement of the alkali solution in a cell by the acid solution and vice versa (transition processes). The wavelength was measured during swelling and transition to the stationary state. In this case, the swelling changes monotonically and approximately exponentially. Figure 3 shows the time dependence of the reflection wavelength in the transition process after the replacement of the citrate buffer by distilled water. The initial state of this sensor was not stationary. The time dependences of the reflection wavelength and intensity are nonmonotonic, their signs being opposite. The nonmonotonic behavior can be explained by the complicated character of variations ionic composition of solution in the emulsion. It can be assumed that at the initial moment there is rapid diffusion of hydrogen ions from the hydrogel matrix. Then the dissociation of aminophenylboronic acid take place and negative charge appear on polymer chains. This leads to an increase in the period of the holographic grating and is accompanied by an increase in the wavelength of reflected light. The larger anion citrate diffuses slowly, and the system is gradually coming to an equilibrium state, which is accompanied by compression of the hydrogel matrix and decreasing the wavelength of the reflected light. The observed change in intensity, appear to reflect the change in the microenvironment of silver particles. This effect requires additional studies.

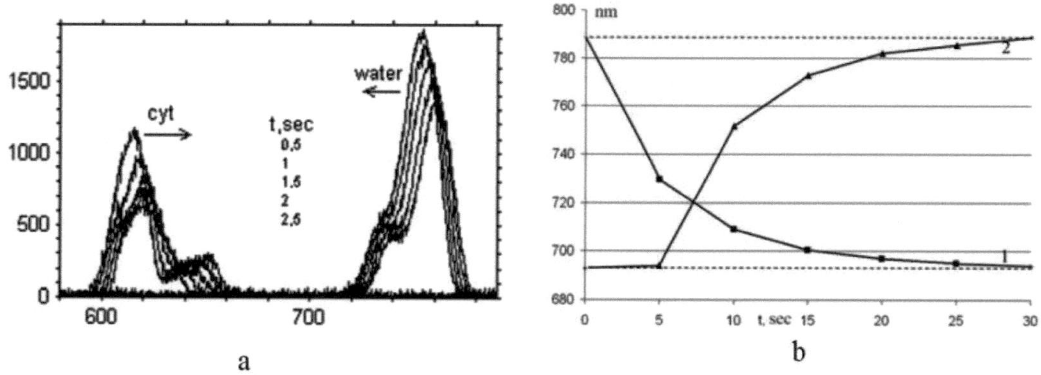

Figure 2. a) Change in the reflection line shape during the transfer of a sensor from the citrate buffer to distilled water (on the right) and back (on the left). The time step is 0.5 s. The arrows indicate the direction of the line shift in time for each group of the lines. b) Refection line wavelengths during the transfer of a sensor based on aminophenylboronic acid from alkali to acid [shrinkage, (1)] and vice versa [swelling, (2)]. (Sensor: AA-AMPh-bis – 87-12-1 mol.%,)

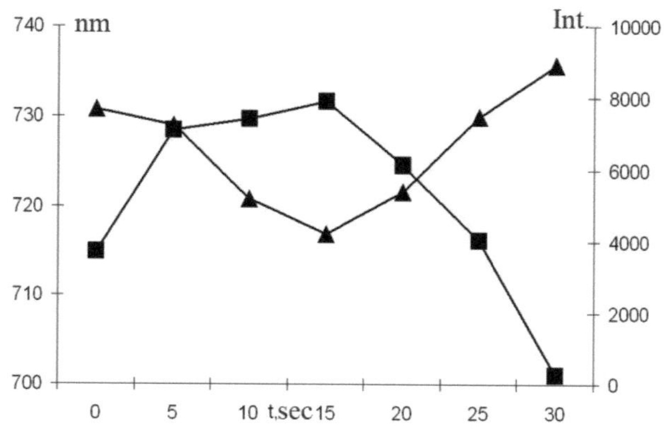

Figure 3. The reflection wavelength line (■) and intensity (▲) during the transfer of the sensor based on aminophenylboronic acid from the citrate buffer to distilled water (b).

Figure 4a shows the response of the sensor located in the NaOH solution titrated hydrochloric acid with (the solution acidity was measured with a usual pH-meter). During titration, the reflected radiation wavelength and diffraction efficiency change drastically at the point where the solution acidity drastically changes. In this case, the diffraction efficiency changed almost by an order of magnitude. This means that the change in the ionic composition is accompanied not only by the swelling of hydrogel matrix of the sensor but also by a strong change in the scattering properties of a holographic layer. This fact was unknown before our studies. Figure 4b presents the dependences from Fig. 4a reduced to the same scale by using the following algorithm. For some dependence $F(m)$, we determined the maximum (A) and minimum (B) of its values for the boundary values of its argument m (in Fig. 4, the volume of the added acid solution): $A = \max(F(0), F(m_{max}))$, $B = \min(F(0), F(m_{max}))$. Then, the dependence $F(m)$ was transformed to the dependence $f(m)$ as $f(m) = (F(m) - B)(A - B)$. One can see from Fig. 4b that all the features of the titration curve are reflected in optical characteristics, i.e. they can be used to control the acidity. Note that the sign of a change in the diffraction efficiency during a change in the amount of added acid is opposite to the sign in the wavelength change.

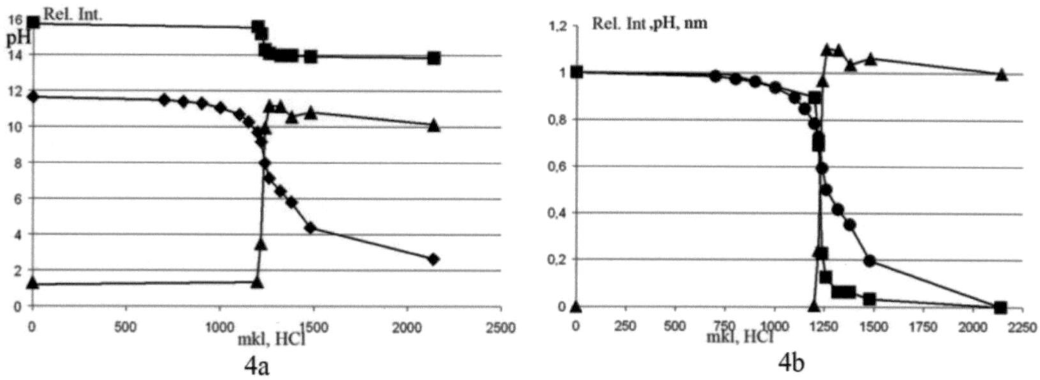

Figure 4. Dependences of the acidity (measured in solution) (♦-a,●-b), the wavelength (■), and intensity (▲) of radiation reflected from a sensor in the NaOH (0,01 N) solution during its titration with hydrochloric acid (0,1 N) (a) and also the so-called reduced dependences (see the text) (b). (Sensor: AA-AC-bis – 96-3-1 mol.%,)

Figure 5 shows the responses of sensors with acrylic acid to metal ions in a broad concentration range from 10^{-7} to 10^{-1}M. They can be divided into three groups: 1- Pb, Co^{+} ions; 2- other bivalent metal ions; 3- alkali metal ions. The sensor is most sensitive to Pb^{2+} and Co^{3+} ions (10^{-5} M). Among the bivalent metal ions (Mg, Sr, Mn, Pb), the presence of Pb^{2+} ions in the solution led to the most noticeable contraction of the hydrogel and changes (542 nm, 37% contraction). The reflection maximum was shifted down by 320 nm with respect to that of the distilled water. The sensor sensitivity to Mg^{2+}, $Sr^{2+}$and Mn^{2+} ions was two orders of magnitude lower. Note that, unlike other metal ions, the sensor's response to the alkali metal ions (Na^{+}, K^{+}) is changed - the first wavelength increases (swelling of hydrogel occurs) and then decreases (shrinkage).

The sensor with acrylic acid can be used for determining the presence of metal ions in water (Fig.6). Figure 6a presents the reflection spectra of the sensor located in different solutions. Stationary response for distilled water is λ=735 nm while response for tap water - λ=615.2 nm which we explain by the presence of metal ions in tap water. The maxima of the reflection lines in water after filtration by household filters are located at 676 nm (Barrier filter) and 711.7 nm (Aquafor filter). The response of sensor on tap water is closer to position for mineral water containing calcium salt at concentration $3 \cdot 10^{-3}$ M (λ=585.4 nm) and to lead salt ($5 \cdot 10^{-3}$ M) in distilled water (λ=542 nm). Sensors can be used repeatedly after regeneration, by washing them, for example, in sodium citrate and then in distilled water. A sensor response rapidly passes to the IR region (λ=860 nm) and then slowly passes to the stationary state (735 nm). Figure 6b shows the typical kinetics of the response maximum.

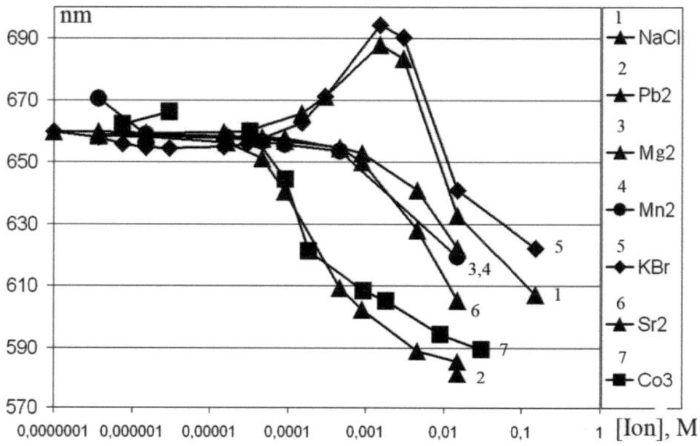

Figure 5. The sensors response (λ_{max}) on different metal ions (1-7) in water solution. (Sensor: AA-AC-bis–96-3-1 mol.%,)

Fig.7 shows the responses of sensors for matrices of two types (with AC or AMPh) for different concentrations of ethanol in water. Figure 7a presents the reflection lines of a sensor based on acrylic acid for different concentrations of ethanol in water, while Fig. 7b shows the dependences of the reflection line wavelength on the ethanol concentration for this sensor and a sensor based on aminophenylboronic acid. The wavelength of reflected light at zero EtOH concentration depends both on the properties of the sensor matrix and on the recording conditions of holograms and can be changed in a controllable way within some range. The concentration dependence in the ethanol solution differs from that upon titration because in this case the decrease in swelling is probably caused by simple dehydration of solution inside the matrix, without ionization.

The spectral region of the sensor's response can be modified in various ways: changing the composition of the solution in the recording hologram (swelling of the hydrogel matrix to change), using a laser at a different wavelength (e.g., instead of the He-Ne laser - semiconductor lasers with an appropriate photosensitizer) or changing the composition of the hydrogel matrix. This can be performed by varying the matrix design and selecting proper co-monomers and their concentrations. Figure 8 shows the dependences of

http://dx.doi.org/10.5772/53564

the reflection line wavelength on the solution acidity for matrices of different compositions. One can see that the properties of the sensor response can be controlled in a broad range. Differences in the response of these sensors at titration of HCl solution correspond to pK_a of components in polymeric matrices, when the charge changes and matrices swelling (or shrinkage) take place. Thus, we have instruments to influence on wavelength maximal response of the holographic system with aminophenylboronic acid from 450 nm (Lys) to 720 nm (DMA) at pH 7.4 (pH of blood serum). The response of the sensor AA-AMPh-GA pointed to the fast swelling when the pH solution is approaching to pK_a= 8.9 aminophenylboronic acid and following slowly shrinkage of the polymeric matrix, at pH more 9.2 – only the swelling. The optical response can be a consequence of a number of different processes: diffusion of H^+ out the gel, complex formation between GA and AMPh groups, and structural rearrangements of the gel due to the increasing concentration of negative charges resulting in gel hydration and swelling.

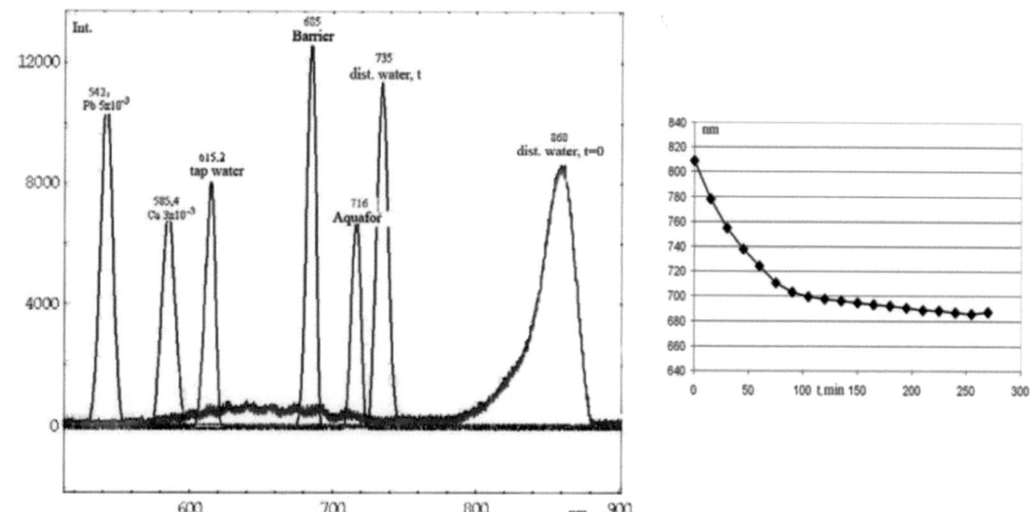

a b

Figure 6. Sensors response to metal ions in water. Reflection spectra in distilled water after the transfer of the sensor from the citrate solution (λ = 860 nm); distilled water (stationary state) (λ = 724 nm); tap water after an Aquafor filter (λ = 711,7 nm); tap water after Barrier filter (λ = 676.3 nm); cold tap water (λ = 615,2 nm); mineral water containing $[Ca^{2+}]$ $3 \cdot 10^{-3}$ M (λ = 585.4 nm); lead salt solution in distilled water $[Pb^{2+}]$ $5 \cdot 10^{-3}$ M (λ = 542 nm) (a) and the shift of the response wavelength of a sensor in distilled water to the stationary state after regeneration (6b). (Sensor: AA-AC-bis – 96-3-1 mol.%,)

It is known that boronic acid can reversibly interact with 1,2-diols or 1,3-diols in aqueous solution to form 5- or 6-membered ring cyclic esters [27-30], (Fig.9). The neutral trigonal form of boronic acid molecules transforms into the anionic tetrahedral form on binding a saccharide, upon which a proton is released. Ester formation by interaction of the corresponding arylboronate with a diol is known to occur very fast and reversibly in aqueous media. Five and six membered cyclic arylboronate esters are formed upon binding between arylboronic acids and cis-1,2- or 1,3-diols respectively. With d-glucose the boronic acid has a choice of binding either the 1,2- or 4,6-diols, but with d-glucosamine hydrochloride, binding with just the 4,6-diol is possible. The stability constant with d-glucose is higher than that observed with d -glucosamine hydrochloride. It may be assumed that this behavior agrees with binding GA with tetrahedron B^{-}-atoms of boronic acid that carry into effect of additional crosslinking.

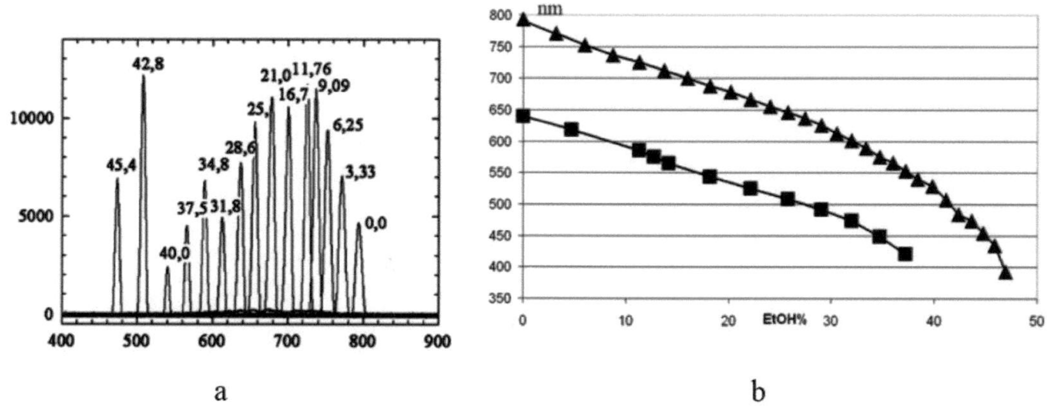

Figure 7. Reflection spectra of sensor based on acrylic acid (AA-AC-bis – 97.8-1.3-0.9 mol.%) at different concentrations of ethanol solutions (a) and the reflection line wavelengths for sensor based on acrylic acid (AA-AC-bis - 97.8-1.3-0.88 mol.%) (upper curve) and aminophenylboronic acid (AA-AMPh-bis – 98-1-1 mol%) (lower curve) (b).

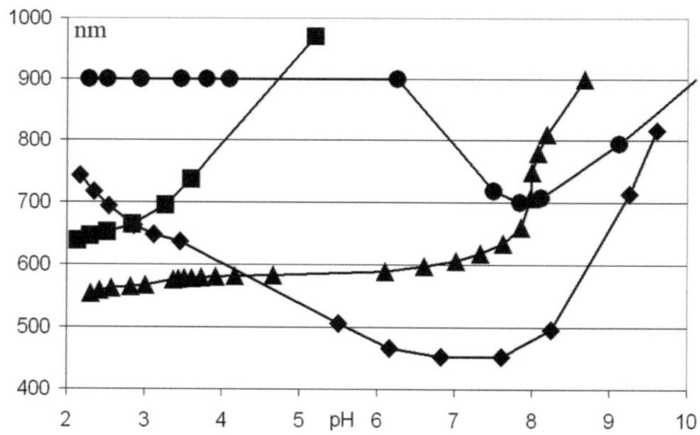

Figure 8. Dependences of the reflection line wavelength on the solution acidity for matrices of different compositions. (sensors: AA-AMPh(12 mol.%)-X-bis; X: ■-AC (5.8, bis-3 mol.%) ●-DMA (3.6, bis -3 mol.%, ▲-GA(3.6, bis-1, mol. %), ◆-Lys (5.8, bis-1 mol.%))

The quantitation of glucose is among the most important analytical tasks. It has been estimated that about 40% of all blood tests are related to it. In addition, there are numerous other situations where glucose needs to be determined, for example in biotechnology, in the production and processing of various kinds of feed and food, in biochemistry in general, and other areas. The significance of glycemic control for the prevention of diabetes complications is well established [30]. The market for glucose sensors probably is the biggest single one in the diagnostic field, being about 30 billion $ per year today. Given this size, it is not surprising that any real improvement in glucose sensing (in whole blood and elsewhere) represents a major step forward. Holographic glucose sensors represent a comparatively new development [9-12, 18, 26]. The advantage of the holographic method over other optical techniques is the long-term stability of the sensor and the ease with which the wavelength may be tuned to suit the application.

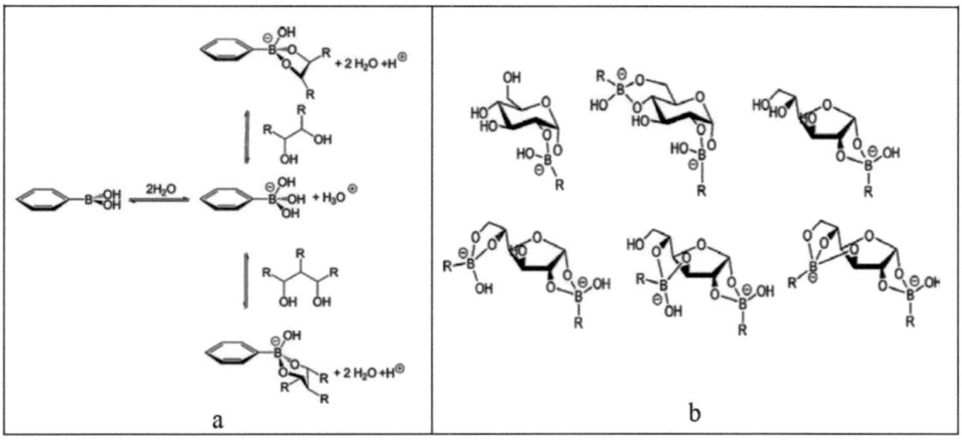

Figure 9. The spontaneous ester formation between phenylboronate and cis-1,2-diol or 1,3-diol compounds (a), aryl-boronate complexes formed with d-glucose (b) [29]

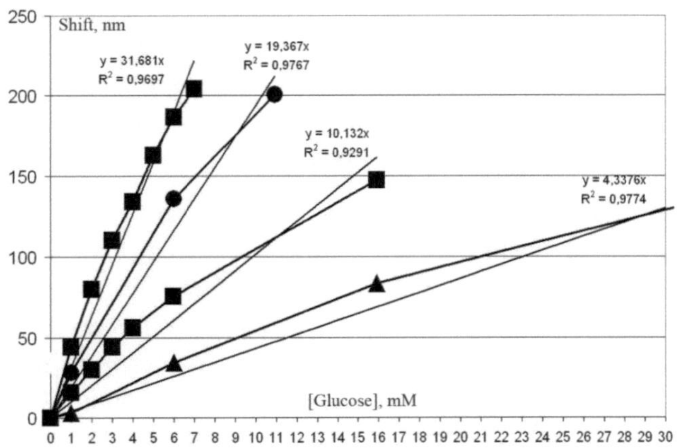

Figure 10. Dependences of the reflection line wavelength on the glucose concentration for different sensors. The straight lines are approximations of experimental curves by proportional functions described by presented equations with determination coefficients R^2. (sensors: AA with AMPh- GA-bis, mol.%:▲- 4-1-0.5, ■- 4-1-0.1, ● -12-0-1, ◙ -6-6-0.1mol.%; 0,01 M glycine, pH 7.4)

Sensors with aminophenylboronic acid were sensitive to glucose concentrations in the solution. The reflection (λ_{max}) and the shift (λ_0-λ_{max}) were influenced on the additive to polymer net, the buffer solution and pH. The shift of λ_{max} is changed from 10 to 200 nm when glucose concentration was increased (0-30 mM). By investigating the properties of sensors in detail, we optimized responses of sensors to glucose. Their concentration dependences are shown in Fig.10.

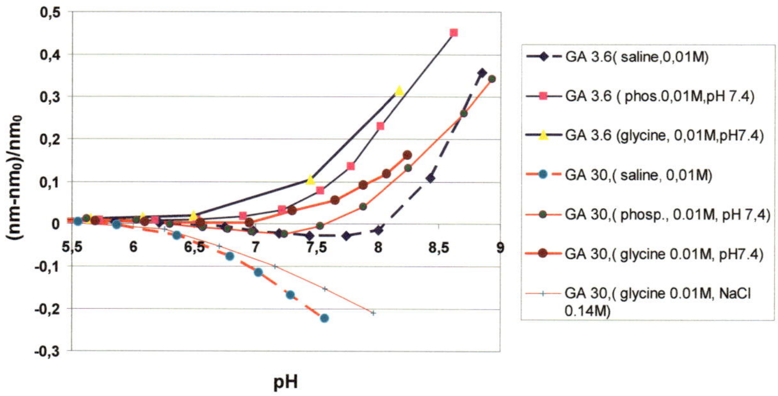

Figure 11. The influence of ionic strength on the hydrogels shrinkage in solutions. (Sensors: AA with GA-AMPh-bis-3.6-12-1; 30-12-1, mol.%)

One can see that the sensor sensitivity changes from 4.3 to 32 nm/(mmol·L^{-1}). Copolymer of acrylamide containing 6 mol.% glucosamine, 6 mol.% boronic acid, 0.1 mol.% bis shows the most sensitivity in glycine solution, pH 7.4. The response of sensor to glucose in blood serum is lower but allows to distinguish changes in 1 mM glucose concentration. A possible reason for reducing the sensitivity of sensors to glucose in the blood serum is a contraction of the matrix caused by ionic strength. According to Fig. 11 at pH = 7.4 for all sensors including the GA and AMPh with increasing content of sodium ions to 0.14 M in the solution, there is a significant contraction of the hydrogel (20%). Therefore swelling of the hydrogel due to the presence of glucose occurs in the already highly compressed hydrogel

Holographic sensors give an interesting object in study of light scattering by an ensemble of nanoparticles, since one can change the environment of the particles almost preserving their mutual location. In these systems (see Fig. 4) we found that when the concentration of alkali changes in the titration, at the same time a sharp change in pH occurs, as well as a sharp change in the position of maximum reflection and a sharp and significant (almost by an order of magnitude) change in the diffraction efficiency of the holographic sensor. This indicates a significant change of the optical characteristics of the holographic layer [28, 33]. These characteristics include diffraction effectivity (DE), transmission, spectral form of the reflection line (in particular, its width) and wavelength distribution over the hologram surface. The line shape reflects homogeneity of the layer period into depth of the hologram. Its study allows investigating the transition processes in emulsion under change of solution.

The transmittance and the line width together allow one to determine the effective number of layers and the weak inhomogeneity of the period. The processes in the sensitive hologram layer when changing solution parameters are complicated due to changing the molecular and ion structure in the solution within the hydrogel, to re-constructing the gel matrix, to interaction of the light-scattering grains with the solution components and matrix elements. Hologram based on silver nanoparticle layers is a typical nanoplasmonics object which scatters light in a complicated environment of ions of different kinds, of water molecules and of polymer matrix elements. The emulsion matrix interacts with the tested compounds by changing the density of crosslink in the polymer mesh. This may change as the charge distribution in the matrix and the composition of ions and other components in the solution. All of these elements (matrix elements, ions, molecules of the solution), interacting with each other and with silver nanograins, can alter the dynamic characteristics of electronic subsystems that match the light field, which leads to a change in optical characteristics. The research of these characteristics would help to understand the processes inside the emulsion and in the vicinity of nanograins.

If the period of layers is constant in depth and the modulation is weak (transmittance of a layer at the resonant wavelength λ is close to unity), the spectral width $\Delta\lambda$ of the reflection line is inverse proportional to the thickness H of the sensitive layer, or to the number of periods N:

$$\Delta\lambda = 0.866\lambda^2 / 2n_0H = 0.866\lambda / N$$

where n_0 is the mean index refraction of holographic layer. The accuracy of determination of wavelength depends on this value. This formula is valid only when the conditions described above. In all other cases require special methods of calculation [33].

The mode of sensor operation is very important. A good resolution is obtained when all the sensitive layer work effectively. If the falling radiation cannot penetrate sufficiently deep, the effective thickness of the hologram decreases. It reduces the resolution. Typically, the sensor sensitive layer contains silver nanograins, which have a high refractive index and a high absorption coefficient in the visible region of the spectrum. This leads to the elimination of radiation from the plane wave of light illuminating the hologram, due to absorption and scattering. This also reduces the number of effectively operating layers and, consequently, leads to the broadening of the reflection spectral line and to the deterioration of accuracy. The increase of the amplitude of modulation of the refractive index, which is introduced to increase the diffraction efficiency of the hologram, leads to the same effect. On the other hand, a strong decrease of the modulation amplitude narrows the line to the limit, but decreases the diffraction efficiency and, consequently, the measurement accuracy. Obviously, the parameters can be optimized. Therefore one needs a rather accurate method of determining the parameters of the hologram.

One of the important reasons to study optical properties of holographic sensors is to provide the proper work regime of the sensor. That means that the holographic sensor should work in the whole working range of concentrations as a thin photonic crystal (the reflectance is weak).

The hologram functioning depends seriously upon the light scattering properties. In its turn, these depend on both the type (metal or dielectric) and properties of the scattering center, and on its environment (mixture and ion concentration of the solution and of the hydrogel). The light scattering is the Raleigh one and can essentially limit the working range from the short wavelength side. Another important issue is to check the quality of the holographic layer, in particular, its homogeneity. To this purpose, we developed a colorimetric method of determination of the wavelength with the digital camera [34-36]. On the other hand, one can check the emulsion homogeneity by the distribution of the light scattering parameters.

The computer model of propagation in a layered medium for one-dimensional case was developed. The case of bleached holograms, where absorption is neglected and the refractive index is not depending from wavelength is included. At the same time is neglected and light scattering. Generalization to the dispersion of the refractive index is not an issue. The model allows determining the amplitude of modulation of the refractive index and effective thickness of the holographic layer by fitting the spectrum of the transmission hologram in the presence of the dip near the resonant frequency.

To measure the homogeneity of response of sensor properties over its surface have been applied the colorimetric method with the help of common camera [34-36]. Spatial inhomogeneity can emerge due either to inhomogeneities of the object under consideration, or to those of the sensor properties. The sensor is a thick layer hologram with width of few tens of micrometers. Its reflection spectrum has the spectral width 5-20 nm. Because of it, one suffices to use response from two color channels.

Hence, the problem is reduced to the following. Assume there is a set of emitters on a plane. We are interested in obtaining the spectra of each emitter preferably simultaneously. It is not easy especially if the sources are closely packed and produce almost continuous radiating surface. The situation is simpler if radiation from each point is spectrally narrow. Then, the distribution of the average radiation wavelength over the surface can be found by the colorimetric method. At each surface point one should determine with the required resolution the magnitudes of three components of a colour vector, i.e., obtain a colour image of the surface under study. Presently, the solution of this problem by using digital devices has no principal difficulties. The aim of our work is to solve the problem by means of conventional digital cameras. Each pixel of the colour image presents a particular colour vector in the RGB system. In order to find the distribution of the average wavelength from the image it is necessary to know how the particular digital camera represents radiation of different wavelengths.

The colorimetric method [34, 35] suggested for finding this distribution is as follows. Radiation passes to at least two detecting channels differing in spectral sensitivity. If in a certain spectral range (call it the working range) the ratio of spectral sensitivities of at least two channels is monotonous then one can determine the average wavelength of narrowband radiation from the signal ratio in the channels (see Fig. 12). At the selective sensitivity of the i-th channel $S_i(\lambda)$ its signal is $J_i=\int d\lambda\ S_i(\lambda)\Phi(\lambda)$, where $\Phi(\lambda)$ is the source brightness. For the δ-shape spectral source with brightness Φ_0, which emits at the wavelength λ_x, the signal in this channel is $J_i=I_0S_i(\lambda_x)$. If the ratio of the spectral sensitivities for two chosen channels is $a(l)$, then the sought-for wavelength is the solution of the equation $\alpha(\lambda)=S_1(\lambda)/\ S_2(\lambda)$:

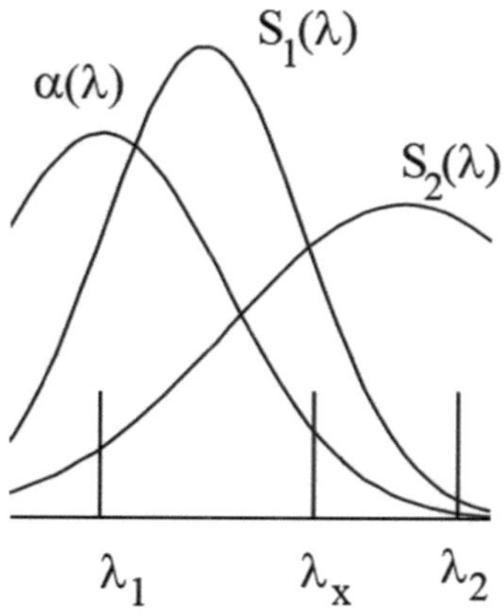

Figure 12. Qualitative view of the spectral sensitivities $S_1(\lambda)$ and $S_2(\lambda)$ of working channels and their ratio $\alpha(\lambda)$: λ_1 and λ_2 are the limits of working range, λ_x is the wavelength of a monochromatic radiation source.

$$\lambda_x = \alpha^{-1}(J_1 / J_2).$$

where α^{-1} is the function inverse to $\alpha(\lambda)$. If the sought-for wavelength is outside the working range, i.e., outside the range of monotonous ratio of sensitivities in two channels, then the unique wavelength determination necessitates an additional (third) channel.

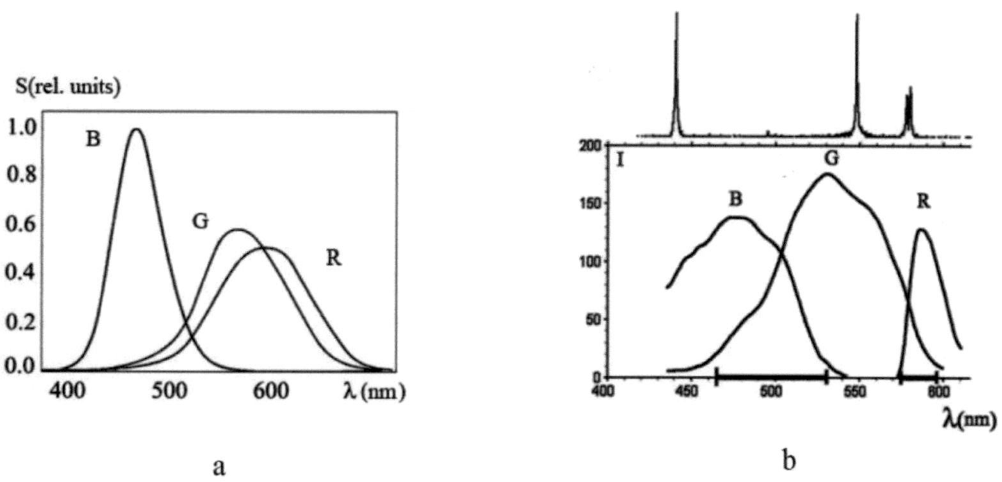

Figure 13. a). The spectral sensitivity of the human eye: signals of red (R) green (G), and blue (B) receptors [37].b). The spectrum of the mercury lamp (top) and signals of red (R), green (G), and blue (B) sensors of Sony F717 digital camera obtained from the photograph of the incandescent lamp spectrum taken by a colour digital camera (bottom).

The case of a finite spectral width is not as simple as that of a δ-like source. In our case the spectrum of reflection from a holographic layer may widen due to several reasons. First, due to a small number of efficiently reflecting layers, which can be related either to a small thickness of the holographic layer or to a short depth of radiation penetration into the layer because of the high reflection caused by high amplitude of the variable part of refractive index or by strong scattering of light. Second, the spectrum may widen due to the non uniform periodicity of layers in depth. We are interested in layer swelling, which is a reason for period variations and is related to the position of reflection maximum. In the latter case it is important to find the average period of layers, which is related to some average wavelength. Obviously, at moderate broadening this parameter can also be determined by means of the procedure described above using the signal relation in different spectral channels. However, in the general case the period obtained in this way from the position of maximum in the measured reflection spectrum differs from the average period. The difference depends both on a particular shape of reflection spectrum and on spectral sensitivities of the channels. The criterion for acceptable line broadening should be the permissible distinction of determined average period from its actual average value. If the sensitivity of sensors is almost constant within the line width of radiation illuminating a single pixel of the array, then radiation actually behaves as monochromatic one. If the spectral sensitivities of the sensor linearly vary within the width of the line that is symmetrical in shape, then the average period determined is the same as that in the case of a monochromatic source. If this condition is ruled out, then in the general case the determined wavelength is distinct from average one.

In the general case, the colorimetric measurements imply a projection of the surface under study to the detecting array through two (or, for expanding the range, a greater number) types of light filters, i.e., it is necessary to create a colorimetric device with a sufficient spatial resolution. A digital camera is just such a device.

In Fig.13a, the spectral sensitivities are shown for three types of human eye cones responsible for colour recognition [37]. A digital camera also distinguishes colours but the spectral sensitivity of its sensors is distinct. For example, we will show below that in the spectral range 540 – 575 nm a digital camera does not discriminate different colour hues at all. In Fig. 13b, the signals of red (R), green (G), and blue (B) sensors of Sony F717 digital camera are shown that were obtained from a digital photograph of the incandescent lamp spectrum. The spectrum was detected from a spectrograph with a diffraction grating (~ 800 lines mm^{-1}). This and all the following results were obtained at the sensitivity ISO 100 and switched-off automatic white balance. If the emission spectrum under study fits one of the two marked working ranges then the digital camera is appropriate for measurements. Note that we studied about ten various cameras and have found that their sensor characteristics are qualitatively similar. Figure 14 shows how a continuous spectrum (colour hue) is represented by digital cameras of various brands. Nevertheless, we did not study the characteristics of particular cameras as we wanted to understand the situation as a whole. Only the basic working Sony F717 digital camera was thoroughly studied. The spectrum of the incandescent lamp with an added calibrating spectrum of the mercury lamp was photographed. The shots used for the comparison were not overexposed, i.e., the maximal signal amplitude in channels was not above 150 – 200 digital units (the maximal admissible signal is 255 digital units). The colour hue H was determined in a standard way as the polar angle in the cylindrical coordinate system of a three-dimensional colour space. Its value was from 0 to 360. For convenient work in red, green, and blue colour ranges we chose the reference point for the colour hue in the blue range (H = 0 at R = 0, G = 0, B = 255). In this case, the break of the colour hue (0 – 360) fits the blue range and introduces no additional difficulties in data processing. The purely red colour (R = 255, G = 0, B = 0) corresponds to H = 120 and purely green colour (R = 0, G = 255, B = 0) corresponds to H = 240. A more thorough analysis of various digital cameras is interesting but is beyond the framework of the present paper. Anyway, some general information may be obtained from Fig. 13. The principal conclusion important for our work is that all the digital cameras used have a defect of colour sensitivity in the green range.

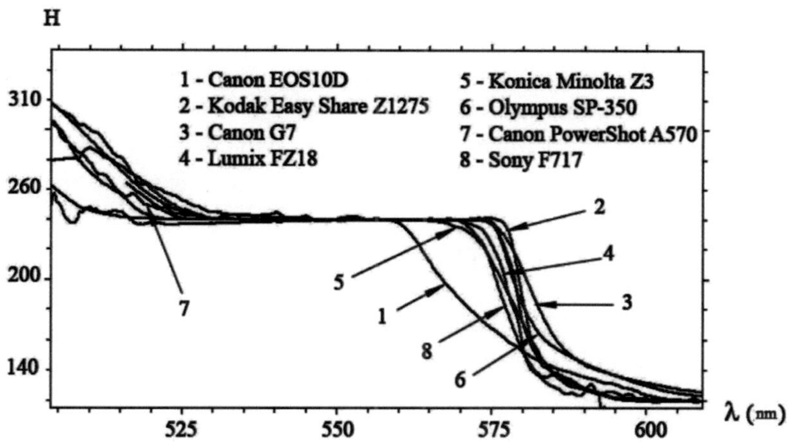

Figure 14. The colour hue (H) versus wavelength for some digital camera types.

Some modern cameras provide the possibility for extracting unprocessed data in the RAW format. Preliminary experiments show that the situation with the colour sensitivity in this case is better. The processor of the digital camera does not distort data but further investigations are necessary for using the RAW format. At the first stage, we limited our study to simplest (mass) formats (JPEG, BMP) by the following reasons. Creation of holographic sensors was assumed for mass consumer and our aim was to develop not only a simple method for checking the quality of sensors but for reading data from them also. The method should be available for mass users, i.e., should rely on simplest digital cameras, in which the RAW format is not presented now. In addition, the processing of the image of the holographic sensor surface should be maximum simple.

A particular procedure for camera spectral calibration was developed because the responses of the three sensor types of the detecting array intricately depend not only on the radiation wavelength but on the exposure as well. The camera to be calibrated takes shots of a continuous spectrum superimposed on the mercury lamp spectrum with various exposures. Then, this spectrum is used for calibrating each image with respect to the wavelength. The images calibrated in this way are then processed together. The result is information on the relationship between the wavelength and sensor responses. The range 570 – 605 nm is considered in which the red and green sensors are sensitive. The signal in the blue channel in this range is not above the noise level. On the basis of all the obtained dependences the characteristic surface is plotted for the camera under study, which gives the sought-for wavelength as a function of the colour hue and the average value of I. Once the characteristic surface is plotted the camera can be used as a spectral device in the working range of wavelengths and sensor responses. Applicability of the method was verified on the yellow doublet of the mercury spectrum and on a continuous spectrum of the incandescent lamp (sees Fig. 15). Clearly visible color distortion of the short wavelength doublet line (too green hue, what can assess spectroscopist) in the picture are associated with the mention above defect of JPEG-format of digital camera.

Note that in the case of the mercury spectrum image and continuous spectrum of the incandescent lamp each pixel is illuminated by an almost monochromatic light source, because the fraction of the continuous spectrum per single pixel of the image is less than 1 nm. Having processed the image of spectrum (in Fig. 15a, the domain is shown fitting the working wavelength range) we obtain the map of the wavelength distribution over the image (Fig. 15b); only the image domains from the processing system working ranges are taken into account. Domains with too low values of I, in which the signal is close to noise, are neglected. Also neglected are the domains with high I in which, probably, noticeable redistribution of signals over different colour channels occurs and domains with almost a zero sensitivity of one of the two sensors. This explains the complicated contour of the wavelength distribution map over the image in the continuous spectrum range. It is interesting that due to different intensities of sources one can see in Fig. 15a the domain with superimposed continuous spectrum and mercury lines. On the wavelength distribution map there is no such superimposed domain, which proves that the recovered wavelengths are equal despite the different intensities. In Figs 15c and d the distributions of various characteristics are shown for horizontal cross sections of the image. It is known that a spectral device with a diffraction grating has a linear dispersion, i.e., the wavelength should linearly vary with the coordinate (Fig. 15d), whereas the colour hue changes obviously nonlinearly (Fig. 15c). The distribution columns (Figs 15e, f, g, and h, i, j) correspond to vertical cross sections of the image along the yellow doublet lines. In Figs 15e and h, the responses of red and green sensors are presented varying along the coordinate in a vertical cross section according to changing I. The colour hue H also varies despite the constant wavelength (Figs 15f, i). Nevertheless, in vertical cross sections of the wavelength distribution map coinciding with the mercury spectrum lines (579 nm and 577 nm) the recovered wavelength is constant to a high accuracy both in the domain of mercury lines and in continuous spectrum (Figs 15g and j).

http://dx.doi.org/10.5772/53564

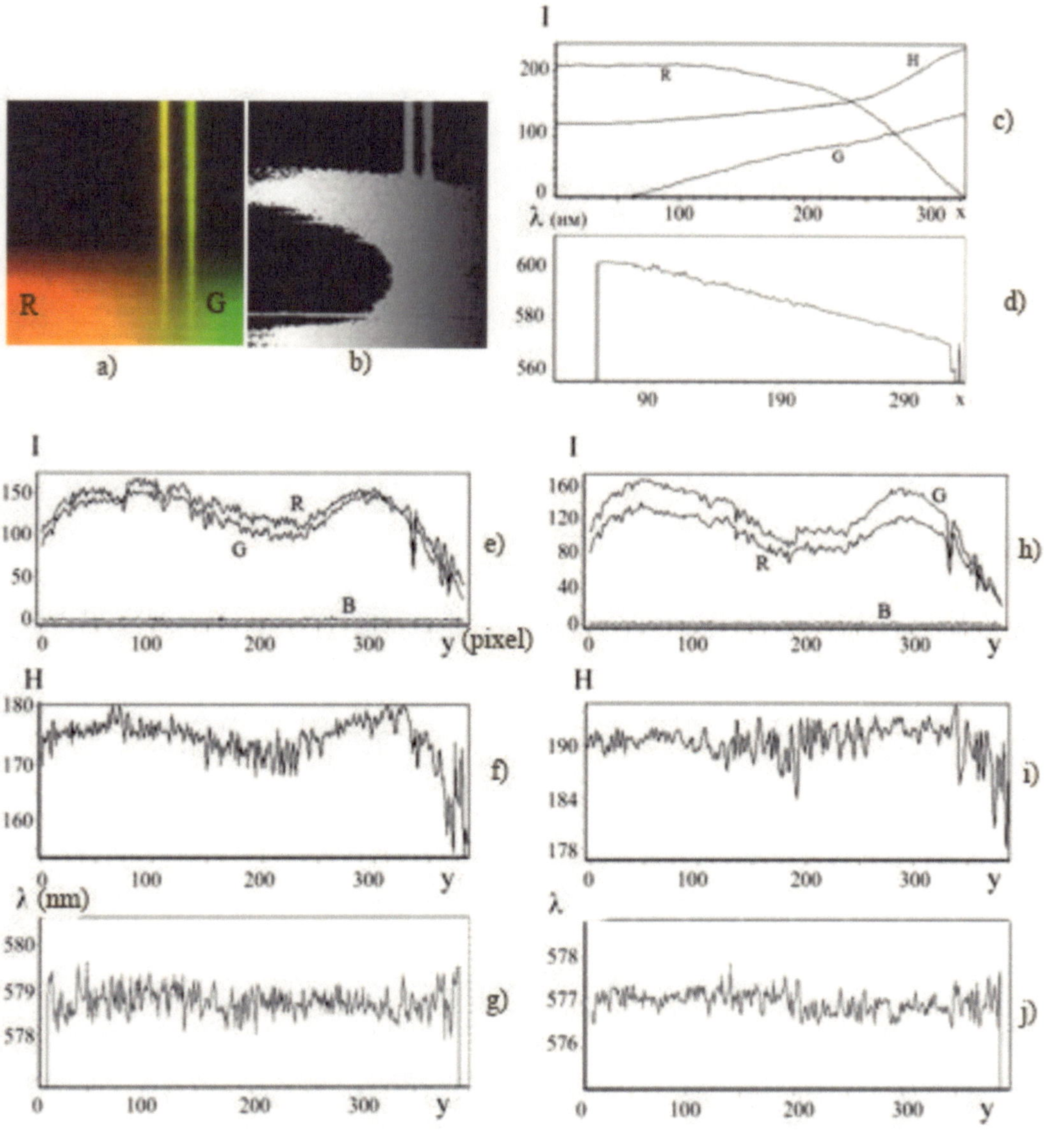

Figure 15. Illustration for an operating test of the method. Shot of spectrum fragment (a); the map of wavelength distribution over the image (b); the distribution of signals in red (R) and green (G) channels and colour hue (H) in a horizontal cross section of the shot (c); the horizontal cross section of the wavelength map (d); the distribution of signal in colour channels (e, h), colour hue (f, i), and calculated wavelengths (g, j) in a vertical cross section of the shot along the mercury doublet lines 579 nm (e, f, g) and 577 nm (h, i, j). The black color on the wavelength map marks the domains in which the signals are beyond the working range and, hence, are excluded from calculation.

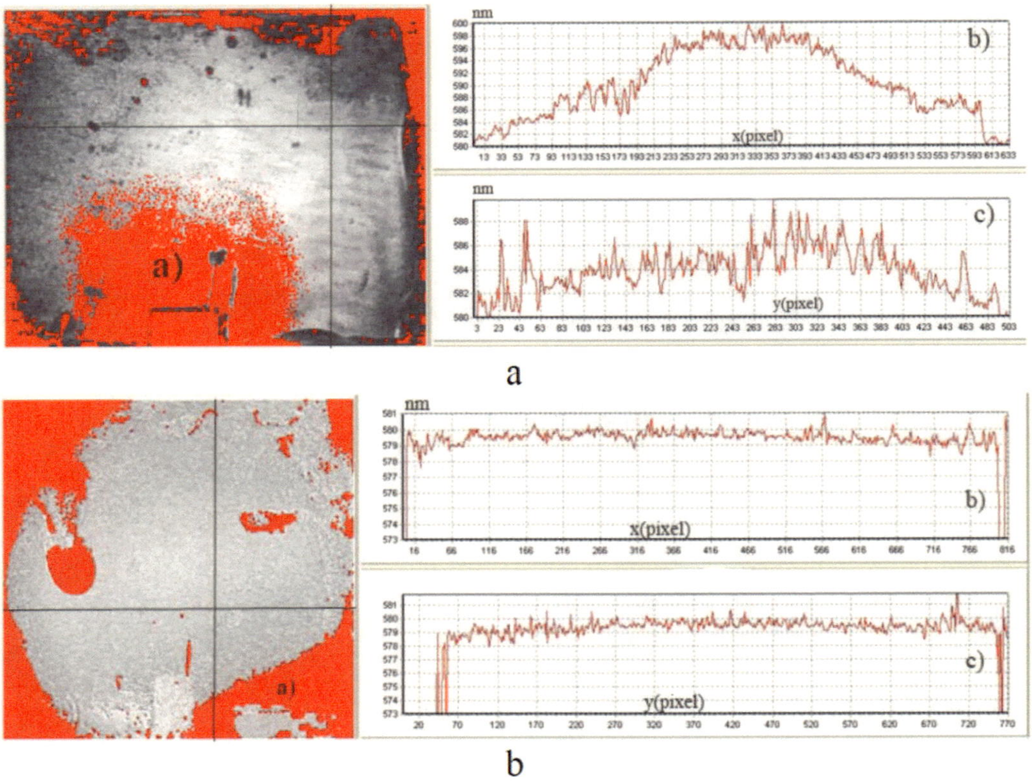

Figure 16. a)The map of wavelength distribution over image (a) and its horizontal (b) and vertical (c) cross sections for a transient process of holographic layer shrinking and b) for a stationary state of sensor AA-AMPh-bis – 87-12-1 mol. %.(JPEG-format) The lines on the maps show the cross-section directions.

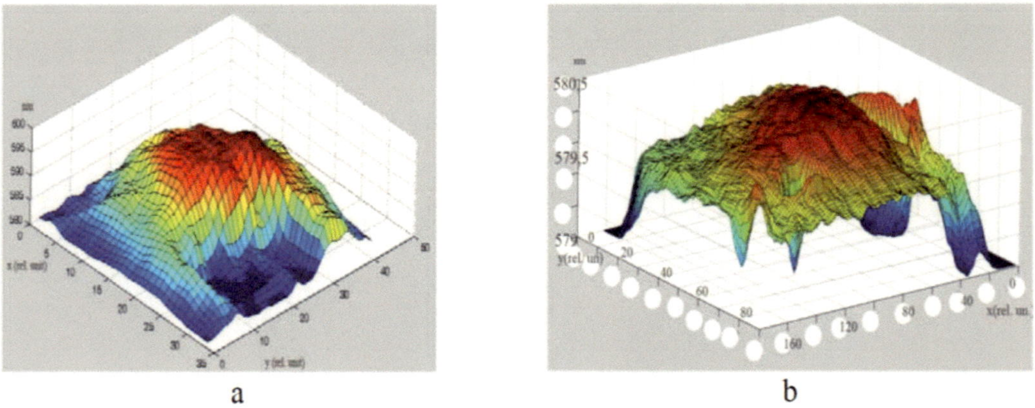

Figure 17. Isometric presentation of the wavelength distribution map (a) in the case of transient shrinkage of the holographic layer of sensor AA-AMPh-bis – 87-12-1 mol.% and for the hologram in a stationary state (b).

http://dx.doi.org/10.5772/53564

By the digital image of the mercury spectrum for the yellow doublet lines and for underlying continuous spectrum we determined the standard deviation of the recovered wavelength in the limits of a narrow window oriented along the central (with respect to the spectrum) part of the mercury line. The window width was 4 pixels, which was less than the line width. The window height was 350 pixels and covered almost all the image of the mercury line and the whole corresponding part of the continuous spectrum. For the mercury doublet lines the wavelengths of 577 nm (the standard deviation is 0.16) and 579 nm (the standard deviation is 0.19) were obtained.

The developed method was employed for studying holographic sensors. The results are shown in Figs 16, 17. The spectrum of radiation reflected from a holographic sensor is wider and the problem of possible inaccuracy in determining the wavelength requires particular investigations. One should keep in mind that in using holographic sensors it is important to know the shift of the wavelength under the action of solution surrounding the sensor rather than the absolute value of the wavelength itself. Data presented in Figs 16a and 17a refer to a transient process to the hologram initially reflecting in the red range. Data for this hologram in ending stationary state is presented in Figs.16b. and 17b. One can see that the spread of wavelengths is noticeably reduced as compared to the transient process, and is less than 2 nm over the whole sensor surface. The local spread also strongly reduced and was less than 1 nm. The map comprises approximately 500 000 points.

The hologram quality and uniformity of the processes occurring during swelling can be estimated from their noise characteristics. In Fig. 18, the standard deviation of the calculated wavelengths is shown versus the width of the averaging window. The standard deviation of wavelength from mean $\bar{\lambda}$ is:

$$A_k = \sqrt{\frac{\sum_i^m (\lambda_i - \bar{\lambda})^2}{m}}$$

where λ_i is the calculated wavelength in the i-th pixel of the image and m is the number of points fitting the window, was averaged over N image points covering the whole studied domain of the sensor. The parameter $S = \frac{1}{N}\sum_k^N A_k$ we will term the noise value. Data presented in Fig. 18 correspond to variation of m from 4 to 2500 pixels. The standard deviation was averaged over the image domain of 500x500 points. With increasing m in the transient process the standard deviation varied from 0.5 to 1.8 nm. A steady increase in noise with the increasing window is related to a large-scale hologram inhomogeneity. In the steady state it was 0.16 – 0.32 nm at the same values of m. An increase in noise at the initial part of the dependence is explained by small-scale inhomogeneity, and the saturation at large m is related to the absence of large-scale inhomogeneity. The ratio of nonstationary noise to stationary level in this range of m increases from 3.4 to 5.6. These facts bear witness that, first, the hologram in the steady state is highly uniform and, second, variations of its swelling over the surface in the nonstationary state are noticeably inhomogeneous.

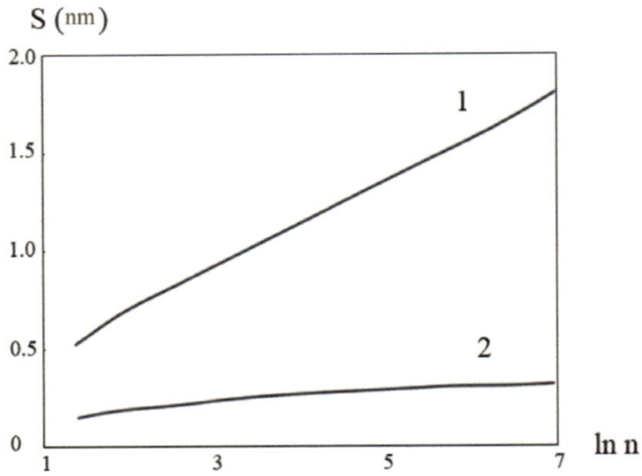

Figure 18. The standard deviation of the calculated wavelength versus the number of points in the averaging window for the transient process (1) and stationary sensor state (2).

Further development of the colorimetric method with the use of RAW-format can significantly increase the working range of wavelengths (440-620 nm), which can be seen from Fig. 19.

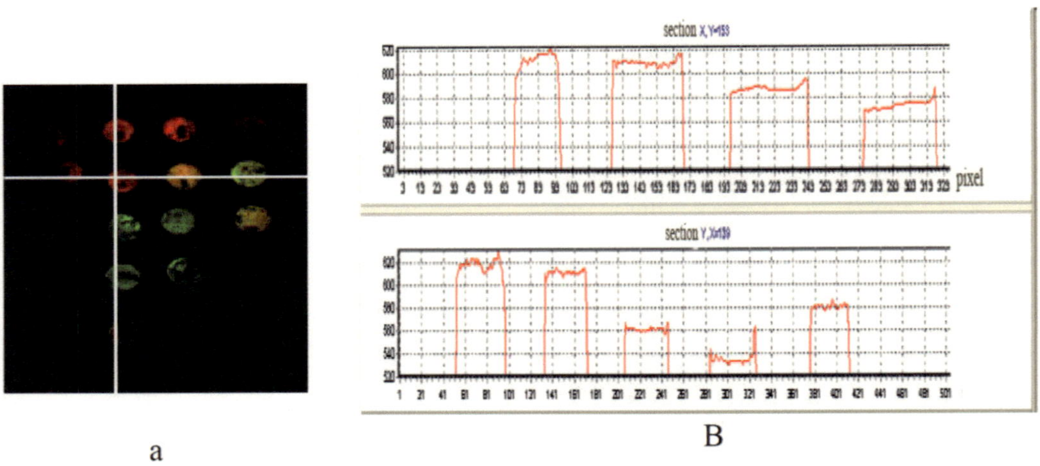

Figure 19. a) The photograph of the hologram in the steady state. b) In the upper right-hand column shows the horizontal and vertical cross-section of the distribution of responses. (RAW-format)

Thus, here is described the method for measuring the distribution of the average wavelength for narrow-band radiation over the source surface by means of a commercial digital camera. There are the following limitations in using the method (without RAW-format): the radiation spectrum should be narrow (the average wavelength is determined); measurements are performed in the spectral range in which at least two sensor types of detecting array are simultaneously sensitive (for the most of cameras

http://dx.doi.org/10.5772/53564

studied these ranges are 470 – 540 nm and 570 – 600 nm). The accuracy of the determined wavelength is not worse than 1 nm. The method was tested on the yellow doublet of the mercury spectrum and on a continuous spectrum of the incandescent lamp covering the working interval 570 – 600 nm. By using this method the uniformity of holographic sensor swelling was studied both in a stationary state and in dynamics.

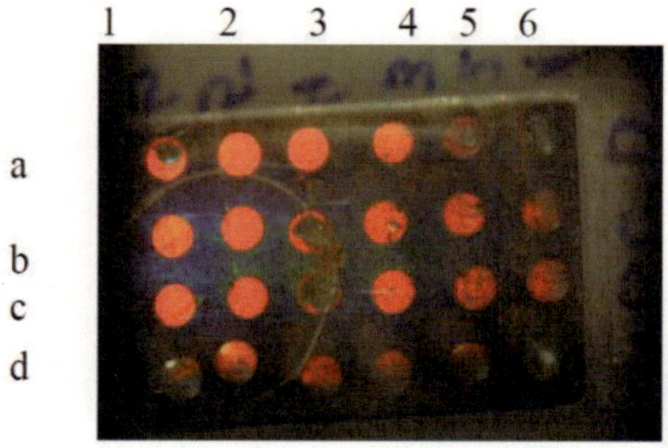

a

	AcOH					
	1	2	3	4	5	6
a	645,6	642,4	643,1	641,0	640,6	643,4
b	645,4	640,6	641,7	640,9	640,6	641,4
c	645,4	644,0	641,1	640,4	640,6	642,2
d	644,5	642,6	641,2	642,6	640,1	641,9
Mean, nm						
642,2	645,2	642,4	641,8	641,2	640,5	642,2
±1,7	0,5	1,7	0,9	1,0	0,3	0,8

b

Figure 20. a) The photograph of the hologram. b) The distribution of samples of 0.5% acetic acid on the sensors surface and wavelength of reflected light in cells (fiber-optic spectrometer).

The design of holographic sensors allows their use in multi-channel mode, when one sensor can simultaneously analyze multiple samples of the same type or define a few parameters of a sample. The holographic sensor is actually a thick hologram plane mirror about the size of a square centimeter. By placing such plate in a special cuvette, containing 24 cells of 2 mm diameter, each contains 50 μL of fluid to be analyzed; it can be used in a multi-channel mode for the simultaneous determination of all samples. The response of the sensor - the wavelength of reflected light - from the cell is easily determined by means of small-sized fiber-optic spectrometer (Fig. 20, 21) or in combination with the developed colorimetric method; it can greatly simplify and speed up the analysis (Fig. 19). As can be seen from Fig. 20, the wavelength of the reflected light at different points on the surface is almost the same (the standard deviation is 1.7 nm). This way you can see the spatial pattern of

kinetics of the holographic sensor, to conduct research of the spatial distribution of processes, with the help of special devices to conduct simultaneous analysis of different components or different samples. Fig. 21 presents the results of the determination of glucose in the blood serum of diabetic patients with glucose sensor (see Fig.) based on aminophenylboronic acid. Despite a significant decrease in the sensitivity of the sensor to the glucose concentration in blood plasma, determined by glucose clearly distinguished spectrometrically.

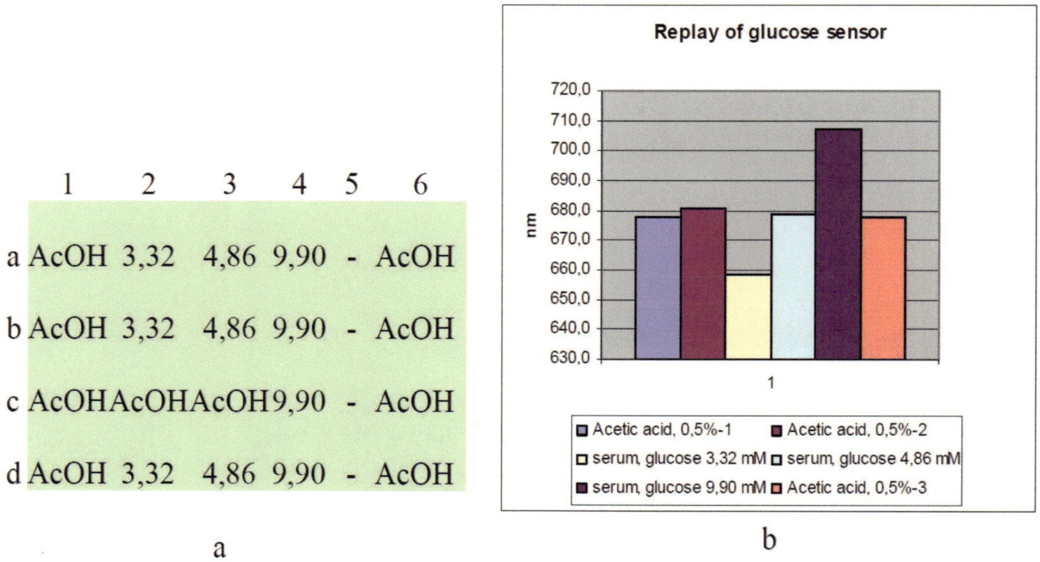

Figure 21. a). The distribution of blood serum (*) [glucose], mM) samples with different glucose concentrations and 0.5% acetic acid on the sensors surface. b). Response (λ_{nm}) of glucose sensor (AA-GA- AMPh - bis: 87,5 - 6 – 6 - 0.5 mol. %) (fiber-optic spectrometer).

3. Conclusion

Thus, we have developed a colorimetric method of determination of the wavelength with the digital camera to study processes in inhomogeneous systems and to check the quality of the holographic layer. On this basis we revealed the multichannel simultaneous methods of analysis of spatially inhomogeneous objects and processes. We have found that the change in the ionic composition of solution is accompanied by the change in the distance between silver nanograin layers and in the diffraction efficiency of holograms. Based on this, we are formulated conditions for optimization of the operating mode of the holographic layer. Transition processes revealed variations in the reflection line shape, caused by the inhomogeneity of the sensitive layer, and non-monotonic changes in the emulsion thickness and diffraction efficiency. In this relation it was developed the computer model of propagation in a layered medium for one-dimensional case 33.

We have developed the method for manufacturing holographic sensors of different types and selected the composition of components of the hydrogel medium for the systems that can be used as bases for glucose sensors. The maximum mean holographic response in the mmol·L^{-1} region concentrations of glucose (1-20 mmol·L^{-1}) per 1 mmol·L^{-1} of glucose in model solutions achieves ~40 nm/(mmol·L^{-1}). It has been shown that holographic sensors can be used to determine the quality of water, in particular, for drinking, the acidity of media, ethanol concentration, ionic strength, metal ions and glucose in blood serum.

http://dx.doi.org/10.5772/53564

Acknowledgements

This work was supported by grant of the Program of Fundamental Studies "Fundamental Sciences for Medicine" of the Presidium of RAS.

Author details

Vladimir A. Postnikov[1*], Aleksandr V. Kraiskii[2] and Valerii I. Sergienko[3]

*Address all correspondence to: vladpostnikov@mail.ru

1 Laboratory of Medical Nanotechnology, Scientific Research Institute of Physical-Chemical Medicine, Moscow, Russia

2 G.S. Landsberg Optical Department, P.N.Lebedev Physical Institute of the Russian Academy of Sciences, Moscow, Russia

3 Department of Biophysics, Scientific Research Institute of Physical-Chemical Medicine, Moscow, Russia

References

[1] Millington R, Mayes A, Blyth J, and Lowe C. A Holographic sensor for Proteases. Anal. Chem. 1995; 67,4229-4233

[2] Mayes A, Blyth J, Kyrollo1inen-Reay M, Millington R. and Lowe C. A holographic alcohol sensor. Anal. Chem. 1999; 71, 3390-3396

[3] Holtz J, Asher S. Polymerized colloidal crystal hydrogel films as intelligent chemical sensing materials. Nature. 1997; 389, 829–32.

[4] Reese E, Baltusavich M, Keim J, Asher S. Development of an intelligent polymerized crystalline colloidal array colorimetric reagent. Anal Chem. 2001; 73, 5038–42.

[5] Marshall A, Young D, Kabilan S, Hussain A, Blyth J. and Lowe C. Holographic sensors for the determination of ionic strength. Analytica Chimica Acta. 2004; 527(1), 13-20

[6] González B, Christie G, Davidson C, Blyth J. and Lowe C. Divalent metal ion-sensitive holographic sensors. Analytica Chimica Acta. 2005; 528(2), 219-228

[7] Alexeev V, Sharma A, Goponenko A, Das S, Lednev I, Wilcox C, et al. High ionic strength glucose-sensing photonic crystal. Anal Chem 2003; 75, 2316–23.

[8] Asher S, Alexeev V, Goponenko A, Sharma A, Lednev I, Wilcox C, et al. Photonic crystal carbohydrate sensors: low ionic strength sugar sensing. J Am Chem Soc 2003; 125, 3322–9.

[9] Kabilan S, Marshall A, Sartain F, Lee M.-C, Hussain A, Yang X, Blyth J, Karangu N, James K, Zeng J, Smith D, Domschke A. and Lowe C. Holographic glucose sensors. Biosensors and Bioelectronics. 2005; 20(8), 1602-1610

[10] Yang X, Lee M.-C, Sartain F, Pan X, Lowe C.R. Designed Boronate Ligands for Glucose-Selective Holographic sensors. Chem. Eur. J. 2006; 12, 8491-8497

[11] Horgan A, Marshall A, Kew S, Dean K, Creasey C. and Kabilan S. Crosslinking of phenylboronic acid receptors as a means of glucose selective holographic detection. Biosensors and Bioelectronics. 2006; 21(9), 1838-1845

[12] Worsley G, Tourniaire G, Medlock K, Sartain F, Harmer H, Thatcher M, Horgan A, and Pritchard J. Continuous Blood Glucose Monitoring with a Thin-Film Optical Sensor. Clinical Chemistry. 2007; 53(10), 1820-26

[13] Yang X, Pan X, Blyth J, Lowe C.R. Towards the real-time monitoring of glucose in tear fluid: Holographic glucose sensors with reduced interference from lactate and pH. Biosensors and Bioelectronics. 2008, 23, 899–905

[14] Alexeev VL, Das S, Finegold DN, Asher SA. Photonic crystal glucose-sensing material for noninvasive monitoring of glucose in tear fluid. Clin Chem. 2004; 50, 2362–9.

[15] Bhatta D, Christie G, Madrigal-González B, Blyth J. and Lowe C.R. Holographic sensors for the detection of bacterial spores. Biosensors and Bioelectronics. 2007; 23(4), 520-527

[16] Bhatta D, Christie G, Blyth J, Lowe C.R.. Development of a holographic sensor for the detection of calcium dipicolinate-A sensitive biomarker for bacterial spores. Sensors and Actuators. 2008; B 134, 356–359

[17] Marshall AJ, Young DS, Blyth J, Kabilan S, and Lowe CR. Metabolite-Sensitive Holographic Biosensors. Anal. Chem. 2004; 76 (5), 1518-1523

[18] Lee M-C, Kabilan S, Hussain A, Yang X, Blyth J, and Lowe CR. Glucose-Sensitive Holographic sensors for Monitoring Bacterial Growth. Anal. Chem. 2004; 76 (19), 5748-5755

[19] Bell LL, Seshia AA, Davidson CA, Lowe CR. Integration of holographic sensors into microfluidics for the real time pH sensing of L. casei metabolism. Procedia Engineering. 2010; 5, 1352-1355

[20] Naydenova I, Jallapuram R, Toal V, Martin S. Characterisation of the humidity and temperature responses of a reflection hologram recorded in acrylamide-based photopolymer. Sensors and Actuators. 2008; B 139(1) , 35-38

[21] Cody D, Naydenova I, Mihaylova E. New non-toxic holographic photopolymer material. J. Opt. 14 (2012) 015601 (4pp)

[22] Sartain FK, Yang X, Lowe CR. Holographic lactate sensor. Anal Chem. 2006;78(16), 5664-70

[23] Postnikov VA, Kraiskii AV, Sultanov TT, Tikhonov VE. Hydrogel holographic sensors sensitive to an acid media. In Proceedings of XVIII Intenational scool-seminar "Spectroscopy of molecules and crystals" 20.09-28.09.2007, Beregove, Crimea, Ukraine, Abstracts p.261

[24] Postnikov VA, Kraiskii AV, Tikhonov VE, Sultanov TT, Khamidulin AV. Hydrogel holographic sensors for detection of components in biological fluids. In Proceedings of CAOL 2008: 4th International Conference on Advanced Optoelectronics and Lasers ,2008,), Alushta, Crimea South Coast, Ukraine, September 29 – October 4, art. no. 4671956, 369-371

[25] Postnikov VA, Kraiskii AV, Tikhonov VE, Sultanov TT, Khamidulin AV. Hydrogel holographic sensors for detection of components in biological fluids. In Proceedings of CAOL 2008: 4th International Conference on Advanced Optoelectronics and Lasers ,2008,), Alushta, Crimea South Coast, Ukraine, September 29 – October 4, art. no. 4671956, 369-371

[26] Postnikov VA, Kraiskii AV, Sultanov TT, Deniskin VV. Holographic sensors of glucose in model solution and serum. In Conference Proceedings - 5th International Conference on Advanced Optoelectronics and Lasers, CAOL' 2010, September 10 -14, 2010, Sevastopol, Crimea, Ukraine, art. no. 5634191, 257-258

[27] Postnikov VA, Kraiskii AV, Sultanov TT. Holographic sensors. In Conference Proceedings - 11th International Conference on Laser and Fiber-Optical Networks Modeling, LFNM 2011, Kharkov, Ukraine, September 5 – 8, 2011, art. no. 6145033, 369-371

[28] Kraiskii AV, Postnikov VA, Sultanov TT, Khamidulin AV. Holographic sensors diagnostics of solution components. Quantum Electronics. 2010; 40 (2), 178 -182

[29] Hansen J, Christensen J, Petersen J, Hoeg-Jensen T, Norrild J. Arylboronic acids: A diabetic eye on glucose sensing. Sensors and Actuators. 2012; B 161, 45– 79

[30] Steiner M-S, Duerkop A, Wolfbeis O. Optical methods for sensing glucose. Chem. Soc. Rev. 2011; 40, 4805–4839

[31] Christopher R. Cooper and Tony D. James. Synthesis and evaluation of D-glucosamine-selective fluorescent sensors. J. Chem. Soc., Perkin Trans. 2000; 1 ,963–969

[32] Egawa Y, Seki T, Takahashi S, Anzai J-i. Electrochemical and optical sugar sensors based on phenylboronic acid and its derivatives. Materials Science and Engineering 2011; C 31, 1257–1264

[33] Kraiskii AV, Postnikov VA, Sultanov TT, Mironova TV, Kraiskii AA. On optical properties of holographic sensors based on silver emulsions. In Conference Proceedings - 11th International Conference on Laser and Fiber-Optical Networks Modeling, LFNM 2011, Kharkov, Ukraine, September 5 – 8, 2011 , art. no. 5634214, 191-192

[34] Kraiskii AV, Mironova TV, Sultanov TT, Postnikov VA, Sergienko VI, Tikhonov VE. Sposob izmereniya dliny volny…, Pat. RF No. 2390738, prior. 21.05.2008.

[35] Kraiskii AV, Mironova TV, Sultanov TT. Measurement of the surface wavelength distribution of narrow-band radiation by a colorimetric method. Quantum Electronics. 2010; 40 (7), 652 – 658 36.

[36] Kraiskii AV, Mironova TV, Sultanov TT, Postnikov VA. Measuring surface distribution of narrowband radiation wavelength by colorimetric method. In Conference Proceedings - 5th International Conference on Advanced Optoelectronics and Lasers, CAOL' 2010, September 10 -14, 2010, Sevastopol, Crimea, Ukraine, art. no. 5634214, 191-192

[37] Judd D.B., Wyszecki G. Color in Business, Science and Industry (New York: Wiley, 1975; Moscow: Mir, 1978).

Chapter 6

Photopolymer Holographic Optical Elements for Application in Solar Energy Concentrators

Izabela Naydenova, Hoda Akbari, Colin Dalton, Mohamed Yahya so Mohamed Ilyas, Clinton Pang Tee Wei, Vincent Toal and Suzanne Martin

Additional information is available at the end of the chapter

http://dx.doi.org/10.5772/55109

1. Introduction

Making use of the sun's radiation as an alternate energy resource has become increasingly worthwhile in recent years both on a domestic and large industrial scale. Rooftop solar collectors for domestic water heating are now common even in regions where direct sunlight is somewhat limited, and large installations for commercial electricity generation are increasing in sunnier climates. In 2010 in the US there was a 45% increase in the number of grid connected photovoltaic systems installed compared to the preceding year, raising the cumulative grid-connected capacity to 2.15 GW_{dc}. In the same year, the largest solar concentrating plant since the 1980s (75 MW_a) was completed in Florida [1].

There are three key technologies for the conversion of solar energy; thermal heating, photovoltaic and thermal to electric.

In thermal heating systems, water is heated directly or indirectly by the sun, typically in insulated tubing on the premises roof, and used for domestic or sometimes for commercial water heating. Photovoltaic cells generate electricity directly and are widely used in domestic and commercial applications.

Thermal to electric involves mechanical heat engines and requires higher temperatures, so to date it has been mostly used in large scale commercial generation plants where concentrating collectors can be used.

However availability of new materials and technologies currently under development may well change the applicability of each technology. For example, a recent paper in Nature[2] describes the use of nanostructured thermoelectric materials and spectrally selective solar absorbers in a solar thermal to electric power conversion system. This has efficiency 7–8 times greater than the previously reported best value for a flat-panel solar thermal to electric (STEG) system and could lead to a much wider use of STEG systems.

Solar collector technologies in current use can be divided into concentrating and non-concentrating types. Concentrators have obvious advantages where the solar conversion surface is expensive (photovoltaics) or requires high temperatures to work efficiently (thermal to electric systems). The most common concentrators currently used in commercial systems are either cylindrical or hemispherical reflectors. They concentrate the light by reflectance off a curved surface either to a line or spot where the solar energy is converted.

The holographic equivalent is a concentrating diffractive optical element, or holographic lens, which will focus the collected light in a similar fashion.

2. Solar application for holographic optical elements

Holographic Optical Elements (HOE) have also been studied for controlling and directing the radiation of the sun with high potential for energy saving.

Photovoltaic energy conversion is very suitable for solar energy generation but the main disadvantage of photovoltaic electrical energy generation is the cost.

In order to solve this problem a significant amount of expensive photovoltaic material can be replaced by an optical concentrator. By providing complex optical functions in thin, low cost layers which can be used with other PV components, benefits could be expected.

HOEs are very good examples of optical concentrators and have been suggested for use as solar concentrators [3]. HOEs are produced by dividing coherent light into monochromic waves with the same polarization and equal intensities. An optical lens is placed in one of the beams and focuses the incident beam; the HOE can be recorded where two beams overlap with each other. HOEs have several unique features such as ability to diffract light through a large angle, and Bragg selectivity. They also have the potential for multifunctionality by multiplexing a number of optical components in the same layer. They are thin, flat and lightweight, making HOEs attractive for solar collector/ concentrator devices.

Another type of HOE has been used for window shading in buildings with a defined orientation [4, 5]; the holograms have been designed and produced to shade the windows of a building with a facade facing 56º east of south. HOEs were recorded at 45º and 60º and tested in a solar simulator for an entire year. The test revealed that the maximum illumination took place at 11 a.m. Comparison of the spectral characteristics proved that the HOES recorded at 45 º are more suitable for window shading. Due to the ammonium dichromate in the HOEs they showed some absorption in the blue spectral range and due to iron ions (which can be found in standard green glass) they showed some absorption in the red.

3. Advantages of HOE solar energy concentrators

The collection of light from a moving source (such as sun) which exhibits a broad spectral range of wavelengths is a complex process. HOEs have the capability to perform a range of functions in one element thus providing a potential solution to this problem without the need for tracking or mechanical movement.

Holographic solar concentrators can use flat optics for the collection of sunlight because they can be designed to have a very wide field of view which would make them attractive for improving power conversion efficiencies in energy conversion devices which have fixed orientations and locations.

HOEs can be designed to redirect, concentrate or block the incident light, such as that from the sun. They may also be designed for wavelength selectivity, so a range of wavelengths can be directed to one position while other wavelengths go to another position and the diffracted light can be focussed in one spot [6, 7].

4. Types of HOEs

Depending on their effect on the incident light holographic optical elements for use in solar energy collection can be classified as:

- Non focussing elements: optical elements that are used simply to redirect light;
- Focussing elements: optical elements that produce a converging wavefront, having the same effect as spherical or cylindrical lenses. The focal length can vary depending on the devices; they can have a dual role in solar collectors by focusing the light and redirecting the beam.

Depending on the geometry of the recording, HOEs can be classified as:

- Reflection HOEs: The incident beam and the diffracted beam propagate on the same side of the hologram; they allow diffuse light to be transmitted whilst the direct beam is diffracted.

In this type of HOE the fringes due to interference between the recording light beams, form planes that are usually parallel to the recording material surface. The spacing between fringes depends on the angular separation between the reference beam and the object beam and on the wavelength of the recording light.

- Transmission HOEs: In a transmission HOE the incident and the diffracted beams are both transmitted through the optical element. The fringes due to interference between the recording light beams can be perpendicular to the layer surface (unslanted gratings) or at an angle (slanted gratings). As in the case of the reflection gratings the spacing between the interference fringes depends on the angle between the two recording beams and the wavelength of recording light.

5. HOEs used in solar concentrators

Prism Solar Technologies manufacture a solar cell concentrator which at present has a limited bandwidth and low conversion efficiency [8]. The sunlight is reflected and concentrated onto the photovoltaic cell (PV) with all components supported by a substrate. The HOE reflector is placed in a waveguide. The waveguide has been used in this application to receive the sunlight and redirect it to the PV cell. The concentrators produce uncompensated aberration such as dispersion and wavelength shift produced by the reflector, so that the spectral bandwidth of reflected band may not be precisely matched to the energy band gaps of the PV solar cells.

Another application of HOEs in light harvesting that could be useful in solar energy collection is reported in [9]. Holographic diffractive optical elements were used in order to increase the light collection from fluorescence-based biochips. The HOEs increased the transmitted fluorescence intensity and also served to filter out the undesired wavelengths. This was possible due to their high angular selectivity. The diffracted intensity of the HOE was measured to be about 50% of that of the incident beam. The diffraction efficiency was relatively low due to a complexity of the recording process that covers a large spatial frequency range (0-2800 lines/mm). It was found that the HOE can collect fluorescent light coming from a spot with the same size as that of the HOE.

Another example of holographic solar application described in [10] uses a sensor and feedback system to maintain 0.5 degree tracking accuracy with one-axis tracking holographic planar concentrators (HPCs). It was found that in the polar one-axis tracking HPC system the efficiency increases by 43.8% compared to non tracking HPC systems due to high overall module optical efficiency and higher levels of irradiance.

Dispersive concentrating systems based on transmission phase HOEs for solar applications are reported in [2]. The authors demonstrate that volume based transmission HOEs can be used advantageously in solar concentrators due to their high diffraction efficiency, low absorption and adjustable dispersion. The ratio of diffracted intensity to incident beam intensity is defined as diffraction efficiency. In solar applications the measurement of the diffraction efficiency as a function of wavelength is essential. The transmissivity of HOEs as a function of wavelength was measured when white light illuminated the phase holograms and due to diffraction the light was split spatially and spectrally. It was determined that a minimum angle of 20° is required between the recording beams for achieving high diffraction efficiency in one diffraction order so that only an off-axis zone plate was suitable. A zone plate with diameter of 8 cm and a focal length of 25 cm was recorded at 488 nm wavelength. The diffraction of efficiency of the recorded zone plate was about 70% for monochromatic light. The shrinkage of the gelatin layer caused a change in the Bragg angle depending on the shape of recorded interference patterns and the intensities of the recording beams.

Volume HOES are suitable for multiplexing; a range of HOES with various angles between the recording beams can be recorded in one photosensitive layer and this allows spatial separation of the red and the blue spectral ranges of sunlight into different areas. Three solar cell systems with various band gaps and multiplexed HOEs were tested [3]. The maximum efficiency achieved was 42% since the concentration ratio for diffracted wavelengths was about c= 100.

Holographic solar concentrators have been theoretically modelled [11] and several useful aspects of holographic gratings have been investigated for use in solar concentrator applications. The basic relationships for designing holographic elements have also been presented.

A solar radiation receiver is described in [12]. This combined system uses a holographic film to concentrate the solar radiation and to optimize the efficiency of the sensor. A mathematical model is used to calculate the Volt-Ampere behaviour and the thermal and photovoltaic efficiencies to demonstrate the advantages of the suggested system.

The design and optimization of photopolymer based holographic solar concentrators was recently reported in [13]. The authors demonstrated the recording of broad band spectrally splitting holographic solar concentrator in HoloMer photopolymer material with an efficiency of 70% and an average efficiency of 56.6% for a wavelength range from 633nm to 442 nm. The recorded elements showed a narrow angular selectivity hence tracking would be required for an effective photovoltaic concentrator system.

A simple technique to realize a compact and nearly all-angle solar energy concentrator using a volume holographic element is presented in [14]. The theoretical modelling of the HOE predicts up to a fivefold concentration of energy per unit area of photovoltaic material.

In the following section we present experimental results from the recording of simple focusing holographic optical elements in a photopolymer layer, namely a spherical lens and a cylindrical lens. Furthermore we have explored the possibility of multiplexing a number of elements in the same layer.

6. Experimental

6.1. Photopolymer solution preparation

The photosensitive layer was prepared as previously described [15]. Briefly, 2ml of triethanolamine was added to 17.5 ml stock solution of polyvinyl alcohol (PVA) (10% w/w). Then the monomers, 0.6g acrylamide and 0.2 g of N,N Methylene bisacrylamide and 2ml of initiator, TEA, were added. Finally, 4ml of Erythrosin B dye was added (stock solution concentration - 1.1mM) to sensitise at 532 nm. The solution was made up to 25ml by adding distilled water. Methylene blue sensitised samples of thickness 50 μm were used to record at 633nm.

6.2. Layer preparation

Different amounts of photopolymer solution were spread evenly on a 50x50 mm^2 glass plate placed on a levelled surface and allowed to dry. This resulted in layers of thickness varying between 50 and 120 μm. The drying time was usually 18-24 hours.

6.3. Recording of HOE consisting of a single optical component

A standard holographic optical setup (Fig.1) was used to record transmission gratings and lenses using a 532nm Nd:YVO_4 laser. The recording intensity was controlled by a variable neutral density filter. The inter-beam angle was adjusted to be 9 degrees in order to obtain a spatial frequency of recording of 300 lines/mm. At the end of the holographic recording, the focusing beam was blocked and the collimated beam was used to probe the recorded HOE. The intensity of the diffracted beam was measured using an optical power meter (Newport 1830-C) to determine the diffraction efficiency of the recorded grating or lens respectively.

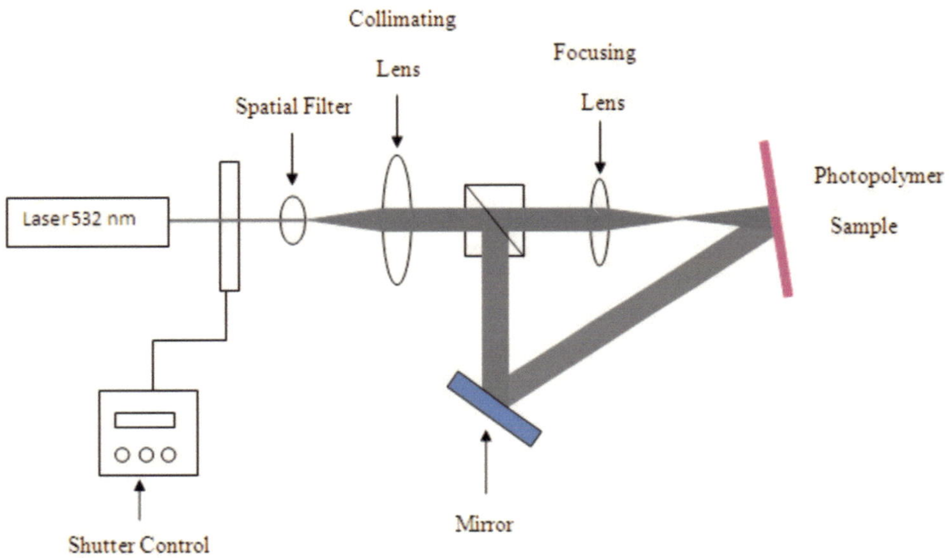

Figure 1. Optical set-up for recording of a single lens HOE.

The recording set up at 633 nm was similar to that shown in Fig. 1. A single off-axis HOE of focal length 5 cm was recorded. The recording intensity of the beams was 1 mW/cm^2 and the average spatial frequency of recording was 650 l/mm.

6.4. Recording of HOEs by multiplexing

The aim of this experiment was to record a holographic optical element which would direct the light in a fixed direction independently of the direction of incoming light.

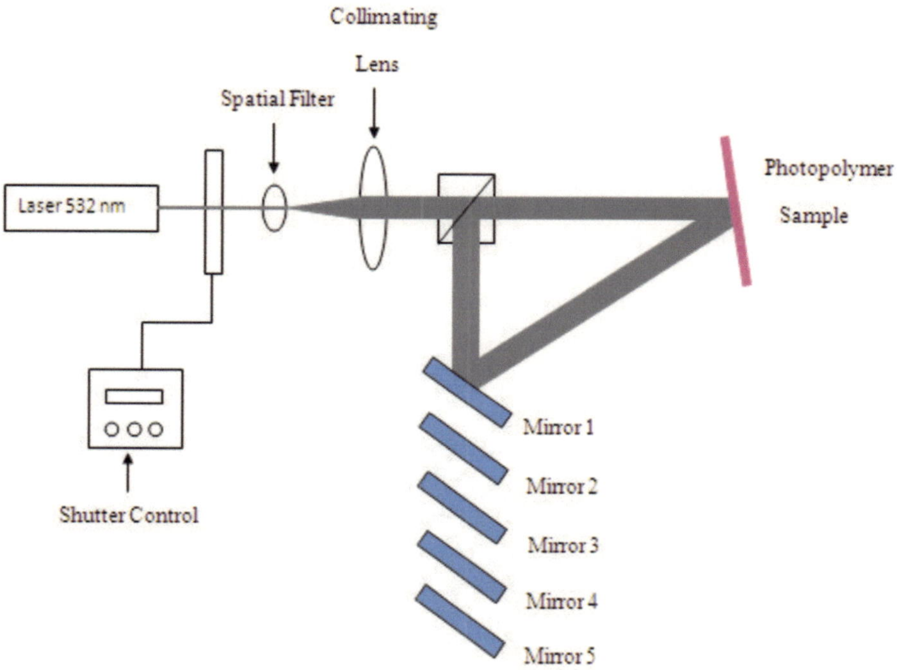

Figure 2. Optical set-up for recording multiplexed HOEs in this case - diffraction gratings of different spatial frequencies. B S (Beam Splitter), C L (Collimating Lens), S F (Spatial Filter), P S (Photopolymer Sample)

Figure 2 shows the experimental set up for the recording of multiplexed transmission gratings. The photopolymer sample was kept at a fixed distance from the beam splitter and the reference beam was varied in direction by using five mirrors fixed at different distances from the beam splitter to reflect the light onto the photopolymer layer. The photopolymer sample was adjusted so that the object beam and the reference beam from mirror 5 overlapped in the plane of the photosensitive medium with the sample normal bisecting the interbeam angle. This ensured the grating was unslanted when recorded by the beam reflected by mirror 5 and the beam transmitted by the beam splitter. The gratings were recorded in the same photopolymer layer starting with the lowest spatial frequency (mirror1). Mirror 1 was then removed and the next grating was recorded in the same area by the light reflected onto the photopolymer layer from mirror 2 and the light transmitted by the beam splitter. This procedure was repeated for the other three mirrors, with mirror 5 corresponding to the largest spatial frequency. Cylindrical lenses were also recorded in the same volume of the recording medium using a cylindrical lens of 15 cm focal length placed in the path of the beam transmitted by the beam splitter so that this light was focused into a thin line just behind the photopolymer sample. In order to find the optimum recording conditions for HOEs with equal diffraction efficiencies the transmission gratings were recorded in two ways. First, the intensity was kept constant and the exposure time varied from one recording to the next. The second approach was to keep the exposure time constant and vary the intensity. The recorded HOEs initially consisted of three gratings utilising mirrors M1, M2 and M5 and then five gratings utilising all five mirrors (M1, M2, M3, M4 and M5).

The spatial frequencies of the recorded gratings using the different mirrors in the recording set up were respectively: M1- 450 lines/mm; M2 - 1065 lines/mm; M3 -1295 lines/mm; M4 -1470 lines/mm and M5 -1700 lines/mm.

6.5. Characterisation of the recorded HOEs

Two procedures were used in order to measure the maximum diffraction efficiencies (η) of the HOEs at different spatial frequencies.

Probing the recorded holograms using Nd:YVO_4 laser beam (532nm)

After the recording of the transmission gratings with the photopolymer sample fixed in the same position, one of the recording beams was stopped and the HOE was illuminated only with the other recording beam, but with intensity much less than that used to record the grating, in order to avoid further polymerization. A photo detector was used to measure the intensities of the diffracted beam, the incident beam and the beam reflected from the photopolymer surface.

The percentage diffraction efficiency (η) was calculated from the equation

$$\eta = \frac{I_d}{I_1 - I_r} \times 100. \tag{1}$$

where I_1 is the intensity of the incident beam, I_d is the intensity of the diffracted beam and I_r is the intensity of the beam reflected from the front photopolymer surface.

Probing the recorded holograms using a Helium-Neon laser (633nm)

Figure 3 shows the experimental set up for measuring the diffraction efficiencies using a Helium-Neon laser beam that has a much smaller diameter than that of the HOE. The Helium-Neon laser was positioned so that it probed the centre of the HOE that was recorded on the photopolymer layer. The photopolymer is not sensitive to light of wavelength 633 nm, therefore further polymerisation does not occur. The photopolymer sample was rotated until the maximum diffracted intensity of the laser beam was observed on a screen behind the photopolymer. The angle of incidence of the probe beam at which the maximum diffraction efficiency is obtained is known as the Bragg angle.

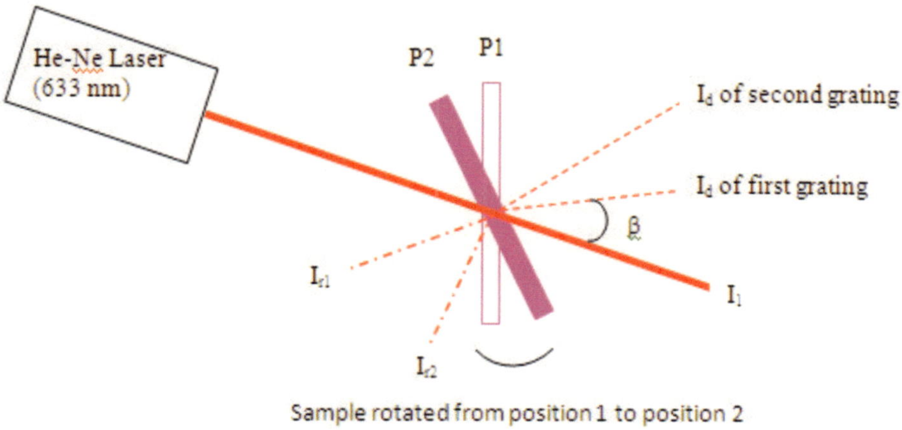

Figure 3. Characterisation of the HOE at 633nm. I_1 is the intensity of the probe beam,

I_d the intensity of the reconstructed or diffracted beam and I_r the intensity of the beam reflected from the photopolymer surface.

The intensity I_d was measured using a photo detector, and equation (1) was used to calculate the diffraction efficiency. In the case of multiplexed gratings the value of I_d for each grating was measured in turn by further rotation of sample until the diffracted intensity maximum for each was obtained at the appropriate Bragg angle.

7. Results and discussion

7.1. Recording of focusing HOEs

The diffraction efficiency of a single lens recorded in a red sensitive layer of thickness of 50 μm as a function of recording time is presented in Fig. 4. It is seen that the maximum diffraction efficiency is nearly 45 % and it is reached after 100 s exposure time.

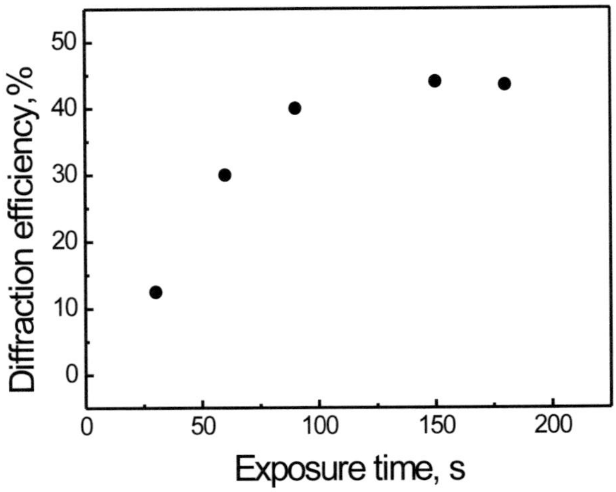

Figure 4. Diffraction efficiencies of single lenses recorded in 50 micrometer layers. Recording wavelength was 633 nm. Recording frequency was 650 l/mm and recording intensity was 1 mW/cm^2.

Much higher diffraction efficiency was achieved in green sensitised layers of thickness 50 μm (Fig.5). The total recording intensity of the beams was 1 mW/cm^2. The spatial frequency of recording was 300 l/mm.

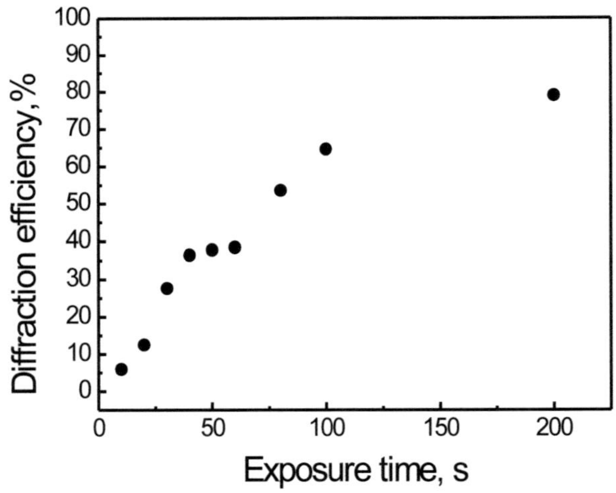

Figure 5. Diffraction efficiency of gratings recorded in 50 μm layers. Recording wavelength was 532 nm.

7.2. Recording of three multiplexed holographic gratings

Initial experiments were carried out in layers of thickness of 100 μm. In order to find the optimum exposure times required to obtain gratings with diffraction efficiency above 50 %, gratings were separately recorded at 1000, 1500 and 2000 l/mm. At the next stage of the experiment, three gratings of spatial frequencies 2000, 1500 and 1000 l/mm were recorded in the same volume of the recording medium, first by using the measured recording times required to achieve 50% diffraction efficiency at each of the spatial frequencies. This produced gratings with unequal diffraction efficiencies. In order to equalize the diffraction efficiency of the gratings the recording time was varied. The diffraction efficiencies of previously recorded gratings were measured after each exposure to observe how the recording of the gratings at 1500lines/mm and 1000 lines/mm affected the grating recorded at 2000 lines/mm.

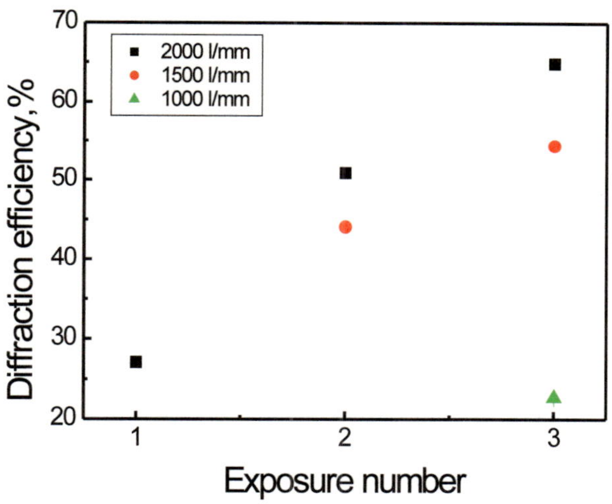

Figure 6. Diffraction efficiency of three gratings multiplexed in the same region of a photopolymer layer of thickness 100 μm.

It is seen from Fig. 6 that the recording of the grating at 1500 lines/mm had a large effect on the diffraction efficiency of the grating previously recorded at 2000 lines/mm. The diffraction efficiency at 2000 lines/mm increased by 23.8% after the recording of the second grating at 1500 lines/mm. It increased a further 14% due to the recording of the third grating at 1000 lines/mm. This shows that the recording of a grating affects the diffraction efficiency of a previously recorded grating. This must be taken into account when the exposure schedule for equalization of the diffraction efficiencies is developed.

This procedure was repeated several times by varying the exposure times, but it was not possible to equalise the diffraction efficiencies of the three gratings and to achieve diffraction efficiency above 50% for all three of them.. From Fig. 6 is seen that the maximum diffraction efficiencies measured at spatial frequencies of 1500 lines/mm and 2000 lines/mm were greater than the set target of 50%. The lower diffraction efficiency at 1000lines/mm was assumed to be due to the dynamic range of the photopolymer layer being consumed.

In order to achieve gratings with diffraction efficiency higher than 50% layers with greater thickness and dynamic range were prepared. The next set of gratings was recorded in layers of 120 μm thickness.

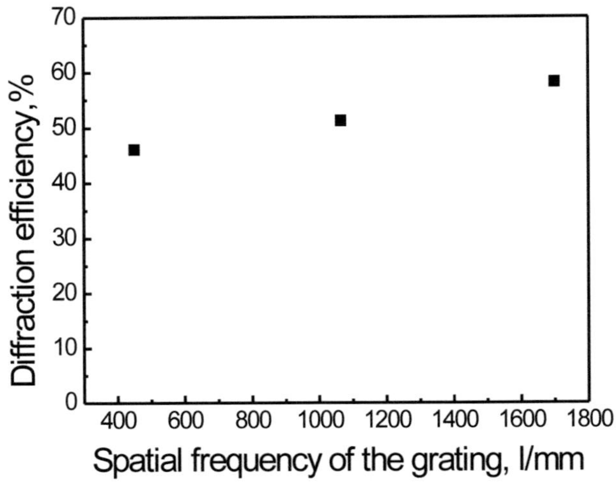

Figure 7. Diffraction efficiency of three gratings multiplexed in the same region of a photopolymer layer of thickness 120 μm.

It can be observed in Fig.7 that the three gratings of different spatial frequencies were successfully recorded with nearly equal diffraction efficiencies around 50%. This confirmed the assumption that in the thinner layers the main obstacle to equalising the gratings with diffraction efficiencies above 50% was insufficient dynamic range of the photopolymer layer. The order of recording and corresponding exposure times for the three gratings were 450, 1065 and 1700 l/mm and 2, 4 and 18 seconds.

7.3. Recording of five multiplexed holographic gratings

After successfully multiplexing three gratings in the same layer the next step was to try to increase the number of holograms and in this way to increase the number of solar light incidence angles that can be exploited. The aim of this experiment was to obtain optimum diffraction efficiencies from five gratings recorded in the same volume of the recording medium. This was achieved by using two different recording conditions, constant intensity with variable expsosure time and constant exposure time with variable intensity. The experimental set-up used was as shown in Fig. 2. The diffraction efficiencies were measured using a He-Ne laser.

The results of these experiments are represented in Fig. 8.

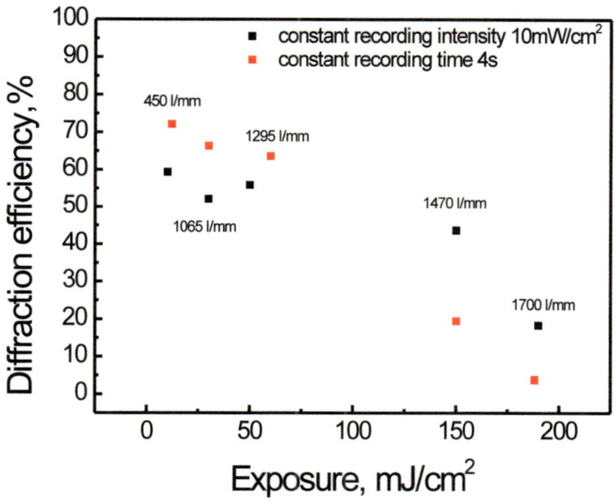

Figure 8. Diffraction efficiencies of five multiplexed gratings recorded by using two exposure schedules- constant exposure intensity of 10 mW/cm² (black symbols) with variable exposure time and constant exposure time of 4s (red symbols) with variable intensity. The order of recording and the exposure times and intensities are given in Table 1.

		Constant Intensity of 10mW/cm²		**Constant Exposure time of 4 s**	
Grating No.	**Spatial Frequency l/mm**	**Exposure time, s**	**Exposure energy mJ/cm²**	**Exposure energy mJ/cm²**	**Exposure Intensity, mW/cm²**
1	450	1	10	12	3
2	1065	3	30	30	7.5
3	1295	5	50	60	15
4	1470	15	150	150	37.5
5	1700	19	190	188	47

Table 1. Exposure time and intensity for recording of the five multiplexed gratings.

From Fig.8 it is seen that recording the gratings with constant intensity produced less variation in the diffraction efficiencies of the recorded gratings. In both cases the dynamic range of the layer is insufficient to produce all five gratings with high diffraction efficiency..

7.4. Recording of five multiplexed holographic lenses

The method of varying the exposure time for the recording of the gratings was repeated with a cylindrical lens in the path of the beam transmitted by the beamsplitter focussing the beam into a long narrow line. The diffraction efficiencies were measured using the He-Ne laser and compared with the diffraction efficiencies measured for gratings recorded under the same conditions with two collimated beams (Fig. 9).

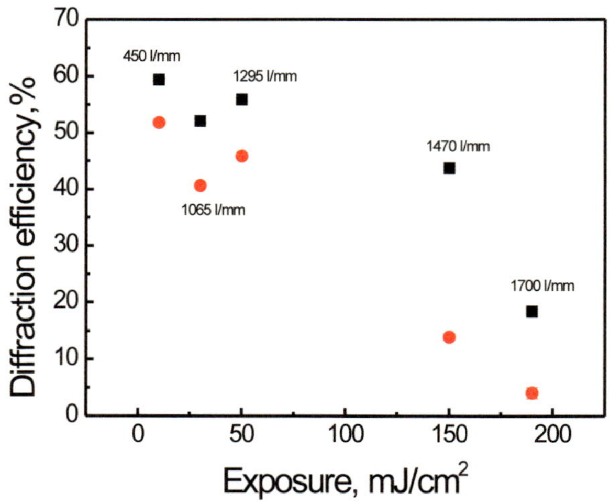

Figure 9. Comparison of the diffraction efficiencies of HOEs of five multiplexed gratings (squares) and five multiplexed lenses (circles).

From Fig. 9 it is seen that the diffraction efficiencies of the first three gratings (recorded at low spatial frequencies) were around the same value above 50% and that the diffraction efficiency is lower for the last two gratings recorded at larger spatial frequencies.

In a further experiment just four lenses instead of five were recorded to reduce the risk of the dynamic range being consumed. The recording conditions were optimised again (Table 2) and are presented in Fig. 10.

		Constant Exposure time of 4 s	
Lenses No.	Spatial Frequency l/mm	Exposure energy mJ/cm²	Exposure Intensity, mW/cm²
1	450	6	1.5
2	1065	13	3.2
3	1295	60	15
4	1700	160	40

Table 2. Recording conditions for multiplexing of four cylindrical lenses in a 120 μm thick photopolymer layer.

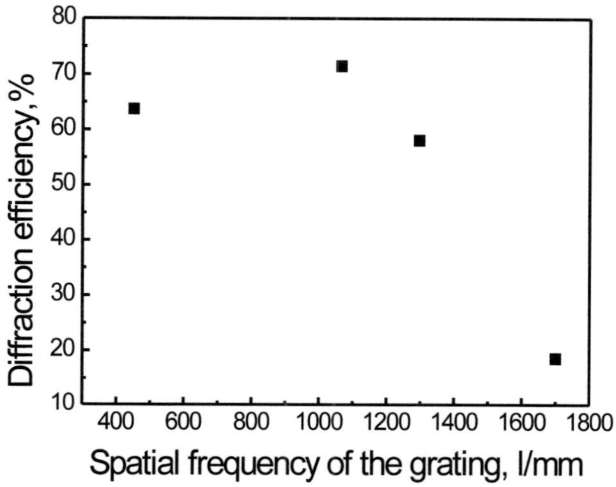

Figure 10. Diffraction efficiencies of multiplexed holographic cylindrical lenses.

8. Conclusions

It was demonstrated that high diffraction efficiency HOE consisting of a single spherical lens can be recorded in a relatively thin photopolymer layer of 50 μm thickness. The advantage of using thin layers and lower spatial frequency of recording in this application is the larger acceptance angle of the optical component.

It was possible to equalise the diffraction efficiencies of three multiplexed gratings at 51.9±3.5 %.

A study of the influence of the exposure schedule – keeping the intensity constant and changing the time or keeping the exposure time constant and varying the intensity, revealed that the first schedule delivered better equalisation of the diffraction efficiency.

Three HOEs - containing five gratings with a range of spatial frequencies from 450 to 1700 l/mm, five cylindrical lenses and four cylindrical lenses, were successfully recorded in the same photopolymer layer. These can be considered as successful first steps in the design and fabrication of holographic solar concentrators fabricated in acrylamide based photopolymer.

Author details

Izabela Naydenova[1], Hoda Akbari[1], Colin Dalton[1], Mohamed Yahya so Mohamed Ilyas[2], Clinton Pang Tee Wei[2], Vincent Toal[1] and Suzanne Martin[1]

1 Centre for Industrial and Engineering Optics, School of Physics, College of Sciences and Health, Dublin Institute of Technology, Kevin Street, Dublin, Ireland

2 School of Chemical & Life Sciences, Singapore Polytechnic, Singapore

References

[1] U.S. Solar market Trends 2010, Larry Sherwood, IREC (Interstate Renewable Energy Council) June 2011

[2] Daniel Kraemer, Bed Poudel, Hsien-Ping Feng, J. Christopher Caylor, Bo Yu, Xiao Yan, Yi Ma, Xiaowei Wang, Dezhi Wang, Andrew Muto, Kenneth McEnaney, Matteo Chiesa, Zhifeng Ren & Gang Chen , "High-performance flat-panel solar thermoelectric generators with high thermal concentration", Nature Materials, Volume 10, 532 – 538, (2011)

[3] Bloss, W. H., Griesinger, M. and Reinhardt, E. R., "Dispersive concentrating systems based on transmission phase holograms for solar applications", Appl. Opt., 21, 3739-3742 (1982)

[4] C.G. Stojanoff, "Holographic optical elements for window shading in buildings", Holography, 13.2, p.5 (2002)

[5] P.A.B. James, A.S. Bahaj, "Holographic optical elements: various principles for solar control of conservatories and sunrooms", Solar Energy 78, 441- 454 (2005)

[6] Ludman, J.E., Riccobono, J., Semenova, I.V., Reinhand, N.O., Tai, W., Li, X., Syphers, G., Rallis, E., Sliker, G., Martin, J., "The optimization of a holographic system for solar power generation", Solar Energy 60(1), 1-9 (1996)

[7] R. K. Kostuk, and G. Rosenberg, "Analysis and design of holographic solar concentrators", Proc. SPIE 7043, 70430I (2008)

[8] R.K. Kostuk, J. Castillo, and J.M. Russo and G. Rosenberg "Spectral-shifting and holographic planar concentrators for use with photovoltaic solar cells", Proc. of SPIE vol 649, 64901 (2007)

[9] P. Macko and M.P. Whelan, "Fabrication of holographic diffractive optical elements for enhancing light collection from fluorescence-based biochips", Optics Letters, vol. 33, 22, 2614 (2008)

[10] D. Zhang, J.M. Castro and R.K. Kostuk, "One-axis tracking holographic planar concentrator system", Journal of Photonics for Energy, 1947-7988 (2011)

[11] A. Kumar, N. Deo, H.L. Yadav, "Analysis of design parameters for wavelength selective holographic solar concentrators", IEEE conference paper 978-1-4244-1641 (2008)

[12] O. Iurevych, S. Gubin, M. Dudeck, "Combined receiver of solar radiation with holographic planar concentrator", IOP Conference paper, Materials Science and Engineering 29 (2012) 012016, doi:10.1088/1757-899X/29/1/012016

[13] S. Sam Tl, A. Kumar PT, "Design and Optimization of Photopolymer Based Holographic Solar Concentrators", American Institute of Physics conference *Optics: Phenomena, Materials, Devices, and Characterization,* Conf. Proc. 1391, 248-250 (2011); doi: 10.1063/1.3646844

[14] M. Hsieh, S. Lin, K. Y. Hsu, J. Burr, and S. Lin, "An Efficient Solar Concentrator using Volume hologram", in CLEO:2011 - Laser Applications to Photonic Applications, OSA Technical Digest (CD) (Optical Society of America, 2011), paper PDPB8, http://www.opticsinfobase.org/abstract.cfm?URI=CLEO: A and T-2011-PDPB8

[15] S. Martin, C.A. Feely and V. Toal, "Holographic recording characteristics of an acrylamide-based photopolymer", Appl. Optics 36, 5757-5768, (1997)

Optically Accelerated Formation of One- and Two-Dimensional Holographic Surface Relief Gratings on DR1/PMMA

Xiao Wu, Thi Thanh Ngan Nguyen,
Isabelle Ledoux-Rak, Chi Thanh Nguyen and
Ngoc Diep Lai

Additional information is available at the end of the chapter

http://dx.doi.org/10.5772/53788

1. Introduction

Polymer-based periodic structures nowadays are very useful for many applications in optoelectronics and photonics, such as optical filters, distributed-feedback laser, wave-guide coupling, photonic crystals, etc. [1-3]. Different methods based on photoinduced transformation of photosensitive materials have been used to fabricate the desired periodic structures. A common point of these fabrication technologies is the use of a so-called photoresist to record the light pattern following by a development process. The later one allows to wash out the remaining unpolymerized photoresists, resulting in a polymerized structure, which is a duplication of the light pattern. However, development techniques based on solvent dissolutions affect the fabrication process, leading often to a deformation of the fabricated structures. Recently, new organic materials named azobenzene-containing polymers (azopolymers) have attracted much attention for the fabrication of sub-micrometer structures, thanks to a particular mass transport effect under a modulated light irradiation. This phenomenon allows to fabricate a so-called surface relief grating (SRG) by a simple one-step process, without development process [4-5]. Figure 1 shows the chemical structure of one typical commercial azopolymer named Disperse Red 1-poly-methyl-methacrylate (DR1/PMMA). Here, the DR1 molecule is attached to the polymer backbone MMA monomers through covalent bonds with a 30/70 molar ratio between them. This copolymer presents very good thermal and temporal stability with high glass transition temperature (T_g = 125°C). Experimental results have been shown that the SRG formation on an azopolymer film depends on different parameters: sample temperature, light polarization, intensity of the interference beams, etc. Many theoretical models have been proposed to explain the mechanism of SRG formation [6-10] on DR1/PMMA azopolymer. Despite these efforts, the mechanism is still not fully explained. The most plausible and widely used model is the gradient force model [7]. According to this model, the pressure and resultant force can be achieved thanks to the light irradiation, which induces a *trans*-form ↔ *cis*-form photoisomerization effect in azobenzene molecules. Inset of the Fig. 1 illustrates the photoisomerization process between the *trans*-form and *cis*-form of a DR1 chromophore molecule. At room temperature, the *trans*-form is fundamentally stable as compared with the *cis*-form. When the DR1 molecule is subjected to a visible illumination, the *trans*-form will be transformed to a *cis*-form, which later relaxes back to the *trans*-form by thermal relaxation (slow process) or by UV irradiation (fast process). Under a spatially modulated irradiation, the DR1 molecules, after many *trans*-form ↔ *cis*-form cycles, will move from the position of highest intensity to the position at which the light intensity is lowest. Therefore, the necessary condition to form the SRG is a photoisomerization process under the irradiation of a modulated light intensity.

This chapter presents the fabrication of one- and two-dimensional (1D and 2D) holographic SRGs based on one- or multi-exposure of the azobenzene copolymer (DR1/PMMA) to two- and/or three-beam interference patterns. A single exposure of the two-beam interference pattern is used to form 1D SRG. 2D periodic structure then can be fabricated either by two exposures of the sample to a two-beam interference pattern or by only a single exposure to a three-beam interference pattern. Also, the formation of SRGs is optically accelerated by assisting it with an independent UV or VIS laser.

Section 2 shows the fabrication of SRG by using the two-beam interference technique. Because of the important role of the intensity and polarization modulations during the formation of SRG, the theory of two-beam interference will be presented in detail. The diffraction efficiency (DE) and the depth of SRGs fabricated with different polarization configurations have been characterized and discussed. The relationship between the depth and period of SRG was also studied and reported. The 2D holographic SRG is realized by using two exposures to the two-beam interference pattern. This fabrication method is simple and easy to control the SRG periodicity, but it is time consuming and the 2D SRG structures are not symmetric.

In order to rapidly fabricate uniform and symmetric 2D SRG structures, the three-beam interference technique has been used as shown in Section 3. The theory of three-beam interference is first studied, analysing in particular the influence of polarizations of the three laser beams on the intensity and polarization modulations. Then, 2D hexagonal structures have been fabricated by this fabrication technique with a particular polarization configuration (circular-circular-circular). Comparison with the results obtained by the multiple-exposure two-beam interference technique and discussions of the advantages of this technique will also be presented.

In Section 4, we investigate experimentally the optimization of 1D SRG formation by using an additional laser to assist the photoisomerization process. First, an UV beam (355 nm-wavelength) is used to accelerate the photoisomerization from the *cis*-form to the *trans*-form. Second, a VIS beam (532 nm-wavelength), of the same wavelength as the interference beams, is used to accelerate the photoisomerization from the *trans*-form to the *cis*-form. Both techniques allowed to enhance the SRG formation, resulted in a better DE and a larger depth of the SRGs. The mechanisms of these two methods are different but both of them are polarization dependent.

Finally, we will make some conclusions of our work and also release some prospects.

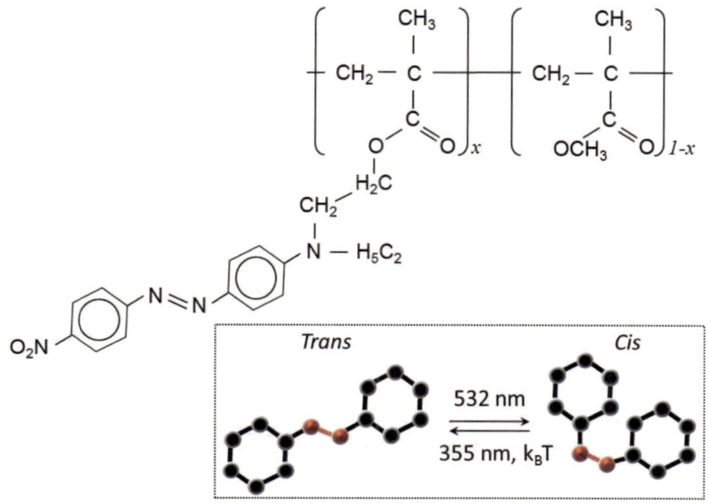

Figure 1. Chemical structure of the DR1/PMMA copolymer. Insert shows the *trans*-form↔*cis*-form photoisomerization process induced by different optical excitations and thermal relaxation.

2. Two-beam interference

Laser interference technologies have been widely used to fabricate polymer-based periodic and quasi-periodic micro- and nano-structures with large areas. We propose to use the two-beam interference technique to fabricate 1D and 2D SRG structures by one- and two-exposure. Indeed, two-beam interference is the simplest configuration (Fig. 2(a)), which allows to create a spatial modulation of light intensity in one dimension.

2.1. Theory of two-beam interference

Considering two-beam interference as illustrated in Fig. 2(a). Two coherent laser beams of the same profiles and same intensities and coming from the same laser source propagate toward the same sample area. These laser beams are symmetrically oriented around the sample normal direction and make an angle θ with respect to this axis. The electric fields, $\mathbf{E}_1(\mathbf{r}, t)$ and $\mathbf{E}_2(\mathbf{r}, t)$, of the two plane waves corresponding to these two laser beams are given by

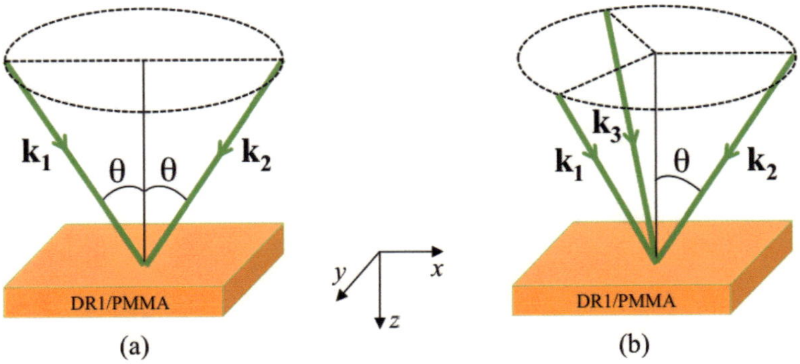

Figure 2. Optical arrangement of two-beam (a) and three-beam interference (b) techniques. Each laser beam is symmetrically oriented around the vertical axis by an angle θ. $\mathbf{k}_i$ (i = 1, 2, 3) represents the wave vector of each laser beam.

$$\mathbf{E}_1(\mathbf{r},t)=\mathrm{Re}\left[E_{01}\exp\left(i\left(\mathbf{k}_1\bullet\mathbf{r}-\omega t\right)\right)\mathbf{e}_1\right], \tag{1}$$

$$\mathbf{E}_2(\mathbf{r},t)=\mathrm{Re}\left[E_{02}\exp\left(i\left(\mathbf{k}_2\bullet\mathbf{r}-\omega t\right)\right)\mathbf{e}_2\right], \tag{2}$$

where $\mathbf{k}_1$ and $\mathbf{k}_2$ are the corresponding wave vectors, $\mathbf{r}$ is the position vector in the overlapping space, E_{01} and E_{02} are the real electric field amplitudes, and $\mathbf{e}_1$ and $\mathbf{e}_2$ are the unit vectors of the polarizations. At the overlapping area of the two beams, the interference electric field is the sum of the electric fields of individual plane waves

$$\mathbf{E}_T(\mathbf{r},t)=\mathbf{E}_1(\mathbf{r},t)+\mathbf{E}_2(\mathbf{r},t). \tag{3}$$

The interference intensity distribution of the resultant wave is given by

$$I_T(\mathbf{r},t)=\left\langle \mathbf{E}_T^*(\mathbf{r},t)\bullet\mathbf{E}_T(\mathbf{r},t)\right\rangle_t, \tag{4}$$

where $\langle ... \rangle_t$ represents the time average of the resultant electric field.

Using equations (3) and (4), we can easily calculate both the intensity distribution and the polarization distribution of the interference pattern. The periodicity of the interference pattern depends on the angle θ and the laser wavelength (λ), and it is determined by

$$\Lambda=\frac{\lambda}{2\sin\theta}. \tag{5}$$

In this work, all numerical calculations were realized by using Matlab software with personal codes, which allowed to investigate all properties of the interference pattern as a function of different polarizations of the laser beams.

2.1.1. *Intensity distribution*

Figure 3 shows the simulation results of the intensity modulation of the two-beam interference pattern, obtained with different polarization configurations and at different incident angles θ. We have considered four particular polarization configurations of the two laser beams: S-S, P-P, S-P, and RC-LC (right circular and left circular). Since the interference cannot be realized with S-P polarization configuration, this particular case is not shown here. For the three other polarization configurations, we can see that intensity modulation depends not only on the polarization configuration, but also on the incident angle θ. Namely, for a S-S polarization configuration, the polarizations are the same for both laser beams at any angle θ, resulting in a maximal amplitude modulation (100%) of the intensity interference pattern. However, the amplitude modulation increases from 0 to 100% when θ increases in the case of RC-LC polarization configuration. Also, for the P-P configuration, the amplitude modulation firstly decreases then increases when θ varies from 0° to 90°. We note that for the last case, there is a position shifting the interference pattern by a distance of Λ/2 along *x*-axis for θ = 45°, but this does not affect the fabrication of SRGs.

In order to evaluate the influence of polarizations configurations on the intensity modulation, we introduce a well-known parameter called visibility (interference contrast), C

$$C = \left| \left(I_T^{\max} - I_T^{\min} \right) / \left(I_T^{\max} + I_T^{\min} \right) \right|, \tag{6}$$

where $I_T^{\max}$ and $I_T^{\min}$ are the maximum and minimum of the intensity, respectively.

Figure 4 shows the interference contrast as a function of θ (from 0° to 85°) for different polarization configurations. It is clear that the interference contrast is constant for S-S polarization configuration and keeps increasing with θ for the RC-LC polarization configuration. On the other hand, for the P-P case, the interference contrast decreases from 100% to 0 when the incident angle is varied from 0° to 45°, then increases again from 0 to 100% when θ increases from 45° to 90°. The reason is that in the case of P-P polarization configuration, two polarizations tend to be orthogonal when θ approaches 45°. At this particular angle, two polarizations are perpendicular and there is no interference. Therefore, for a standard optical lithography, a two-beam interference pattern with S-S polarization configuration is used in order to ensure the best intensity modulation contrast.

2.1.2. *Polarization modulation*

However, when the two-beam interference technique is applied to SRG formation, the modulation condition of the interference intensity is not enough, since the photoisomerization of DR1 molecules depends also on the illuminated light polarization. The polarization

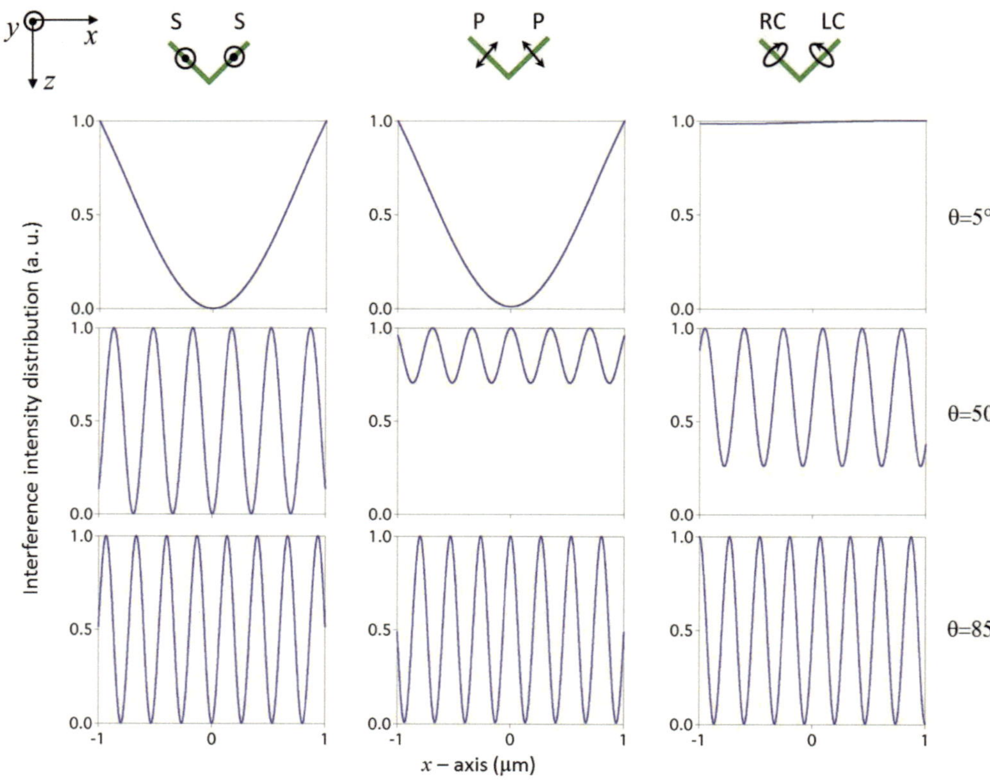

Figure 3. Interference intensity distributions along the *x*-axis, calculated for different polarizations configurations (S-S, P-P, RC-LC) at θ = 5°, 50° and 85°, respectively. S and P represent two orthogonal linear polarizations; RC and LC are right and left circular polarizations, respectively. Note that: i) the intensity modulation keeps the same shape (except periodicity) for any θ–value in the case of S-S polarization configuration; ii) there is a Λ/2 switching position of the interference pattern for θ = 45° in the case of P-P polarization configuration, and iii) there is no intensity modulation at any θ–value in the case of S-P polarization configuration (not shown).

distribution of the resultant field of the two laser beams has been then evaluated. Figure 5 represents the polarization distributions of the two-beam interference pattern in the *xy*-plane for different polarization configurations and for different incident angles. The background illustrates the intensity pattern where the deep colour corresponds to high intensity and the light colour corresponds to low intensity. The polarization of the resultant field is calculated for several particular positions, corresponding to $x = \pm\Lambda/2; \pm\Lambda/4; 0$. For the S-S polarization configuration, the interference polarization keeps the same direction, as those of the two laser beams, for any position and for all incident angles. In the case of the P-P polarization configuration, the interference polarization direction is also the same for different θ-values, but the polarization amplitude decreases with increasing θ. In fact, when θ increases, the polarizations of both laser beams become parallel to the *z*-axis, i. e. perpendicular to the *xy*-plane, resulting in a diminution of the interference polarization amplitude in this plane. For the two other polarization configurations, the interference polarization varies periodically between linear,

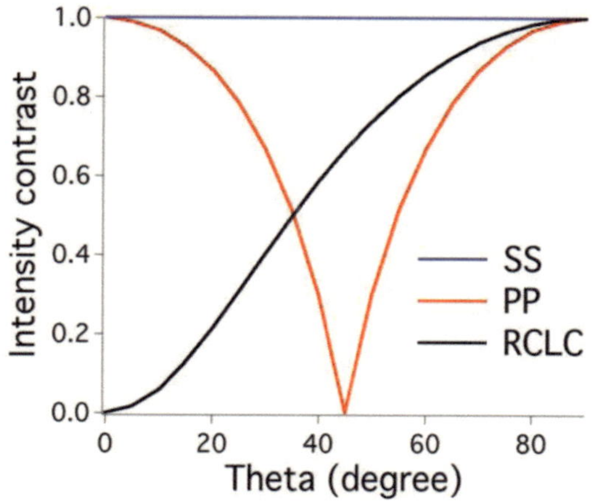

Figure 4. Interference contrast or visibility of the two-beam interference pattern as a function of the angle θ. Three curves are obtained by using different polarizations configurations (S-S: blue line, P-P: red line, RC-LC: black line). There is a Λ/2 switching position of the interference pattern for θ = 45° in the case of P-P polarization configuration, corresponding to a minimum contrast at this angle.

elliptic and circular forms, as seen in Fig. 5. In particular, for the S-P polarization configuration, a periodical modulation of the resultant polarization is obtained, while the resultant intensity modulation cannot be achieved, as discussed above. That will explain why SRG can be realized with such polarization configuration, thanks to the interference polarization modulation. Finally, for the case of RC-LC polarization configuration, the resultant polarization becomes a linear polarization for any θ-value, but the polarization direction changes periodically in the xy-plane. We note that, similar to the case of P-P polarization configuration, the polarization amplitude in the xy-plane decreases when θ increases. Besides, the interference polarization pattern is shifted by a distance of Λ/4 along the x-axis with respect to the interference intensity pattern, as shown in Fig. 5.

As discussed before, the formation of SRG on azo-copolymer depends on the modulation of the irradiating light pattern and also on its resultant polarization. Therefore, polarization modulation and intensity distribution of the interference pattern are two necessary conditions, complementary and also competitive, for creating SRG. In this work, different SRGs were experimentally realized and the polarization dependence in the formation of SRG was also investigated.

2.2. Experimental demonstration

SRGs were fabricated by the following procedure: i) preparation of a thin film sample by spin-coating DR1/PMMA on cleaned glass substrate and baking in the oven at a temperature of 120°C for 2 hours to remove the solvent; ii) exposure by a two-beam interference pattern.

In order to build-up the fabrication technique, we have first recorded the UV–Visible absorption spectrum of the DR1/PMMA thin film. The absorption band ranges from 400 nm to 570

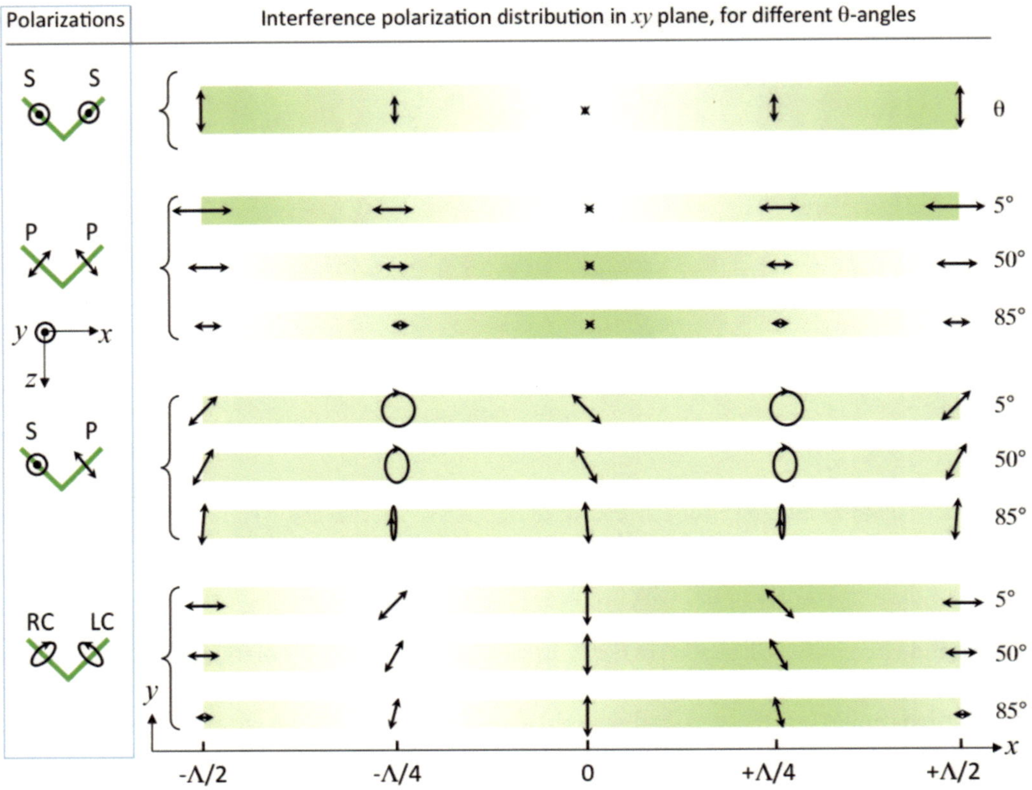

Figure 5. Polarization distributions in *xy*-plane of the two-beam interference pattern, obtained with different polarization configurations. The interference pattern is calculated for one period (from -Λ/2 to +Λ/2). The polarization modulation varies as a function of θ-values (5°, 50° and 85°). The white-green colour of the background represents intensity interference pattern.

nm, with an absorption peak at 480 nm. A green laser is therefore suitable for the SRG formation.

The experimental setup for two-beam interference can be realized easily according to Fig. 2 (a). A green laser ($\lambda = 532$ nm) beam is split into two identical secondary beams by a 50/50 non-polarized beam splitter. The two beams were then combined, by using two mirrors, and interfered on the azo-copolymer film. The polarizations of the two laser beams were controlled independently by using different wave plates (quarter-wave plate and half-wave plate). The incident angle θ was adjusted by tuning the two mirrors symmetrically, and the SRG periodicity varied from several micrometers to hundreds nanometers. The intensity of each interference beam was fixed to about 84 mW/cm^2 at the sample position. In order to monitor the dynamics of SRG formation, a red laser beam ($\lambda = 633$ nm, power = 1 mW) was sent into the interference area, and the first-order diffraction intensity was measured as a function of time, indicating the formation of SRG. The fabricated SRGs were then examined by using an atomic force microscope (AFM) and/or a scanning electron microscope (SEM).

2.2.1. *Formation of SRG with different polarization configurations*

Figure 6 shows experimental results of the SRGs formation. The incident angle θ is 9°, corresponding to a grating period of 1.7 μm. Figure 6(b) shows the AFM image of a 1D SRG obtained by the RC-LC polarization configuration, which is perfectly consistent with the simulation result of the interference pattern illustrated in Fig. 6(a). Actually, the shape of the interference intensity pattern and that of SRG are similar, with a sinusoidal form of the same period. However, we note that the highest intensity of the interference pattern corresponds to the valley of SRG, due to the mass transport effect, which induces the transfer of the DR1 molecule from high intensity to low intensity area.

Figures 6(c) and (d) show the first-order diffraction efficiency (DE) and the amplitude of the SRGs fabricated using different polarization configurations. Note that the probing beam (red laser) applied to the film surface during the whole formation process has no influence on the sample structure because its wavelength is out of the absorption band of the DR1 molecules [11]. Figure 6(c) shows the time dependence of the DE, which is obviously polarization dependence. The diffraction signal indicates the creation of the SRG and depends on the exposure time. For all the polarization configurations, DE increases as a function of time, except for the RC-LC polarization configuration for which DE saturates and decreases after 10 min of exposure. However, we note that during the light irradiation process, the DE results from the formation of three different gratings for the azobenzene copolymer: two gratings were caused by refractive index change in the bulk copolymer material because of the different refractive index values between *trans*-form and *cis*-form of DR1, and only the third one is related to SRG [12]. An investigation of the SRG amplitude is necessary to fully analyse the polarization dependence of the SRG formation.

Figure 6(d) shows the amplitude of the SRGs measured by AFM. The time-dependence of the SRG depth is similar to that of the first-order diffraction intensity, except in the case of RC-LC polarization configuration, for which SRG depth doesn't decrease after saturation. This explains the behaviour observed in Fig. 6(c) for RC-LC polarization configuration, in which there is an exchange of the DE between the three different gratings, i. e. while the DE of two other refractive gratings increases then decreases, the DE of the SRG just continues to increase. We conclude that the SRG formation plays a dominant role in DE evolution.

Besides, we also found that the RC-LC polarization configuration is the best case, which allows to achieve SRGs with the largest amplitude, as seen in Fig. 6 (d). On the other hand, the S-S polarization configuration, theoretically providing 100% of intensity modulation, allows obtaining SRGs with a depth of only several tens nanometers. Surprisingly, even in the case of S-P polarization configuration, which does not create any intensity modulation, allows to obtain SRGs with large depth, similar to those obtained by using a P-P polarization configuration. The formation of SRGs therefore depends strongly on the polarization distribution, or more precisely, it depends on the compromise between the intensity and the polarization modulations. Furthermore, we observed that the SRG depth reaches to a saturation level and remains unchanged after. This saturation level depends mostly on the thickness of the sample, on the light irradiation intensity, and also on the periodicity of the interference pattern. The dependence of the SRG formation with respect to the two first parameters has been studied

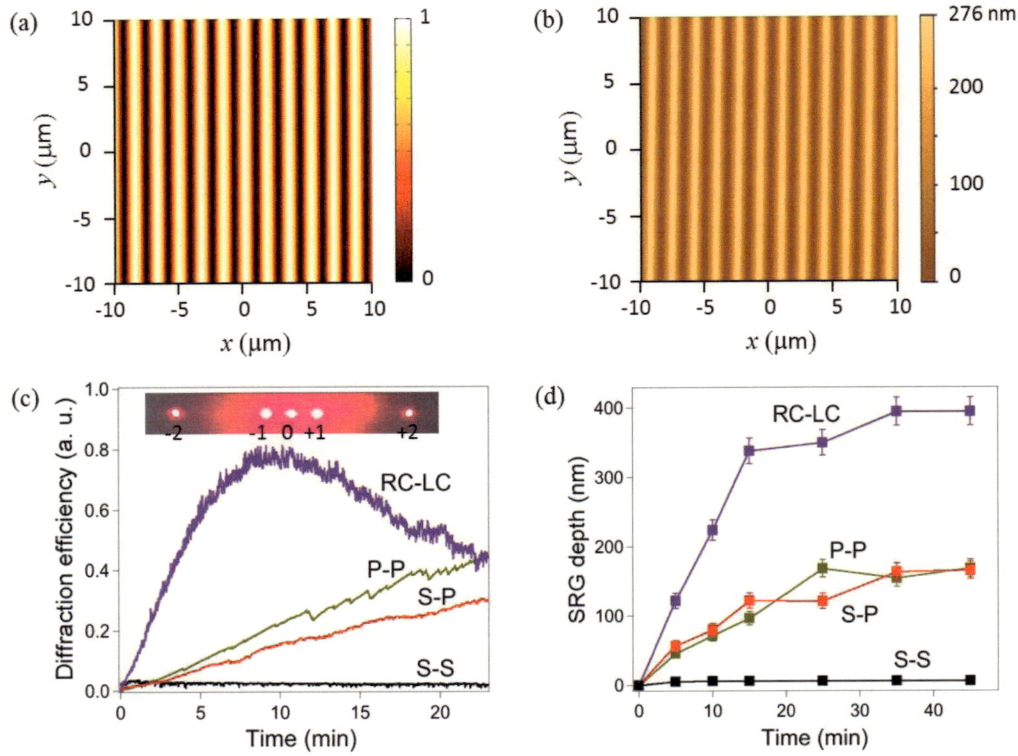

Figure 6. Surface relief grating inscribed on DR1/PMMA by two-beam interference technique. (a) Theoretical calculation of the light intensity distribution of the two-beam interference pattern. (b) AFM image of a fabricated 1D SRG. (c) Time evolution of the first-order diffraction intensity, obtained by sending a red laser beam at a normal incidence to the 1D SRG. Insert shows the experimental diffraction pattern. (d) SRG depths measured as a function of exposure time for different polarization configurations.

before [13, 14], and those parameters are kept unchanged in our case. In the next section, we will show the influence of the periodicity of the interference pattern on the SRGs depth, in order to find out the best SRG, i.e. the smallest period with large amplitude, for our applications in nanophotonic domain.

2.2.2. SRG depth versus interference periodicity

The periodicity of the two-beam interference was varied and all other parameters were kept the same for this investigation. The thickness of the azo-copolymer film is about 1.7 μm. The exposure time is fixed at 40 min, which is long enough to achieve the saturation of the grating formation. The polarizations of the two laser beams are RC-LC configuration to ensure the best SRGs amplitude. According to equation (5), the SRG period can be adjusted with the incident angle θ to a minimal value of $\lambda/2$, equivalent to approximately 270 nm. Figure 7 shows the experimental results of the relationship between the SRG period and depth.

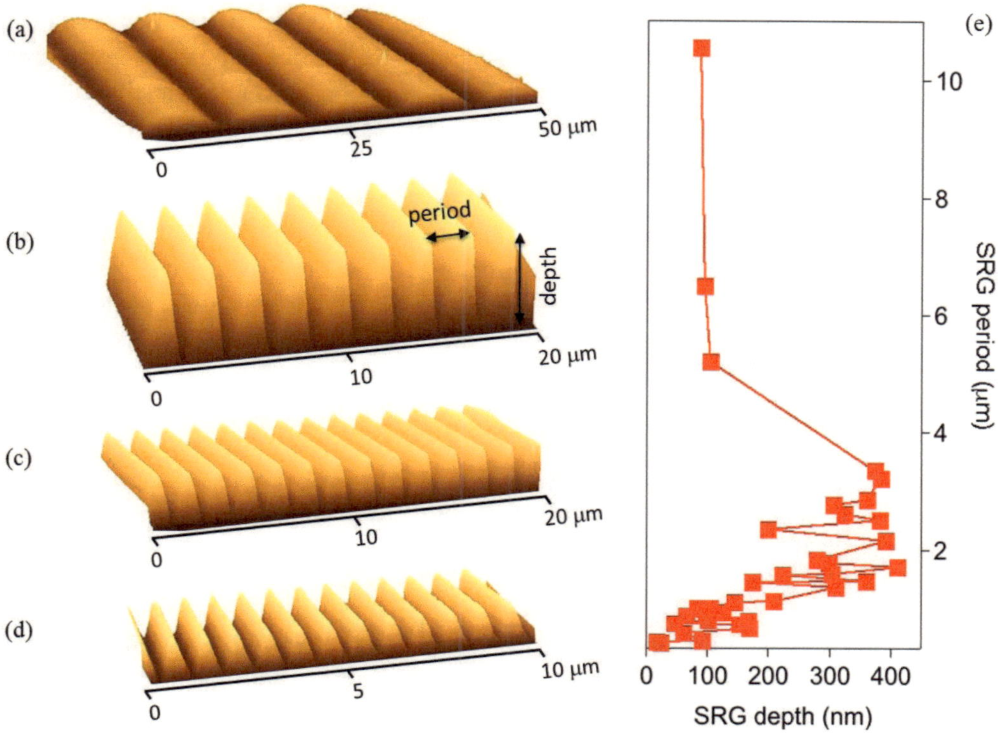

Figure 7. The dependence of SRG depth on the interference periodicity. (a-d) AFM images of SRG structures obtained with different θ-values. (e) SRG depth as a function of the SRG period.

Figures 7(a-d) show the AFM images of several examples of 1D SRGs with different periods ((a): 10 μm, (b): 2 μm, (c): 1.5 μm, and (d): 0.7 μm). As expected from the intensity modulation (Fig. 4) and polarization modulation (Fig. 5), the SRG amplitude is not constant, but varies as a function of the θ-value. Figure 7(e) shows how the SRG amplitude depends on the grating period. The best SRG with the largest amplitude, of about 400 nm, was obtained with Λ between 1.5 μm and 3 μm. The SRG amplitude decreases outside of this period range (>3 μm or < 1.5 μm), but SRG can be still created with Λ values as large as 10 μm, or as small as 0.38 μm. In literature [15-16], people tried to explain this phenomenon including of a compromise of the intensity and the polarization modulation. However, it is quite difficult to explain the dependence of SRG depth on its period. Various elements should be considered to explain this dependence. For example, Kim et al. [15] suggested that the thermal effects resulting from absorption of light contribute to this phenomenon. But it cannot explain the sharp drop of the depth for smaller periods (< 0.8 μm). Barret et al. [17] have used the photoisomerization pressure model to explain the mass transport effect, which led to a relationship between the SRG period and depth. However, their theoretical prediction and the experimental observations do not match well.

In our point of view, the dependence of the SRG depth on period should be explained by taking into account the effective movement distance of the azo-copolymer material under light irradiation. Actually, light induces the photoisomerization effect and pushes the azo-copolymer material away from high exposure intensity to dark areas over an effective distance of several hundred nanometers [18]. For a large period, this movement distance is too short to match with Λ, and cannot help to create a SRG with large amplitude. When the SRG period is smaller than the movement distance, the azo-copolymer will move from highest intensity to lowest intensity areas, and even to the next highest intensity area. A mixing movement in different areas happens and the barrier between lowest and highest intensity is not clearly identified, leading to a decrease of the SRG amplitude. Finally, there exists a range of periods, in which the movement distance of the azo-copolymer is matched with the distance between highest and lowest intensities of the interference pattern, leading to a best formation of the SRG with largest amplitude. These arguments are well consistent with our experimental observations. We note also that the movement distance of the azo-copolymer, accordingly the optimum SRG period and depth, depends strongly on different experimental parameters, such as the sample thickness, the light wavelength and intensity, the temperature, etc.

2.2.3. Formation of 2D SRG by two exposures

Recently, the multi-exposure of two-beam interference technique has been demonstrated to be very powerful to fabricate desired 2D and 3D structures on photoresists [19-20]. Here, the same method was used to realize 2D structures on DR1/PMMA. In practices, after the first exposure, the sample was rotated by an α-angle around the z-axis, and then was exposed for a second time to the same interference pattern.

Figure 8 shows the simulation and the corresponding experimental results by setting the rotational angle of 90° or 60° between two exposures to the two-beam interference pattern. As can be seen in Fig. 8 (a, b), we predicted a fabrication of a square or hexagonal structure with symmetric form. Figures 8 (c, d) show that 2D square and hexagonal structures were effectively fabricated on the DR1/PMMA. The corresponding diffraction patterns shown in Fig. 8 (e, f) also explain the periodicities of fabricated 2D structures. However, as can be seen in Fig. 8(c-f), the 2D structures fabricated in DR1/PMMA, by using two exposures of two-beam interference technique, are not symmetric with respect to the two directions of fabrication, as indicated by the 1 and 2 axis. AFM results also show that the SRG depths are different in these two directions. It is clear that the mechanism of the SRG formation is different from that of the fabrication of 2D structures on photoresists. Indeed, after the first inscription, a 1D SRG was created and the thickness of DR1/PMMA in the regions of peaks was increased with respect to the thickness of original film. The second exposure therefore dealt with a non-uniform film, which makes the lubrication of a final symmetric 2D structure difficult. In order to obtain such a 2D symmetric SRG, the exposure time of the second exposure should be much longer than that of the first exposure. The control of the exposure dose ratio between two exposures has been considered [21], but this method lacks of reproducibility. Indeed, the SRG formation depends on many experimental parameters and the SRG depth does not reach the same value for different samples or different fabrication times.

http://dx.doi.org/10.5772/53788

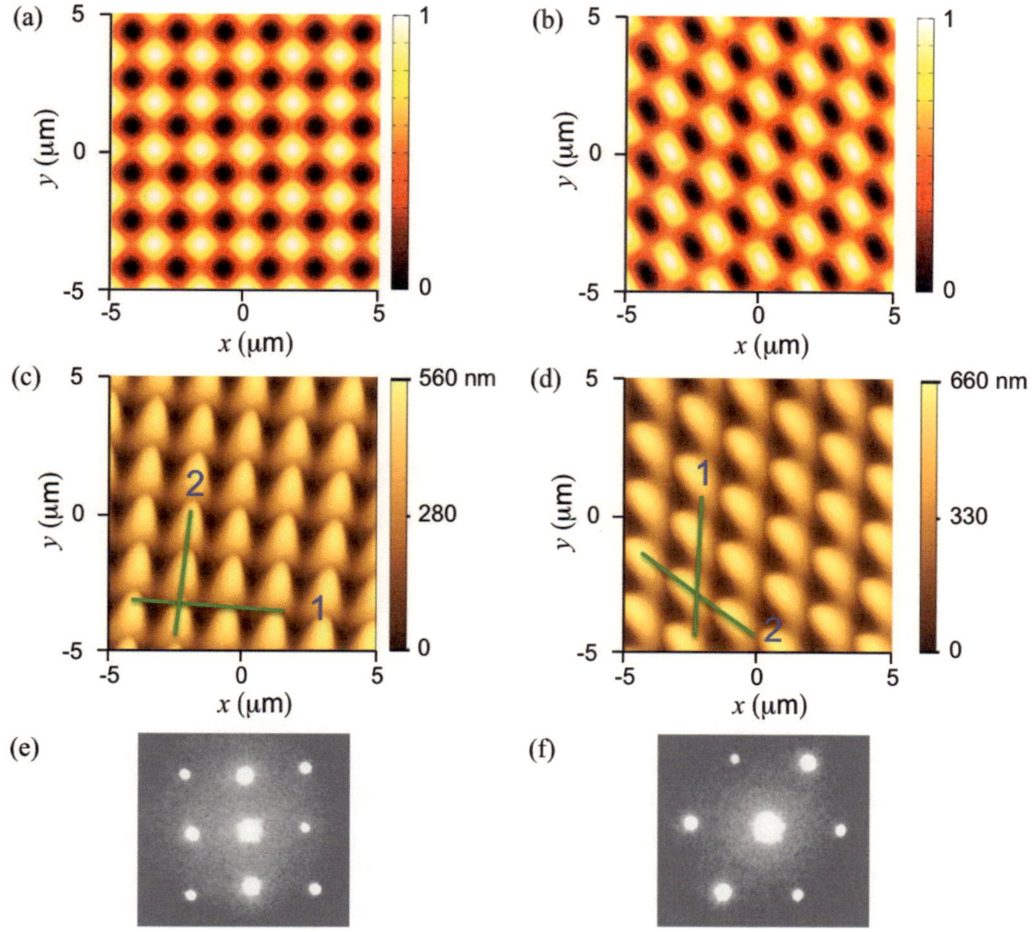

Figure 8. Square and hexagonal SRG structures fabricated by two exposures of two-beam interference pattern with a rotation angle of 90° and 60° between the two exposures, respectively. (a), (b) Theoretical calculation of light intensity distribution, and (c), (d) corresponding experimental results, respectively. (e), (f) Diffraction patterns of the square and hexagonal structures, respectively.

Therefore, in order to create 2D symmetric SRGs on an azo-copolymer material, a single exposure of a three-beam interference pattern is necessary. In the next section, we report our investigations on the use of this interference technique.

3. Three-beam interference

Three-beam interference has been successfully employed to fabricate hexagonal periodic structures [22]. In the case of a standard fabrication on photoresist, the information of three-beam interference resultant polarization is often ignored. However, when this method is applied to the formation of SRG, both intensity distribution and polarization distribution of the interference pattern play important roles. In this section, we present in detail the properties of the three-beam interference technique, using different possible polarization configurations.

3.1. Theory of three-beam interference

Figure 2 (b) shows the beams geometry of the considered three-beam interference. The three laser beams are symmetrically aligned around the z-axis with the same incident angle θ. Similar to the case of two-beam interference, the three beams are associated to three plane waves $\mathbf{E}_1(\mathbf{r}, t)$, $\mathbf{E}_2(\mathbf{r}, t)$ and $\mathbf{E}_3(\mathbf{r}, t)$, whose electric fields are given by

$$\mathbf{E}_1(\mathbf{r},t)=\mathrm{Re}\left[E_{01}\exp\left(i\left(\mathbf{k}_1\bullet\mathbf{r}-\omega t\right)\right)\mathbf{e}_1\right], \tag{7}$$

$$\mathbf{E}_2(\mathbf{r},t)=\mathrm{Re}\left[E_{02}\exp\left(i\left(\mathbf{k}_2\bullet\mathbf{r}-\omega t\right)\right)\mathbf{e}_2\right], \tag{8}$$

$$\mathbf{E}_3(\mathbf{r},t)=\mathrm{Re}\left[E_{03}\exp\left(i\left(\mathbf{k}_3\bullet\mathbf{r}-\omega t\right)\right)\mathbf{e}_3\right], \tag{9}$$

where $\mathbf{k}_1$, $\mathbf{k}_2$ and $\mathbf{k}_3$ are the corresponding wave vectors, $\mathbf{r}$ is the position vector in the overlapping space, E_{01}, E_{02} and E_{03} are the real electric field amplitudes, and $\mathbf{e}_1$, $\mathbf{e}_2$ and $\mathbf{e}_3$ are the unit vectors of the polarizations. In our simulations, we assumed that $|\mathbf{k}_1| = |\mathbf{k}_2| = |\mathbf{k}_3| = k$ and $E_{01}=E_{02}=E_{03}=E_0$. At the overlapping area of the three beams, the interference electric field is the sum of the electric fields of individual plane waves, $\mathbf{E}_T(\mathbf{r}, t)=\mathbf{E}_1(\mathbf{r},t) + \mathbf{E}_2(\mathbf{r},t) + \mathbf{E}_3(\mathbf{r},t)$. The interference intensity is calculated by using equation (4). A 2D periodic structure was then generated with a periodicity determined by $\Lambda=\lambda/(1.5\sin\theta)$, where λ is the wavelength of laser beam.

Similar to the case of two-beam interference, we have investigated the intensity distribution and the polarization distribution of the three-beam interference pattern as a function of the polarizations of the three laser beams. We considered four particular polarizations configurations, namely, three random polarizations (R,R,R), three p-polarizations (P,P,P), three s-polarizations (S,S,S), and three circular polarizations (C,C,C), as shown in the top of Fig. 9.

3.1.1. Intensity distribution

Figure 9 represents the intensity distributions of the three-beam interference pattern with different polarization configurations. All simulated hexagonal structures are symmetric and have the same period, but their forms change for different polarization configurations. For example, we obtained air-hole structures (low intensity spots) with P,P,P or S,S,S polarization configuration, and dielectric-cylinder structures (high intensity spots) with C,C,C polarization configuration. The intensity contrast varies from this case to the other. The bottom line of Fig. 9 shows the intensity distributions along the x-axis of each case. Note that the contrast also

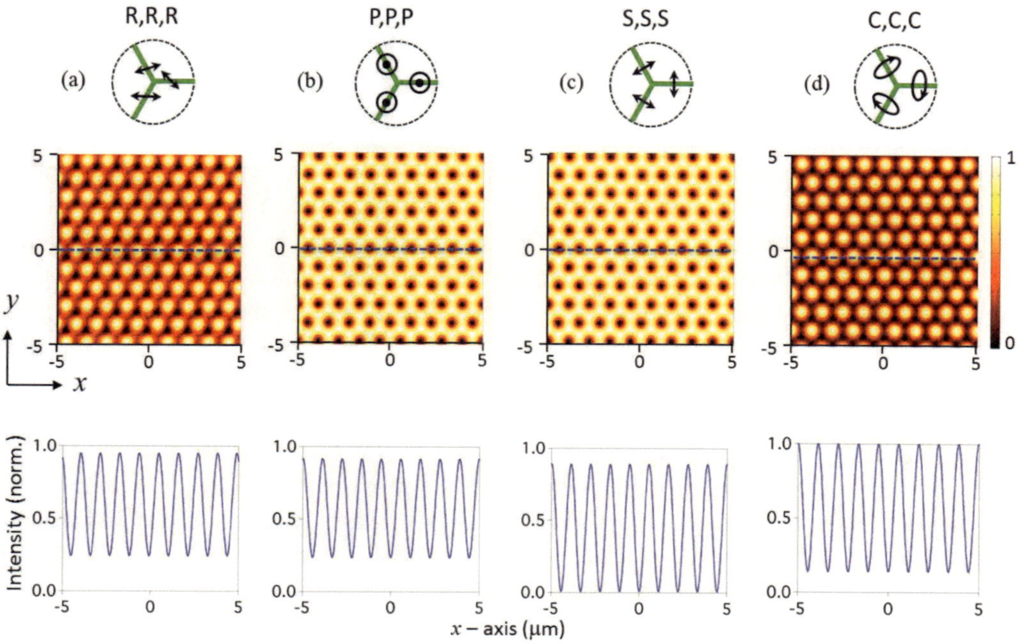

Figure 9. Theoretical calculation of the three-beam interference intensity patterns with different polarization configurations. Polarization arrangements: (a) three random polarization beams; (b) three p-polarization beams; (c) three s-polarization beams; and (d) three circular polarization beams. The interference patterns are all symmetric in *xy*-plan, but the intensity modulation never reaches 100% for all the cases.

varies as a function of the incident angle θ. However, we show here only results corresponding to the case of θ=17.65°, as it will be realized experimentally and shown in the next section. Theoretically, we expected that this three-beam interference technique allows to create 2D symmetric SRG, by using any polarization configuration.

3.1.2. Polarization modulation

We now consider only three particular polarization configurations, i.e., P,P,P, S,S,S and C,C,C. Because of the periodicity of the interference pattern, it is necessary to calculate the resultant polarization for only one particular area corresponding to a so-called Wigner-Seitz primitive cell. Figure 10 shows thus polarization distributions in the *xy*-plane for the three cases. We can see that the resultant polarization changes as a function of the considered position. The polarization distributions are also different from this configuration to the other. However, the interfering polarizations are all symmetrically distributed around the origin of Wigner-Seitz primitive cell. Concretely, for P,P,P and S,S,S cases, the resultant polarization is changed from linear to elliptic and to circular. But for the C,C,C case, the resultant polarization keeps the same polarization (circular) throughout the interference pattern. With the SRG samples obtained using the two-beam interference technique, it is difficult to predict the best polarization configuration enabling the fabrication of SRGs with the largest amplitude. However, from the point of view of fabrication setup, it is quite easy to build-up a three-beam interference technique with C,C,C polarizations, as it will be demonstrated in the next section.

3.1.3. Experimental demonstration

Figure 11 shows the experimental setup of the three-beam interference and the experimental results of 2D hexagonal SRG realized on the DR1/PMMA material. A large and uniform laser beam with circular polarization was split into three sub-beams by a non-polarized multi-surface prism. These three sub-beams, corresponding to three surfaces denoted as A_1, A_2, and A_3, respectively (Fig. 11(a)), show different propagation directions after passing through the prism and then overlap on the surface of the sample. These three beams have the same intensities and same polarizations (circular). This compact system allows to realize a 2D hexagonal structure by only one exposure, which corresponds to the theoretical calculation of the C,C,C polarization configuration shown before. We note that other polarization configurations could be also realized from this setup, but it requires the use of three other mirrors and also different wave plates (quarter-wave and half-wave plates) to control the polarization of each laser beam. In this work, we experimentally demonstrated the fabrication of 2D SRG by using only the simple C,C,C polarization configuration.

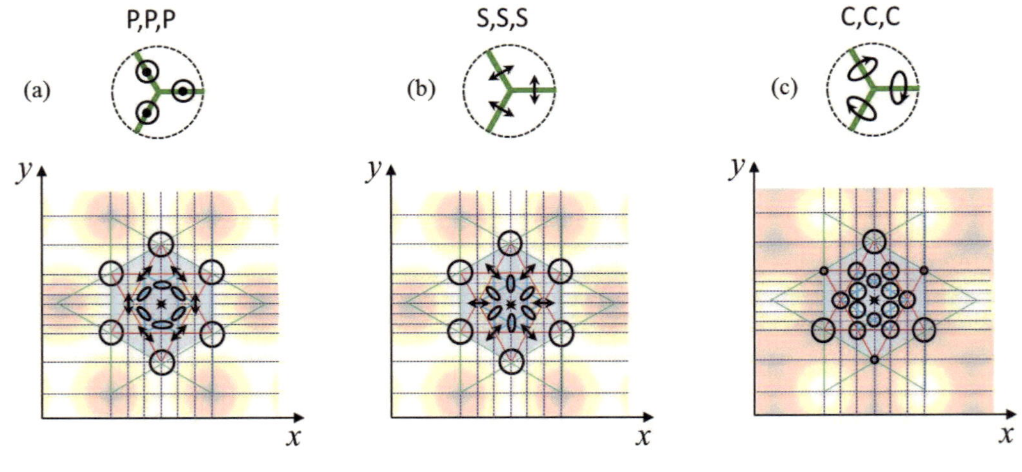

Figure 10. Polarization distributions of the three-beam interference pattern, calculated for one Wigner-Seitz primitive cell. The polarizations vary in different ways for three particular polarization configurations, but all distributions display a 3-fold ~ 6-fold symmetry.

The special design of the tri-prism results in a hexagonal structure with a period of 1.2 μm (corresponding to θ=17.65°). With only one exposure of a green laser (532 nm) via the multi-surface-prism, a 2D hexagonal SRG was then created, as shown in Fig. 11(b). The 2D SRG is quite uniform and symmetric. Actually, Fig. 11(c) shows a symmetric diffraction pattern of fabricated structure. The surface modulation along different directions was also characterized, and possessed the same modulation depth, as illustrated in Fig. 11(d). However, we remark

http://dx.doi.org/10.5772/53788

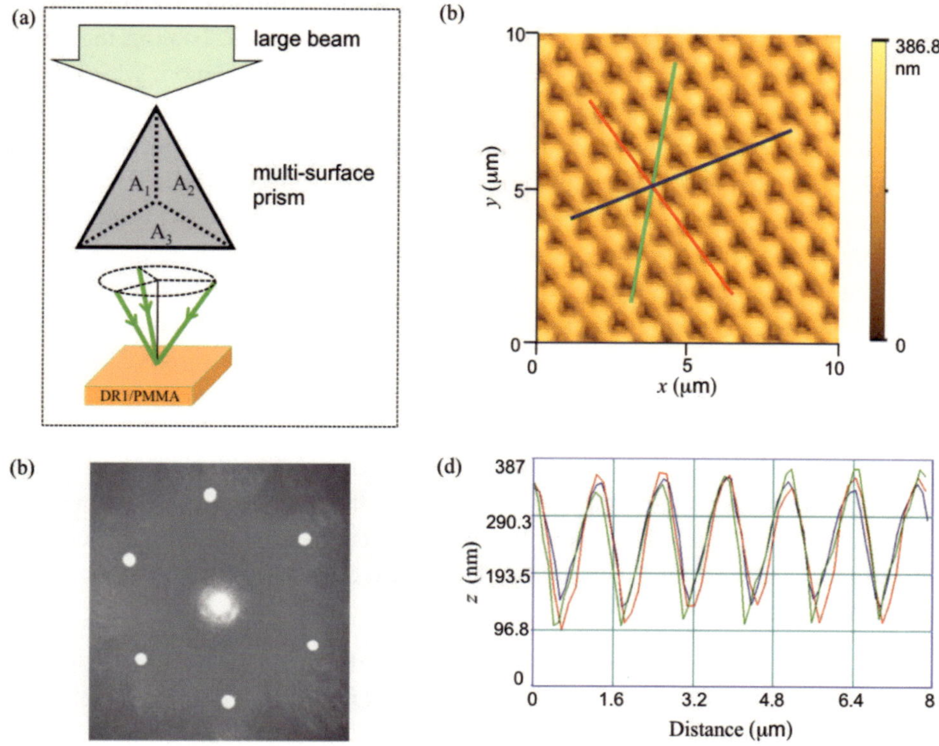

Figure 11. Realization of 2D periodic and symmetric SRG structure by one exposure to the three-beam interference pattern with C,C,C polarization configuration. (a) A large and uniform laser beam comes into a multi-surface prism and is divided into three sub-beams corresponding to surfaces denoted as A_1, A_2, and A_3, respectively. The three beams overlap in an area in which a DR1/PMMA film is placed for the fabrication. (b) AFM image of a 2D SRG structure produced by three-beam interference with C,C,C polarization configuration. (c) Experimental diffraction pattern of the fabricated 2D SRG structure. (d) Surface modulation along three particular directions, as shown in figure (b), of the fabricated 2D SRG structure.

that, since the period belongs to the range for which the SRG depth is weak (see Fig. 7), the formation of the structure strongly depends on the relative ratio of the intensity of the three laser beams. A small difference of the intensities of the laser beams induces a deformation of the 2D SRG. Identical intensities of the three laser beams are therefore necessary for obtaining a perfect symmetry of the SRGs. The dependence of the symmetry of the 2D SRGs on the relative intensities and on different polarizations (S,S,S and P,P,P) of the laser beams is under investigation.

4. Optimization of SRG formation

Besides the realization of SRGs on azo-copolymer materials, it is also interesting to optimize the SRGs depth. Indeed, for a best choice of experimental parameters, the SRG amplitude is obtained only about 30% of the thickness of the sample. Several methods have been proposed to improve the DE and the modulation depth of the SRGs, such as electrical poling, temperature effect, etc. [23-24]. In this work, we demonstrated a simple optical method, which allowed increasing rapidly the formation of the SRGs. This method is based on the control of the photoisomerization process between *trans*- and *cis*-forms of the DR1 molecules. We have demonstrated, as shown in the insert of the Fig. 1, that the use of an additional UV or VIS laser beam assists the *trans-cis-trans* cycle, resulting in a rapid rotation of the DR1 molecules. This optical assistance leads to the formation of SRGs with a large modulation depth. To understand the mechanism of this assisting effect, we describe the photoisomerization process of DR1 molecules (insert of Fig. 1) as follow: DR1 molecules undergo photoisomerization process from *trans*-form to *cis*-form by applying a green light. If we apply an assisting UV light beam simultaneously with the green beam, the *trans*-form becomes the *cis*-form (green excitation), and the *cis*-form rapidly returns to the *trans*-form (UV excitation). On the other hand, if we apply an assisting VIS light beam simultaneously with the green beam, the *trans*-form becomes the *cis*-form (green excitation), and the *cis*-form relaxes to the *trans*-form in the perpendicular direction, which is then transferred back to the *cis*-form thanks to the excitation of the assisting VIS beam. The *trans-cis-trans* cycle is therefore accelerated and multiplied, resulting in a SRG with larger amplitude.

Figure 12 (a) shows the optical arrangement of two interfering beams with an assisting beam. Two coherent green beams interfere and create SRG on DR1/PMMA sample. Another laser beam, whose wavelength is 355 nm (UV) or 532 nm (VIS), comes into the sample, at the interfering area to improve the formation of SRG. Here again, different polarization configurations of the writing and assisting beams are investigated, as shown in Fig.12 (b). All other parameters, such as the thickness of samples (about 1.7 μm), the writing time (long enough to reach the maximum SRG depth), the intensities of the writing beams and of the UV or VIS assisting beam, were kept unchanged.

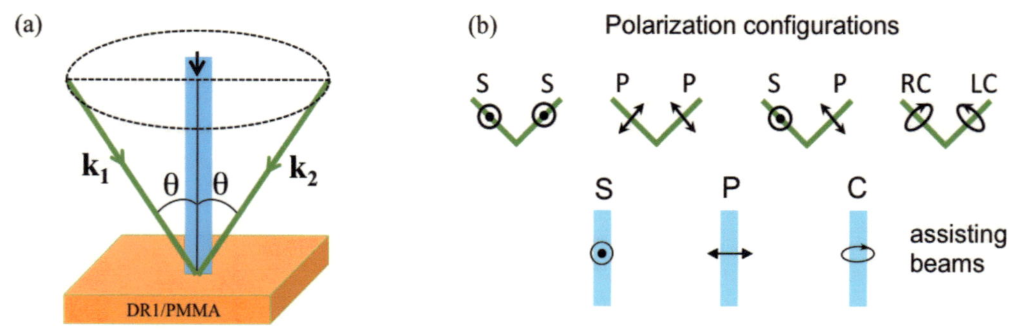

Figure 12. a) Optical arrangement of two-beam interference experiment with an additional assisting beam. Two green (VIS) beams interfere on the surface of the DR1/PMMA and an assisting beam comes into sample at normal incidence. (b) Different possibilities of polarization configurations of writing (VIS) and assisting beam (UV or VIS).

4.1. Assisting by UV beam

Figure 13 shows the intensity of the first-order diffraction and the modulation depth of the SRGs created with the assistance of the UV beam. We can observe clearly that the DE increases immediately and rapidly when the UV assisting beam is turned on (Figs. 13(a-c)) and reaches a maximum value, which is much higher than that obtained without the UV assisting beam. We also found that the assisting effect is polarization dependent, for both writing beams and assisting beams. The best polarization configuration for the improvement of SRG formation was identified, corresponding to the case in which the polarization of the UV assisting beam is same as the polarizations of the writing beam. The reason why such a polarization configuration is optimum could be found from the photoisomerization process. Indeed, the green beam transfers the *trans*-form to the *cis*-form, and the *cis*-form rapidly returns to the *trans*-form via the UV excitation. The polarization of the UV laser therefore should be as same as that of the green laser beam in order to act on the same molecule oriented in the same direction. Figures 13(d-f) show the SRG depths obtained in such an optimized polarization configuration. The SRG amplitude was improved from several nanometers to several hundred nanometers. The evolution of the SRG depth is similar to that of the DE, but is not exactly the same, in particular for the case of RC-LC writing beam polarization configuration.

4.2. Assisting by VIS beam

Another additional VIS beam, of the same wavelength as the writing beams (532 nm), was used instead of the UV beam to assist the formation of SRG. The DE also immediately increases and accordingly a SRG with large amplitude is obtained, similar to the results obtained from the UV assisting. Figure 14 shows the improvement of DE and the SRG depth for different polarization configurations. Considering only two particular polarizations, s-and p-polarizations, contrary to the case of UV assisting, the best improvement of SRG formation was obtained when the polarization of the VIS assisting beam is perpendicular to the polarizations of the writing beams. Here again, the mechanism of the VIS assisted SRG formation should be explained using the photoisomerization process. Indeed, when an assisting VIS light beam is simultaneously applied with the writing green beams, the *trans*-form is transferred to the *cis*-form (green excitation), the *cis*-form relaxes to the *trans*-form, which is oriented in perpendicular direction to the original *trans*-form (angular hole burning effect). The assisting VIS beam, whose polarization is perpendicular to those of the writing beams, therefore excites the new *trans*-form and enhances the photoisomerization process and consequently the SRG formation.

As compared with UV assisting, this VIS assisting technique is quite interesting for SRGs fabrication. Effectively, on one hand, a low cost VIS laser such as a green laser diode is sufficient to help the SRGs formation. On the other hand, a single green laser could be also split and delayed in time into two independent lasers sources, each one playing a role as writing and assisting beams, resulting in a simple and compact fabrication setup.

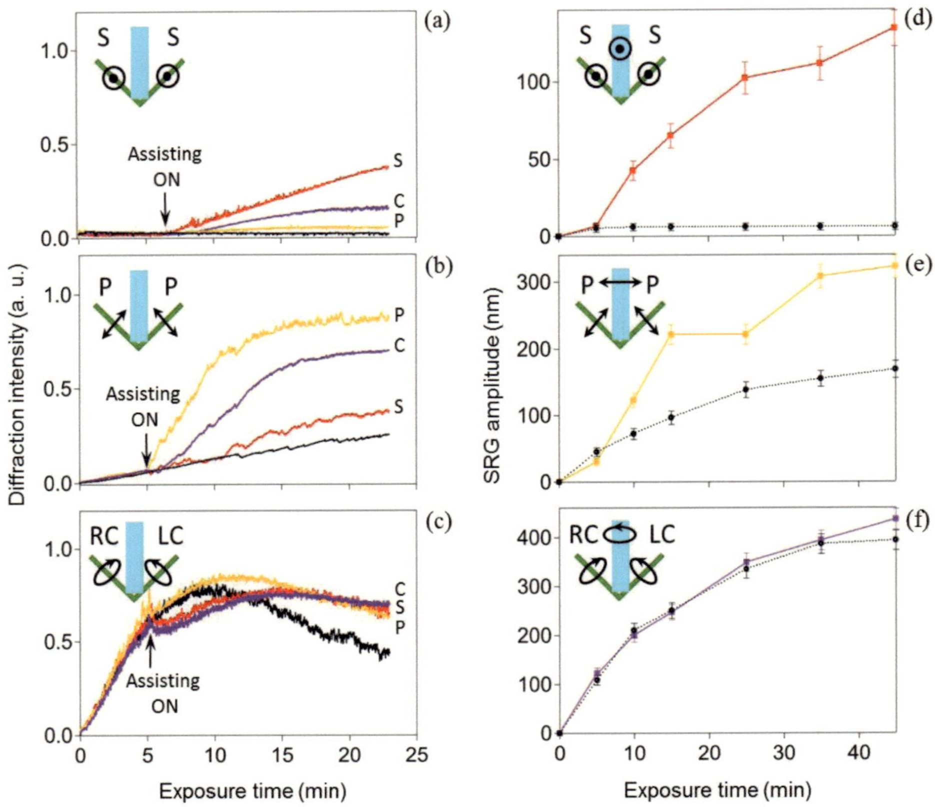

Figure 13. Optimization of SRG formation by an UV assisting beam. Left: time dependence of the first-order diffraction intensity. Right: improvement of the SRG depth as a function of time. The polarization configurations are illustrated in each figure. The black curves (left) and dots (right) show the results obtained without UV assisting beam, which are plotted in each figure in order to compare with those obtained with assisting beam.

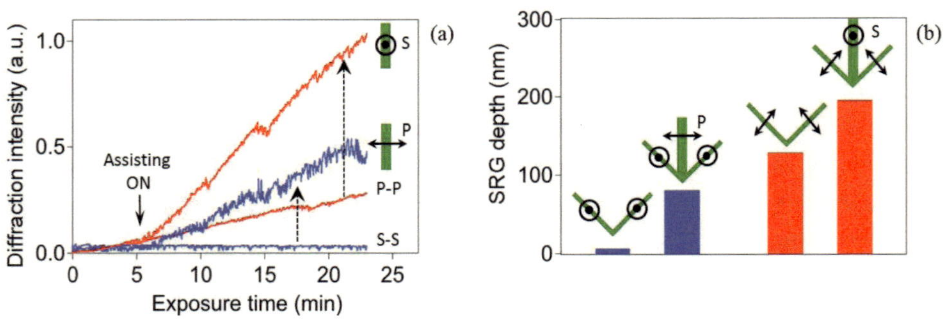

Figure 14. Optimization of SRG formation by a green incoherent beam. (a) Time dependence of the first-order diffraction intensity. (b) Comparison of the depth of the SRGs inscribed with and without green assisting beam for two particular polarization configurations, P-P (red) and S-S (blue).

5. Conclusion

The realization and optimization of 1D and 2D surface relief grating made of on azopolymer materials are in high demand for the use in many applications, such as holographic data storage, active waveguides, electro-optic modulators and also distributed-feedback lasers. In this chapter, simple fabrication techniques based on two-beam and three-beam interferences were theoretically and experimentally demonstrated as efficient methods for creation of desired SRGs on azo-copolymer. The interference patterns were theoretically analysed in detail for both intensity and polarization distributions. These two parameters are competitive and complementary for the formation of SRG. The polarization modulation is however experimentally demonstrated to be more important. Depending on the desired applications, 1D and 2D SRG could be fabricated by two-beam or three-beam interference, respectively. 2D SRGs with different configurations, e.g., hexagonal or square, have been fabricated by using a simple two-exposure of the two-beam interference pattern. The shape of the fabricated structures is however not symmetric due to the mechanism of the SRG formation. 2D hexagonal SRGs with perfect symmetry have been then fabricated by a single exposure of the three-beam interference pattern. We expect that a symmetric 2D square SRG could be also fabricated by using a four-beam interference pattern. Furthermore, it will be possible to fabricate quasi-periodic SRGs on demand by using a two-exposure of the three-beam interference or four-beam interference patterns.

Besides, two efficient optical methods were also proposed to enhance the formation of SRGs, employing an incoherent UV or VIS beam. These lasers assist the photoisomerization process of DR1 molecules, resulting in a rapid inscription and large amplitude of SRG. The polarization analysis has been experimentally investigated, showing different mechanisms of the two assisting laser beams. SRGs with largest amplitude were obtained when the polarizations of the writing beam and the UV beam are same and when the polarizations of the writing beam and the VIS beam are orthogonal. These properties help to understand the mechanism of the formation of SRG that is obviously not clear till now.

These periodic and quasi-periodic SRGs can be very useful for many photonic applications [25]. Application of 2D SRGs as nonlinear photonic crystals is under investigation. Fabrication of large-area 3D photonic crystals and nonlinear photonic crystals is also the objective of future work.

Acknowledgements

We would like to thank J. Lautru and A. Brosseau for invaluable help and access to the cleaning room and atomic force microscope. We also thank M. Dumont and Q. Li for useful discussion. This work was partially supported by Institute d'Alembert of the ENS Cachan. X. Wu acknowledges the fellowship from the China Scholarship Council, and T. T. N. Nguyen acknowledges the fellowship from the Vietnam International Education Development "322 program".

Author details

Xiao Wu[1,2], Thi Thanh Ngan Nguyen[1,3], Isabelle Ledoux-Rak[1], Chi Thanh Nguyen[1] and Ngoc Diep Lai[1*]

*Address all correspondence to: nlai@lpqm.ens-cachan.fr

1 Laboratoire de Photonique Quantique et Moléculaire, UMR 8537 CNRS, Ecole Normale Supérieure de Cachan, France

2 Condensed Matter Physics, East China Normal University, Shanghai, China

3 Institute of Materials Sciences, Vietnam Academy of Science and Technology, Cau Giay, Hanoi, Vietnam

References

[1] Goldenberg L. M., Lisinetskii V., Gritsai Y., Stumpe J., and Schrader S. Second Order DFB Lasing Using Reusable Grating Inscribed in Azobenzene-containing Material. Optical Materials Express 2012; 2 11-19.

[2] Yariv A. Periodic Structures for Integrated Optics. IEEE Journal of Quantum Electronics 1977; 13 233-253.

[3] Goldenberg L. M., Gritsai Y., Kulikovska O., and Stumpe J. Three-dimensional Planarized Diffraction Structures Based on Surface Relief Gratings in Azobenwene Materials. Optics Letters 2008; 33 1309-1311.

[4] Viswanathan N. K., Kim D. Y., Bian S., Williams J., Liu W., Li L., Samuelson L., Kumar J., and Tripathy S. K. Surface Relief Grating on Azo Polymer Films. Journal of Materials Chemistry 1999; 9 1941-1955.

[5] Natansohn A., and Rochon P. Photoinduced Motions in Azo-Containing Polymers. Chemical Reviews 2002; 102 4139-4175.

[6] Pedersen T. G., Johansen P. M., Holme N. C. R., Ramanujam P. S., and Hvilsted S. Mean-Field Theory of Photoinduced Formation of Surface Reliefs in Side-chain Azobenzene Polymers. Physical Review Letters 1998; 80 89-92.

[7] Kumar J., Li L., Jiang X. L., Kim D. Y., Lee T. S., and Tripathy S. K. Gradient Force: The Mechanism for Surface Relief Grating Formation in Azobenzene Functionalized Polymers. Applied Physics Letters 1998; 72 2096-2098.

[8] Sumarua K., Yamanaka T., Fukuda T., and Matsuda H. Photoinduced Surface Relief Gratings on Azopolymer Films: Analysis by A Fluid Mechanics Model. Applied Physics Letters 1999; 75 1878-1880.

[9] Fiorini C., Prudhomme N., Veyrac de G., Maurin I., Raimond P., and Nunzi J.-M. Molecular Migration Mechanism for Laser Induced Surface Relief Grating Formation. Synthetic Metals 2000; 115 121-125.

[10] Baradaa D., Itoh M., and Yatagai T. Computer Simulation of Photoinduced Mass Transport on Azobenzene Polymer Films by Particle Method. Journal of Applied Physics 2004; 96 4204-4210.

[11] Loucif-Saibi R., Nakatani K., Delaire J. A., Dumont M., and Sekkat Z. Photoisomerization and Second Harmonic Generation in Disperse Red One-doped and -functionalized Poly(methyl methacrylate) Films. Chemistry of Materials 1993; 5 229-236.

[12] Sobolewska A., and Bartkiewicz S. Three Grating Coupling during the Holographic Grating Recording Process in Azobenzene-functionalized Polymer. Applied Physics Letters 2008; 92 253305(1-3).

[13] Munakata K., Harada K., Itoh M., Umegaki S., and Yatagai T. A New Holographic Recording Material and Its Diffraction Efficiency Increase Effect: The Use of Photoinduced Surface Deformation in Azo-polymer Film. Optics Communications 2001; 191 15-19.

[14] Bian S. P., Williams J. M., Kim D. Y., Li L., Balasubramanian S., Kumar J., and Tripathy S. Photoinduced Surface Deformations on Azobenzene Polymers Films. Journal of Applied Physics 1999; 86 4498-4508.

[15] Kim D. Y., Li L., Jiang X. L., Shivshankar V., Kumar J., and Tripathy S. K. Polarized Laser Induced Holographic Surface Relief Grating on Polymer Films. Macromolecules 1995; 28 8835-8839.

[16] Barrett C. J., Rochon P. L., and Natansohn A. L. Model of Laser-driven Mass Transport in Thin Films of Dye-Functionalized Polymers. Journal of Chemical Physics 1998; 109 1505-1516.

[17] Barrett C. J., Natansohn A. L., and Rochon P. L. Mechanism of Optically Inscribed High-efficiency Diffraction Gratings in Azo Polymer Films. Journal of Physics Chemistry 1996; 100 8836-8842.

[18] Lambeth R. H., Park J. Y., Liao H. W., Shir D. J., Jeon S. Rogers J. A., and Moore J. S. Proximity Field Nanopatterning of Azopolymer Thin Films. Nanotechnology 2010; 21 165301.

[19] Lai N. D., Liang W. P., Lin J. H., Hsu C. C., and Lin. C. H. Fabrication of Two- and Three-dimensional Periodic Structures by Multi-exposure of Two-beam interference Technique. Optics Express 2005; 13 9605-9611.

[20] Lai N. D., Liang W. P., Lin J. H., and Hsu C. C. Rapid Fabrication of Large-area Periodic Structures Containing Well-defined Defects by Combining Holography and Mask Techniques. Optics Express 2005; 13 1094-4087.

[21] Lee S., Jeong Y. C., and Park J. K. Facile Fabrication of Close-packed Microlens Arrays Using Photoinduced Surface Relief Structures as Templates. Optics Express 2007; 15 14550-14559.

[22] Berger V., Gauthier-Lafaye O., and Costard E. Photonic Band Gaps and Holography. Journal of Applied Physics 1997; 82 60-64.

[23] Jager C., Bieringer T., and Zilker S. Bicolor Surface Reliefs in Azobenzene Side-chain Polymers. Applied Optics 2001; 40 1776-1778.

[24] Yu H. F., Okano K., Shishido A., Ikeda T., Kamata K., Komura M., and Iyoda T. Enhancement of Surface-relief Gratings Recorded on Amphiphilic Liquid-crystalline Diblock Copolymer by Nanoscale Phase Separation. Advanced Materials 2005; 17 2184-2188.

[25] Lee S., Kang H. S., and Park J. K. Directional Photofluidization Lithography: Micro/Nanostructural Evolution by Photofluidic Motions of Azobenzene Materials. Advanced Materials 2012; 24 2069-2103.

Chapter 8

Holographic Printing of White-Light Viewable Holograms and Stereograms

Hoonjong Kang, Elena Stoykova, Jiyung Park,
Sunghee Hong and Youngmin Kim

Additional information is available at the end of the chapter

http://dx.doi.org/10.5772/53412

1. Introduction

Denis Gabor [1] invented the holographic method to improve the resolution of an electron microscope in 1948. Following the invention of the coherent light sources a decade later, the holographic techniques proved their unique potential in many fields as three-dimensional (3D) display technology [2], optical metrology [3], medicine [4], commerce etc. Among them, full-color and full parallax high resolution holographic printing as a technique for recording of 3D objects and scenes which are reconstructed under white light illumination is experiencing extensive development. The holographic printing, being a part of the research on 3D imaging of 3D objects from sampled data sets by holographic means, also followed the two main approaches in this area: i) computation of the holographic fringes by numerical simulation of the interference and encoding the resulting pattern onto a suitable medium for further optical display; ii) digital acquisition or computation of a set of discrete perspectives of a scene and their optical multiplexing in a holographic medium for building a stereoscopic pseudo 3D image.

A holographic stereogram (HS) has received much research attention since it can reduce the bandwidth of the hologram by defining a viewing scope, while the holography is a technique to reconstruct the real wavefront of the light field coming from the object. That's why the HSs form a separate region in the field of holographic printing. However, more studies of this innovative method had to be navigated because of the inherent characteristics of holographic recording. A two-step method, spatially-multiplexing technique, horizontal-parallax-only (HPO) method, and HS' exposure geometry were instances of such valuable efforts. Figure 1 shows the historical events of the important technical developments related to the HS.

The early experiment on a HS was conducted by R. V. Pole in 1967. Pole's experiment included recording of multiple perspectives by means of two-dimensional (2D) fly's eye lenslet array with incoherent white light, and then transfer of the perspectives onto the holographic material [5]. De Bitetto's spatially-multiplexed technique via sequential exposure of a fine grain film (such as Panatomic-X) provided a clue to overcome the resolution limitation of Pole's original approach to the HS [6]. The intensive research on printing HSs had been conducting since 1970s [7]. In [7], a large HS was recorded from a sequence of computed perspective images of a 3D object taken from multiple viewpoints equidistantly placed on a part of a circle. Benton's "Rainbow" hologram [8] and Lloyd Cross's "Multiplex(TM)" [9], which were developed with a HPO holographic technique, were the expression of the efforts for the reduction of the bandwidth and the simple acquisition of perspective images.

In 1974, Yatagai [10, 11] proposed a method to accelerate producing of computer-generated HSs. According to this method, computer calculated not only the perspective images but also the elemental hologram through Fourier transform of these images to build the composite hologram. The research was pushed forward in 1990 for a straightforward process with the help of a spatial light modulator (SLM) and the introduction of a pulsed laser, when an one-step printer for full parallax holographic stereograms was invented [12, 13]. The essence of the method was successive recording of multiple volume-type elemental holograms by displaying on a SLM the angular distribution of the light field for each elemental hologram built from a sequence of perspective 2D images. The result is a stereoscopic vision at a varying viewing angle. In 1998 a holographic printer for one-step color full parallax HSs was patented [14], which was further improved by Geola group [15-17] by proposing much faster and more stable pulsed RGB lasers implementation of the holoprinting technique. Nowadays the advanced HS printers with CW or pulse laser illumination can produce white-light viewable large format digital color holograms [18]. Recently, promising results have been reported when the holographic stereogram technique was applied to realize a quasi-real-time 3D display by printing on a newly developed erasable dynamic photorefractive material [19] by using pulsed lasers illumination. The principle of the HS was implemented in a curved array dynamic holographic display built from many SLMs [20].

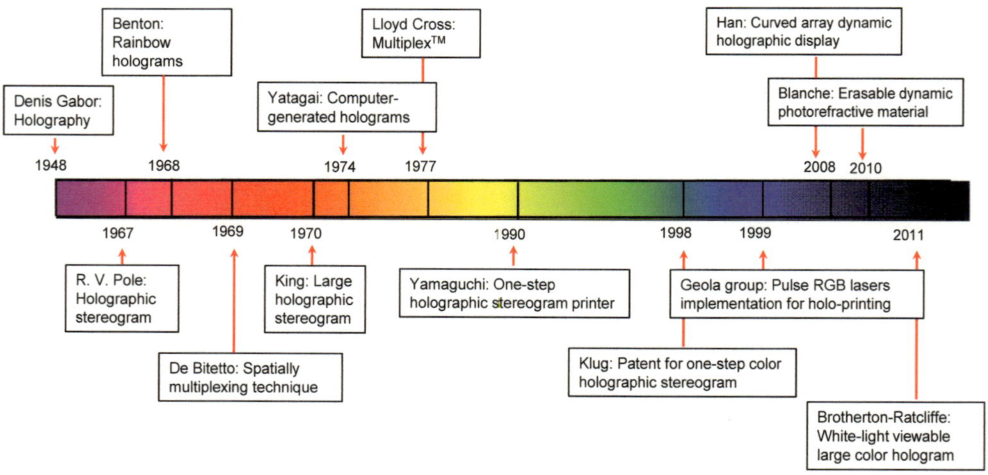

Figure 1. Historical events of the technical developments for a holographic stereogram.

http://dx.doi.org/10.5772/53412

In 2004, a device for direct printing of the holographic fringe pattern was proposed and developed [21, 22]. The holographic fringe pattern is computer generated from the 3D information extracted from a 3D object and further printed onto a photo-sensitive holographic plate. The SLM displays in this case a fractional part of the fringe pattern for recording an elemental hologram. Since then a lot of efforts have been focused on direct printing of various types of computer generated holograms which can be reconstructed under laser or white-light illumination.

The structure of the Chapter is as follows: **Section 2**, which consists of five subsections, gives a critical analysis of the research on printing HSs and a survey of the recent achievements in printing large-format full-color HSs. **Subsection 2.1** describes the principle of the HS printing. **Subsection 2.2** considers advantages and drawbacks of different methods for acquisition of perspective images and explains forming of the parallax related images. **Subsection 2.3** provides analysis of distortions which worsen the quality of the reconstructed image. **Subsection 2.4** presents a simulation tool developed by us for numerical reconstruction of the HS from the formed parallax images as a quality check before printing. **Subsection 2.5** presents the main blocks of the printer set-up and describes the main requirements set on the photo-sensitive materials used for panchromatic holographic recording of volume reflection holograms. **Section 3** consists of three subsections and is dedicated to direct printing of a holographic fringe pattern on a photo-sensitive material. **Subsection 3.1** introduces briefly the dedicated acceleration methods for generation of fringe patterns for various holograms which can be manufactured by holographic printing techniques. Furthermore, **Subsection 3.2** focuses on the technique for direct printing of the generated holographic fringe pattern onto the holographic emulsion. **Subsection 3.3** treats a wave-front recording technique which is novel technology. The essence of the method is to record as a volume hologram the wave field diffracted from a holographic fringe pattern displayed on a suitable SLM. As a result, a digitally designed volume hologram is recorded whose quality is comparable to a conventional analog hologram. The conclusion of the Chapter gives the future trends in the holographic printing.

2. Printing of holographic stereograms

2.1. Holographic stereograms — Principle of the holographic printing

Holographic stereograms are popular autostereoscopic display devices with a strong visual impact [23]. They implement the idea of displaying a 3D scene by using stereo-images and the property of the holographic medium to record 3D wavefront through interference and to reconstruct it by diffraction. The underlying technology behind the HS stems from the off-axis display holography and the autostereoscopic approaches in lenticular and parallax barrier displays [24]. This technology allows high-quality quasi-holographic 3D imaging of large objects. To make a HS, a sequence of 2D images of the scene is incoherently acquired from multiple views. The directional information carried by these perspective images is processed to form parallax-related images which after displaying on a projection screen are recorded onto a holographic photo-sensitive material by a coherent source in a two-beam recording scheme. The parallax-related images modulate the intensity of the object beam. The whole hologram is divided into elemental holograms which are sequentially exposed to the parallax-related images. Illumination of the fringe pattern recorded in the hologram for reconstruction of the 3D scene ensures spatial multiplexing of the perspective views.

Stereoscopy reduces substantially the huge amount of information encoded in a hologram, since this information is recorded from a finite discrete set of viewpoints. The bandwidth of the HS, which presents a sequence of discrete apertures to the viewer, is reduced through a predetermined viewing scope by the HS viewing window. Each aperture yields information for a single 2D image of the scene. The viewer's left and right eyes observe different perspectives of the scene, as viewed from different directions, so the viewer perceives stereoscopic vision due to the binocular parallax. When the viewer moves from one image to the other, the motion parallax is observed at discrete steps. The viewer is able to verge on an object but accommodation occurs either at infinity or at a certain virtual observation plane, i.e. the HS does not provide the accommodation cue.

The HSs can be divided into HPO stereograms and full parallax stereograms in accordance with the exhibited parallax properties. The HPO stereograms are recorded by a cylindrical lens which focuses the laser light within a narrow vertical slit and preserves intact propagation in the vertical plane. The HS of this type are often called multiplex stereograms [25]. Horizontal orientation of human eyes allows to discard the vertical parallax and still to obtain adequate perception of the shape of the objects and their location in space. This makes HPO HSs an effective approach for imaging 3D objects. If perspective views are taken from slowly moving objects, the HPO stereogram can display this motion by linking it to the parallax recording. Animated HSs can be also produced by sacrificing the vertical parallax to encode the motion of the object [26].

In the first produced HPO HS [27] the distance between the plane of perspective images capture and the tracking camera should correspond to the distance between the projection screen and the hologram plane. To view a non-distorted image produced by such a HPO HS the viewer eyes should coincide with the elemental holograms. To alleviate this requirement a two-step recording process has been invented in which the recorded HS becomes a master for optical transfer by using a phase conjugated illumination source into a second HS which is recorded to allow a more convenient viewing distance. One can spare the two-step recording process by creating pre-distorted images in the computer from the directional information encoded in the perspective images; thus the so called Ultragram HPO stereogram was invented [28, 29]. A variety of different methods has been developed for composing a HS. However, independently of the method, the HS can be considered as an array of Fourier transformed perspective images of the scene. Thus, the HS exhibits only one phase term which is related to direction of propagation [30]. Following the description of diffractive properties of a HS given in [31], the perspective images are composed from pixels (picture elements) which send light with equal intensity in all directions. The stereograms encode directional information. They can be composed by direls (directional elements) which emit a spherical wave with a controllable amount of intensity in each direction or from hogels (holographic elements) in the case of HS which emit a set of plane waves with controllable intensity in different directions [32]. In order to ensure an accommodation and to improve a smooth motion parallax presentation in HSs a wafel (wavefront element) is introduced in [31] that send a controllable intensity of light with a controllable wavefront curvature in each direction. The HS composed from wafels is called Panoramagram [31].

The modern digital holographic printers, based on the HS principle, ensure an automated one-step printing process to produce full-color full parallax output which is viewable under white light illumination. The main steps of the printing process include i) acquisition of the perspective images; ii) post-processing of the acquired images to form parallax-related images for distortion free reconstruction; iii) holographic recording of the elemental holograms. The principle of HS printing is schematically depicted in Figure 2 for the case of a full parallax hologram adopting the optical scheme of the holographic printer proposed in [12, 13]. The authors coined a name a multidot recording method for the proposed technique. The parallax-related image, composed from information taken from different perspectives, is displayed by means of a SLM. The SLM can be transparent or reflective liquid crystal display (LCD) [33] or digital micro-mirror device (DMD) [34]. Holographic recording corresponds to a Denisyuk type reflection hologram. The illuminating coherent light beam from a laser source is split into mutually coherent object and reference beams. The object beam illuminates the image displayed on the SLM. It is focused by a high numeric aperture lens on the exposed area of the hologram plate that comprises the elemental hologram. The other names have been introduced for the elemental holograms as hogels [32] or holopixels [35]. In this chapter we adopt the name hogel. The hologram plate is positioned close to the focal plane of the lens. To improve the illumination conditions on the hologram plate, a diffuser can be introduced in the object beam [6, 36, 37]. Exposure of the remaining part of the hologram is prevented by using a masking plate. The reference beam illuminates the exposed area from the opposite side to form a thick reflection hologram in the photo-sensitive layer of the plate. The light is reflected from the hologram in accordance with Bragg's diffraction which makes possible reconstruction under white light illumination. A full color HS can be recorded onto a panchromatic recording material with three lasers which emit at the wavelengths of the primary colors [38]. The lasers emit in a longitudinal mode and provide a beam with a TEM00 spatial structure. In some set-ups there is a masking plate with an aperture size equal to the hogel size between the light-sensitive layer and the reference beam. The hologram plate is sequentially translated in the horizontal and vertical planes with a X-Y stage until its whole surface is exposed. Thus both horizontal and vertical parallaxes can be recorded. Exposure time of each hogel and translation of the holographic plate are controlled by computer. The hogel encodes the directional information and intensity which comes from all points of the 3D scene to be imaged. This directional information varies with the location of the hogel in the hologram plane. When illuminated, the hogel creates an image of a small color patch with a given intensity for a certain viewing direction. The color patches reconstructed by all hogels in a given direction form one of the acquired perspective images. The reconstructed perspective image changes with the change in viewer's position. The acquisition and post-processing of the perspective images can be entirely separated in space and time from the holographic recording. The hogel encodes information from a large number of pixels which correspond to the number of perspective images.

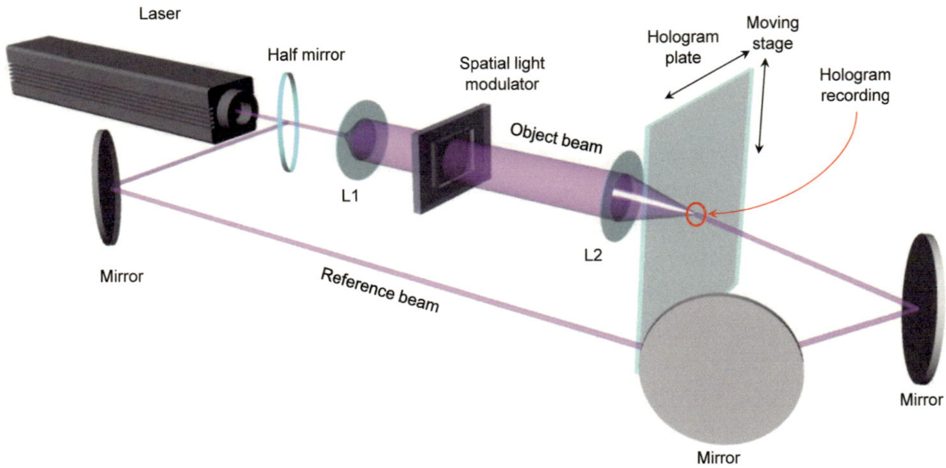

Figure 2. Schematic of the holographic stereogram printer.

Different improvements of this classical scheme for printing HSs have been proposed. The multidot printing method in [13] has been extended for printing HS of a rainbow hologram type and multicolor HS [39] as well as for 3D imaging by using a specially designed holographic screen and a transparency printed by a laser printer with a parallax information [40]. Taking in view the difficulty to obtain recording with a high diffraction efficiency in the Fourier plane of the lens due to the relatively narrow spectrum carried by the object beam, pseudo-random diffusers have been invented independently by [36, 41]. An ordinary ground glass diffuser spreads the light outside the hogel both in horizontal and vertical directions. This causes a light loss and hence entails increasing of exposure time. In addition, for HPO stereograms such a diffuser may worsen the image quality in vertical direction. A digitally designed pseudo-random band-limited diffuser in the object beam path improves uniformity of illumination of the hogel [41]. Two holographic diffusers, which can redirect up to 100% of the falling light, are proposed in [37] to be used with HPO stereograms. The first one is manufactured by recording a hologram of the strip diffuser. The second type is produced by recording a HPO stereogram of a rectangular point diffuser. The holographic diffuser is mounted in a close contact with the SLM to project the real image of the diffuser on the hogel. In the second case a multiple-point holographic diffuser is reconstructed. In [14] a special lens is introduced in the path of the object beam close to the holographic plate to control the HS resolution. The same authors also proposed to replace the masking plate by a specially designed holographic optical element which acts as a variable band-limiting diffuser that redirects the object beam to uniformly illuminate only the area of the hogel. The latter together with a changeable reference beam masking plate allows to record hogels of variable size. The proposed printer can be also used for production of animated stereograms. A special system of an aperture and a 2D microlens array is used in Geola printers [35] to form hogels or holopixels of variable size and shape. HS technology is applied in Zebra Imaging [42] in USA using DuPont photopolymers, 3D Holoprint [43] in France using Ultimate' silver halide materials, Inline holography Inc. in Canada and others. A holographic printer which produces an animated HS in vertical direction with preserving the full parallax information in the horizontal direction is proposed and tested in [44]. The animation effect is observed by scrolling the hologram in vertical direction. The holographic printers developed and patented by Geola [15,16] are fully described in [18,35]. The color HSs can be recorded by using a multiple exposure method [45] or primary color mosaic method. In the first method the beams from the RGB lasers are combined to form a single beam and expose simultaneously each hogel. The quality of the recording depends on the dynamic range of the photo-sensitive material [38]. The main disadvantage of this method is the cross-talk between the separate color channels [46]. In the second method a space division of exposures for the primary colors is applied which, however, decreases three times the diffracted intensity. A method of color management for a full-color holographic 3D printer for HSs under RGB lasers illumination is proposed in [47] through the spectral measurement of the reconstructed light. Different hogel sizes have been reported from 0.4 mm × 0.4 mm up to > 2 mm × 2 mm in [18] and 0.2 mm × 0.2 mm in [47]. Decrease of the hogel size to make it comparable to the pixel size of the digital displays entails rise in printing time. To speed the recording process more powerful CW lasers and SLMs with higher refreshing rate should be used. Pulsed lasers are more suitable for this task from the point of view of stability of the printing system. Parallel exposure of several hogels is tested in [48].

2.2. Acquisition and post-processing of perspective images

Acquisition of the perspective images needs a tracking camera or modeling by a computer using different rendering methods. It is also possible to combine captured images with digitally rendered. The images are further processed to be recorded as hogels. At proper acquisition of the perspective images the HS can provide the viewer with an animated image. Image acquisition for the case of a HPO is shown in Figure 3(a), where the camera takes images along the horizontal axis only, and no acquisition is made along the vertical axis. The main advantage is a strongly alleviated requirement for the number of the required 2D images at the expense of viewer's eyes location only in the horizontal plane. The capture procedure for a full parallax HS is shown in Figure 3(b), where the camera takes images along both horizontal and vertical axes. The number of the acquired images is squared which is the most essential drawback of this approach. The nowadays HSs, printed by the modern holographic printers, can boast with size up to 1 m × 1.5 m and field of view (FOV) about 100 degrees [18]. The recent advances in laser technique, computers and SLMs make possible fabrication of HSs with a very high spatial resolution. This entails capture or modeling of thousands of perspective images. For real-life scenes these images should be acquired for a short time on the order of a few seconds.

In the dawn of the holographic printing, the systems for capture of perspective images comprised a camera facing an object which was placed on a rotating stage [7]. Such a system introduced a keystone distortion in the captured images, but this distortion was considered as a minor drawback because of the low quality of the printing itself. Later, two methods for acquisition of perspective images were developed as the simple camera method and the recentering camera method [27]. The simple camera method provides the simplest geometry for acquisition and rendering due to the invariable FOV of the camera during the capture process, as is shown in Figure 4. The forward facing camera, preferably with a large FOV, captures perspective images, while being translated equidistantly along the horizontal (or vertical) axis. The leftmost camera C_{LM} and rightmost camera C_{RM} take images, which are shown in Figure 5. The acquired images give different perspective representation of the object. The shortcoming of the simple camera method is that the object in the images is surrounded by a large non-informative area, and the number of pixels used for object representation is reduced leading to possible decrease of resolution too. Thus, the simplicity of rendering of the simple camera method is counter-balanced by worsened resolution and unavoidable non-informative area in the images. In addition, the camera with a large CCD is required and the lens of the camera should obligatory have a large FOV which may introduce severe distortions in the captured images.

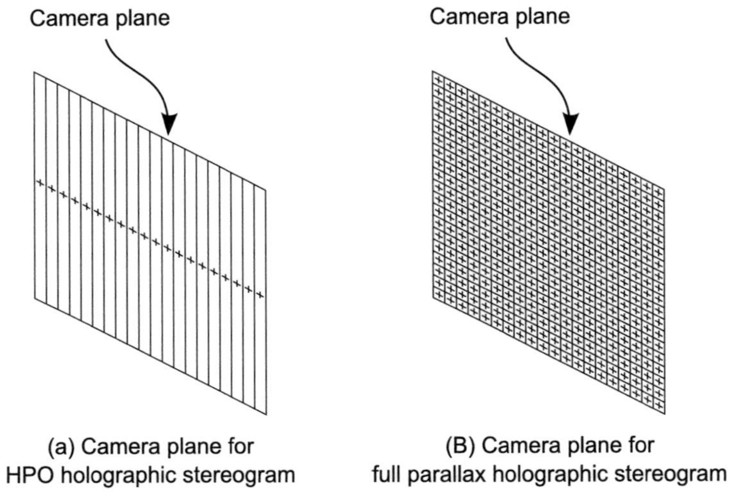

Figure 3. Acquisition of perspective images for a holographic stereogram.

The main drawback of the simple camera method is removed by a recentering camera method, whose acquisition geometry is shown in Figure 6. It is similar to the simple camera capture of the perspective images along the horizontal axis at equidistant intervals, but in this case the camera is provided with a recentering camera configuration to position the acquired objects in the center of the images. The acquired images by the recentering camera in the leftmost and rightmost positions in Figure 6 are presented in Figure 7(a) and (b). The non-informative area is reduced. Although implementation of this approach is more complicated, it enables taking higher resolution images. The figures depict translation only along the horizontal axis; generalization to translation in the vertical plane is straightforward. The recentering camera method is a good model to be used for computer generation of the perspective images. However, for capture of real-time scenes this method requires sophisticated expensive equipment and puts severe demands on the speed of the movement of the CCD array inside the camera. The required lens with a large FOV may also distort the captured images.

An effective solution for improvement of image acquisition while keeping the advantage of a simple camera method rendering has been recently proposed [49]. In the proposed solution the camera with an ordinary FOV rotates while being translated. The captured image is undistorted in a vertical plane which is normal to the central ray passing through the camera, but it is distorted in a plane parallel to the hologram plane. That's why the proposed image capture is a two-stage process. The sequence of the captured images is further preprocessed to transform them into images corresponding to a virtual forward-facing non-rotatable camera with a substantially wider FOV as if it is translating along a rail. The second sequence of images is used to compose the HS. The transformation procedure and the interpolation algorithm developed to decrease the noise which may be introduced by the pixel swapping transformations are thoroughly patented [49].

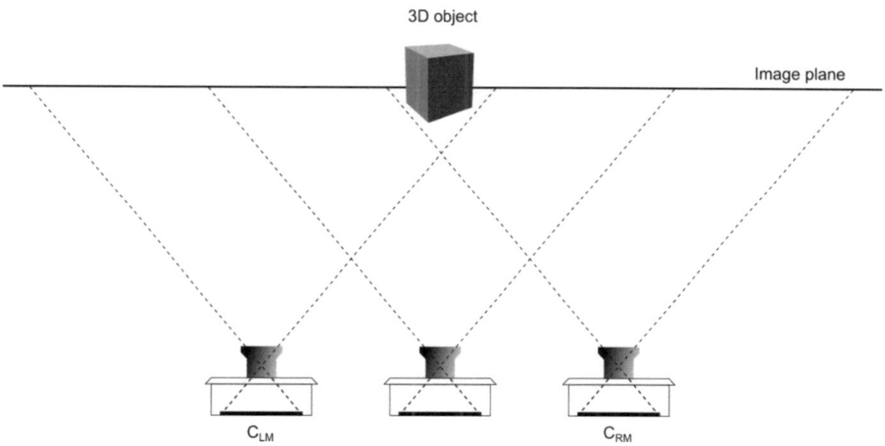

Figure 4. Simple camera method.

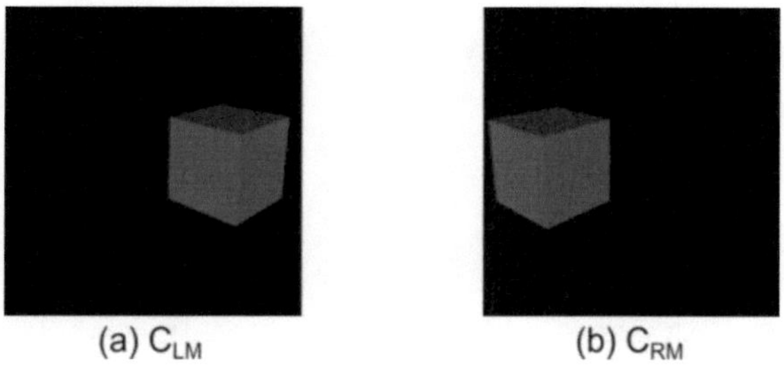

Figure 5. Image capture by the simple camera method.

To view distortion-free reconstruction comparatively far from the hologram [27], perspective images should be rearranged to form the separate parallax or "hogel" images corresponding to different hogels in the hologram plane, as it is shown in Figure 8. Both perspective and hogel images are 2D arrays with, in general, different dimensions. The perspective images

P_{kl}, $k=1..n$, $l=1..m$, compose a stack Φ of $n \times m$ images, where n and m are the number of images captured in horizontal and vertical directions, and k and l are indices which give the camera position at image capture in 1D or 2D grid in Figure 3. Each perspective image consists of $N \times M$ pixels. The size of the hogel images is $n \times m$ whereas their number is given by $N \times M$. The pixels in the hogel images are arranged in the order of capture of perspective images along horizontal and vertical axes. The hogel image h_{ij} is composed from (*i,j*)-th pixels in all perspective images in Φ as follows:

$$h_{ij}(k,l) = P_{kl}(i,j), k = 1..n, l = 1..m; i = 1..N, j = 1..M \tag{1}$$

The hogel image h_{ij} is displayed on a SLM and recorded in a focal plane of a lens as an elemental hologram by means of a reference beam in the (*i,j*)-th hogel in the hologram.

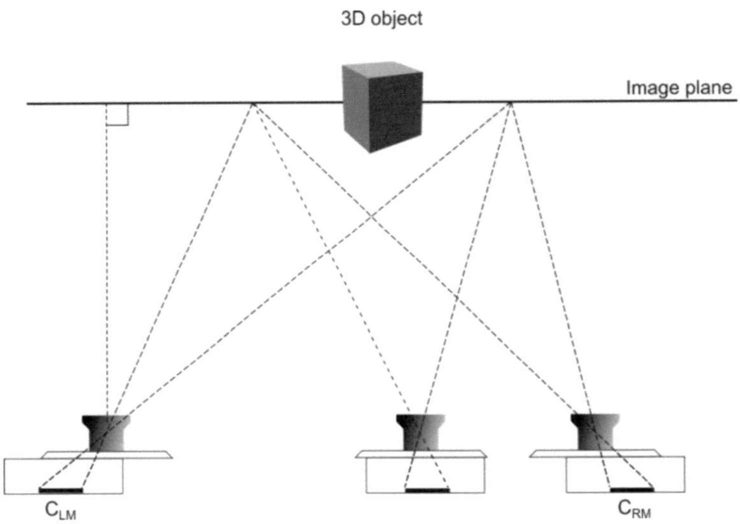

Figure 6. Recentering camera method.

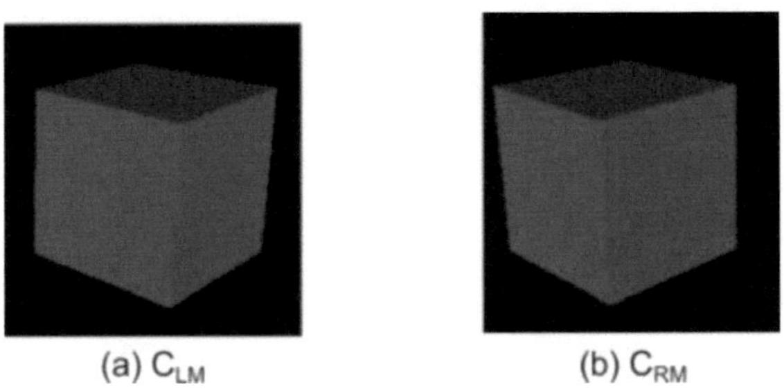

Figure 7. Image capture with the recentering camera.

http://dx.doi.org/10.5772/53412

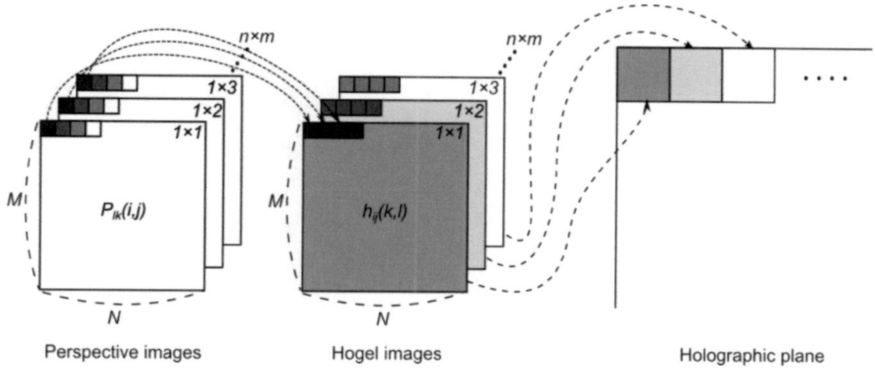

Figure 8. Rearrangement of perspective images into hogel images.

2.3. Distortions deteriorating the reconstructed image

The light modulated by the hogel image displayed on the SLM passes through optical components, such as objective or telecentric lenses, which may cause radial distortion [50]. As shown in Figure 9, the radial distortion can be categorized by two ways - a pincushion distortion and a barrel distortion. In the case of an "ideal" optical system the hogel image is recorded without any distortion, and it shows uniform angular intensity distribution within a FOV. When the hogel image is recorded with pincushion distortion, the angular intensity distribution is dense at the center and sparse at the edges of the viewing zone, and vice versa in the case of barrel distortion. Figure 10 depicts angular distributions corresponding to different distortions. The distortions cause changes in direction and range of the angular intensity distribution of the hogel image, which means the observer will see a distorted image. Figure 11 shows the shifted position of the observer by radial distortion. The radial distortion is given by

$$X_u = X_d\left(1 + kr_d^2\right),\ Y_u = Y_d\left(1 + kr_d^2\right),\ r_d = \sqrt{X_d^2 + Y_d^2} \tag{2}$$

where X_u and Y_u give the original position of the pixel, X_d and Y_d correspond to the shifted position of the pixel due to the radial distortion, r_d is the radius of the radial distortion, and k is a distortion coefficient.

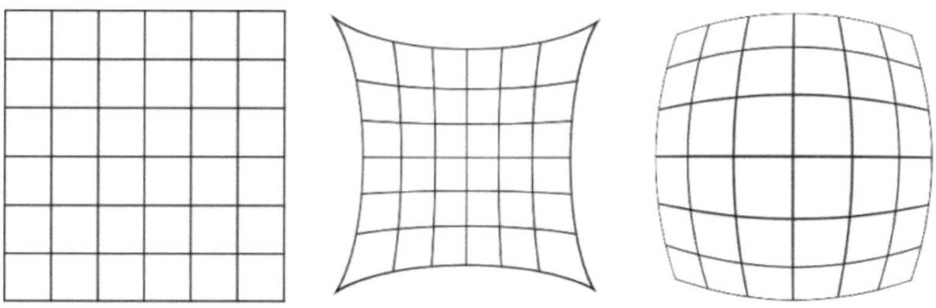

Figure 9. Examples of radial distortion: (a) none distortion, (b) pincushion distortion, (c) barrel distortion.

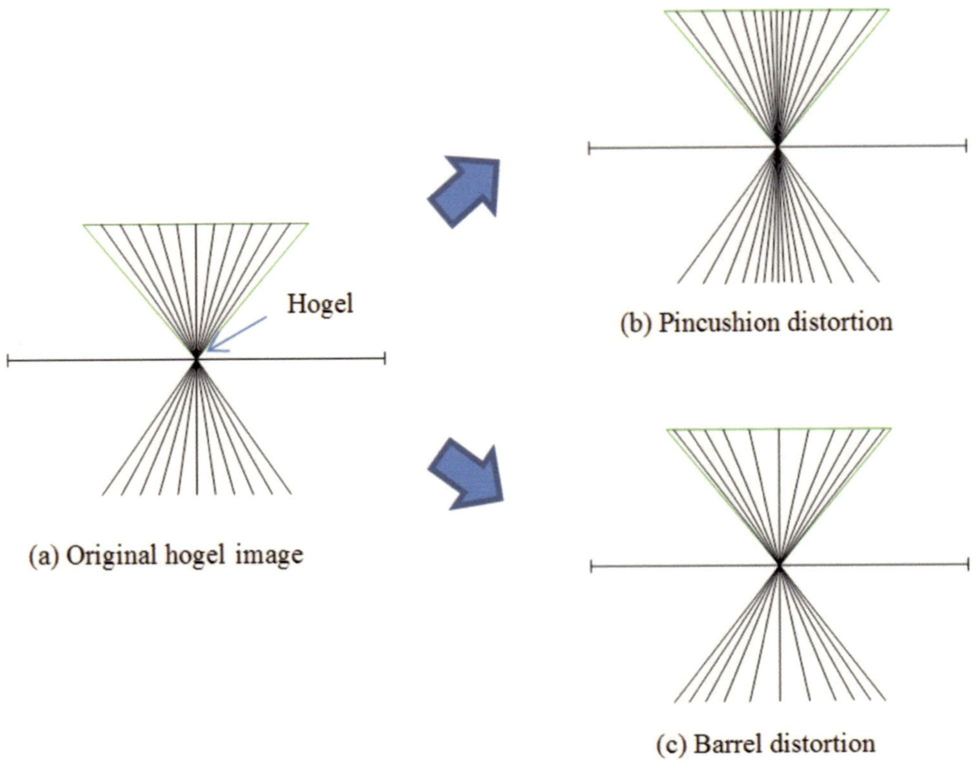

Figure 10. Angular distributions of rays at different radial distortions.

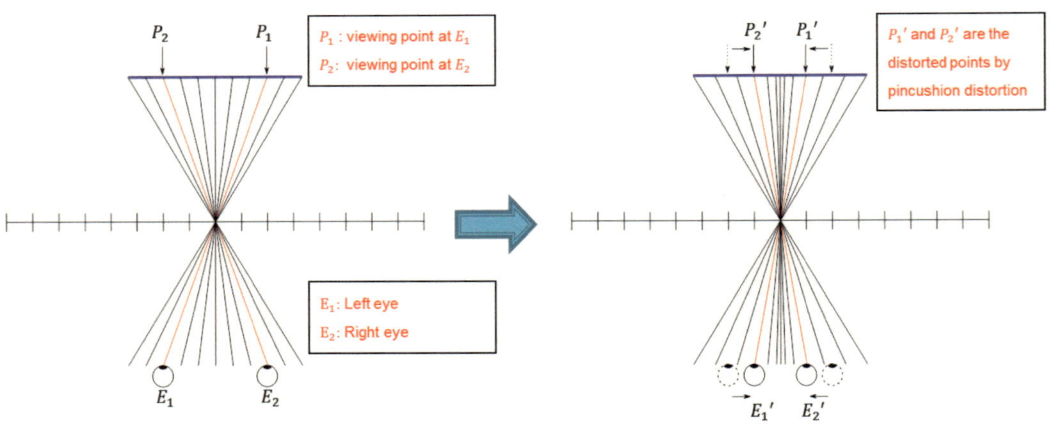

Figure 11. Movement of viewing point by pincushion distortion.

The pixelated structure of the HS and the way of building the reconstructed 3D image make them discrete imaging systems which can exhibit aliasing artifacts. The HS is characterized with an angular sampling and spatial sampling of the reconstructed image. Both sampling rates are related. Angular spectrum depends on the spectrum of the object to be imaged and is determined by the SLM parameters. In the holographic plane the sampling is given by the size of the hogel. The view-based analysis which is usually applied to HSs is an effective tool to predict forming of the 3D images but it is not always capable to explain their distortions. The study of these distortions needs to apply both wavefront analysis and sampling theory [24,27]. The wavefront analysis is based on the incoherent imaging. Analysis of image artifacts of HPO HSs based on imaging of a single point which creates a spherical wavefront is made in [24]. To the contrast with a hologram, the HS creates piecewise approximations to the wavefronts of the spherical waves emitted by the object's points. If the size of the hogel is too large the piecewise approximation is undersampled which results in visual artifacts as e.g. jumping of the reconstructed image when the viewer is moving along the HS. Quantization of the wavefront introduces phase errors. They are due to the fact that a wavefront from a point with an arbitrary depth is reconstructed as a wavefront of a point localized in the image plane of the HS. For a point which is located in front of the image plane of the HS the segmented wavefront has a less curvature than the real one and vice versa for a point behind the image plane. In [51,52] an expression for the optical transfer function of the HPO HS is derived which relates together the size of the hogels, the depth of the imaged scene and the resolution of the reconstructed image. The modulation transfer function falls rapidly with the spatial frequency for hogel sizes below 1 mm [52] which shows that some optimum size should be found to preserve the good quality of the reconstructed images. The optimum hogel size depends on the requirements of the human visual system, viewing distance, object depth and proper sampling of perspectives in the viewing angle. The hogel size should ensure smooth perception of the motion parallax and smooth spatial reconstruction of images. These are to a certain degree contradictory requirements. The decrease of the hogel size inevitably leads to lower number of reproduced directions due to the diffraction limit. Measurement of the angular resolution of diffracted light for a full-color HS was undertaken in [53] with sizes of the elemental hologram varying from 50μ m× 50 μm up to 400μ m × 400 μm. It is shown that the size 50μ m× 50 μm provides angular resolution of 1.08 deg., which can satisfy the angular resolution required by the human visual system.

2.4. Simulation of reconstruction of full-parallax holographic stereograms

Despite the progress made in the recent years, the holographic printing of large format digital holograms is expensive and in most of the cases time consuming undertaking. Separated by location and time capture and holographic recording require replaying of the composed HS by computer. In other words, to have freedom during the design process one should be able to check the quality of reconstruction from the designed HS by simulation before it is fed to the actual physical device. This makes development of appropriate simulation tools a pressing task. Software for obtaining a preview for a HPO HS produced from a web camera video stream is reported in [54].

The viewer perceives intensity provided by all printed hogels within the angular intensity distribution related to the particular viewer location. Each hogel encodes angular distribution of intensity corresponding to a certain small part of the visualized 3D object or scene when this part is viewed from multiple angles. The inputs from different hogels come from different pixels of the corresponding hogel images, as is depicted in Figure 12. For convenience, we derive the simulation algorithm for a single horizontal line of the hologram which is oriented along the X axis. Derivation of the algorithm for the whole hologram is straightforward. We assume that the viewing point $E(x, z)$ is located at a certain observation distance, D, from the hologram plane (Figure 12a). The Z axis points to a virtual observation plane (image plane) which is parallel to the hologram and contains the overlapping inputs from all hogels. The virtual observation plane is also located at distance D from the hologram plane. Let us consider the input to the viewer from a given hogel on the hologram plane. The size of the hogel is so small in comparison to the distance D that we can consider it as a point which creates angular distribution of intensities in the virtual observation plane, as it is shown in Figure 12b. The input from the hogel is determined by the angle, θ, corresponding to the line which passes through the viewer location and the hogel. We choose the hogel position as an origin of the (X, Z) coordinate system. From the point $E(x,z)$ the viewer gets the intensity from the point P in the cross-section of the virtual observation plane with the angular spread of intensities provided by the hogel. The value of this intensity is found from the hogel image pixel which encodes the direction given by θ. We introduce an auxiliary axis ξ in the observation plane that is parallel to the X-axis. The width of the patch in the observation plane with intensity input from this hogel is calculated by

$$W = 2D\tan\left(\frac{\phi}{2}\right) \tag{3}$$

where φ is the angle which gives the spread of the angular intensity distribution attached to the hogel. The sampling step, $\Delta\xi$, of the intensity values distribution in the observation plane is given by $\Delta\xi = W/n$, where n is the number of samples of the intensity distribution encoded in the hogel along a single row. The index of the pixel, n_P, which encodes the intensity at point P is determined by

$$n_P = \mathrm{I}\left\{\frac{W/2 + \xi_P}{\Delta\xi}\right\} \tag{4}$$

where ξ_P is the coordinate of P, and $I\{\}$ is an operator which takes the closest integer value of the expression in the brackets. Since the sampling step, $\Delta\xi$, is constant in the virtual observation plane, the uncertainty in estimation of direction of the hogel input varies along the auxiliary axis, ξ. It is maximum at the center of the hogel at $x = 0$, where it is approximately equal to $2\tan(\phi/2)/n$ radians, and decreases to its ends becoming $\approx 2\sin(\phi/2)/n$. Actually, $|\xi_P|$ is the distance from the point at which the normal from $E(x, z)$ to the hologram intersects its plane. Thus, for an arbitrary viewer location one easily calculates the resulting intensity of rays coming from all hogels at a given point of the virtual observation plane, which makes the numerical reconstruction of the HS for any location of the viewer feasible.

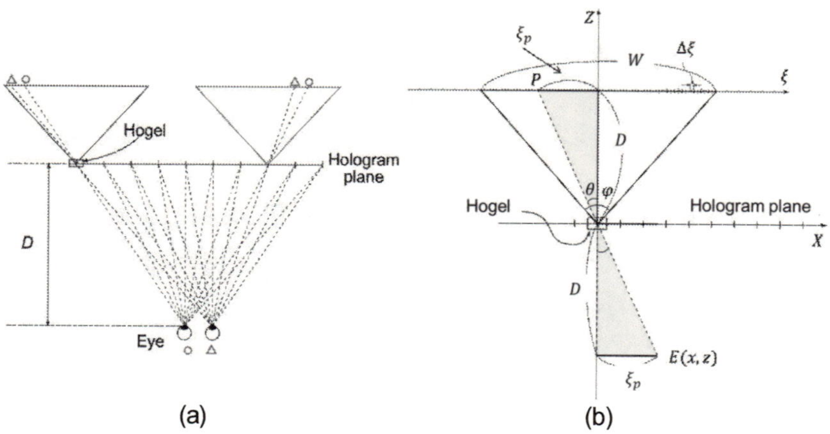

Figure 12. a) Geometric relation between the viewer and the hologram plane, (b) intensity input from a hogel to the viewer's location.

Figure 13. a) Perspective images from different views, (b) example of a hogel image.

To check the developed approach, we made simulation of all steps involved in the synthesis of a HS with its further numerical reconstruction. We assumed that hologram plane was composed from 100× 100 hogels and each hogel image consisted of 100× 100 pixels, which means that capture of 10,000 perspective images of a 3D object was simulated by using computer. In this test, we used a computer simulated 3D scene. The perspective images were rearranged to form 10,000 hogel images. The perspective images were captured by the recentering camera method, and some of them are shown in Figure 13(a). For illustration, examples of the composed hogel images are presented in Figure 13(b). The generated 10,000 hogel images were used as an input data for numerical reconstructions of the holographic stereogram which was supposed to be recorded. The numerical reconstructions for some arbitrary viewer's locations along the horizontal and vertical directions are shown in Figure 14. The good quality of reconstruction from the synthesized stereogram is obvious.

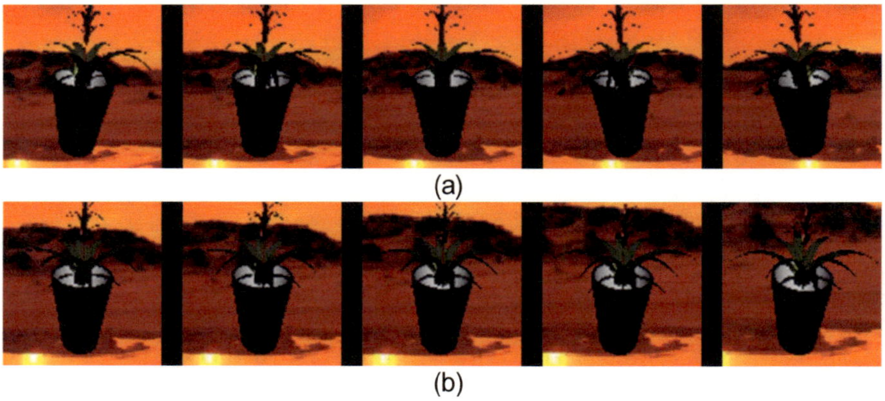

Figure 14. a) Numerical reconstruction results at 500 mm (angle interval 10 degree), (b) numerical reconstruction results at fixed *X* and *Y* coordinates.

2.5. Hardware issues and light-sensitive materials

To illustrate in practice printing of HSs we give the description of the developed by us holographic printer (Figure 15). The specifications of the main system's components are given in Table 1. The beam from a laser emitting at 532 nm is divided by the first polarizing beam splitter (PBS) into two optical paths, and the intensity ratio of two beams can be adjusted by a half-wave plate. The laser beam which passes through the PBS1 is the reference beam, whereas the other one reflected by the PBS1 is the object beam. The object beam is expanded by two lenses, L1 and L2, and illuminates the amplitude type SLM by using the PBS2. The beam is spatially modulated by the hogel image which is fed to the SLM as a bmp file. The modulated beam is focused onto the holographic emulsion by the lens, L3. The reference beam is also expanded by two lenses L4 and L5, in order to provide a beam width, which covers the hogel in the hologram. The reference beam impinges the holographic plate at 45 degrees. The interference pattern produced by the object beam and the reference beam in the holographic emulsion is recorded as a volume hologram. The holographic plate is moved by a X-Y stage along horizontal and vertical axes at a given spatial step, which coincides with the hogel size. Through such a procedure, each hogel is recorded at the desired hogel position. The shutter controls the exposure time of the hologram which is a product of the material's sensitivity and the laser power. The accuracy of the shutter is crucial. The time sequence of shutter operation is shown in Figure 16. The shutter goes into an open state after the shift of the X-Y stage, the time, required for the system to settle and for loading the hogel image on the SLM. The X-Y stage coordinates the shift of the optical header. The moving precision of the device is about 1 μm. Typically the stage can be driven by two types of motors: i) a step motor which is cheap and easy to handle but with a lower precision; ii) a linear motor which is more complicated and expensive but with higher precision. We use a step motor in our set-up. Due to the advances in modern computers and software a personal computer can be used as a holographic printer controller. However, it is still recommendable to use a microprocessor for a high-speed and real-time system.

http://dx.doi.org/10.5772/53412

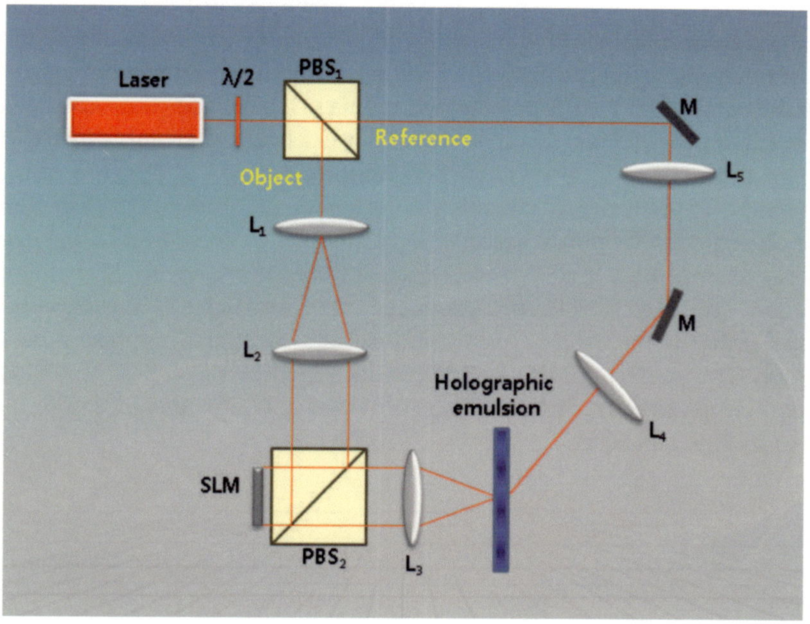

Figure 15. Schematic of the holographic printer.

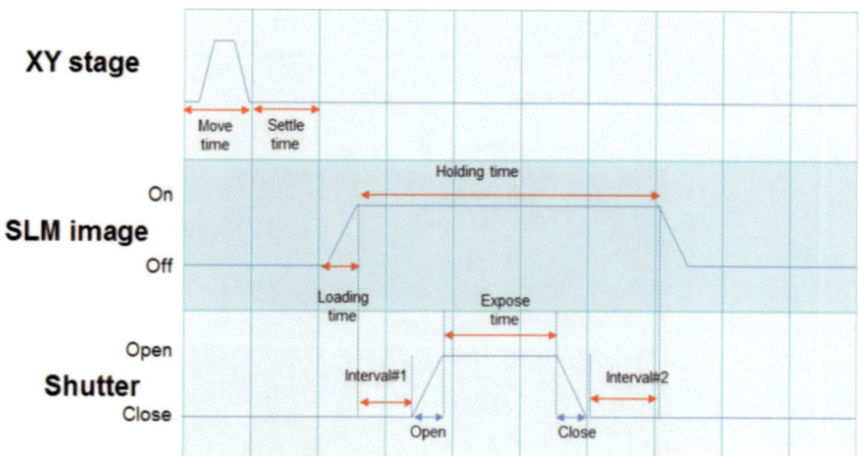

Figure 16. Time sequence of shutter operation.

Production of stable reproducible hard-copies by a holographic printing, based on recording of volume holograms, requires reliable medium for permanent multicolor (RGB) holographic recording with high diffraction efficiency, sensitivity, resolution and signal-to-noise ratio across the visible region. The dichromate gelatin, photopolymers and silver halide provide parameters close to the requirements [55]. The non-satisfactory spectral response and low sensitivity of the dichromate gelatin exclude it from the list of candidates despite its low losses and high diffraction efficiency. The photopolymers, in which the phase modulation is formed due to photoinduced changes, allow simple rapid processing and practically 100% diffraction efficiency, but they still exhibit comparatively low sensitivity, resolution and dynamic range. The silver halide emulsions are discrete carriers media in which recording occurs in nano-sized particles dispersed in a carrying gelatin matrix. They can boast with high sensitivity in a broad spectral range, diffraction efficiency of 80-98%, high resolution and dynamic range as well as long-term storage [55]. The drawback of the silver-halide emulsions is the low signal to noise ratio in the blue spectral region due to the light scattering. Recording of volume reflection holograms needs resolution > 6000 mm^{-1} which is realized only with ultra-fine-grain silver halide materials. The materials PFG-03C produced by the firm Slavich, Russia [35, 56] has about 12 nm size of initial silver halide crystals and exhibit low signal-to-noise ratio in the blue spectral region. The scattering in this region is decreased by nanosized emulsions with the average grain size about 8 nm. Such quality is provided in Ultimate holographic plates [57] or in the plates HP-P [55], Bulgaria.

SLM	Type	Amplitude type (liquid crystal on silicon)
Number of pixels	1920 × 1080 pixels	
Pixel interval	7 µm	
Laser	Power	100 mW
	Wavelength	532 nm
Holographic emulsion	Emulsion	ULTIMATE-08
	Grain size	8 nm

Table 1. Specifications of the holographic printer

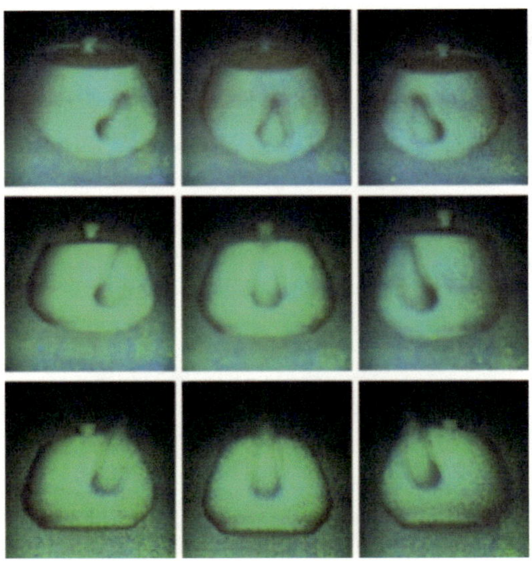

Figure 17. Optical reconstruction from a printed holographic stereogram along the horizontal and vertical directions.

http://dx.doi.org/10.5772/53412

We used in our printer system the Ultimate 08 emulsion with exposure 200 μJ/cm². We summarized the specifications of this emulsion in Table 2 [57]. The typical exposure time of this emulsion for He-Ne laser varies from 4-5 s at 5 mW power and 6.1 cm × 6.1 cm size of the holographic plate to 30-40 s at 25 mW for a 30 cm × 40 cm plate. Developing time is about 6 minutes at 20 C° - 25°C, and a bleaching agent is also used. The calculated hogel images were expanded 10 times before being applied to the SLM. Thus, a matrix of hogels is formed in a hologram plane. Figure 17 presents the photos taken from different locations of the image reconstructed at white light illumination from the HS of a computer graphic model of a teapot.

Emulsion	Application	Sensitivity (uJ/cm²)	Grain size (nm)/ Resolution (lines/mm)	Lasers	Lifetime (at 4°C)
Ultimate 08-mono-chrome	For transmission and reflection holograms	150-200	8/10000	Continuous and pulsed: all colors	> 2 years
Ultimate 08-color	For reflection holograms (RGB)	120-150/ color	8/10000	Continuous : R+G +B	> 2 years
Ultimate 15	For transmission and reflection holograms (RG)	75-100	15/7000	Continuous and pulsed : R+G	> 1 year
Ultimate 25	For transmission holograms (pulsed lasers), Brighter and much less noise, U25 needs more energy.	10-30	25/5000	Pulsed lasers: Ruby, YAG	> 2 years

Table 2. Ultimate hologram emulsion specification

3. Printing of holographic fringes

The white viewable HSs spatially multiplex 2D images and hence do not reconstruct a real 3D image. Computer-generated holograms (CGHs) based on modeling of a holographic interference pattern create a true 3D impact [58]. That's why a lot of efforts have been dedicated to printing of CGHs whose calculation is based on rigorous diffraction. Two problems must be overcome when solving this task – the time-consuming calculation of the fringe pattern and the requirement for high spatial resolution of the printer in order to ensure a large viewing angle. Increase in resolution entails rise in the computation time.

3.1. Methods for computer generation of holographic fringe patterns

A fast holographic fringe pattern generation algorithm is required for the wavefront printing. The Rayleigh-Sommerfeld (R-S) integral gives an exact fringe pattern corresponding to a desired object. The object is represented as a set of self-emitting points giving a light field with a complex amplitude which at the point (x, y) in the plane of the hologram is the sum of the spherical waves coming from all points of the object:

$$O(\xi, \eta) = \sum_{p=1}^{N} \frac{a_p}{r_p} \exp\left[j(kr_p + \varphi_p)\right], \quad r_p = \sqrt{(\xi - x_p)^2 + (\eta - y_p)^2 + z_p^2} \tag{5}$$

where (x_p, y_p, z_p) are the Cartesian coordinates of the object's point, a_p and φ_p are the amplitude and the phase of the light field emanated by this point, and r_p is the distance between this point and the point on the hologram; $k = 2\pi / \lambda$ is a wave number, λ is the wavelength. Since in the equation of the hologram intensity, $H = |O + R|^2$, where $R(\xi, \eta) = a_r \exp(j\varphi_r)$ is the reference wave with an amplitude a_r and phase φ_r, the only relevant term is $H = 2Re\{OR^*\}$, the so called bipolar intensity approach has been invented [32] that allows to calculate the fringe pattern

$$H_{bi}(\xi, \eta) = \sum_{p=1}^{N} \frac{a_p}{r_p} \cos(kr_p + \varphi_p + \varphi_r), \tag{6}$$

by using only the real numbers where we assume that $a_r = 1$. However, one of the substantial drawbacks of the R-S method is its quite high computational complexity. To overcome this bottleneck, different fast algorithms for implementation of (6) have been developed for flat holograms and more sophisticated geometries as a cylindrical or a disk hologram which provide an increased viewable area [59,60]. The fast algorithms for computer generation of cylindrical ordinary and rainbow holograms [61, 62], for generation of a master disk hologram [63] and image plane hologram [64] have been reported. Although these holograms are based on the same underlying optical principal, the associated computer generation algorithms undergo different modifications according to the characteristics of each hologram. A successful approach, especially for holographic printing, is the partitioning based algorithm for computer hologram generation. The hologram plane is divided into $M \times N$ multiple segments with $m \times n$ elements each, and a set of approximations to calculate the distance in (5) is applied to each segment. For example, the distance between the object and the hologram in the case of a cylindrical hologram is practically fixed and not large enough to use the Fresnel approximation. In this case the distance, r_p, is computed by means of two look-up tables which are composed for each segment in such a way as to give the distance between the object point and the point located along the vertical and horizontal central lines in the segment. To decrease the spatial frequency in the plane of the hologram, the computation is performed with a spherical reference wave in a Fourier lenless geometry when the reference point source is positioned close to the object and at the same distance from the hologram [61]. The same approach with two look-up tables has been applied for generation of the disk hologram [63]. For a rainbow hologram the computation is made for 1D hololine. Calculation of the image-plane hologram requires introduction of a small positive value in the denominator in (6) to avoid the high divergence of fringes for object points which are too close to the hologram plane [64,65]. In this case the sign of the phase of the object beam depends on which side of the hologram is the object's point. 360 degrees viewable hologram requires removal of hidden surfaces to ensure proper reconstruction of the object [66]. This problem is solved by forming the correct object data for generation of the hologram for different viewpoints. For the purpose, perspective images from different viewpoints are taken. The acquired intensity distributions are combined with the depth information provided by a computer graphics model to yield 3D coordinates, amplitudes and phases corresponding to all point sources that constitute the object.

There have been developed a series of algorithms such as phase-added stereogram (PAS) [30, 67], compensated phase-added stereogram (CPAS) [68, 69], accurate phase-added stereogram (APAS) [70], and accurate compensated phase-added stereogram (ACPAS) [71]. Although the ACPAS gives a better quality, still it has some unwanted noise which is due to the inaccurate numerical model. As an improved version, we propose a novel digital hologram generation algorithm which we call fast phase-added stereogram (FPAS). The numerical model of the FPAS is expressed as,

$$H_{FPAS}(\xi,\ \eta)=F^{-1}\{I(\upsilon,\ \nu)\}, \tag{7}$$

$$I(\upsilon,\ \nu)=\sum_{p=1}^{N}\frac{a_p}{r_p}\exp\left(jkr_p+\varphi_p\right)\exp\left\{j2\pi\left[\upsilon_p(\xi-x_p)+\nu_p(\eta-y_p)\right]\right\}, \tag{8}$$

where, $H(\xi,\ \eta)$is the holographic fringe pattern, $I(\upsilon,\ \nu)$is the spatial frequency distribution in the spatial frequency domain, p is the index of points, N is the number of points, $r_p$is given by (6), a_p is complex amplitude of the p-th point, $\exp\left(jkr_p\right)$ is the phase, and last term in the sum is a complex sinusoidal function. The spatial frequencies u_p and v_p are determined as

$$\upsilon_p=\frac{\sin\theta_{\xi p}-\sin\theta_{\xi\mathrm{ref}}}{\lambda},\qquad \nu_p=\frac{\sin\theta_{\eta p}-\sin\theta_{\eta\mathrm{ref}}}{\lambda}, \tag{9}$$

where, $\theta_{\xi p}$and $\theta_{\eta p}$ are the incident angles from the associated object point, and $\theta_{\xi\mathrm{ref}}$ and $\theta_{\eta\mathrm{ref}}$ are the illuminating angles of the reference wave forξ and ηaxes.

The geometry of the coherent stereogram calculation is shown in Figure 18. In the first step the hologram plane is partitioned into suitable square shape segments. The fringe pattern over each segment is approximated as a superposition of 2D complex sinusoids, where each such sinusoid approximates the contribution of each object point to the hologram pattern over one segment. Therefore, a spectrum associated with each segment is easily constructed by placing the amplitudes of complex sinusoids to correspond to frequency locations. The spatial frequencies associated with the contributions of points in a point cloud are quantized to a discrete domain by moving them to their nearest allowed discrete frequency value without changing their complex amplitudes. This modification is an additional source of distortion in the reconstruction. In the second step, the spectrum of a segment, that is composed of complex amplitudes of 2D complex sinusoids, is transformed by IFFT to convert the spectrum to the associated fringe pattern. This procedure is repeated for each segment to complete the computation. An arbitrary hologram function over one segment, representing the spatial coordinates in a plane, can be written as a superposition of harmonic functions. Each harmonic function is the inverse Fourier transform of a single impulse function which corresponds to a single object point with a complex amplitude. Due to the linearity of the Fourier transform, the IFFT of the spectrum of a segment, which is composed of contributions from all 3D object points, yields the hologram over that segment.

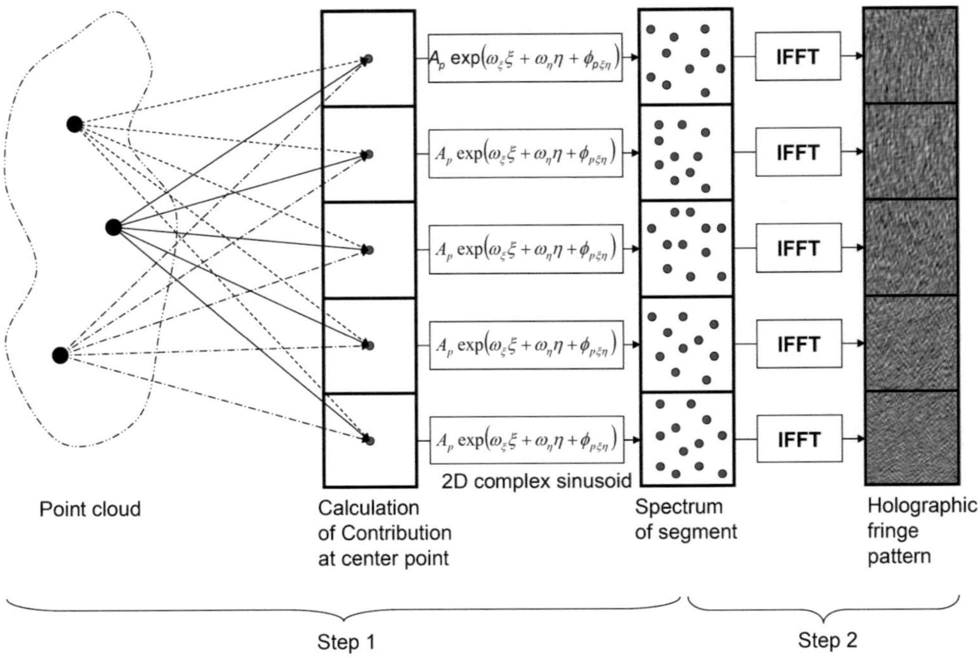

Figure 18. Geometry of fast phase-added stereogram calculation.

Three holographic fringe patterns generated by using R-S integral, ACPAS and FPAS algorithms corresponding to a single self-illuminating object are shown in Figure 19. For the ACPAS and the FPAS, the used segmentation size and FFT size are 4 × 4 pixels and 8 × 8 pixels, respectively. As shown in Figure 19, the R-S integral gives exact fringe pattern, and even at the initial phase difference about 68 degrees between Figure 19(a) and 19(c), the fringe pattern from the FPAS algorithm is comparable to the R-S fringe pattern. However Figure 19(b) which is generated by using ACPAS algorithm looks worse when compared to the fringe patterns obtained by the R-S integral and the FPAS algorithm. This means that fine phase matching cannot be done by the ACPAS algorithm. Contrary to the ACPAS, the numerical model of the FPAS is acceptable, and fine phase matching can be done by the exact phase distribution determination.

http://dx.doi.org/10.5772/53412

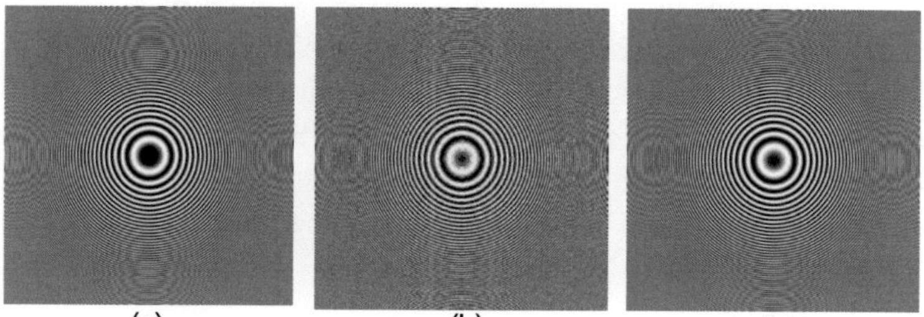

Figure 19. Generated holographic fringe patterns corresponding to a single self-illuminating object; (a) Rayleigh-Sommerfeld integral, (b) ACPAS, (c) FPAS.

3.2. Direct printing of fringes

Micro-processing techniques as e-beam writing or lithography, which provide excellent resolution and can be used for printing of holographic fringes, are too expensive for everyday use. This inspired development of low-cost fringe printers. Using of a laser printer for recording of a CGH is proposed in [72]. Printing of a CGH by using optical disk writing equipment is described in [73]. Printing of the fringe pattern by using a CD-R writer is proposed in [74, 75]. The printed hologram is reconstructed with a white light. Printing of the fringe pattern dot by dot of 3 μm in a diameter by scanning a laser spot on a holographic plate is reported in [76]. To increase the speed of printing the holographic film is placed on a rolling drum. A direct fringe printer in which a small part of the fringe pattern is displayed on a SLM and its demagnified version is recorded as a thin hologram is proposed in [21,22]. The demagnification on the order of 1/12 or 1/16 is achieved with a telecentric system of lenses. The SLM is illuminated with a laser light. In [62] a Nd:YAG+LBO DPSS laser emitting at 473 nm with power 5 mW is used. After the exposure the hologram is shifted with a highly accurate X-Y stage with a stepping motor. Precision of the X-Y stage is 4 μm. Resolution of the printed fringe pattern depends on the quality of optics used to transfer the image from the SLM onto the holographic film. A fringe pitch of 0.44 μm has been reported. The fringe printer was used for printing of a laser reconstructed cylindrical hologram with radius of 69.5 mm and pixel pitch 0.867 μm [61]. The produced CGH required 45 h computation time. The printer was used also for production of a computer generated master 360 degrees viewable portable disk hologram which was used for optical recording of a reflection hologram viewable with white light [63]. Recently, image-plane full-parallax hologram has been printed [64]. Fringe printing of an animated computer-generated cylindrical hologram which is calculated to show animation in horizontal direction is reported in [77].

3.3. Holographic recording of the wave-front diffracted from the fringes

The direct fringe printer records partitioned digital holographic fringe patterns into a holographic emulsion repeatedly in order to make a large SLM. Although the holographic fringe pattern is recorded into a holographic emulsion, it can be regarded as a thin hologram because it does not record the interference pattern with a reference wave. Due to such reasons, it should be reconstructed under laser illumination. A volume hologram printer is proposed in [78] which records an interference pattern with a reference wave of the optical reconstruction from the holographic fringe pattern displayed over an electrically addressed SLM. This method provides several advantages such as fine wavelength selectivity for reconstruction with a white light, manufacturing large hologram without large collimating system, fine full color hologram etc. as in the case of a conventional analog reflection hologram.

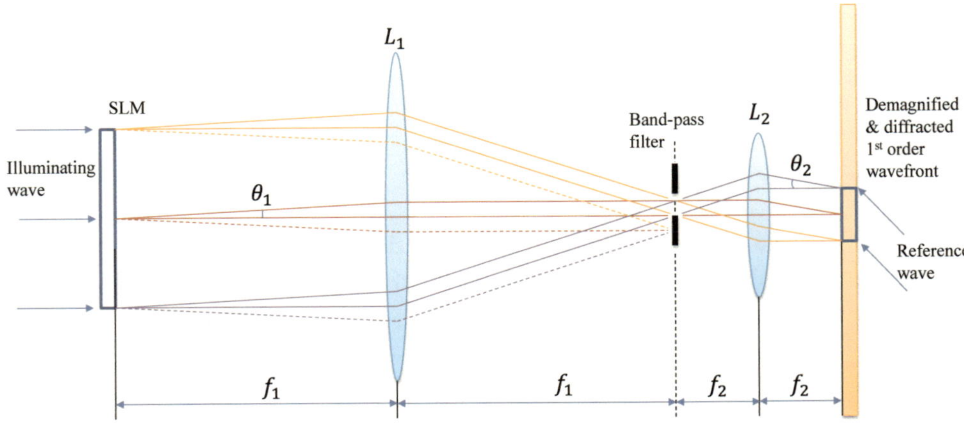

Figure 20. An optical schematic of a wavefront printer.

Below we describe the principle of the proposed by us wavefront printer for production of white-light viewable CGHs. In case of a conventional analog hologram, the scattered wave from a real object propagates to the holographic emulsion and interferes with an illuminating reference wave. The formed interference pattern is recorded as a hologram. In other words, the wavefront coming from the object is recorded onto the holographic emulsion. In the same way, the wavefront from a virtual object, which is generated by computer graphic tools, can be recorded by a wavefront printer. Actually, this is the only printer capable to record a wavefront coming from a virtual object and encoded as a CGH.

An optical schematic of a wavefront printer is shown in Fig. 20. A holographic fringe pattern generated by computer is displayed by a SLM, and an illuminating wave is diffracted by the SLM. The diffracted wave passes through the first lens, L_1. This wave is filtered by a band-pass filter which cuts off the undesired components such as the -1st order diffracted wave and non-diffracted wave. Therefore, only the desired 1st order diffracted wave goes through the filter, and is demagnified by the two lenses, L_1 and L_2. The demagnified wavefront interferes with an illuminating reference wave in a holographic emulsion placed at the focus of the lens L_2. The interference pattern is recorded as a holographic element. The fringe pattern on the SLM is updatable, and the recording location over the holographic emulsion is also changed accordingly. Therefore, the holographic fringe pattern corresponding to different hogel locations is recorded as a volume reflection hologram. Thus, a hologram is formed which encodes the wavefront of light coming from the object. The hologram can be reconstructed under white light illumination.

The hologram can be used also as a master hologram to make a transfer hologram by using the reference wave as that in the recording step for illumination of the whole area of the recorded master hologram as is shown in Figure 21. The holographic emulsion of the second hologram is placed at the location of the reconstructed image. The second hologram is illuminated with a reference wave. After recording of the second hologram, it can be reconstructed under white light illumination. Thus we can see a hologram with a naked eye. The optical reconstruction is shown in Figure 22. A virtual object, the logo of the Korea Electronics Technology Institute, is recorded digitally by the proposed wavefront printing technique, and the obtained hologram reconstructs the image like a conventional analog hologram under illumination with a point light source (a LED).

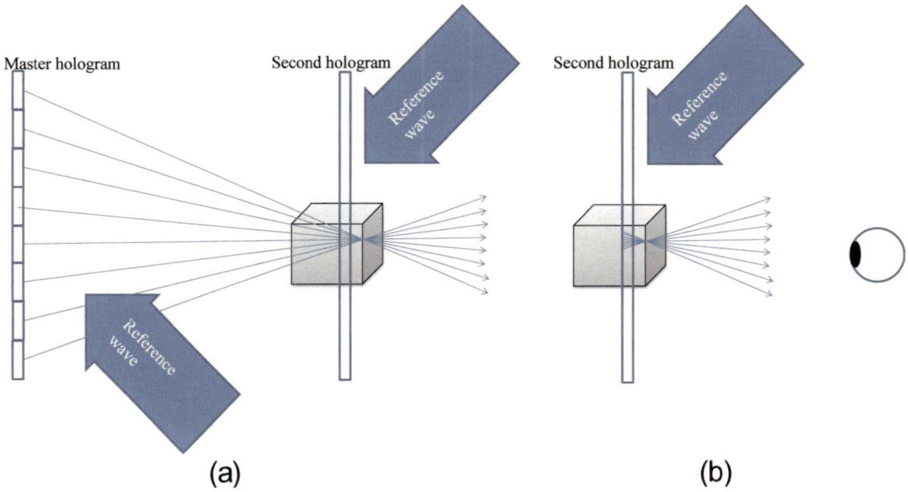

Figure 21. a) Recording schematic for second hologram, (b) holographic display.

Figure 22. The optical reconstruction of the second hologram.

4. Future trends

The holographic printer has the potential to be useful equipment for industry, medicine, cultural heritage protection, commerce and entertainment because of its capability to represent exact 3D space without any distortion and visual fatigues. However, although numerous attractive printed holograms have been created in the recent years, the market is still not populated with holographic printers due to some technical difficulties. There are a lot of unsolved issues which should be overcome. Among them, the most important are the time consuming holographic recording procedure, a rather bulky recording system with extremely high price and quality of the printed hologram. Generally, the frame per second (fps) rate of a conventional SLM is about 30 fps, therefore, a conventional holographic printer is able to record 30 hogels per one second. If a hogel size is 1 mm × 1 mm and a hologram place size is 1 M × 1 M, then the recording procedure will take approximately 10 hours. This issue might be a serious obstacle for market realization. The recording time can be reduced with a tuned mass damper or active vibration control, but this solution also has a limitation. The ultimate solution of the problem by using pulsed laser is, however, very expensive. High-end components such as SLMs with high frame rate, wide angle objectives, lasers with single longitudinal mode, lenses etc. are required to build a holographic printer. Moreover, such optical and electrical components are mounted on a vibration insulated optical table. For industrialization and commercialization, further improvement of the holographic printer is mandatory to facilitate its use in office and conventional places. The final issue is the quality of the printed hologram. In case of a holographic stereogram, multiple perspectives are used as an input data, and angular intensity distributions which are made using the multiple perspectives are recorded onto a holographic emulsion. Because the perspectives already have unwanted distortions from the used optics such as radial distortion, depth distortion etc. the represented 3D space is also distorted. This means that an observer may not be able to experience a true 3D perception even at properly encoded information about the 3D scene. The unsolved issues put a lot of challenges to be overcome in the near future to make the holographic printer a conventional equipment in our everyday life, industry, education, and cultural exchange.

Author details

Hoonjong Kang[1], Elena Stoykova[1,2*], Jiyung Park[1], Sunghee Hong[1] and Youngmin Kim[1]

*Address all correspondence to: e.stoykova@keti.re.kr

1 Broadcasting &ICT R&D Division, Korea Electronics Technology Institute, F8, Sangam-dong, Mapo-gu, Seoul, Korea

2 Institute of Optical Materials and Technologies, Bulgarian Academy of Sciences, Sofia, Bulgaria

References

[1] Gabor D, A new microscopic principle. Nature 1948;161: 777-778.

[2] Schnars U, Jueptner W. Direct recording of holograms by a CCD target and numerical reconstruction Applied Optics 1994; 33(2):179-181.

[3] Kreis T, editor. Handbook of holographic interferometry: Optical and Digital Methods, Wiley-VCH GmbH&Co.KGaA: Weinheim; 2006.

[4] Boyer K, Solem J, Longworth J, Borisov A, Rhodes C. Biomedical three-dimensional holographic microimaging at visible, ultraviolet and x-ray wavelengths, Nature medicine 1996; 2(8): 939-941.

[5] Pole RV. 3-D imagery and holograms of objects illuminated in white light. Applied Physics Letters 1967; 10(1): 20-22.

[6] De Bitetto D. Holographic panoramic stereograms synthesized from white light recordings. Applied Optics 1969; 8(8): 1740–1741.

[7] King M, Noll A, Berry D. A new approach to computer-generated holography. Applied Optics 1970; 9(2): 471-475.

[8] Benton S. Hologram reconstructions with extended incoherent sources. Journal of the Society of America 1969; 59(10): 1545-1546.

[9] Pizzanelli D. The development of direct-write digital holography. Proc. of 'Holography, Art and Design' Conference, Royal College of Art, London. (23 March 2002). http://www.holography.co.uk/events/eventindex.htm

[10] Yatagai T. Three-dimensional display using computer-generated holograms. Optics Communications 1974; 12(1): 43-45.

[11] Yatagai T. Stereoscopic approach to 3-D display using computer-generated holograms. Applied Optics 1976; 15(11): 2722-2729.

[12] Yamaguchi M, Ohyama N, Honda T. Holographic 3-D printer. Proc. SPIE 1990; 1212: 84-92.

[13] Yamaguchi M, Ohyama N, Honda T. Holographic three-dimensional printer: new method. Applied Optics 1992; 31(2): 217-222.

[14] Klug M, Holzbach M, Ferdman A. Method and apparatus for recording 1-step full color full parallax holographic stereograms. U.S. Patent 1998; No.US630088B1.

[15] Brotherton-Ratcliffe D, Vergnes F, Rodin A, Grichine M. Method and apparatus to print holograms. Lithuanian Patent 1999a; No.LT4842.

[16] Brotherton-Ratcliffe D, Vergnes F, Rodin A, Grichine M. Holographic Printer. U.S. Patent 1999b; No. US7800803B2.

[17] Rodin A, Vergnes FM, Brotherton-Ratcliffe D. Pulsed multiple colour laser. EU Patent 1236073; 2001.

[18] Brotherton-Ratcliffe D, Zacharovas S, Bakanas R, Pileckas J, Nikolskij A, Kuchin J. Digital holographic printing using pulsed RGB lasers. Optical Engineering 2011; 50(9): 091307-091307-9.

[19] Blanche PA, Bablumian A, Voorakaranam R, Christenson C, Lin W, Gu T, Flores D, Wang P, Hsieh WY, Kathaperumal M, Rachwal B, Siddiqui O, Thomas J, Norwood RA, Yamamoto M, Peyghambarian N. Holographic three-dimensional telepresence using large-area photorefractive polymer. Nature 2011;468: 80-83.

[20] Hahn J, Kim H, Lim Y, Park G, Lee B. Wide viewing angle dynamic holographic stereogram with a curved array of spatial light modulators. Optic Express 2008; 16(16): 12372-12386.

[21] Yoshikawa H, Takei K. Development of a compact direct fringe printer for computer-generated holograms. Proc. SPIE 2004; 5290: 114-121.

[22] Yoshikawa H, Tachinami M. Development of direct fringe printer for computer-generated holograms. Proc. SPIE 2005; 5742: 259-266.

[23] Benton S. Survey of holographic stereograms. Proc. SPIE 1983; 367: 15-19.

[24] Halle M. Holographic stereograms as discrete imaging systems. Proc. SPIE 1994; 2176: 73-84.

[25] Leith E, Voulgaris P. Multiplex holography: some new methods. Optical Engineering 1985; 24: 171-175.

[26] Aebischer N, Carquille B. White light holographic portraits (still or animated). Applied Optics 1978; 17(23): 3698-3700.

[27] Halle M. The Generalized holographic stereogram. PhD thesis. MIT Dept. of Electrical Engineering and Computer Science, Cambridge MA, USA; 1993.

[28] Halle M, Benton S, Klug M, Underkoffler J. The Ultragram: A Generalized Holographic Stereogram. Proc. SPIE 1991; 1461 "Practical Holography V" (SPIE, Bellingham,WA, February) paper #21

[29] Klug M, Halle M, Hubel P. Full color ultragrams. Proc. 1992; SPIE 1667: 110-119.

[30] Yamaguchi M, Hoshino H, Honda T, Ohyama N. Phase added stereogram: calculation of hologram using computer graphic technique. Proc. SPIE 1993; 1914, 25-33.

[31] Smithwick Q, Barabas J, Smalley D, Bove V. Interactive holographic stereograms with accommodation cues. Proc. SPIE 2010; 7619: 761903-1-761903-13.

[32] Lucente M. Diffraction-Specific Fringe Computation for Electro-Holography. PhD thesis, MIT Dept. of Electrical Engineering and Computer Science, Cambridge MA; 1994.

[33] Honda T, Yamaguchi M, Kang D.-K, Shimura K, Tsujiuchi J, Ohyama N. Printing of holographic stereograms using liquid-crystal TV. Proc. SPIE 1989; 1051: 186-191.

[34] Benton S. Real Image Holographic Stereograms. U.S. Patent 4834476 (issued 30 May 1989).

[35] Zacharovas S. Advances in digital holography. In: Proceedings of the International Workshop on Holographic Memories, IWHM2008, 20-23 October 2008, Aichi, Japan; 55-67.

[36] Klug M, Halle M, Lucente M, Plesniak W. A compact prototype one-step ultragram printer. Proc. SPIE 1993; 1914: 15-23.

[37] Hellseth L, Singstad I. Diffusers for holographic stereography. Optics Communications 2001; 193(1): 81-86.

[38] Bjelkhagen H, Mirlis E. Color holography to produce highly realistic three-dimensional images. Applied Optics 2008; 47(4): A123-A133.

[39] Yamaguchi M, Honda T, Ohyama N, Ishikawa J. Multidot recording of rainbow and multicolor holographic stereograms. Optics Communications 1994; 110 (5-6): 523-528.

[40] Yamaguchi M, Koyama T, Ohyama N, Honda T. A stereographic display using a reflection holographic screen. Optical Review 1994; 1(2): 191-194.

[41] Yamaguchi M, Endoh H, Honda T, Ohyama N. High quality recording of a full-parallax holographic stereogram with a digital diffuser. Optics Letters 1994; 19(2): 135-137.

[42] Zebra Imaging Inc. Company (2012) http://www.zebraimaging.com/.

[43] 3D Holoprint. Company (2012) http://www.3d-holoprint.com/.

[44] Yamaguchi M, Sugiura H, Honda T, Ohyama N. Automatic recording method for holographic three-dimensional animation. Journal of the Optical Society of America A 1992; 9(7): 1200-1205.

[45] Takano M, Shigeta H, Nishihara T, Yamaguchi M, Takahashi S, Ohyama N, Kobayashi A, Iwata F. Fullcolor holographic 3D printer. Proc. SPIE 2003; 5005: 126-136.

[46] Frey S, Thelen A, Hirsch S, Hering P. Generation of digital textured surface models from hologram recordings. Applied Optics 2007; 46(11): 1986-1993.

[47] Yang F, Murakami Y, Yamaguchi M. Digital color management in full-color holographic three-dimensional printer. Applied Optics 2012; 51(19): 4343-4352.

[48] Yamaguchi M, Endoh H, Koyama T, Ohyama N. High-speed recording of full-parallax holographic stereograms by a parallel exposure systems. Optical Engineering 1996; 35(6): 1556-1559.

[49] Brotherton-Ratcliffe D, Nikolskij A, Zacharovas S, Pileckas J, Bakanas R. Image capture system for a digital holographic printer. U.S. Patent 2009; No.US20090147072A1.

[50] Okada K, Honda T, Tsujiuchi J. A method of distortion compensation of multiplex holograms. Optics Communications 1983; 48(3): 167-170.

[51] Hilaire P. Optimum sampling parameters for generalized holographic stereograms. Proc. SPIE 1993; 3011: 96-104.

[52] Hilaire P. Modulation transfer function and optimum sampling of holographic stereograms. Applied Optics 1994; 33(5): 768-774.

[53] Maruyama S, Ono Y, Yamaguchi M. High-density recording of full-color full-parallax holographic stereogram. Proc. SPIE 2008; 6912: 12-22.

[54] Zacharovas S, Nikolskij A, Kuchin J. DYI digital holography. Proc. SPIE 2011; 7957:79570A-79570A-5.

[55] Sainov S, Stoykova E. Display holography – status and future. In: Osten W, Reingand N. (eds.) Optical Imaging and Metrology. Advanced Technologies, Wiley-VCH; 2012. p 93-115.

[56] Zacharovas S, Rodin A, Ratcliffe D, Vergnes F. Holographic materials available from Geola. Proc.SPIE 2001; 4296: 206-212.

[57] Gentet Y, Gentet P. "Ultimate" emulsion and its applications: a laboratory-made silver halide emulsion of optimized quality for monochromatic pulsed and full-color holography. Proc. SPIE 2000; 4149: 56-62.

[58] Plesniak W, Halle M, Bove V, Barabas J, Pappu R. Reconfigurable Image Projection Holograms. Optical Engineering 2006; 45(11): 115801-1-115801-15.

[59] Yoshikawa H. Computer-generated holograms for white light reconstruction. In: Ting-Chung Poon (ed.) Digital Holography and Three-dimensional Display: Principles and Applications. Springer Verlag; 2006. part 2, p235-255.

[60] Yoshikawa H, Yamaguchi T. Computer-generated holograms for 3D display. Chinese Optics Letters 2009; 7(12): 1079-1082.

[61] Yamaguchi T, Fujii T, Yoshikawa H. Fast calculation method for computer-generated cylindrical holograms. Applied Optics 2008; 47(19): D63-D70.

[62] Yamaguchi T, Fujii T, Yoshikawa H. Computer-generated cylindrical rainbow hologram, Proc. SPIE 2008a; 6912: 69121C-1-69121C-10.

[63] Yamaguchi T, Fujii T, Yoshikawa H. Disk hologram made from a computer-generated hologram. Applied Optics 2009; 48(34): H16-H22.

[64] Yamaguchi T, Yoshikawa H. Computer-generated image hologram. Chinese Optics Letters 2011; 9(12): 120006.

[65] Yoshikawa H, Yamaguchi T, Kitayama R. Real-time generation of full color image hologram with compact distance look-up table. In: Digital Holography and Three-Dimensional Imaging, April 30, 2009, Vancouver, Canada; DWC4.

[66] Fujii T, Yoshikawa H. Improvement of Hidden-Surface Removal for Computer-Generated Holograms from CG. In: Digital Holography and Three-Dimensional Imaging, June 18, 2007, Vancouver, Canada; DWB3.

[67] Kang H, Yamaguchi T, Yoshikawa H. Processing techniques for quality improvement of phase added stereogram. Proc. SPIE 2007; 6488: 6488-41.

[68] Kang H, Fujii T, Yamaguchi T, Yoshikawa H. A Compensated Phase-Added Stereogram for Real-Time Holographic Display. Optical Engineering 2007; 46 (9): 095802-1-095802-11.

[69] Kang H, Yamaguchi T, Yoshikawa H. Accurate phase-added stereogram to improve the coherent stereogram. Applied Optics 2008; 47(19): D44-D54.

[70] Kang H, Yamaguchi T, Yoshikawa H. Accurate phase-added stereogram. In: Digital Holography and Three-Dimensional Imaging, June 18, 2007, Vancouver, Canada; DTuB5.

[71] Kang H, Yamaguchi T, Yoshikawa H, Kim SC, Kim ES. Acceleration method of computing a compensated phase-added stereogram on a graphic processing unit. Applied Optics 2008; 47(31): 5784-5789.

[72] Lee A. Computer-generated hologram recording using a laser printer. Applied Optics 1987; 26(1): 136-138.

[73] Yatagai T, Camacho-Basilio J, Onda H. Recording of computer-generated holograms on an optical disk master. Applied Optics 1989; 28(6): 1042-1044.

[74] Cable A, Mash P, Wilkinson T. Production of computer-generated holograms on recordable compact disk media using a compact disk writer. Optical Engineering 2003; 42(9): 2514-2529.

[75] Sakamoto Y, Morishima M, Usui A. Computer generated holograms on a CD-R disk. Proc. SPIE 2004; 5290: 42-49.

[76] Matsushima K, Kobayashi S, Miyauchi H. A high-resolution fringe printer for studying synthetic holograms. Proc. SPIE 2006; 6136: 347-354.

[77] Yamaguchi T, Maeno Y, Fujii T, Yoshikawa H. Animated computer-generated cylindrical hologram. NICOGRAPH International 2008. [CD-ROM].

[78] Miyamoto O, Yamaguchi T, Yoshikawa H. The volume hologram printer to record the wavefront of a 3D object. Proc. SPIE 2012; 8281: 82810N-82810N-10.

Chapter 9

Microscopic Interferometry by Reflection Holography with Photorefractive Sillenite Crystals

Eduardo Acedo Barbosa,
Danilo Mariano da Silva and Merilyn Santos Ferreira

Additional information is available at the end of the chapter

http://dx.doi.org/10.5772/53416

1. Introduction

The continuous growth of the development and production of micro- and nano-scaled devices requires the employ of compatible measurement techniques which fulfill the increasing demands of this new field. Despite the several very well established microscopy techniques, the potentialities of measuring the dynamic behavior of devices like microelectromechanical systems (MEMS) or capacitive micromachined ultrasonic transducers (CMUTs) were not sufficiently explored so far. In this framework, microscopic holographic interferometry and microscopic DSPI (digital speckle pattern interferometry) have been demonstrated to be very promising techniques for micro-scaled device measurement, due to its whole-field character, precision and accuracy. Due to its incomparable resolution and to the possibility of performing real-time testing with a minimum of computational image processing, photorefractive holography is a powerful tool for this task.

Photorefractive materials comprise a class of materials which present an interesting combination of physical properties. They combine light sensitivity with photoconductivity and the linear electrooptic effect. This effect was first observed in the years 1960 at Bell Laboratories [1, 2], in second harmonic generation experiments in ferroelectric crystals. At the time the effect was classified as "optical damage" by their observers, in function of localized variations in refractive index of the crystal with laser incidence.

Among the photorefractive crystals there are the ones from the sillenite family, namely: $Bi_{12}GeO_{20}$ (BGO), $Bi_{12}SiO_{20}$ (BSO), and $Bi_{12}TiO_{20}$ (BTO) [3, 4]. These crystals have a cubic lattice with symmetry group 23, with only the elements r_{14}, r_{52} and r_{63} electro tensors being nonzero. They are optically active and become linearly birefringent in the presence of an electric field.

As observed in other photorefractive materials working as holographic media, the sillenites have attractive characteristics for holographic applications such as infinite cycles of simultaneous, real-time holographic recording and reconstruction, all without fatigue or need of chemical processing.

The BTO crystal presents a lower optical activity for red light if compared to BSO and BGO, which makes it more appropriate for holographic applications, providing the highest possible diffraction efficiency for this wavelength range and enabling holography with the easily available and cost-effective He-Ne and red diode lasers. Its low diffraction efficiency can be compensated by its anisotropic diffraction properties [5, 6]. Due to this characteristic, under certain conditions the transmitted beam and diffracted beam propagate with orthogonal polarization at the crystal output, so that the signal-to-noise ratio of the output image can be increased by eliminating the beam transmitted by means of a linear polarizer.

All these features make this crystal an extremely interesting medium for many applications like real-time interferometry [7, 8, 9], spatial light modulation [10, 11, 12], nonlinear optical signal processing [13, 14], coherent image processing [15], edge detection [16], phase conjugation [17, 18], pattern recognition [19, 20], information storage [21] as well as phase conjugation in optical resonators [22]. Two-wave mixing with transmission holography configuration is the most employed arrangement with photorefractive sillenite crystals. However, reflection holography with these materials have been received relatively few attention, in spite of the fact that this sort of holographic configuration has been proved to be quite effective and powerful for interferometry and image processing [23].

The first study of a sillenite crystal for applications in interferometry was performed by Kukhtarev et al by using a [111]-cut BTO crystal and employing anisotropic diffraction in order to read the diffracted wave only [24]; the influence of the input polarization on the coupling of the interfering beams in reflection holograms with BTO and BSO crystals was developed by Mallick et al; Weber et al analyzed the gain and the diffraction efficiency as a function of the input polarization angle for BTO and BSO crystals with the grating vector parallel to the [001]-axis [25]. Salazar et al recorded a speckle pattern in sillenite crystals in a reflection holography configuration [26] in order to develop a four wave-mixing optical correlator through reflection holography [27]. Regarding recent applications of selenite crystals in reflection holography we can mention Erbschloe et al, which investigated the intensity and the phase of two optical beams in a photorefractive material, showing the implications of a reflection holography geometry [28]; Shepelevich et al investigated the dependence of maximum diffraction efficiency of volume reflection holograms recorded in BSO crystals [29]; Shandarov et al studied the interaction of two light waves in a network formed in a dynamic reflection holography scheme [30].

The lensless Denisiuk configuration [31] for reflection holography allows obtaining high resolution holographic images in very compact and simple setups, which is a particularly valuable characteristic for microscope construction. This optical conception consists in placing the studied object close to the holographic medium through which the image can be collected in a wide angular range, favoring the image resolution. A sillenite-based optical setup for reflection holography aiming practical purposes like holographic interferometry must basically combine the simplicity of such arrangement and the high image quality obtainable through the anisotropic diffraction properties of the sillenite crystals. In this framework, it has been proposed a novel optical display for holographic imaging and interferometry using a $Bi_{12}TiO_{20}$ crystal and red lasers as light source. This optical arrangement employed as a key-element a polarizing beam splitter (PBS) positioned at the BTO input for polarization selection [23]. The potentialities of the setup for holographic imaging, double exposure holography and time average holography of small diffusely scattering objects are theoretically studied and experimentally demonstrated in this chapter. Aiming the development of a measurement device which allows the dynamic characterization of small components, this chapter analyzes the combination of three optical features: the Denisiuk configuration, the holographic recording and readout with sillenite crystals and the compound microscope geometry. The performance of the holographic microscope in the characterization of microscopic transducers and MEMs is described and potencial applications in the study of other micro-components are pointed out.

2. Denisiuk setup with photorefractive crystals

The Denisiuk configuration is the simplest geometry for reflection holography. The original setup comprises a light source, an object, and a recording medium between them. Since the object is usually positioned right behind the holographic medium, when both are illuminated the medium works also as a beam splitter: the laser beam hitting the front face of the medium is the reference wave, while the beam transmitted through the medium illuminates the object. The light scattered by the object illuminates the holographic medium through its rear face - the object beam – and interferes with the reference wave, thus generating the hologram.

The typical low diffraction efficiency of the sillenite crystals make them not suitable for real-time holography in an original Denisiuk configuration, since the transmitted object beam is much more intense than the holographic image, leading to a very small signal-to-noise ratio (SNR). In transmission holography setups this low-diffraction efficiency limitation is usually overcome by exploring the anisotropic diffraction properties of those crystals: by properly setting the input polarization angle of the incoming waves with respect to the crystal [001]-axis, the diffracted and transmitted waves emerging from the sample become orthogonally polarized [5,6]. Hence, a conveniently positioned analyzer can block the transmitted wave and enable the propagation of the diffracted wave only, which is the holographic reconstruction of the object. However, this arrangement cannot be made in reflection holography because a polarizer behind the crystal adjusted to eliminate the transmitted beam would block the reference beam also.

Due to the reasons above, Denisiuk-type reflection holography experiments using anisotropic diffraction in sillenite crystals require an unusual approach and a novel optical display, which should obey the following requirements often adopted for interferometry design in order to avoid spurious elliptical polarization and consequent losses in the hologram diffraction efficiency: a - the light beam propagation occurs in a plane parallel to the table top; b - the beam polarization must be kept whether perpendicular or parallel to this plane, except when the light polarization undergoes a rotation inside the BTO crystal due to its optical activity; c – the hole setup must be simple and compact, in order to enable the construction of rugged and portable holography microscopes.

Those requirements are achieved by using a polarizing beam splitter (PBS) cube. With this configuration, anisotropic diffraction can be optimally observed by tilting the sillenite crystal with respect to the axis perpendicular to the table top. The tilting angle is selected in order to enable the diffracted wave to be orthogonally polarized with respect both to the incident reference wave and to the transmitted object wave. In such a configuration the signal-to-noise ratio is maximized.

The PBS cube separates the *s*-polarized (whose electric field is perpendicular to the plane of incidence) from the *p*-polarized (electric field parallel to the plane of incidence) components of the incident light and generates two linearly polarized beams propagating in mutually perpendicular directions. The *s*-polarized beam emerges from the PBS at a right angle, while the *p*-polarized is transmitted through it.

Figure 1 schematically shows a setup for reflection holography with a BTO crystal with thickness d and a PBS cube as the polarizing component. The x-y plane is parallel to the table top. The s-polarized light coming from the laser hits the PBS and is 90º deviated, hitting the BTO crystal as the reference wave, whose propagation vector $\vec{k}_R$ is shown in figure 1. Due to the crystal optical activity, the wave polarization is rotated by an angle ρd (counterclockwise rotation, looking towards the negative X-axis in fig. 1) where ρ is the optical rotatory power. The beam transmitted through the crystal illuminates the object and is scattered by it, forming the object wave. This wave has a propagation vector $\vec{k}_S$, parallel to the positive X-axis, and is polarized at an angle ρd with respect to the z-axis. The object beam travels back through the crystal and again undergoes a polarization rotation of $-\rho d$, such that both reference and object beams present the same polarization orientation throughout the whole holographic medium and propagate in opposite directions. At the output (left side in fig. 1) of the BTO crystal there are two beams emerging with the same propagation vector: the transmitted object beam (with electric field $\vec{S}'$ parallel to the Z-axis) and the diffracted reference beam, which in turn is the holographic reconstruction of the object wavefront (shown as the electric field $\vec{U}$). If the polarization directions of both beams are mutually orthogonal, or as close as possible to it, the hologram SNR is highest. This can be accomplished by properly rotating the crystal around its [100]-axis, which is parallel to the X-axis shown in figure 1.

When the optimal angle between the the [001]-axis and the input reference beam polarization is achieved, the diffracted wave with amplitude $\vec{U}$ at the BTO output is p-polarized due to anisotropic diffraction, as shown in figure 2: while figure 2a shows the reference wave polarization $\vec{R}$ at the BTO crystal input $x = d$ ("solid" vector) and at the sample output at $x = 0$ ("dashed" vector), figure 2b shows the object wave amplitude vector $\vec{S}$ ("dashed" vector) hitting the BTO crystal and the polarization states of the transmitted ($\vec{S}$) and the diffracted ($\vec{U}$) waves at $x = d$. Notice that $\vec{U}$ and $\vec{S}$ in figure 2b are nearly orthogonal, which provides the condition of highest SNR. In the next sections the photorefractive recording and readout will be analyzed in order to allow these conditions to be achieved.

http://dx.doi.org/10.5772/53416

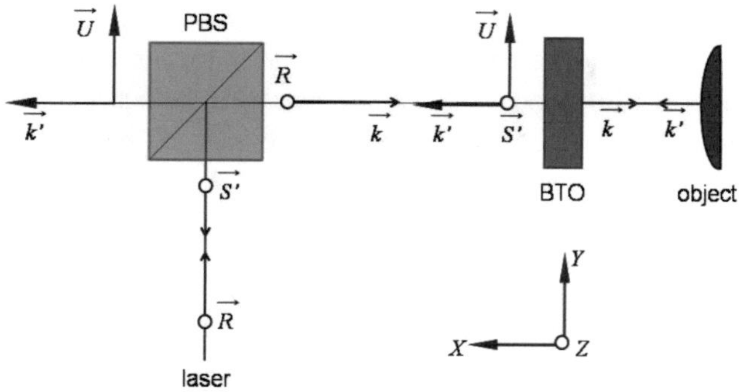

Figure 1. Sillenite-based Denisiuk holographic setup

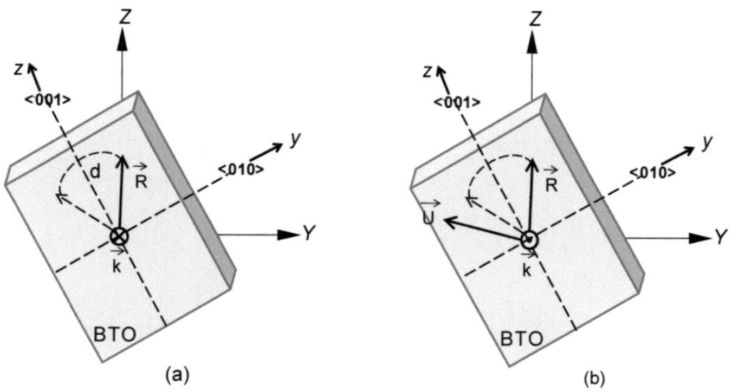

Figure 2. a - reference wave polarization $\vec{R}$ and its propagation vector $\vec{k}_R$ at the BTO input *x*=*d*; b - transmitted ($\vec{S}'$) and the diffracted ($\vec{U}$) beam polarizations propagating along positive *x*-axis at *x*=*d*.

3. Photorefractive effect in sillenite crystals

The photorefractive effect consists basically on the combination of two mechanisms: charge migration and electrooptic effect. In the former, charge carriers, say, electrons, are excited from occupied donor states to the conduction band due to the incidence of an interference pattern of light and then trapped by empty centers. In the latter, the resulting spatially non-uniform electric field due to the charge distribution modulates the refractive index, thus generating a phase index grating [3].

3.1. Charge carrier migration

Let us consider the incidence of a light interference pattern onto an impurity-dopped photorefractive crystal given by $=I_0(1+m\cos Kx)$, where K is the pattern spatial frequency and m is the modulation due to the interacting beams intensities. In the literature several models describe the migration process [32], and among them, the band transport model has been more widely adopted. In the illuminated areas of the sample, photoelectrons from ionized donors indergoe a transition to the conduction band. In this band the electrons migrate by diffusion and/or drift, i. e., under the influence of an externally applied electrical field. After relaxation the electrons are captured by acceptor centers. This process of excitation to the conduction band and posterior recombination is repeated until the photoelectrons are trapped in dark regions of the sample (interference pattern minima). Correspondingly, holes can be excited from filled acceptors to the valence band.

In typical experimental conditions for holographic imaging, $I_R \gg I_S$, so that $m \ll 1$. In this case, the low-modulation interference pattern can be expressed in terms of the first harmonic of its Fourier expansion according to

$$I = I_0 + \frac{I_0}{2}\left(me^{iKx} + m^* e^{iKx}\right) \tag{1}$$

where $m = 2(I_S I_R)^{1/2} e^{-ti\theta} / (I_S + I_R)$, and ϕ is the arbitrary phase of the signal (object) wave. The correspondent space charge electric field is written as

$$E(x) = E_0 + \frac{E_{SC}}{2} e^{iKx} + \frac{E_{SC}^*}{2} e^{iKx} \tag{2}$$

Through Poisson equation $div(\varepsilon \vec{E}) = \rho / \varepsilon_0$, the continuity equation $\partial\rho / \partial t = -\partial j / \partial x$ and the equation for the current density $j = \mu en(x) + eD\partial n / \partial x$, where D is the diffusion coefficient and $n(x)$ is the electron concentration in the conduction band, the amplitude E_{sc} of the steady-state space charge field in the holographic recording by diffusion (E_0=0) is given by

$$E_{SC} = \frac{-imE_D}{1 + K^2 L_S^2} \tag{3}$$

where L_s is the Debye screening length and the E_D is the diffusion electric field given in terms of Boltzmann´s constant k_B and the temperature T as $E_D = Kk_B T / e$.

3.2. Electrooptic effect

The propagation of the electromagnetic wave in a medium can be described with the help of the index ellipsoid, which provides the wave velocity according to its polarization state:

$$\frac{x^2}{n_x^2} + \frac{y^2}{n_y^2} + \frac{z^2}{n_z^2} = 1 \tag{4}$$

where x, y and z are the principal dielectric axes. If the medium is isotropic, $n_x = n_y = n_z$, and the light velocity does not depend on its polarization state in this case.

http://dx.doi.org/10.5772/53416

When a crystal without inversion simmetry is under the influence of an electric field, there is a change in the index ellipsoid, now represented by

$$\left(\frac{1}{n^2}\right)_1 x^2+\left(\frac{1}{n^2}\right)_2 y^2+\left(\frac{1}{n^2}\right)_3 z^2+2\left(\frac{1}{n^2}\right)_4 yz+2\left(\frac{1}{n^2}\right)_5 xz+2\left(\frac{1}{n^2}\right)_6 xy=1 \tag{5}$$

The terms $(1/n^2)_i$ are determined as a function of an arbitrary electric field through the matrix relation

$$\left(\frac{1}{n^2}\right)_i=\sum_{j=1}^{3} r_{ij}E_j \tag{6}$$

where the electrooptic coefficients r_{ij} are the elements of the 6 x 3 electrooptic tensor. By finding a new coordinate system x', y', z' through which equation (5) assumes the form of equation (4), the refractive index modulation along these axes can be determined. Since the symmetry group of the sillenite crystals is 23 and the only nonzero elements of the electrooptic tensor are r_{14}, r_{52} and r_{63} ($r_{41} = r_{52} = r_{63} = 5 \times 10^{-12}$ m/V for BTO), the electrooptic tensor of such crystals is written as

$$\begin{bmatrix} 0 & 0 & 0 \\ 0 & 0 & 0 \\ 0 & 0 & 0 \\ r_{41} & 0 & 0 \\ 0 & r_{41} & 0 \\ 0 & 0 & r_{41} \end{bmatrix} \tag{7}$$

From relations (6) and (7) one obtains the coefficients for the crossed terms:

$$\begin{aligned} \left(\frac{1}{n^2}\right)_1 &= r_{41}E_X \\ \left(\frac{1}{n^2}\right)_2 &= r_{41}E_Y \\ \left(\frac{1}{n^2}\right)_3 &= r_{41}E_Z \end{aligned} \tag{8}$$

Since $n_x = n_y = n_z = n_o$, the index ellipsoid expression takes the form

$$\frac{x^2}{n_0^2}+\frac{y^2}{n_0^2}+\frac{z^2}{n_0^2}+2r_{41}E_{SC}yz+2r_{41}E_{SC}xz+2r_{41}E_{SC}xy=1 \tag{9}$$

From equation (9) the refractive index modulation can be obtained, as it will be seen in detail in the next sections. Figure 3 summarizes the photorefractive mechanism, showing the incident light pattern (3a), the consequent steady-state charge distribution due to diffusion (3b), the space-charge electric field (3c) and the resulting refractive index modulation via electrooptic effect (3d). Notice that, in this case the electric field and the refractive index modulation are $\pi/2$-shifted with respect with the light intensity pattern.

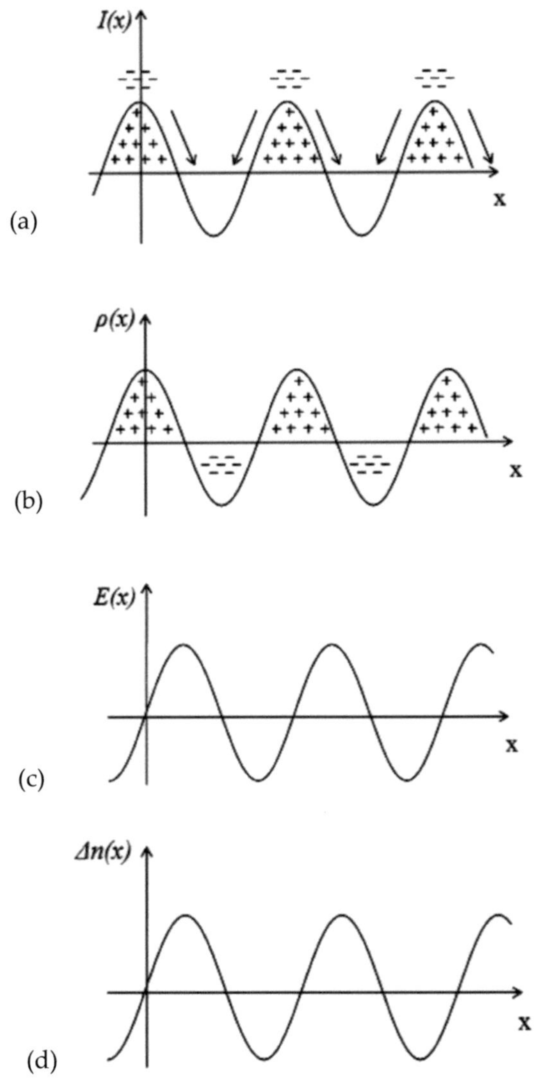

Figure 3. The photorefractive process; a – Intensity pattern; b – charge distribution; c – space-charge electric field and d – spatial refractive index modulation.

4. Reflection holography in photorefractive sillenite crystals

4.1. Recording

In this section the holographic recording in a photorefractive sillenite crystal is studied considering the interference of two counterpropagating monochromatic coherent waves with wavelength λ. The resulting interference pattern rearranges the charge carriers by diffusion, leading to a spatially nonuniform electric field E_{SC} inside the sample, as described in the previous section. Through the electrooptic effect this electric field gives rise to a phase grating due to local modulation of the refractive index. The crystal is cut in the transverse electrooptic configuration, in which its input facets are parallel to the crystalline (110) plane, as shown in figure 4. Since the counterpropagating interfering waves (with propagation vectors $\vec{k}_S$ and $\vec{k}_R$ shown in this figure) incide normally to this facet, both the grating vector and the induced electric field are parallel to the [100]-axis, referred as to the x-axis in figure 4. The index ellipsoid of equation (9) due to E_{sc} is then given by

$$\frac{x^2}{n_0^2}+\frac{y^2}{n_0^2}+\frac{z^2}{n_0^2}+2r_{41}E_{SC}YZ=1 \tag{10}$$

where n_0 is the bulk refractive index. If the BTO crystal is rotated around the X-axis by an angle θ, equation (10) can be conveniently expressed according to the coordinate system whose x-, y- and z-axes are parallel to the principal crystalographic axes of the sample. In the rotation, x and X are parallel, so that the transformation relations are given by

$$X=x;\quad Y=y\cos\theta - z\sin\theta;\quad Z=y\sin\theta+z\cos\theta \tag{11}$$

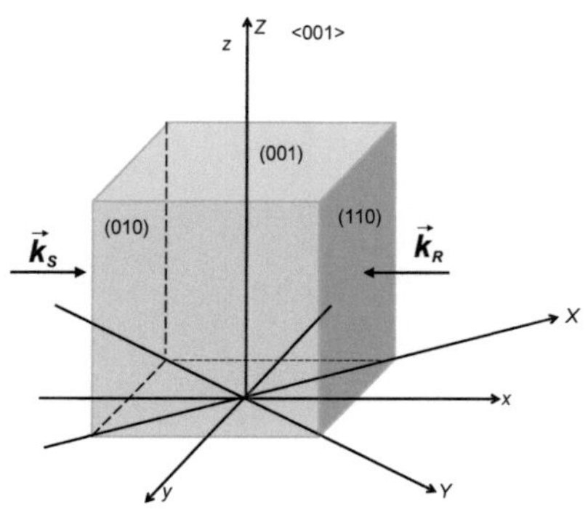

Figure 4. Electrooptic transverse-cut BTO crystal

By substituting Y and Z from eq. (11) into eq.(10), the index ellipsoid in the x, y, z system is written as

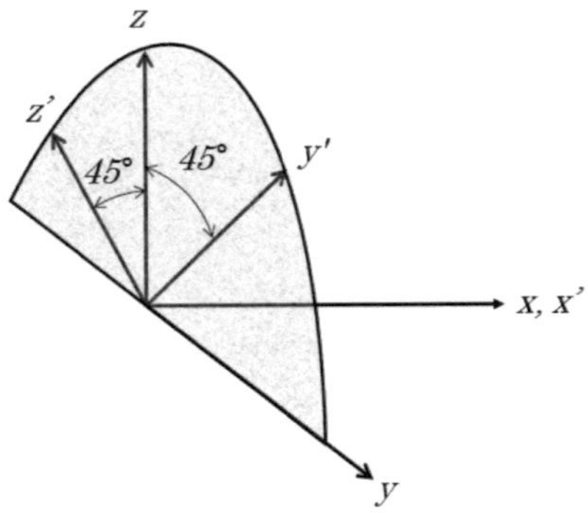

Figure 5. Rotation of the coordinate system around the *x*-axis

$$\frac{x^2}{n_0^2} + \frac{y^2}{n_0^2} + \frac{z^2}{n_0^2} + 2r_{41}E_{SC}yz = 1 \tag{12}$$

Notice that eqs. (10) and (12) have the same form, regardless the rotation angle θ. The ellipsoid major axes x', y', z' can be determined by performing another coordinate transformation by a 45°-rotation around the x-axis, as shown in figure 5, such that

$$x = x'; \; y = y'\cos 45° - z'\sin 45°; \; z = y'\sin 45° + z'\cos 45° \tag{13}$$

Hence, upon substitution in eq. (12) this coordinate transformation yields

$$\frac{x'^2}{n_0^2} + y'^2\left(\frac{1}{n_0^2} + r_{41}E_{SC}\right) + z'^2\left(\frac{1}{n_0^2} + r_{41}E_{SC}\right) = 1 \tag{14}$$

which corresponds to the following ellipsoid with x', y' and z' axes:

$$\frac{x'^2}{n_0^2} + \frac{y'^2}{n_{y'}^2} + \frac{z'^2}{n_{z'}^2} = 1 \tag{15}$$

By comparing eqs. (14) and (15) one obtains

$$\frac{1}{n_{y'}^2} = \frac{1}{n_0^2} + r_{41}E_{SC}; \; \frac{1}{n_{z'}^2} = \frac{1}{n_0^2} + r_{41}E_{SC} \tag{16}$$

With the help of relation $d(1/n^2) = -2/n^3\, dn$ equation (16) provides the refractive index modulations along y′ and z′ axes:

$$\Delta n_{y'} = -\frac{n_0^3}{2} + r_{41}E_{SC}; \; \Delta n_{z'} = -\frac{n_0^3}{2} + r_{41}E_{SC} \tag{17}$$

The results above evidence an anisotropy in the photorefractive phase gratings generated in the sillenite crystals, since $\Delta n_{y'} \neq \Delta n_{z'}$, which will be analysed in the next section.

4.2. Readout; anisotropic diffraction

In this section the experiment to confirm the theoretical predictions on the holographic process is performed by using a BTO crystal as holographic medium and a He-Ne laser as light source. In the setup the PBS is used in order to separate the diffracted and the transmitted beams and simultaneously allow the incidence of the reference wave onto the crystal. The intensity of the diffracted wave was measured as the BTO crystal was rotated, so that the dependence of the diffracted wave on the direction of the incident light polarization with respect to the crystal (001)-axis was studied. The experimental results very satisfactorily agreed with the theoretical analysis, showing that there is an optimal input polarization configuration through which the background noise generated by the transmitted object beam can be totally eliminated by the PBS, thus enabling the detection of the holographically reconstructed signal wave only [33]. From the theory presented in the previous section the amplitude of the wave diffracted by a reflection hologram in a self-diffraction process can be obtained. Due to the refractive index modulation anisotropy, the diffracted wave presents two different orthogonal components. This is the most important consequence of anisotropic diffraction. The dependence of the angle between the diffracted and the transmitted waves – a feature of crucial importance in this work – will be both theoretically and experimentally studied. In this section the angle between both polarization states can be theoretically obtained and the conditions to provide the best holographic image visibility will be analyzed.

The reference wave polarization at the BTO input with respect to the coordinate systems involved and the rotation angle γ is shown in figure 6. The components of the reference wave relatively to the y'- and z'-axis are written as

$$R_{y'}(x) = R_0 \cos[\theta - \rho(d - x)]; \quad R_{z'}(x) = R_0 \sin[\theta - \rho(d - x)] \tag{18}$$

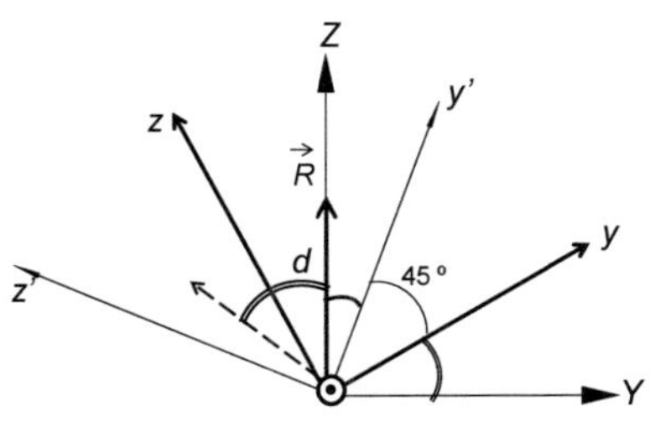

Figure 6. Reference wave polarization at the BTO input and the coordinate systems *X-Y-Z*, *x-y-z* and *x´-y´-z´*.

where θ is the angle between the reference wave polarization direction and the y'-axis at the crystal output and R_0 is the amplitude of the reference beam at $x = 0$. As mentioned earlier, the object beam and the reference beam polarizations are parallel throughout the crystal. The fringe contrast m as a function of the crystal depth x takes into account the changes of the interacting beams as they propagate along the sample [25]:

$$m(x)=m_0 exp\left\{2\frac{\beta}{\rho}\cos\left[2\theta - \rho(2d - x)\right]\sin(\rho x)\right\} \tag{19}$$

where $\beta \equiv \pi r_0^3 r_{41} E_{SC} / 2\lambda$ and $m_0 \approx 2S_0 / R_0$ for $R_0 \gg S_0$, where S_0 is the object beam amplitude at $x=0$. The elementary components of the diffracted amplitude at $x=d$ are given by [25]

$$dU_{y'}(x) = -\beta m(x) R_0 \cos(\theta - 2\rho d + \rho x)dx; \quad dU_{z'}(x) = -\beta m(x) R_0 \sin(\theta - 2\rho d + \rho x)dx \tag{20}$$

where the sign of $dU_{y'}(x)$ is due to the negative sign of $\Delta n_{y'}$ in equation (17). Since $m_0 \ll 1$ and $|\beta / \rho| < 0.4$, $m(x)$ can be expanded into a Taylor series, so that from equation (19) one obtains

$$m(x)=m_0 exp[-\beta / \rho \sin(2\theta - 2\rho d)][1 + \beta / \rho \cos(2\theta - 2\rho d + 2\rho x)] \tag{21}$$

By substituting $m(x)$ from equation (21) into equation (22) and integrating along the crystal thickness, the components of the diffracted amplitudes parallel to y' and z' are written as

$$\begin{aligned} U_{y'}(d) &= -\beta R_0 m_0 exp[-2\beta \sin(2\theta) / \rho] \times \left\{\frac{\sin \rho d}{\rho}\cos(\theta - \rho d) + \frac{\beta}{8\rho^2}[\sin(4\rho d - 3\theta) + \sin(3\theta) + 4\rho d \cos\theta]\right\} \quad (a) \\ U_{z'}(d) &= -\beta R_0 m_0 exp[-2\beta \sin(2\theta) / \rho] \times \left\{\frac{\sin \rho d}{\rho}\cos(\theta - \rho d) + \frac{\beta}{8\rho^2}[\cos(4\rho d - 3\theta) - \cos(3\theta) - 4\rho d \sin\theta]\right\} \quad (b \end{aligned} \tag{22}$$

At the front face of the crystal the y′ and z′ components of the object wave amplitude are given by $S_{y'}(d)=S_0 \cos\theta$ and $S_{z'}(d)=S_0 \sin\theta$, respectively. Since this wave does not carry any relevant information and constitutes a noise to the holographically reconstructed wavefront, it is worthy cutting off the transmitted object beam by a polarizing element in order to provide the diffracted wave only. The maximal holographic signal I_U corresponding to the holographic image must then be proportional to $\sin^2\varphi$, where φ is the angle between the vectors $\vec{U} = U_{y'}(d)\hat{y}' + U_{z'}(d)\hat{z}'$ and $\vec{S} = S_{y'}(d)\hat{y}' + S_{z'}(d)\hat{z}'$:

$$I_U \propto \sin^2 \sin^2\varphi = 1 - \left(\frac{\vec{U}.\vec{S}}{|\vec{U}||\vec{S}|}\right)^2 \tag{23}$$

It is convenient to make the substitution $\theta = \pi / 4 - \gamma$, where γ is the angle between the [001]-axis and the Z-axis, as shown in figure 6. With the help of equations (22a), (22b) and (23) one obtains the signal I_U :

http://dx.doi.org/10.5772/53416

$$I_U \propto \sin^2 \varphi \approx 1 - \frac{\left\{\sin(\rho d)\sin(2\gamma + \rho d) + \frac{\beta}{8\rho}\left[\sin 4\gamma - \sin(4\rho d - 4\gamma) + 4\rho d\right]\right\}^2}{\sin^2(\rho d) + \frac{\beta}{4\rho}\sin(\rho d)\left[4\rho d \sin(2\gamma + 4\rho d) + \cos(2\gamma - \rho d) - \cos(2\gamma + 3\rho d)\right]} \tag{24}$$

For typical diffusely scattering objects, $\beta \ll \rho$, so that the signal I_U from equation (10) can be satisfactorily written as

$$I_U \approx \cos^2(2\gamma + \rho d) \tag{25}$$

Through equation (25) the optimal angle between the crystal [001]-axis and the input polarization can be obtained to be $\gamma \approx -\rho d / 2 + N\pi / 2$, where $N = 1, 2, 3, \ldots$. In practical terms, since the polarization of the incident beam is perpendicular to the table top, the crystal must be tilted such that its [001]-axis makes an angle of $\gamma \approx -\rho d / 2$ with respect to the Z-axis, as shown in figure 7.

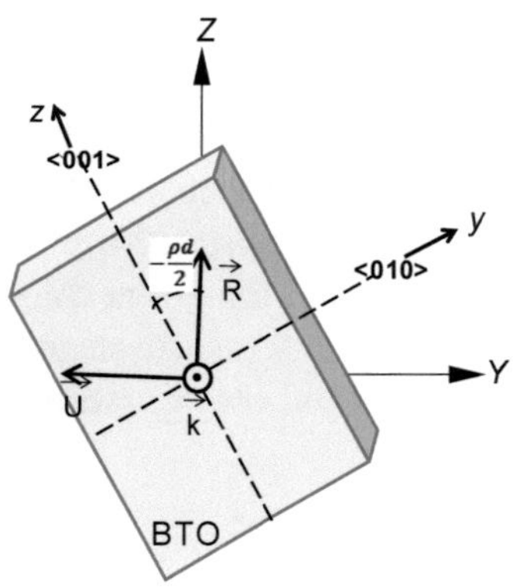

Figure 7. Optimal BTO orientation for maximum holographic image SNR.

5. Experiments

5.1. Dependence of the diffracted beam intensity on the crystal tilting

The intensity of the holographically reconstructed object beam as a function of the tilting angle γ is investigated in order to confirm the theoretical prediction of equation (25). Figure 8 shows the optical setup for this purpose. The setup was illuminated by a 20-mW He-Ne laser emitting at 632.8 nm. The s-polarized reference beam coming directly from the laser is expanded by lens L1. The crystal is cut in the electrooptic transverse configuration. The BTO sample is rotated around the X-direction by a goniometer. The transmitted object beam wave is deviated by the PBS, while the diffracted beam passes through it to be sent to the photodetector PD through lens L2. The sensitive area of the photodetector is larger than the diffracted beam cross section. The rotatory power of $Bi_{12}TiO_{20}$ is $\rho = -0.11\ mm^{-1}$ for 632.8 nm. For $m_0 \approx 0.1$ and $n_0 \approx 2.6$, β was estimated to be ~10^{-2} mm^{-1}.

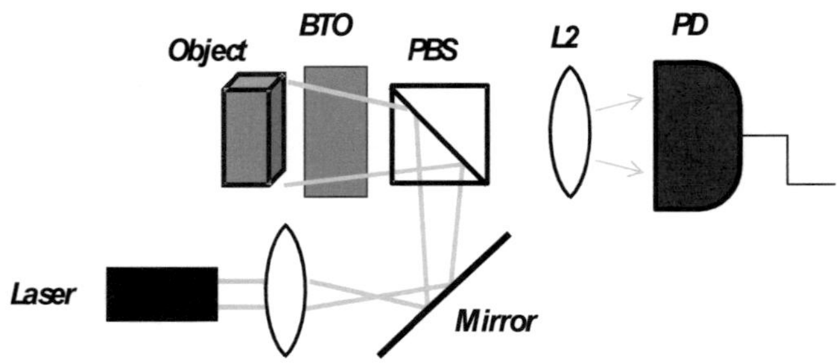

Figure 8. Optical setup: L1 and L2, lenses, M, mirror, PD, photodetector

Two BTO samples with sizes 10 × 12 × 10 mm^3 (BTO 1), and 8 × 7 × 7 mm^3 (BTO 2) were used. A 10×10-mm^2 flat metallic bar placed right behind the crystal was used as the opaque scattering object surface. Figure 9a shows the dependence of I_U on the orientation of the BTO 1 [001]-axis. The solid curve is the fitting of the experimental data with equation (25), showing maximum I_U values for $\gamma \cong 30^o$ and 120°, showing a very good agreement with the optimal values theoretically obtained for the sample 1 thickness (10 mm) and the crystal rotatory power. Figure 9b shows the same measurement for the 8-mm thick BTO 2 sample. The hologram buildup time was τ ~15s for both cases. Those measurements confirm the theoretical predictions and provide information to an optimal configuration in order to achieve holographic images with the best signal-to-noise-ratio.

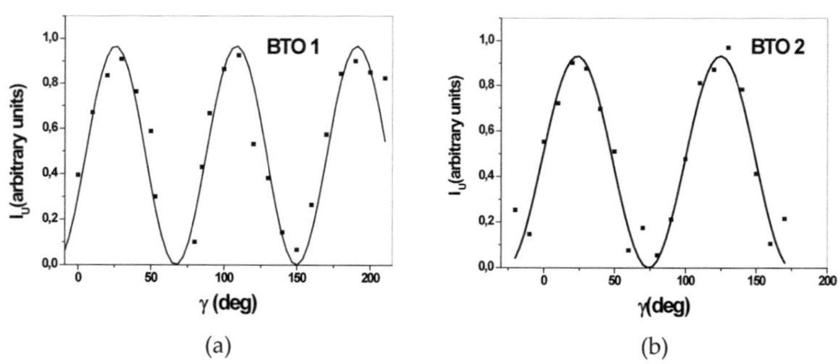

Figure 9. Signal I_U as a function of the orientation angle γ; dotted curve, measured values; solid curve, fitting with equation (10), for a – BTO 1 and b – BTO 2 samples [23].

5.2. Denisiuk-type reflection holography configurations for microscopy and interferometry

In this section two geometries for reflection holography microscopes using a BTO crystal cut in the electrooptic transverse configuration for the characterization of microscopic devices are studied and analyzed. The polarizing beam-splitter did enable blocking the transmitted object beam and reading the diffracted wave, thus allowing for the reconstruction of the holographic image of the object in quasi real-time processes.

5.2.1. *First optical configuration*

In this optical setup a red diode laser emitting at 660 nm was employed as light source. A variation of the original Denisiuk optical scheme was developed by positioning the objective lens between the object and the holographic medium, so that the lens is used both to illuminate the object and to build its real image in front of the ocular lens. The beam coming from the laser is slightly expanded by lens L1, is reflected by mirror M and impinges the PBS. Since the direction of the beam polarization is perpendicular to the table top, it is totally reflected by the PBS and hits the BTO crystal, thus constituting the reference beam. The part of the beam transmitted through the crystal is focused by the 3-mm focal length objective lens L2 and illuminates the object; the light scattered by the diffuse object forms the object beam, as described earlier. Between the objective lens and the crystal a polarizer is positioned in order to compensate for the partial depolarization caused by the diffusely scattering surface. The holographic recording occurs by diffusion. The 28-mm focal length ocular lens L3 was positioned at a distance from the crystal which is nearly its front focal length, in order to display an enlarged holographic object image at a CMOS camera. The 8x8x8-mm^3 PBS cube was placed between the ocular lens and the holographic medium. The holographic compound microscope is shown in figure 10. The size of the whole setup is 30 X 20 cm^2 approximately. This setup allows the degree of freedom to conveniently place the BTO crystal whether closer to the objective lens or to the PBS in order to get a more intense object beam, which may provide a shorter hologram buildup time. The fastest hologram recording was achieved by placing the BTO crystal at the image plane of lens L2.

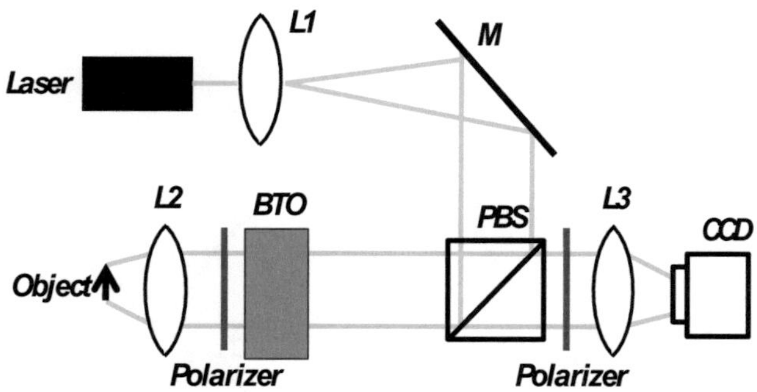

Figure 10. First configuration of the holographic compound microscope

As described in section 4.2, the crystal [001]-axis was oriented with respect to the Z-direction by setting $\gamma = |\rho d|/2$ in order to maximize the diffracted wave intensity. Figure 11 shows the holographic image of a pattern chart while figure 11b shows its corresponding. The distance between two neighboring bars of the chart is 100 μm.

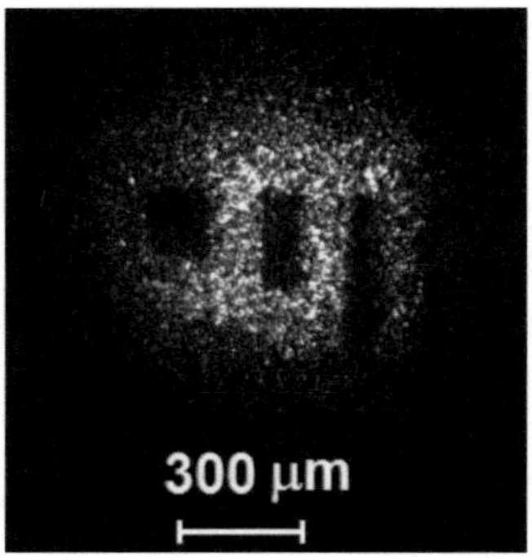

Figure 11. Holographic image of the test chart formed by the first microscope configuration

5.2.2. Second optical configuration

In the second microscope configuration the holographic medium is positioned between the objective lens and the object, such that the object wave at the crystal is originated directly from scaterring by the object surface, as shown in figure 12. The real holographic image built by the objective lens lays in a plane between the PBS and the ocular lens, which in turn forms the enlarged image onto the CMOS target.

This configuration requires the illuminating beam to be tightly focused onto the object surface and the crystal front face to be placed as close as possible to the object. This assures the highest possible object beam intensity inside the crystal. In addition, this small distance allows the object beam to be collected by the BTO in a very broad angular range, which increases the image resolution due to diffraction and therefore allows a higher holographic image quality. Figure 12a shows the holographic image of a chart of a 2-mm high "x" letter.

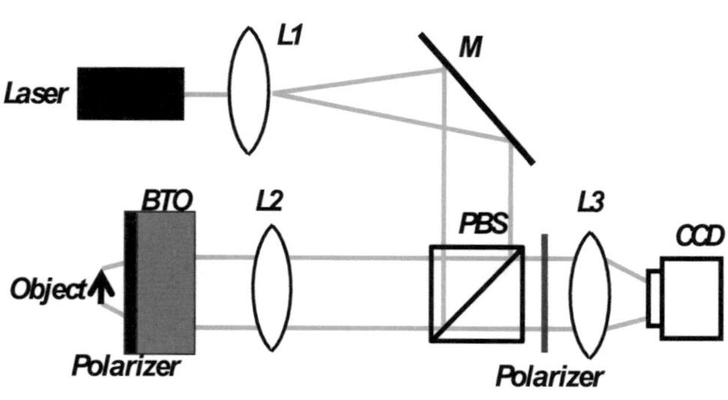

Figure 12. Second compound microscope configuration

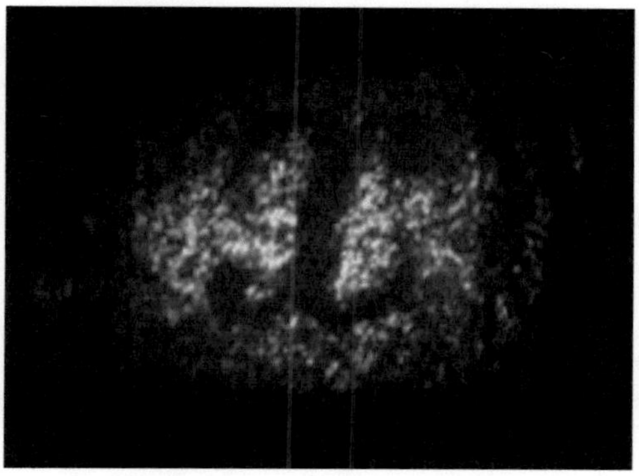

Figure 13. Holographic image built by the second optical configuration

6. Applications

In this section the performance of both configurations are tested and compared as well as the potentialities of the microscopes in the field of device testing and material characterization are pointed out. The most important aspects of the technique are also compared with other characterization processes.

6.1. Microcomponent characterization by double-exposure holographic interferometry

As a preliminary example, figure 14 shows double exposure interferograms resulting from mechanical loads. Figure 14a shows a 2.5 x 2.5-mm^2 illuminated area of a flat metallic bar obtained with the first microscope configuration, while figure 14b shows the chart of figure 13 submitted to a small mechanical perturbation, obtained with the second microscope geometry. In both cases the characteristic double-exposure interferograms can be visualized. Those interference patterns can be mainly attributed to a partial wave depolarization which occurs when the illuminating beam strikes the diffusely scattering object and to domains in the crystal bulk which also partially depolarize the transmitted object beam. Since part of these depolarized waves become p-polarized as they are reflected by the PBS, they interfere with the diffracted waves. While the transmitted object wavefront changes instantaneously with the perturbation, the diffracted wavefront remains unchanged in a period of the order of the hologram buildup time, so that the resulting interference between both waves generates the well-known cos^2-fringe pattern. By whether qualitatively or quantitatively evaluating this interferogram, the deformation map undergone by the object can be determined.

The performance of the reflection holography microscope for holographic interferometry was investigated by studying the response of a 2.96 x 0.6 – mm^2 a-SiC piezoresistor (PZR) through double exposure holography. The sample was bonded to the edge of a 125 x 25-mm^2 tip made of stainless steel. The side containing the PZR was fixed by a massive holder, while the free opposite side was submitted to forces applied normally to the tip. By slightly bending the plate,

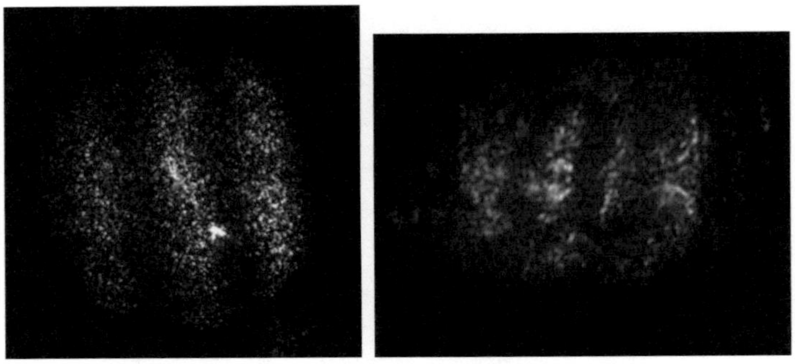

(a) (b)

Figure 14. Double exposure interferograms obtained through: a – the first and b – the second microscope configuration

typical $\cos^2$-fringes are instantaneously visualized. The interference pattern results from the interference between the wave carrying the object holographic reconstruction and the partially transmitted object wave. The consequent deformation of the PZR can be noticed by examining the interferograms shown in figures 14a, b and c, for applied forces of 0.3, 0.5 and 0.7 N, respectively.

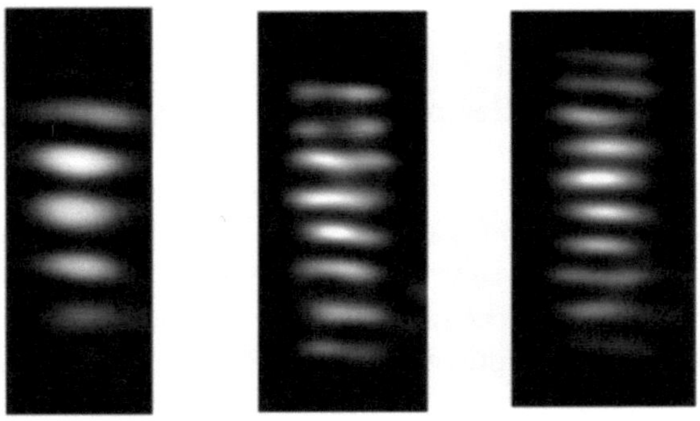

(a) (b) (c)

Figure 15. The deformation map of the partially bended, partially twisted PZR is shown in figure 15.

6.2. Time average holography of a transducer

The second configuration of the holographic microscope was also used for vibration analysis through time average holography. For this purpose a 20x15-mm^2 piezoelectric ceramic and a 12.7x12.7- mm^2 transducer were excited by dither signals. The illuminated area of the transducer is 2x2 mm^2. Figures 17a, 17b and 17c show the nodal regions of the piezoelectric ceramic vibrating at 6 kHz, 11 kHz and 14 kHz, respectively; figure 18 shows the time average pattern of the piezoelectric ceramic vibrating at 1 kHz. Remarkably in figures 17a, 17b and 18 the nodal regions can be clearly noticed. These brightest regions correspond to loci of zero vibration

http://dx.doi.org/10.5772/53416

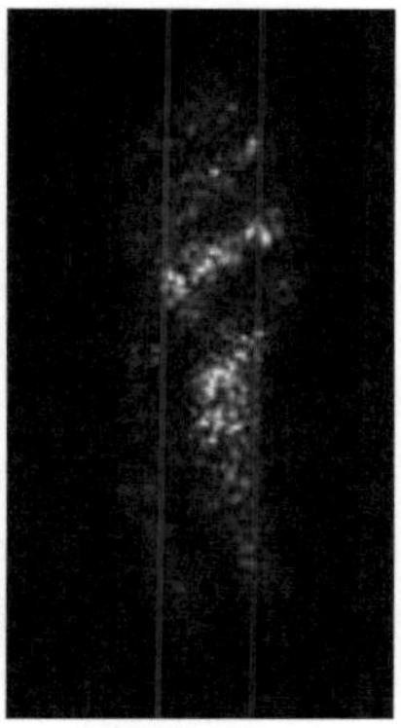

Figure 16. Double-exposure interferogram of the PZR

amplitude, as widely reported in the literature [34]. The thin dark fringes surrounding the nodal regions (denoted by "P" and "Q" in figures 17 and 18) correspond in turn to the roots of the zeroth-order Bessel function whose argument is given by $4\pi A/\lambda$, where A is the vibration amplitude and λ is the light wavelength.

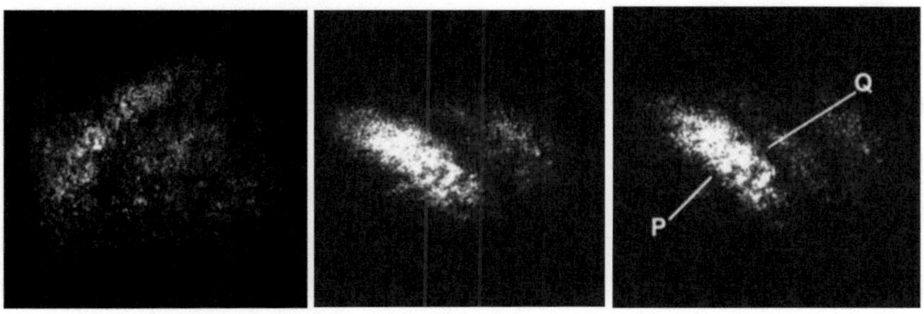

(a) (b) (c)

Figure 17. Time average holograms of a vibrating transducer.

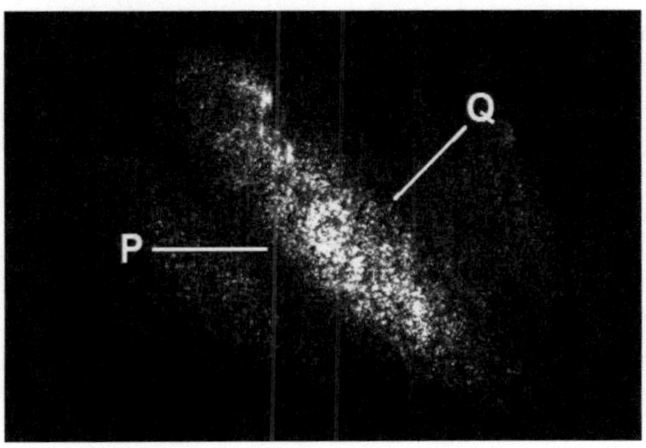

Figure 18. Time average hologram of a vibrating piezoelectric ceramic.

7. Conclusion

The Denisiuk-type reflection holography microscope has been demonstrated to be very suitable for double-exposure and time average holographic interferometry. Due to the use of the PBS cube and the tilting applied to the BTO crystal, the transmitted object beam and its holographic reconstruction emerged from the crystal orthogonally polarized, thus providing high-visibility interferograms in spite of the typically low diffraction efficiency of those media. This novel conception allowed the construction of very simple and compact inline microscopes, with the objective lens working simultaneously as an illuminating lens and an imaging one. In the first optical configuration the BTO crystal is placed at the image plane of the objective, while in the second configuration the BTO was positioned between the object surface and the objective lens. Since the object wave at the holographic medium is higher in the first geometry, the hologram buildup time is shorter, as well as the diffracted wave intensity is higher, resulting in if higher-visibility interferograms, if compared to the second case. The interferograms generated in both cases points out the possibility for construction of compact and portable instruments for microscopic device characterization.

Author details

Eduardo Acedo Barbosa, Danilo Mariano da Silva and Merilyn Santos Ferreira

Laboratório de Óptica Aplicada, Faculdade de Tecnologia de São Paulo, CEETEPS – UNESP, Pça Cel Fernando Prestes, São Paulo – SP, Brazil

References

[1] Ashkin, A, Boyd, G, Dziedzic, J, Smith, R, Ballman, A, Levinstein, J, & Nassau, K. Optically induced refractive index inhomogeneities in LiNbO3 and LiTaO3. Applied Physics Letters (1996)., 9(1), 72-74.

[2] Chen, F. La Macchia J., Fraser D. Holographic storage in Lithium Niobate. Applied Physics Letters (1968)., 13(7), 223-225.

[3] Günter, G, & Huignard, J. Photorefractive Materials and Their Applications II. Topics Applied Physics, 62. Berlin, Heidelberg: Springer Verlag; (1989).

[4] Frejlich, J. Photorefractive Materials. New York: Wiley & Sons; (2007).

[5] Kamshilin, A, & Petrov, M. Continuous reconstruction of holographic interferograms through anisotropic diffraction in photorefractive crystals. Optics Communications (1985)., 53(1), 23-26.

[6] Mallick, S. Roue`de D. Influence of the polarization direction of two-beam coupling in photorefractive Bi12SiO20: Diffusion regime. Applied Physics B: Lasers Optics (1987)., 43(4), 239-245.

[7] Huignard, J, Herriau, J, & Valentin, T. Time average holographic interferometry with photoconductive electrooptic Bi12Si0 20 crystals. Applied Optics (1977). , 16(11), 2796-2798.

[8] Georges, M. Lemaire Ph. Phase-shifting real-time holographic interferometry that uses bismuth silicon oxide crystals. Applied Optics (1995)., 34(32), 7497-7506.

[9] Barbosa, E, & Muramatsu, M. Mapping of vibration amplitudes by time average holography in Bi12SiO20 crystals. Optics Laser Technology (1997)., 29-359.

[10] Horwitz, B, & Corbett, F. The PROM-theory and applications for the Pockels readout optical modulator. Optical Engineering. (1978)., 17-353.

[11] Marrakchi, A, Tanguay, A, Yu, J, & Psaltis, D. Physical characterization of the photorefractive incoherent-to-coherent optical converter. Optical Engineering (1985). , 24-124.

[12] Mccahon, S, Kim, S, & Tanguay, A. Optically modulated linear-array total-internal-reflection spatial light modulator. Journal of the Optical Society of America A (1984).

[13] White, J, & Yariv, A. Real-time image processing via four wave mixing in a photorefractive medium. Applied Physics Letters (1980)., 37-5.

[14] Herriau, J, & Micheron, F. Coherent Selective Erasure of Superimposed Volume Holograms in LiNbO3. Applied Physics Letters (1975). J.P Herriau, F. Micheron, "Coherent Selective Erasure of Superimposed Volume Holograms in LiNbO3" Appl. Phys. Lett. 26, 256 (1975), 26(5), 256-258.

[15] Poon, T, & Banerjee, P. Contemporary Optical Image Processing With Matlab, Elsevier Science (2001)., 1

[16] Feinberg, J. Real-time Edge Enhancement Using the Photorefractive effect. Optics Letters (1980)., 5(8), 330-332.

[17] Chang, C, Chen, T, Yau, H, & Ye, P. Two-way two-dimensional pattern transferring upon requesting with BaTiO3 crystal. Optical Materials (2001)., 18(1), 103-106.

[18] Fischer, B, Cronim-golomb, M, White, J, & Yariv, A. Passive (self-Pumped) Phase Conjugate Mirror: Theorical and Experimental Investigation. Applied Physics Letters (1982)., 41(8), 689-691.

[19] Santos, P, Faria, S, & Tagliaferri, A. Photorefractive optical holographic correlation using a Bi12TiO20 crystal at λ=0.633 μm. Optics Communications (1991). , 86(1), 29-33.

[20] Alam, M, & Khoury, J. Proceedings of the Spie Conference on Photorefractive Fiber and Crystal Devices: Materials, Optical Properties and Applications, San Diego, California (2000).

[21] Chuang, E, & Psaltis, D. Storage of 1000 holograms with use of a dual-wavelength method. Applied Optics (1997). , 36(32), 8445-8454.

[22] Yeh, P, Khoshnevisan, M, Ewbank, M, & Tracy, J. Possibility of relative position sensing by using double phase-conjugate resonators. Optics Communication (1986). , 57(6), 387-390.

[23] Barbosa, E, Preto, A, Silva, D, Carvalho, J, & Morimoto, N. Denisiuk-type reflection holography display with sillenite crystals for imaging and interferometry of small objects. Optics Communications (2008). , 281(3), 408-414.

[24] Kukhtarev, N, Chen, B, Venkateswarlu, P, Salamo, G, & Klein, M. Reflection holographic gratings in [111] cut Bi12TiO20 crystal for real time interferometry. Optics Communications (1993).

[25] Mallick, S, Miteva, M, & Nikolova, I. Polarization properties of self-diffraction in sillenite crystals: reflection volume gratings. Journal of the Optical Society of America B (1997). , 14(5), 1179-1186.

[26] Salazar, A, Lorduy, H, Tebaldi, M, & Bolognini, N. Analysis of reflection speckle holograms in a BSO crystal. Optics Communications (2006). , 262(2), 157-163.

[27] Salazar, A, Goez, R, Sierra, D, Garzón, J, Pérez, F, & Lorduy, H. Optical wavelet correlator by four-wave mixing via reflection holograms in a BSO crystal. Optics Communications (2004).

[28] Erbschloe, D, Solymar, L, Takacs, J, & Wilson, T. Two-wave mixing in reflection holograms in photorefractive materials. IEEE Journal of Quantum Electronics (1988). , 24(5), 820-826.

[29] Shepelevich, V, & Naunyka, V. Effect of optical activity and crystal symmetry on maximal diffraction efficiency of reflection holograms in cubic photorefractive piezocrystals.Applied Physics B (2009). , 95(3), 459-466.

[30] Shandarov, S, & Burimov, N. Kul'chin Y., Romachko R., Tolstik A., Shepelevich V. Dynamic Denisyuk holograms in cubic photorefractive crystals. Quantum Electronics (2008). , 38(11), 1059-1069.

[31] Denisyuk, Y. On the reflection of optical properties of an object in a wave field of light scattered by it. Doklady Akademii Nauk SSSR (1962). , 144(6), 1275-1278.

[32] Buse, K. Light-Induced Charge Transport Processes in Photorefractive Crystals I: Models and Methods. Applied Physics B (1997). , 64(3), 273-291.

[33] Miridonov, S, Kamshilin, A, & Barbosa, E. Recyclable holographic interferometer with a photorefractive crystal: optical scheme optimization. Journal of the Optical Society of America A (1994). , 11(6), 1780-1788.

[34] Hariharan, P. Optical Holography: Principles, techniques and applications. Cambridge Studies in Modern Optics, (1996).

Chapter 10

Bifurcation Effects Generated with Holographic Rough Surfaces

G. Martínez Niconoff, G. Díaz González,
P. Martínez Vara, J. Silva Barranco and
J. Munoz-Lopez

Additional information is available at the end of the chapter

http://dx.doi.org/10.5772/54512

1. Introduction

The holographic research is related to the coded storage and the ulterior decoded of optical information [1]. The holographic processes involved had extended its application to almost all the optical areas; such that nowadays is not possible to conceive the development of the modern optics without this powerful tool [2-5]. The development of this area implies the generation of optical fields with suitable structure also as the research and synthesis of novel holographic materials with large refractive index values and sensible to a wide frequencies range [6-8].

In the present study, we are interested in to generate holographic rough surfaces, such that the scattered field can be amplitude self-correlated. Until our best knowledge, almost all works related to the speckle pattern are irradiance correlated. However, in order to understand the physical features of the speckle pattern is necessary to obtain the amplitude correlation function, which must be manifested in the interference features between speckle motes. This is possible because for the same illumination configurations, the roughness parameters may obey two probability density functions. Other important effect occurs during the recording process, making possible to generate regions with cusped geometry. The behavior of the electric field in the neighborhood of these cusped regions generates evanescent waves [9,10], and it is used to generate surface plasmon fields. This occurs when a metal thin film is deposited on the holographic rough surface [11]. The surface plasmon fields appears when the power spectrum associated to the cusped region, is matched with the dispersion relation function of the surface plasmon. In the context of the angular spectrum model the cusped regions correspond to the Gibbs phenomenon [12].

The holographic rough surface proposed is generated by recording a set of optical fields kind cosine, the register media consists in a photo-resist film deposited on a glass substrate, using the periods of the optical field as the control parameter. This construction allows us to design the power spectrum of the holographic surface. Consequently, during the reconstruction process, the scattered field consists in a well localized speckle band.

The holographic rough surface thus generated is implemented as a beam splitter in an amplitude-correlation interferometer, which allows the interference between two speckle bands. The main feature is that the two speckle patterns coming from the same holographic rough surface obey different probability density functions; however a certain amplitude correlation function between the speckle patterns is preserved.

From the experimental results for the interference, very interesting features can be identified, one of them consists in the generation of bifurcation effects kind pitchfork [13,14]. The physical origin of this effect is explained from the boundary condition to the electromagnetic field. Since the theoretical point of view, the bifurcation effects allow to determinate the interaction between the irradiance distributions and can be interpreted as amplitude four order correlations. The geometry of the bifurcation suggests as application to be used as a kind of speckle tweezers. Another possible application consists in the alignment of nanoparticles and nanotubes inducing resonance effects close related to tunable spectroscopy [15-17]. Since the theoretical point of view, behavior such as Anderson localization can be implemented [18].

The structure of this chapter is as follows. In section *2*, we describe the synthesis of the rough surface, using as prototype cosine beams of different periods. When some consonance occurs between maximum or minimum values of the cosine beams, randomly distributed cusped points are generated. In the section *3*, we show the design of a very stable four arms interferometer by using the holographic rough surface as a beam splitter to generate two optical fields. In each arm, the optical field consists in a speckle pattern where each mote contains a set of cosine fringes. In section *4*, we show that controlling the size of the illumination beam, the mean size of the motes is also controlled, obeying an inverse relation, i.e. by decreasing the size of the illumination beam, the size of the mote increase. This property allows us to control the relative transversal separation between motes generating an interaction between interference fringes, the set of fringes presents similar behavior to wave-guide, allowing to explain the physical origin of the bifurcation effects. In section *5*, we describe the general conclusions remarking the property of the cusped points to generate surface plasmon fields and some potential applications are mentioned.

2. Holographic generation of rough surfaces

The holographic rough surfaces are generated by means of a superposition of cosenoidal patterns resulting of the interference between two plane waves, whose amplitude distribution is given by

$$\phi(x,z) = a\exp\left[ik\left(xsen\theta + z\cos\theta\right)\right] + a\exp\left[ik\left(-xsen\theta + z\cos\theta\right)\right], \tag{1}$$

where k is the wave number, θ is the incidence angle measured respect the normal vector n to the surface as it is sketched in Fig. 1.

The irradiance distribution takes the form

$$I(x,z) = \left|\phi(x,z)\right|^2 = 2a^2\left(1 + \cos\left(kxsen\theta\right)\right). \tag{2}$$

By changing the incidence angle we generate a set of cosine patterns

$$I_q(x,z) = \left\{S_q\left(1 + \cos\left(kxsen\theta_q + \delta_q\right)\right)\right\}. \tag{3}$$

with q=1,2,…n and $S_q=2a_q^2$. The phase term δ_q appears when a lateral shift in the maximum values is implemented.

These irradiance distributions are recorded on the holographic material. The experimental details are as follows. The holographic plate was made by depositing a photo-resist film using a spin-coating technique on a glass substrate. The number of irradiance distributions recorded were N=300 and it was excited using a *He-Cd* laser with a wavelength of 442 *nm*.

Assuming a lineal response of the holographic material, the mathematical representation to the resultant profile is

$$h(x) \approx \sum_{i=1}^{N}\left[1 + \cos\left(K_n x + \delta_n\right)\right]S_n. \tag{4}$$

By considering that S_n is a random variable that depends on the exposition time of each register, and δ_n is a random phase controlled by shifting the holographic plate along the x-coordinate, then the holographic surface acquires a one dimensional random profile, whose height distribution satisfies a Gaussian probability density function as a consequence of the limit central theorem.

The transmittance function associated to the holographic surface is obtained by normalizing the height distribution in Eq. (4), and it is given by

$$t(x) = h(x) - \sum_{i=1}^{N} S_n = \sum_{i=1}^{N} S_n \cos\left(K_n x + \phi_n\right). \tag{5}$$

The statistical parameters of the surface are the following, the mean value of the rough surface profile is $\langle t(x) \rangle = 0$.

The variance of the height distributions is given by

$$\sigma^2 = \frac{1}{2}\sum_{i=1}^{N} S_n^2. \tag{6}$$

Another important parameter is the length of correlation. This can be obtained following the classical definition of correlation, but it implies to lose the geometrical point of view, for this reason, we prefer to use an approximated relation. This can be done by noting that the maximum correlation of a cosine term with itself is $\pi/2$; with this interpretation, the correlation length depends geometrically on the initial and final recording angles, and can be expressed as

$$\Delta x = x_0 - x_0^{'} = \frac{\lambda}{4}\left(\frac{1}{sen\theta_i} - \frac{1}{sen\theta_f}\right). \tag{7}$$

Equations (5-7) are the expressions that carry on the information of the statistical properties of the holographic rough surface.

To generate the surface, we use a holographic system as it is sketched in Fig. (1). The mirrors and the holographic plate are placed on displacement mountings whose movements are controlled with a computer. This setup allows us to control the fringe period and the phase term δ_n. The recording times are random variables with uniform probability density function in the interval [0,2] sec., and it is controlled with the shutter shown in Fig. (1).

As a final remark of this section, during the recording process, some regions with geometrical cusped may be generated by the consonance in the maximum/minimum values of the cosine terms, as it is shown in Fig. 2.

The importance of these cusped regions appears during the reconstruction process, because they have the capacity to generate evanescent waves. We consider that the number of cusped regions follows a Poisson distribution. The amplitude value to the electric field in the neighborhood of these points can exceed in several magnitude orders the value respect other regions.

So far we have described the synthesis of holographic rough surfaces with controlled statistical parameters. To understand the physical features of the scattered field is necessary to study the amplitude distribution, this can be done by analyzing the interference effects as it is described in the following section.

http://dx.doi.org/10.5772/54512

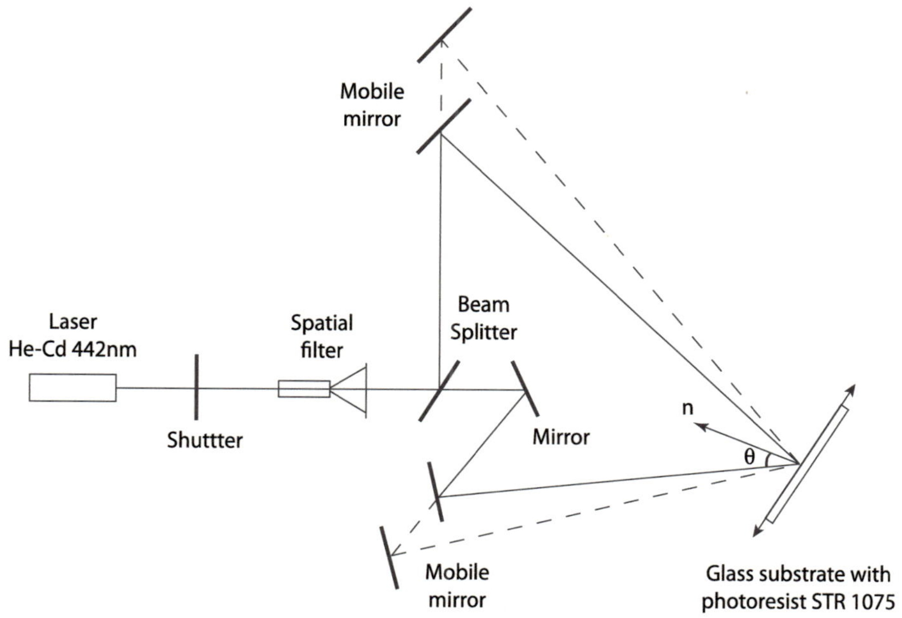

Figure 1. Schematic set up to generate the holographic rough surface.

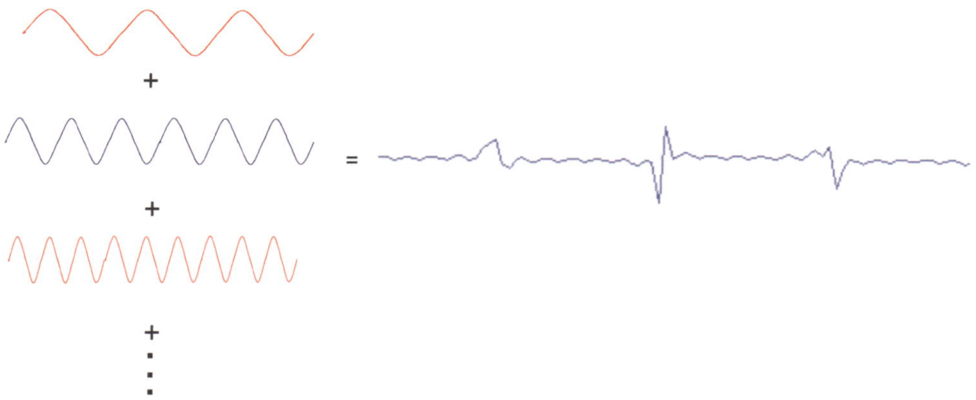

Figure 2. Consonance between maximum/minimum values of the cosine beams to generate cusped points.

3. Interference between speckle patterns

During the reconstruction process, the scattered field emerging from the rough surface, when it is illuminated with a plane wave has the structure of a speckle pattern. The speckle pattern is spatially bounded as a consequence of the recording process. This is because the recording incident angles of the plane waves take values in an established range, for the presented case the angular range is *[30º-45º]*. However, the reconstruction wavelength used was of 632.8 *nm* emerging from a He-Ne laser.

It is a knowing fact that the amplitude function of a speckle pattern satisfies a Gaussian probability density function, and the irradiance distribution follows an exponential function [19]. In both cases, the statistical parameters such as the variance can be controlled with the transversal size of the illumination beam. This parameter will be used to control the bifurcation effects generated during the interference process, as it is shown below.

The holographic rough surface is implemented as a beam splitter to perform a four arm interferometer as it is sketched in Fig.3.

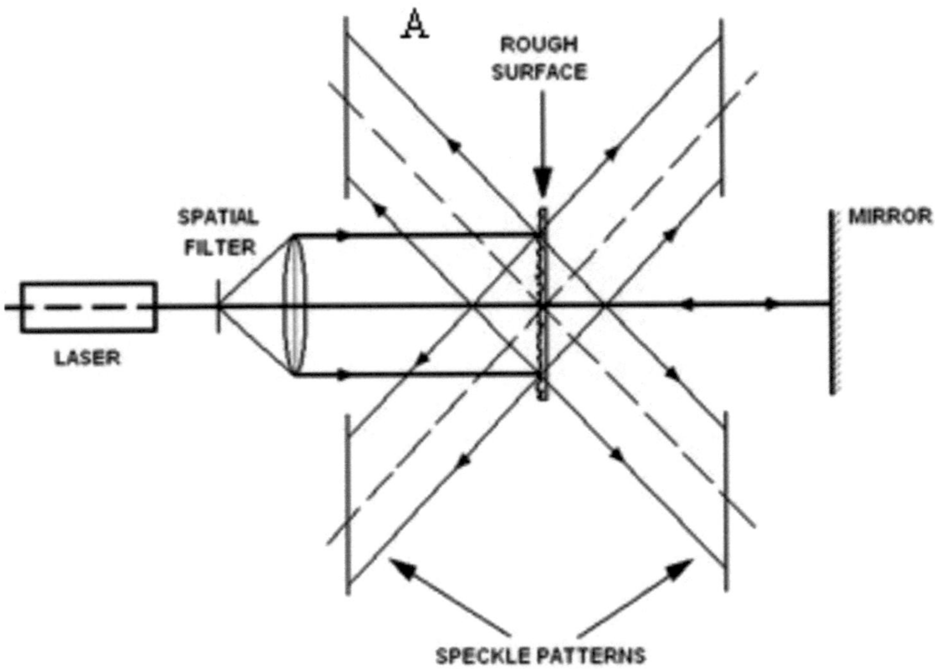

Figure 3. Experimental set up to generate the interference between speckle patterns.

The interference effects, on the arm *A* are generated by means of the amplitude superposition between the field emerging by reflection and the field emerging by the illumination of the zero order diffraction reflected in the mirror. Both fields are shifted each other, because the mean thickness of the holographic rough surface and the difference of the wavelengths. Then we have that, the structure of the interference pattern is locally similar to the Young experiment. This comment is reinforced by the experimental results showed in Fig4. In Fig. 4.a we show the speckle pattern and in Figs. 4.b, 4.c, we show the interference between two amplitude correlated speckle patterns for two configurations of illumination.

http://dx.doi.org/10.5772/54512

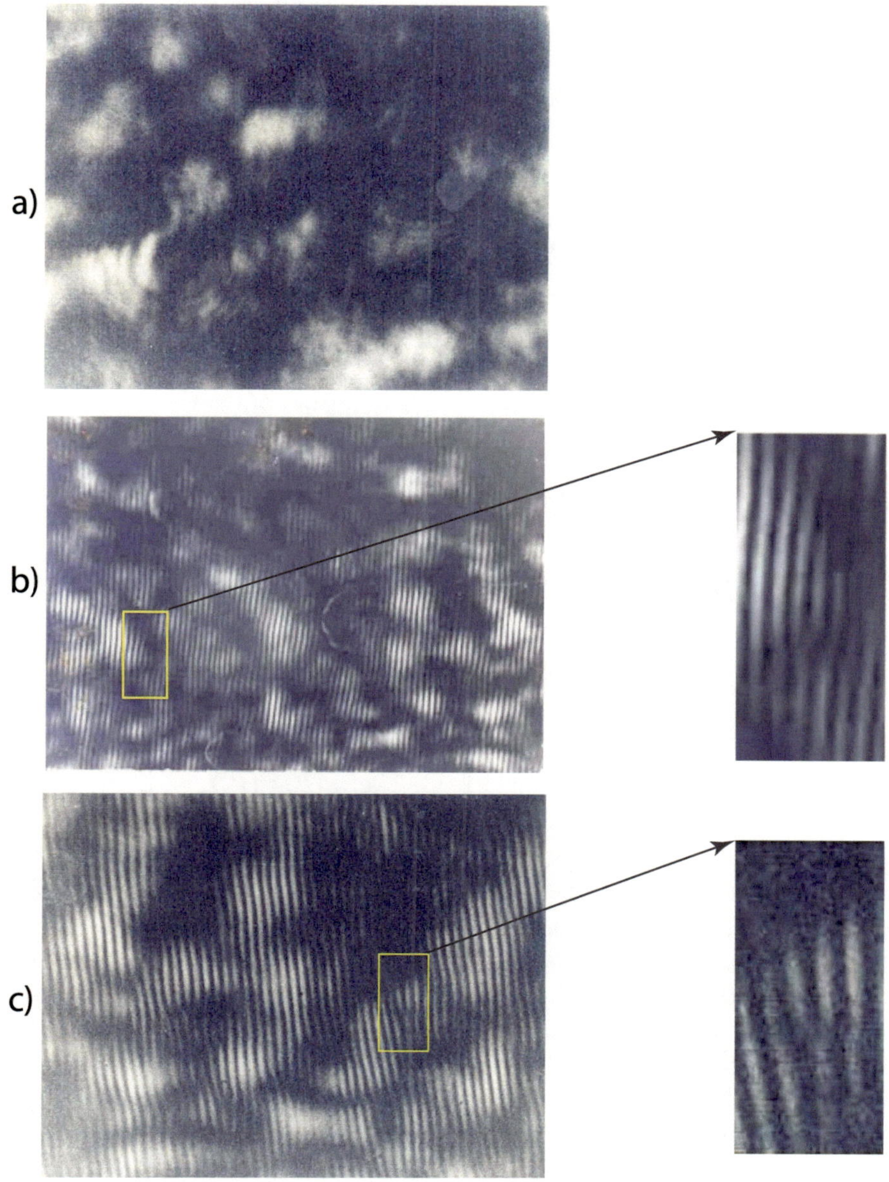

Figure 4. a) Speckle pattern generated by illuminating a rough surface with bounded power spectrum. The image was amplified *400X* using a microscope. b) and c) Interference between speckle patterns for two configurations of illumination. In both cases, the interference pattern presenting bifurcation effects kind pitchfork.

The expression for the interference is described as follows. The amplitude on an arbitrary point P is given by

$$\phi(P) = \phi_r(P) + \phi_t(P), \tag{8}$$

where the amplitude terms for reflected and transmitted fields can be approximated as

$$\begin{aligned}\phi_r(P) &\approx \sum_{n=1}^{N} A_n \exp\left[ikr_{np}\right]\\ \phi_t(P) &\approx \sum_{i=1}^{M} A_i \exp\left[ikr_{ip}\right].\end{aligned} \tag{9}$$

An important parameter is the number of trajectories N, M emerging from each surface, which in general are different because each optical field obey different probability density functions, this due to the zero order diffraction after reflection in the mirror illuminates the holographic rough surface with a wavelength of λ_t, this is a consequence of the propagation in a media with a refractive index corresponding to the holographic material.

The irradiance associated to the scattered field, takes the form

$$I(P) = \left|\phi_r(P)\right|^2 + \left|\phi_t(P)\right|^2 + 2\mathrm{Re}\,\phi_r(P)\phi_t^*(P), \tag{10}$$

and the mean irradiance is given by

$$\left\langle I(P)\right\rangle = \left\langle \left|\phi_r(P)\right|^2 \right\rangle_r + \left\langle \left|\phi_t(P)\right|^2 \right\rangle_t + 2\mathrm{Re}\left\langle \phi_r(P)\phi_t^*(P)\right\rangle. \tag{11}$$

A remarkable feature is that the interference area is controlled by means of the size of the illumination beam. This means that the N and M parameters in the sum term in Eq. (9) have an implicit dependence on the number of trajectories emerging from each holographic rough surface as sketching in Fig. 5.

The fact that the holographic rough surface exhibits two probability density functions is easily understood because the roughness profile is depending on the illumination wavelength. When the illuminating light is coming from free space, the probability density function for the amplitude field is $f(x,\lambda_0)$, and for the light reflected in the mirror through the photo-resist, the probability density function is $f_t(x,\lambda_t)$, meaning that both functions have the same functional dependence except a scale factor associated to the wavelength. This justifies that the scattered fields, given by Eq. (9), must present a certain correlation between the amplitude functions allowing the interference effects.

The average size of the speckle pattern is greater for the scattered field generated by reflection, this is because the refractive index, expressed as quotation between the wavelength implies that $n=\lambda_0/\lambda$. The typical values for the photo-resist refractive index are in the range [1.5-1.7]. A consequence of this fact is $\lambda_t<\lambda_0$.

http://dx.doi.org/10.5772/54512

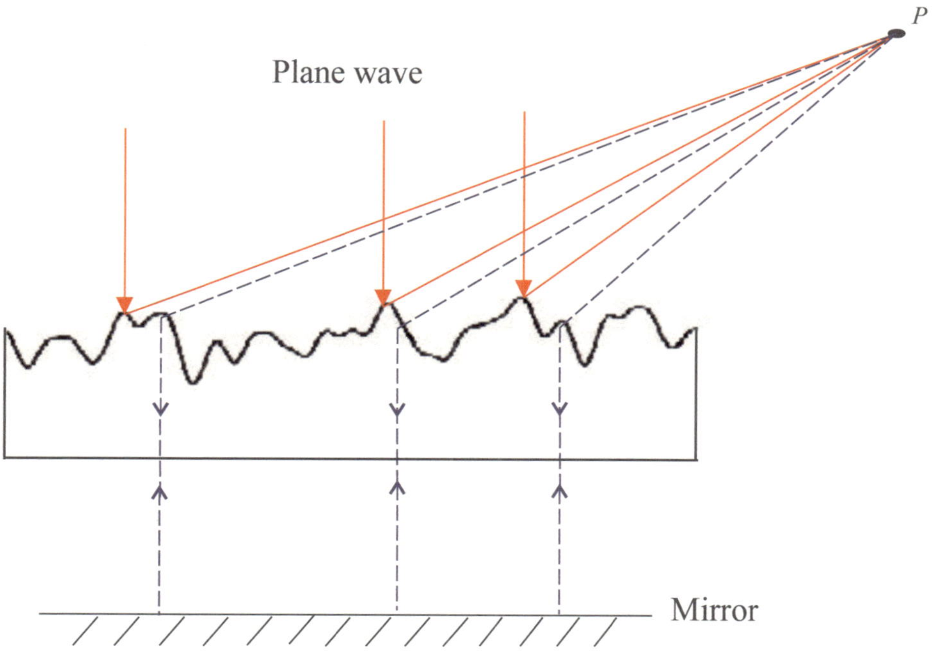

Figure 5. Generation of the interference effects on an arbitrary point *P*. The bold line represents light generated by the reflection on the rough surface coming from free space. The dot lines represent light from rough surface coming from the holographic media. The number of trajectories that arrives to point *P* may be different in each case.

The sub-index in the square brackets in Eq. (11) means that the mean value for the interference term must be calculated using the joint probability density function, which is an unknown function. However an approximate expression can be proposed by noting that one of the amplitude values can be scaled, such that the mean interference term may be calculate by using a Gaussian probability density function whose arguments depends on the relative difference between two arbitrary points $(x_2\text{-}x_1)$. This previous comments allows to describe completely the interference effects.

As a finally remark, by a visual analysis of the interference pattern it is easily to detect the existence of regions where the interference fringes are "branched", which corresponds to the bifurcation effects under study. The experimental shown in Fig. 4 are for normal incidence illumination and for angle of 5º respect the normal *n*.

4. Description of bifurcation effects

The bifurcation effects are generated when one or more parameters that characterize the system change continually, such that, when they acquire some critical value, modify and generate new physical properties of the system. For the present study, this parameter is the size of the transversal section of the illumination beam, which allows controlling the size of the speckle motes and then generates in a controlled way a transversal interaction between two or more speckle motes. The influence of this parameter is implicit in the number of trajectories *N* and *M* given in Eq. (9) that emerges from the rough surface and arrives on the same point p in the scattered field generating the interference effects. Each speckle mote has associated an interference fringes pattern, and the bifurcation effects are associated to the changes in the interference fringes when two or more speckle motes becomes closer. These comments are sketched in Fig. 6. In Fig. 6.a) we sketch two speckle motes, where the cosine interference fringes are bounded by the size and geometry of the mote. The size of the motes is controlled by changing the transversal size of the illumination beam, when this decreases, the size of the motes increase, and vice versa, as it is sketched in Fig. 6.b).

The transversal interaction between the interference fringes bounded by the speckle motes is shown in Fig. 6.c). The interaction between two interference fringe is the responsible of the generation of the bifurcation effects. The physical origin of this effect is in the boundary condition of the electromagnetic field which are dependent on the phase value in the contact point, in general, exists a discontinuity in the phase value when the interference fringes becomes closer. In order to satisfy the continuity of the tangential components of the electric field and the normal components of the electric displacement, a balance in energy and phase between the interference fringes occurs. This means that, when the two motes are far away no interaction occurs, when they become closer part of the energy must be transferred between the fringes, i.e. the energy flows through the fringes acquiring a final equilibrium value, modifying the interference fringes geometry. In general the fringes associated to each mote has different values in the phase function, which means that the fringes are shifted one respect to other. When a jump in the phase value of $\pi/2$ occurs between two fringes, geometrically means that a bright fringes is aligned with a dark fringes, the capacity of energy transfer is maximum, and the interference fringes splits generating the bifurcation effects kind pitchfork sketched in Fig. 6.c). This explanation agrees with the electromagnetic models and it is supported by the experimental results shown in Fig. 4.

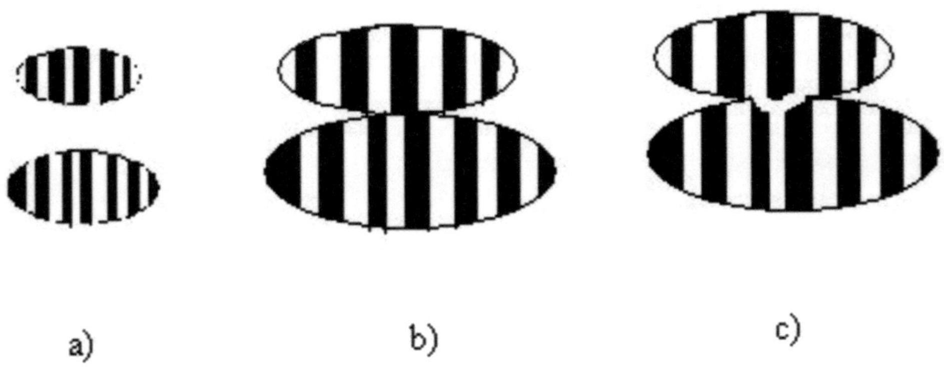

Figure 6. Description of bifurcation effects. In a) The two motes are independent and no interaction between the interference fringes occurs. In b), and c), when the motes become closer, an interaction between the fringes occurs unfolding the fringes structure. The splitting of the fringes is a consequence of the continuity of the electromagnetic field.

To describe the transversal interaction between interference fringes, we assume that two speckle neighborhood motes has irradiance I_1 and I_2 respectively, the energy transfer satisfies

$$\begin{aligned} \nabla_{\perp} I_1 &= \boldsymbol{a} I_2 \\ \nabla_{\perp} I_2 &= \boldsymbol{b} I_1, \end{aligned} \tag{12}$$

where $\nabla_{\perp} = \left(\hat{i}\frac{\partial}{\partial x} + \hat{j}\frac{\partial}{\partial y} \right)$ and ***a, b*** are coupling constants vectors, in general case, ***a, b*** may be function of position and time whose analysis is out scope of the present work. This two expressions are equivalent to have a single Helmholtz equation given by

$$\nabla^2 \left(I_1 - I_2 \right) = \left(\boldsymbol{a} \cdot \boldsymbol{b} \right) \left(I_1 - I_2 \right). \tag{13}$$

The nature of the solutions for the Helmholtz equation, depends on the difference between the irradiance values on a contact point, also as the sign of the dot product between the coupling vectors. The simplest case occurs when $\boldsymbol{a.b} = 0$ corresponding to orthogonal polarization states. For this case, the Eq. (13) acquires the form of Laplace Equation and no interaction between irradiance distributions is expected.

When the dot product is negative, $\boldsymbol{a.b}<0$ the equation corresponds to the traditional Helmholtz equation used in classical optics. The physical implication is that, the interference fringes may be extended on a bigger region, because energy can flows troughs the interference fringes and the optical field presents a wave behavior, this effect corresponds to the interference fringes which are easely identified in Fig.(4).

When the dot product is positive, $\boldsymbol{a.b}>0$ the solutions has a decreasing exponential solution in some coordinate, i.e. the solution may have a wave behavior along one coordinate and an exponential decreasing in the other coordinate, this kind of solution, delimits a well identified interference region. All previous comments are in well agreement with the experimental results shown in Fig.4.

The study presented offers the possibility to generate local optical vortex by controlling in an alternating way the size of the illuminating beam, i.e. we pass from regions with bifurcation to region without bifurcation, controlling locally the geometry of the interference fringes. An important application of this effect is the possibility to transfer angular moment to particles placed in the neighborhood of the contact point of two speckle motes.

5. Final remarks and conclusions

In order to have a complete description of the scattered field generated by the holographic rough surface is necessary to describe the optical field emerging from the neighborhood of the cusped points. We approximate the effects by noting that the cusped point can be consider as a quasi-point source, its representation, using the angular spectrum model, can be obtained using the Weyl representation given by [10]

$$\frac{\exp\left[ikr\right]}{r}=\frac{ik}{2\pi}\int_{-\infty}^{\infty}\frac{1}{m}\exp\left[ik\left(xu+yv+zp\right)\right]dudv, \tag{14}$$

where (u,v,p) are the spatial frequencies that satisfies

$$u^2+v^2+p^2=\frac{1}{\lambda^2}. \tag{15}$$

It must be noted that the representation consists in two kinds of waves. One of them occurs when $u^2+v^2\leq\frac{1}{\lambda^2}$ and it corresponds to homogeneous plane waves. Another case occurs when $u^2+v^2>\frac{1}{\lambda^2}$, the spatial frequency p associated to the z-coordinate becomes imaginary, this corresponds to evanescent waves. More details concerning this representation can be founded in [10]. This evanescent character is implemented to generate other interesting physical features such as enhanced backscattering. When the holographic rough surface is covered with a metal thin film, the evanescent waves induce surface charge oscillations that propagate along the surface as a non-radiative inhomogeneous wave. These waves are known as surface plasmon waves. The important parameter is the relative separation between to cusped points. Then we have that incident light on the surface is coupled with the power spectrum of the cusped point generating a surface plasmon field. The propagation of the surface plasmon field when it meets another cusped point generates radiative optical field. This field interferes constructively with the incident light, this effect is known as enhanced backscattering, more detailed information to this effect can be found in [11].

In general the surface plasmon waves propagate short distances, typically 100 μm. [20], however long range surface plasmon waves can be generated by controlling the thickness of the metal film. When the thickness is in the range *[20 nm-60 nm]*, the length of propagation can reach until to 2000 μm [21], this allows to implement a two-dimensional surface plasmon optics. We assume that the thickness of the film does not change the roughness statistical parameters. The parameter that determinates the length of propagation of the surface plasmon is known as the dispersion relation function. For a semi-infinite media it is given by

$$\beta=\frac{\omega}{c}\left(\frac{\varepsilon_1\varepsilon_2}{\varepsilon_1+\varepsilon_2}\right)^{1/2}, \tag{16}$$

and for a metal thin film of thickness *[20 nm-60 nm]*, it acquires the form

$$\beta = \frac{\omega}{c}\left\{\left(\frac{\varepsilon_1\varepsilon_2}{\varepsilon_1+\varepsilon_2}\right)^{1/2} + 2an_1\left(\frac{\varepsilon_1\varepsilon_2}{\varepsilon_1+\varepsilon_2}\right)^{-1/2}\exp\left[-2\alpha d\right]\right\}. \tag{17}$$

From last representation, we have that to generate the coupling of illumination light-surface plasmon fields-scattered light, the mean distance between two cusped points L_c must be less than the length propagation of the plasmon field, i.e. $L_c < \beta^{-1}$, which is a necessary condition to improve the enhanced backscattering.

As a conclusion, in this chapter, we described the generation of a holographic rough surface using an incoherent convergence of holograms kind cosine. The surface was implemented to perform an interferometer that allows correlating two speckle patterns. The structure of the interference fringes shows the generation of bifurcation effects kind pitchfork. The splitting of the interference fringes is related with the size of the speckle motes and it is a consequence of the boundary conditions of the electromagnetic field. The superposition of cosine patterns generates cusped points randomly distributed and during the reconstruction process this cusped points generates evanescent waves. When the holographic rough surface is covered with a metal film, the cusped points generate surface plasmon fields.

Author details

G. Martínez Niconoff[1], G. Díaz González[1], P. Martínez Vara[2], J. Silva Barranco[1] and J. Munoz-Lopez[1]

1 Instituto Nacional de Astrofísica Óptica y Electrónica, Luis Enrique Erro No. , Tonantzintla, Puebla, México

2 Benemérita Universidad Autónoma de Puebla, Ciudad Universitaria, Facultad de Ingenierías, Puebla, México

References

[1] Hariharan, P. (1983). Colour Holography, *Progress in optics* 20, North-Holand, Amsterdam.,, 263-324.

[2] Yamaguchi, I, Ida, T, Yokota, M, & Yamashita, K. (2006). Surface shape measurement by phase-shifting digital holography with a wavelength shift. *Appl. Opt.* 45, , 7610-7616.

[3] Weidong MaoYongchun Zhong, Jianwen Dong, and Hezhou Wang, ((2005). Crystallography of two-dimensional photonic lattices formed by holography of three noncoplanar beams. *JOSA B*, 22(5), , 1085-1091.

[4] Matsushima, K. (2005). Computer-generated holograms for three-dimensional surface objects with shade and texture. *Appl. Opt.* 44, , 4607-4614.

[5] Parshall, D, & Kim, M. K. (2006). Digital holographic microscopy with dual-wavelength phase unwrapping. *Appl. Opt.* 45, , 451-459.

[6] Martinez-niconoff, G. Ramirez San Juan J.C., Muñoz-Lopez J., Martinez-Vara P., Carbajal-Dominguez A., and Sanchez-Gil J.A., ((2008). Spatial filtering dark hollow beams. *Opt. Comm.*, 281 , 3237-3240.

[7] Korolev, E. (1996). Dynamic holography in alkali metal vapour. *Optics and Laser Technology*, 28(4), , 277-284.

[8] Demetri PsaltisFai Mok, and Hsin-Yu Sidney Li, ((1994). Nonvolatile storage in photorefractive crystals. *Opt. Lett.* 19, , 210-212.

[9] Jackson, J. D. (1998). *Classical Electrodynamics.* 3rd. Edition, *John Wiley & Sons, Inc., New York*, 047130932, 29-47.

[10] Mandel, L, & Wolf, E. (1995). *Optical Coherence and Quantum Optics.* Cambridge University Press., 0-52141-711-2, 120-125.

[11] West, C. S, & Donnell, K. A. O. (1995). Observations of backscattering enhancement from polaritons on a rough metal surface. *J. Opt. Soc. Am.* A,12, , 390-397.

[12] Shizgal, B, & Jung, J. H. (2003). Towards the Resolution of the Gibbs Phenomena, *J. Comput. Appl. Math.* 161, , 41-65.

[13] Beltrami, E. J. (1987). *Mathematics for dynamic modeling.* 2nd Edition, New York, *Academic Press Inc.* 0-12085-555-0, 171-202.

[14] Jyoti Champanerkar and Denis Blackmore(2007). Pitchfork bifurcations of invariant manifolds, *Topology and its Applications.*, 154, , 1650-1663.

[15] Tal, R. V, Roze, G. A, Shandryuk, A. S, Merekalov, A. M, & Shatalova, O. A. Otmakhova, ((2009). Alignment of Nanoparticles in Polymer Matrices. *Polymer Science*, Ser. A 51, , 1194-1203.

[16] Miguel, A. Correa-Duarte, Marek Grzelezak, Veronica Salgueiriño-Maceira, Michael Giersig, Luis M.Liz-Marzan, Michael Farle, Karl Sierazdki, and Rodolfo Diaz, ((2005). Alignment of Carbon Nanotubes under Low Magnetic Fields through Attachment of Magnetic Nanoparticles. *J. Phys. Chem. B* 109 (41), , 19060-19063.

[17] Nahum Gat(2000). Imaging Spectroscopy Using Tunable Filters: A Review. *Proc. Spie* , 4056, 50-64.

[18] Sheng, P. (1991). Scattering and Localization of Classical Waves in Random Media,World Scientific, Singapore.

[19] Goodman, J. P. (1985). *Introduction to statistics optics*. John Wiley & Sons, 0-47101-502-4, 7-55.

[20] Raether, H. (1988). Surface plasmons on smooth and rough surfaces and on gratings. of *Springer tracts in modern physics*, Springer-Verlag, Berlin, 3-54017-363-2, 111, 4-37.

[21] Martínez, G, Niconoff, P, Martínez-vara, J, Muñoz-lopez, J. C, Juarez, M, & Carbajal-domínguez, A. (2011). Partially coherent surface plasmon modes. *Journal of the European Optical Society* 6,1109, , 1-6.

Chapter 11

Holography at the Nano Level With Visible Light Wavelengths

Cesar A. Sciammarella, Luciano Lamberti and
Federico M. Sciammarella

Additional information is available at the end of the chapter

http://dx.doi.org/10.5772/53346

1. Introduction

Microscopy was invented in the 17th century, and after four centuries the methodology to get information at increasingly small distances has become a complex multidisciplinary science. Abbe, towards the middle of 1870s, introduced the fundamental idea that, due to the wave nature of light, the resolving power of a microscope was constrained by its angular aperture that limited the number of components of an image. Almost at the same time, Lord Rayleigh introduced his criterion based on the work of Airy dealing with the optical astronomy problem of the separation of two stars.

An optical method to overcome the classical limits of resolution was initiated by Toraldo di Francia in the late 1940s, about 65 years ago, utilizing evanescent fields [1]. The motivation came from the solutions of the Maxwell's equations and the theory of antennae. He foresaw the possibility of increasing resolution to a limit only constrained by the indetermination principle that connects the energy available in an observation process to the spatial resolution that can be achieved.

The authors [2], following this line of research, reported in 2006 the successful detection of information well beyond the optical resolution limit getting down to 4 nm, that is 1/79 of the classical resolution limit $\lambda/2$. The experiments conducted by the authors yielded later on very important developments that connect super-resolution with an optical method very similar in its formalism to Fourier transform holography.

This chapter will cover the following topics: 1) basic definitions on evanescent fields and fundamental relationships; 2) generation of super-oscillatory fields; 3) processes involved in the transformation of super-resolution near fields, that are well known and extensively researched, into propagating fields that can be observed in the far field; 4) similarity between the observed images and FT holography but in the context of a different type of diffraction effect; 5) extraction of 3-D information from the 2-D image of the pseudo-FT hologram; 6) digital reconstruction of the pseudo-FT holograms of simple objects such as prismatic nano-crystals and nano-spheres; 7) verification of the obtained results; 8) numerical issues entailed by the reconstruction process; 9) discussion and conclusions.

2. Evanescent fields

2.1. Evanescent wave's solution of Maxwell equations

Let us consider the solution of the Maxwell equations for planar propagating waves, the vectorial Helmholtz equation. By taking an exponential function as a solution of the Maxwell equations of the form $\exp(i\omega t)$ one gets the following vector equation:

$$(\nabla^2 + \omega^2 \mu_0 \varepsilon_0)\left\{ \begin{matrix} \vec{E} \\ \vec{B} \end{matrix} \right\} = 0 \tag{1}$$

The electric and the magnetic field vectors $\vec{E}$ and $\vec{B}$ satisfy the above equation (1). The notation ∇^2 indicates the Laplace operator, $\omega=2\pi f=2\pi/T$ is the temporal angular period, ε_o and μ_o are the permittivity and permeability of vacuum, respectively. By introducing the argument $\exp(\vec{k} \bullet \vec{r} - i\omega t)$, the periodicity in space is included in the wave solution. The quantity k is the wave number $2\pi/\lambda$, $\vec{r}$ is the position vector. The vector $\vec{r}$ is characterized for a plane wave by the equation, $\vec{r} = r\,(\alpha\,\vec{i} + \beta\,\vec{j} + \gamma\,\vec{k})$, where α, β, γ are the direction cosines of the considered vector. A general solution of Eq. (1) is possible, by assuming that α, β, γ are complex quantities that have real and imaginary components. By defining:

$$\begin{aligned} \alpha &= a_1 + i\,a_2 \\ \beta &= b_1 + i b_2 \\ \gamma &= c_1 + i c_2 \end{aligned} \tag{2}$$

the dotted $\vec{k} \bullet \vec{r}$ product gives:

$$\vec{k} \bullet \vec{r} = k\left[-(a_2 x + b_2 y + c_2 z) + i(a_1 x + b_1 y + c_1 z)\right] \tag{3}$$

Let us apply the above derivations to the problem of total reflection, Figure 1. For simplicity, the analysis is reduced to a two dimensional problem, by analyzing the process in the incidence plane of a propagating beam from medium 1 to medium 2 such that $n_1>n_2$, where n_1 and n_2 are the indices of refraction of the two media. Considering the total internal reflection condition, introducing the refraction equation and calling θ_i the angle of incidence and θ_t the angle of the transmitted light one arrives to the following conclusions:

1. There is a surface wave that propagates in the X-direction as a plane wave.
2. The planes of constant phase and constant amplitude are orthogonal to each other.
3. The electromagnetic field penetrates the second medium but decays very rapidly in the Z-direction.
4. If the electric vector is contained in the plane of incidence, the evanescent field electric vector becomes elliptically polarized in the plane of incidence, (p-polarization).
5. If the electric vector is orthogonal to the plane of incidence (s-polarization), the polarization does not experience changes.
6. If one computes the Poynting vector of the field on the upper half of the plane, one concludes that no energy is transmitted to the second medium.
7. Computing the modulus of the component k_z of the $\vec{k}$ vector (see Figure 1b) one arrives to the conclusion that this component oscillates with spatial frequencies $2\pi/\lambda_e$, much higher than the spatial oscillation of all ordinary electromagnetic waves. Berry [3] showed that such a field is a super-oscillatory field that through scattering in a medium can be transformed into an actual near field. This approach leads to the near-field microscopic detection that is well documented in the literature.

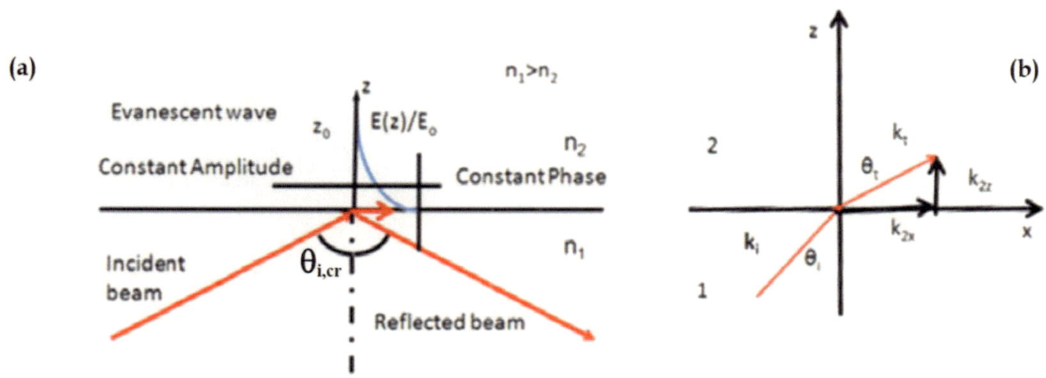

Figure 1. Characteristics of evanescent field: (a) Orthogonality of the vectors of constant phase and constant amplitude and exponential decay of the vector amplitude in the z-direction; (b) Resultant $\mathbf{k_t}$ vector penetrating in the second medium.

3. Improvement of the optical resolution of an optical instrument via evanescent illumination

Scanning probe devices are currently utilized to collect local information on the electromagnetic field lying near a surface of different geometrical configurations. Over the past decade, optical experiments based on near field observations have been developed via scanning probe devices. These experiments demonstrated the actual realization of optical resolutions well beyond the classical λ/2 limit mentioned in the Introduction section. In this work, we are concerned with the problem of how the electromagnetic field interacts with nano-sized objects producing propagating light waves capable of carrying information generated in the near field up to the far field where this information is retrieved. This phenomenon involves in the near field what is called in the literature "confined electromagnetic fields" since the near field electromagnetic fields exist in nano-objects that are smaller than the wavelength of the illuminating light.

Reference [4] addresses the relationship between the field generated by the evanescent illumination in the case of an array of objects similar to the one depicted in Figure 2a, a prismatic nano-crystal lying on a microscopic slide. Figure 2b shows the field resulting from TM polarization for such an array, the k_x component is a super-oscillatory component. The objects are 25 nm tall and the field is represented at 30 nm from the plane x-y; the field resembles the geometry of the objects. However, the TE polarization provides patterns that indicate the edges of the protrusions. The results provided in [4] indicate the increasing resolution of the field in following the shape of the objects, as the objects become sub-wavelength in dimensions and this field has its source of energy in the electro-magnetic field created by the evanescent waves.

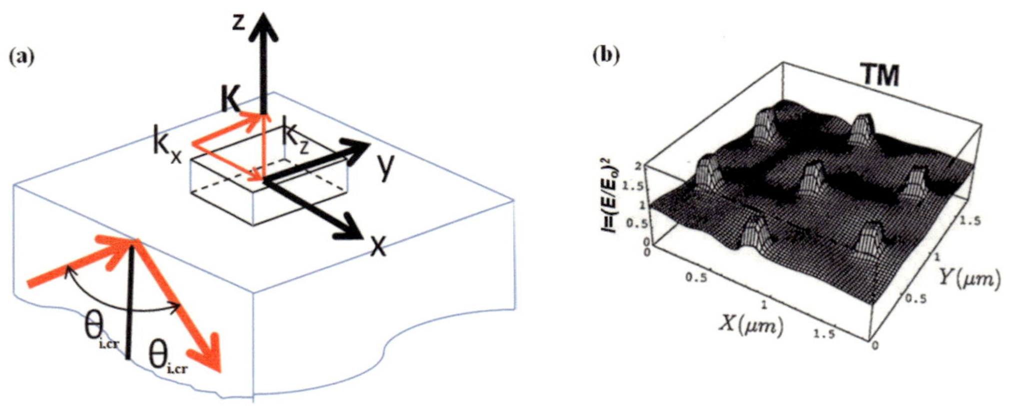

Figure 2. (a) Example of one of the observed objects in this work, a prismatic nano-crystal lying on a microscope slide. The k vector of the propagating wave front and its components are indicated. The object dimensions are sub-wavelength, of the order of magnitude close to λ/10; (b) Electric field intensity lines in the neighborhood of array of objects similar to the one depicted in Figure 2a.

Having summarized the basic properties of the evanescent waves, and from reference [4] concluded that the presence of a dielectric object in the evanescent field produces a scattering field that when the dimensions of the object are sub-wavelength resembles the object's geometry, it is necessary to look further to the relationship existing between evanescent waves and super-resolution. The presence of super-oscillations in the near field was postulated by Toraldo di Francia [1,5]. A formal approach relating evanescent fields and super-resolution is due to Vigoureux [6]. It is interesting to look back to this argument for the implications that it has in the retrieval of information from the geometry of the near field. The starting point of the argument is the uncertainty principle of FT. From the uncertainty principle of FT [7] applied in the x-direction, and applied to the pair of complementary quantities position and wave vector component, Δx and Δk_x respectively, Vigoreux shows that the uncertainty principle leads to the inequality,

$$\Delta x\,\Delta k_x > 2\pi \tag{4}$$

From the above inequality, one can conclude that to obtain the smallest spatial resolution Δx it is necessary that the interval Δk_x must be as large as possible. The classical solution of the Maxwell equation for propagating waves in vacuum (approximately in air) provides a limit. This limit can be computed by observing that the limit imposed by the condition of total reflection from a material of index of refraction n with respect to vacuum gives values of $k_x = -\omega/c, +\omega/c = -2\pi/\lambda, +2\pi/\lambda$, resulting in a $\Delta k_x = 4\pi/\lambda$. Replacing this value in Eq. (4) one obtains $\Delta x = \lambda/2$, which brings the Rayleigh limit.

If we consider now evanescent waves as sources of electromagnetic energy capable to excite a medium and create super-oscillating fields, the values Δk_x are no longer limited to the above mentioned interval. When the diffracted waves corresponding to the plane wave fronts with real direction cosines arrive to the limit $\lambda/2$, the solutions of the evanescent plane wave fronts with complex direction cosines add new frequencies to the spectrum. In order to estimate the actual Δk_x interval, let us introduce a simple mathematical argument that will allow making an estimate of the values of k_x for evanescent waves without a more extensive derivation.

A one-dimension model is sufficient for this purpose. By utilizing the scalar theory of light wave propagation, one can start from the Fourier solution of Maxwell equations:

$$E(x,\tau) = \frac{1}{\sqrt{2\pi}} \int_{-\infty}^{+\infty} E(k)\, e^{ikx - i\omega(k)\tau}\, dk \tag{5}$$

where: $E(x,\tau)$ is the scalar representation of the propagating electromagnetic field; x is the spatial coordinate; τ is the time; E(k) is the amplitude of the electric field of angular frequency $\omega(k)$. $E(k)$ provides the linear superposition of the different waves that propagate and can be expressed as $E(k) = \sqrt{2\pi}\,\delta(k-k_o)$, where $\delta(k-k_o)$ is the Dirac's delta function.

$E(k)$ corresponds to the monochromatic wave $E(x,\tau)=e^{ikx-i\omega(k)\tau}$. If one considers a spatial pulse of finite length L_{wt} at the time $\tau=0$, E(x,0) represents a finite wave-train of length L_{wt}, where E(k) is not a delta function but a function that contains an angular spread Δk. The dimension of L_{wt} depends on the size of the analyzed object. If L_{wt} and Δk are defined as the RMS deviations from the corresponding average values $|E(x,0)|^2$ and $|E(k)|^2$ evaluated in terms of intensities, it can be shown that $L_{wt} \bullet \Delta k \geq 1/2$. If L_{wt} is very small, the spread of wave numbers must be large. Hence, there is a quite different scenario with respect to the classical context where the length L_{wt} is large compared to the wavelength of light. Again, there will be super-oscillatory waves. A nanometric object will support super-oscillatory evanescent waves and the spectrum of diffraction will be wider as the dimension of the object becomes smaller.

Some conclusions can be drawn from the above derivations. The interval of Δk_x is no longer limited to $-2\pi/\lambda \leq k_x \leq +2\pi/\lambda$, but can be extended to $2\pi/\lambda \leq k_x \leq +\infty$. There are practical limitations but one can obtain evanescent waves with increasing k_x and accordingly increasing the interval Δk_x. The resolution can be increased well beyond the Rayleigh limit. However, as the values of Δk_x increase, the values of Δk_z are reduced since the sum of the two components is the vector $\vec{k}_t$: therefore, as Δk_z decreases, the depth of penetration of the field in the second medium is reduced. Hence, the high frequency components of the observed objects that are located at the interface of the plane of separation of the two media remain limited at distances very close to the separation plane. All the above derivations are in agreement with the near field microscopy methods. Another important point that can be extracted from the above considerations is the following. If we consider the case of a single element shown in Figure 2, one single beam will generate a single k_x and hence the resolution will be limited to this particular value. To increase the Δk_x it will be necessary to increase the angle θ shown in Figure 2a. A practical way to achieve this objective will be described in what follows.

In summary, objects as the one depicted in Figure 2 supported by a surface where an evanescent wave is propagating generate confined electromagnetic fields. Results presented in [4] show that if the dimensions of the surface elements are varied, the interaction between the objects and the electromagnetic field changes. Larger objects produce both real waves with real direction cosines and evanescent waves with imaginary direction cosines. The evanescent component becomes predominant as the dimensions of the object are reduced and the confinement is increased. Increasing confinements lead to fields that, depending on their state of polarization, resemble the geometry of the objects.

4. Generation of multiple k-vectors evanescent fields with TE and TM polarizations

In order to understand the generation of multiple **k** vectors with TE and TM illuminations, we need to introduce the optical set up utilized to perform the observations. Following the classical arrangement of total internal reflection (see Figure 3), a helium-neon (He-Ne) laser beam with nominal wavelength 632.8 nm sends a beam in the direction of the normal of a penta-prism designed to produce limit angle illumination at the interface between a microscope slide and a saline solution of sodium-chloride contained in a small cell.

The prism is supported in the platina of a microscope utilized to record the images of the observed objects. Inside the cell filled with the NaCl solution there is a polystyrene microsphere of 6 μm diameter. The microsphere is fixed to the face of the slide through chemical treatment of the contact surface in order to avoid Brownian motions. The polystyrene sphere plays the role of a relay lens that collects the light wave fronts generated by the observed nano-sized objects resting on the microscope slide. Table 1 provides information on the spherical particle and the index of refraction of the saline solution.

The microscope has a NA=0.95. Two CCD sensors are attached to the microscope. A monochromatic CCD is a square pixel camera with 1600 x 1152 pixels. At a second port, a color camera records color images. The analysis of the image recorded in the experiment is performed with the Holo Moiré Strain Analyzer software (HoloStrain™) [8], developed by C.A. Sciammarella and his collaborators.

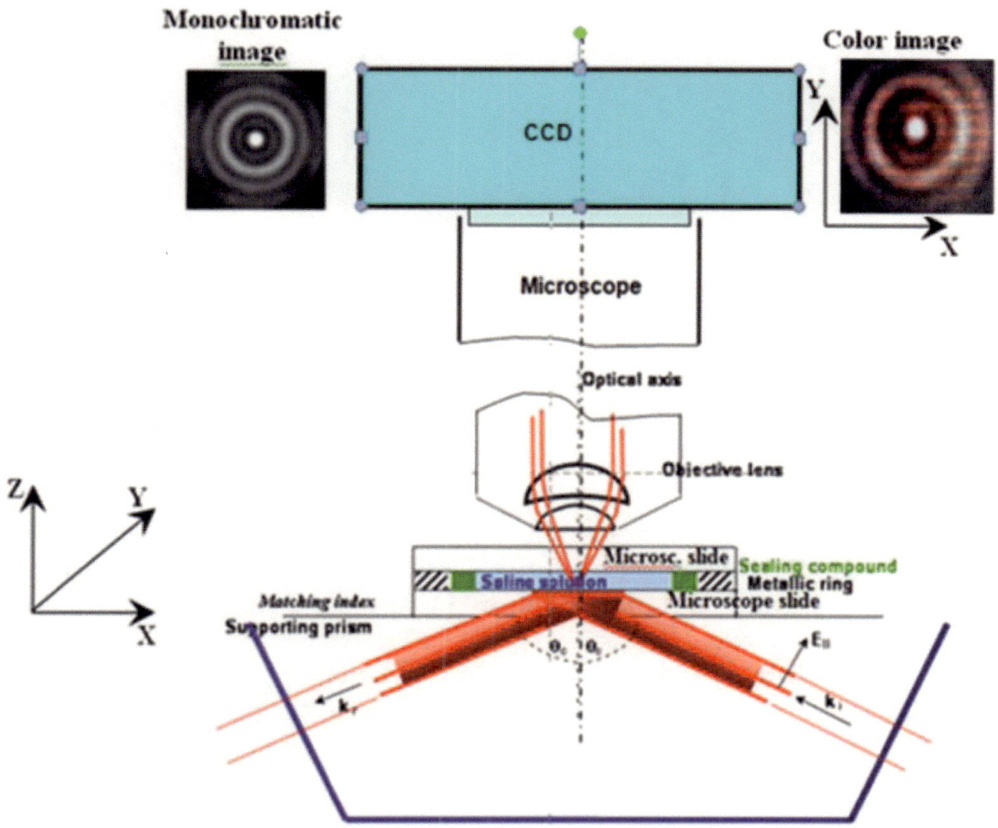

Figure 3. Optical set up utilized to observe the nano-objects.

Parameter	Value	Note
Polystyrene microsphere diameter D_{sph}	6 ± 0.042 μm	Tolerance specified by the manufacturer
Refraction index of polystyrene sphere n_p	1.57 ± 0.01	Value specified by the manufacturer
Refraction index of saline solution n_{so}	1.35	Computed from NaCl concentration for λ=590 nm

Table 1. Details on polystyrene microsphere and saline solution.

It will be shown that the above described optical set up provides the multiple **k** vectors. The initial polarization as indicated in Figure 2 is TE. Multiple illumination beams travelling in the penta-prism are generated by the residual stresses in the outer layers of the prism that hence acts as a volume grating. In Refs. [9,10], there are two attempts to analyze the formation of interference fringes originated by evanescent illumination in presence of residual stresses on glass surfaces. Before proceeding to further analyze generation of multiple **k** plane waves, some properties of the scattered light must be recalled.

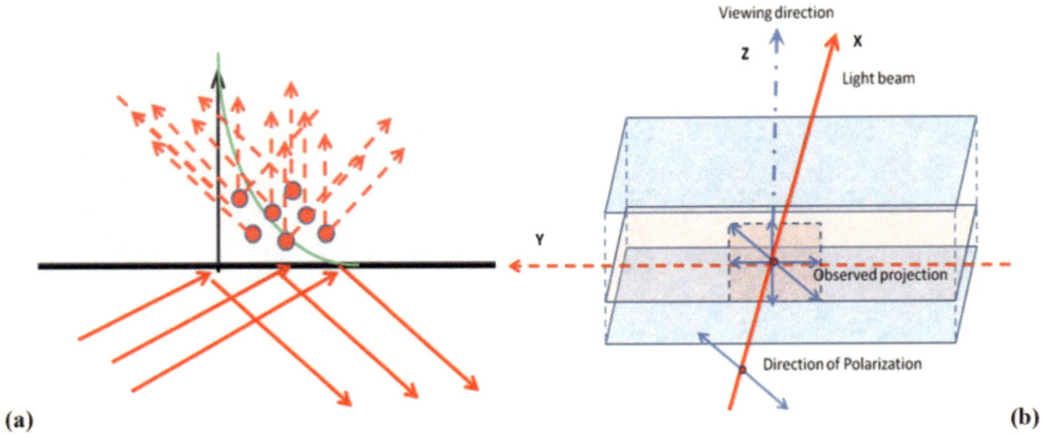

Figure 4. (a) Illustration of the effect of the electromagnetic evanescent field penetrating into a dielectric medium; (b) Observation of events that take place in the X-Y plane in the direction perpendicular to a scattered light beam propagating in the dielectric medium.

Figure 4a illustrates the scattering (diffraction effect) of the evanescent field entering in a dielectric medium. The actual problem is very complex [11] and the main properties of interest for the present derivation will be summarized in what follows. At this point, an additional element must be introduced that has to do with the recording of the information generated in the X-Y plane. Because the observation of the field is done in the Z-direction (see Figure 4b), it is necessary to have a mechanism that transforms the changes taking place in the X-Y plane into observable quantities in the Z-direction. The process of light scattering achieves this objective. The observer sees the projection of the vector $\vec{E}$ in the direction perpendicular to the observation vector. If non-polarized light enters the medium, the electromagnetic field becomes polarized. In Figure 4b it is shown the case of plane-polarized light entering the scattering medium: the observer sees the projected polarization vector; this conclusion applies to all types of polarization. Another important property that is relevant for the present analysis is the phenomenon of scattered light photoelasticity. In a stressed medium and observing the medium in the direction perpendicular to the propagating beam, fringes will be observed that are given by the following equation,

$$d\delta_s / dx = C(\sigma_1^s - \sigma_2^s) \tag{6}$$

where: σ_1^s and σ_2^s are the principal secondary stresses acting in the plane of the propagating beam, C is the photoelastic constant expressed in m^2/N, $d\delta_s/dx$ is the gradient of the retardation in the X-direction. The existence of these fringes on the surface of artificially birefringent media is a well known phenomenon. The existence of scattered light fringes on the surfaces has been known for a very long time, and has been used to measure residual stresses in glass surfaces since the early 1960s [12–15]. A comprehensive analysis of the formation of the fringes can be found in [15]. An important fact pointed out in [15] is that the observed fringes are multiple order interference fringes and the frequency composition depends on the profile of the residual stresses in the neighborhood of the surface.

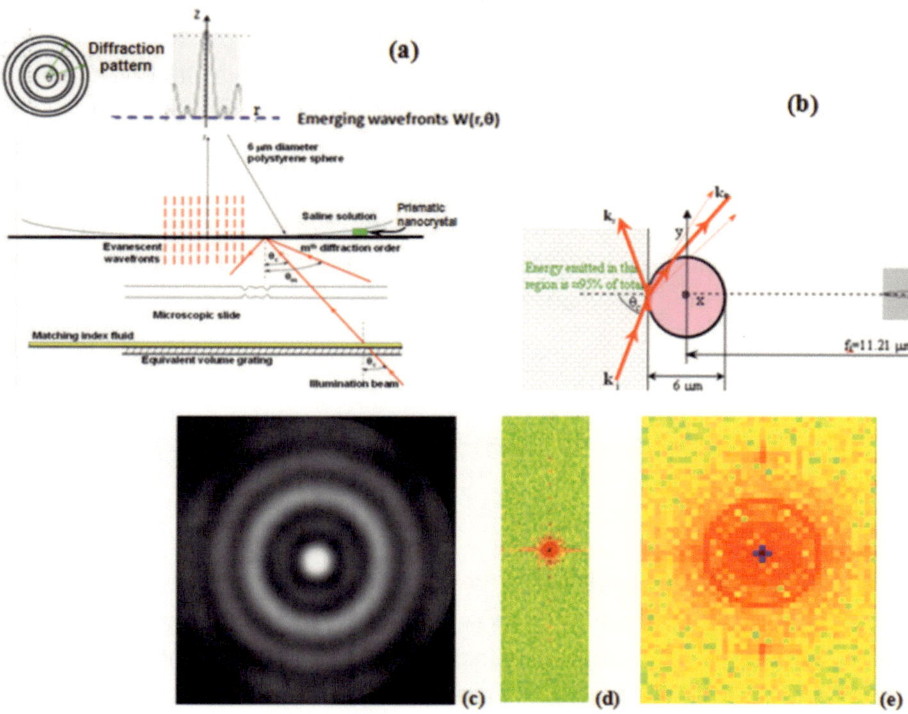

Figure 5. (a) Overall illustration of the set up geometry involved in the formation of observed fringes; prismatic nanocrystals lay on the microscope slide; (b) Relay lens (microsphere) illuminated by the evanescent field and diffraction pattern of the lens formed at the focal distance of the lens; (c) Observed pattern of the relay lens (microsphere) filtered to show average intensities; (d) FT pattern of the observed image; (e) Enlarged central portion of the FT pattern shown in Figure 5d.

Figure 5a shows the laser light incident at the interface between the upper face of the prism and the microscope slide that forms the lower face of the small cell containing the polystyrene microsphere that acts as a relay lens. The stressed upper layer of the prism is a volume diffraction grating that produces multiple diffraction orders. Between the prism and the microscopic slide there is a matching index fluid that insures the continuity of the optical path of the incident beams in the interface prism-microscope slide. In correspondence of the equivalent volume grating, different wave fronts emerge and continue their path to the interface microscope slide-saline solution where the evanescent field is generated. Because of the birefringence two wave fronts emerge from the equivalent grating: the ordinary and the extraordinary beams that have orthogonal polarizations. Figure 5b shows the interface of the microscope slide and the arriving illuminating laser beam. The total reflection at this interface produces the evanescent field that produces the diffraction pattern of the spherical relay lens. Figure 5c shows the diffraction pattern of the sphere that has been filtered to extract the pattern intensity distribution. Figure 5d shows the FT of the diffraction pattern of the captured image. Figure 5e shows the enlarged central part of the FT of the diffraction pattern.

An analysis of the pattern shown in Figure 5c that deals with its formation has been presented in [16,17]. The obtained results have been confirmed by a formal solution of the problem of a sphere illuminated by evanescent illumination utilizing Debaye's potentials [18]. There are two important aspects of the analysis of the formation of the sphere's diffraction pattern to be highlighted. The results presented in references [16–18] through the scale of the fringes diffraction pattern confirm the assumption that the microscope is focused at the focal plane of the sphere. The results also support the model of the interface between the prism and the microscope glass slide acting as a diffraction grating that causes the impinging beam to split into different diffraction orders. In [16,17] utilizing the plane wave complex solutions of the Maxwell equations and applying a method outlined by Toraldo di Francia in [5] the following equation was derived:

$$\sin\theta_n = \frac{n_o}{n_{so}}\sin\theta_i + \frac{\lambda}{n_{so}\dfrac{p_o}{N}} \tag{7}$$

In equation (7), θ_i is the angle of incidence of the laser beam shown in Figure 2; n_{so} is the index of refraction of the saline solution (see Table 1); n_o is the index of the refraction of the microscope slide (see Table 2 and Figure 8); θ_n is the angle of the evanescent diffraction order N; λ is the actual wavelength of the light generating the plane evanescent wave fronts; the integers N_o=1,2,3,... represent the fraction of the wavelength generating interference fringes. Upon total reflection, Eq. (7) can be rewritten as:

$$\sin\theta_n = 1 + \sin\theta_{en} \tag{8}$$

The value of the first term is equal to one because it corresponds to the total reflection of the beam. We introduce the notation $\sin\theta_{en}$ for the second term where the subscript "en" indicates the evanescent order N. With this notation,

$$\sin\theta_{en} = \frac{\lambda}{n_{so}\frac{p_o}{N}} \tag{9}$$

By defining the effective wavelength,

$$\lambda_e = \frac{\lambda}{n_{so}} \tag{10}$$

and the pitch corresponding to the Nth evanescent order, we get

$$p_n = \frac{p_o}{N} \tag{11}$$

Using the notation reported above, equation (9) can be written as:

$$\sin\theta_{en} = \frac{\lambda_e}{p_n} \tag{12}$$

The results of the model including equations (7-12) are plotted in Figure 6a for two families of rectilinear fringes observed in the FT pattern shown in Figure 5d. Point and triangle dots in the figure correspond to order values measured experimentally. The continuous curves represent the correlation between the experimental results and the theoretical model.

Figure 6b shows an excellent correlation between the fringe spacing obtained by dividing the whole field of view of the recorded image by the order and Eq. (11). The values of the resulting hyperbolic laws written in Figure 6b provide, for each order N, the pitch p_n of the equivalent grating pitch for the corresponding order as a function of the fundamental pitch p_o of each of the two families of rectilinear fringes generated by the p-polarized and the s-polarized waves, respectively.

There is a third family of fringes that has been detected in Figure 5d and it is shown in Figure 7. Because the microscope slide acts like an interferometer, it is possible to observe two families of fringes of absolute retardation and the third family of fringes of relative retardation. Figure 7 shows that the fundamental spatial frequency of the fringes of relative retardation is equal to the difference between the fundamental spatial frequencies of the fringes of absolute retardation: that is, $p_3 = p_1 - p_2$. Replacing values, one gets: $p_3 = (3.356 - 2.238)$ μm=1.118 μm.

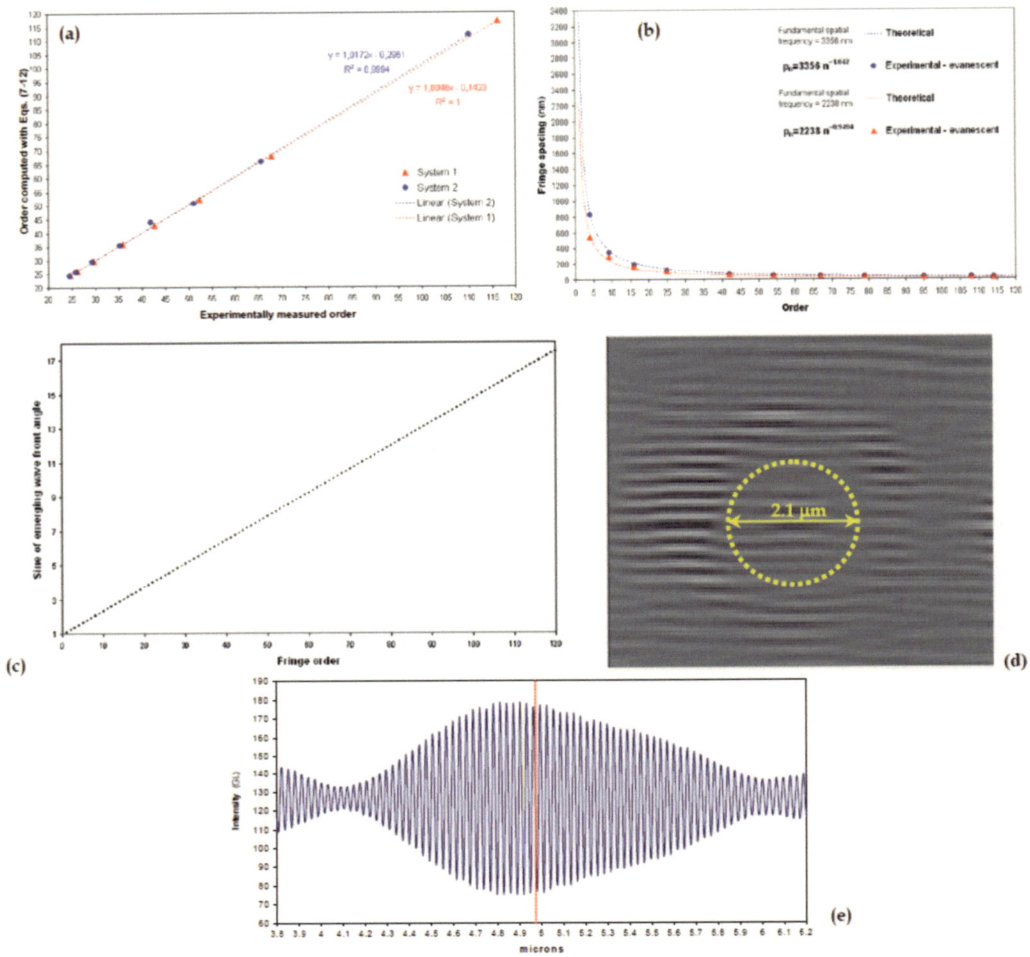

Figure 6. (a) Correlation between experimental fringe order values extracted from Figure 5d and theoretical values computed with Eqs. (7-12); (b) Two families of fringes can be extracted from the FT in Figure 5d; (c) Plot of the complex sine vs. fringe order according to Eq. (7); (d) Fringes observed in the image field of the sphere: they are modulated by the microsphere diffraction pattern (the dotted circle of diameter 2.1 µm represents the first dark ring in the diffraction pattern shown in Figure 5c; (e) Cross-section of the fringe pattern of Figure 6d.

The rectilinear fringes are modulated by the diffraction pattern of the particle (see Figure 6d). Figure 6e shows the cross-section of these fringes in the region corresponding to the central crown of the diffraction pattern of the sphere. In this cross-section, it is possible to observe the modulation of a system of parallel fringes produced by the presence of the polystyrene microsphere.

Figure 8 shows the wave fronts involved in the formation of the observed fringes. The illuminating beam as it arrives at the interface between the prism and the microscope slide is diffracted because of the residual stresses existing in the surface layer of the prism. At the interface prism-microscope slide, the incident beam is diffracted by the residual stresses that act as a diffraction grating. In order to analyze the effect of the diffraction, it must be realized that due to the birefringence of the upper layer of the prism the incident beam is split into two beams: (i) the ordinary beam that has an index of refraction n_{sp} very close to the glass of the prism and also to the microscope slide; (ii) the extraordinary beam that has an index of refraction lower than the ordinary beam because birefringent glass is equivalent to a negative crystal. Both beams are orthogonally polarized hence they cannot interfere with each other. Consequently two zero order beams propagate in the slide with slightly different directions.

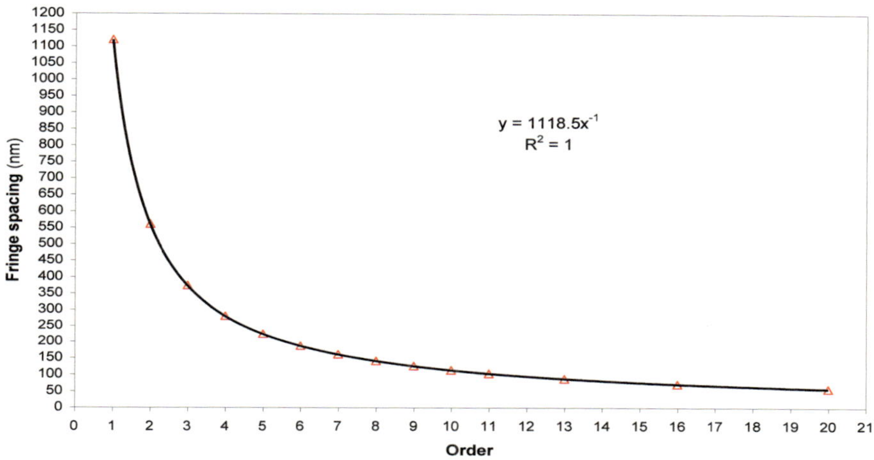

Figure 7. Third family of fringes present in the FT of the diffraction pattern of the microsphere captured by the CCD camera.

Each beam produces its own diffraction order and in Figure 8 the angles of each zero order beam are called θ_{s0} and θ_{p0}, while the angles corresponding to the first orders are called θ_{p1} and θ_{s1}, respectively. The symmetrical orders corresponding to the diffractions ±1 are not indicated. Upon arrival to the interface between the microscope slide and the saline solution all the orders experience total reflection and produce electromagnetic evanescent fields that, interacting with the solution, produce, through scattering, propagating beams. Due to the preservation of the momentum, the resultant vectors corresponding to the different evanescent waves continue with their trajectory in the saline solution and are indicated with the symbol $\vec{k}$ with the subscripts corresponding to the different wave fronts. There is one important point to remark here: no fringes exist before the evanescent field is converted into propagating waves at the level of the interface between the microscope slide and the saline solution. The values of the pitches measured through the process of taking a FFT of the image captured by the microscope correspond to the scattered light beams produced in the saline solution. Specifically, they correspond to the gradients of the retardation of the fringe families in the direction of the coordinate axis X, as it is shown in Figure 2a. These fringes are observed at the FT plane of the spherical relay lens (i.e. the polystyrene microsphere) and the numerical FT provides the pitches of the fringes which are themselves equivalent to diffraction gratings of equation $(\sin\theta_i+\sin\theta_n)=np$, where θ_i is the angle of incidence of the illuminating beam and θ_n is the angle that the diffraction order n makes with the direction of the illumination beam. The grating equation is in agreement with the generalization made by Toraldo Di Francia which has been formalized by Eq. (7).

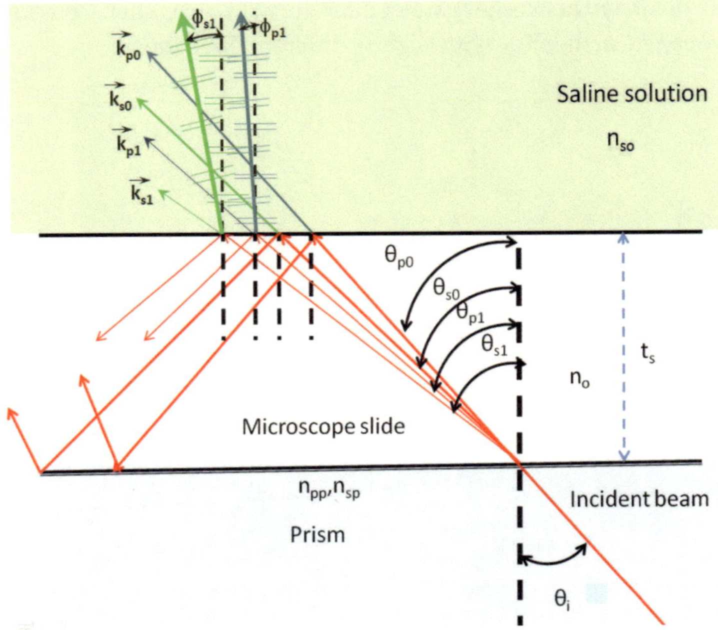

Figure 8. Beams forming the system of rectilinear fringes observed with the optical microscope

Unlike an ordinary diffraction grating, the residual stresses from one incident beam produce two sets of diffraction orders, one corresponding to the ordinary beam and another corresponding to the extraordinary beam. Furthermore, these two beams are orthogonally polarized. The law of refraction at a boundary with a uniaxial birefringent material can be written (see Figure 9):

$$\begin{cases} \vec{k}_i \sin\theta_i = \vec{k}_o \sin\theta_{p0} \\ \vec{k}_i \sin\theta_i = \vec{k}_o \sin\theta_{s0} \end{cases} \tag{13}$$

While the first equation of Eqs. (13) corresponds to the classical Snell's law, the second relationship does not because the extraordinary beam does not obey this law. As illustrated in the insert of Figure 9, the wave front of the extraordinary beam is not normal to the ray. In the case of the uniaxial crystal, the ordinary and extraordinary beams are parallel to each other and the ray velocity of the extraordinary beam is different from the wave front velocity.

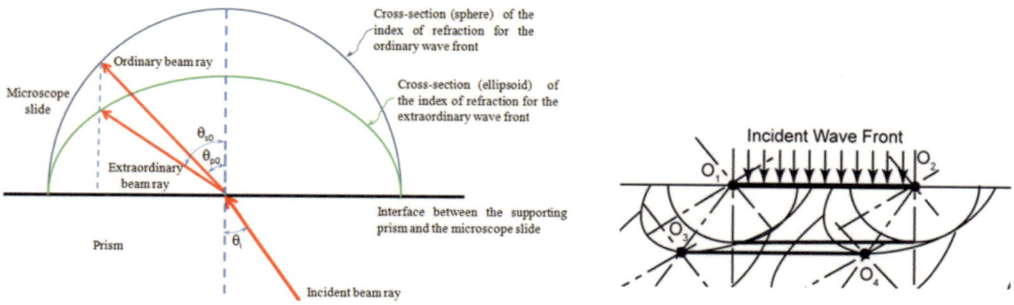

Figure 9. Interface of the prism with the slide rays corresponding to the ordinary and extraordinary beams. The insert in the right side of the figure shows that in the case of an uniaxial crystal the ordinary and extraordinary wave fronts are parallel.

All the diffraction beams that are produced in the interface prism-microscope slide have separate trajectories in the microscopic slide and upon arriving at the interface of the saline solution-microscope slide are totally reflected and produce evanescent wavefronts that generate the families of observed fringes. In view of the conservation of momentum of the photons, the resulting vectors $\vec{k}_{p0}$, $\vec{k}_{s0}$, $\vec{k}_{p1}$ and $\vec{k}_{s1}$ continue their trajectories in the saline solution. The vectors $\vec{k}_{p0}$ and $\vec{k}_{s0}$ are the limit beams that experience total reflection. The vector $\vec{k}_{p1}$ has components,

$$k_{p1x} = \frac{2\pi}{\lambda_e} n_0 \sin\theta_{p1} \tag{14}$$

$$k_{p1z} = \frac{2\pi}{\lambda_e} i\sqrt{n_0^2 \sin\theta_{p1}^2 - n_{so}^2} \tag{15}$$

where λ_e is given by equation (10). The modulus of the k-vector is

$$\left\| \vec{k}_{p1} \right\| = \frac{2\pi}{\lambda_e}\sqrt{2n_0^2 \sin^2\theta^2_{1p} - n_{so}^2} \tag{16}$$

It is possible to see that as the orders increase, the k-vector component k_{pnz} in the Z-direction decreases while the k-vector component k_{pnx} in the X-direction increases, and the two components are super-oscillatory. The diffraction orders that are observed in the FT of Figure 5d were indicated in Figure 8 by the angles ϕ_{p1} and ϕ_{s1} that they make with the direction of observation, Z-direction. The corresponding sines of the above mentioned angles are:

$$\begin{cases} \sin\phi_{pm} = \dfrac{\lambda}{n_{so} p_{pm}} \\ \sin\phi_{sm} = \dfrac{\lambda}{n_{so} p_{sm}} \end{cases} \tag{17}$$

where p_{pm} and p_{sm} are extracted from Figure 5d in correspondence of the order m currently being considered. The experimental values hence are:

$$\begin{cases} \sin\phi_{pm} = \dfrac{0.6328}{1.36x3.356} = 0.13683 \\ \sin\phi_{sm} = \dfrac{0.6328}{1.36x2.238} = 0.20791 \end{cases} \Rightarrow \begin{cases} |\ \phi_{pm}\ | = arc\sin(0.136834) = 7.9693^{o} \\ |\ \phi_{sm}\ | = arc\sin(0.20791) = 12.0^{\circ} \end{cases}$$

The above angles define two families of scattered light photoelastic fringes that give the gradients of the absolute retardation of the beams traveling parallel to the surface of the prism. The upper face of the prism has a state of residual stresses generated during the fabrication of the glass slab where the glass of the prism was extracted. Residual stresses are created in the process of cooling of the slab. These residual stresses are compressive in the faces of the slab and tensile inside the slab. The compressive stresses are located in a small region across the total height of the slab. Because the field observed by the microscope is very small and the stresses are uniform in this field, the gradient is lineal and the observed fringes must have a uniform pitch. The pitches that have been observed can be related to the gradient of the uniform stresses of the outer layer of the prism. These gradients can be expressed as follows:

$$\frac{d\delta_{px}}{dx} = n_{pp} - n_{o} = A\sigma_1 + B\sigma_2 \tag{18}$$

$$\frac{d\delta_{sx}}{dx} = n_{sp} - n_{o} = B\sigma_1 + A\sigma_2 \tag{19}$$

The second terms of the equations (18,19) are the Maxwell-Neumann equations that relate the absolute retardations to the principal stresses σ_1 and σ_2. In the current case, since residual stresses are both compressive, it holds $\|\ \sigma_1\| < \|\ \sigma_2\|$.

By subtracting Eq. (19) from Eq. (18), one gets:

$$\frac{d\delta_{px}}{dx} - \frac{d\delta_{sx}}{dx} = \frac{d\delta_3}{dx} = (A - B)(\sigma_1 - \sigma_2) = C(\sigma_1 - \sigma_2) \tag{20}$$

This last equation corresponds to the family of fringes plotted in Figure 7. Approximate solutions for these equations were presented in references [9,10]. A new set of values are given in Table 2. The index of refraction of the microscope slide was corrected to 1.51509 from the value of 1.5234 originally indicated by the manufacturer. This was done because the experimental measurements required the use of red light (i.e. λ=0.6328 μm). The indices of refraction n_{pp} and n_{ps} of the ordinary and extraordinary beams travelling in the optical system were determined by combining equations (18-20) and optimization techniques. The photoelastic constants of glass were taken from values obtained for optical glass by H. Favre, Polytechnic Institute of Zurich, Switzerland.

p_{pm}	3.356±0.060 (μm)	n_{pp}	1.52082	n_{so}	1.36	A	$-0.565 \cdot 10^{-11} m^2/N$	σ_1	-147 MPa
p_{sm}	2.238±0.0019 (μm)	n_{sp}	1.52061			B	$-3.160 \cdot 10^{-11} m^2/N$	σ_2	-155 MPa
p_{ps}	1.118±0.0025 (μm)	n_o	1.51509			C	$2.571 \cdot 10^{-11} m^2/N$	$\sigma_1-\sigma_2$	8 MPa

Table 2. Determination of residual stresses and indices of refraction from measured values of diffraction angles and retardations.

The obtained results support the assumptions concerning the presence of systems of lines in the captured images and their source in the residual stresses present on the glass of the prism.

5. Diffraction patterns of the observed objects

In Figure 2a, it was illustrated one of the geometrical configurations observed in this research wok (i.e. a prismatic object), the type of field originated by the evanescent illumination and, from the literature, it was described the near field configuration in the neighbourhood of a prismatic nano-crystal. In the obtained images there are diffraction patterns produced by the presence of NaCl nano-crystals on the microscope slide. However, these diffraction patterns are not classical patterns of diffraction produced by illuminating the object with wave fronts originated at a source and diffracted by the object. In this case, the object interacts with an electromagnetic field (i.e. the evanescent field) and such interaction causes the object to emit light. This light propagates through diverse media and arrives to a sensor that captures the image. The image captured is the diffraction pattern of the object. Figure 10 shows the light path from the source to the sensor.

From the preceding developments, the scattered light is produced at the interface between the microscope slide and the saline solution. Figure 2 shows right the main beam arriving to the interface, the vector $\vec{k}$ and its components k_x and k_z. From the preceding section, we know that there are many other evanescent plane wave fronts that also impinge in the observed object and hence will produce scattered patterns that will be present in the formed image of the object in a similar way to the description provided for the effect of the beams in the saline solution but will experience different path changes because the index of refraction of the sodium-chloride nano-crystals is higher than the index of refraction of the saline solution. The observed diffraction patterns in the collected images have a structure shown in Part 4 of Figure 10. The images show a diffraction pattern that outlines the object contour in a similar way to the outline depicted in Figure 2by the near field (this pattern can be assumed to be a zero order of diffraction), and two shifted images that can be assumed to be diffraction orders ±1. These images are generated in the object itself (nano-crystal) that emits light through the scattering process since no light passes from the microscope slide to the crystal but there is only an evanescent electromagnetic field penetrating in the nano-crystal. It is possible to understand then that the observed pattern is not a classical diffraction pattern and hence what we observe is not the classical FT of the object as it occurs in the case of an illuminated object.

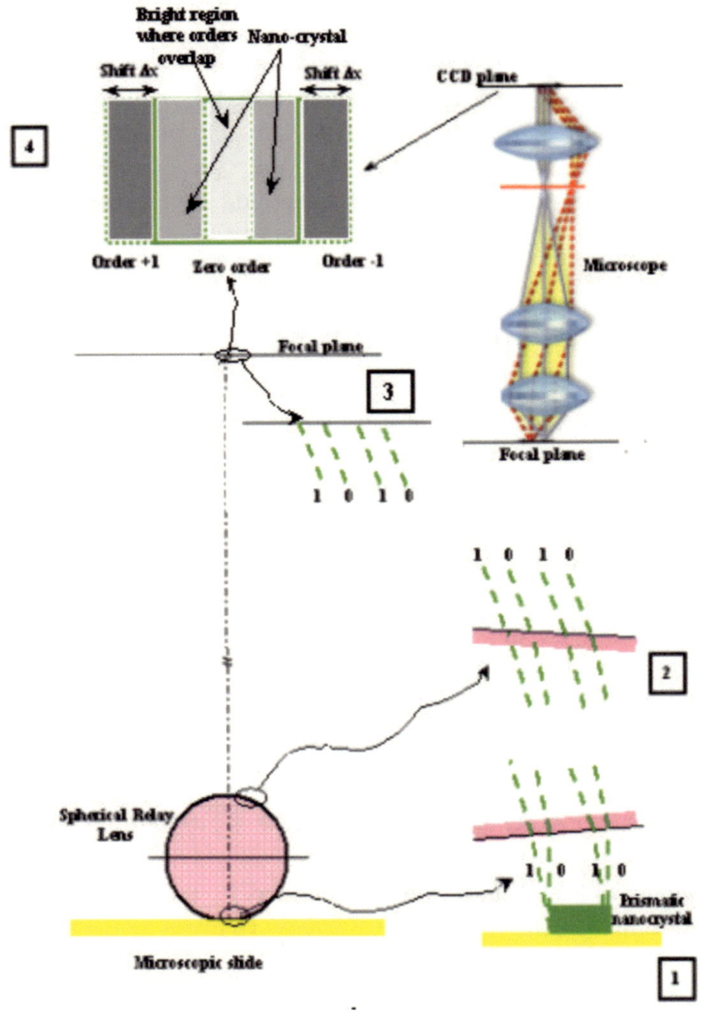

Figure 10. Schematic representation of the optical system leading to the formation of lens hologram: 1) Prismatic nano-crystal; 2) Wave fronts entering and emerging from the polystyrene microsphere acting as a relay lens; 3) Wave fronts arriving at the focal plane of the spherical relay lens; 4) Wave fronts arriving at the image plane of the CCD. The simulation of the overlapping of orders 0, +1 and -1 in the image plane of the CCD is also shown.

The same point brought in the case of the observed scattered light photoelastic fringes applies to the crystals. The fringes are present in the interface microscope slide-saline solution and are captured by the microscope through the small sphere acting as a relay lens. To get the diffraction pattern of the fringes required a numerical FT of the image (Figure 5d). The same concept applies to the diffraction pattern of the nano-crystals, to get their diffraction patterns it is necessary to perform a numerical FT. Hence, the observed images have a direct connection with the geometry of the object as shown in Figure 2, but the traditional relationships between the object and the optical FT of the object do not apply.

In [19], the conversion of the evanescent field into scattered light waves is explained in terms of Brillouin-Raleigh scattering. The evanescent field through resonance causes the crystals to vibrate in their eigenmodes. These vibrations cause phonon-photon interactions that produce the light emission. The eigenmodes depend on the crystal sizes and hence the different crystals emit light of different frequencies. There is a correlation between light color and crystal size and the emitted frequencies are present in the reflectance energy spectrum of NaCl [19]. The color camera images provided approximate image frequencies through a graphical plot of frequency vs. color for the camera sensor.

All the observed objects are localized in a region that is very close to the vertical axis of the relay lens in a radius smaller than one micron. Hence, the boundary conditions of the problem concerning the diffraction patterns of the observed prisms and nano spheres are very complex. An analysis of the electrical field amplitude [2,16] shows that the energy of the field is concentrated in a very small region (see Figure 11).

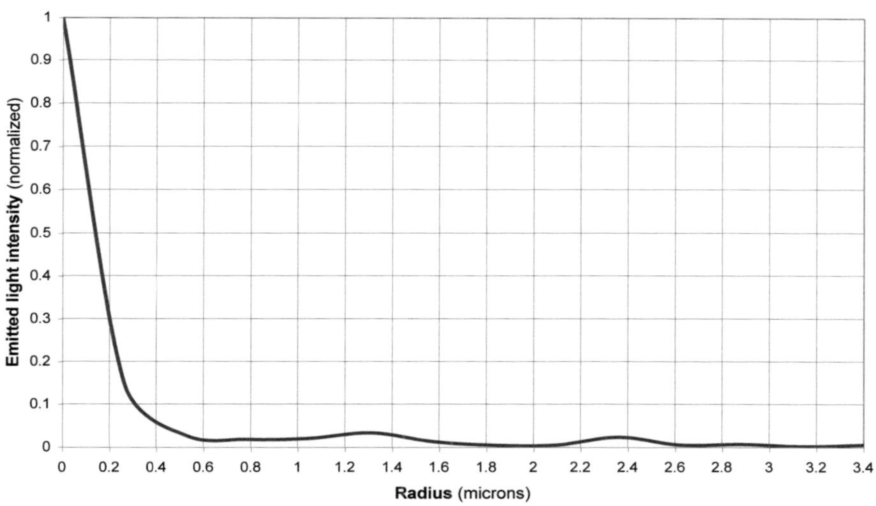

Figure 11. Intensity light distribution at the contact plane between the polystyrene microsphere and the supporting microscope slide

As is shown in Figure 2, the intensity of the field in the neighborhood of the particle is very complex but tends to resemble the object itself. In the present case, there is a resonance phenomenon that causes the emission of wave fronts that are captured by the microscope camera sensor.

6. Propagation of the wave fronts emerging from the observed object to the camera sensor

The diffraction wave fronts generated by the observed objects reach the sensor by propagating through the relay lens that concentrates the beams in its focal region, then through the saline solution, air, and finally through the microscope optical path to arrive to the sensor. Since the propagating wave fronts are beyond the resolution limit, this fact implies that we are dealing with the propagation of solitons.

Following the arguments presented in reference [20] and referring to the coordinate system shown in Figure 2a, a wave front propagating in the Z-direction can be represented as:

$$\vec{E}(x,y,z,t) = E_o(x,y)e^{i(\vec{k}z-\omega t)} \tag{21}$$

where $E_o(x,y)$ is the transversal amplitude profile of the wave front. If the temporal component is removed the amplitude reduces to:

$$\vec{E}_s(x,y,z) = E_o(x,y)e^{i(\vec{k}z)} \tag{22}$$

The spatial component must satisfy the stationary Helmholtz equation:

$$(\nabla^2 + \vec{k}^2)\left\{\vec{E}_s\right\} = 0 \tag{23}$$

Since the amplitude $E_o(x,y)$ is independent of Z, the intensity $\vec{E}_s \vec{E}_s^* = I$ of the propagating wave is constant. Utilizing the method of variables separation, the solution of the partial differential equation (23) can be separated into the transversal component and in the longitudinal component. By expressing this solution in cylindrical coordinates one gets:

$$\vec{E}_{sc}(r,\theta,z) = \vec{E}_{sr}(r)\vec{E}_{s\theta}(\theta)e^{i(\vec{k}z)} \tag{24}$$

The $\vec{E}_{s\theta}(\theta)$ is a periodic function of θ of the form $\vec{E}_{s\theta}(\theta)= E_{s\theta}e^{im\theta}$ (m=0,1,2,…). By replacing this solution in (24) and introducing Eq. (24) in the Helmoltz's equation (23), it is obtained a partial differential equation of the second order in r whose solution is formed by a combination of Bessel function of the first kind and Neumann functions.

From the above outlined mathematical model a number of different kinds of propagating beams can be derived. In the present case discussed in this chapter, the propagating waves correspond to super-resolution electromagnetic fields. The particular problem that we are considering is extremely complex. It can be shown that this type of solitons require polarization in the direction of propagation. Hence, the solution of the problem requires functions that provide longitudinal polarization propagating in free space with super-resolution and uniform amplitude along the direction of propagation. A partial answer to this problem can be found in [21,22] where it is shown that such a type of wave fronts can be obtained by phase modulation and beam focusing by a high aperture focusing lens. In the particular problem dealt with in this chapter the relay lens has this property and it will generate this type of wave front in the focal plane. The experimental results obtained in the present study seem to support this model for the propagation of the diffraction patterns of the observed objects to the microscope camera sensor. For example, Figure 11 shows that the intensity pattern $I = \vec{E}_{sr}^2 + \vec{E}_{s\theta}^2$ at the interface between the microscope slide and the polystyrene microsphere that acts as relay lens presents a very strong axial field.

7. Observation of prismatic nano-objects

The process of observation of the objects present in the central spot of the image shown in Figure 5c was the following. First, the objects are located by observing the image. The portion of the image that includes the object to be analyzed is then extracted. The cropped image is magnified and then repixelated via bicubic spline either to 512x512 or 1024x1024 increasing thus numerically the resolution.

Figures 12 and 13 show two examples of the captured nano-crystals images, the isophote lines (lines of equal intensity) and the FT of the images. The isophote lines are similar to the field intensity lines shown in Figure 2. In Figures 12a and 12b, there are respectively shown the monochromatic image and the color image of a particle with a square cross-section in the plane of the image. A detailed analysis of the particle of Figure 12 a will be presented later in the chapter. Figure 13e includes the theoretical isomeric structure of the NaCl nano-crystal [23] corresponding to the structure observed experimentally.

The dimensions of the crystals can be obtained by utilizing a Sobel filter to detect the edges in the corresponding images as shown in Figure 14. In these figures, the zero and the first orders are outlined following the schematic representation of Part 4 of Figure 10. One nano-crystal has a square cross-section of side length 86 nm. The dimensions of the other nano-crystal in the plane of the image are 120x46 nm.

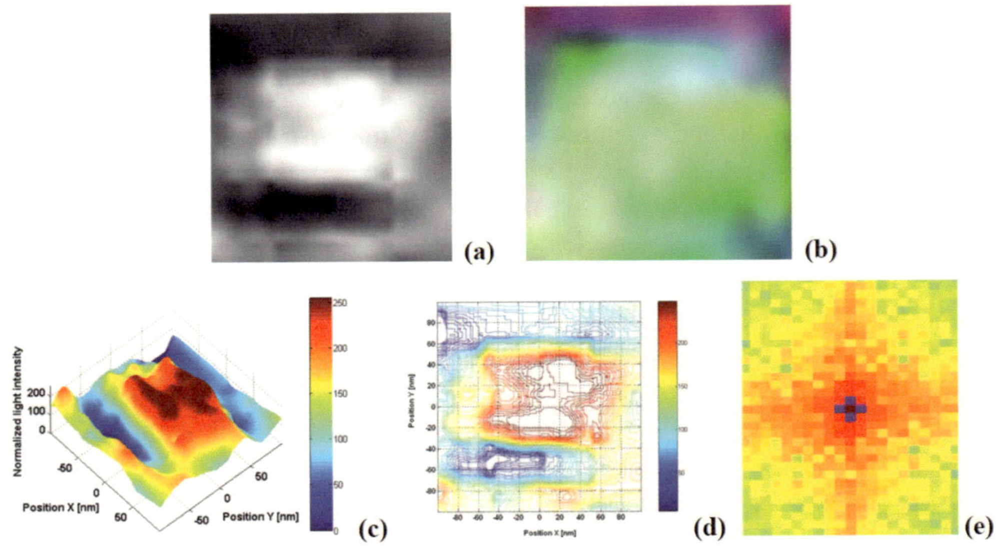

Figure 12. NaCl nano-crystal of length 86 nm: (a) gray-level image (1024 x 1024 pixels); (b) Image of the nano-crystal captured by a colour camera; (c) 3-D distribution of light intensity; (d) Isophote lines; (e) FT pattern of the image of the nano-crystal recorded by the sensor.

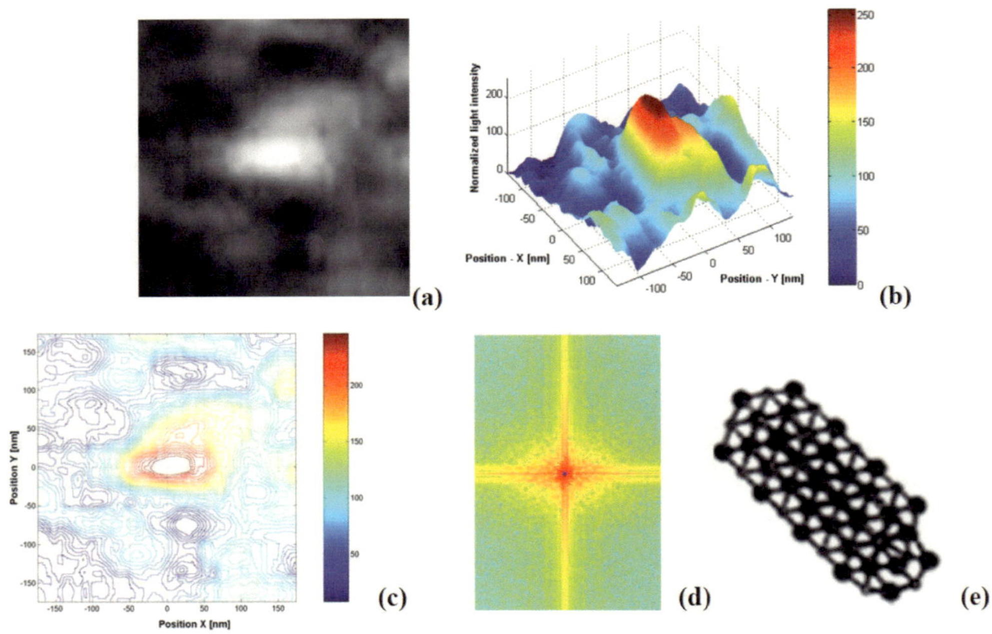

Figure 13. NaCl nano-crystal of length 120 nm: (a) Gray-level image properly repixelated; (b) 3-D distribution of light intensity; (c) Isophote lines; (d) FT pattern of the image of the nano-crystal recorded by the sensor; (e) Theoretical crystal structure [23].

http://dx.doi.org/10.5772/53346

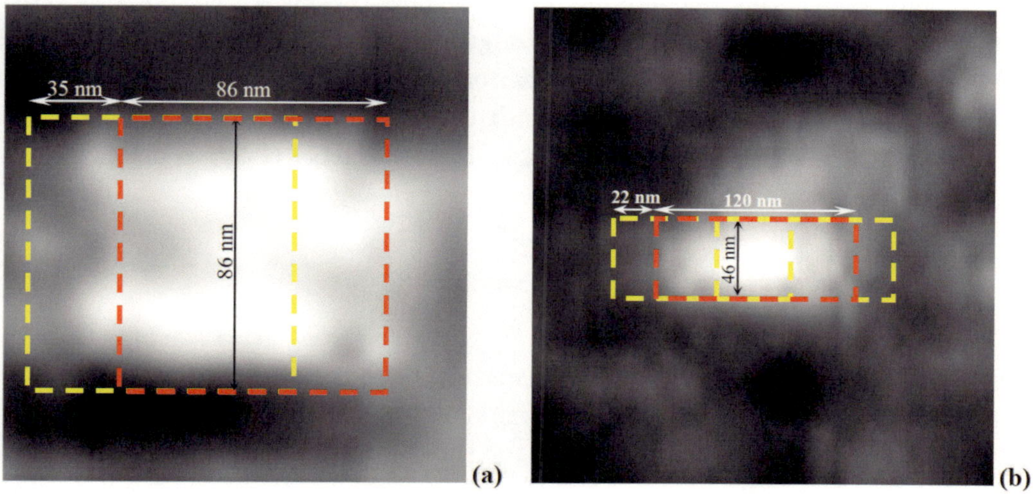

Figure 14. Edge detection process for determining main geometric dimensions of NaCl nano-crystals: a) L=86 nm; b) L=120 nm.

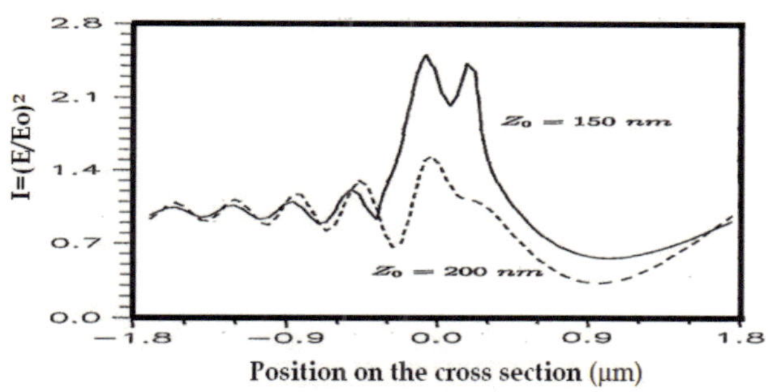

Figure 15. Cross-section of the electromagnetic field intensity in the neighborhood of a particle of prismatic shape as those indicated in Figure 2b. z_0 gives the level of the cross-section with respect to the plane supporting a particle of 150 nm depth.

Figure 15, taken from reference [4], shows the intensity of the electromagnetic field in the neighborhood of a prismatic particle illuminated by an evanescent field. As it can be seen, the intensity gradient is sharp at the edges of the prism and, hence, the edge detection filter is a useful tool to locate the prism edges.

8. Recovery of the depth information

As mentioned previously, the photoelastic gradient fringes produced by the different diffractions orders at the interface of the prism-microscope slide experience phase changes that provide depth information. These fringes are carrier fringes that can be utilized to extract optical path changes. This type of setup to observe phase objects has been used in phase hologram interferometry as a variant of the original set ups proposed by Burch et al. [24] and Spencer and Anthony [25]. When the index of refraction in the medium is constant, the rays going through the object are straight lines. If a prismatic object is illuminated with a beam normal to its surface, the optical path s_{op} through the object can be determined by computing the integral:

$$s_{op}(x,y) = \int n_i(x,y,z)dz \tag{25}$$

where the direction of propagation of the illuminating beam is the Z-coordinate and the analyzed plane wave front is the plane X-Y; $n_i(x,y,z)$ is the index of refraction of the medium.

The change experienced by the optical path is given by:

$$\delta_{op}(x,y) = \int_0^t \left[n_i(x,y,z) - n_o \right] dz \tag{26}$$

where t is the thickness of the medium. Assuming that:

$$n_i(x,y,z) = n_c \tag{27}$$

where n_c is the index of refraction of the observed nano-crystals. By replacing Eq. (27) in Eq. (26), the latter becomes:

$$\delta_{op}(x,y) = \int_0^t \left[n_i(x,y,z) - n_o \right] dz = (n_c - n_o)t \tag{28}$$

By transforming Eq. (28) into phase differences and making n_o=n_{so}, where n_{so} is the index of refraction of the saline solution containing the nano-crystals, one can write:

$$\Delta\phi = \frac{2\pi}{p_{fr}}(n_c - n_{so})t \tag{29}$$

where p_{fr} is the pitch of the fringes generated as the light goes through the specimen thickness. In general, the change of path is small and no fringes are observed. In order to solve this problem carrier fringes can be added. An alternative procedure is the introduction of a grating in the illumination path [26]. In the case of the nano-crystals, the carrier fringes can be obtained from the FT of the lens hologram of the analyzed crystals. Details of the procedure to carry out this task are given in [19].

9. Example of the digital reconstruction of a nano-crystal

Having obtained the shape of the section of the prism and the depth it is possible to reconstruct a crystal. The results of this process are summarized in Figure 16. The 5x4x4 nano-isomer of NaCl (Figure 16b) is interesting because has one step in the upper part of the crystal [23]. This step is correctly recovered in the numerical reconstruction. Figure 16a shows the numerical reconstruction of this crystal, consistent with the theoretical structure; Figure 16c shows the level lines of the top face; Figure 16d shows a cross-section where each horizontal line corresponds to five elementary cells of NaCl. Since the upper face of the nano-crystal is not very likely to be exactly parallel to the camera plane, there is an inclination which can be corrected by means of an infinitesimal rotation. By performing this operation, the actual thickness jump in the upper face of the crystal (see the theoretical structure in Figure 16b) is obtained. The jump in thickness is 26 nm out of a side length of 86 nm: this corresponds to a ratio of 0.313 which is very close to theory. In fact, the theoretical structure predicts a vertical jump of one atomic distance vs. three atomic distances in the transverse direction: that is, a ratio of 0.333.

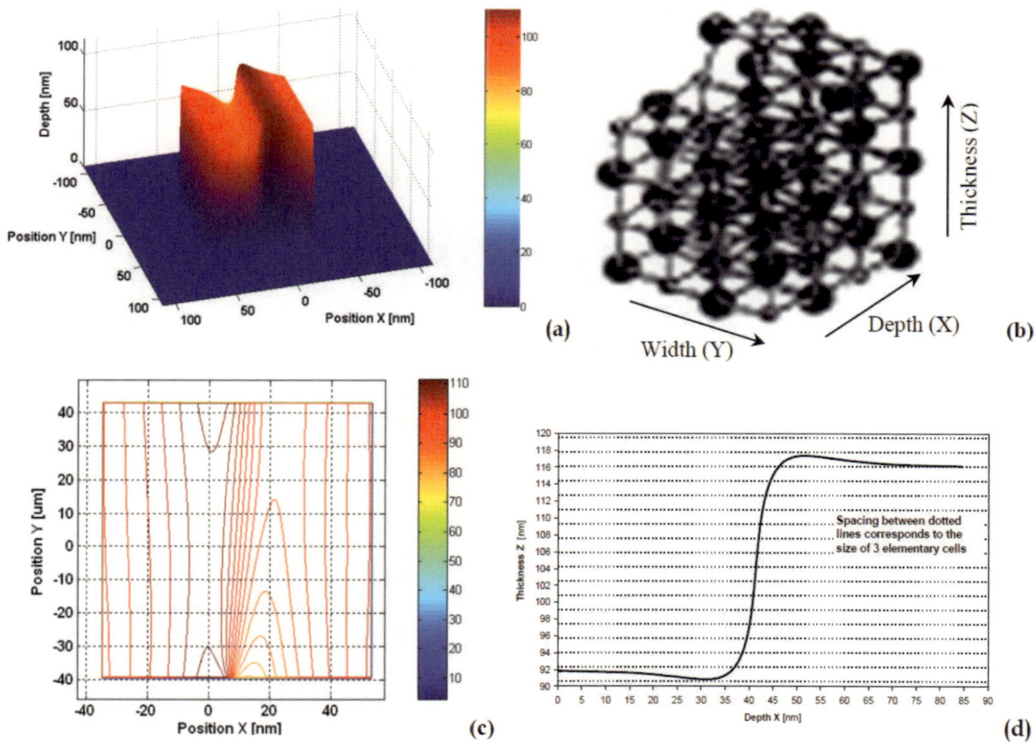

Figure 16. (a) Numerical reconstruction of the NaCl nano-crystal of length 86 nm, the crystal is inclined with respect to the image plane; (b) 5x4x4 theoretical structure of the nano-crystal; (c) Level lines; (d) Rotated cross-section of the upper face of the nano-crystal: the spacing between dotted lines corresponds to size of three elementary cells.

10. Verification of some of the assumptions of the developed model to observe nano-size objects

A further analysis of the image of the 86 nm prismatic nano-crystal provides more insight on the process of formation of the recorded images. In Figure 12a, it is possible to see the image of the particle and the presence of background fringes that go across the image. A partial simulation of the image in the X-direction was carried out by adding to a uniform illumination zero order two shifted orders in the X- and in the Y-directions and adding the image of a sinusoidal background fringe. The results of the simulation are presented in Figure 17. The simulated image (Figure 17a) is very similar to the image of the nano-crystal recorded by the CCD camera (Figure 17b).

Figure 18 is obtained by considering only the zero order of the FT pattern of the nano-crystal. By adopting a 4x4 low-pass filter centered in (0,0) one obtains the filtered image shown in Figure 18a. By masking the image with a mask corresponding to the position of the nano-crystal in the recorded image, Figure 18b is obtained. The isophote lines for the filtered-unmasked zero order image and for the filtered-masked image are shown in Figures 18c and 18d, respectively. It can be seen that there is a strong resemblance between the two images indicating the plausibility of the adopted interpretation supported by the developed models of the image formation process. The masked zero order has an almost uniform intensity distribution that is not completely uniform because the crystal is not symmetric in the X-direction but the intensity distribution is almost uniform as it was assumed in Part 4 of Figure 10.

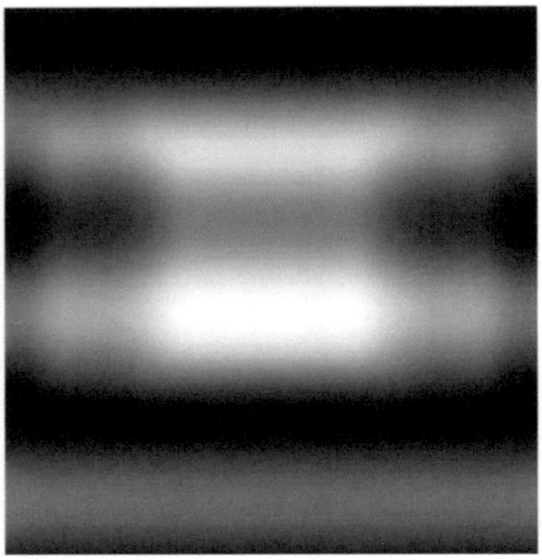
(a)

(b)

Figure 17. (a). Simulated image of the 86 nm nano-crystal obtained by adding up the zero order, two shifted orders in the X-direction and a sinusoidal background fringe pattern; (b) Actual image of the nano-crystal recorded by the CCD camera.

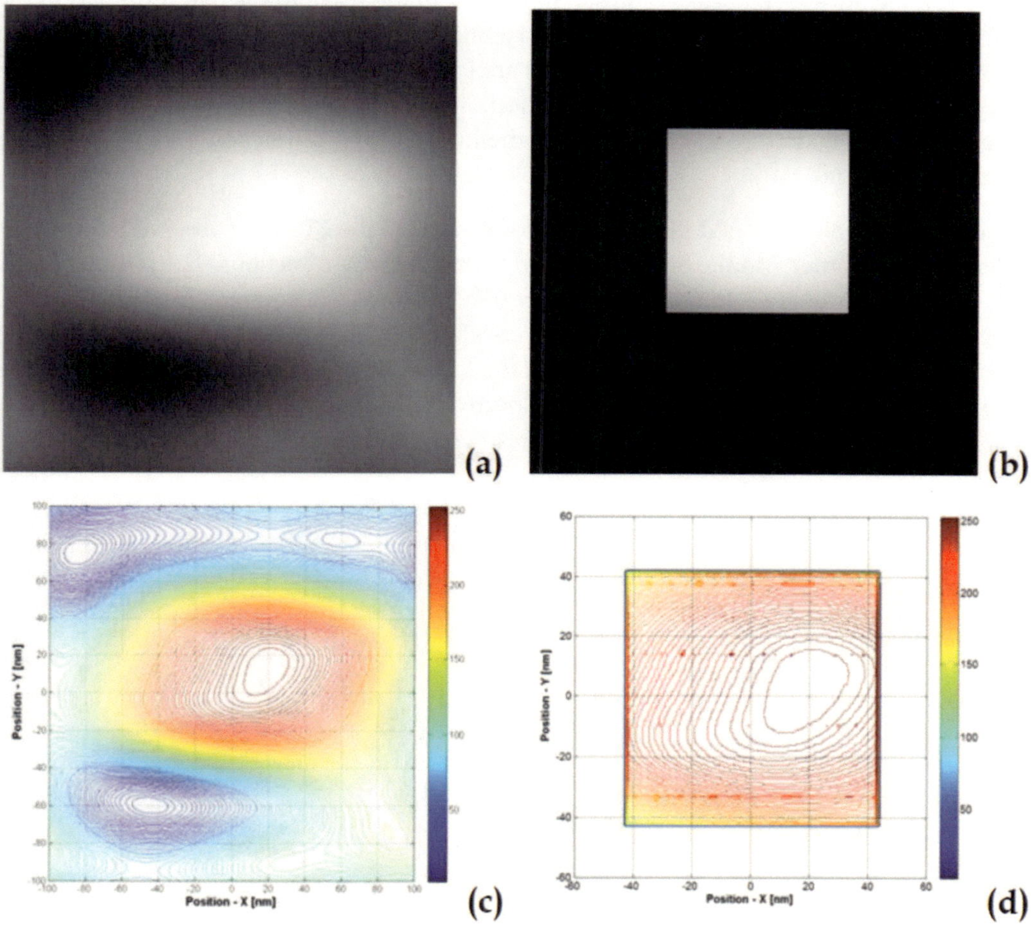

Figure 18. (a) Filtered zero order of the 86nm nano-crystal image (Figure 12a) obtained by using a 4x4 low-pass filter; (b) Masking of the filtered zero-order of Figure 18a with a mask corresponding to the region occupied by the nano-crystal; (c) Isophote lines of the filtered image shown in Figure 18a; (d) Isophote lines of the masked filtered image shown in Figure 18b.

The recorded images are originated in scattered wave fronts that, as shown in Figure 4b, are observed in the Z-direction but provide information of events that occur in the X-Y plane. Hence, in order to analyze the information coming from the X-Y plane, one needs to deal with the real part of the FT pattern shown in Figure 12e (i.e. that relative to the 86 nm nano-crystal). The FT of the real part of the FT of Figure 12e was computed. Figure 19a shows the FT of the real part of the FT of Figure 12e. The pattern presents different diffraction orders with a complex structure. These orders contain information concerning features of the recorded image of the nano-crystal. This information can be retrieved by filtering the orders and getting the inverse FT. Figure 19b is the result of filtering the zero order of Figure 19a and taking the inverse FT. This figure provides information concerning the sources that contribute to form the zero order of the image.

Figure 19b includes seven peaks representing the FT of the wave fronts that form part of the image of the diffraction pattern of the nano-crystal. The two peaks recorded farther apart in the Y-direction correspond to the fringes that are in the background of the image and represent the system of fringes discussed in the section *"Generation of multiple k-vectors"*. These fringes are independent of the formation of the image of the diffraction pattern of the observed nano-crystal.

The other five peaks included in Figure 19b correspond to the FT of the observed diffraction orders, the zero order and the orders ±1 in the X- and in the Y-directions. The filtering of the two diffraction orders ±1 indicated in Figure 19a provides the components that form the structure of the orders ±1. These components are shown in Figure 19c and Figure 19d for the X-direction (i.e. the harmonics are selected in the f_x-direction) and in the Y-direction (i.e. the harmonics are selected in the f_y-direction), respectively.

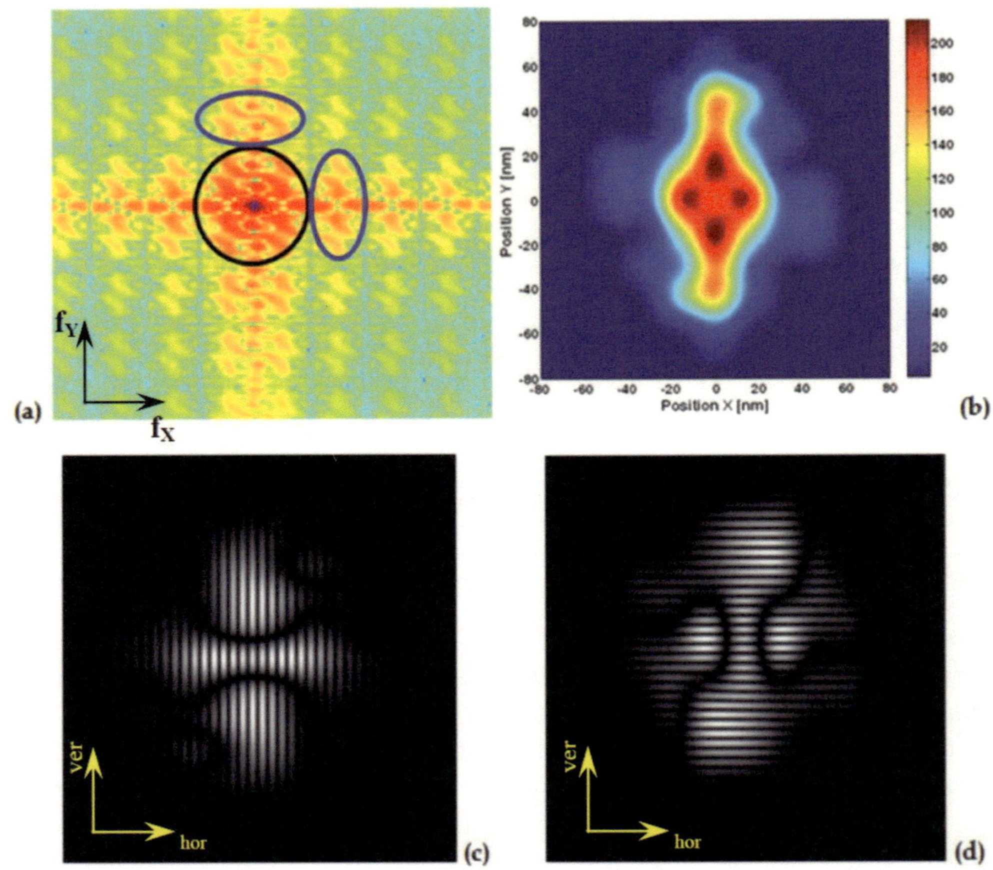

Figure 19. (a) FT of the real part of the FT of the 86 nm prismatic nano-crystal and filtered components; (b) 2-D view of the filtered zero order extracted from the real part of the FT pattern of the nano-crystal; (c) Result of filtering first order in the f_x-direction of the FT pattern shown in Figure 19a; (d) Result of filtering first order in the f_y-direction of the FT pattern shown in Figure 19a.

The cross-sections of the filtered components shown in Figures 19c-d are plotted in Figure 20a-d. Figure 20a corresponds to the cross-section in the horizontal direction (i.e. "hor" in Figure 19c) of the pattern obtained by filtering the f_x–orders ±1. Figure 20b corresponds to the cross-section taken in the vertical direction (i.e. "ver" in Figure 19c). While the filtered pattern is modulated in amplitude along the horizontal direction (see Figure 20a), we see in the vertical direction a central peak at Y=0 and two lateral peaks located at Y=17.6 nm from this central peak (see Figure 20b).

Figure 20c corresponds to the cross-section in the horizontal direction (i.e. "hor" in Figure 19d) of the pattern obtained by filtering f_y–orders ±1. Figure 20d corresponds to the cross-section in the vertical direction (i.e. "ver" in Figure 19d). While the filtered pattern is now modulated in amplitude along the vertical direction (see Figure 20d), we see in the horizontal direction a central peak in X=0 and two lateral peaks located at X=13.8 nm from this central peak (see Figure 20c). Since the crystal is not symmetric in X- and Y-directions, one should expect some difference between the two resonant frequencies.

The distance between the central peak and the lateral peaks in the cross-section represented in Figure 20c coincides with the spatial frequency of the vibration nodes of the nano-crystal in the X-direction resulting from the model introduced in Ref. [19] and that at the same time is a multiple of the elementary cell of the NaCl, 24 d, where d=0.573 nm is the size of the elementary cell.

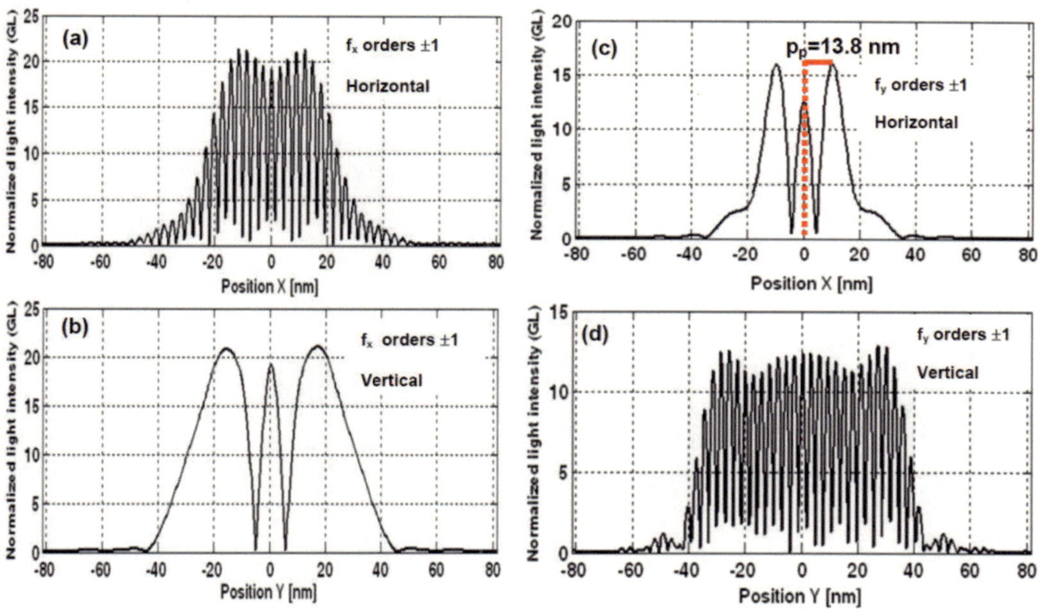

Figure 20. (a) Cross-section in the horizontal direction of the filtered pattern shown in Figure 19c (i.e. that obtained by selecting f_x-orders ±1); (b) Cross-section in the vertical direction of the filtered pattern of Figure 19c; (c) Cross-section in the horizontal direction of the filtered pattern shown in Figure 19d (i.e. that obtained by selecting f_y-orders ±1); (d) Cross-section along the vertical direction of the filtered pattern of Figure 19d.

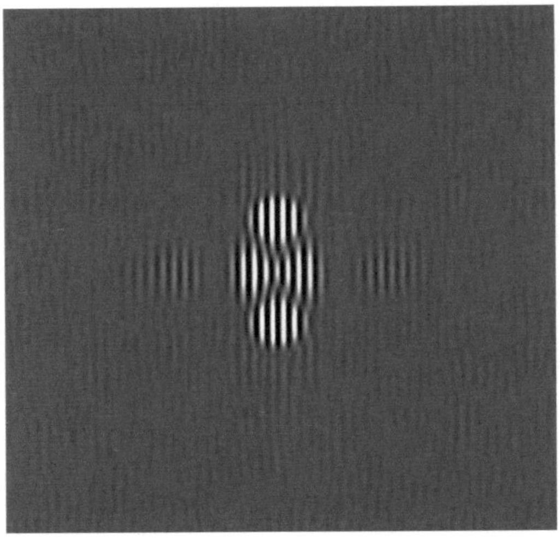

Figure 21. Result of the same processing operations utilized for the 86 nm nano-crystal actual image and then applied to the numerically reconstructed image pattern shown in Figure 17a.

If the same processing sequence utilized for the actual image recorded by the CCD sensor is applied to the simulated image, one regains the same structure of the inverse FT (see Figure 21). This indicates that the components are connected to the square shape of the cross-section of the nano-crystal and to the shifts between the 0 and the ±1 orders, which in turns are determined by the vibration mode of the crystal. The vibration mode of the nano-crystal is directly related to the diffraction pattern of the nano-crystal.

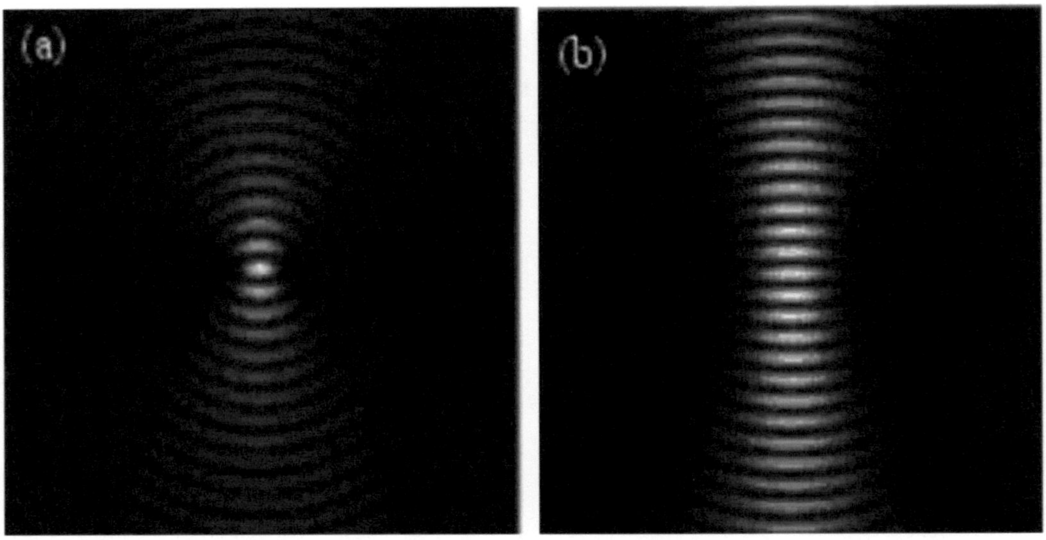

Figure 22. Transverse intensity profiles of non-diffracting Mathieu beams obtained for different values of wave solution parameters [20].

http://dx.doi.org/10.5772/53346

The obtained intensity profiles are similar to the intensity profiles of Mathieu non-diffracting wave fronts simulated in [20] (see Figure 22). The preceding analysis provides a strong evidence that the adopted models for the observed phenomena are supported by the analysis of the structure of the recorded images.

The assumption made in the *"Diffraction patterns of the observed objects"* section that the recorded images are diffraction patterns of the NaCl nano-crystals is validated by all the material presented in the analysis of the images of the nano-crystals. Since the observed nano-crystals lay in the vertex plane normal to the optical axis of the spherical relay lens, following the classical interpretation given in FT optics one would say that the observed intensity distribution in the focal plane of the lens is the FT of the intensity distribution in the vertex plane. Although this concept corresponds to a two dimensional transparency (X-Y) intensity distribution, it is commonly extended to the case of thin objects located in the vertex plane. If one adds a reference point source in same plane of the object or a plane reference wave front, the resulting intensity in the focal plane of the lens is called a FT hologram.

In the measurements discussed in this chapter, there is a difference with respect to classical FT holography: the diffraction pattern of the observed object is not the FT of the field distribution of the observed objects. The formation of the diffraction pattern obeys to different equations than those of the classical case. However, the final result is the same: one gets a hologram containing the diffraction pattern of the observed objects. Actually, because of the presence of many reference plane wave fronts, it corresponds to the Tanner [26] type of holograms of transparent objects. Hence, we are in presence of a different kind of hologram but that from the point of view of application has the same final result: it provides information on the geometrical configuration and optical properties of the observed object. These holograms share a common feature with classical FT holograms: they are formed by the diffraction pattern of the observed objects. The difference between the two types of holograms is that the diffraction pattern produced by the evanescent illumination is not a FT of the electromagnetic field of the observed object.

11. Observation of the polystyrene nano-spheres

The preceding sections described the different aspects involved in the retrieval of the information concerning the geometry of isomers of NaCl nano-crystals. However, the analyzed images contain other objects besides NaCl nano-crystals: among these objects, nano-spheres are investigated.

Micro/nano-spheres made of transparent dielectric media are excellent optical resonators. Unlike the NaCl nano-crystals whose resonant modes to our knowledge have never been analyzed in the literature, both theoretical and experimental studies on the resonant modes of micro/nano-spheres are available in the literature. Of particular interest are the modes localized on the surface of the sphere, along a thin ring located on the equator. These modes are called *whispering gallery modes* (WGM). WGM result from light confinement due to total internal reflection inside a high index spherical surface immersed in a lower index medium and from resonance as the light travels a round trip within the cavity with phase matching [27]. The WG modes are included in the Mie's family of solutions for resonant modes in light scattering by dielectric spheres. The WG modes can be also derived from Maxwell's equations by imposing adequate boundary conditions [28]. WG modes can also be obtained as solutions of the Quantum Mechanics Schrodinger-like equation describing the evolution of a complex angular-momentum of a particle in a potential well (see, for example, references [29, 30] and the other references cited therein).

Figure 23a shows the image of a spherical nano-particle of diameter 150 nm. This image presents the typical whispering gallery mode intensity distribution. Waves are propagating around the diameter in opposite directions thus producing a standing wave with seven nodes and six maxima. The light is trapped inside the particle and there is basically a surface wave that only penetrates a small amount into the radial direction.

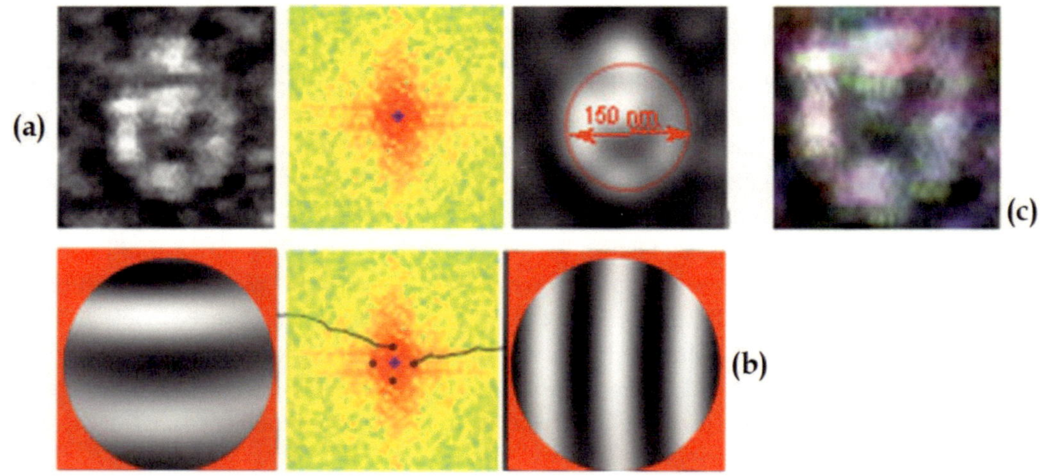

Figure 23. Spherical nano-particle of estimated diameter 150 nm: (a) FT and zero order filtered pattern; (b) Systems of fringes modulated by the particle; (c) Color image of the particle.

Similarly to the case of nano-crystals, the observed images are diffraction patterns of the electromagnetic field and are not actual images of the resonant modes of the spheres. As it can be seen in the images, different diffraction orders are present in the recorded images thus creating an effect that looks similar to an out-of-focus image. However, the changes between maxima and minima are preserved and can be utilized to ascertain the characteristics of the WG mode. As it occurs with the nano-crystals, the edges of the sphere image can be detected and analyzed.

The method of depth determination utilized for the nano-crystals can be applied also to the nano-spheres. While in prismatic bodies made out of plane surfaces the pattern interpretation is straightforward, in the case of curved surfaces the analysis of the patterns is more complex since light beams experience changes in trajectories determined by the laws of refraction. In the case of a sphere, the analysis of the patterns can be performed in a way similar to what is done in the analysis of the Ronchi test for lens aberrations. Figure 23b shows the distortion of a grating of pitch 83.4 nm that passes through the nano-sphere. The appearance of the observed fringes is similar to that observed in a Ronchi test. Through this analysis, the radius of curvature of the sphere is derived to be equal to 150 nm. The detailed description of this process is not included in this chapter for the sake of brevity.

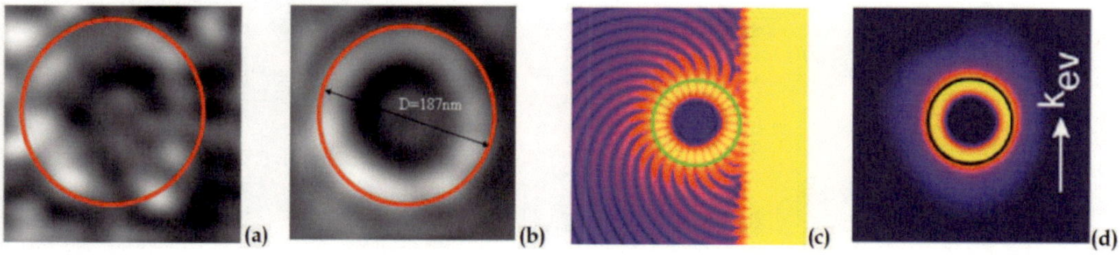

Figure 24. Spherical nano-particle of estimated diameter 187 nm and numerical simulations: (a) Original image; (b) Average intensity image; (c) Numerical simulation of whispering gallery modes [31]; (d) Average intensity of numerical simulation represented in Figure 24c.

Figure 24 shows a spherical particle of diameter 187 nm. The diameter has been obtained from the average intensity shown in Figure 24b. Figure 24c is taken from Ref. [31]. In [31], the WGM of a polystyrene microsphere of diameter 1.4 μm has been determined numerically. Figure 24c shows the pattern of the intensity of the electromagnetic field for the sphere equator. The average intensity corresponding to Figure 24c is represented in Figure 24d. The black circle included in Figure 24d corresponds to the green contour shown in Figure 24c that represents the surface of the microsphere. This boundary line also corresponds to the red line sketched in Figure 24b. In both cases, the field extends beyond the boundary of the sphere equator. There is a very good agreement between the experimental results and the numerical simulation. The electromagnetic resonance occurs at the wavelength λ=386 nm which corresponds to UV radiation. The color camera sensor is sensitive to this frequency and Figure 23c shows the color picture of the D=150 nm nano-sphere. Both the observed sphere and the sphere analyzed in the numerical example are made of polystyrene which has a resonance peak at the wavelength λ=386 nm.

The same procedure to determine geometry and shape applied to the nano-crystals has been applied to four spheres with radius ranging between 150 and 228 nm. For example, Figure 25 illustrates the different steps of the process for the 150 nm diameter particle shown in Figure 23a. The Fourier transform of the image is shown in Figure 25a. Figure 25b shows the Fourier transform of the real part of the FT of the image. Figure 25c presents the intensity distribution of the inverse transform of the filtered zero order shown in Figure 25b. Figure 25d and Figure 25e show the cross-sections of Figure 25c, respectively, in the X- and Y-directions. The structure of the zero order is complex. The gray level intensity decays from 255 to 20 within 75 nm: this quantity corresponds to the radius of the nano-sphere.

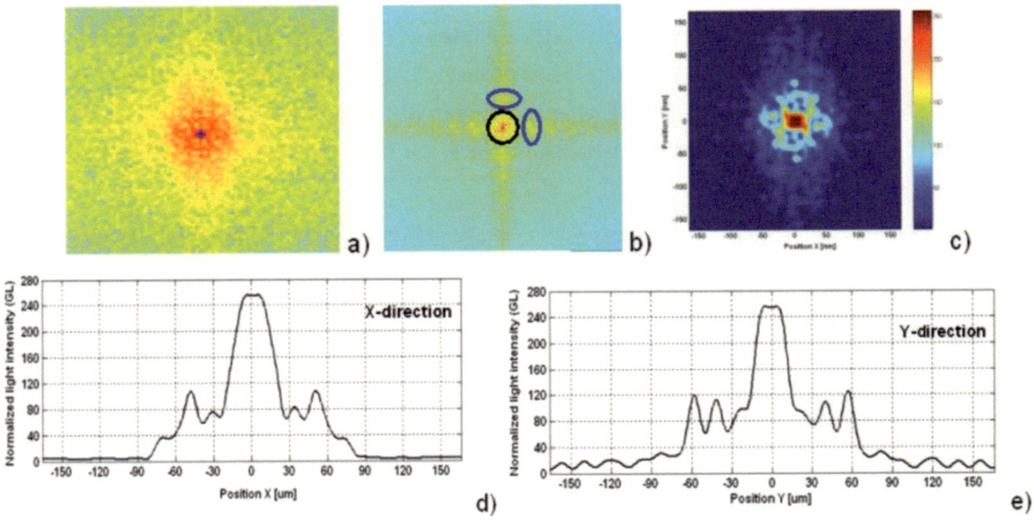

Figure 25. a) FT pattern of the image of the 150 nm polystyrene nano-sphere shown in Figure 23a; (b) Fourier transform of the real part of the FT of the nano-sphere; (c) 2-D view of the filtered zero order extracted from the real part of the FT pattern of the nano-sphere; (d) Cross-section of the filtered zero order in the X-direction; e) Cross-section of the filtered zero order in the Y-direction.

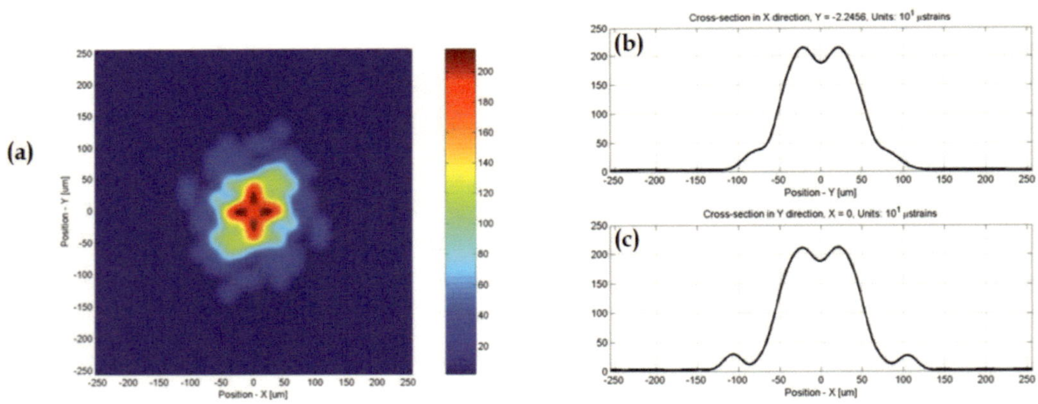

Figure 26. a) 2-D view of the filtered zero order extracted from the real part of the FT pattern of the polystyrene nano-sphere of diameter 187 nm shown in Figure 24a; (b) Cross-section of the filtered zero order in the X-direction; (c) Cross-section of the filtered zero order in the Y-direction.

The filtered zero order extracted from the real part of the FT pattern of the nano-sphere of diameter 187 nm is shown in Figure 26a. The structure of the order is far more symmetric than for the 150 nm diameter particle previously analyzed. Figures 26b-c show the cross-sections in the X and Y-directions of the filtered zero order, respectively. As in the preceding example, the intensity level drops sharply at the boundary of the equatorial region outlining the diameter of the sphere.

http://dx.doi.org/10.5772/53346

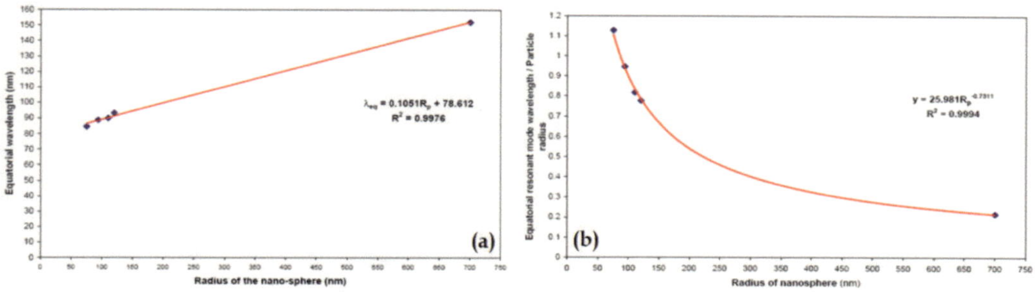

Figure 27. Relationships between nano-sphere radius and (a) equatorial wavelength of the WGM, (b) normalized equatorial wavelength of the WGM.

In order to verify that the pattern interpretation is in agreement with the presence of WGM modes, the experimentally determined equatorial wavelength of the WGM mode has been correlated with the sphere radius. Numerical results given in reference [31] also are included in the correlation. Two alternative correlation parameters have been considered following [32]. Figure 27a shows the variation of the equatorial wavelength vs. the radius of the sphere. Figure 27b shows the variation of the equatorial wavelength divided by the sphere radius vs. the sphere radius. Both models show a very high correlation coefficient R^2.

12. Numerical issues involved in the reconstruction process of nano-objects

There is a very important point to be made concerning the process of elaboration of the optically recorded data. The final results are a consequence of both optical and numerical super-resolution techniques [33]. These procedures have their foundations in two basic theorems of analytic functions. The FT of the images of nano-objects extended to the complex plane are analytical functions. If the FT of a function is known in a region of the domain under analysis, then, by analytic continuation the FT can be extended to the entire domain. The resolution obtained in this process is determined by the frequencies f_{sc} contained in the captured image. The images can be reconstructed by a combination of phase retrieval and suitable algorithms. The images can be reconstructed from a FT such that, if we call f_{sc} the maximum frequency that has been retrieved and $f_{sc,max}$ the maximum frequency content of the image, $f_{sc} \leq f_{sc,max}$.

The bi-cubical interpolation of pixels is a standard procedure utilized also in numerical super-resolution that allows getting sub-pixel resolutions. Furthermore, the fact that the process of image formation includes different replications of the image due to the different diffraction orders present in the image is an additional factor that increases the amount of information contained in an image. The effect of the successive images depends on the structure of the image plane array of the CCD, that is on the factor of fullness of the detector array, but it is equivalent to micro-scanning, which is to obtain successive frames of displaced images. Finer sampling procedures produce higher accuracies and better modulation transfer functions (MTF) together with higher Nyquist frequencies [34].

13. Summary and conclusions

This chapter presented a new method to analyze the near field super-oscillatory field generated by evanescent illumination at the nano-scale by imaging the near field in the far field. This approach was successfully applied to measure the topography of nano-sized simple objects such as prismatic sodium-chloride crystals and spherical polystyrene particles. The obtained results are supported by additional experimental evidence that independently provides confirmation of the different applied procedures and adopted models.

The recorded images are nano-sized lens holograms of the diffraction patterns of the observed objects. In a manner of speaking, they are similar to FT holograms that are also lens holograms of the diffraction patterns of the observed objects but the process of formation of the diffraction patterns follows very different mechanisms. While the FT holograms are the result of illuminating the observed object with an external source, the diffraction of the observed objects in the proposed method is a consequence of self illumination caused by electromagnetic resonance produced by the electromagnetic field generated by multiple evanescent fields. The wave fronts that contain the diffraction patterns of the observed objects are solitons solutions of the Maxwell equations that are generated by the presence of a relay lens that converts the local super-oscillations in non-diffracting Bessel waves that to go through the whole process of image formation without the restrictions imposed by diffraction-limited optical instruments.

The degree of accuracy achieved in measurements is ascertained on the basis of the observed sodium-chloride nano-crystals. The actual sizes of the observed crystals are known from theoretical and independent experimental verifications [23]. The actual measured values and the error analysis of the obtained results can be found in [19]. Two types of correlation are established, one correlation corresponds to the theoretically formulated proportion rations of the nano-crystal contained in [23]. The mean error of the measured aspects ratios is 4.6% with a standard deviation of ±6.6%. The other correlation corresponds to the actual dimensions of the nano-crystals. The mean absolute error in the length measurements is of the order of 3 nm and the standard deviation is ±3.7 nm. The measured lengths of the crystals agree very well with the lengths computed from the sodium-chloride elementary cell size (d=0.573 nm at room temperature). The overall measurements performed show an overall standard deviation that is of the order of ±5 elementary cells.

In the case of the nano-spheres, trends of variation of the observed equatorial wavelength of the confined photons with respect to particle radius are in good agreement with numerical results reported in the literature.

The developed methodology is an effective tool to perform with visible light measurements in the nano-range in the far field with a traditional optical microscope thus overcoming the diffraction-limited resolution of optical microscopes that currently limits their use.

Author details

Cesar A. Sciammarella[1*], Luciano Lamberti[2] and Federico M. Sciammarella[1]

*Address all correspondence to: csciammarella@niu.edu

1 College of Engineering & Engineering Technology, Northern Illinois University, DeKalb, USA

2 Dipartimento di Meccanica, Matematica e Mananagement, Politecnico di Bari, Bari, Italy

References

[1] Toraldo di Francia G. Super-gain antennas and optical resolving power. *Nuovo Cimento* 1952; 9(S3): 426-435.

[2] Sciammarella CA, Lamberti L. Optical detection of information at the sub-wavelength level. In: *Proceedings of the* NANOMEC06 *Symposium on Materials Science and Materials Mechanics at the Nanoscale. Modeling, Experimental Mechanics & Applications,* November 2006, Bari, Italy.

[3] Berry MV. Evanescent and real waves in quantum billiards and Gaussian beams. *Journal of Physics A: Mathematical and General* 1994; 27: 391-398.

[4] Girard C, Dereux A, Martin OJF, Devel M. Generation of optical standing waves around mesoscopic surface structures: scattering and light confinement. *Physical Review B* 1995; 52(4): 2889-2898.

[5] Toraldo di Francia G. *La Diffrazione della Luce*. Torino (Italy): Edizioni Scientifiche Einaudi; 1958. (In Italian)

[6] Vigoureux JM. De l'onde évanescente de Fresnel au champ proche optique. *Annales de la Fondation Luis de Broglie* 2003; 28(3-4): 525-548.

[7] Papoulis A. *The Fourier Integral and Its Applications*. New York (USA): McGraw-Hill; 1962.

[8] General Stress Optics Inc. *Holo-Moiré Strain Analyzer (Holostrain) Version 2.0*, Chicago (USA), 2007. http://www.stressoptics.com.

[9] Sciammarella CA, Lamberti L. Observation of fundamental variables of optical techniques in the nanometric range. In: Gdoutos EE (Ed) *Experimental Analysis of Nano and Engineering Materials and Structures*. Springer (The Netherlands); 2007. ISBN 978-1402062384

[10] Sciammarella CA, Lamberti L, Sciammarella FM. Light generation at the nano-scale, key to interferometry at the nano-scale. In: Proulx T. (Ed) *Conference Proceedings of the*

Society for Experimental Mechanics Series; Experimental and Applied Mechanics 6: 103-115. New York (USA): Springer; 2010. ISSN: 2191-5644.

[11] van de Hulst HC. *Light Scattering by Small Particles*, 2nd Edition. Mineola (USA): Courier Dover Publications; 1981.

[12] Guillemet C, Aclocque P. *Compte Rendue du Colloque sur la nature des surfaces vitreuses polies*. Charleroi (Belgium): Union Scientifique Continentale du Verre; pp. 121-134; (1959).

[13] Acloque P, Guillemet C. *Comptes Rendues de la Academie des Sciences* 1960; 250: 4328-4330.

[14] Ansevin RW. *Non Destructive Measurement of Surface Stresses in Glass*. Pittsburgh Plate Glass Company, Glass Research Center, Pittsburgh (USA), 1964.

[15] Guillemet C. *L'Interférométrie à Ondes Multiples Appliquée à Détermination de la Répartition de l'Indice de Réfraction Dans Un Milieu Stratifié*. PhD Dissertation, University of Paris. Paris (France): Imprimerie Jouve; 1970. (In French)

[16] Sciammarella CA. Experimental mechanics at the nanometric level. *Strain* 2008; 44(1): 3-19.

[17] Sciammarella CA, Lamberti L, Sciammarella FM. Optical holography reconstruction of nano-objects. In: Rosen J. (Ed.) *Holography, Research and Technologies*. Rijeka (HR): InTech; 2011. p191-216

[18] Ayyagari RS, Nair S. Scattering of P-polarized evanescent waves by a spherical dielectric particle. *Journal of the Optical Society of America, Part B: Optical Physics* 2009; 26(11): 2054-2058.

[19] Sciammarella CA, Lamberti L, Sciammarella FM. The equivalent of Fourier holography at the nanoscale. *Experimental Mechanics* 2009; 49(6): 747-773.

[20] Bouchal Z. Non diffracting optical beams: physical properties, experiments, and applications. *Czechoslovak Journal of Physics* 2003; 53(7): 537-578.

[21] Wang H, Shi LP, Lukyanchuk BS, Sheppard CJR, Chong TC, Yuan GQ. Super-resolution and non-diffraction longitudinal polarized beam, 2007. http://arxiv.org/ftp/arxiv/papers/0709/0709.2748.pdf (Accessed 16 August 2012)

[22] Wang H, Shi LP, Lukyanchuck BS, Sheppard CJR, Chong TW. Creation of a needle of longitudinally polarized light in vacuum using binary optics. *Nature Photonics* 2008; 2: 501-505.

[23] Hudgins RR, Dugourd P, Tenenbaum JN, Jarrold MF. Structural transitions of sodium nanocrystals. *Physical Review Letters* 1997; 78: 4213-4216.

[24] Burch JW, Gates C, Hall RGN, Tanner LH. Holography with a scatter-plate as a beam splitter and a pulsed ruby laser as light source. *Nature* 1966; 212: 1347-1348.

[25] Spencer RC, Anthony SAT. Real time holographic moiré patterns for flow visualization. *Applied Optics* 1968; 7(3): 561-561.

[26] Tanner LH. The scope and limitations of three-dimensional holography of phase objects. *Journal of Scientific Instruments* 1966; 44(12): 774-776.

[27] Johnson BR. Theory of morphology-dependent resonances - shape resonances and width formulas. *Journal of the Optical Society of America, Part A: Optics Image Science and Vision* 1993; 10(2): 343-352.

[28] Bohren CF, Huffman DR. *Absorption and Scattering of Light by Small Particles*. New York (USA): Wiley; 1998.

[29] Fan X, Doran A, Wang H. High-Q whispering gallery modes from a composite system of GaAs quantum well and fused silica microsphere. *Applied Physics Letters* 1998; 73(22): 3190-3192.

[30] Shopova SI. *Nanoparticle-Coated Optical Microresonators for Whispering-Gallery Lasing and Other Applications*. PhD Dissertation, Oklahoma State University, Stillwater (USA), 2007.

[31] Pack A. *Current Topics in Nano-Optics*. PhD Dissertation, Chemnitz Technical University, Chemnitz (Germany), 2001.

[32] Collot L, Lefèvre-Seguin V, Brune M, Raimond JM, Haroche S. Very High-Q Whispering-Gallery Mode resonances observed on fused silica microspheres. *Europhysics Letters* 1993; 23(5): 327-334.

[33] Borman S, Stevenson R. *Spatial Resolution Enhancement of Low Resolution Image Sequences, a Comprehensive Review with Directions for Future Research.* Laboratory for Image and Signal Analysis, IM 46556, University of Notredame (USA), 1998

[34] Boreman GD. *Modulation Transfer Function in Optical and Electro-Optical Systems.* Bellingham (USA): SPIE Press; 2001.

Section 3

Digital Holography

Chapter 12

Digital Hologram Coding

Young-Ho Seo, Hyun-Jun Choi and Dong-Wook Kim

Additional information is available at the end of the chapter

http://dx.doi.org/10.5772/53904

1. Introduction

In this section, the overall process to code a digital hologram video and the whole architecture of the service system for digital holograms are explained.

1.1. Overview of holographic signal processing

A digital hologram includes not only the light intensity but also the depth information of the 3D (dimensional) object. That is, both the whole amplitude and the phase information are necessary to reconstruct the original 3D object, which are included in the interference pattern between the reference light and the object light. Since a digital hologram signal has much different characteristics from general 2D signal, a particular data processing technique is required. In spite, both have the same goal to acquire image information from 3D world and to display it as realistic as possible to human visual system (HVS). Thus, if the techniques based on the 2D-image are modified and some proper techniques for 3D image are added, they can be efficient enough to be applied to digital holograms [1, 2].

Fig. 1 shows an overall simplified scheme to process digital holographic signals. A digital hologram video is captured from a moving 3D object by an optical system using CCD (Charge Coupled Device) or by generating with a computer calculation (Computer-Generated Hologram, CGH) [3]. The acquired information (Fresnel field or fringe pattern) shows a noise-like feature. The fringe pattern is converted into a different data type to be applied to a developed image processing tool in *Data Processing* step. The result is encoded with properly designed coding tools in *Video Coding* step, for which this section uses standard techniques of H.264/AVC [4], entropy coder, and a lossless coder [5, 6].

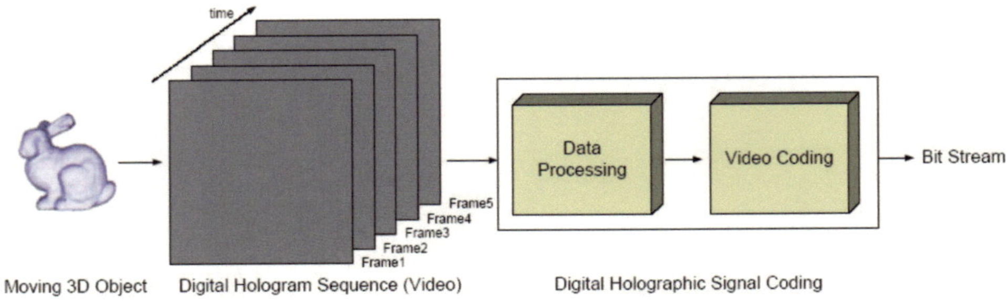

Figure 1. Overall data process scheme for digital hologram videos

1.2. Digital hologram service system

A digital hologram service system can be organized with 3D information acquisition, compression (or encoding), transmission, decompression (or decoding), and holographic display, as shown in Fig. 2. In the data acquisition, 3D information of a real object is acquired as the types of a digital hologram, a depth-and-texture image pair, or a graphic model. A digital hologram is generated by a scanning-based holographic system or components of optical system. A depth-and-texture image is extracted from an advanced imaging system such as the infrared sensor-based depth camera that captures 8-bit depth information for each gray-level pixel. The 3D model is formed by IBMR (Image Based Model Rendering) using multi-view information that is captured by several 2D cameras.

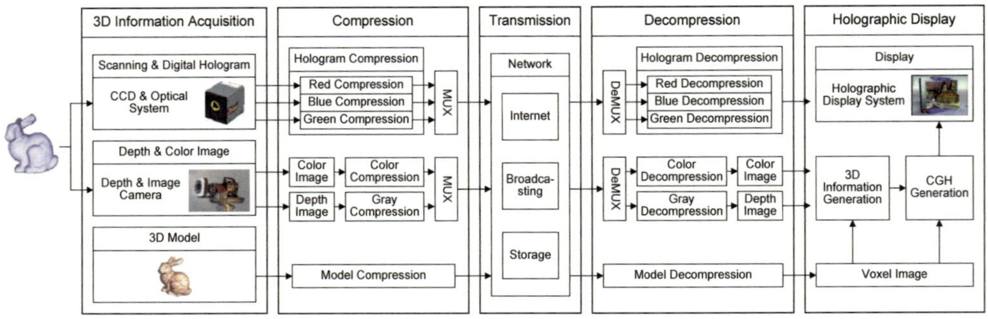

Figure 2. Digital hologram video service system

The acquired 3D information is encoded with various coding algorithms according to the characteristics of the 3D information in the data compression steps. Basically the holographic image is a color image. Some proposed a scheme to process a color hologram without separating the color components [5]. But in this book, each color component (R, G, or B) of a digital hologram is processed separately because each component has different frequency band and different importance level, which are very important factors in our scheme. The encoded data is transmitted through a network and the received data is decoded with the decoding algorithms that are dependent of the encoding process. The decoded data which retains the digital holographic information such as fringe pattern can be easily displayed in a holographic display system. If the decoded data is a 3D model or a depth-and-texture image, the adequate 3D information to the corresponding display system must be extracted.

2. Characteristics of digital holograms

A digital hologram is a 2D data even though it retains 3D information such as intensity and phase of the interference pattern between object wave and reference wave. Also, a digital hologram is a kind of a transformed result (Fresnel transform, for example) from the spatial domain to a frequency domain. But we regard it as a 2D spatial data throughout this book. In this section, we analyze the characteristics of a digital hologram in a viewpoint of a 2D image to use the techniques for 2D image.

2.1. Sub-sampling

First, we examine the pixel, a basic element of a 2D digital hologram. As a methodology of examination, we took the sub-sampling method as follows: A digital hologram, CGH is divided into fixed-sized blocks, one out of two blocks in both direction is discarded, and the remaining blocks are re-assembled to form a reduced digital hologram whose size are one-fourth of the original one.

Fig. 3 shows the example results of the Rabbit image for various sizes of the sub-sampling blocks. As can see in the figures, a hologram shows totally different characteristics from a natural 2D image. The reconstructed image after sub-sampling one out of two pixels totally loses the original information, as Fig. 3(b). As the size of the sub-sampling segment increases as Fig. 3(c) and (d), the 3D information is getting perfect. Note that the size of the reconstructed image is proportional to the size of the digital hologram. It means that, differently from 2D image, a pixel in a digital hologram retains a piece of inter-dependent information for the whole image, not the localized one. Thus a certain amount of neighboring pixels can reconstruct the original information and the quality is getting better as the number of neighboring pixels increases [6].

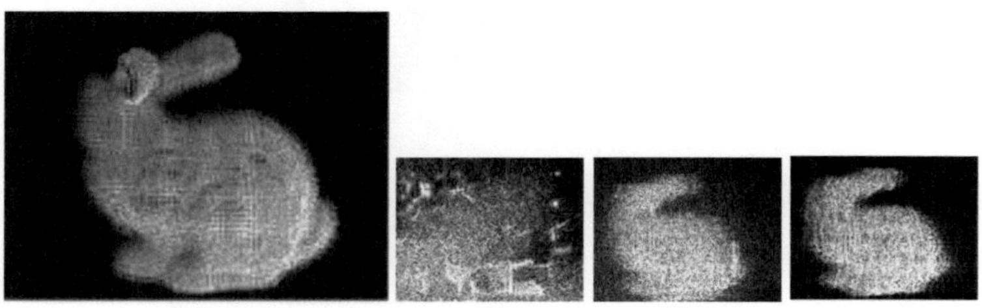

(a) (b) (c) (d)

Figure 3. Example of reconstructed images after sub-sampling; (a) original 3D object, by the block size of (b) 1×1 pixel^2 (one pixel), (c) 32×32 pixel^2, (d) 128×128 pixel^2.

2.2. Localization

This inter-dependent property of each pixel can be clearer by taking a part of a digital hologram (cropping) and reconstructing the image. Fig. 4 shows several cropping examples, in which various sizes of co-centered parts of a fringe pattern are cropped out and each of which is converted to reconstruct the image. As in the figures, the reconstructed holographic image is getting larger and clearer as the cropped size increases. This property is similar to the previous result from sub-sampling, which shows entirely different characteristics from the case of 2D image: a local region of a natural 2D image retains only the specified information that is defined by the position of the region, while a local region of a hologram retains the information of the entire image [6].

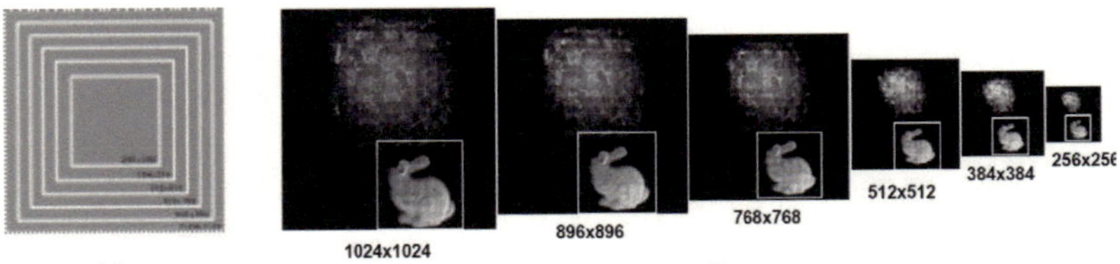

(a) (b)

Figure 4. Examples of localization by cropping a digital hologram; (a) cropping scheme for digital hologram, (b) reconstructed images.

This inter-dependent property of a local region in a hologram can also be ascertained by dividing the whole fringe pattern into several segments and reconstructing the holographic image with each part or segment, as shown in Fig. 5, where segmentation into four 512×512 segments and sixteen 256 ×256 segments are depicted. In these figures, the dotted lines are the vertical and horizontal center lines for each locally reconstructed image to show the difference in the location and shape in each local image.

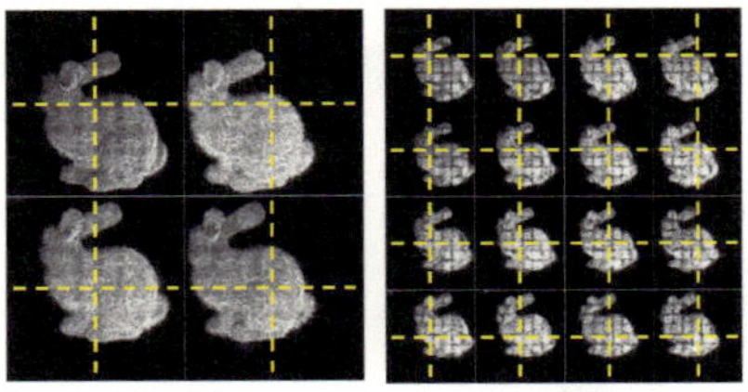

(a) (b)

Figure 5. Reconstructed objects in local regions after segmentation with the size of; (a) 512×512 size, (b) 256×256 size.

This property provides a possibility that a digital hologram can be processed as a multi-view image. That is, each of the segmented local regions can be treated as an individual 2D image. Because each of the segments resulting from a fringe pattern has similar information, we can convert each segment into a proper type of data to find correlation among them and efficiently encode them by eliminating the redundancies.

2.3. Frequency characteristic

As shown in Fig. 4, a fringe pattern has noise-like feature and frequency property of it has different tendency from that of a 2D image. Fig. 6 shows the scheme to examine the energy distribution of results from DCT (Discrete Cosine Transform) [7] and DWT (Discrete Wavelet Transform) [8], the two representative frequency-transform methods for 2D natural images, where the whole fringe pattern is 2-dimensionally processed as one processing unit for DCT to retain a consistency in both transform. That is, the regions of frequency bands are matched to compare the energies for each band. In both transforms, the left top band retains the lowest-frequency coefficients and the frequency is getting higher as goes to right and bottom.

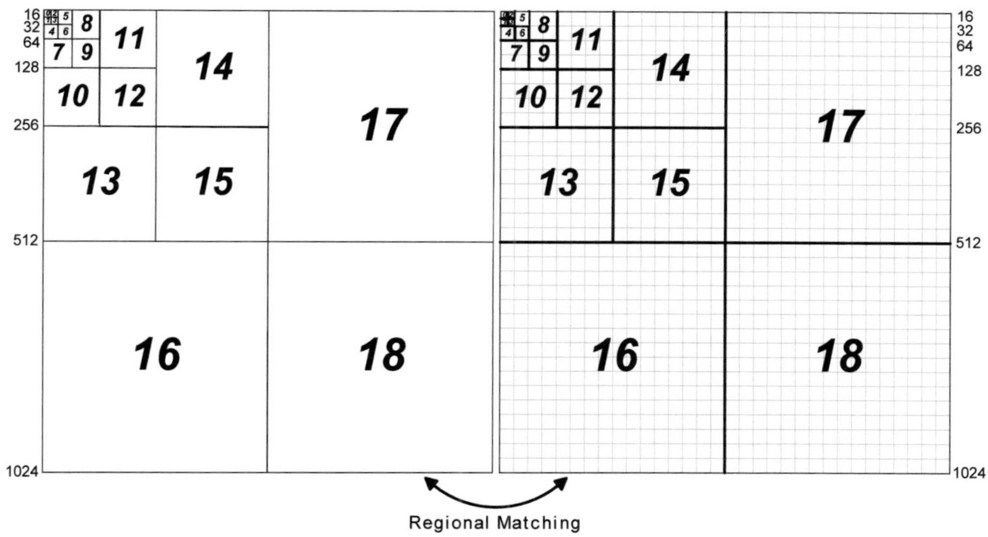

Figure 6. The scheme to examine the coefficient energy for DCT and DWT

The average energies of the coefficients in the frequency bands are depicted in Fig. 7, which was obtained by experimenting various test digital holograms. Note that the energy values of the lowest frequency band are the numbers on the graph, not the quantity the graph scale shows, because they are too large to show in a same graph with others. It is quite similar to a 2D image in that the lowest-frequency coefficient or region has very large energy. The difference in energy distribution for a digital hologram is quite different from that of a natural 2D image is in that some of the high-frequency bands have quite high energy distribution. It implicitly shows that to deal with the frequency-transformed coefficients with an image processing technique for natural 2D images without an additional processing or modification is not efficient for a digital hologram.

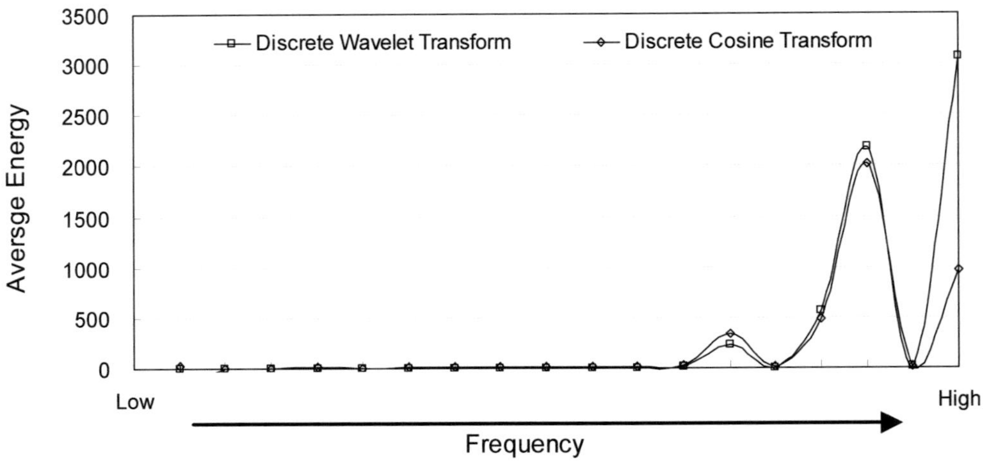

Figure 7. Average coefficient energies at the frequency bands for both DCT and DWT.

3. Lossless compression of a digital hologram

One of the classifications divides the source coding algorithms into lossless coding and lossy coding. During coding processing, a lossless coding method retains perfect information of the original data. But lossy coding method removes a part of it with a permissible limit according to application. In this section, digital hologram is compressed by the following lossless coding methods [9].

3.1. Run length encoding

RLE, or Run Length Encoding, is a very simple method for lossless compression. It encodes how many times each coefficient repeats (a pair of codes with each coefficient and the number of repetitions) [10]. Although it is simple and obviously very inefficient for general purpose compression, it can be very useful at times (it is used in JPEG compression [11], for instance).

http://dx.doi.org/10.5772/53904

3.2. Shannon-Fano coding

Shannon-Fano coding was invented by Claude Shannon (often regarded as the father of information theory) and Robert Fano in 1949 [12]. It is a very good compression method. But since David Huffman improved it later, the original Shannon-Fano coding method has almost never used.

The Shannon-Fano method replaces each symbol with an alternate binary representation, whose length is determined by the probability of the particular symbol such that more common symbol uses less bits. The Shannon-Fano algorithm produces a very compact representation of each symbol that is almost optimal (it approaches optimum when the number of different symbols approaches infinite). However, it does not deal with the ordering or repetition of symbols or sequence of symbols.

3.3. Huffman coding

The Huffman coding method was presented by David A. Huffman, a graduate student of Robert Fano, in 1952. Technically, it is very similar to the Shannon-Fano coder, but it has the nice property of being optimal in the sense that changing any binary code of any symbol will result in a less compact representation [13].

The only real difference between the Huffman coder and the Shannon-Fano coder is the way of building the binary coding tree: in the Shannon-Fano method, the binary tree is built by recursively splitting the histogram into equally weighted halves (i.e. top-down), while in the Huffman method, the tree is built by successively joining the two least weighting nodes until there is only a single node left - the root node (i.e. bottom-up).

Since Huffman coding has the same complexity as Shannon-Fano coding (this also holds for decoding) with always better compression (although only slightly), Huffman coding is almost always used instead of Shannon-Fano coding in reality.

3.4. Rice coding

For data consisting of large words (e.g. 16 or 32 bits) and mostly low data values, Rice coding can be very successful to achieve a good compression ratio [14]. This kind of data is typically audio or highly dynamic range images that have been pre-processed with some kind of prediction (such as delta to neighboring samples). Although Huffman coding should be optimal for this kind of data, it is not a very suitable method due to several reasons (for instance, a 32-bit word size would require a 16 GB histogram buffer to encode the Huffman tree). Therefore a more dynamic approach is more appropriate for data consisted of large words.

The basic idea behind Rice coding is to store as many words as possible with less bits than in the original representation just as with Huffman coding. In fact, one can think of the Rice code as a fixed Huffman code. The coding is very simple: Encode the value X with X '1' bits followed by a '0' bit.

3.5. Lempel-Ziv coding

There are many different variants of the Lempel-Ziv compression scheme. The Basic Compression Library has a fairly straight forward implementation of the LZ77 algorithm (Lempel-Ziv, 1977) [15]. The LZ coder can be used for general purpose compression, and performs exceptionally well for text. It can also be used in combination with the provided RLE and Huffman coders to gain some extra compression in most situations.

The idea behind the Lempel-Ziv compression algorithm is to take the RLE algorithm a few steps further by replacing sequences of bytes with references to previous occurrences of the same sequences. For simplicity, the algorithm can be thought of in terms of string matching. For instance, in written text certain strings tend to occur quite often, and can be represented by pointers to earlier occurrences of the string in the text. The idea is, of course, that pointers or references to strings are shorter than the strings themselves.

The coding results for some example images by above algorithms are shown in table 1.

	Bunny	**Duck**	**Spring**	**Bramhs**
	Ratio (%)	**Ratio (%)**	**Ratio (%)**	**Ratio (%)**
Huffman Coding	85.810	84.816	84.287	91.373
LZ77	99.935	99.862	99.917	100.000
RICE 8-bit	100.000	100.000	100.000	100.000
RLE	99.992	99.986	99.889	100.000
Shannon-Fano	86.332	85.395	84.899	91.717

Table 1. Lossless compression results

4. Lossy compression of a digital hologram

As shown in the previous section, it is identified that lossless coding methods don't give enough compression efficiency. To get more efficient compression for a digital hologram, a lossy coding method can be used. In this section, we try code a digital hologram into a very small amount of bitstream [5, 6].

4.1. Pre-processing

In general, a fringe generated from a 3-D object image has color components. To code it, the fringe pattern should be separated into R, G, B or Y, U, V components. Fig. 8 shows this process. Each of the separated components (RGB or YUV) is coded as an independent channel. Since the YUV format shows more degradation than the RGB format, we decided to use the RGB format. Because the G (green) component shows superior results to the others, we use it to explain the scheme from now on.

http://dx.doi.org/10.5772/53904

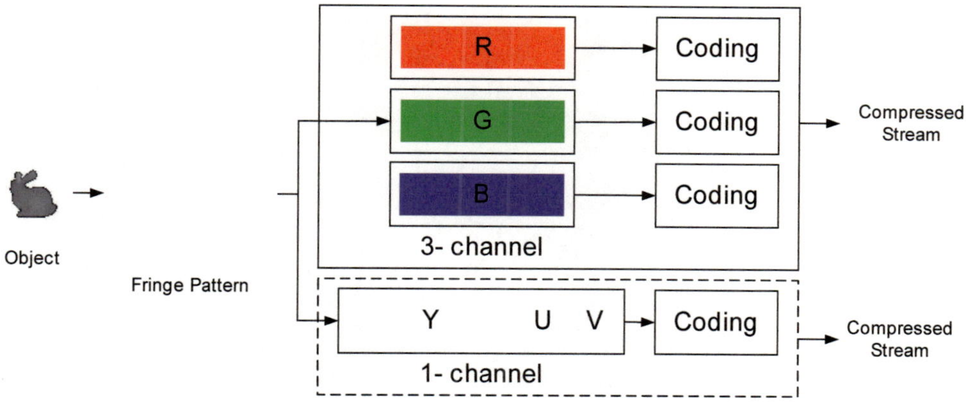

Figure 8. Pre-process to code a digital hologram.

4.2. Data formatting

Each separated component (fringe component) of a fringe pattern is segmented and transformed by 2-D DCT to be applied to a video compression tool.

4.2.1. Segmentation of a digital hologram

The first step in lossy coding for each color component is to divide it into several segments. The size of the segment can be determined arbitrarily but the feature by the different size of the segment is different, which is related to the explanation in section 2. This feature is discussed in next sub-section. Here, we examine various size of segment from 8×8 [pixel^2] to 512×512 [pixel^2]. The segment size is exactly the same block size of 2D DCT. If the horizontal and vertical size of a fringe component cannot be divided by the segments size, a fringe component us extended with "0" values (zero-padding technique). The segmentation and extension method of a fringe component for the block-based DCT is depicted in Fig. 9.

4.2.2. Frequency transform of each segment

As shown in Fig. 9, each separated segment $I_{m,n}(x,y)$ from a fringe pattern $I(x,y)$ is separately transformed using 2D DCT [7] of Eq. (1), which is for $M \times N$ block size, where C_k is $1/\sqrt{2}$ (k=0) or 1 (otherwise).

$$z_{m,n}(x,y) = \frac{1}{4}\sum_{u=0}^{M}\sum_{v=0}^{N} C_u C_v I_{m,n}(u,v)\cos[\pi(2x+1)u/16]\cos[\pi(2y+1)v/16] \quad (1)$$

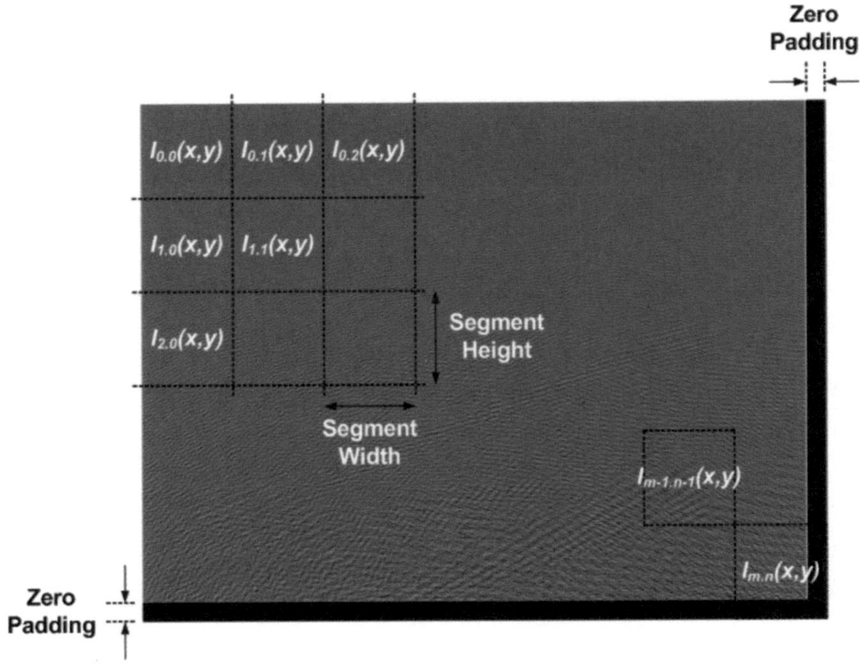

Figure 9. Fringe segmentation and extension for 2D DCT

Fig. 10 shows the results from 2D DCT for the divided segments that have the sizes from 512×512 [pixel^2] to 64×64 [pixel^2]. A fringe pattern itself is the result of a frequency transform, but we treat it an ordinary 2D image. Thus, 2D DCT makes double transform for each segment, which results in the somewhat similar shape to the original object for each segment, as can see in the figures. In other words, we can treat a fringe segment as a video frame because the local characteristic of the divided fringe component is very similar to the temporal variation characteristics in 2D video. In addition, the differences among the fringe segments are minimal, because the patterns are similar to each other. Therefore, it can be treated as temporal redundancy and compressed efficiently by a coding system for a moving picture [5, 6, 16, 17].

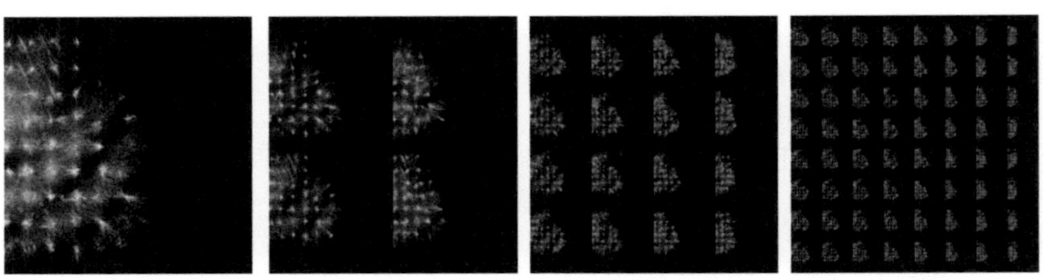

(a) (b) (c) (d)

Figure 10. The results from 2D DCT of a fringe with the segment size of (a) 512×512 [pixel^2], (b) 256×256 [pixel^2], (c) 128×128 [pixel^2], and (d) 64×64 [pixel^2].

http://dx.doi.org/10.5772/53904

4.2.3. *Feature of fringe by segmentation*

Fig. 11 shows peak signal-to-noise ratios (PSNRs) of the reconstructed fringe and normalized correlation (NC) of a reconstructed object image after applying only 2D DCT. As shown in Fig. 11(a), PSNR increases as the block size increases, but NC does not show any specific relationship as in Fig. 11(b). From the experiment, the segment size of 64× 64 [pixel^2] shows best NC values of the reconstructed object images [5].

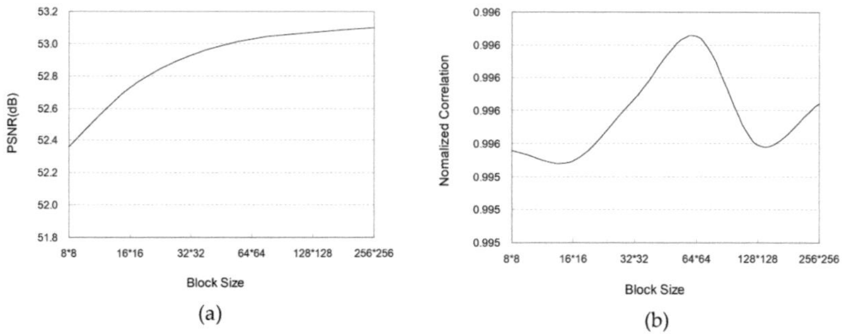

Figure 11. Simulation results for segmentation and DCT; (a) PSNR of the reconstructed fringe, (b) NC of the reconstructed object image.

4.2.4. *Sequence formation*

As mentioned above, the segmented and 2D DCTed fringe segments can be treated as the video frames with motion. To make a video sequence with those frames, we impose timing information to the segments by ordering them. We call this process as *scanning*. The concept of video streaming including hologram generation is shown in Fig. 12. The object that is projected at a segment or a part of the hologram film (the fringe pattern) has the information of the entire original object with different optic angles. It is similar to the multi-view stereoscopic display method. To use this property in compression coding, a video sequence is generated by segmentation, transformation, and scanning a fringe pattern.

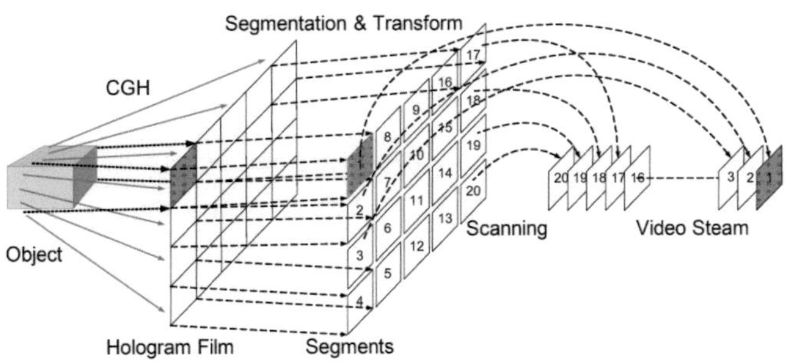

Figure 12. Conceptual description of the scanning

4.3. Segment-based coding

From this sub-section, the lossy coding techniques are explained. First, a scheme based on the segmentation itself is explained, in which a video sequence is formed on the basis of each fringe pattern frame. Many components of this scheme are used in the next coding schemes which will be explained in the next sections [5, 6, 17].

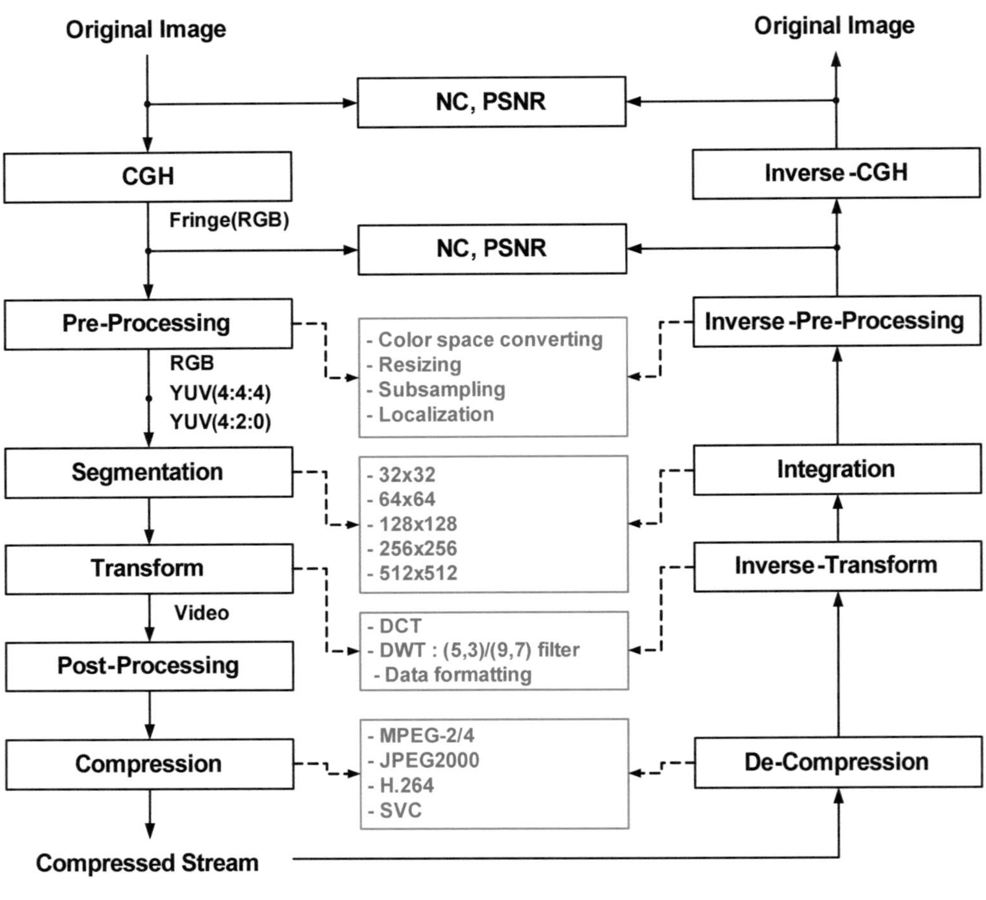

Figure 13. Process flow of digital hologram coding

The first coding scheme is a hybrid coding scheme for hologram compression which includes the proper treatment of the intermediate data. We use the international standard 2D video coding techniques for main compression coding. Thus, it includes the some data manipulation steps to convert the fringe data to fit those standards.

Fig. 13 shows the whole flow to code and decode a digital hologram. It consists of pre-processing, segmentation, transform, post-processing, and compression. During the process, the fringe pattern is divided into several segments (*segmentation*) for 2D DCT (*transform*), as explained

http://dx.doi.org/10.5772/53904

above. The DCT coefficients are rearranged into a video sequence by a data scanning. Therefore, a compression system for 2D moving picture is applied to compress the hologram data.

4.3.1. Scan method

If the segmented fringes are transformed independently by 2D DCT, they have similar property to 2D video frames. Therefore, to apply the 2D video coding tools, they have to be scanned to form a frame sequence in a temporal ordering. Fig. 14 shows the possible scan methods. After 2D DCT, the choice of scan method is related with temporal characteristic and efficiency. That is, each scanning method determines how the object moves, and how much correlation (or redundancy) the two consecutive frames have.

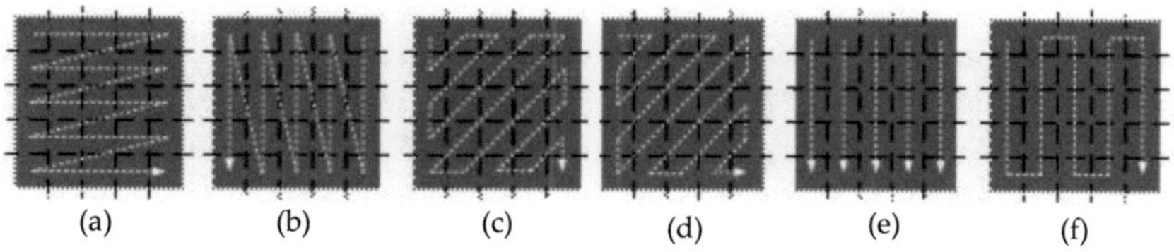

Figure 14. Scanning methods for the segmented fringe images

We analyzed the cost and performance for various scanning methods in Fig. 14 after applying the DS (Diamond Searching)-based ME (Motion Estimation) and MC (Motion Compensation). Two items were compared and the results are shown in Fig. 15 for various sizes of the segmented images. The first item is the number of search points (Fig. 15(a)) which represent the amount of calculation to find the best-matched point. The other is the error value that is the difference between the original image and the ME/MC result, for which the SAD (Sum of Absolute Differences) values are used (Fig. 15(b)).

Both the number of search points and the SAD value decrease as the size of segment increases. In both items, Method f shows the best performance although all the methods showed similar results for the number of search points.

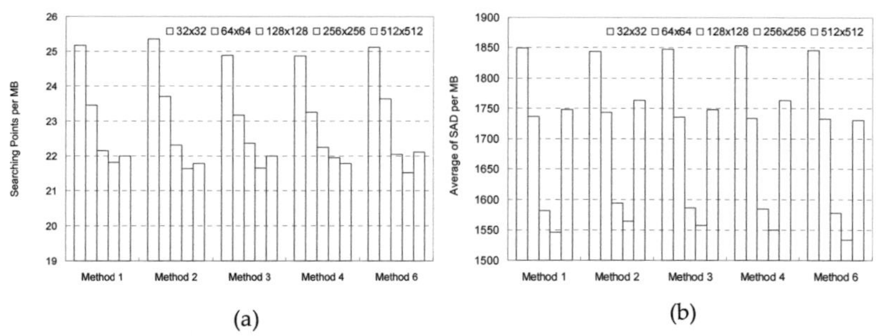

Figure 15. Comparison of (a) searching points in DS, (b) SAD in DS for the scanning methods in Fig. 14

4.3.2. Data renormalization

We classify the transformed data into three kinds according to the characteristics of the data and they are treated differently. The basic classification is shown in Fig. 16. First, the DC coefficients are separated from the other AC coefficients because the DC coefficients have very large energy portion of the DCT block. The DC and several AC coefficients may have the absolute value over 255 and usually they are discarded during quantization. These coefficients have very low possibility to occur (as shown in Table 2, they are less than 0.1%) but their values are so large that they might affect quite amount of image quality. Thus, we treat them especially as will be explained in the next subsection with the name of *exceptional coefficients* (ECfs), while the coefficient with absolute value lower than 256 is named as *normal coefficient* (NCf).

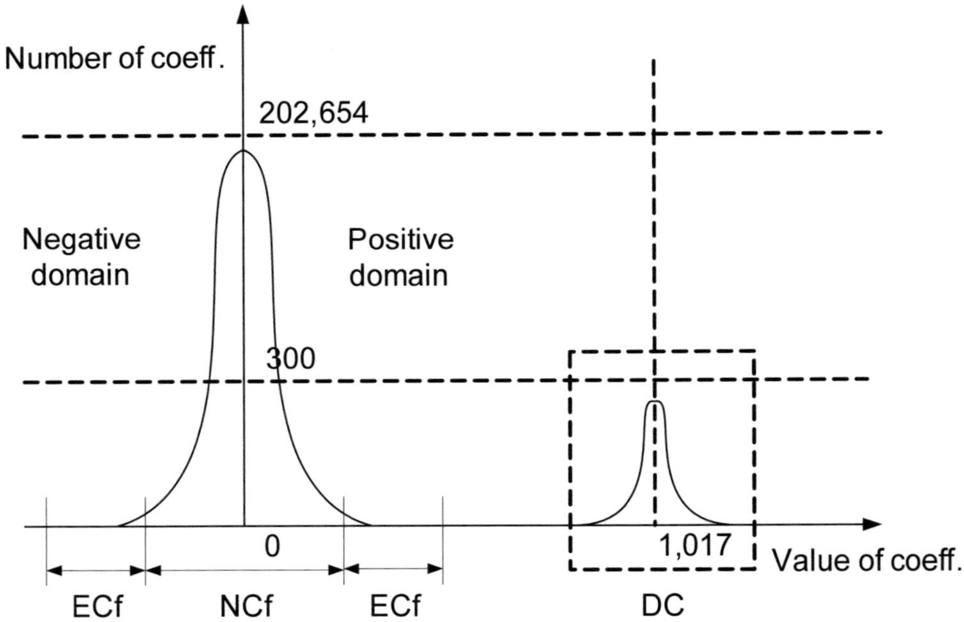

Figure 16. Classification of DCT coefficients

NC can also have a negative value. However negative values are not suitable as the input of general 2D compression tools such as MPEGs. Thus, we change the expression of each coefficient into a signed-magnitude format as shown in Fig. 17. That is, each coefficient has a sign bit and its magnitude. The sign bits are assembled as a bitplane named as *sign bitplane* (SB), in which each sign bit lies in the corresponding position to the original coefficient. As the result, all the coefficients have positive values and a separate SB is produced.

Segment Size	DC Coefficient	AC Coefficient		Sign Bitplane	
		NCfs	ECfs	Plus	Negative
8×8	16,384 (1.5625%)	1,032,192 (98.4375%)	0 (0%)	531,796 (50.7203%)	516,780 (49.2797%)
16×16	4,096 (0.3906%)	1,044,480 (99.6094%)	0 (0%)	526,922 (50.2533%)	521,654 (49.7467%)
32×32	1,024 (0.0976%)	1,047,526 (99.8999%)	26 (0.0024%)	524,825 (50.0521%)	523,751 (49.9479%)
64×64	256 (0.0244%)	104,378 (99.9543%)	223 (0.0213%)	524,926 (50.0652%)	523,650 (49.9348%)
128×128	64 (0.0061%)	1,047,611 (99.9079%)	883 (0.0842%)	524,264 (49.9878%)	524,312 (50.0122%)
256×256	16 (0.0015%)	1,047,677 (99.9143%)	901 (0.0859%)	526,878 (50.2509%)	521,698 (49.7491%)
512×512	4 (0.0004%)	1,047,866 (99.9322%)	706 (0.0673%)	523,328 (49.9085%)	525,248 (50.0926%)

Table 2. Coefficient distribution of the results from 2D DCT

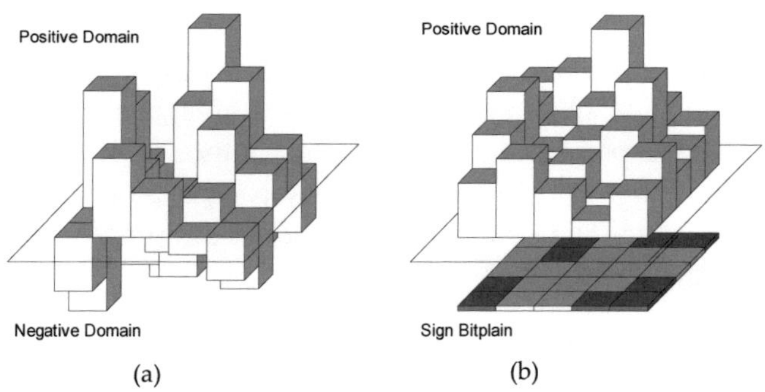

Figure 17. Rearrangement of DCT coefficients; (a) original coefficient plane, (b) signed-magnitude format.

4.3.3. Video coding standard-based compression

As shown in Fig. 18, three compression schemes are involved for compression coding. NCfs of AC coefficients are compressed with an MPEG encoder for 2D video. The MPEG Encoder corresponds to one of MPEG-2 [18], MPEG-4 [19], and H.264/AVC [4]. The ECfs are compressed by DPCM (Differential Pulse Code Modulation) method and the results are applied to an entropy encoder such as Huffman encoder or arithmetic encoder. The SB is very important to recover the image. So it is compressed by a conventional binary compression method such as ZIP [20] etc.

The results of the three compression scheme are assembled to a bit stream to send or store.

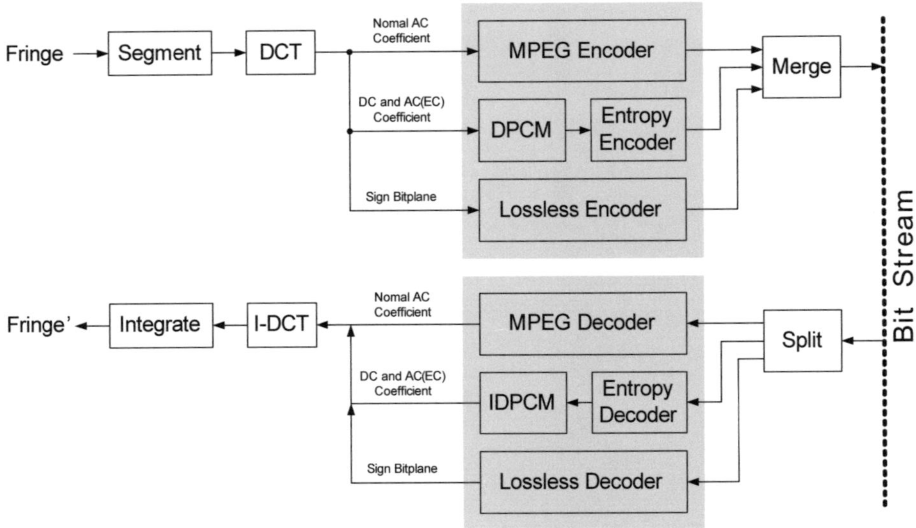

Figure 18. A hybrid coding algorithm for digital hologram compression

4.3.4. Coding characteristics

For the MPEG encoder in the hybrid coding scheme in Fig. 19, we applied MPEG-2, MPEG-4, and H.264/AVC with other tools fixed. The size of segment was from 16×16 [pixel^2] to 512×512 [pixel^2]. The experimental results from compression and reconstruction are shown in from Fig. 19 to Fig. 31, which are the lossy compression results without lossless compression. Since the reduced amount of data by lossless compression is negligible to lossy compression, it has little influence on the compression ratio.

Fig. 19 and 20 show the example results with Rabbit image after compression and reconstruction by MPEG-4 and H.264, respectively for various compression ratios. In visual examination, there is little performance difference between the results of MPEG-4 and H.264/AVC.

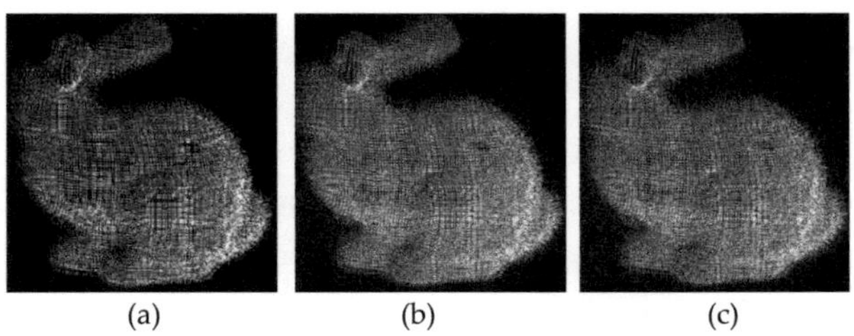

Figure 19. Reconstruction results of object image by MPEG-4 (64×64 segment): (a) original object image, (b) 30:1 compression, and (c) 50:1 compression.

http://dx.doi.org/10.5772/53904

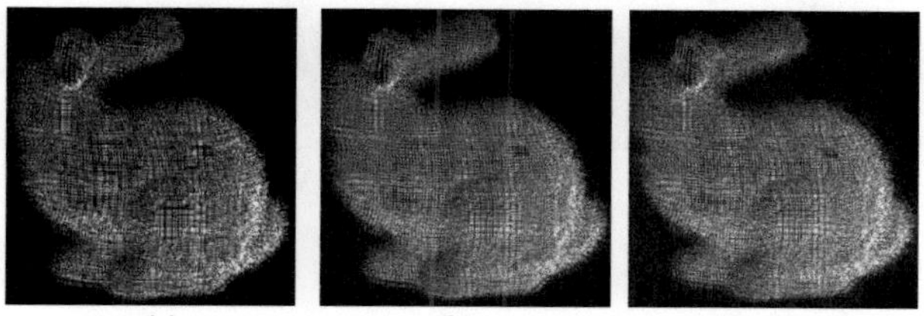

(a) (b) (c)

Figure 20. Reconstruction results of object image by H.264/AVC (64×64 segment): (a) original object image, (b) 30:1 compression, and (c) 50:1 compression.

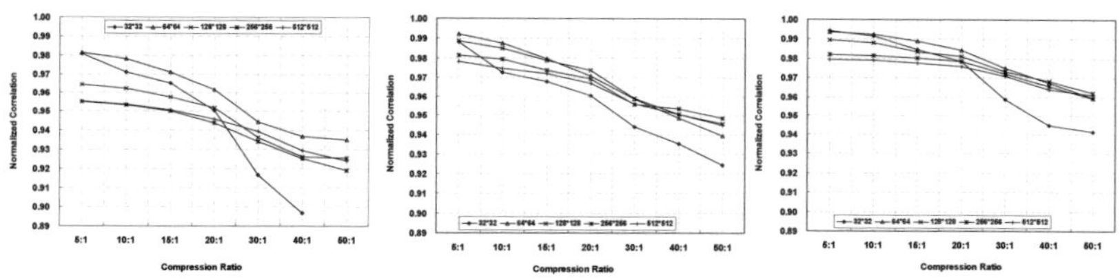

(a) (b) (c)

Figure 21. NC values of reconstructed images: (a) MPEG-2, (b) MPEG-4, and (c) AVC.

In Fig. 21, the average image qualities after reconstruction are graphically summarized for the various coding tools as the function of compression ratio. Here, we used the NC value as the measure for the image quality. As seen in Fig. 21, segmented results of the size of 64×64 pixels showed the best quality, as expected by the explanation above. Among the compression tools, H.264/AVC shows the best image quality at the same compression ratio. In the case of H.264/AVC, the NC value of the reconstructed image retained over 0.94, even at the compression ratio of 50:1, except for the segment size of 16×16. Consequently, the scheme shows the best quality when the segment size of 64×64 pixels and H.264/AVC tool are used. In the compression ratio with the same image quality, this scheme shows from four to eight times better performance than the previous schemes whose compression ratios were between 8:1 and 16:1 at 0.94 of NC value.

Fig. 22 and 23 are additional results for other 3-D object images, which are Spring and Duck. The experiment used H.264/AVC for a 64×64 segment. As shown in these figures, the reconstructed images have little difference from the original images in visual inspection, and the values of NC are more than 0.95. Also the reconstructed digital holograms are optically captured and they are shown in Fig. 24.

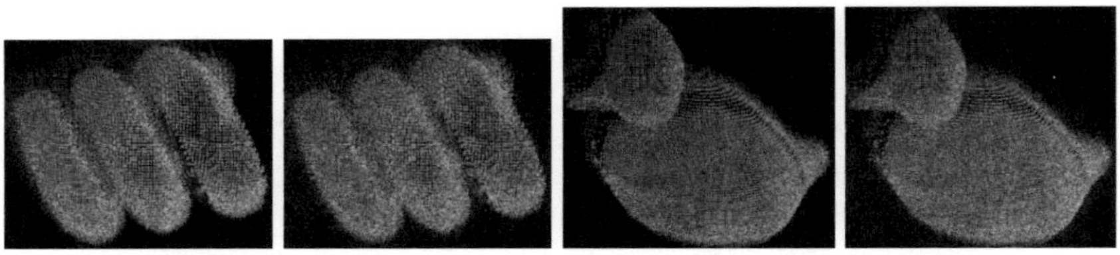

(a) (b) (c) (d)

Figure 22. Reconstruction results by H.264/AVC (64×64 segment); (a) original spring image, (b) 50:1 compression, (c) original duck image, and (d) 50:1 compression.

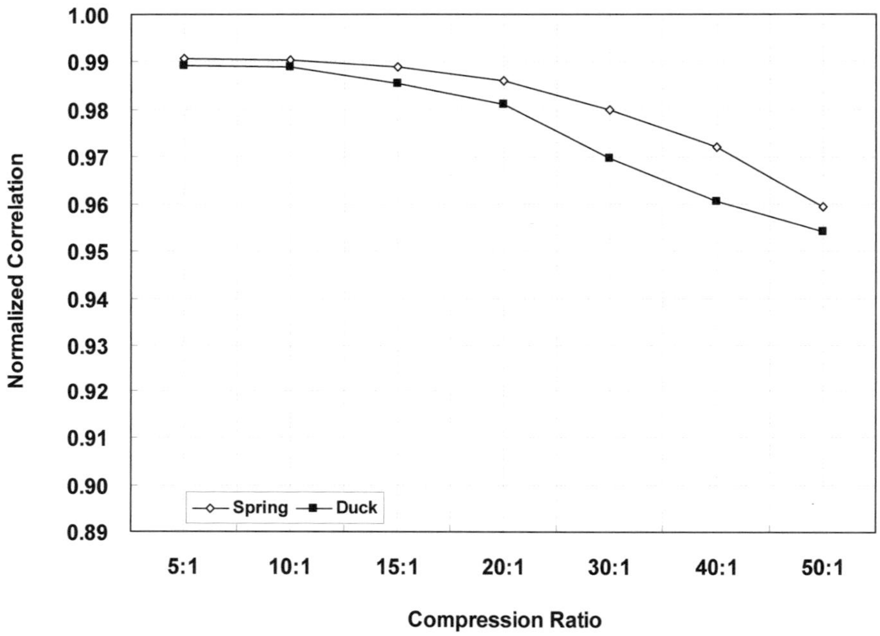

Figure 23. NC values of reconstructed results for the Spring and Duck images in Fig. 22.

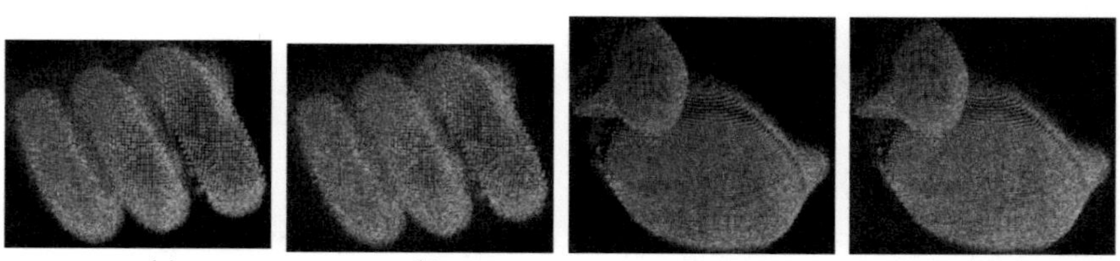

(a) (b) (c) (d)

Figure 24. Optically-captured results; (a) original spring image, (b) 50:1 compression, (c) original duck image, and (d) 50:1 compression.

http://dx.doi.org/10.5772/53904

4.4. 3D Scanning-based coding

In this section, we introduce a coding technique based on the properties explained in the previous section. Fig. 25 shows the whole flow to encode a digital hologram, which is for digital hologram videos. It consists of capturing, segmentation, transform, scanning the 3D segments, and lossy/lossless compression. A fringe pattern is divided into several blocks that are defined as segments. After transformed by 2D DCT, the segments are rearranged by 3-dimensional scanning into a video sequence, in which a segment corresponds to a frame. The coefficients of each segment are classified and normalized to fit to the standard 2D coding tools. Finally, the video sequence is compressed with tools for moving picture [6].

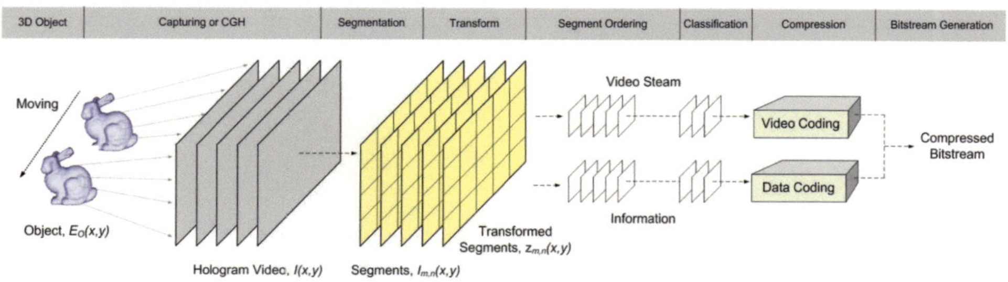

Figure 25. The 3D scanning-based coding procedure for digital hologram videos.

4.4.1. 3D Scanning method

A hologram video consists of several frames of digital holograms and a frame consists of several segments. After rearranged, each segment is treated as a frame to form a new video sequence. Three such sequencing methods with several fringe frames can be considered [6].

- Method 1: it scans all the segments frame by frame, by a predefined order in a frame, to form a sub-sequence (as shown in Fig. 26(a)). The scanning order in a frame is defined to maximize the inter-frame redundancy. This method focuses on the correlation between the segments in the same frame.
- Method 2: it scans segments in the same positions of frames in a GOH in turn (as shown in Fig. 26(b)). The scanning order for the positions is predefined. This method focuses on the correlation for the segments of the same positions in the fringe frames throughout the GOH.
- Method 3: it is a combined form of method 1 and method 2 (shown in Fig. 26(c)) Part of scanning sequence is taken frame by frame.

Method 1 is based on visual similarity between segments in a hologram frame. It is the extended version of coding technique for still object. The scanning order of segments consists of up-scanning and down-scanning in vertical direction to generate a video sub-sequence, which is similar method with the previous section. It connects the frames by the unit of the frame. Meanwhile, in Method 2, the inter-frame connection is drawn by the unit of segment in the same position. It is based on the similarity between segments in successive frames of GOH. The positions are ordered up and down as Method 1. Method3 is to combine Method 1 with Method. It is based on the similarity between a bundle of segments in the same columns of frames in a GOH.

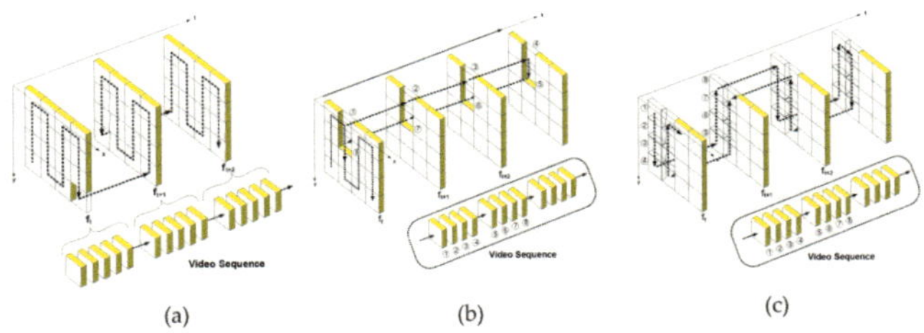

Figure 26. segment scanning methods; (a) Method 1, (b) Method 2, (c) Method 3.

4.4.2. Video coding standard-based compression

Fig. 27 shows a hybrid encoding architecture that depicts the detailed of the compression process in Fig 25. After classification and normalization, NCf, ECf, and SBP are inputted into the compression process. NCfs of AC coefficients are compressed by H.264/AVC, while ECfs are compressed by DPCM (differential pulse code modulation) and the results are applied to an entropy encoder such as Huffman encoder or arithmetic encoder. The SBP is very important to recover the image. So it is compressed by a conventional binary compression method. The results of the three compressed results are assembled to a bit stream to send or store [6].

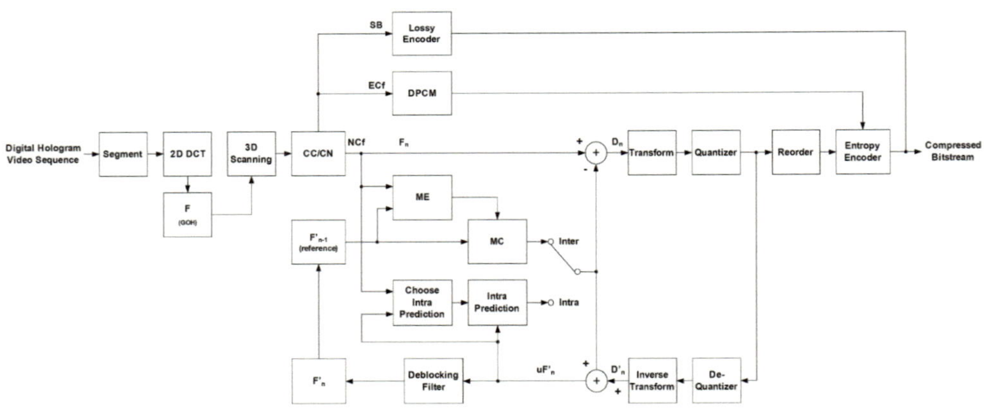

Figure 27. hybrid compression coding scheme for digital hologram.

4.4.3. Coding characteristics

In this section, we introduce the experimental results from applying various digital hologram videos to our scheme and discuss about the compression/reconstruction performance.

The fringe patterns with the size of 1,024×1,024 [pixel²] were used, and the size of segment was 64×64 and 128×128 [pixel²]. The bit rate of the generated video stream compressed by H. 264/AVC was adjusted to satisfy the requirement of the amount of data. The options of H. 264/AVC used for encoding and decoding are as follow.

- Profile: Baseline (High quality)
- Search range: 16
- Incorporate Hadamard transform
- Reference frames: 5
- Variable macro-block: from 16×16 to 4×4
- Entropy coding: CAVLC
- Bit rate: fixed (10:1~120:1)

4.4.3.1. Still object

First, we applied several still object to our technique. The experimental results are shown in Fig. 28 through Fig. 32, which are the lossy compression results without lossless compression. Since the reduced amount of data by lossless compression is negligible to lossy compression, it has little influence on the compression ratio. In Fig. 28, the average image qualities after reconstruction are graphically summarized for the various images as the function of compression ratio. Here, we used normalized correlation (NC) value as the measure for the image quality. Fig. 29 through Fig. 32 show visual image examples.

As can see from Fig. 28, segmentation results by the size of 64×64 [pixel²] showed the better quality than the size of 128×128 [pixel²]. The NC values of the reconstructed image were over 0.90 even at the compression ratio of 120:1.

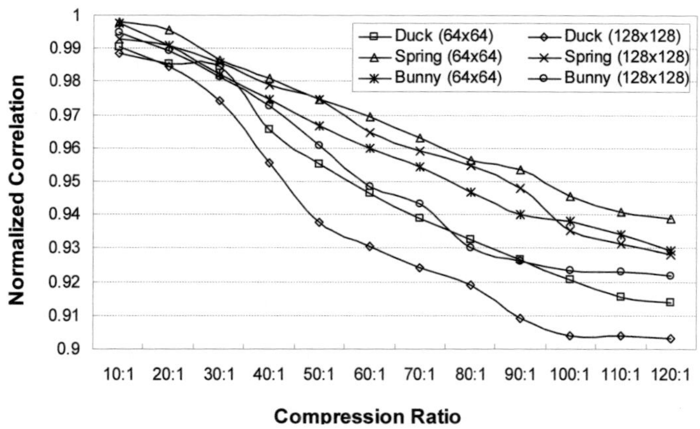

Figure 28. Estimated NC results of reconstructed object images

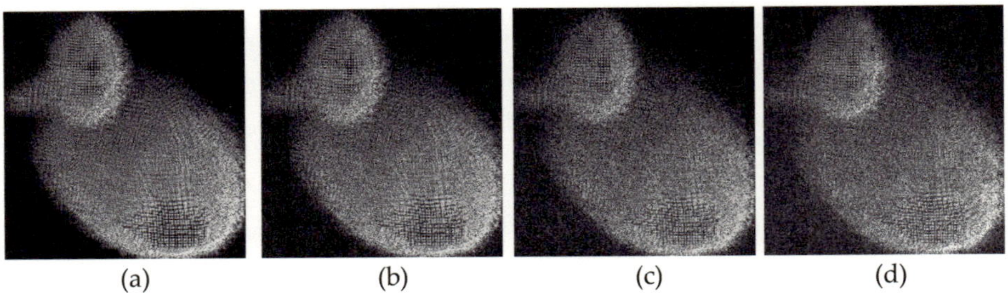

Figure 29. Example of the reconstructed duc object after compression with ratio of (a) 1:1, (b) 40:1, (c) 80:1, (d) 120:1.

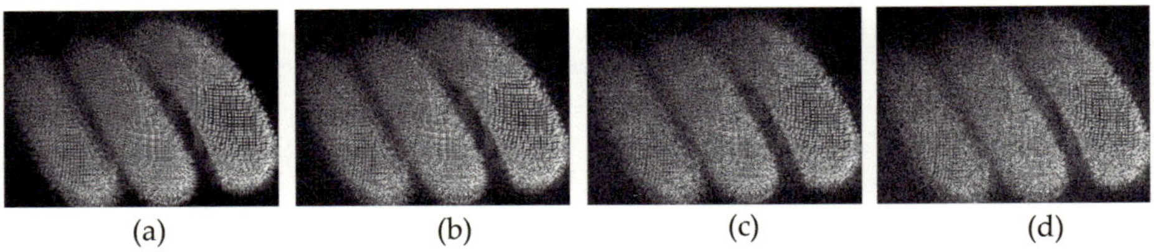

Figure 30. Example of the reconstructed spring object after compression with ratio of (a) 1:1, (b) 40:1, (c) 80:1, (d) 120:1.

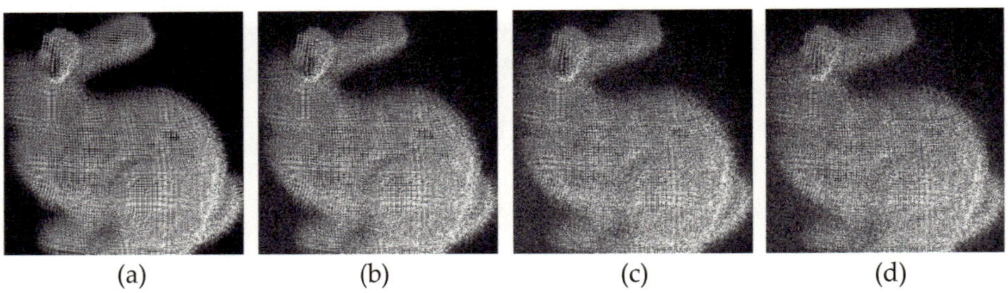

Figure 31. Example of the reconstructed rabbit object after compression with ratio of (a) 1:1, (b) 40:1, (c) 80:1, (d) 120:1 compression

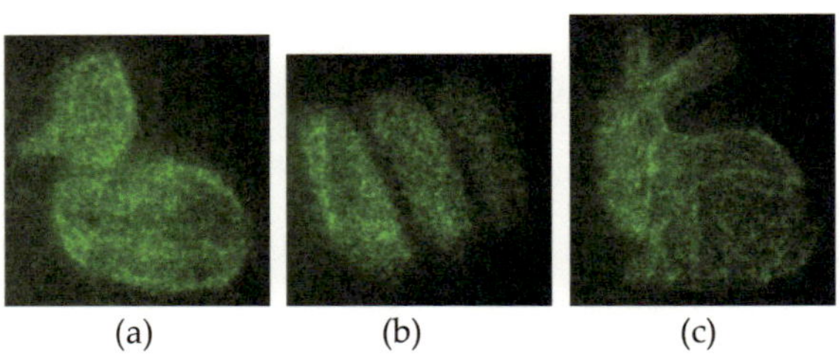

Figure 32. Optically-captured reconstructed objects after compression with 120:1 ratio (a) duck, (b) spring, (c) rabit

4.4.3.2. Moving object

We compressed two digital hologram videos, which consist of several frames, with the proposed 3D segment-scanning technique. The compression ratio is the same as the case of still hologram. Fig. 33 and Fig. 34 are the NC results, and Fig. 35 is a visual example. The object for Fig. 33 shifts in parallel to 2D axes, and the one for Fig. 34 rotates at the same position. The NC value for the shifting object is better than for the rotating object. For the scanning methods, Method 2 showed the best performance in average, but the differences were not much. Comparing them to the result of the still object, the compression efficiency of our scheme for a moving object is better than a still object.

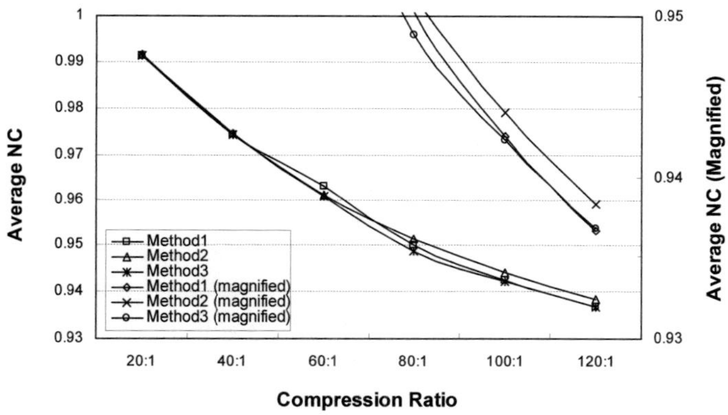

Figure 33. Estimated NC results of the reconstructed video stream for shifting movement

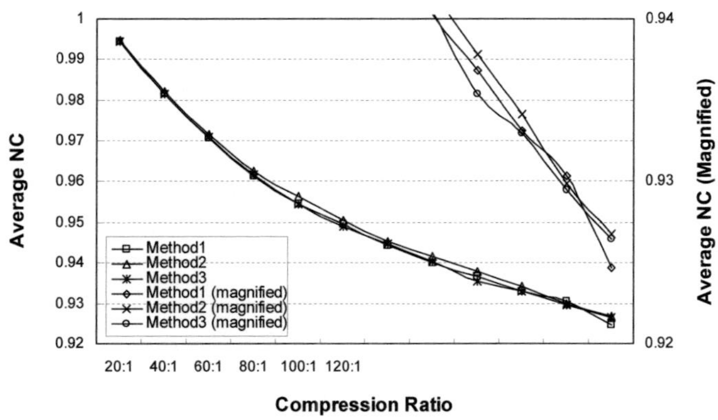

Figure 34. The NC result of the reconstructed video stream for rotating movement

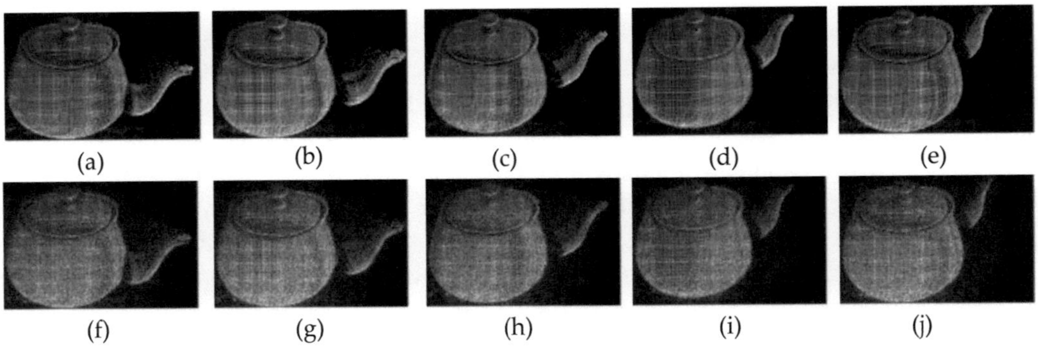

Figure 35. Reconstructed digital hologram video (teapot, 64×64 [pixel^2] segment with 120:1 compression), (a) through (e): original frames, (f) through (j): reconstructed frames

4.5. MVC-based coding

In this section, a different kind of coding method for digital holograms is introduced. Fig. 36 shows the coding procedure based on the Multi-View Coding (MVC) technique. It includes various signal processing techniques, prediction techniques, and coding techniques. It is based on the assumption that the local area (segment) in a digital hologram has the similar feature to a view in a 3D multi-view image. As the previous sections, a digital hologram is applied to pre-processing, segmentation, conversion, classification, and normalization in order to deriving correlation between the segments. The difference in the method in this section lies on the multi-view prediction to remove the redundancy among the segments. Thus, this section focuses on this process [21].

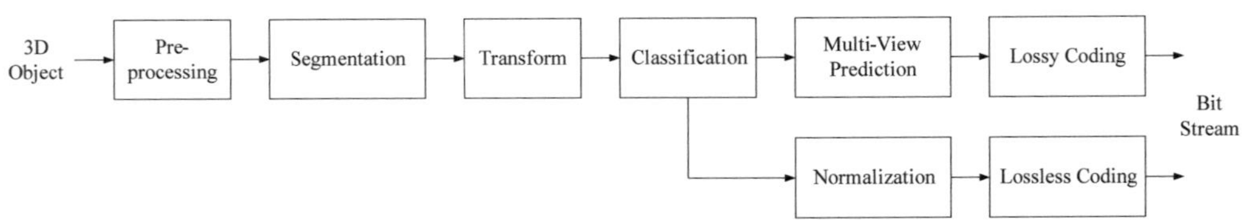

Figure 36. The MVC-based coding scheme.

4.5.1. Multi-view prediction

As explained above, we use a multi-view prediction algorithm to remove the spatial redundancy among the segments and thereby to obtain a high coding performance. Considering the characteristics of a digital hologram, the camera arrangement is limited to 1×N, as an example. The processing order of the multi-view prediction is shown in Fig. 37.

http://dx.doi.org/10.5772/53904

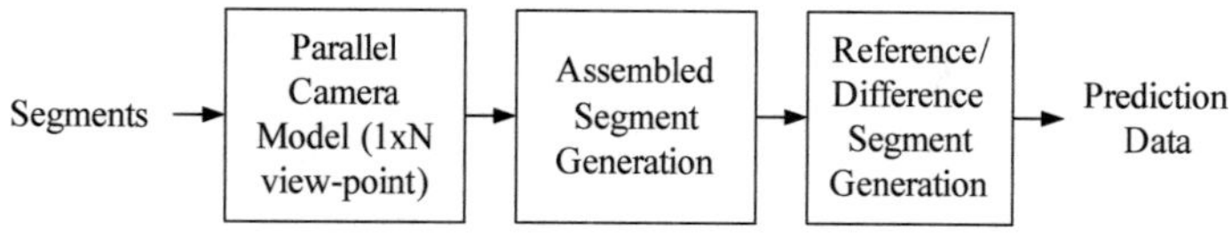

Figure 37. Multi-view prediction scheme

4.5.1.1. Assembled segment

As mentioned above, the transformed segments show visual characteristics similar to images obtained by parallel cameras. For each segment in a segment group (1×N segments), a global disparity is calculated for a base segment in the group with a general matching technique, and an assembled segment (AS) is generated with a method similar to the image mosaic technique. A matching function used in the assembling algorithm to find the global disparity (GD) is,

$$GD_{v+1} = \left\{ X_{r,v+1} \mid \min \sum_{i} \sum_{j} \left| I_v(i,j) - I_{v+1}^{T(r,X_{r,v+1})}(i,j) \right|, r \in R \right\} \tag{2}$$

where, R represents the area of the AS and r is the area for a segment to be assembled. $I_v(i,j)$ is the coefficient value of a pixel in (i, j) of segment v. The superscripted $T(r,X)$ indicates that the area r is moved by the disparity vector X. In this equation, v is the base segment and v+1 is a segment to be assembled to v. The AS generation algorithm described above is shown in Fig. 38. AS is generated for the segments of a column direction and the third segment is defined as the base segment, which generally has the smallest disparity.

Fig. 39 shows an example of AS generation. An AS may become larger than the original resolution of a segment depending on the camera model, and contains all the information about other segments as well as the base segment (the third image in a column in this example). If N=4 as the example, the size of AS is about 1.5 times of the original segment.

4.5.1.2. View-point prediction by AS

For general video coding, coding efficiency is improved through motion prediction between images to be coded, using temporally adjacent images as the reference images. In case of multi-view prediction, disparity prediction technique is used to remove redundancy between images in various view-points. Segment at each view-point is coded using the reference segment that is re-separated from AS using MPEG-2.

Fig. 40 shows the scheme to separate the reference segments from AS's with the corresponding GD and to generate difference (residual) segments (DS) using motion estimation and compensation (ME/MC) between the transformed original segments and the reference segments. When the AS is created through global disparity prediction, the values of global disparities are preserved together with the resultant AS. The difference segments are generated by compensating the transformed segments to the predicted segments with the reference segments.

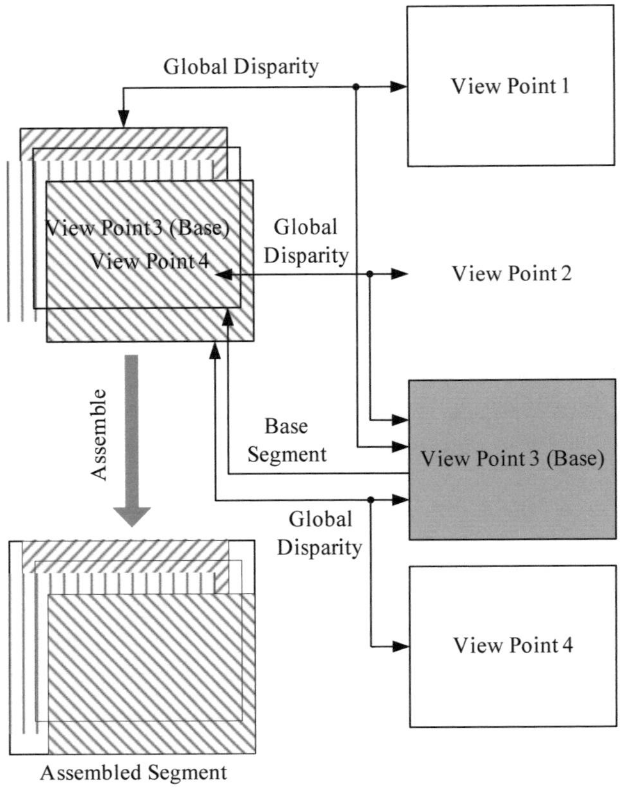

Figure 38. Procedure to generate an AS

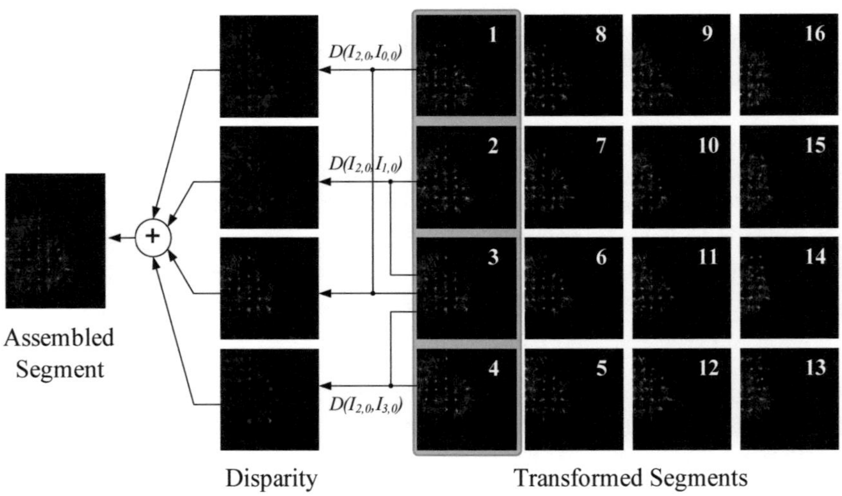

Figure 39. An example of AS generation when fringe pattern (1,024×1,024 pixels) is divided into 4×4 segments

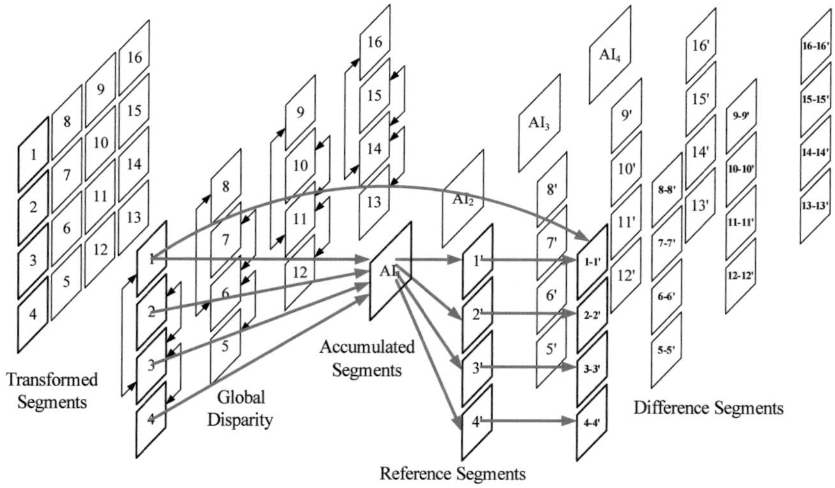

Figure 40. View-point prediction technique to generate AS and DS

4.5.1.3. Temporal prediction

By extending the view-point prediction scheme in the previous sub-section, a temporal prediction technique is applied to a digital holographic video consisting of multiple frames. For each DS generated through the MVP method, prediction in a view is performed in the temporal order. For temporal prediction in each view-point, motion prediction and compensation techniques are used. The scheme is shown in Fig. 41. The detailed are omitted to prevent duplicated explanation.

4.5.2. Video coding standard-based compression

After pre-processing, segmentation, classification and normalization, the segments is converted to DS through GDC (global disparity calculator), ASG (accumulated segment generator), and RSG (reference segment generator) according to the algorithm described above. AS's and DS's are inputted to the corresponding parts of a 2D video coding tool, which is MPEG-2 encoder as an example tool. The modified MPEG-2 encoder with predicting facility for multi-view is shown in Fig. 42. Other information such as, global disparities, motion vectors, and sign bit-planes are encoded by a lossless coding technique.

4.5.3. Coding characteristics

Fig. 43 shows an example of the part of the experiments: (a) is an original 3D object generated by CG, (b) is the hologram reconstructed from the fringe patterns created by the CGH technique, and (c) is an AS produced with the 4 segments in a column direction (when a fringe pattern with 1,024×1,024 in size are segmented into segments with 256×256 in size). Fig. 44 (a) through (d) show the four segments in a column after 2D DCT and Fig. 44(e) through (h) are the corresponding reference segments separated from AS.

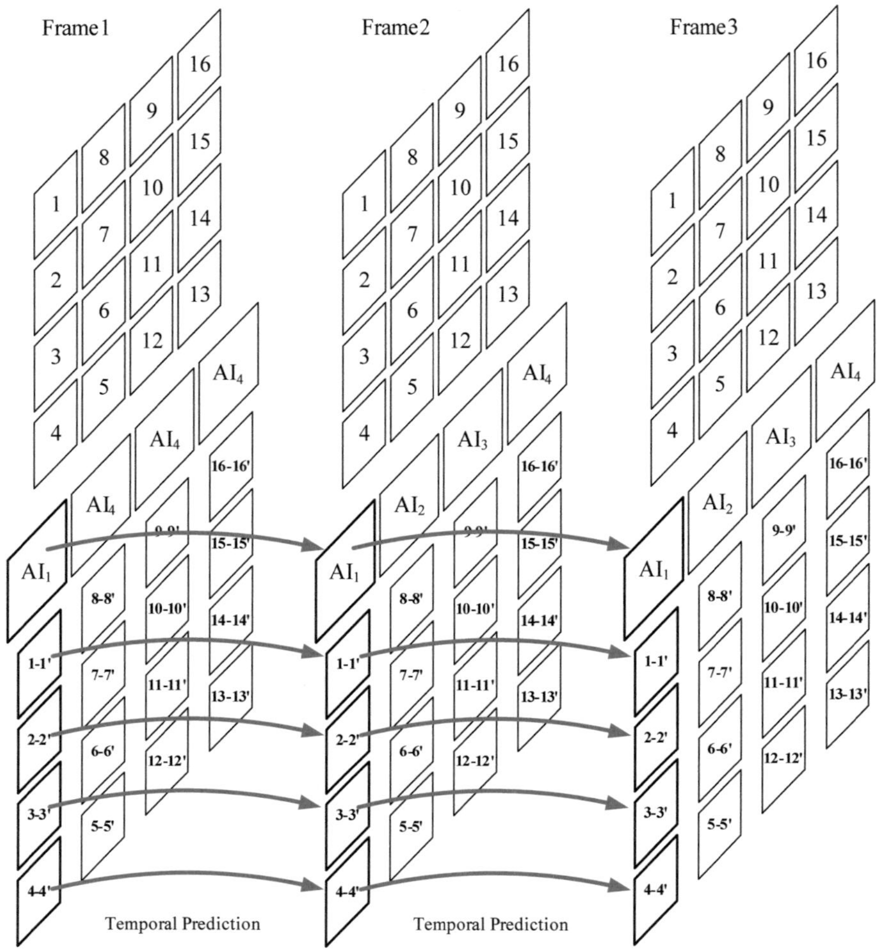

Figure 41. Temporal prediction technique of hologram video

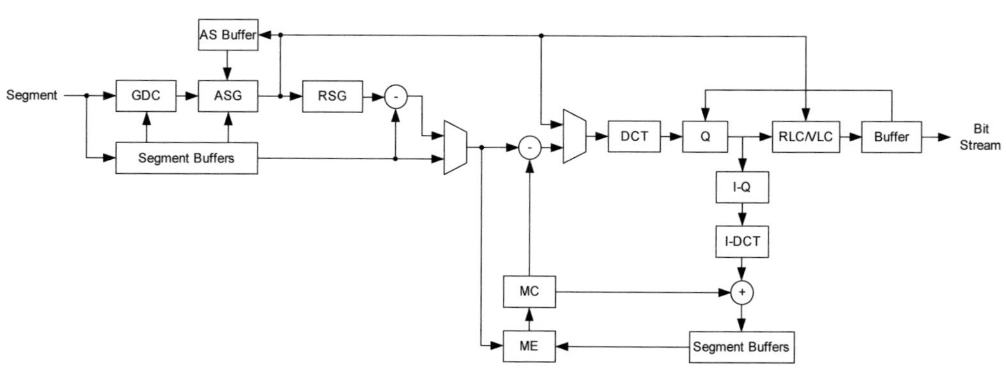

Figure 42. Modified MPEG-2 encoder

http://dx.doi.org/10.5772/53904

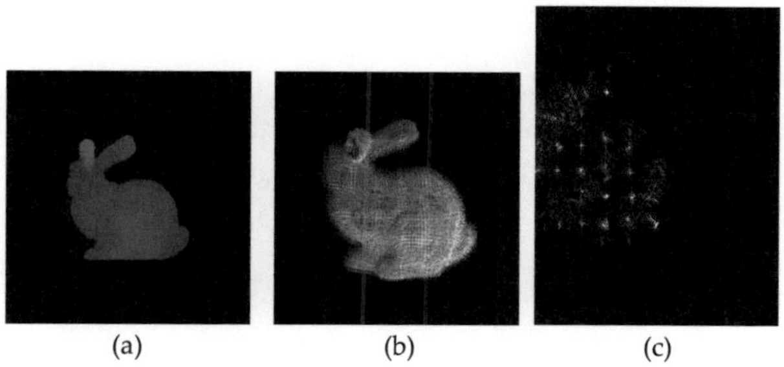

Figure 43. An example of (a) 3D object, (b) reconstructed hologram, (c) accumulated image

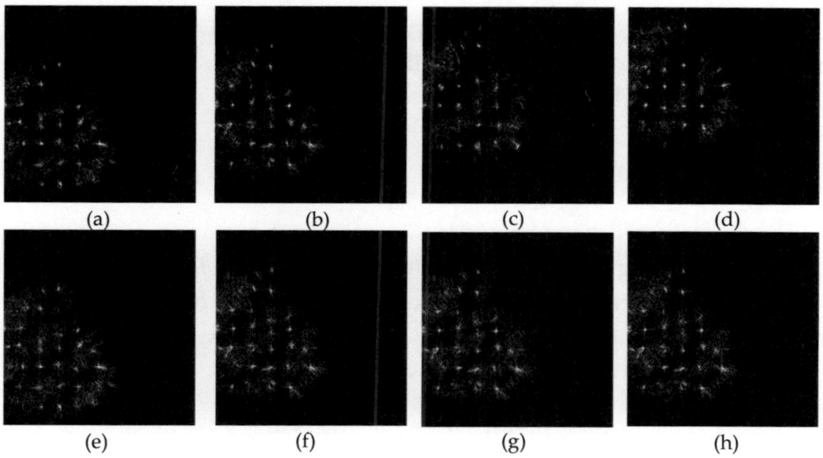

Figure 44. One column of fringe pattern segments after frequency transform (a~d) and the corresponding reference segments (e~h)

Fig. 45. shows the results after applying the multi-view prediction technique based on the AS's. With the proposed method with MPEG-2, the NC value was 0.0349 (approximately 3.6%) higher at a compression rate of 25:1 than the method of section 4.3.

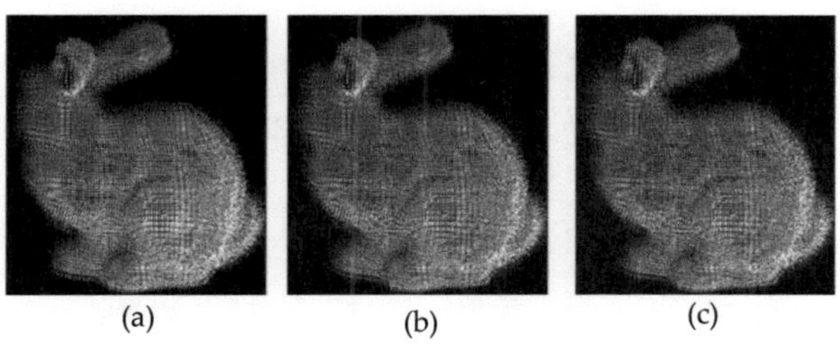

Figure 45. Reconstruction results by the proposed technique: (a) original, (b) 15:1 (NC:0.981842), (c) 25:1(NC: 0.975114)

4.6. Still image coding standard-based compression

Among the still image coding algorithm, the representative methods are JPEG and JPEG2000 standard. Since digital hologram is different from a natural 2D image, although they are used in compressing digital hologram, it is not a good method. In this section, we compress digital hologram using JPEG and JPEG2000 standard, and compare the results with the previous techniques.

4.6.1. JPEG

JPEG (Joint Photographic Experts Group) is the most commonly used still image compression method for photographic images. JPEG has 20:1 compression ratio for a natural image, but we rarely expect its property to be kept because of different visual characteristic of a digital hologram. The property is identified by the coding results, which showed that the maximum compression ratio is 6:1 with NC value of 0.927586. It shows that JPEG is not the powerful tool for digital hologram coding.

4.6.2. JPEG2000

JPEG2000 [22], the new still-image compression standard, was also examined for test, and the results are shown in Figs. 46 and 47. Fig. 46 shows an example of the compression/reconstruction results, which were processed for the color format of RGB. The compression ratio more than 10:1 degrades the image quality quite a lot. Fig. 47 shows the average NC values for each color component as the compression ratio increases.

One can identify that the coding performance has the nearly linear relationship with the algorithm cost. In the case of the compression rate of 20:1, the result of H.264/AVC has more than 0.975 in NC. But the result by JPEG2000 has between 0.73 and 0.83. Also, the object reconstructed by inverse CGH in Fig. 46 has more degradation than the previous results. If we identify the visual difference between Fig. 46 (c) and Fig. 31(d) that are the results from the compression rate of 50:1 and 80:1, Fig. 31(c) shows the clear shape of the object, but Fig. 46(c) is indistinguishable. By comparing the proposed scheme, it shows much better quality than JPEG2000. For reference, a lossless compression that can be reconstructed perfectly shows a compression ratio of about 1.3:1 in average.

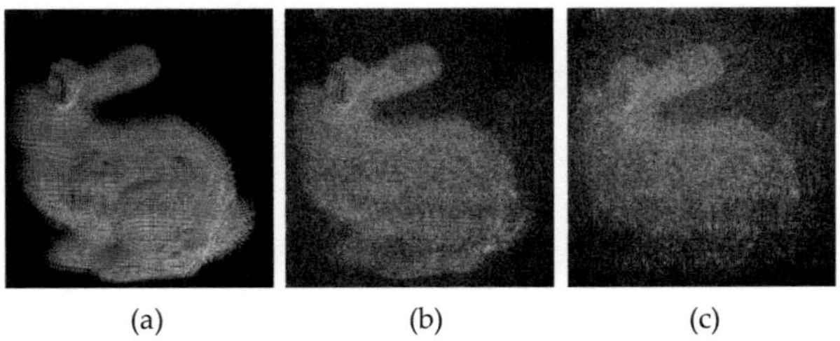

Figure 46. Reconstruction result of object image by JPEG2000 compression (a) Original object image (b) 30:1 (c) 50:1

http://dx.doi.org/10.5772/53904

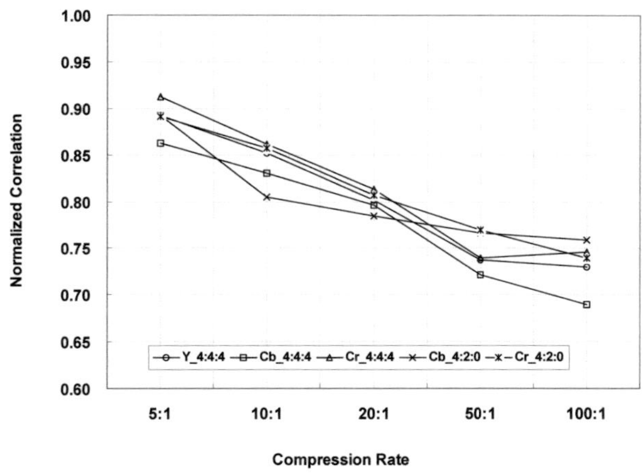

Figure 47. Reconstruction result using JPEG2000

Acknowledgements

This research was supported by Basic Science Research Program through the National Research Foundation of Korea (NRF) funded by the Ministry of Education, Science and Technology (MEST). (2010-0026245).

Author details

Young-Ho Seo[1], Hyun-Jun Choi[2] and Dong-Wook Kim[3*]

*Address all correspondence to: dwkim@kw.ac.kr

1 College of Liberal Arts, Kwangwoon University, Seoul, Republic of Korea

2 Division of Maritime Electronic & Communication Engineering Mokpo National Maritime University, Mokpo, Republic of Korea

3 Department of Electronic Materials Engineering, Kwangwoon University, Seoul, Republic of Korea

References

[1] B. Javidi and F. Okano eds, "Three Dimensional Television, Video, and Display Technologies," Springer Verlag Berlin, 2002.

[2] P. Hariharan, Basics of Holography, Cambridge University Press, 2002.

[3] H. Yoshikawa, "Digital holographic signal processing," Proc. TAO First International Symposium on Three Dimensional Image Communication Technologies, pp. S-4-2, 1993.

[4] Joint Video Team of ITU-T and ISO/IEC JTC 1. "Draft ITU-T Recommendation and Final Draft International Standard of Joint Video Specification(ITU-T Rec. H.264 ISO/IEC 14496-10 AVC)", Joint Video Team(JVT) of ISO/IEC MPEG and ITU-T VCEG, JVT-G050, 2003.

[5] Young-Ho Seo, Hyun-Jun Choi, and Dong-Wook Kim, "Lossy Coding Technique for Digital Holographic Signal", SPIE Optical Engineering, Vol. 45, No. 6, pp. 065802-1~065802-10, Jun. 2006.

[6] Young-Ho Seo, Hyun-Jun Choi, and Dong-Wook Kim, "3D Scanning-based Compression Technique for Digital Hologram Video", Elsevier Signal Processing - Image Communication, Vol.22, Issue 2, pp. 144-156. Feb. 2007.

[7] K. R. Rao and P. Yip, "Discrete cosine transform - algorithms, advantage, applications," New York, Academic Press, 1990.

[8] R. M. Rao ad A. S. Bopardikar, Wavelet Transforms, Introduction to Theory and Applications, Addison-Wesley Inc., Reading, MA, 1998.

[9] T. J. Naughton, Y. Frauel, B. Javidi and E. Tajahuerce, "Compression of digital holograms for three-dimensional object recognition," SPIE Proc. Vol 4471, pp. 280-289, 2001.

[10] http://en.wikipedia.org/wiki/Run-length_encoding

[11] ISO/IEC 10918-1:1994, "Information technology -- Digital compression and coding of continuous-tone still images: Requirements and guidelines," 1994.

[12] http://en.wikipedia.org/wiki/Shannon%E2%80%93Fano_coding

[13] http://en.wikipedia.org/wiki/Huffman_coding

[14] http://en.wikipedia.org/wiki/Golomb_coding

[15] http://en.wikipedia.org/wiki/Lempel%E2%80%93Ziv%E2%80%93Markov_chain_algorithm

[16] H. Yoshikawa and J. tamai, "Holographic image compression by motion picture coding," editor, SPIE Proc. vol 2652 Practical Holography, pp. 2652-01, 1996.

[17] Y.-H. Seo, H.-J. Choi, J.-S. Yoo, G.-S. Lee, C.-H. Kim, S.-H. Lee, S.-H. Lee and D.-W. Kim, "Digital hologram compression technique by eliminating spatial correlations based on MCTF", Optics Communication, 283, pp. 4261~4270, Jul. 2010

[18] ISO/IEC 13818-1:2000 "Information technology -- Generic coding of moving pictures and associated audio information: Systems", 2000.

[19] ISO/IEC 14496-1 MPEG-4 "Coding of Audio -Visual Objects - Part 2 : Visual", Aug. 2002.

[20] http://en.wikipedia.org/wiki/Zip_(file_format)#cite_note-1

[21] Young-Ho Seo, Hyun-Jun Choi, Jin-Woo Bae, Hoon-Chong Kang, Seung-Hyun Lee, Ji-Sang Yoo and Dong-Wook Kim, "A New Coding Technique for Digital Holographic Video using Multi-View Prediction", IEICE Transactions on Information and Systems, Vol.E90-D, No.1, pp.118-125, Jan. 2007.

[22] JPEG2000 Final Part I: Final Draft International Standard. ISO/IEC FDIS 15444-1, ISO/IEC JTC1/SC29/WG1 N1855 (2000).

Chapter 13

Applications of Holographic Microscopy in Life Sciences

Iliyan Peruhov and Emilia Mihaylova

Additional information is available at the end of the chapter

http://dx.doi.org/10.5772/56176

1. Introduction

Imaging of microscopic objects is an essential art, especially in life sciences. Rapid progress in electronic detection and control, digital imaging, image processing, and numerical computation has been crucial in advancing modern microscopy. At present the 3D imaging of biological samples is done by confocal microscopes. Their ability to image biological events in real time is limited by the time necessary to capture stacks of images taken through a certain plane in cells or tissues from which a 3D view is calculated. Digital holographic microscopy is a new imaging technology applied to optical microscopy. The digital holographic microscopy is a very advanced imaging technique because it yields a 3D volume image from a single image capture.

Holography is a technique by which a wavefront can be recorded and subsequently reconstructed in the absence of the original wavefront i.e. a 3D image is observed just as if the object was still present and being illuminated in the same way as when the holographic recording was made [1]. In conventional holography, invented by Gabor [2], the holograms are photographically recorded and optically reconstructed. Both the amplitude and phase information of the light wave are recorded in a hologram. Because the holographic image retains the phase as well as the amplitude information, a variety of interference experiments can be performed, and this is the basis of many interferometric applications in metrology.

Digital holography does not require wet chemical processing of a photographic plate, although at some expense of resolution. However, once the amplitude and phase of the light wave are recorded numerically, one can easily subject these data to a variety of manipulations, and so digital holography offers capabilities not available in conventional holography. The remarkable aspect of the digital reconstruction – its possibility to refocus at different depths inside a transparent object, depending on the reconstruction distance, makes this technique very suitable for biological cells studies and could have many applications in life sciences.

In digital holography the reconstruction process is implemented by multiplication of the CCD captured and PC stored digital hologram by the numerical description of the reference wave, and convolution of the result with the impulse response function of the optical system. The diffracted field in the image plane is given by the Rayleigh-Sommerfield diffraction formula [3]

$$\psi(x',y') = \frac{1}{i\lambda}\iint h(\xi,\eta) r(\xi,\mu) f(x',y',\xi,\eta)\cos\Theta dxdy \tag{1}$$

with $f(x',\ y',\ \xi,\ \eta) = \dfrac{\exp(ik\rho)}{\rho}$ and $\rho = \sqrt{d'^2 + (\xi - x')^2 + (\eta - y')^2}$

where d' is the reconstruction distance, i.e. the distance measured from the hologram plane ξ-η to the image plane; $h(\xi,\eta)$ is the recorded hologram; $r(\xi\text{-}\eta)$ represents the reference wave field; k denotes the wave number and λ is the wavelength of the laser source. Due to the small angles between the hologram normal and the rays from the hologram to the image points, the obliquity factor cosΘ can normally be set = 1.

Equation (1) is the basis for numerical hologram reconstruction. Because the reconstructed wavefield $\Psi\ (x',\ y')$ is a complex function, both the intensity as well as the phase can be calculated [1].

Digital holographic microscopy (DHM) can provide quantitative marker-free imaging that is suitable for high resolving investigations of transparent and reflective surfaces as well as for fast analysis of living cells under usual laboratory conditions. One of many interesting applications of DHM is to study cells without staining or labeling them and without affecting them in any way.

This chapter is divided in two parts. The first part reviews the recent advances in the application of digital holographic microscopy to biological specimen. The second part of the chapter describes the development of a digital holographic microscope at the Agricultural University of Plovdiv and reports some of its life science applications.

2. Recent advances in the application of digital holographic microscopy to biological specimen

Kim M. K. [4] has proposed a novel digital holographic method that allows axial resolution of objects by superposition of a number of numerically reconstructed optical diffraction fields of digital holograms that are optically recorded with a number of wavelengths. The principle of wavelength-scanning digital interference holography is applied to imaging of 3D objects with diffuse surfaces, such as a biological specimen. The head of a small insect of a few millimeters in size is imaged with 120 μm axial resolution and ~20 μm lateral resolution. An animated 3D numerical model of the object surface structure is generated from the tomographic data with good fidelity. The experiments are performed using a standard holographic apparatus. Approximately 50 mW of ring dye laser output is expanded to about 10 mm diameter and spatially filtered. The object beam is apertured to about 5 mm diameter and illuminates the sample object. The scattered light from the object is combined with the reference beam. The magnifying lens images the optical field at infinity. The digital camera is focused at infinity, so that it records a magnified image of the optical intensity. It is important to aperture the object beam so that it only illuminates the area of the object that is to be imaged, otherwise spurious scattering can seriously affect the quality of the picture.

A digital holographic microscope (DHM) in a transmission mode has been developed in Rappaz, B. et al. [5], adapted to the quantitative study of cellular dynamics. Living cells in culture are optically explored by calculating the phase shift they produce on the transmitted wave front. The high temporal stability of the phase signal and the low acquisition time makes it possible to monitor cellular dynamics processes. An experimental procedure allowing calculating both the integral refractive index and the cellular thickness (morphometry) from the measured phase shift is presented. Specifically, the method has been applied to study the dynamics of neurons in culture during a hypotonic stress. Such stress produces a decrease of the phase which can be entirely resolved by applying the methodological approach described in the article; in fact the method allows determining independently the thickness and the integral refractive index of cells. The phase signal depends on both the thickness and the refractive index of the specimen. To decouple these two contributions, a procedure named "decoupling procedure" is applied. The dynamic quantitative phase images, containing information about both the cell morphometry and the integral refractive index, can be unambiguously interpreted thanks to the decoupling procedure presented. Quantitatively, the local cellular thickness measurement can be performed with accuracy of 1 μm. Spatial averaging allows measuring mean thickness of cellular regions corresponding to the area of typical neuronal bodies, i.e. 170 μm^2, with an accuracy of a few tens of nanometers. On the other hand, the spatial variations of the integral refractive index have been estimated at 0.005 and the mean integral refractive index can be measured with an accuracy of 0.0003. The cellular refractive index is a poorly documented parameter which is related to the intracellular content and which is relevant for the interpretation of the functional light imaging signal resulting from a multiple scattering process in biological tissues.

Marquet, P. et al. [6] present for the first time DHM images of living cells in culture. They represent the distribution of the optical path length over the cell, which has been measured with subwavelength accuracy. These DHM images are compared with those obtained by use of the widely exploited phase contrast and Nomarski differential interference contrast techniques. The developed digital holographic microscope presents a simplified and easy-to-operate technique compared with classical interferometry. The authors show that digital recording and numerical reconstruction of holograms, offers new perspectives in imaging, because numerical processing of a complex wave front allows one to compute simultaneously the intensity and the phase distribution of the propagated wave. Digital holography has made it possible to focus numerically on different object planes without using any opto-mechanical movement. Moreover, different lens aberrations can be corrected by a numerical procedure. In the article for the first time absolute phase distribution images of living neurons in a culture are obtained by use of DHM with accuracy in the 2–4º range. To compare the DHM with the standard and widely used techniques of phase contrast (PhC) and differential interference contrast (DIC) microscopy in biology, images of living neurons obtained with PhC, DIC, and DHM are presented.

In an article of Garcia-Sucerquia J. et al. [7] some significant characteristics of (digital in-line holographic microscopy) DIHM and the underwater DIHM have been emphasized:

1. Simplicity of the microscope: DIHM is microscopy without objective lenses. The hardware necessary for the desktop version is a laser, a pinhole, and a CCD camera. For the underwater DIHM version, they use the same elements contained in a submersible hermetic shell.

2. Maximum information: a single hologram contains all the information about the 3D structure of the object. A set of multiple holograms can be properly added to provide information about 4D trajectories of samples.

3. Maximum resolution: optimal resolution, of the order of the wavelength of the laser, can be obtained easily with both versions.

4. Simplicity of sample preparation: this is mainly true for biological samples, because no sectioning or staining is required, so that living cells and specimens can be observed in depth. Indeed, for the underwater DIHM, there is no sample preparation at all, and real-time information of living organisms can be retrieved.

It is shown [7] that high-resolution tracking of many particles in 4D can be obtained from just one difference hologram. Since resolution of the order of a wavelength of the light has been achieved with DIHM, tracking of organisms as small as bacteria is possible, as would be the motion of plankton in water or, at lower resolution, the trajectories of flying insects. DIHM can also be used on macroscopic biological specimens, prepared by standard histological procedures, as for a histological section of the head of the fruit fly, *Drosophila melanogaster*. Such images reveal the structure of the pigmented compound eye and different neuropile regions of the brain within the head cuticle, including the optic neuropiles underlying the compound eye. DIHM, with its inherent capability of obtaining magnified images of objects, unlike conventional off-axis holography, is therefore a powerful new tool for a large variety of research fields.

The optical arrangement described by Parshall D. et al. [8] provides a straightforward means for high-resolution holographic microscopic imaging. There is no need for elaborate processing such as magnification by using a reconstruction wavelength that is compared with the recording wavelength, which inevitably introduces aberration, or using an aperture array in front of the camera and scanning it to artificially increase the CCD resolution. Also the phase image appears less noisy than the amplitude image. The amplitude image reflects the intensity variations in the reference wave, whereas the phase noise comes mostly from the quality of the optical surfaces in the imaging system. The former is much more difficult to control. The phase images have less noise than the amplitude image, and one can readily discern the index variation over the nucleus as it is done for an onion cell.

In this article [8] a number of experimental results has been presented that reveal the effectiveness of digital holography in high-resolution biological microscopy. In particular, phase-imaging digital holography offers a highly sensitive and versatile means to measure and monitor optical path variations. The authors have offered biological microscopy by two-wavelength phase-imaging digital holography and proposed its extension to three-wavelength phase imaging for longer axial ranges with undiminished resolution.

Jeong, K. et al. [9] show that coherence-gated digital holography detects motility as deep as 10 optical thickness lengths inside tissue. This opens prospects to use motility as a contrast agent when imaging at depths inaccessible to conventional motility assay approaches. Coherence-gated digital holography is an interferometric imaging approach that measures motility with displacement sensitivity below a fraction of a wavelength, over a macroscopic lateral field of view up to 1 mm. Motility at depth appears in real-time holograms as dynamic speckle. Furthermore, the authors define a motility metric based on the coefficient of intensity variance per pixel that becomes a novel imaging contrast agent. The authors demonstrate that the motility metric enables direct visualization of the effect of cytoskeletal anti-cancer drugs on tissue inside its natural three-dimensional environment, allowing measurements of tissue and cellular response to drugs. The reconstructed *en face* image of the rat tumor spheroid is striking. The rat osteogenic sarcoma tumor spheroids are grown *in vitro* in a rotating bioreactor. The spheroids may be grown up to several mm in diameter, and thus are large enough to simulate the thickness of different mammalian tissue. As tumor spheroids are cultured, they undergo cell apoptosis and necrosis in their center and so consist of an inner necrotic core with low activity and an outer shell with a thickness of 100 to 200 μm of viable proliferating cells with high motility. The speckle images of the tumor spheroids shimmer due to motility in tissue, and statistical properties of the dynamic speckle are obtained by capturing successive images at a fixed depth.

A method of quantitative phase microscopy with asynchronous digital holography has been suggested by Chalut K. J. et al. [10]. An essential requirement that must be met to apply a phase microscopy system to imaging the dynamics of live cells is that the system can acquire quantitative phase images of the sample at a high rate (>100 Hz). Although modern CCDs are capable of >100 Hz image acquisition rates, multiple interferograms are often necessary to extract the phase information, which reduces the acquisition rate considerably. Additionally, if multiple inteferograms are used, they must be recorded fast enough so that instabilities in the system and the dynamics of the cells themselves do not vary appreciably during acquisition. The authors [10] demonstrated that the system is capable of obtaining quantitative phase measurements on millisecond time scales. The inclusion of acousto-optic modulators in each arm of the interferometer permits to use phase-shifting interferometry. The system is innovative in the field of digital holography, because the phase shift is easily evaluated, which greatly simplifies the experimental setup. In addition, the algorithm requires only two phase-shifted interferograms, compared to the usual 4 interferograms required in most phase shifting algorithms. A potential increase in speed can be realized by utilizing frame transfer CCD devices, which can record two images on a microsecond time scale. By transferring frames without reading them out, the latency between two interferograms is greatly reduced and the quantitative phase imaging frame rate is then nearly the frame rate of the camera, of the order of 100 Hz. It is demonstrated, with a red blood cell sample, and a smooth muscle cell sample, that this system is capable of obtaining quantitative phase images of live cells.

Kemper, B. & von Bally, G. [11] carried out an analysis of living pancreas tumor cells (Patu8988T) to reveal the prospective of digital holographic microscopy for the visualization of drug induced morphology changes. The authors exposed the tumor cells to an anticancer drug (Taxol). Digital holograms of selected cells were recorded continuously every 120 s over 16 h in a temperature stabilized environment with an inverse digital holographic microscopy setup. DHM has clearly shown that Taxol first induces morphological changes as cell rounding that effects an increase in cell thickness. Afterward, for all the specimens, the final cell collapse is detected precisely by a significant decrease of the phase contrast. The authors also demonstrate that the subsequent numerical focus adjustment reduces unwrapping artifacts that are caused by diffraction patterns in the defocused phase contrast images. For investigation of suspension cells this feature is of particular advantage because cells in different focal planes can be investigated by the evaluation of a single captured hologram. The results show that digital holographic phase contrast microscopy can be applied for quantitative long-term observation of living cells. The studies show new ways for marker-free dynamic monitoring of cell morphology changes to access new parameters, e.g., for quantitative observation of the time-dependent reactions of cells to drugs. In addition, for investigation of cells, the scattering properties of the cell culture medium and the optical quality of the cell handling equipment (e.g., glass carrier, coverslip, or Petri dishes) must be considered. In summary, the presented results demonstrate that digital holographic microscopy can be applied for noncontact, marker-free, and quantitative phase contrast imaging. The method allows a high resolution multifocus reconstruction of amplitude and phase data from a single recorded digital hologram. It enables hologram capture time in the millisecond range. The hologram acquisition rate is limited by the digital recording device.

A phase-imaging technique to quantitatively study the three-dimensional structure of cells is presented by Khmaladze A. et al. [12]. The method, based on the simultaneous dual-wavelength digital holography, allows for higher axial range at which the phase imaging can be performed. The technique is capable of nanometer axial resolution. The method compares favorably to software unwrapping, as the technique does not produce non-existent phase steps. Curvature mismatches between the reference and an object beam is numerically compensated. The 3D images of SKOV-3 ovarian cancer cells are presented. The measurements of the optical thickness of cells can then be performed. One also needs to make an assumption of the cells refractive index, which is taken to be 1.375. While it may not be possible to precisely determine the refractive index of the cell at each individual point, this number is always close to the refractive index of water and unlikely to deviate by more than a few percent. As a result, the accuracy and the level of details of the dual-wavelength images of cells, presented here, are superior to what has been previously demonstrated. In comparison to the software unwrapping, dual-wavelength optical unwrapping method is advantageous, as it requires no intensive computation procedures and can handle complex phase topologies. The proposed method of curvature correction is simple and effective to easily implement the experiment without the microscope objectives in the reference arms of the Michelson interferometer. This greatly simplifies the optical setup and makes it much easier to achieve the initial adjustments of the apparatus. Simultaneous dual wavelength setup utilized together with the angular spectrum algorithm provides an easy way to acquire single frame images in real time, which can be used to study cell migration.

Langehanenberg P. et al. [13] propose autofocusing in digital holographic phase contrast microscopy on pure phase objects for live cell imaging. Common passive optical autofocus techniques are based on axial scanning of the image space by mechanical adjustment of a lens element or a stage to find the maximum image definition. In digital holography, this scanning process is performed numerically by variation of the propagation distance in the convolution-based propagation. The main task in passive autofocusing is the determination and maximization of the image sharpness. Pure phase objects with negligible absorption such as technical reflective specimens or biological cells are sharply focused at the setting with the least contours in the amplitude distributions. In contrast to the bright-field case, in digital holography this setting is of particular interest, as the amplitude and phase distributions are accessible simultaneously, and the focal setting with the least-contrasted amplitude image corresponds to the best-resolved structures in the quantitative phase contrast distribution. Four numerical methods are compared in order to identify best autofocus method for application in digital holographic microscopy.

Remmersmann C. et al. [14] present research for the optimization of a temporal phase-shifting (TPS) - based digital holographic microscopy setup. In order to enable a phase-shift-dependent investigation a variable three-step algorithm is applied. First, the phase error of the reconstructed object wave is evaluated theoretically. In a second step the results obtained from the calculations are compared to the measured phase noise. Finally, the applicability for noise reduction is demonstrated by quantitative phase contrast imaging of a pancreas tumor cell sample. Theoretical and experimental investigations on phase errors in temporal phase-shifting-based digital holographic reconstruction have been performed in order to minimize the noise within the reconstructed object wave. Coherent as well as partially coherent light sources were applied and compared. The application example of LED and laser-based digital holographic microscopy on fixed pancreas tumor cells demonstrates that disturbances in the reconstructed amplitude and phase distributions due to multiple reflections within the experimental setup can be effectively reduced by partially coherent light sources.

Choi Y. S. and Lee S. J. [15] apply digital holographic microscopy (DHM) for three-dimensional volumetric measurement of red blood cells in motion. Currently, various particle image velocimetry (PIV) measurement techniques have been applied to numerous hemorheological studies. Standard PIV methods provide two-dimensional (2D) planar information confined in a thin depth of field. Holography is capable of recording 3D volumetric field information in a single hologram. The recent development of digital holography enables the volumetric measurement of particle fields without the use of any chemical or physical processes. In this technique, a digital hologram of the particles distributed in a flow is directly recorded digitally. The 3D flow information can be subsequently obtained through the numerical reconstruction and the particle tracking procedure. The authors applied DHM to measure the 3D motion of human red blood cells (RBCs) in a microtube flow. DHM requires only a pair of particle hologram images to get complete 3D flow information and this is of great advantage in motion analysis of individual blood cells. The viability and uncertainty of the established DHM system in the detection of 3D RBC position were evaluated by a planar test target. The position in depth of a RBC was located by applying focus functions that quantify the sharpness of its reconstructed image. Five focus functions were evaluated to find the suitable function that provides minimum uncertainty. Finally, the sample trajectories as well as the 3D velocity profiles of RBCs inside the microtube flow are presented and the measurement uncertainties are discussed.

Warnasooriya N. et al. [16] captured pictures of gold nanoparticles in living cell environments using heterodyne digital holographic microscopy. With recent developments in the fields of nanotechnology and modern optical microscopy, the use of nanometric particles as biomarkers in biological specimens has been rapidly increased. The paper describes an imaging microscopic technique based on heterodyne digital holography where subwavelength-sized gold colloids can be imaged in cell environments. Surface cellular receptors of 3T3 mouse fibroblasts were labeled with 40 nm gold nanoparticles, and the biological specimen is imaged in a total internal reflection configuration with holographic microscopy. Due to a higher scattering efficiency of the gold nanoparticles versus that of cellular structures, accurate localization of a gold marker is obtained within a 3D mapping of the entire sample's scattered field, with a lateral precision of 5 nm and 100 nm in the x,y and in the z directions respectively, demonstrating the ability of holographic microscopy to locate nanoparticles in living cell environments. However, in order to apply these techniques to biological specimens, important issues must be considered. In biological samples, the particle holographic signal is superimposed with the light scattered by cell refractive index fluctuations, which yields a speckle field. This paper studies the possibility of 3D holographic imaging in a biological context. Since the cell-scattered speckle field cannot be avoided, it is important for future cell labeling applications, to scale the particle signal with respect to the scattered speckle. The authors show that the amplitude of the 40 nm gold particle signal is much larger than the cell-scattered field. NIH 3T3 mouse fibroblasts are used (quoted as 3T3 cells) with integrin surface receptors labeled with 40 nm gold particles. Streptavidin-coated gold nanoparticles were attached to the cell surface integrin receptors via biotin and fibronectin proteins. Fibronectin proteins were labeled with biotin. The illumination source is a single-mode near infrared laser diode. A polarizing beam splitter cube (PBS) is used to split the original illumination laser light into two beams, a reference beam and an object illumination beam forming the two arms of a Mach- Zehnder interferometer. A CCD camera detects the interference pattern (hologram) and sends it to a computer. The hologram is then reconstructed numerically. Using a parabolic approximation for the local field, the location of the gold particle can be calculated by fitting the data points that are above half maximum. The accuracy of the measurement made by this method is ±5 nm in the x and y directions. The authors show that the acquisition of a single image is sufficient to localize in 3D the nanoparticle within a 90 micrometer thick sample, with localization accuracy similar to that obtained in conventional light microscopy. This method provides significant progress towards the development of 3D microscopy in living cell environments,

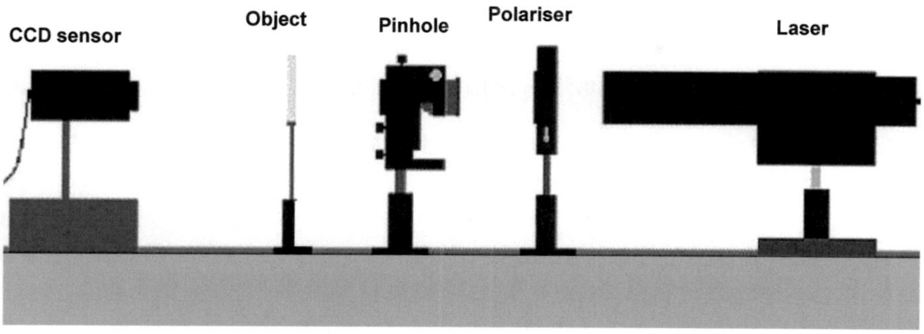

Figure 1. Optical setup of the digital in-line holographic microscope

since the 3D reconstruction of such a thick sample by conventional light microscopy would require the acquisition of a stack of hundreds of slices.

The traction force produced by biological cells has been visualized by Yu X. et al. [17]. Quantitative phase microscopy by digital holography (DH-QPM) has been utilized to study the wrinkling of a silicone rubber film by motile fibroblasts. Surface deformation and the cellular traction force have been measured from phase profiles in a direct and straightforward manner. DH-QPM is shown to provide highly efficient and versatile means for quantitatively analyzing cellular motility. The traction force has been measured as ~4×10^{-3} dyn/cell based on the degree of wrinkling determined from phase information. Fourier transformation and the angular spectrum methods were applied to the complex hologram obtained to calculate the phase-contrast, dark-field, Zernike and differential interference contrast (DIC) images. The basic principles of DH have been applied to quantitative imaging of wrinkles on silicone rubber due to cell adhesion and motility. The approach is sensitive to cellular forces and it can detect and quantify variations in force within the adhesion area of a cell over time. DH-QPM is shown to be an effective approach for measuring the traction forces of cells. A time-lapse phase movie of the migration of cells was recorded every 3 min over a period of 2 hours. The traction force for NHDFs is a factor of five smaller than for chick heart fibroblast cited in literature. This is a substantial achievement in the quantitative profiling of substrate deformation and wrinkling under cellular traction force achieved by the quantitative phase microscopy of digital holography.

3. Digital in-line holographic microscopy for life science applications at the Agricultural University Plovdiv

A digital in-line holographic microscope (DIHM) was developed at the Agricultural University of Plovdiv. The light source is 20 mW He-Ne laser. The emerging spherical wave illuminates the object, and the hologram is recorded on a CCD sensor and stored in a computer.

DIHM was applied to visualise live algae cells of two different species (*Pseudokirchneriella subcapitata* and *Chlorella vulgaris*) without any preliminary preparation. Digital reconstruction of the recorded interference patterns is performed using the "HoloVision 2.2" software [18].

Figure 2 and Figure 3 show the holograms and the reconstructed intensities to represent the object. Four wavefront intensities of each digital hologram (2a and 2b) are reconstructed at different consecutive planes with the distance between them changing by 2 μm. The reconstructed intensities illustrate the possibility of observation of different layers in a live cell obtained from one digital hologram only. In that way many cuts of one live object can be done and observed from one hologram of the whole object.

These experiments illustrate the capability of DHM for non-invasively visualizing and quantifying biological cells and tissues. That's why DHM can be successfully used for:

- cell counting
- measuring cell viability directly in the cell culture
- label-free viability analysis of adherent cell cultures etc.

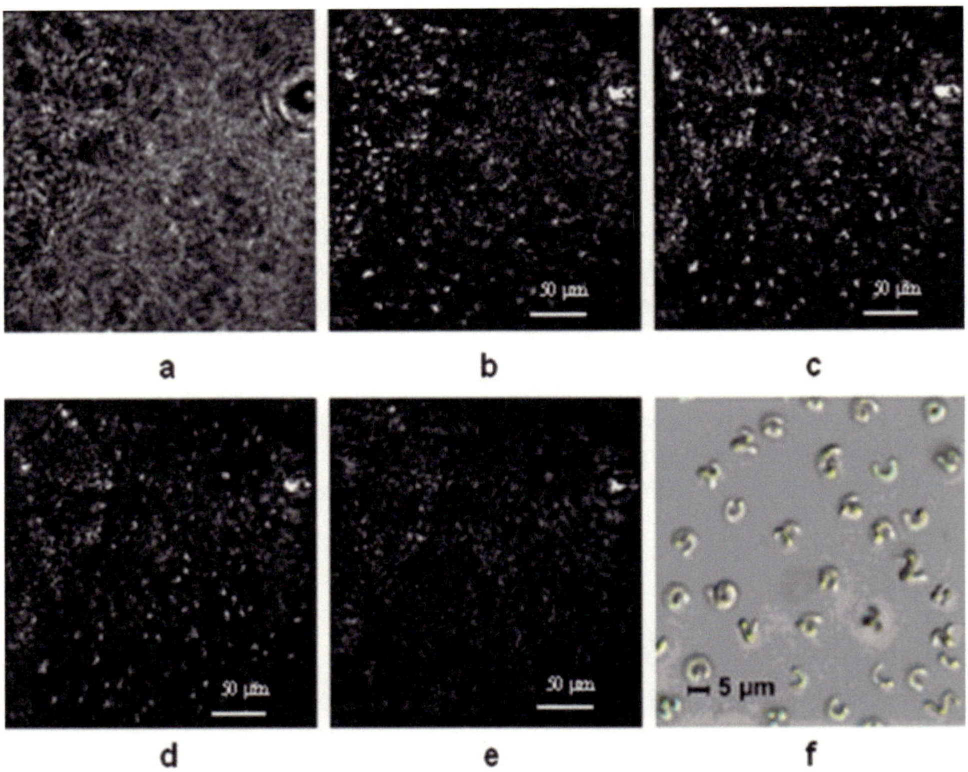

Figure 2. Images of algae *Pseudokirchneriella subcapitata:* a) digital hologram; b-e) the wavefront intensity at four consecutive planes with the distance between them changing by 2 μm; f – image from electron microscope

http://dx.doi.org/10.5772/56176

Clearly, DIHM is capable of visualising live cells with dimensions 5 – 10 μm without any preliminary preparation. It can be applied to dynamic quantitative visualisation of live cell deformations to study their interactions with other particles as well as the surrounding environment. This makes the DIHM a valuable technique for many life science applications. Further development of the technique is envisaged in order to overcome the limited pixel resolution of a CCD sensor, which is the major drawback of DIHM at present.

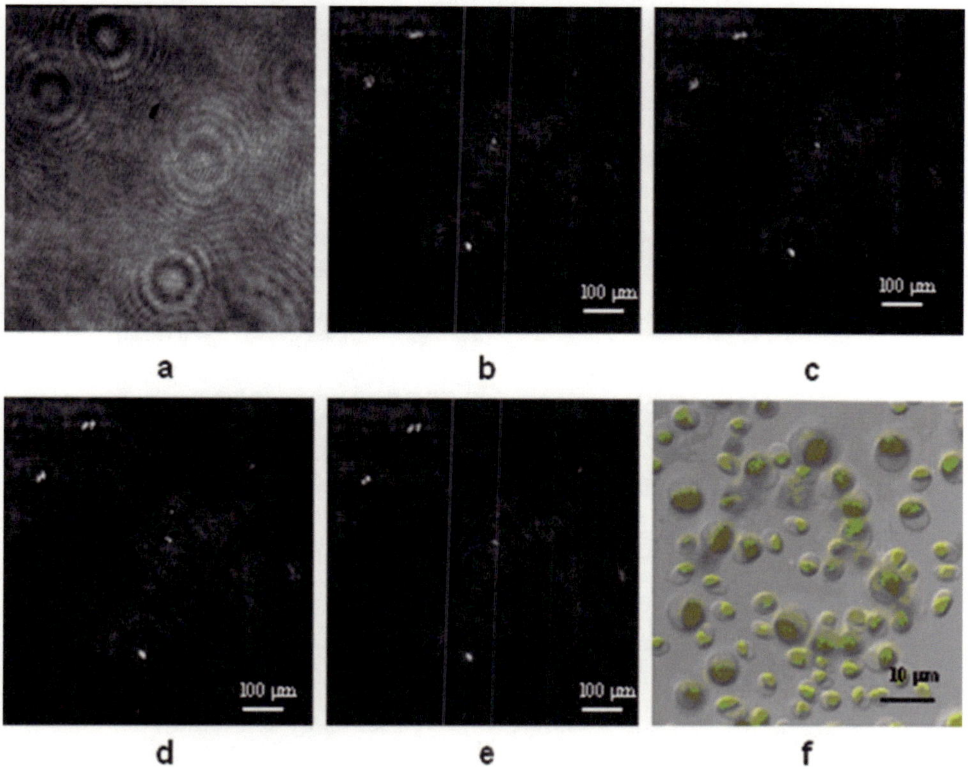

Figure 3. Images of algae *Chlorella vulgaris:* a) digital hologram; b-e) the wavefront intensity at four consecutive planes with the distance between them changing by 2 μm; f – image from electron microscope

Figure 4 and Figure 5 present digital holograms of algae cells *Pseudokirchneriella subcapitata* and *Chlorella vulgaris* taken at different stages of their life cycle and the reconstructed intensities of these holograms. The cells morphology is visible on the images showing the reconstructed intensities.

These experiments illustrate the capability of DHM for:

- label free morphology analysis of cells
- label free studies of cell division and migration
- label-free analysis of subcellular motion in living tissues etc.

By combining several images reconstructed from the same digital hologram, but at different focal planes, an increased depth of field can be obtained, which is vastly superior to the depth of field achieved with traditional light microscopy.

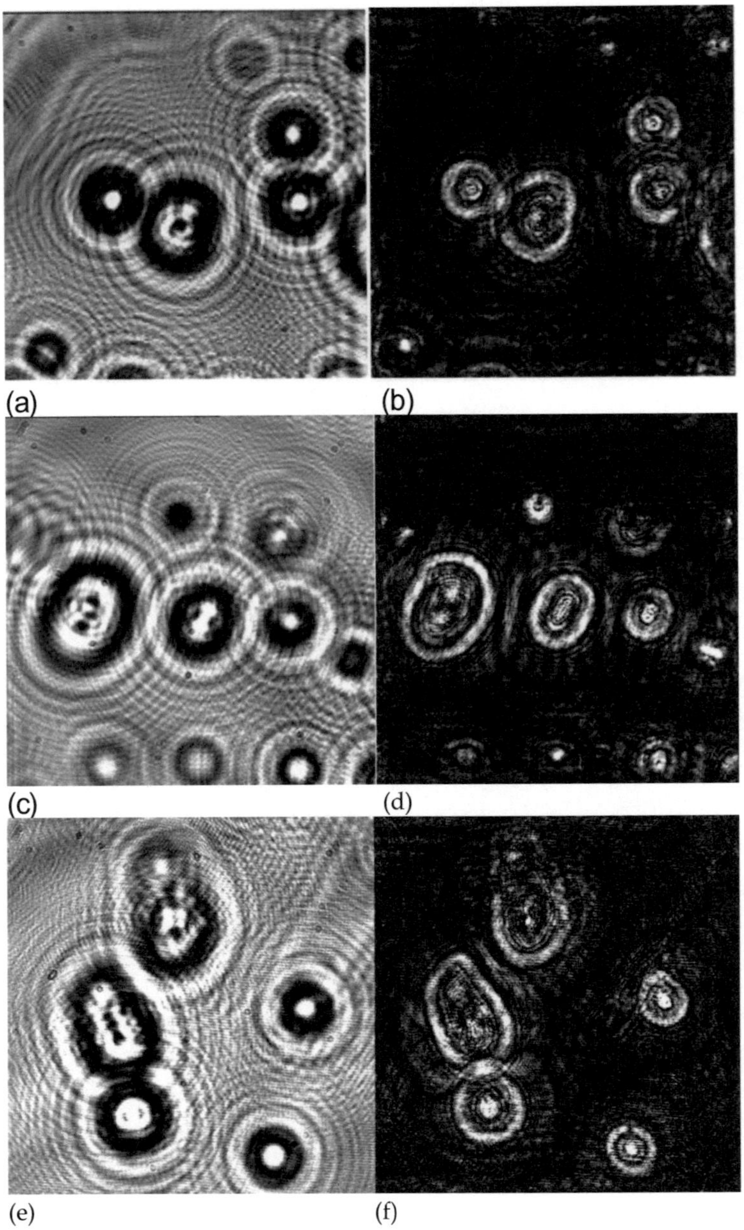

Figure 4. Images of algae *Pseudokirchneriella subcapitata,* approximately 10 μm in a sickle: a) digital hologram of two days old cells; b) the wavefront intensity of a) c) digital hologram of 4 days old cells; d) the wavefront intensity of c) e) digital hologram of 9 days old cells; f) the wavefront intensity of e).

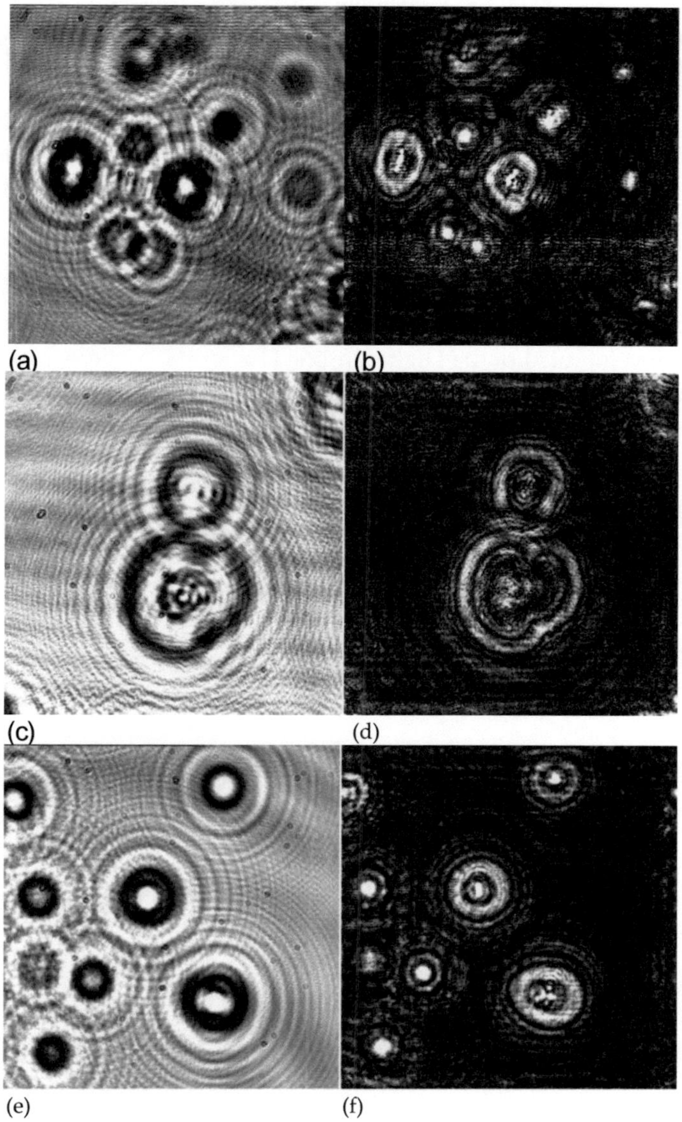

Figure 5. Images of algae *Chlorella vulgaris,* approximately 3 μm in diameter: a) digital hologram of two days old cells; b) the wavefront intensity of a) c) digital hologram of 4 days old cells; d) the wavefront intensity of c) e) digital hologram of 9 days old cells; f) the wavefront intensity of e).

4. Conclusion

DIHM imaging is very advanced method because digital holography yields a 3D volume image from a single interferogram capture. This makes the development of a dynamic microscope capable of fast 3D imaging an achievable objective.

The attractive features of DHM are: a very high acquisition rate (limited only by the video acquisition frequency), monitoring of physiological and pathological activity of cell and tissue culture, non contact, non destructive, marker free in vivo imaging.

DIHM is capable of label free morphology analysis of cells and label free studies of cell division and migration. It is a very attractive technique for application in biological research and in the agricultural science. Other life science and medical applications are also envisaged.

Further development of this technique will involve the use of lasers with shorter wavelength and CCD cameras with higher resolution. These developments will allow the application of DIHM for study of cell features having dimensions below 100 nm.

The work on the development of the Digital In-line Holographic Microscope was financially supported by the Agricultural University of Plovdiv.

Author details

Iliyan Peruhov and Emilia Mihaylova

Department of Mathematics, Informatics and Physics, Agricultural University — Plovdiv, Bulgaria

References

[1] Jones, R, & Wykes, C. *Holographic and Speckle Interferometry*, Cambridge University Press, Cambridge, UK (1989).

[2] Gabor, D. *Nature* 161, 777-778 (1948).

[3] Palacios, J, Ricardo, D, Palacios, E, Goncalves, J, & Valin, R. De Souza, "3D image reconstruction of transparent microscopic objects using digital holography", *Optics Communications* 248, 41-50 (2005).

[4] Kim, M. K. Tomographic three-dimensional imaging of a biological specimen using wavelength-scanning digital interference holography", *Optics Express* 7 (9), 305-310 (2000).

[5] Rappaz, B, Marquet, P, Cuche, E, Emery, Y, Depeursinge, C, & Magistretti, P. J. Measurement of the integral refractive index and dynamic cell morphometry of living cells with digital holographic microscopy", *Optics Express* 13, 9361-9373 (2005).

[6] Marquet, P, Rappaz, B, & Magistretti, P. J. Digital holographic microscopy: a noninvasive contrast imaging technique allowing quantitative visualization of living cells with subwavelength axial accuracy", *Optics Letters* 30, 468-470 (2005).

[7] Garcia-sucerquia, J, Xu, W, Jericho, S. K, Klages, P, Jericho, M. H, & Kreuzer, H. J. Digital in-line holographic microscopy", *Applied Optics* 45 (5), 836-850 (2006).

[8] Parshall, D, & Kim, M. K. Digital holographic microscopy with dual-wavelength phase unwrapping", *Applied Optics* 45 (3), 451-459 (2006).

[9] Jeong, K, Turek, J. J, & Nolte, D. D. Volumetric motility-contrast imaging of tissue response to cytoskeletal anti-cancer drugs", *Optics Express,* 15 (21), 14057-14065 (2007).

[10] Chalut, K. J, Brown, W. J, & Wax, A. Quantitative phase microscopy with asynchronous digital holography", *Optics Express* 15 (6), 3047-3052 (2007).

[11] Kemper, B, & Von Bally, G. Digital holographic microscopy for live cell applications and technical inspection", *Applied Optics* 47 (4), AA61(2008)., 52.

[12] Khmaladze, A, Kim, M, & Lo, C. M. Phase imaging of cells by simultaneous dual-wavelength reflection digital holography", *Optics Express* 16 (15), 10900-10911 (2008).

[13] Langehanenberg, P, Kemper, B, Dirksen, D, & Von Bally, G. Autofocusing in digital holographic phase contrast microscopy on pure phase objects for live cell imaging", *Applied Optics* 47(19), DD182 (2008)., 176.

[14] Remmersmann, C, Stüwald, S, Kemper, B, Langehanenberg, G, & Von Bally, G. Phase noise optimization in temporal phase-shifting digital holography with partial coherence light sources and its application in quantitative cell imaging", *Applied Optics* 48 (8), 1463-1472 (2009).

[15] Choi, Y. S, & Lee, S. J. Three-dimensional volumetric measurement of red blood cell motion using digital holographic microscopy", *Applied Optics* 48 (16), 2983-2990 (2009).

[16] Warnasooriy, N, Joud, F, Bun, P, Tessier, G, Coppey-moisan, M, Desbiolles, P, Atlan, M, Abboud, M, & Gross, M. Imaging gold nanoparticles in living cell environments using heterodyne digital holographic microscopy", *Optics Express* 18 (4), 3264-3273, (2010).

[17] Yu, X, Cross, M, Liu, C, Clark, D. C, Haynie, D. T, & Kim, M. K. Measurement of the traction force of biological cells by digital holography", *Biomedical Optics Express* 3 (1), 153-159 (2012).

[18] Oysen Skotheim and Vegard LTuft, "HoloVision 2.2.1" software package for numerical reconstruction and analysis of digitally sampled holograms, Norwegian University of Science and Technology, Norway (2001).

Chapter 14

Cells and Holograms – Holograms and Digital Holographic Microscopy as a Tool to Study the Morphology of Living Cells

Kersti Alm, Zahra El-Schich, Maria Falck Miniotis, Anette Gjörloff Wingren, Birgit Janicke and Stina Oredsson

Additional information is available at the end of the chapter

http://dx.doi.org/10.5772/54505

1. Introduction

Digital holographic microscopy (DHM) is an emerging high-resolution imaging technique that offers real-time imaging and quantitative measurements of physiological parameters without any staining or labeling of cells. The first DHM images of living cells were obtained 8-10 years ago [1, 2]. Analysis of human hepatocytes showed that DHM was a versatile tool for *in vivo* cell analysis by using quantitative amplitude and phase-contrast imaging with very high resolution [1]. Another study showed that the quantitative distribution of the optical path length created by transparent specimens contained information concerning both morphology and refractive index of the observed mouse cortical neurons [2]. This could only be measured by DHM and not by phase contrast and Nomarski's differential interference contrast (DIC) microscopy. In addition, the high sensitivity of these phase-shift measurements enables sub-wavelength axial accuracy, offering attractive possibilities for the visualization of cellular dynamics.

Since the first studies on living cells were performed, DHM has been used to study a wide range of different cell types, *e.g.* protozoa, bacteria and plant cells, mammalian cells such as nerve cells, stem cells, various tumor cells, bacterial-cell interactions, red blood cells and sperm cells [3-18].

The phase shift caused by cells is dependent on the amount of nonaqueus material, which affects the refractive index [19]. Thus, changes in cellular water concentration will dilute or concentrate the nonaqueus material resulting in phase shift changes. Jourdain et al., exploited this in a study of water fluxes in neurons elicited by stimulation of glutamate receptors in cultures of cortical neurons isolated from mouse embryos [17]. Glutamate receptor stimulation results in neuronal depolarization with a rapid Na^+, Ca^+ and Cl^- and concomitantly water inflow. Using DHM they found three types of glutamate-induced phase shifts in individual neurons. They also showed that one of these phase shifts resulted in cell death. The role of the two cotransporters NKCC1 and KCC2 was also investigated. These phase shifts were only found in older cultures of neurons but not in young neuronal cultures, which was correlated to the expression of glutamate receptors. Kemper et al., presented a set-up for DHM and algorithms for digital holographic reconstruction, which they used to investigate the shape of three human pancreatic duct adenocarcinoma cell lines [3]. By comparing scanning electron microscopy with DHM, they concluded that DHM gives fast and reliable results on live cell morphology. They also used DHM to investigate cellular dynamic changes taking place during 3 minutes after addition of an actin cytoskeleton-disrupting toxin, showing distinct changes in the cellular refractive index correlating with cell collapse.

There are several diseases where the number of immature red blood cells (reticulocytes) increases. The determination of reticulocyte numbers requires staining with different markers, thus, noninvasive methods would yield faster results. Mihailescu et al., recently developed a code for automated simultaneous individual label free cell image separation using DHM to distinguish between reticulocytes and mature erythrocytes [13]. Red blood cells are imaged as donut-like structures using DHM [5] and the obtained data can be used to calculate erythrocyte volume. Hemoglobin is the main nonaqueus material in erythrocytes which causes a phase shift. The resulting phase signal can be directly related to the mean corpuscular hemoglobin [20]. Rappaz et al., showed that DHM could in fact be used to calculate the mean corpuscular hemoglobin concentration of erythrocytes [5]. Similar results have also been presented by Jin et al. [14].

Sperm morphology has been identified as a characteristic that can be useful in the prediction of fertilizing capacity. Recently it has been shown that DHM can be used to monitor the structure and composition of sperm heads [11-12] and that there can be significant differences between individuals [12]. The data are interesting and should stimulate further research into the use of DHM in assessing fertility.

A new tool for the study of bacterial-cell interaction has been described very recently, such as adherence and invasion, which is an interesting application in order to advance diagnostic tools for evaluating infection scenarios [15]. Holographic optical tweezers were used to select, move and align multiple rod shaped *Bacillus subtilis* DB 630 on top of human pancreatic ductal adenocarcinoma cells and the interaction were subsequently monitored with off-axis DHM. The authors were able to reproduce the alignment of bacteria on the cell surface with very high accuracy, while bacterial morphology and viability remained unaffected.

Excitingly, a portable holographic pixel super-resolution lens-free on-chip microscope has been developed to be used in remote locations, for the purpose of monitoring and diagnosing pathogens in samples such as blood and water [21]. The 95 g microscope features less than 1 μm resolution over a wide field-of view of ~24 mm^2. A digital sensor-array acquires holograms and pixel super-resolution algorithm post-processing yields high resolution images with retained wide field-of view. A digital micro-processor that enables step-wise LED illumination for lens-free transmission holograms was employed for this purpose. Reconstructed holograms of the human malaria parasite *Plasmodium falciparum* in smears showed that infected red blood cells can be identified using a combination of amplitude and phase images.

A key feature of DHM is the ability to study cell morphological changes associated with differentiation. In a recent study, Chalut and colleagues set out to investigate the physical changes that are associated with cellular differentiation [22]. They used a rapidly differentiating sub-line of human promyelocytic leukemic cell line HL-60, HL-60/S4, which were induced to differentiate into various mature blood cells; neutrophils, monocytes and macrophages. As shown by off-axis DHM and confocal microscopy, neutrophil and monocyte differentiation displayed a decrease in overall refractory index and a change in the distribution of cellular material towards the nucleus, hence these cells were becoming less dense during differentiation. On the contrary, macrophage differentiation showed no change in the distribution pattern of cellular material, although overall refractory index increased. Moreover, the use of a laser trap technique, optical stretching, showed that neutrophils and monocytes became more compliant (soft), while macrophages became stiffer after just one day of differentiation. The study shows that DHM together with optical stretching can be used as novel approach to monitor and distinguish cellular differentiation of myeloid precursor cells.

The common denominator of all these described studies is that DHM is used to analyze the morphology of living cells in a way that is automatic, cost efficient and causes the cells no harm. Moreover, the method will contribute with large amounts of cell data in a high throughput manner.

2. Cell death and DHM

The balance between cell growth and controlled cell death is very crucial for many physiological processes such as embryogenesis, differentiation, in the immune system and in diseases such as stroke, heart failure and neurodegeneration [23]. Cells can die in two ways in vertebrates, either by cell disintegration, necrosis, or by a process of programmed cell death, apoptosis, that play a central role in development and homeostasis. On the contrary, necrosis is a fast induction of cell death that induces an inflammatory response. Late necrosis is characterized by extensive DNA hydrolysis, organelle breakdown, and finally cell lysis. Morphologically, dying cells differ from viable cells in many ways. Apoptosis begins with a variety of morphological alterations: cell membrane changes such as loss of membrane asymmetry and attachment, cell shrinkage, formation of small blebs, nuclear fragmentation, chromatin condensation, chromosomal DNA fragmentation and finally the cell breaks into several apoptotic bodies [24]. One of the earliest indications of apoptosis is the translocation of the membrane phospholipid phosphatidylserine (PS) to the outside of the plasma membrane [25].

The most commonly used assays to differentiate between viable and non-viable cells today are trypan blue and propidium iodide, both laborious and time-consuming methods. Khmaladze and colleagues used DHM to measure, with high time and volume resolution and in real-time, cell volume changes induced by apoptosis [26]. Adherent human epithelial KB cells were treated with 1 - 2 μM staurosporine for 4 hours (h). By measuring the phase change of light passing through cells, an early stage morphological feature of apoptosis were observed in treated cells - a marked decrease in cell volume. These observations were consistent with previous studies using standard population-based techniques. The ability to analyze individual cells in a given cell population by using DHM was successfully demonstrated, as individual treatment-induced cell responses could be monitored. Moreover, with the high time resolution that can be obtained using DHM, one can also study initial cell responses. Accordingly, the authors did indeed note time-dependent fluctuations in cell volume, which increased in the earlier phases of treatment.

Excessive stimulation of neurotransmitters through addition of L-glutamate was used to induce cell death in primary cultures of mouse cortical neurons [16]. Cell volume regulation was monitored by DHM phase response, which allowed the researchers to estimate in a very short time-frame, if a neuronal cell would survive or die. By varying the concentration and exposure time of glutamate, the authors could identify reversible phase responses corresponding to phase recovery though an efficient ionic homeostasis. Moreover, they could also observe irreversible phase responses, indicating a constant change of intracellular ionic homeostasis, related to cell volume regulation alterations and suggested as a marker of glutamate induced cell death in neurons. By monitoring the phase shift, the authors were also able to distinguish nuclear condensation and "blebbing" induced by treatment which could indicate that cells were apoptotic rather than necrotic. Importantly, cells recognized within minutes by their DHM phase signal as unable to regulate their ionic homeostasis, were only several hours later identified as dead by trypan blue staining.

3. The technique

As opposed to traditional microscopy imaging, DHM is a technique that does not directly result in cell images. Instead, the technique measures the effects on light exerted by a cell. Light that has passed through the cell, and which is affected by the cell, is combined with identical light that has bypassed the cell (Figure 1). This results in the formation of an interference pattern, which is captured by a sensor. From this interference pattern a computer can reconstruct the object (*e.g.* a cell) that caused the pattern. The creation and capture of an interference pattern requires very low light intensity, thus making the system free from photo toxicity [27].

As the objects are reconstructed in the computer, focusing does not need to be as exact as when capturing cell images directly. The interference pattern, which is the base of the image reconstruction, enables the computer to collect object data from a series of focal planes comprising a calculation span. If the object is within the calculation span, the computer will be able to reconstruct a focused object.

http://dx.doi.org/10.5772/54505

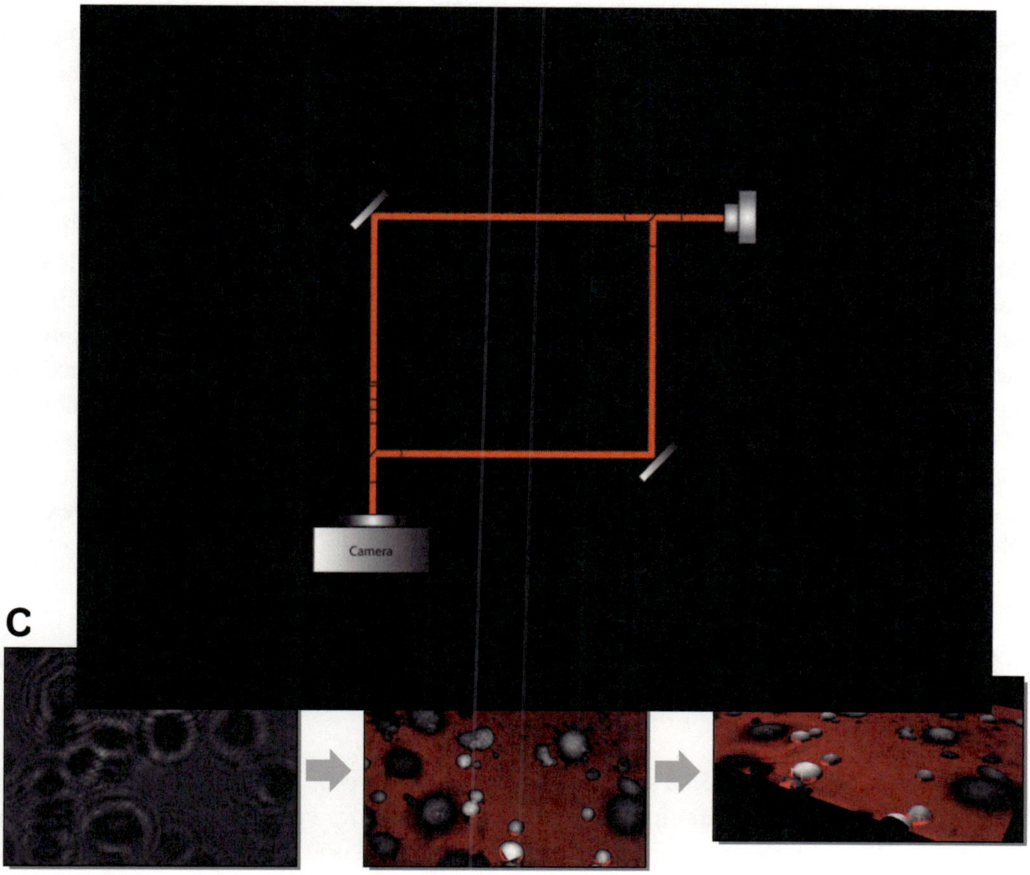

Figure 1. A digital holographic setup. (A) A laser beam is split into two identical beams. One beam passes through an object (in this case the cells) while the other beam travels undisturbed. (B) The two beams are merged again and focused on a camera sensor. (C) The sensor will capture an interference image which is. (D) A computer algorithm reconstructs the objects, which in this figure are L929 mouse fibroblast cells. (E) As the reconstruction will give 3D-information, 3D-images can be displayed.

The transmission of light can be compared to the transmission of waves over water. The waves come with different heights and with different intervals. The intensity of light is determined by the height of the light-wave, called the amplitude of the wave. The color of light is determined by the distances between the wave tops, called the wave-length. The human eye can detect the intensity of the light and its color. An additional characteristic of light is of importance, namely in which phase of the light wave the light is detected. In light from a laser source, all light-waves are produced synchronously and simultaneously, *i.e.* they are coherent and all waves are in the same phase. Regular sunlight on the other hand is non-coherent as the light-waves are not synchronized but come with various patterns of deviation resulting in differences in the phases of the light waves. The human eye cannot detect whether light is coherent or non-coherent.

If light passes through an object that can absorb light, the amplitude will decrease and thus the intensity decreases. If light passes through an optically dense object, the light will be delayed, and the phase of the light will shift. Using digital holography it is possible to measure the shifts in the phases of light.

As the reconstructed holographic cell images are based on the phase shifts of the light, it is easier to quantify cell characteristics. The area is obtained from the total number of pixels covering the cell being imaged. By determining the edge, the shape of the cell can be disclosed. The shift in the phase of light that occurs when the light passes though the cell can be translated into cellular thickness. The phase shift is related to optical path length and the wavelength of the light. As a consequence, the optical path length is directly correlated to the thickness and the refractory index of the cell. In short, if the phase shift is measured and the wavelength of the light as well as the refractive index of the cell is known, the thickness of the cell can be calculated. Lastly, the volume of the cell can be calculated from the area and the thickness. In other words, DHM enables its user to quantify cellular characteristics without causing photo toxicity. Moreover, as mechanical focusing does not need to be exact, DHM makes time-lapse studies more convenient.

4. Quantitative imaging of cell morphology

4.1. Cell division

Cells reproduce by division in a process called mitosis. All cells go through a series of well-documented stages, which are the same for all cells except for egg and sperm cells. The duration of each stage however, differs between cell types and is also due to the environmental conditions and external and internal growth signals.

We have studied the morphology of an individual cell division over time using DHM (HoloMonitor M3, Phase Holographic Imaging AB, PHIAB, Lund, Sweden). The pancreatic cancerous cells, PanC-1 (ATCC CRL-1469), were grown on a IBIDI-micro slide (IBIDI, Martinsried, Germany) in their normal growth medium during the entire study and the micro slide was placed on a heating plate (IBIDI) to retain 37°C. A time-lapse movie was created with one capture taken every 5 minutes for 72 h in total, and thereafter one cell was selected for a morphological study, which spanned over 24 h.

In Figure 2, the selected cell is presented as an artificially colored image. The 12 individual sequence images represent a time span of 24 h, starting at 5 h and ending at 29 h within the total time lapse. After the division of the mother cell, the two daughter cells were followed in the study.

The first three images show how the mother cell rounds up and organizes its chromatin. The "white bar" on top of the cell at time point 12 h 45 min corresponds to the chromatin just before the separation of the two sets of genes. Twenty minutes later (at time point 13 h 05 min) there are two distinct sets of chromosomes moving away from each other. Seen at the same time point is a small elongation of the cell as it continues its path of mitosis. The next three images spanning over two hours show how the cell continues the separation of its two sets of chromosomes leading to further elongation, until the cell has become two cells. The daughter cells are still connected to each other via their outer membranes, but are clearly two individual cells. Finally the cells adopt the appearance of mature cells. The spreading out of the daughter cells is not synchronized as the daughter cell to the left in the image spreads out at 17 h 25 min and the right daughter cell at 29 h.

From the vast amount of morphological parameters stored for the cell in each image, we chose here to analyze the change in cell area, average optical thickness and cell volume of the mother cell (red) and daughter cells (black and blue, respectively) over time (Figure 3). The cell area for the mother cell decreases markedly, whereas the thickness increases until mitosis. The two daughter cells, on the other hand, show increasing cell area and decreasing thickness. The volume for all cells is relatively uniform (Figure 3).

Pan et al., [28] have exemplified the technique by studying the effects of microgravity-induced bone-loss by using DHI for long-term studies on dividing living cells in culture. A DHM was connected to a superconducting magnet for observing cell division in real-time in living cells under conditions of simulated zero gravity. A large gradient high magnetic field was used to achieve magnetic levitation of murine MLO-Y4 osteocytes inside the bore of a superconducting magnet. A mixed gravity environment inside the bore was achieved which enabled environments with both hypo- as well as hyper-gravity. Quantitative phase contrast images were recorded from cells subjected to zero gravity for a total period of 10 h. Pixel intensity profiles were obtained from recorded phase images. Significant changes in cell division and cell optical thickness was observed under varying gravity conditions, which the authors believe to be caused by microgravity induced reorganization of cell structures such as cytoskeleton, cytosol and organelles.

4.2. Cell death

Cell death can be categorized as apoptosis, necrosis or as stages in between [23-24, 29-30]. Here we show two different types of cell death as detected with DHM (HoloMonitor M3, Phase Holographic Imaging AB, PHIAB, Lund, Sweden). DU145 prostate cancer cells and L929 mouse fibroblasts were seeded on IBIDI-micro slides (IBIDI, Martinsried, Germany). After 24 h of incubation, the cells were treated with 50 μM etoposide. The cells were followed from the beginning of treatment and images were captured every four minutes using the HoloMonitor M3. The cells were kept at 37°C with a heating plate (IBIDI).

DU145 cells contracted, became dense and rounded up after approximately 4 h of treatment (Figure 4). Then the cells became very uneven and approximately 5.5 h (i.e. 330 minutes) after the beginning of etoposide treatment, the cells fragmented. Interestingly, the remnants of the cell body contracted into a smaller cell-like structure that resembled an apoptotic body. The fragmentation of the cell is a classic hallmark of apoptosis [30].

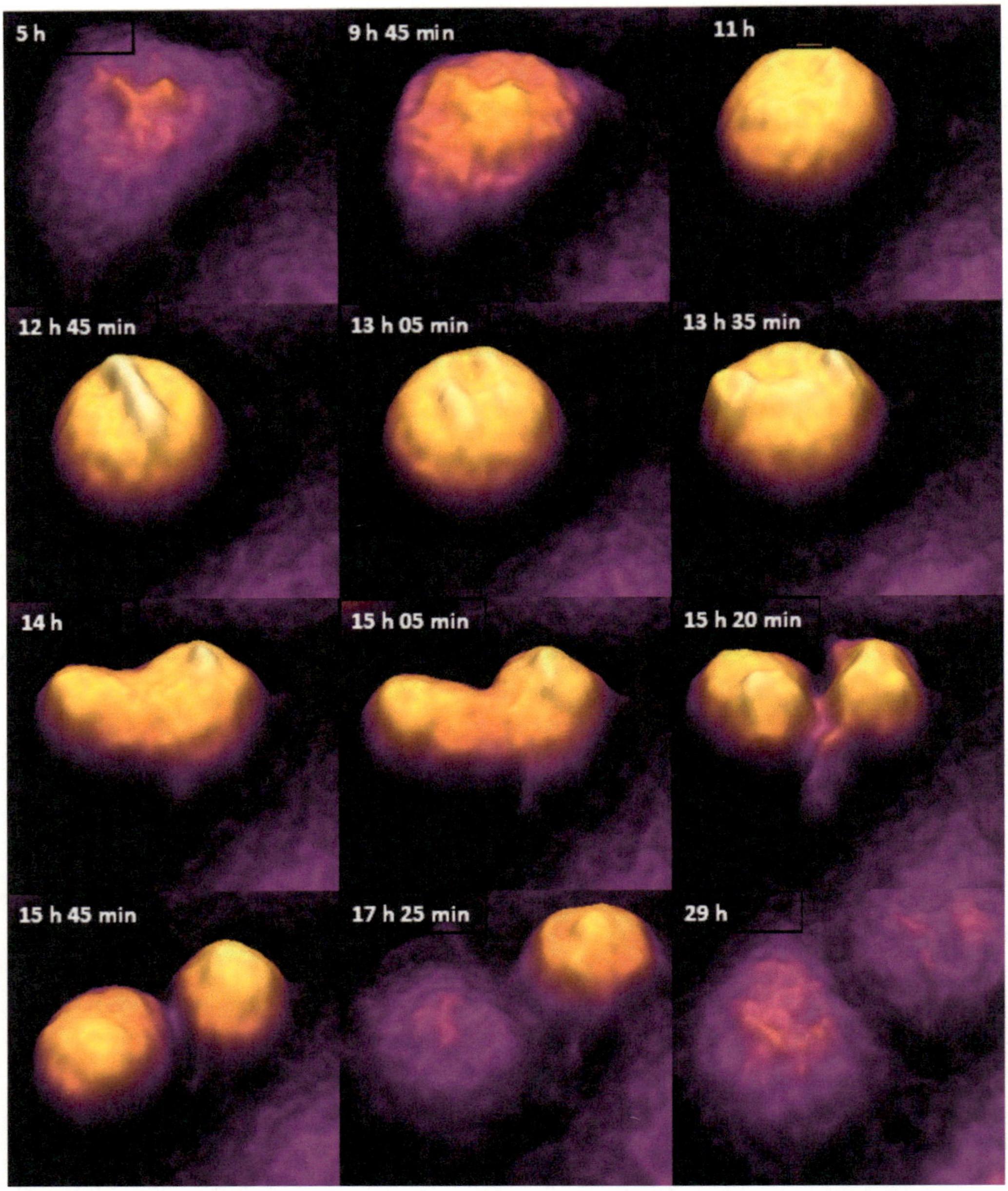

Figure 2. Twelve selected images representing a dividing PanC-1 pancreatic cancer cell from a DHM time-lapse. The image sequence represents 24 h. The images were artificially colored. Note that the interval between the selected images varies, showing the different morphological features of the mitotic events that occur at various rates. As seen in upper part, the mother cell rounds up, the chromatin separates followed by the total division and finally, in the lower part, the two daughter cells achieve the morphology of a mature adherent cell.

http://dx.doi.org/10.5772/54505

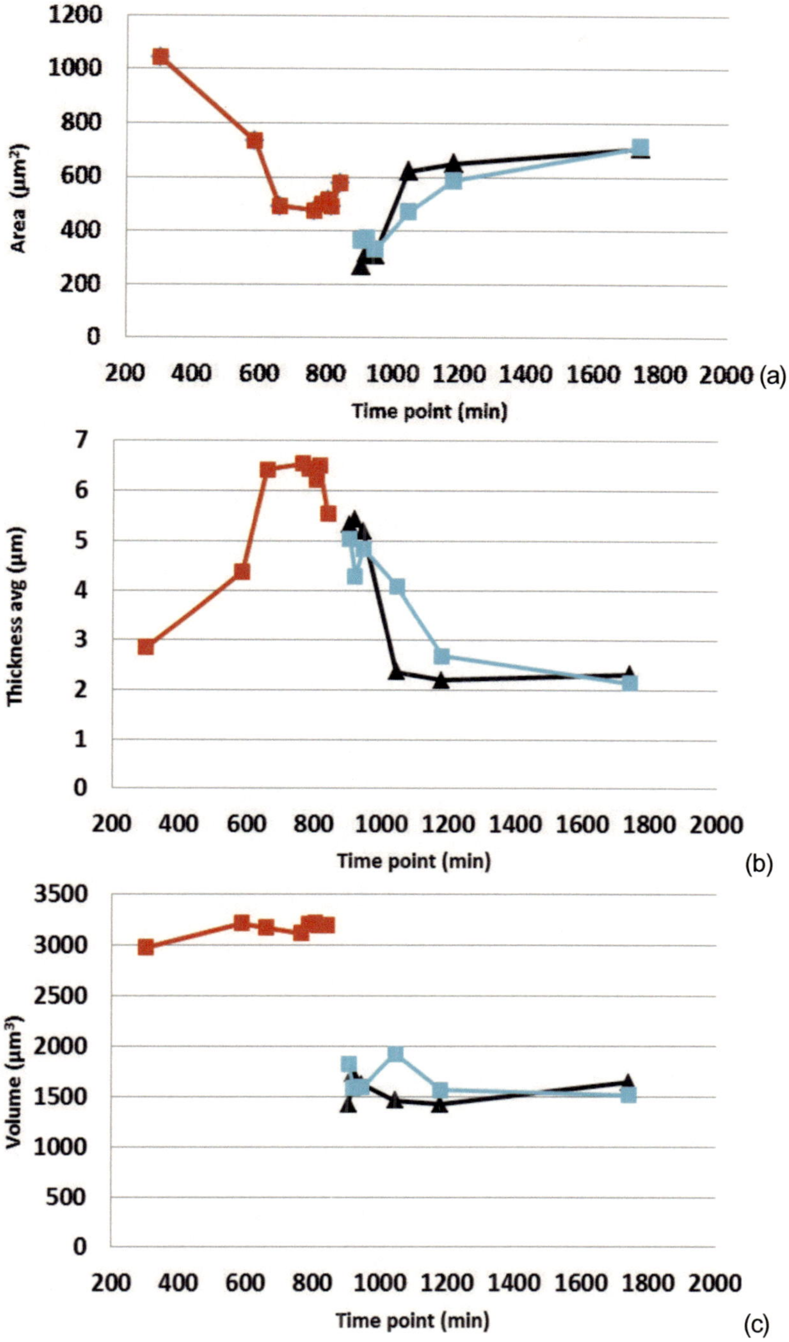

Figure 3. Cell area, thickness and volume define the division of a PanC-1 pancreatic cancer cell into two daughter cells. The mother cell (red) divides after 905 minutes (X-axis, 15 h 05 min) and the values for the daughter cells (left cell: black, right cell: blue) are shown at the subsequent time points.

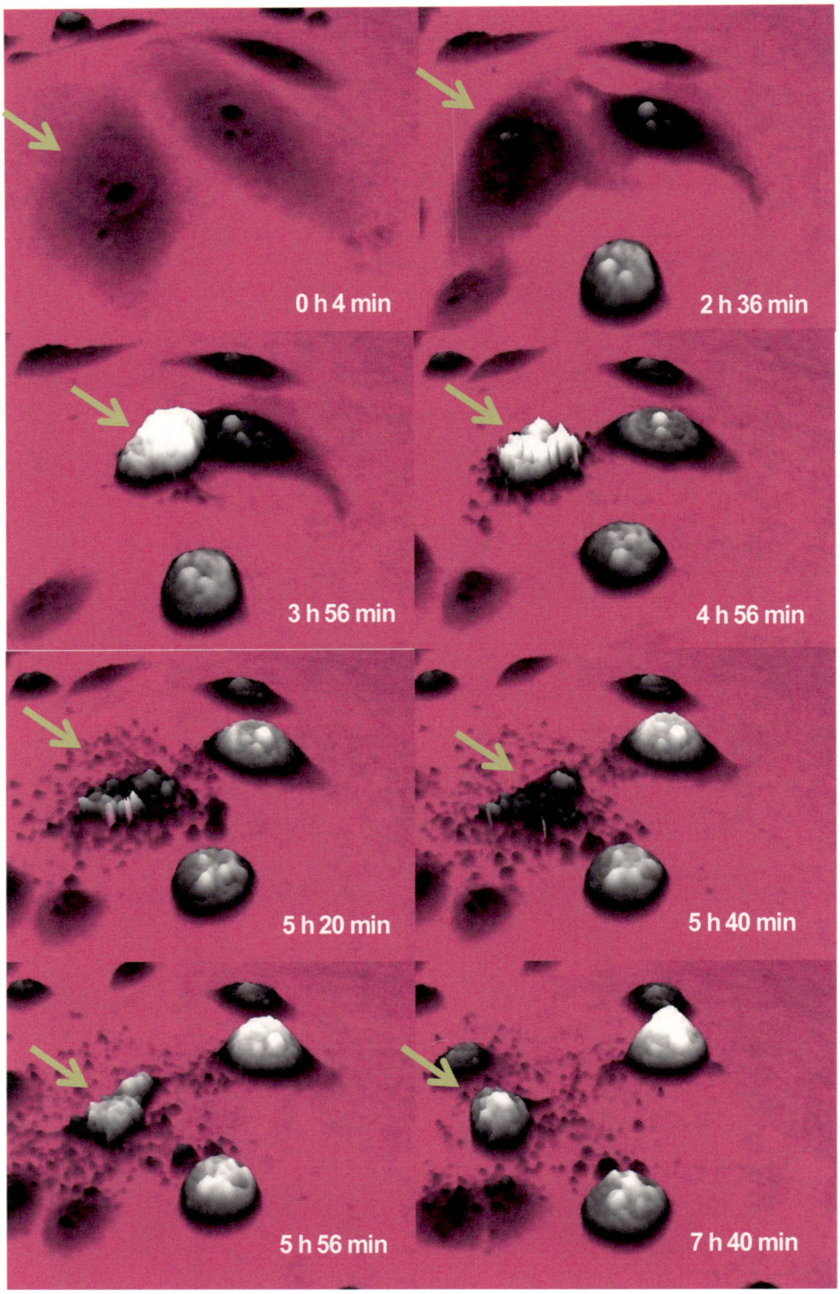

Figure 4. A dying DU145 prostate cancer cell. DHM images were captured every four minutes from the beginning of etoposide treatment (50 μM). The green arrows point to a cell, which starts the death process by contracting markedly. The cell then becomes uneven, and breaks apart. The cell death process displays the hallmarks of apoptosis and the cell remnants are gathered in a structure similar to an apoptotic body.

http://dx.doi.org/10.5772/54505

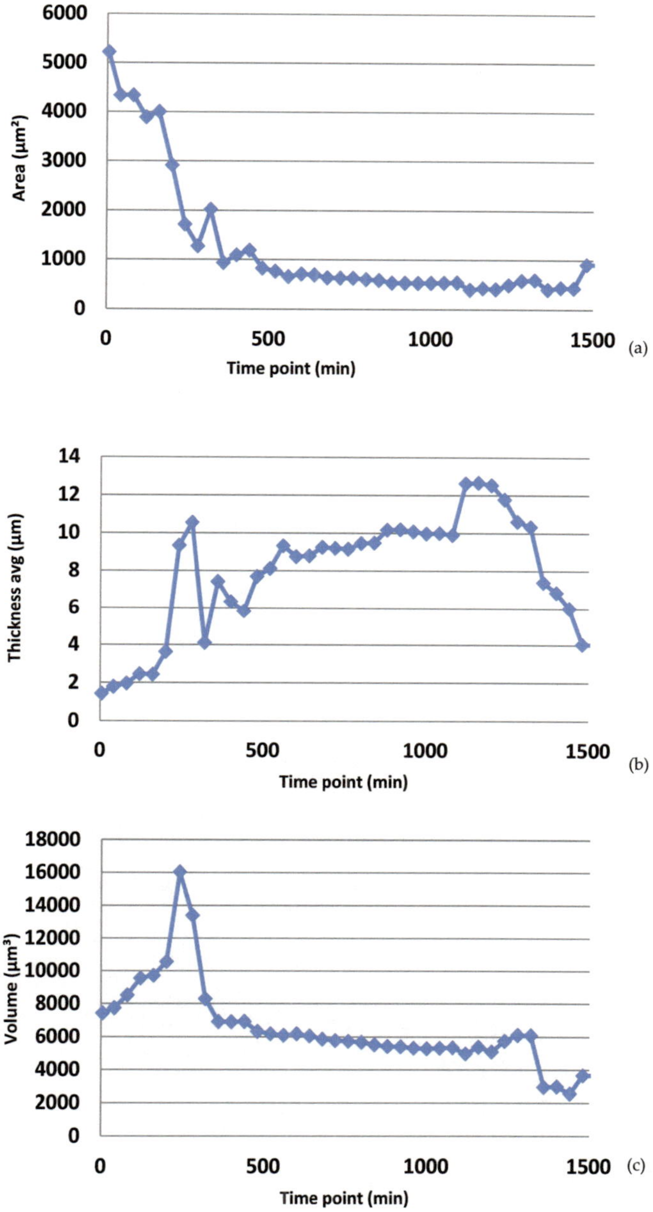

Figure 5. Cell area, thickness and volume changes during etoposide-induced cell death in DU145 cells. The diagrams show how the area, thickness and volume of the DU145 cell in Figure 4 vary over time. The X-axis shows the time after treatment in minutes and the Y-axis shows the measuring units.

When using DHM, each cell can be analyzed regarding morphology. The morphological analysis of the DU145 cell death shown in Figure 4 is displayed in Figure 5. The area of the cell steadily decreased as the cell contracted and rounded up. The cell reached a maximum thickness after approximately 4 h (240 min). The cell volume peaked after approximately 3.5 h, *i.e.* somewhat later than the thickness, and before the cell fragmented.

The L929 cells behaved very differently. Some cells in this culture started dying within hours of treatment, and others started to die several hours later (Figure 6). The individual cell we followed in this study, started to contract approximately 14 h after treatment (i.e. 840 minutes). Approximately 50 minutes later, the cell content had become much less optically dense and the cell displayed a morphology that we have previously observed in dead cells (unpublished). After further incubation, the cell remnants became thinner and thinner, and eventually disappeared, as seen in the image where the surrounding cells turn into small cell remnants. The death process was similar for all cells in this sample. It has previously been shown that L929 cell death can take very different forms depending on treatment [31].

The morphological analysis of the L929 cell death shown in Figure 6 is displayed in Figure 7. After 14 h and 10 minutes (850 minutes) as the cell started to contract, the area decreased and the thickness increased. Thereafter the thickness and volume decreased while the area increased. The dead cell was very thin and large before it started to break down into fragments. The nucleus first condensed and then slowly disintegrated. This particular cell death did not show any of the hallmarks of apoptosis, but rather those of necrosis. We have not confirmed our results with other methods.

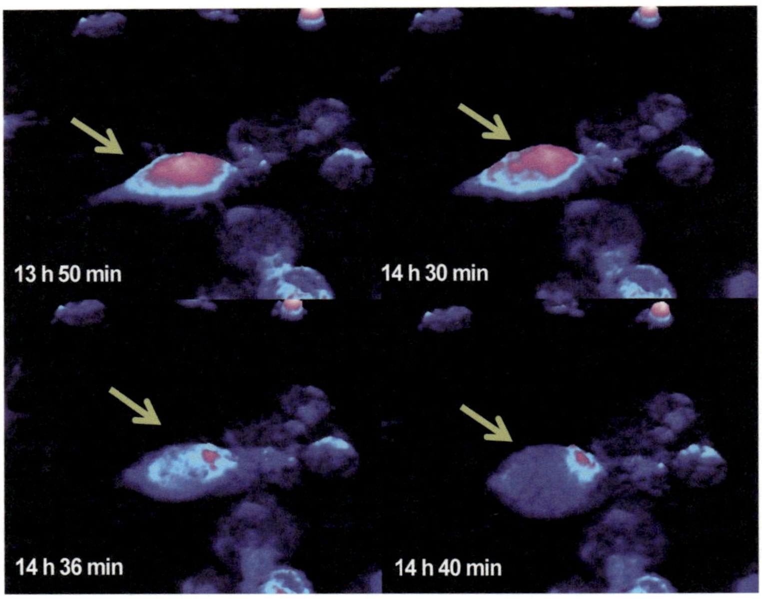

Figure 6. A dying L929 mouse fibroblast cell. Images have been captured every four minutes from the beginning of etoposide (50μM) treatment. The green arrows point to a cell, which starts the death process by contracting slightly. Optically, the cell content becomes thin and finally the cell remnants start to dissolve. The cell death process displays the hallmarks of necrosis.

The possibility to compare morphological data from individual cells makes it feasible to determine the proportion of dead cells in a culture by capturing an image. If the cells are followed with a timelapse, it is possible to determine the course of cell death, but also to determine the type of cell death.

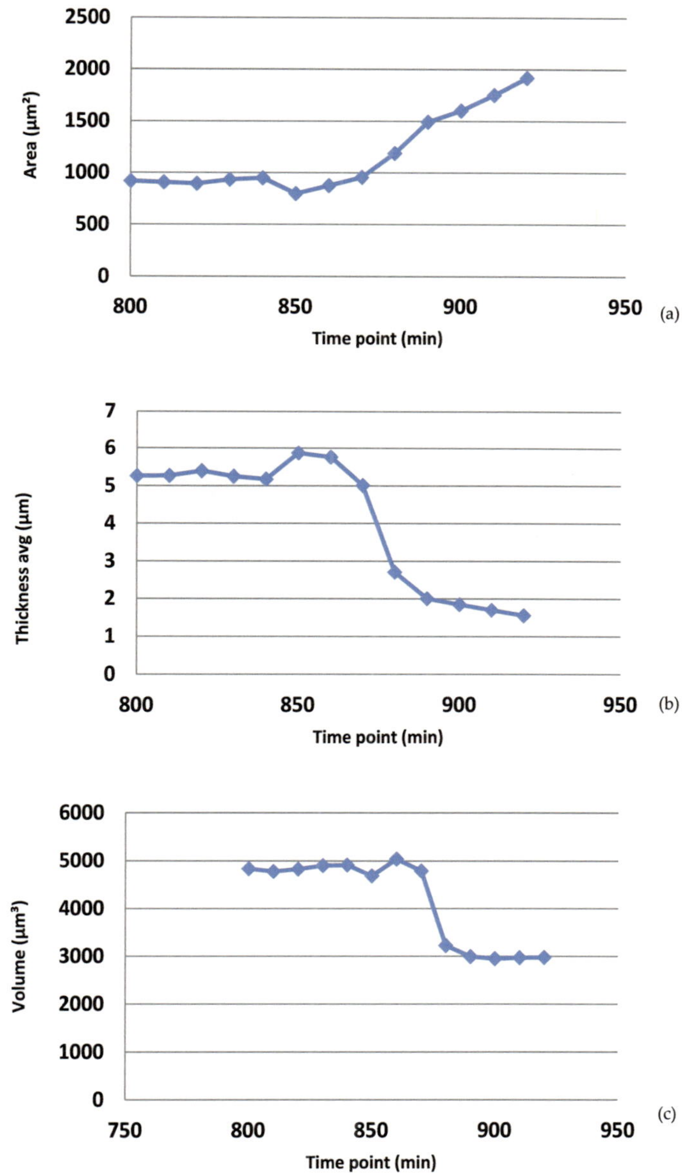

Figure 7. The diagrams show how the area, thickness and volume of the L929 cell in Figure 6 vary over time. The X-axis shows the time after treatment in minutes and the Y-axis shows the measuring units.

5. Conclusion

We present a method to study the morphology of living, dividing and dying cells using DHM. DHM is a non-invasive, non-destructive and non-phototoxic method which allows the user to perform both qualitative and quantitative measurements of living cells over time.

We show here our results on cell division and cell death in single cells. The morphological analyses performed here show changes caused by cell death and cell division, and indicate the possibilities to discriminate between different types of cell death. Cells dying in an apoptosis-like manner display different cell area and cell thickness profiles over time compared to cells dying in a necrosis-like manner, although their volume profiles are very similar. Dividing cells show a characteristic dip in the volume profile, which makes them easily distinguishable. Also, several previous studies show the versatile abilities of DHM. Different cell types have been studied and the morphology has been used to determine cell functionality as well as changes in morphology related to the environment. Cell morphology parameters can be very useful when following the effects of different treatments, the process of differentiation as well as cell growth and cell death. Cell morphology studied by DHM can be useful in toxicology, stem cell and cancer research.

Further research

Several research groups are now using DHM for cell biological studies. A future goal might be to use the morphological analysis ability of DHM as a fast, automatic, and cost efficient evaluation tool for different cancer treatments. This could make it possible to classify cells and to determine cell morphology and differentiation, cell proliferation, cellular changes of cells transfected with DNA or siRNA, cell death and effects on cell movement, all in a high throughput manner. The traditional methods to detect proteins by cell labelling are all disruptive to the cells both due to the labelling methods and to the photo toxicity caused by the detection methods such as fluorescence microscopy, flow cytometry and multi-well assays. To increase the scope of digital holography it would be useful to develop cell labels that can be detected in a non-invasive, non-destructive way.

Author details

Kersti Alm[1], Zahra El-Schich[2], Maria Falck Miniotis[2], Anette Gjörloff Wingren[2*], Birgit Janicke[1] and Stina Oredsson[3]

*Address all correspondence to: anette.gjorloff-wingren@mah.se

1 Phase Holographic Imaging, Lund, Sweden

2 Biomedical Science, Malmö University, Malmö, Sweden

3 Department of Biology, Lund University, Lund, Sweden

References

[1] Carl D, Kemper B, Wernicke G, von Bally G. Parameter-optimized Digital Holographic Microscope for High-Resolution Living-Cell Analysis. Applied Optics 2004;43(36) 6536-6544.

[2] Marquet P, Rappaz B, Magistretti PJ. Digital Holographic Microscopy: a Noninvasive Contrast Imaging Technique Allowing Quantitative Visualization of Living Cells With Subwavelength Axial Accuracy. Optics Letters 2005;30(5) 468-470.

[3] Kemper B, Carl D, Schnekenburger J, Bredebusch I, Schäfer M, Domschke W, von Bally G. Investigations on Living Pancreas Tumor Cells by Digital Holographic Microscopy. Journal of Biomedical Optics 2006;11(3) 34005.

[4] Moon I, Javidi B. Three-Dimensional Identification of Stem Cells by Computational Holographic Imaging. Journal of the Royal Society Interface. 2007; 4(13) 305-313.

[5] Rappaz B, Barbul A, Emery Y, Korenstein R, Depeursinge C, Magistretti P.J, Marquet, P. Comparative Study of Human Erythrocytes by Digital Holographic Microscopy, Confocal Microscopy and Impedance Volume Analyzer. Cytometry Part A 2008;73A(10) 895-903.

[6] Mölder A, Sebesta M, Gustafsson M, Gisselsson L, Gjörloff Wingren A, Alm K. Non-Invasive, Label Free Cell Counting and Quantitative Analysis of Adherent Cells Using Digital Holography. Journal of Microscopy 2008;232(2) 240-247.

[7] Kemper B, Bauwens A, Vollmer A, Ketelhut S, Langehanenberg P, Müthing J, Karch H, von Bally G. Label-Free Quantitative Cell Division Monitoring of Endothelial Cells by Digital Holographic Microscopy. Journal of Biomedical Optics 2010;15(3): 036009.

[8] Persson J., Mölder A., Pettersson S.G., Alm K. Cell Motility Studies Using Digital Holographic Microscopy In: A. Méndez-Vilas and J. Díaz Álvarez (Eds.) Microscopy: Science, Technology, Applications and Education. Formatex Research Center. 2010. p1063-1072.

[9] Alm K, Cirenajwis H, Gisselsson L, Gjörloff Wingren A, Janicke B, Mölder A, Oredsson S, Persson J. Digital Holography and Cell Studies. In: Joseph Rosen (ed) Holography, Research and Technologies, In Tech, 2011. p237-252.

[10] El-Schish Z., Mölder A., Sebesta M., Gisselsson L., Alm K., Gjörloff Wingren, A. Digital holographic microscopy – innovative and non-destructive analysis of living cells. In: A. Méndez-Vilas and J. Díaz Álvarez (Eds.) Microscopy, Science, Technology, Applications and Education. Formatex Research Center. 2011. p1055-1062.

[11] Memmolo P, Di Caprio G, Distante C, Paturzo M, Puglisi R, Balduzzi D, Galli A, Coppola G, Ferraro P. Identification of Bovine Sperm Head for Morphometry Analysis in Quantitative Phase-Contrast Holographic Microscopy. Optics Express 2011;19(23) 23215-23226.

[12] Crha I, Zakova J, Huser M, Ventruba P, Lousova E, Pohanka M. Digital Holographic Microscopy in Human Sperm Imaging. Journal of Assisted Reproduction and Genetics. 2011;28(8) 725-729.

[13] Mihailescu M, Scarlat M, Gheorghiu A, Costescu J, Kusko M, Paun IA, Scarlat E. Automated Imaging, Identification, and Counting of Similar Cells From Digital Hologram Reconstructions. Applied Optics. 2011;50(20) 3589-3597.

[14] Jin W, Wanga Y, Ren N, Bu M, Shang X, Xu Y, Chen Y. Simulation of Simultaneous Measurement for Red Blood Cell Thickness and Refractive Index. Optics and Lasers in Engineering. 2011;50 154-158.

[15] Kemper B, Barroso A, Woerdemann M, Dewenter L, Vollmer A, Schubert R, Mellmann A, von Bally G, Denz C. Towards 3D Modelling and Imaging of Infection Scenarios at the Single Cell Level Using Holographic Optical Tweezers and Digital Holographic Microscopy. Journal of Biophotonics. 2012; doi:10.1002/jbio.201200057.

[16] Pavillon N, Kühn J, Moratal C, Jourdain P, Depeursinge C, Magistretti PJ, Marquet P. Early Cell Death Detection With Digital Holographic Microscopy. PLoS One. 2012;7(1):e30912. doi:10.1371/journal.pone.0030912

[17] Jourdain P, Pavillon N, Moratal C, Boss D, Rappaz B, Depeursinge C, Marquet P, Magistretti PJ. Determination of Transmembrane Water Fluxes in Neurons Elicited by Glutamate Ionotropic Receptors and by the Cotransporters KCC2 and NKCC1: A Digital In-Line Holographic Microscopy Study. Journal of Neuroscience. 2011:31(33) 11846-11854.

[18] Jericho MH, Kreuzer HJ, Kanka M, Riesenberg R. Quantitative Phase and Refractive Index Measurements With Point-Source Digital In-Line Holographic Microscopy. Applied Optics. 2012;51(10) 1503-1515.

[19] Rappaz B, Marquet P, Cuche E, Emery, Y, Depeursinge C, Magistretti PJ. Measurement of the Integral Refractive Index and Dynamic Cell Morphometry of Living Cells With Digital Holographic Microscopy. Optics Express. 2005;13(23) 9361-9373.

[20] Barer R. Refractometry and Interferometry of Living Cells. Journal of the Optical Society of America. 1957;47(6) 545-556.

[21] Bishara W, Sikora U, Mudanyali O, Su TW, Yaglidere O, Luckhart S, Ozcan A. Holographic Pixel Super-Resolution in Portable Lensless On-Chip Microscopy Using a Fiber-Optic Array. Lab on a Chip. 2011;11(7) 1276-1279.

[22] Chalut KJ, Ekpenyong AE, Clegg WL, Melhuish IC, Guck J. Quantifying Cellular Differentiation by Physical Phenotype Using Digital Holographic Microscopy. Integrative Biology:Quantitative Biosciences From Nano To Macro. 2012;4(3):280-284.

[23] Reed JC. Mechanisms of Apoptosis. American Journal of Pathology. 2000;157(5) 1415-1430.

[24] Kroemer G, Galluzzi L, Vandenabeele P, Abrams J, Alnemri ES, Baehrecke EH, Blagosklonny MV, El-Deiry WS, Golstein P, Green DR, Hengartner M, Knight RA, Ku-

mar S, Lipton SA, Malorni W, Nunez G, Peter ME, Tschopp J, Yuan J, Piacentini M, Zhivotovsky B, Melino G. Classification of Cell Death: Recommendations of the Nomenclature Committee on Cell Death. Cell Death and Differentiation. 2009;16(1) 3-11.

[25] Martin SJ, Reutelingsperger CP, McGahon AJ, Rader JA, van Schie RC, LaFace DM, Green DR. Early Redistribution of Plasma Membrane Phosphatidylserine is a General Feature of Apoptosis Regardless of the Initiating Stimulus: Inhibition by Overexpression of Bcl-2 and Abl. Journal of Experimental Medicine. 1995;182(5) 1545-1556.

[26] Khmaladze A, Matz RL, Epstein T, Jasensky J, Banaszak Holl MM, Chen Z. Cell Volume Changes During Apoptosis monitored in Real Time Using Digital Holographic Microscopy. Journal of Structural Biology. 2012;178(3):270-278.

[27] Logg K, Bodvard K, Blomberg A, Käll, M. Investigations on Light-Induced Stress in Fluorescence Microscopy Using Nuclear Localization of the Transcriptionfactor Msn2p as a Reporter. Yeast Research. 2009;9(6) 875-884.

[28] Pan F, Liu S, Wang Z, Shang P, Xiao W. Digital Holographic Microscopy Long-Term and Real-Time Monitoring of Cell Division and Changes Under Simulated Zero Gravity. Optics Express. 2012;20(10) 11496-11505.

[29] Formigli L, Papucci L, Tani A, Schiavone N, Tempestini A, Orlandini GE, Capaccioli S, Orlandini SZ. Aponecrosis: Morphological and Biochemical Exploration of a Syncretic Process of Cell Death Sharing Apoptosis and Necrosis. Journal of Cellular Physiology. 2000;182(1) 41-49.

[30] Elmore S. Apoptosis: A Review of Programmed Cell Death. Toxicologic Pathology. 2007;35(4) 495-516.

[31] Humphreys DT, Wilson MR. Modes of L929 Cell Death Induced By TNF-Alpha and Other Cytotoxic Agents. Cytokine. 1999;11(10) 773-782.

Chapter 15

Phase and Polarization Contrast Methods by Use of Digital Holographic Microscopy: Applications to Different Types of Biological Samples

Francisco Palacios, Oneida Font, Guillermo Palacios,
Jorge Ricardo, Miriela Escobedo,
Ligia Ferreira Gomes, Isis Vasconcelos,
Mikiya Muramatsu, Diogo Soga, Aline Prado and
Valin José

Additional information is available at the end of the chapter

http://dx.doi.org/10.5772/54022

1. Introduction

The light that crosses a biological material can contains phase (refractive), amplitude (absorption) and optical activity (state of polarization) information about the material itself. Bright-field microscopy is an invaluable tool for observation of biological material, and microscopists utilize the intensity data either naturally present in the sample or introduced by staining. Differential staining is a complex process enabling certain structures to be distinguished from others, yet staining is not always appropriate for living cells, or for materials that do not absorb the stain. In these cases, phase contrast microscopy is necessary.

Several methods are available to render phase structure visible. Among the numerous modalities of contrast enhancing techniques that have been developed for non-invasive visualization of unstained transparent specimens, phase contrast (PhC), initially proposed by Zernike as a means of image contrast method (Zernike, 1942a,1942b) as well as Nomarski's differential interference contrast (DIC) (Nomarski, 1955), are available for high-resolution light microscopy (Pluta, 1988) and are widely used in biology. These two contrast techniques allow transforming phase information into amplitude or intensity modulation, which can be detected by photosensitive media. Unlike the PhC and DIC microscopy techniques, interferometric techniques present the great advantage of yielding quantitative measurements of parameters, including the phase distribution produced by transparent specimens.

Digital holography (DH) has several features that make it an interesting alternative to conventional microscopy. These features include an improved focal depth, possibility to generate 3D images and phase contrast images (Buraga-Lefebre et al., 2000; Seebacher et al., 2001; Xu et al., 2001). The technique of DH has been implemented in a configuration of an optical microscope (Schilling et al., 1997). The objective lens produces a magnified image of the object and the interference between this image and the reference beam is achieved by the integration of the microscope to one of the arms of a Mach–Zender interferometer. The interference pattern is recorded by a digital camera. This configuration is called Digital Holographic Microscopy (DHM).

DHM has been demonstrated in many applications as in observation of biological samples (Popescu et al., 2004; Palacios et al., 2005; Kim, 2010, Ricardo et al., 2011), living cells analysis (Carl, 2004; Kemper et al., 2006) and cell death detection (Pavillon et al., 2012) because most biological samples are phase objects. Emery (Emery et al., 2007) applied DHM to dynamic investigation of natural and stimulated morphological changes associated with chemical, electrical or thermal stimulation. Hu (Hu et al., 2011), performed a quantitative research with gastric cancer cells in different periods of cell division under marker-free condition in real-time. DHM technique also allows implementing processing methods to perform phase contrast imaging (Cuche et al., 1999), besides possessing unique advantages as non-destructive and non-invasive analysis.

DH with an off-axis configuration has also been applied for polarization imaging by using orthogonally polarized reference waves (Colomb et al., 2002; Colomb et al., 2004). The advantages of DH over the other polarimetries are its relatively simple optical system without any rotating optics and its adaptability to three dimensional objects due to numerical focusing (Nomura et al., 2007). Polarization microscopy can reveal inner structures of cells without the need of contrast agents, and it is possible to give access to intrinsic information about their morphology and dynamics through the phase change quantification in these microscopic structures. An associated technique which uses the phase information for studying the state of polarization of live neurons in culture was developed by (Wang et al., 2008). However, according to recent publications, the Holographic Microscopy for polarization imaging (Polarization Holographic Microscopy, PHM), has been poorly applied to biological specimens analysis but only to fiber optics (Colomb et al., 2005), polymers (Colomb et al., 2002) and other inorganic materials (Tishko et al., 2012). This demonstrates the need of studies using this method for new applications viewing the biomedical field. Besides, in general, the main goal in the applications of DHM, considering the polarization or not, have been to describe methods of calculations of the DHM technique itself. In this study we intend to enlarge the scope of the application considering the specificities that should be kept in mind for a correct application of the DHM technique to biological sample.

In this chapter, is demonstrated a comparative study between image contrast of different types of biological samples using traditional optical microscopy techniques (OM) and the holographic techniques, with polarization (PHM) and the classical one (DHM), showing the

http://dx.doi.org/10.5772/54022

advantages of the holographic methods in visualization and analysis of microscopic structures. Besides, the staining influence in quality of phase and intensity image reconstruction is discussed. An additional study of birefringence and dichroism of anisotropic samples is developed in this chapter, using also traditional methods compared with the holographic polarization technique, being this study of major importance for the inner structure and composition analysis of a variety of biological objects.

2. Experimental set-up and methodology

In this work comparisons between the results obtained with classical techniques of optical microscopy and digital holographic microscopy are shown. In figure 1, the experimental set-up used in this work integrates both techniques.

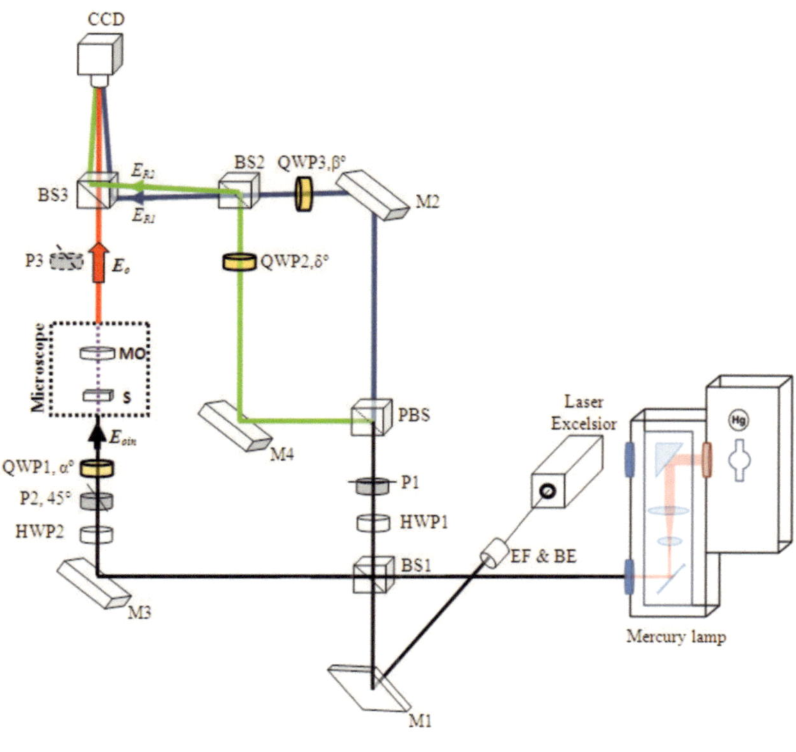

Figure 1. Experimental setup used in this work. In the next items are discussed the symbols.

The optical design allows the implementation of different classical techniques of optical microscopy and recording of single and polarization digital hologram. The same area of the sample is analyzed with classical techniques of optical microscopy using a mercury lamp as the light source. Single and polarization holograms are obtained with a solid state laser combined with an interferometric setup.

2.1. Classical techniques of optical microscopy

2.1.1. *Differential polarization microscopy*

Figure 2, shows optical setup for differential polarization microscopy (DPM).

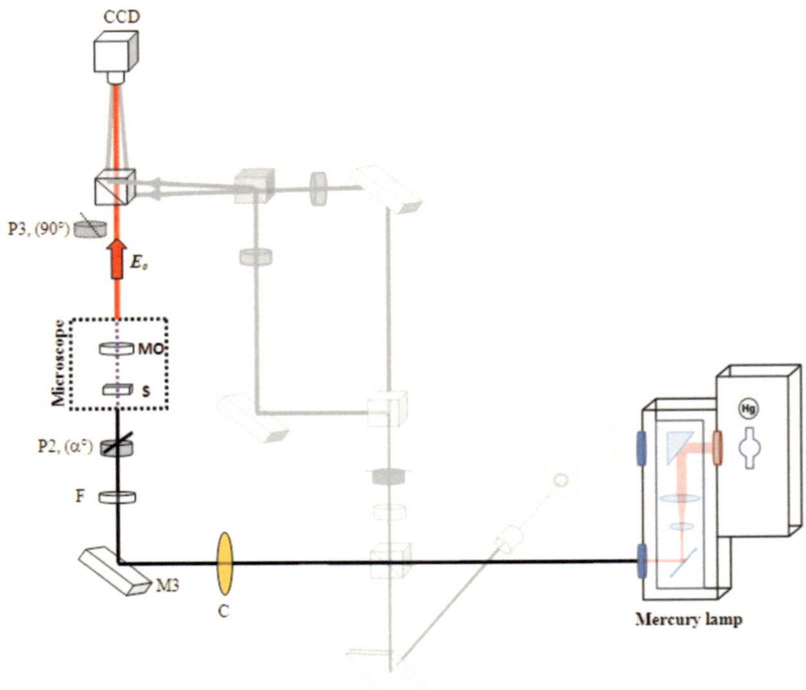

Figure 2. Differential Polarization Microscope. Light source is a mercury lamp, M3 is a mirror, C is the condenser system of the light beam, F is an interferential filter, P2 is a polarizer, S is the sample, MO is the objective lens and CCD is the digital capture device.

The dichroism images I_D can be reconstructed from the digital information. It is the quotient of the transmitted intensity difference by the sum of them,

$$I_D = \frac{I_{||} - I_{\perp}}{I_{||} + I_{\perp}} \tag{1}$$

$I_{||}$ is the intensity of the light beam polarized parallel to a reference direction α and $I_{\perp}$ is the intensity of the light beam polarized perpendicular to α.

To obtain information about orientation and and the average amount of aligned molecules, it is necessary to measure the ratio of the intensities transmitted with polarized perpendicular to α, given in Eq. (1). Two linear differential images are used to perform the numerical image construction dependent of the molecule orientation.

2.1.2. *Bright and polarization microscopy*

Using the experimental setup of figure 2 the bright-field image is capture as the intensity of the light beam that crosses throughout the sample without using any polarizing element in light pathway. For polarization microscopy the polarizer P3 is inserted in the light path with orthogonal polarization with respect to the polarizer P2.

2.2. Digital holographic microscopy techniques

The Digital Holographic Microscopy has two steps to obtain the reconstructed wavefield, the recording and reconstruction of the digital hologram.

2.2.1. *Recording of single digital hologram*

Figure 3 shows the experimental set-up used for recording a single digital hologram. It is a Digital Holographic Microscope designed for transmission imaging with transparent sample.

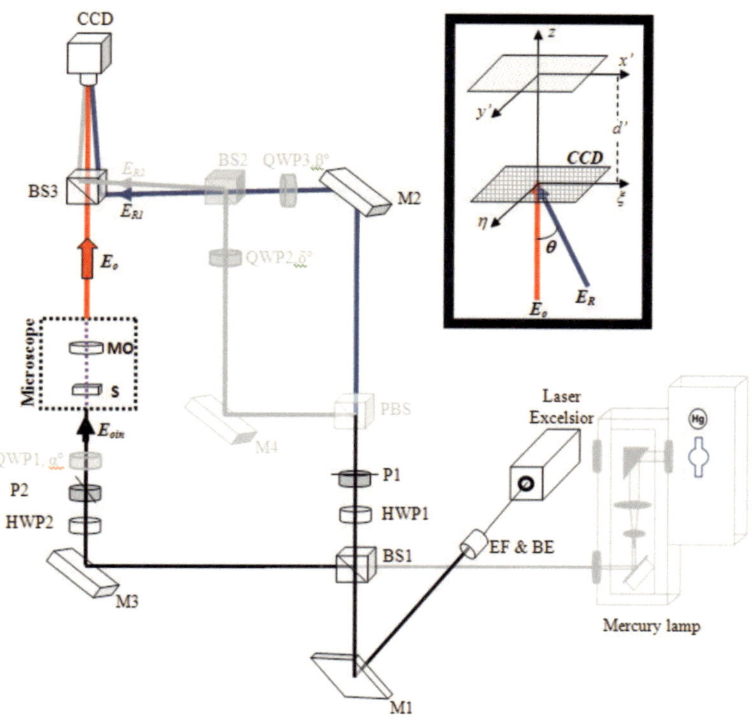

Figure 3. Experimental set-up: EF&BE, beam filter and expander; BS, beam splitter (the splitting ratio of BS1 and BS2 are 10/90 and 50/50 respectively); M, mirror; MO, microscope objective; S, sample; HWP, half wave plate; CCD, digital camera.

The basic architecture is that of a Mach-Zehnder interferometer. A linearly polarized solid state laser (Excelsior, λ=532 nm and 150 mW of power) is used as the light source. The expanded beam from the laser is divided by the beam splitter BS1 into reference and object beams. The microscope produces a magnified image of the object and the hologram plane is located between the microscope objective MO and the image plane $(x'-y')$ which is at a distance d' from the recording hologram plane $(\xi-\eta)$. In digital holographic microscopy we can consider the object wave emerging from the magnified image and not from the object itself (VanLigten & Osterberg, 1966).

With the combinations of the *HWP1, HWP2* and the polarizers *P1* and *P2* the intensities are adjusted in the reference arm and the object arm of the interferometer and the same polarization state is also guaranteed for both arms improving their interference. The specimen S is illuminated by a plane wave and a microscope objective, that produces a wave front called object wave E_o, collects the transmitted light. A condenser, not shown, is used to concentrate the light or focus the light in order that the entire beam passes into the MO, and in this case the wave front is spherical. At the exit of the interferometer the two beams are combined by beam splitter BS2 being formed at the CCD plane the interference pattern between the object wave E_o and the reference wave E_{R1}, which is recorded as the hologram of intensity $I_H(\xi,\eta)$,

$$I_H(\xi, \eta) = |E_o|^2 + |E_{R1}|^2 + E_{R1}^{*}E_o + E_{R1}E_o^{*} \tag{2}$$

where E_{R1}^{*} and E_o^{*} are the complex conjugates of the reference and object waves, respectively. The two first terms form the zero-order, the third and fourth terms are respectively the virtual (or conjugate image) and real image, which correspond to the interference terms. The off-axis geometry is considered; for this reason the mirror M2, which reflects the reference wave, is oriented so that the reference wave reaches the CCD camera with a small incidence angle with respect to the propagation direction of the object wave. A digital hologram is recorded by the CCD camera HDCE-10 with 1024x768 square pixels of size 4.65 μm, and transmitted to the computer by means of the IEEE 1394 interface. The digital hologram $I_H(j,l)$ is an array of $M \times N = 1024 \times 768$ 8-bit-encoded numbers that results from the two-dimensional sampling of $I_H(j,l)$ by the CCD camera,

$$I_H(j, l) = I_H(\xi, \eta) rect\left[\frac{\xi}{L_x}, \frac{\eta}{L_y}\right] \sum_{j=-M/2}^{M/2} \sum_{l=-N/2}^{N/2} \delta(\xi - j\Delta\xi, \eta - l\Delta\eta) \tag{3}$$

where j, l are integers defining the positions of the hologram pixels and $\Delta\xi = \Delta\eta = 4.65\ \mu m$ defines the sampling intervals in the hologram plane.

2.2.2. Recording of the polarization hologram

The experimental configuration for recording of polarization holograms is shown in figure 4. It is a Polarization Holographic Microscope (PHM) for the study of linear dichroism and birefringence of transparent samples.

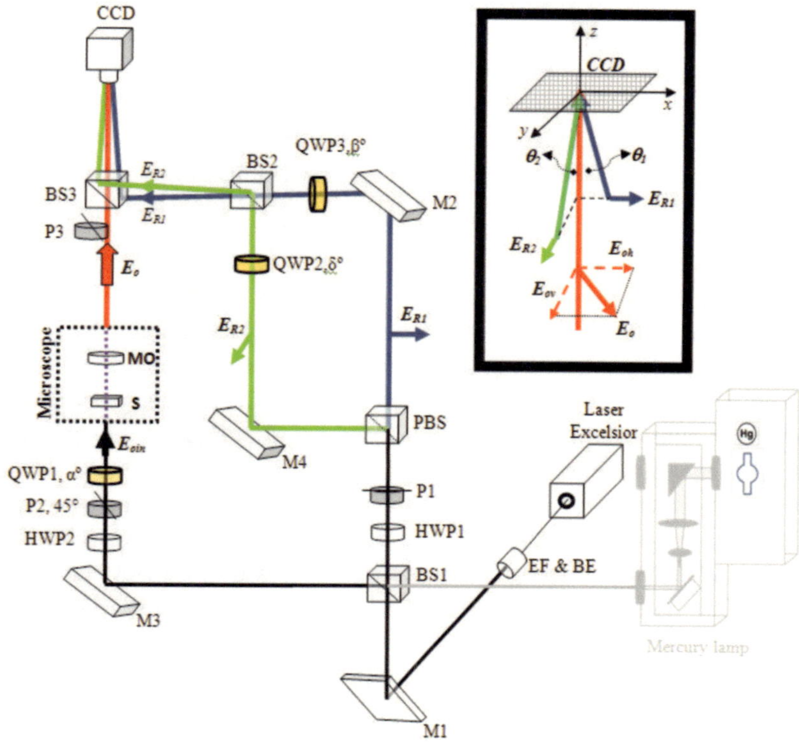

Figure 4. Schematic diagram of the Polarization Holographic Microscope for the study of linear dichroism and birefringence (symbology described in the text).

The experimental setup is composed by two *Mach-Zender* interferometers that form two reference beams E_{R1} and E_{R2}, with orthogonal polarization directions between each other, which interfere in the CCD camera with an object wave E_o in an off-axis geometry. As a light source a solid state laser with wavelenght of 532 nm and 150 mW of power is used. For samples that have some type of anisotropy, the state of polarization of the electric field E_o is different of the state of polarization of the incident electric field E_{oin}. The formation of the two reference waves in an architecture of a *Mach-Zender* interferometer ensures that these beams have the same optical path, becoming this an experimental novelty with respect to schemes reported in the literature. The polarized beam splitter (*PBS*) generates two beams with orthogonal states of polarization as reference waves; this orthogonality avoids any interference among then.

For studies of linear dichroism and birefringence, the polarizer *P2* imposes a 45° of polarization, with respect to reference wave polarization, to the E_{oin} wavefront that illuminates the object *S*. To maintain the linear polarization of the references waves E_{R1} and E_{R2} and incident electric field E_{oin} the fast axis of the quarter wave plates (QWP1, QWP2 and QWP3) are aligned parallel (α=β=δ=0°) with respect to the polarization states of the respective waves. For studies of circular dichroism and birefringence, over the sample, a circularly polarized light is incident. The polarization of the wave which illuminates the sample *S* is controlled by the quarter-wave plate *QWP1*, according to the waveplate's fast axis angle α relative to the polarizer transmission axis $P2$: right-handed circular polarization (α = -45º), left-handed circular polarization (α = +45º). The two reference waves with orthogonal polarization are transmitted by the quarter-wave plates $QWP2$ and $QWP2$ with their fast axis forming angles of -45 ° and +45° with respect to the polarization states of the reference beams E_{R1} and E_{R2}. This configuration transforms the linear polarization of the reference waves E_{R1} and E_{R2} in right and left circular polarization, respectively. The two reference waves are directed by the beam splitter $BS3$ to the CCD surface.

The light transmitted by the object is magnified by the microscopy objective MO producing an object wave E_o with orthogonal components E_{oh} and E_{ov} (detail in figure 4). The state of polarization of the object wave is different from that which illuminates the specimen E_{oin} and results in dichroism and birefringence properties of the specimen integrated along the propagation direction. The interference between the reference and object waves produces the polarization hologram. The hologram is recorded in an off-axis geometry with the three waves propagating along different directions. As shown in detail in figure 4, the object wave E_o has a normal incidence (along Oz) on the Oxy plane of the CCD. The reference waves E_{R1} and E_{R2} propagate symmetrically with respect to the plane Oxz with similar incidence angles θ_1 and θ_2, respectively. The angles of incidence θ_1 and θ_2 of the reference waves are controlled by the mirrors $M2$ and $M4$; these mirrors are dielectric mirrors that do not change the state of polarization during the reference beams reflections. With the rotation of the two half wave plates $HWP1$, $HWP2$ the reference wave intensities E_{R1}, E_{R2} and object wave E_o can be controlled.

With the polarization hologram reconstruction the polarization state of the wave object E_o can be calculated and thus represent the quantitative images of linear dichroism and birefringence. Capturing two polarization holograms, one with right circularly polarized light and the other with left circularly polarized light and then, reconstructing the polarization state of the beam emerging from the sample, the image of circular dichroism can be obtained comparing changes in the polarization state produced by variations when the circularly polarized light is rotated.

2.2.3. *Formal description of polarization hologram formation*

The intensity distribution of the hologram is described by the interference between E_o, E_{R1} and E_{R2}. As E_{R1} and E_{R2} have orthogonal polarization they do not interfere ($E_{R1}E^*_{R2} = E^*_{R1}E_{R2} = 0$). From the Jones formalism, the object wave E_o can be defined by the superposition of two fields E_{oh} and E_{ov} which have the same frequency and the same wave vector $\mathbf{k}_o$ along z, but with orthogonal vibration planes:

$$E_O = \begin{pmatrix} E_{oh} \\ E_{ov} \\ 0 \end{pmatrix} \exp\left[i\left(k_O\hat{l} + \phi_O - \omega t\right)\right] = \begin{pmatrix} |E_O|\exp\left[i\phi_O\right] \\ |E_O|\exp\left[i\phi_O + \Delta\varphi_O\right] \\ 0 \end{pmatrix} \exp\left[i\left(k_O\hat{l} - \omega t\right)\right] \quad (4)$$

where $\hat{l} = (\xi,\eta)$ is a position vector in the plane of the CCD, ϕ_o is the optical phase delay introduced by the specimen and experimented by the horizontally polarized wave and $\Delta\phi_o$ is the phase difference.

Similarly, the reference waves can be described by the relations,

$$E_{R1} = \begin{pmatrix} E_{R1} \\ 0 \\ 0 \end{pmatrix} \exp\left[i\left(k_1 \hat{l} - \omega t\right)\right]. \tag{5}$$

$$E_{R2} = \begin{pmatrix} 0 \\ E_{R2} \\ 0 \end{pmatrix} \exp\left[i\left(k_2 \hat{l} - \omega t\right)\right] \tag{6}$$

where k_o, k_1 and k_2 are the wave vectors:

$$k_o = \frac{2\pi}{\lambda}\begin{pmatrix} 0 \\ 0 \\ 1 \end{pmatrix}, k_1 = \frac{2\pi}{\lambda}\begin{pmatrix} 0 \\ sen\left(\theta_1\right) \\ \cos\left(\theta_1\right) \end{pmatrix}, k_o = \frac{2\pi}{\lambda}\begin{pmatrix} -sen\left(\theta_2\right) \\ 0 \\ \cos\left(\theta_2\right) \end{pmatrix} \tag{7}$$

On the interferometer exit, the interference between E_o, E_{R1} and E_{R2} creates the intensity distribution of the digital hologram, expressed by the equation,

$$\begin{aligned} I_H\left(\xi,\eta\right) &= \left(E_{R1} + E_{R2} + E_o\right)\left(E_{R1} + E_{R2} + E_o\right)^* \\ &= \left|E_{R1}\right|^2 + \left|E_{R2}\right|^2 + \left|E_o\right|^2 + E_{R1}\,E_o^* + E_{R2}\,E_o^* + E_{R1}^*\,E_o + E_{R2}^*\,E_o \end{aligned} \tag{8}$$

The first three terms in Eq. (8) form the zero order diffraction, the fourth and fifth terms produce two real images, corresponding to the horizontal and vertical component of the Jones vector. The last two terms produce the virtual images.

2.2.4. Polarization hologram reconstruction

The numerical reconstruction is realized with the D*ouble* P*ropagation* A*lgorithm* (Palacios et al., 2011). The intensity distribution $\psi(x',y',d')$ on the reconstruction plane (x',y') is obtained from the expression,

$$\psi\left(x',y',d'\right) = \Im^{-1}\left\{G\cdot\Im\left\{I^f\left(\xi,\eta\right)\exp\left[\frac{i\pi}{\lambda D}\left(\xi^2+\eta^2\right)\right]\right\}\exp\left(i d'\sqrt{k^2+k_u^2+k_v^2}\right)\right\} \tag{9}$$

Where $G = A\,exp[i\pi/\lambda D(u^2+v^2)]$ denotes a constant phase factor, d' is the reconstruction distance, D is the distance among the CCD plane and the back focal plane of the objective lens, $\Im^{-1}$ is the inverse Fourier Transform, $k=2\pi/\lambda$, k_u and k_v are the spatial frequencies corresponding respectively to u and v and $I^f(\xi, \eta)$ is the filtered hologram that contains only components of the real image.

Applying two spatial filters on the polarization hologram spectrum, the spatial frequencies components of the real image are selected separately. Calculating the inverse Fourier Transform of the spatial frequency components selected the two filtered and complex holograms, $H_h^f(\xi, \eta) = E_{R1}E_o^*$ and $H_v^f(\xi, \eta) = E_{R2}E_o^*$, can be obtained, corresponding respectively to the horizontal and vertical components of the Jones vector. Applying the numerical method of reconstruction to the holograms H_h^f and H_v^f the complex amplitudes distribution $\psi_h(x', y')$ and $\psi_v(x', y')$ in the reconstructed plane are obtained,

$$\begin{aligned}\psi_h(x',y',d') &= \Im^{-1}\left\langle G\cdot\Im\left\{H_h^f(\xi,\eta)\exp\left[\frac{i\pi}{\lambda D}\left(\xi^2+\eta^2\right)\right]\right\}\exp\left(id'\sqrt{k^2+k_u^2+k_v^2}\right)\right\rangle \\ \psi_v(x',y',d') &= \Im^{-1}\left\langle G\cdot\Im\left\{H_v^f(\xi,\eta)\exp\left[\frac{i\pi}{\lambda D}\left(\xi^2+\eta^2\right)\right]\right\}\exp\left(id'\sqrt{k^2+k_u^2+k_v^2}\right)\right\rangle\end{aligned} \tag{10}$$

The fields $\psi_h(x', y')$ and $\psi_v(x', y')$ correspond to the orthogonal components of the object wave E_{oh} and E_{ov} respectively, therefore they can be represented as follows,

$$\psi_h(x',y') = \begin{pmatrix} I_{R1}(x',y')I_{oh}(x',y')\exp\left(i\left[\phi_h(x',y') - \phi_{R1}(x',y')\right]\right) \\ 0 \end{pmatrix} \tag{11}$$

and

$$\psi_v(x',y') = \begin{pmatrix} 0 \\ I_{R2}(x',y')I_{ov}(x',y')\exp\left(i\left[\phi_v(x',y') - \phi_{R2}(x',y')\right]\right) \end{pmatrix} \tag{12}$$

where I_{R1} and I_{R2} are the intensities of the reference waves; I_{ov} and I_{oh} are the intensities of the orthogonal components of the object beam E_o.

2.2.5. Determination of the parameters that characterizes the state of polarization

Making the intensities of the reference waves equal, $I_{R1}(x', y')=I_{R2}(x', y')$, (this is achieved adjusting the half-wave plates *HWP1*, *HWP2*, figure 4), the amplitude ratio β is calculated as,

$$\beta = \tan\left[\varepsilon(x',y')\right] = \frac{I_{oh}(x',y')}{I_{ov}(x',y')} = \frac{\left|\psi_h(x',y')\right|}{\left|\psi_v(x',y')\right|} \tag{13}$$

Moreover, the phase difference $\Delta\phi\ (x',y')$ between the orthogonal components of the object beam is calculated by,

$$\Delta\phi(x',y') = \phi_h - \phi_v + \Delta\phi_R \tag{14}$$

where $\Delta\phi_R$ is the phase difference on the reference waves used to capture the hologram. Experimentally, this term is time dependent because of vibration and air flow, but this can be suppressed in the phase contrast image by a compensated phase difference $-\Delta\phi_R$. To adjust this phase displacement, is used an image area with known polarization. For that purpose, is inserted in the object beam a polarizer (*P3* in figure 4) oriented in such a way that produces a phase difference of 0 rad in the object beam area.

The corrected value of the phase difference $\Delta\phi_C(x',y')$ is obtained from,

$$\begin{aligned}\Delta\phi_C(x',y') &= \Delta\phi(x',y') + \Delta\phi_R(x',y') = \phi_h(x',y') - \phi_v(x',y') \\ &= \arg\left[\psi_h(x',y')\right] - \arg\left[\psi_v(x',y')\right]\end{aligned} \tag{15}$$

If the parameters "**β**" and "$\Delta\phi$" are experimentally measured, then the modification of the polarization state of the wave transmitted through the specimen is correlated to its structure, composition and optical properties. There are two physical phenomena that can change the polarization state: the **dichroism** and the **birefringence**.

a. **Dichroism**: Several crystalline materials absorb more light at an incident plane of polarization than at another plane, thus as the light travels through the material, its polarization state changes. This absorption anisotropy is called dichroism. The evaluation of the linear dichroism property of a specimen can be made by calculating the ratio of amplitudes of the orthogonal components of the light passing through the specimen.

b. **Birefringence**: Birefringence is a property of materials with refractive index anisotropy. After the polarized light crosses a birefringent sample, there is a relative phase change on the two field components and the beam resulted from the interference of the two wave fields is generally elliptically polarized, i.e. this property can be described through the phase difference in the orthogonal components of light crossing the specimen.

3. Verification of the experimental setup

3.1. Obtainment of the phase contrast image

The verification of the experimental setup of DHM was obtained by processing holograms of an object with well-known parameters. The calibration of the DHM setup in XY dimensions was performed by using USA Airforce standard (USAF 1951). The vertical calibration along Z-axis is intrinsically linked to the phase measurements. Overall performance of DHM was checked using polystyrene beads with refractive index $n_o = 1.59$. Diluted beads suspension in water was put onto a microscopic slide and dried. A drop of glycerol-based mounting media with refractive index of 1.46 was layered up and the slide covered with a glass coverslip. Results of DHM are shown in figure 5.

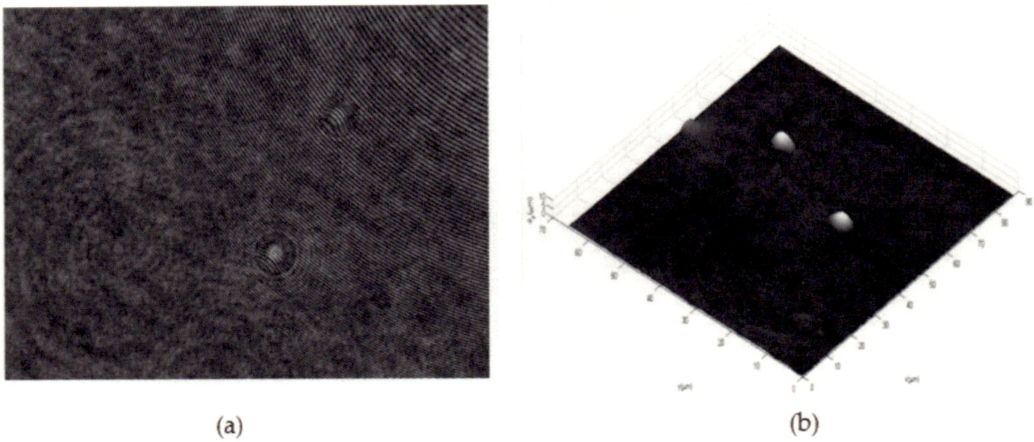

Figure 5. (a) Digital hologram of polystyrene spheres. (b) Phase contrast image reconstruction

The calculated averaged XYZ bead diameter of 6.42 μm is very close to the manufacturer data.

3.2. Measurement of the polarization states

For obtaining the polarization states is used as sample a $\lambda/4$ plate to generate a variety of polarization states of the object wave, see figure 6. The object was placed at a distance of 170 mm from the surface of the CCD. The wave incident on the object is linearly polarized with the polarizer *P2* with an orientation of 45° with respect to the horizontal axis. The polarization state of the light wave transmitted by the $\lambda/4$ plate was analyzed for several orientations α (angle between the fast axis of the quarter-wave plate and transmission axis of the polarizer *P2*) between 0° and 90 ° with a 3° shifts.

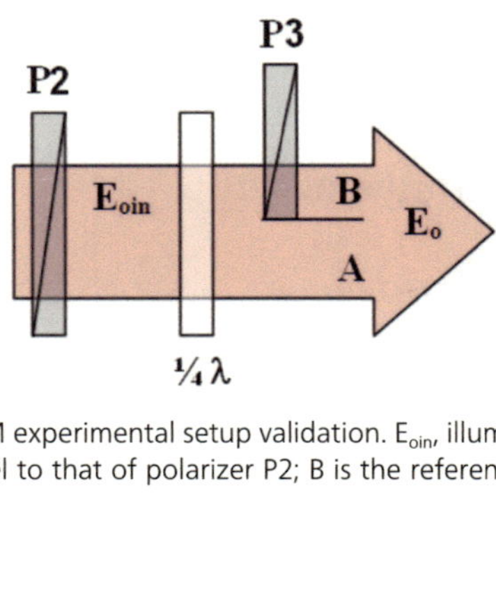

Figure 6. Object arm diagram for PHM experimental setup validation. E_{oin}, illuminating wave; E_o, object wave; polarizer P3 has the transmission axis parallel to that of polarizer P2; B is the reference area, where the phase difference is zero, and A is the area for analysis.

The polarizer *P3* oriented at an angle δ = 45° is used as reference area for determining phase difference of compensation. The area *B* is the reference where the phase difference is zero and *A* is the area for analysis. The calculated mean value in the area *B* is used as compensation value $\Delta\phi_R$.

Figure 7a shows the polarization digital hologram of the λ/4 plate with $\alpha = 0^{\circ}$. In figure 7b and 7c is shown, respectively, the reconstruction of the amplitude ratio and phase difference images. The orientation of the polarizer *P3* is δ = 45º. The area *B* in figure 7b shows the reference area determined by the polarizer *P3* in figure 6 and area *A* shows the area of the examined plate.

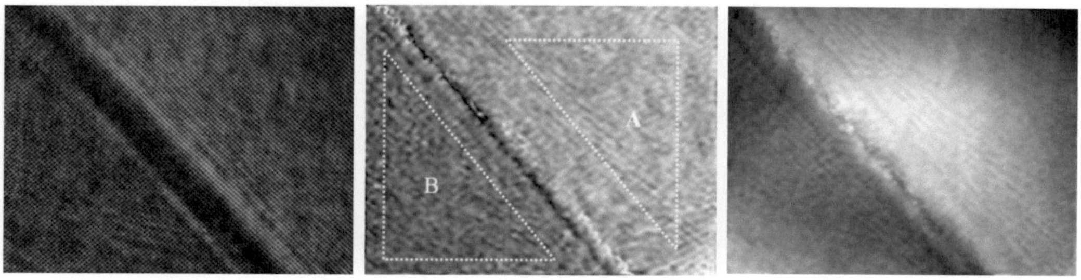

(a) (b) (c)

Figure 7. (a) Polarization hologram. Calculated (b) amplitude ratio, β and (c) phase difference $\Delta\phi_C$ for the quarter wave plate (¼λ in figure 6) with the orientation of $\alpha = 0^{\circ}$ respect to the polarizer transmission axis *P2* in figure 6. Area A is for analysis (¼λ) and area B is for the reference (P3 in figure 6).

Figure 8a and 8b show, respectively, the amplitude ratio β and the corrected phase difference $\Delta\phi_C$. The mean value obtained in area *A* is used as the representative experimental value on the graphic (filled circles).

Using the expressions $\gamma = \frac{1}{2}\,atan[\tan(2atan(\beta))\cos(\Delta\phi)]$ and $\omega = \frac{1}{2}\,asin[\sin(2atan(\beta))\sin(\Delta\phi)]$ there were determined the azimuth γ values, figure 8c, and the deformation of the ellipse ω, figure 8d. The theoretical values calculation for β, $\Delta\phi_c$, γ and ω (continuous curve) were obtained by the following reasoning: the polarization state of the object beam $\psi_T(x,y)$ which emerges from the λ/4 plate is theoretically calculated by the product of the ¼λ plate Jones matrix and the Jones vector of the incident wave linearly polarized with an orientation of 45°,

$$\psi_T(x,y) = \begin{pmatrix} \psi_{Th}(x,y) \\ \psi_{Tv}(x,y) \end{pmatrix} = \begin{pmatrix} \cos\alpha & -sen\,\alpha \\ sen\,\alpha & \cos\alpha \end{pmatrix} \begin{bmatrix} \exp(i\Delta) & 0 \\ 0 & \exp(-i\Delta) \end{bmatrix} \times \begin{pmatrix} \cos\alpha & sen\,\alpha \\ -sen\,\alpha & \cos\alpha \end{pmatrix} \begin{pmatrix} 1 \\ 1 \end{pmatrix} \tag{16}$$

where Δ=π/4 is the phase difference between the orthogonal components of the wave emerging from the ¼λ plate. The theoretical values of the ratio of amplitudes β and the phase differences

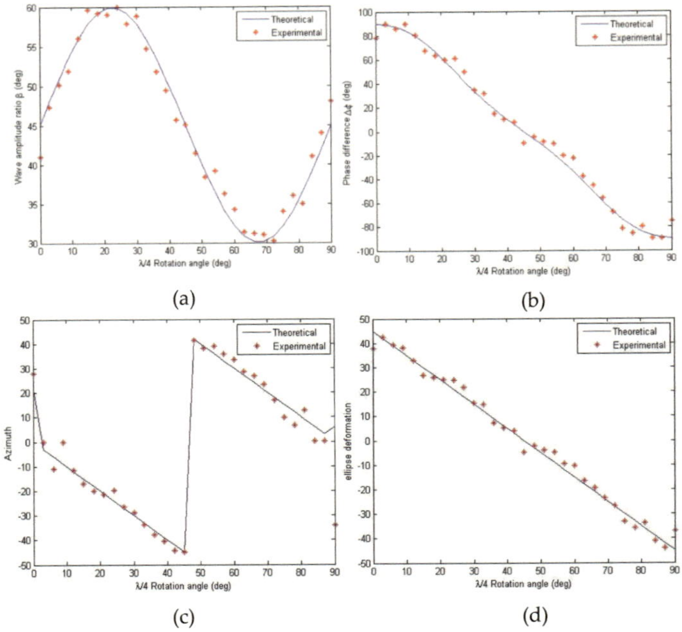

Figure 8. Filled circles) experimental values of (a) amplitude ratio, (b) phase difference (c) azimuth and (d) ellipse deformation of the wave transmitted by the λ/4 plate. (Continuous curve) theoretical values.

$\Delta\phi_C$ were calculated directly by substituting Eq. (16) into Eq. (13) and Eq. (15) respectively. From figure 8, it can be noted that the experimental values are in good agreement with the theoretical values; this ensures the implementation of the designed setup to study objects with distinctive optical activity.

4. Phase contrast method

In this section are presented the results of Digital Holographic Microscopy (DHM) applied to the analysis of different types of biological samples. The advantages of DHM upon bright-field optical microscopy (OM) in visualization and analysis of microscopic structures are illustrated and discussed.

The DHM adds information to the conventional microscopic morphology of isolated cells, obtained either from clinical and research specimens or from cell cultures. Fixative substances and stains were not required, nor essential. Nevertheless, stains were very convenient tools and added some information when conventional morphology and MHD images were considered not equivalent. In general, stained slides analysis succeeded well for three-dimensional image reconstruction of known samples, even if the main Cytology and Histology stains are intended to discriminate structures only through light intensity modification, while light phase effects are not valued or are even minimized by the technical protocols. Then, except for some

http://dx.doi.org/10.5772/54022

particular samples, stains were not of help in increasing the quality of the reconstructed phase images, and staining artifacts were not considered relevant to quantitative phase analysis. Blood smears or body fluid cells prepared by cytocentrifugation or sedimentation techniques were air dryed before being dehydrated with methanol for fixation and stained with Hematological stains (Leishmann, Rosenfeld) with good results. Papanicolaou and Hematoxylin-Eosin (HE) staining procedures were also assayed. As for any microscopic technique, correct fixation and staining procedures were relevant to assure good quality morphology, the technical quality stringency being essentially equivalent for bright field analysis and for MHD. Fixative preserved samples, unstained or only slightly stained consistently gave superior results for phase image reconstruction by the MHD technique than the brilliant and deeply stained samples. Unpreserved and labile fresh specimens stained or not could also be observed. Mounting media changes could evince or veil sample morphology, then mounting media composition and physical properties was carefully considered when phase contrast images were obtained from samples prepared with glycerol, resins or Permount.

The reconstructed topographic profile was determined by the actual expected specimen dimensions, but was also modified by the intrinsic composition of each structure, as can be easily realized in comparing the MHD image of macrophage and lymphocytes in the figure 9. The phase images reconstruction of the cells of rat peritoneal fluid (figure 9) was obtained after an isosmotic PBS wash procedure in a normal and otherwise unmanipulated adult animal. The resulting cell suspension was cytocentrifuged over a glass slide, fixed with methanol and stained with Rosenfeld stain (Eosin/Methylene Blue/Methylene Azures). No mounting media was employed.

(a)

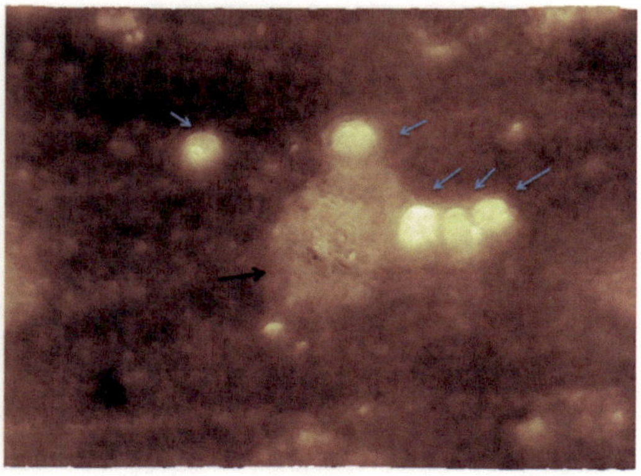
(b)

Figure 9. Rat peritoneal fluid cells obtained after phosphate buffered saline (PBS) flux of the peritoneal cavity, Rosenfeld stain. Slide provided by the researcher Dalila Cunha de Oliveira, from the archives of her graduate student Master Thesis tutored by Dr. Ricardo Ambrosio Foch, (FCF-USP Ethical Committee Protocol number 316/2011). Phase image reconstructions with DHM. Magnification (A) 10x objective, (B) 40x objective.

When low magnification was used, the discrimination of the contours of the distinct cells in the reconstructed image presented some difficulties, as seen in the figure 9-A. Peritoneal fluid lipoproteins and other methanol insoluble molecules produced some background depth fluctuation in the phase reconstructed image. Observed in a greater magnification, as in figure 9-B, the different cells were more clearly defined, showing color intensities proportional to their relative contributions of the refractive index magnitudes and the thickness of the sample structural components. In figure 9-B lymphocytes are presented with light arrows and the monocyte/macrophage with dark arrow. The peculiarities about the topography of the monocyte/macrophage and lymphocyte cells well express how their structural differences, besides their expected dimensions, contribute to the reconstruted image. The dense chromatin and the protein rich cytoplasm of the lymphocytes contributed to produce a bright yellow color, while the lose chromatin and the foamy microvacuolated cytoplasm of the macrophages produced darker orange-brown color.

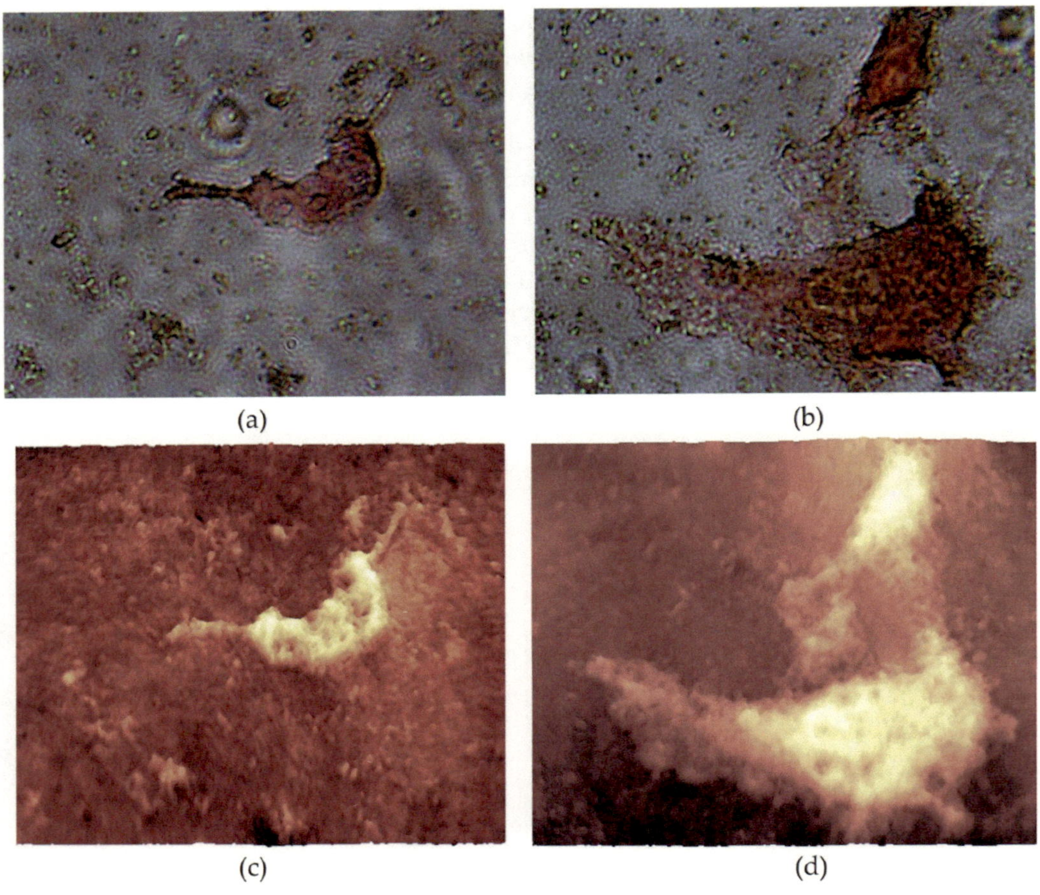

Figure 10. Fibroblast cells of FN1 cell line kindly furnished by Dr. Durvanei Augusto Maria were cultivated by Dr. Sonia E. Will over round coverslides and stained with Picrosirius Red for collagen. (A, B) Optical microscopy images. (C, D) Phase contrast images reconstructed with DHM. Magnification 10x objective.

Syrius Red staining for collagen fibers was used to evaluate MHR performance in the study of extracellular matrix structures and fibroblast physiology. Figure 10A and 10B show the optical microscopy images. Figure 10C and 10D show the phase contrast images of fibroblast

http://dx.doi.org/10.5772/54022

cells stained with the picrosyrius technique (Junqueira et al., 1979). Phase contrast image reconstructed with DHM and bright-filed image under mercury lamp illumination was obtained from the same area of the sample, both are shown for comparison.

As shown in figures 10-C and 10-D the cells structures and the fibers produced by them are better differentiated by means of difference in phase values of each one.

Digital Holographic Microscopy showed suitable for unstained tissue observation. Even unstained sections of paraffin embedded tissues could reveal more details about topography and composition of the samples than did bright field optical microscopy. Archive samples were not destroyed through the observation by the technique and the sample could be subsequently prepared for special molecular biology based on immunological staining procedures, when convenient.

Figure 11 shows an example of this kind of material, from the personal archive of Dr. Bruno Gomes Vasconcelos, in which the structural information on the gustative epithelia could be observed in the paraffin embedded section of the tongue tissue sample, figure 11A-B. On the other hand, fresh and unfixed tissue samples could also be studied. Microcirculation of the chorioallantoic membrane of the chicken embryo (CAM) furnished an example about the possibilities of analysis of capillary mesh structure, applicable to the study of the microcirculation of tissues, figure 11C-D.

Sample	Optical Microscopy	Holographic Microscopy
Histological section of *Cavia porcellus* tongue, Fixation in formaldehyde 10%, embedding in paraffin, cut of 5 μm, stained with HE, magnification of 10x.	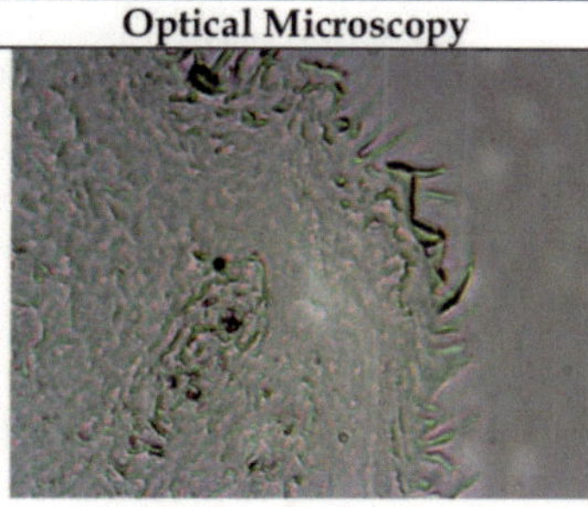 A	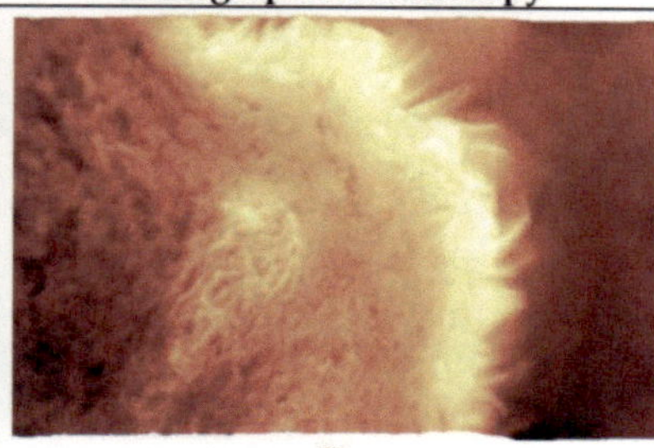 B
Chicken embryo chorioallantoic membrane. Magnification of 10x	 C	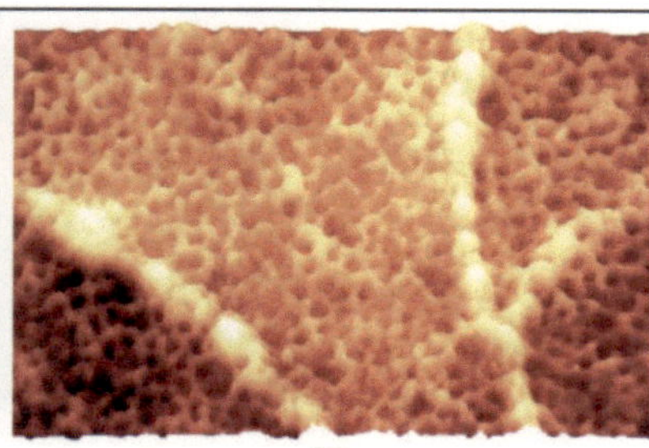 D

Figure 11. (A,B) Histological section of *Cavia porcellus* tongue, Fixation in formaldehyde 10%, embedding in paraffin, cut of 5 μm, stained with HE, magnification of 10x. (C,D) Chicken embryo chorioallantoic membrane distended over glass slides and analysed previously to fixative procedures showing good preservation of the capillary mesh. (FCF-USP Ethical committee protocol no. 274/2010).

White eggs of *Gallus domesticus*, (Granja Hyline) were incubated for 10days in an automatic incubator thermostated (Zagas) at 37.2 º C, relative humidity 50%, with periodical turns at two hour intervals. CAM sampling was carried during the 10th day of incubation, after the eggs were placed for at least 30 min at 4°C before being opened. The shells were cut in the air chamber and the CAM was collected and distended over glass slides for vasculature analysis as previously described (Will et al, 2011). Samples of chorioallantoic membrane could be analyzed previously to fixative procedures showing good preservation of the capillary mesh. (Ethical committee protocol no. 274/2010).

The biochemical composition of the main analyzed structures, the red color of hemoglobin and the fiber rich vasculature ease the direct observation of the unstained specimens. The phase contrast images, reconstructed by DHM, provide an accurate visualization of three-dimensional structures of the sample, in addition provide a quantitative assessment of the refractive index and thickness of the sample that ensure the indirect calculation of specimen intrinsic parameters.

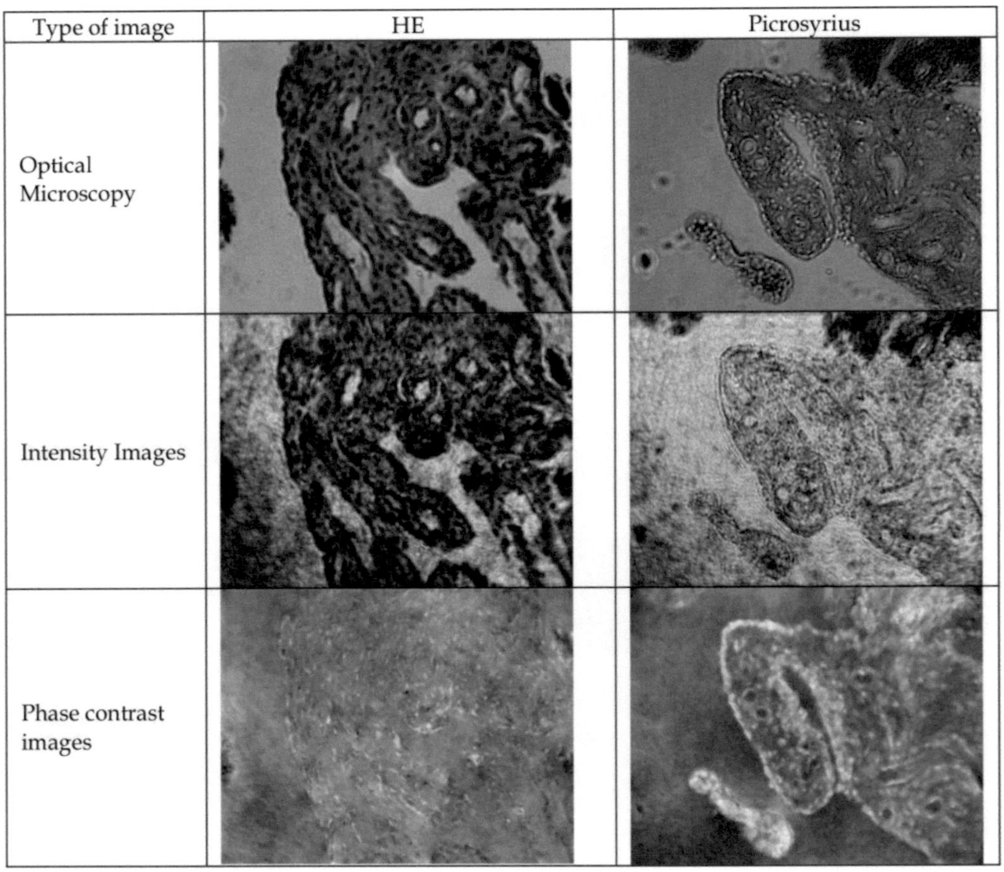

Figure 12. Glass slides with equine dissecating osteochondritis (OCD) synovial membrane material. HE and Picrosyrius stainings, 10x objective. Permount mount. Clinical samples kindly furnished by Aline Ambrogi Franco Prado (FMVZ-USP Ethical Commitee protocol no. 2771/2012)

4.1. Influence of staining and mounting procedures

The effect of sample preparation on the quality of phase and intensity image reconstructions is presented in figure 12. The results of Synovial Membrane samples were obtained using two different staining sorts. The images obtained with optical microscopy display high contrast with the two staining sorts, although the staining influences the contrast quality in the two types of images observed with DHM. Thus, in the case of HE stain it intensifies the contrast of the intensity reconstructed image and decreases it in the phase contrast image. An opposite effect is observed when the Picrosyrius stain is used. This effect was ascribed to the Permount mounting associated to the optimal intensity contrast enhancing staining procedure obtained with HE technique, which relies on the base of its universal and general preference use for routine histological samples. The Picrosirius stain sets for collagen fibers demonstration, and collagen demonstrated to produce good phase image reconstructs, superimposed to Picrosirius stained regions as could be demonstrated below.

5. Polarization contrast method

An orderly material can be selectively detected in the presence of random absorbent. Thus, orderly structures can be detected and quantified and their orientation can be stated in complex objects. The selectivity depends on the polarization direct relation with the chromophores extinction coefficient.

5.1. Visualization of linear dichroism in *Calcium Oxalate*

Figure 13 shows the visualization of linear dichroism in *Calcium Oxalate* sample extracted from *Sansevieria trifasciata* sap.

From figure 13, is possible to compare the results of the dichroism image reconstruction obtained with DPM and PHM. Difference in the intensity images obtained with specific polarization states of the object beam for each technique is possible to notice. The holographic images show a higher contrast for the calcium oxalate samples when compared with those obtained by the traditional method. The dichroism image obtained by the Differential Microscopy, is represented by a color bar distributed between blue and red shades, being the red shades referring to negative dichroism and the blue referring to positive dichroism. Differently, the dichroism image obtained with the holographic method is shown in gray scale, where the lighter shades correspond to positive dichroism values and the dark shades represent negative dichroism values. When these two images are compared is possible to see a correspondence among these images.

5.2. Cell death through dye induced optical activity

Figure 14-A presents optical microscope image of an endothelial cell sample where the presence of undesirable objects (such as air bubbles or particulate material) do not guarantee

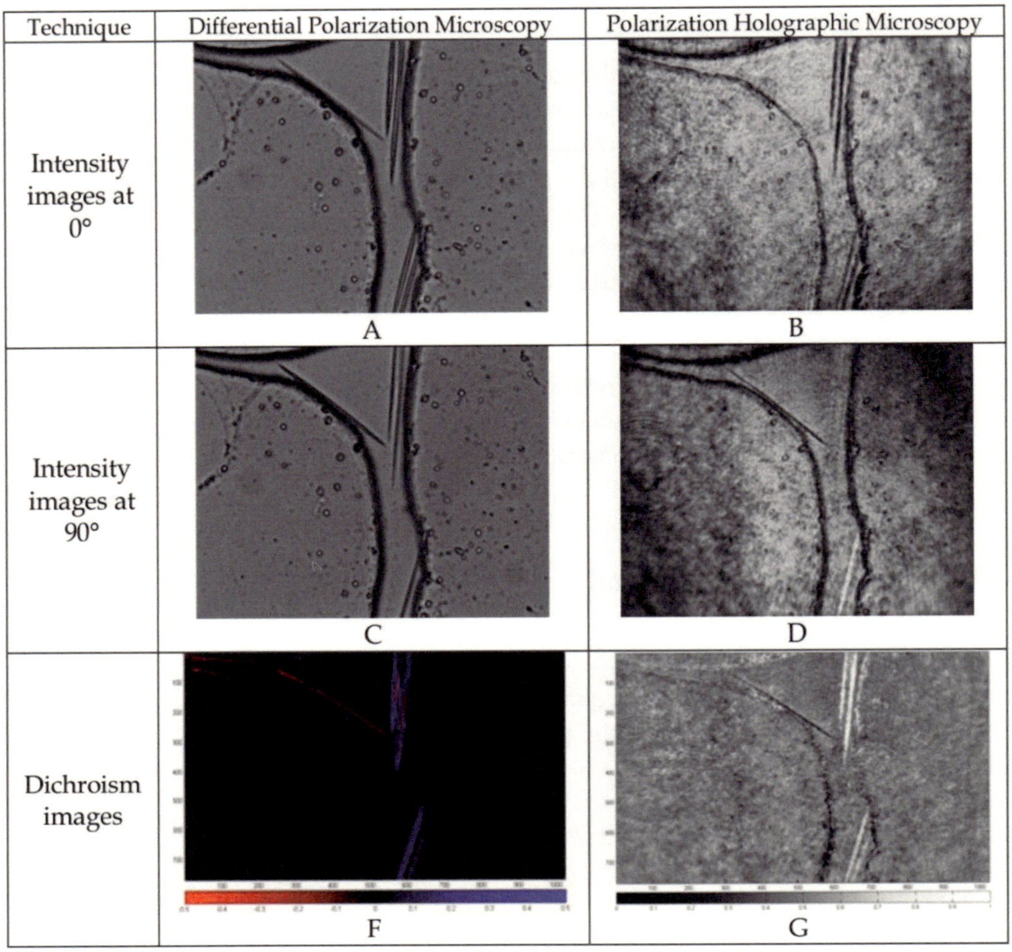

Figure 13. Visualization of linear dichroism in *Calcium Oxalate* sample extracted from *Sansevieria trifasciata* sap. (A,C) Intensity images obtained with polarizer (*P2* in figure 4) oriented at 0° and 90° with the Differential Polarization Microscopy. (B,D) reconstructed intensity image with the Polarization Holographic Microscopy. (F,G) dichroism image reconstruction obtained with Eq. (1) and Eq. (13) respectivelly.

a good visualization of the cells. The phase contrast image (Figure 14-B) obtained with holographic microscopy, still retains the undesirable objects reconstruction.

When the Polarization Holographic Microscopy is used, the possibility of staining (*Picrosirius Red for collagen fibers*) to introduce optical activity in the sample allows a more differentiated study of the cells. Reconstructing the Polarization Digital Hologram, Fig. 14-C, are reconstructed the molecular alignment structure generating birefringence or dichroism, without showing other types of structures, Figure 14-D. Some of these are not displayed in the optical microscopy image. Besides improving the internal structure organization of cell visualization, the Polarization Holographic Microscopy allows observing the molecular alignment within

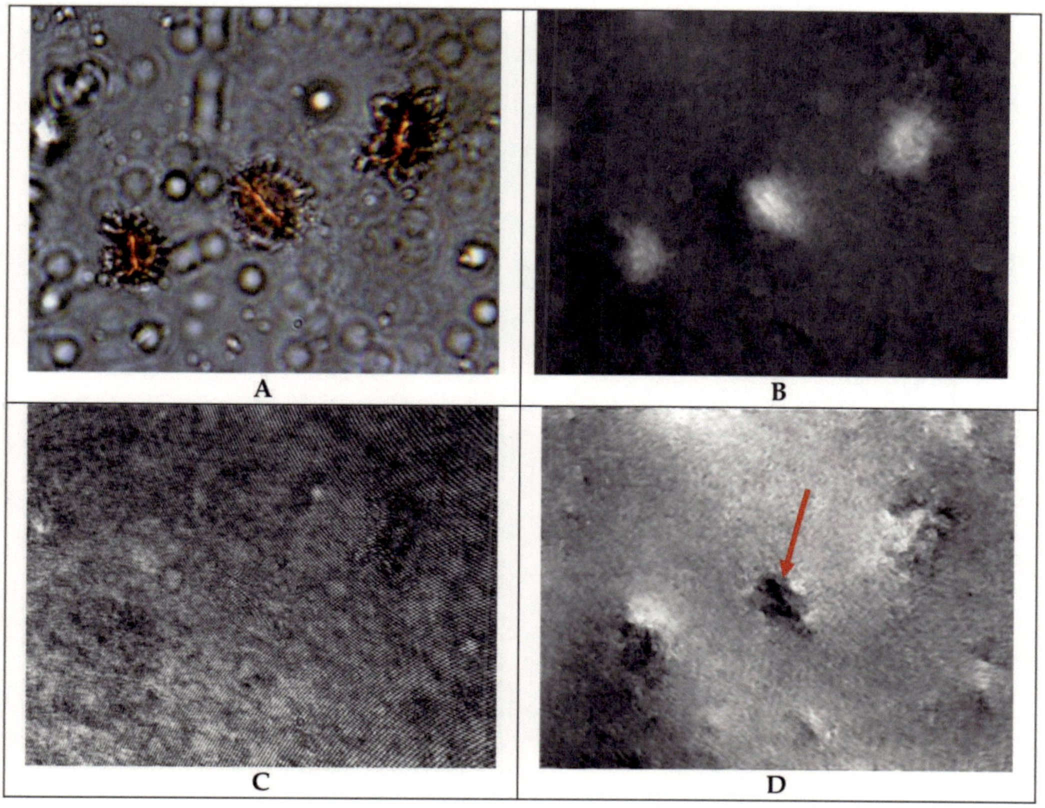

Figure 14. Cell death visualization by polarization staining in the presence of particulates and air bubbles. HUVEC cells (kindly furnished by Dr. Durvanei Augusto Maria) induced to cell death by silver nanoparticles exposure *in vitro* (22ppm, nanosilver Khemia), Picrosyrius stain. (A) Optical microscopy image, (B) Phase contrast image, (C) Polarization hologram (D) Polarization hologram reconstruction. Magnification 10x objective.

the cell. This molecular alignment is well observed in the signed cell with an arrow in Figure 14-D. In this cell, the molecular alignment is most evidently displayed because of their vitality, which is not shown on the less vital neighboring cells.

5.3. Visualization of birefringence in metronidazole

The Polarization Holographic Microscopy is suitable for crystalline and amorphous powder analysis. The sample and mounting media optical properties must be considered, as well as aggregation interference. In the figure 15 it is presented the result of a metronidazole sample processing. The optical microscopy image, figure 15-A, shows the intensity changes in light passing through the sample. The use of holographic microscopy enables to quantify the topographic characteristics the of the powder grains through the phase image reconstruction (figure 15-B) knowing that the metronidazole refractive index is $n_o = 1.618$ and the medium immersion (glycerol) refractive index is $n_m=1.437$.

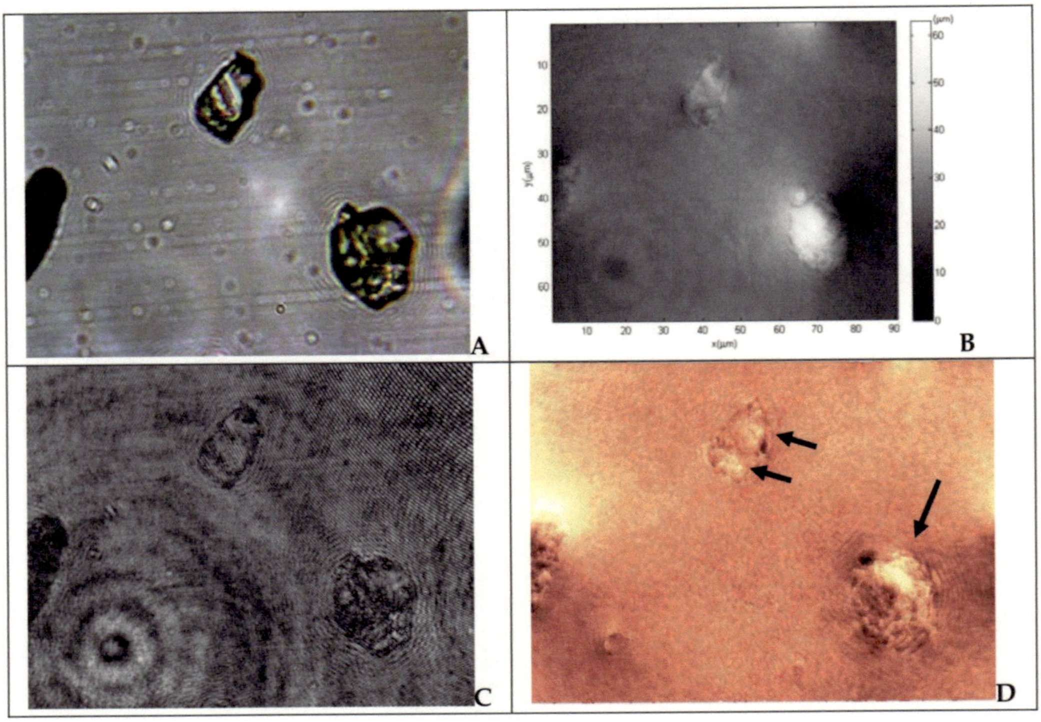

Figure 15. Metronidazole powder material observed in glycerol suspension. Thin film produced by placing a suspension drop between 1mm thick glassslide and 00 coverslip, 10x objective. (A) Optical microscopy image, (B) Phase contrast image obtained with single hologram reconstruction, (C) Polarization hologram, (D) Polarization hologram reconstruction where is observed the linear birefringence of this drug. Sample kindly provided by the researcher Michele Georges Issa, Master degree graduate student tutored by Dr. Humberto Ferraz.

The polarization hologram reconstruction (figure 15-C), reveal the lineal birefringence characteristics from this drug by evidenciating the chemical crystals alignment which comprises the metronidazole structure, figure 15-D (dark arrows).

6. Conclusion

In this chapter were discussed the phase and polarization contrast methods for digital holographic microscopy. Both contrast methods were applied to different types of biological samples. The potentialities of DHM were shown through the comparison with classical techniques of optical microscopy. It was evidenced that the DHM offers a more precise visualization of the structures that compose the samples as well as others characteristics obtained by means of the phase contrast image analysis that contains information about the refractive index and thickness in each portion of the specimen. The effect of sample preparation in the quality of phase and amplitude images reconstruction was shown. There were analyzed different types of biological samples that include different types of tissues, cellular culture, drugs and the Chicken embryo chorioallantoic membrane. The possibilities of the DHM for obtaining the polarization state of the samples were also shown. It was demonstrated that the knowledge of the polarization state allows a wider characterization of the sample, such as the visualization of linear dichroism and birefringence, cell differentiation through special components or dye induced optical activity. It was demonstrated that the use of polarization holographic microscopy provides not only high specificity for the detection of ordered structures, but also for cellular vitality status.

Acknowledgements

This work was supported by the Brazilian research agencies FAPESP and CAPES, University of Oriente, Cuba and São Paulo University, Instituto Nacional de Ciência e Tecnologia de Fluidos Complexos (INCTFcx) , Marcos Roberto da Rocha Gesualdi and Elisabeth Andreoli de Oliveira, Brazil.

Author details

Francisco Palacios[1], Oneida Font[2], Guillermo Palacios[1], Jorge Ricardo[1], Miriela Escobedo[1], Ligia Ferreira Gomes[2], Isis Vasconcelos[2], Mikiya Muramatsu[2], Diogo Soga[2], Aline Prado[2] and Valin José[3]

1 University of Oriente, Cuba

2 University of Sao Paulo, Brazil

3 Polytechnic Institute "José A. Echeverría", Cuba

References

[1] Buraga-Lefebre, C.; Coetmellec, S.; Lebrun D.; & Ozkul C. (2000). Opt. Laser Eng. 33, 409.

[2] Carl, D.; Kemper, B.; Wernicke, G. & Von Bally, G. (2004). Appl. Opt. 43, pp. 6536-6544.

[3] Colomb, T.; Dahlgren, P.; Beghuin, D.; Cuche, E.; Marquet, P. & Depeursinge C. (2002). Appl. Opt. 41, 27–37.

[4] Colomb, T.; Cuche, E.; Montfort, F.; Marquet, P.; & Depeursinge C. (2004). Opt. Commun. 231, 137–147.

[5] Colomb, T.; Dahlgren, P.; Beghuin, D.; Cuche, E.; Marquet, P. & Depeursinge, C. (2002). Appl. Opt., Vol. 41, No. 1, pp.27-37.

[6] Cuche, E.; Bevilacqua, F. & Depeursinge, C. (1999). Opt. Lett. Vol. 24, pp.291-293.

[7] Emery, Y.; Cuche, E.; Colomb, T.; Depeursinge, C.; Rappaz, B.; Marquet, P. & Magistretti, P. (2007). J. of Phys.: Conf. Series 61 (1) , 1317-1321.

[8] Hu, C.; Zhong, J.; Weng, J. & Yan, G. (2011). Proceedings of the ISBB, pp.271-274, doi: 10.1109/ISBB.2011.6107699.

[9] Junqueira, L.; Bignolas, G. & Brentani, R. (1979). Histochem J 11:447–455.

[10] Kemper, B.; Carl, D.; Höink, A.; Von Bally, G.; Bredebusch, I. & Schnekenburger, J. (2006). Proceeding of SPIE, 6191.

[11] Kim, M. (2010). J. Opt. Soc. Korea, Vol. 14, No. 2, pp. 77-89.

[12] Nomarski, G. (1955). J. Phys. Radium 16, 9.

[13] Nomura, T.; Javidi, B.; Murata, S.; Nitanai, E. & Numata T. (2007). Opt. Lett. 32, 481–483.

[14] Palacios, F.; Ricardo, J.;Palacios, D.; Gonçalves, E.;Valin, J. & De Souza, R. (2005). Opt. Commun. 248 41.

[15] Palacios, F.; Font O.; Ricardo, J.; Palacios, G.; Muramatsu M.; Soga, D.; Palacios, D. & Monroy, F.; (2011). Advanced Holography - Metrology and Imaging, Ed. InTech, ISBN 978-953-307-729-1, Chap. 9, pp. 183-206.

[16] Pavillon, N.; Kuhn, J.; Moratal, C.; Jourdain, P. & Depeursinge, C. (2012). PLoS ONE, Vol. 7, No.1, e30912. doi:10.1371/journal.pone.0030912.

[17] Popescu, G.; Deflores, L.; Vaughan, J.; Badizadegan, K.; Iwai, H.; Dasari, R. & Feld, M. (2004). Opt. Lett. 29, pp. 2503-2505.

[18] Pluta, M. (1988). Opt. Laser Techn. 20 (2), 81-88

[19] Ricardo, J.; Muramatsu, M.; Palacios, F.; Gesualdi, M.; Font, O; Valin, J.; Escobedo, M.; Herold, S.; Palacios, D.; Palacios, G. & Sánchez, A. (2011). J. Phys. Conf. Ser. 274, 012066 doi: 10.1088/1742-6596/274/1/012066.

[20] Seebacher, S.; Osten, W.; Baumbach, T. & Jüptner W. (2001). Opt. Laser Eng. 36, 103.

[21] Schilling, B.; Poom, T.; Indebetouw, G.; Storrie, B.; Shinoda, K.; Suzuki, Y.; & Wu, M. (1997). Opt. Lett. 22 1506.

[22] Tishko, T.; Tishko , D. & Titar, V. (2012). J. Opt. Techn. 79 (6), 340-343.

[23] VanLigten, R. F. & Osterberg, H. (1966). Nature, 211, pp. 282-283.

[24] Wang, Z.; Millet, L.; Gillette, M. & Popescu, G. (2008). Opt. Lett., Vol. 33, No. 11, pp. 1270-1272.

[25] Xu, W.; Jericho, M.; Meinertzhagen, I. & Kreuser, H. (2001). Cell Biol. 20, 301.

[26] Zernike, F. (1942). Physica 9, 686.

[27] Zernike, F. (1942). Physica 9, 974.